D1523723

OXFORD CLASSICAL MONOGRAPHS

*Published under the supervision of a Committee of the
Faculty of Classics in the University of Oxford*

The aim of the Oxford Classical Monograph series (which replaces the Oxford Classical and Philosophical Monographs) is to publish books based on the best theses on Greek and Latin literature, ancient history, and ancient philosophy examined by the Faculty Board of Classics.

The Protean Ass

The Metamorphoses *of Apuleius from Antiquity to the Renaissance*

ROBERT H. F. CARVER

OXFORD

UNIVERSITY PRESS

OXFORD

UNIVERSITY PRESS

Great Clarendon Street, Oxford OX2 6DP

Oxford University Press is a department of the University of Oxford.
It furthers the University's objective of excellence in research, scholarship,
and education by publishing worldwide in

Oxford New York

Auckland Cape Town Dar es Salaam Hong Kong Karachi
Kuala Lumpur Madrid Melbourne Mexico City Nairobi
New Delhi Shanghai Taipei Toronto

With offices in

Argentina Austria Brazil Chile Czech Republic France Greece
Guatemala Hungary Italy Japan Poland Portugal Singapore
South Korea Switzerland Thailand Turkey Ukraine Vietnam

Oxford is a registered trade mark of Oxford University Press
in the UK and in certain other countries

Published in the United States
by Oxford University Press Inc., New York

British Library Cataloguing in Publication Data

Data available

Library of Congress Cataloging in Publication Data

Data available

Typeset by SPI Publisher Services, Pondicherry, India
Printed in Great Britain
on acid-free paper by
Biddles Ltd., King's Lynn, Norfolk

ISBN 978-0-19-921786-1

1 3 5 7 9 10 8 6 4 2

For my mother
Mary Fielding Carver
and
in memory of my father
John Henry Carver
(1926–2004)

**

venisti tandem . . . ?

Acknowledgements

Apuleius provides some memorable images of confinement: Lucius toiling blindly in the mill; Charite threatened with being sewn in the belly of an ass; the woman bewitched by Meroe, unable to give birth even after eight years of pregnancy. I am pleased to record that the experience of writing this book has never quite matched any of these torments, though it may have seemed so, at times, to some of my friends, family, and colleagues. My first thanks are due to the late Professor A. D. Nuttall of New College, Oxford, who supervised the D.Phil. thesis from which this monograph emerged. I have also benefited greatly from the comments of my examiners, Professors Emrys Jones and Charles Martindale, and from the generosity and patience of Professor Stephen Harrison, the adviser appointed by the Oxford Classical Monographs Committee. The Association of Commonwealth Universities, in conjunction with the British Council, supported me, during the first three years of my doctoral research at Magdalen College, Oxford, with a Commonwealth Scholarship (1985–88). The Provost and Fellows of Worcester College, the President and Fellows of Trinity College, and the Principal and Fellows of Linacre College, Oxford, made the continuation of the work possible (and certainly more congenial) by electing me to Junior Research Fellowships during the period 1989–96. For much good conversation and many kindnesses, I have to thank John Fuller, Ingrid de Smet, Andrew Laird, and the then President, Mr Anthony Smith, at Magdalen; Dinah Birch, Peter Brown, Bryan Ward-Perkins, and Clive Griffin at Trinity; Tom Earle and the late Mr Paul Turner at Linacre; Glenn Black at Oriel College, and Richard Jenkyns at Lady Margaret Hall.

The long process of transforming the thesis into a book was facilitated by a British Academy Postdoctoral Fellowship held in the Faculty of English Language and Literature in the University of Oxford (1990–3), and by an Arts and Humanities Research Board Research Leave Award at the University of Durham (January to April 2001). I am indebted, also, to the Bodleian Library (particularly the staff of Duke Humfrey's), the British Library, the Vatican's Biblioteca Apostolica, Dr Mariateresa Horsfall Scotti (who kindly supplied me from Rome with *Apuleiana* otherwise unobtainable), Dr Danielle Mal-Maeder, and Professor Michael Reeve at Pembroke College, Cambridge. Like ancient novel scholars the world over, I owe a great debt to Professor James Tatum at Dartmouth College, New Hampshire, to Dr Maaike Zimmerman and her colleagues at the University of Groningen, and to Professors Robin Nisbet,

Michael Winterbottom, Ewen Bowie, and Stephen Harrison at Corpus Christi College, Oxford.

I am grateful to all of my colleagues (past and present) at Durham, especially to Professors Michael O'Neill, J. R. Watson, David Fuller, Patricia Waugh, Gerald Bonner, Tony Woodman, and Edith Hall, and Drs Robin Dix, Barbara Ravelhofer, Corinne Saunders, Alison Shell, Ian Doyle, Regine May, Geoff Bromiley, and Augustine Casiday.

Invaluable bibliographical assistance was rendered by Mike Huxtable and Dr Donata Kick as this book was going to press.

I remember, too, debts contracted in other times and contexts: the inspiration of some of my earliest teachers, Mr J. F. Roe and Dr D. C. C. Daintree in Adelaide, and Dr P. G. Lennox in Canberra; and the example of humane scholarship provided at the Australian National University by Professors C. I. E. Donaldson, G. W. Clarke, and Richard Johnson, Drs Colin Mayrhofer, Douglas Kelly, and John Gillies, and Messrs Robert Barnes and F. H. Langman. Of friends, I would single out the late David Reid and Jim Rogers, Stephen Bennetts (the *condiscipulus* who introduced me to Apuleius in 1983), Orde Levinson, Richard Major, Christopher Miller, Philip T. Crotty, Walter Hooper, the Reverend Dr Ian Ker, Sheridan Gilley, the late Fr. Denis Cleary, Dan Anlezark, and Fr. M. L. Withoos; of family, Commander and Mrs W. M. Norrie, Mr and Mrs H. Jackson, and Mary Ann Carver.

I cannot close without mentioning my wife, Anna Zaranko (who has endured the company of Fotis, Isis, Polia, and Phaedria for more years than she cares to remember), or our children, Clare, Thomas, Anastasia, Helena, and Aleksander, who betray no signs of having lived the whole of their lives 'in the shadow of an ass': *Nocte media uidi solem candido coruscantem lumine.*

The greatest debt of all is recorded in the dedication.

R.H.F.C.

University of Durham
November 2006

Contents

Abbreviations

AA	*Asinus Aureus* (*The Golden Ass* or *Metamorphoses* of Apuleius)
ACME	*Annali della facoltà di lettere e filosofia dell'università degli studi di Milano*
AJA	*American Journal of Archaeology*
AJP	*American Journal of Philology*
ARAST	*Atti della reale accademia delle scienze di Torino*
BBDIH	*Biographical and Bibliographical Dictionary of the Italian Humanists and of the World of Classical Scholarship in Italy, 1300–1800*, by M. E. Cosenza, 6 vols. (Boston: Hall, 1962–7)
BBDIP	*Biographical and Bibliographical Dictionary of the Italian Printers, and of Foreign Printers in Italy from the Introduction of the Art of Printing into Italy to 1800*, by M. E. Cosenza (Boston: Hall, 1968)
BJRL	*Bulletin of the John Rylands Library*
BL	British Library
BM	British Museum
Bod.	Bodleian Library
CAGN	*Collected Ancient Greek Novels*, ed. B. P. Reardon
CCCM	Corpus Christianorum Continuatio Mediaeualis
CCSL	Corpus Christianorum Series Latina
CL	*Comparative Literature*
CP	*Classical Philology*
CQ	*Classical Quarterly*
CR	*Classical Review*
CSCA	*California Studies in Classical Antiquity*
CSEL	Corpus Scriptorum Ecclesiasticorum Latinorum
CW	*Classical World*
CWE	*Collected Works of Erasmus* (Toronto: U of Toronto P, 1974–)
DAI	*Dissertation Abstracts International*
DBI	*Dizionario biografico degli italiani* (Rome: Istituto della Enciclopedia italiana, 1960–)
DLI	*De litteratorum infelicitate*, by Pierio Valeriano
DNB	*Dictionary of National Biography*

EC	*Essays in Criticism*
EETS	Early English Texts Society
EHR	*English Historical Review*
ELH	*English Literary History*
ELLMA	*European Literature and the Latin Middle Ages*, by E. R. Curtius
ELN	*English Language Notes*
ELR	*English Literary Renaissance*
FQ	*The Faerie Queene*, by Edmund Spenser
GCA	Groningen Commentaries on Apuleius
GCN	*Groningen Colloquia on the Novel*
GL	*Gerusalemme liberata*, by Torquato Tasso
Gloss. Lat.	*Glossaria Latina*
GSLI	*Giornale storico della letteratura italiana*
GW	*Gesamtkatalog der Wiegendrucke* (Leipzig: Hiersemann, 1925–)
HL	*Humanistica Lovaniensia*
HLB	*Harvard Library Bulletin*
HLQ	*Huntington Library Quarterly*
ICAN2	International Conference on the Ancient Novel, Dartmouth College, New Hampshire, 23–29 July 1989.
IMU	*Italia medioevale e umanistica*
JEGP	*Journal of English and Germanic Philology*
JMRS	*Journal of Medieval and Renaissance Studies*
JRS	*Journal of Roman Studies*
JWCI	*Journal of the Warburg and Courtauld Institutes*
JWI	*Journal of the Warburg Institute*
KJV	King James Version (Authorized Version) of Bible (1611)
L & S	Liddell and Scott, *Greek-English Lexicon*
LCM	*Liverpool Classical Monthly*
M&H	*Medievalia et Humanistica*
MLN	*Modern Language Notes*
MLR	*Modern Language Review*
MRTS	Medieval and Renaissance Texts and Studies
NA	*New Arcadia*, by Sir Philip Sidney
N&Q	*Notes and Queries*
NCE2	*New Catholic Encyclopedia* (2nd edn., 2003)

OA	*Old Arcadia*, by Sir Philip Sidney
OCD2	*Oxford Classical Dictionary* (2nd edn., 1970)
OCD3	*Oxford Classical Dictionary* (3rd edn., 1996; rev. 2003)
ODNB	*Oxford Dictionary of National Biography* (online edn.)
OF	*Orlando furioso*, by Ludovico Ariosto
OI	*Orlando innamorato*, by Matteo Maria Boiardo
OLD	*Oxford Latin Dictionary*
Pauly-Wissowa	*Paulys Real-Encyclopädie der classischen Altertumswissenschaft*, ed. G. Wissowa et al. (1894–1978)
PBSA	*Papers of the Bibliographical Society of America*
PG	*Patrologiae cursus completus series Graecus*, ed. J.-P. Migne
PIMS	Pontifical Institute of Mediaeval Studies
PL	*Patrologiae cursus completus series Latinus*, ed. J.-P. Migne
PLPLS	*Proceedings of the Leeds Philosophical and Literary Society*
PMLA	*Publications of the Modern Languages Association of America*
PQ	*Philological Quarterly*
PRO	Public Record Office, Kew (UK)
PUP	Princeton University Press
RANL	*Rendiconti Accademia nazionale dei Lincei*
REL	*Revue des études latines*
RES	*Review of English Studies*
RIS	Rerum italicarum scriptores
RPL	*Res publica litterarum*
RQ	*Renaissance Quarterly*
RS	*Renaissance Studies*
S&S3	*Scribes and Scholars*, by L. D. Reynolds and N. G. Wilson (3rd edn.)
SB	*Studies in Bibliography*
SCJ	*Sixteenth Century Journal*
SEL	*Studies in English Literature*
SFN	*Shakespeare's Favorite Novel*, by J. J. M. Tobin
SHA	*Scriptores Historiae Augustae*
SIFC	*Studi italiani di filologia classica*
SP	*Studies in Philology*
SQ	*Shakespeare Quarterly*

SR	*Studies in the Renaissance*
SS	*Shakespeare Survey*
STC	*A Short-Title Catalogue of Books Printed . . . 1475–1640*, by A. W. Pollard and G. R. Redgrave et al. (2nd edn., 1986–91)
SUP	*Studi umanistici Piceni*
TAPA	*Transactions of the American Philological Association*
YCS	*Yale Classical Studies*
ZPE	*Zeitschrift für Papyrologie und Epigraphik*

PROTEUS

sunt, quibus in plures ius est transire figuras,
ut tibi, conplexi terram maris incola, Proteu.
nam modo te iuvenem, modo te videre leonem,
nunc violentus aper, nunc, quem tetigisse timerent,
anguis eras, modo te faciebant cornua taurum;
saepe lapis poteras, arbor quoque saepe videri,
interdum, faciem liquidarum imitatus aquarum,
flumen eras, interdum undis contrarius ignis.

(There are those who have the power of changing into many forms, like you, Proteus, inhabitant of the earth-embracing sea. For now men saw you as a youth, now as a lion; now you were a violent boar, now a snake whom men would fear to touch; now horns made you a bull; often you could seem to be a stone, often also a tree; sometimes, imitating the appearance of flowing water, you were a river; sometimes, the opposite of water—a flame)

(Ovid, *Metamorphoses* 8: 730–7)

verum ubi correptum manibus vinclisque tenebis,
tum variae eludent species atque ora ferarum.
fiet enim subito sus horridus atraque tigris
squamosusque draco et fulva cervice leaena,
aut acrem flammae sonitum dabit atque ita vinclis
excidet, aut in aquas tenuis dilapsus abibit.

(But when you hold him in the grasp of hands and fetters, then various forms and the features of wild beasts will frustrate you. For suddenly he will become a bristling pig, a black tiger, a scaly snake or a lioness with a tawny neck; or he will give out the fierce sound of flame and in this way he will slip out of his fetters; or he will melt away into thin waters)

(Vergil, *Georgics* 4. 405–10)

They are a grett deale more mutable
Then Proteus of forme so variable,
Which coulde hym silfe so disgyse.
They canne represent apes and beares,
Lyons and asses with longe eares,
Even as they list to divyse.

(Barlow, *Rede me and be nott wrothe* (Strasbourg: J. Schott, 1528), sig. i 4^v)

What knot can hould this *Proteus,* that varies thus in hewe?

('Horace his Epistles to Maecenas', trans. Thomas Drant)

Introduction

Mais s'il y a une vérité artistique au monde, c'est que ce livre est un chef-d'
œuvre. Il me donne à moi des vertiges et des éblouissements. La nature
pour elle-même, le paysage, le côté purement pittoresque des choses sont
traités là à la moderne et avec un souffle antique et chrétien tout ensemble
qui passe au milieu. Ça sent l'encens et l'urine, la bestialité s'y marie au
mysticisme.

(Gustave Flaubert to Louise Colet, 27–8 June 1852)[1]

Flaubert is not alone in feeling 'dizzy and dazzled' in the face of Apuleius'
'masterpiece'. *The Golden Ass* (or *Metamorphoses*) has always divided its
readers. What, after all, is one to make of a work which fuses ten books of
witches, slave-girls, bandits, aristocrats, and priests (variously involved in
fornication, adultery, buggery, bestiality, and storytelling) with a final book
in which a sublime vision transforms the asinine narrator into a devout
disciple of the goddess Isis? Critical responses to this problem have traditionally tended towards one of two extremes, with readers classing (or rejecting)
the work as a mere piece of Milesian entertainment, or drawing, paradoxically, from its gutters, a pattern of moral and spiritual edification.[2] Literary
responses have (perhaps inevitably) been rather more complex.

One of the attractions of diachronic studies is a licence to revel in multiplicity, to delight in the varied responses of readers from different times and
places. This monograph is, primarily, a study in the reception of a classical
text over a period of fourteen centuries. *The Golden Ass* has many claims upon
our attention as students of the Western tradition: the only Latin 'novel'

---

[1] ('But if there is any artistic truth in the world, it is that this book is a masterpiece. It leaves
me dizzy and dazzled. Nature for her own sake, the landscape, the purely picturesque side of
things, are treated there in a modern way and with a spirit all at once ancient and Christian
which goes to the very centre. It reeks of incense and urine; bestiality is there married to
mysticism.') See *Œuvres Complètes de Gustave Flaubert*, 16 vols. (Paris: club de l'Honnête
Honne, 1971–6), xiii. 215 (Letter 431). Cf. F. Steegmuller, *Flaubert and Madame Bovary:
A Double Portrait*, 2nd edn. (London: Collins, 1947), 237, 251, 254. The influence of Apuleius
on the development of realism in the 19th-cent. novel is beyond the scope of this monograph,
but we might observe that Colet was one of the models for the eponymous heroine of Flaubert's
own *chef-d' œuvre* (*Madame Bovary*) which was being written at this time.

[2] Lucius (9. 14) compares the soul of the baker's wife to a *caenosa latrina*.

worthy of the name to survive intact from the ancient world, it impressed itself upon the consciousness of thinkers and writers as diverse as Augustine and Martianus Capella, Petrarch, Boccaccio, and Erasmus, Sidney, Spenser, Shakespeare, Jonson, and Milton. But even as we consider individual instances of reception over this long period, our Janus-like gaze is bound to keep in view two terminal points: the circumstances (so far as we can reconstruct them) of the text's original production and consumption, and our own position as early twenty-first-century readers, both of the original text and of other texts that it may have influenced. One does not need to subscribe fully to the tenets of the Konstanz school of *Rezeptionsästhetik* to acknowledge that studying the history of the reception of a text can illuminate its hermeneutic potential.[3] Equally, when approaching the reception of an ancient text, it can be useful to bring to bear a twenty-first-century understanding of the interpretive possibilities generated by that text.

One of the obstacles to our engagement with any 'ancient novel' is the failure of antiquity to accommodate prose fiction within its literary taxonomies. The most famous classical theorists—Aristotle, Horace, Quintilian— are all silent on the subject. We are left, instead, to piece together an account from the surviving examples and a handful of scattered labels: λόγοι, πλάσματα, Μιλησιακά, *historiae*, *fabulae*, *Milesiae*, and so on. Horace does, however, provide a number of leitmotifs to our discussion of Apuleius. 'Imagine', he says, at the beginning of the *Ars poetica*, 'if a painter chose to join a human head to a horse's trunk...Who could forbear to laugh?'[4] He proceeds, by analogy, to an exposition of the demands of congruity and uniformity in the verbal arts: *denique sit quod uis, simplex dumtaxat et unum* ('whatever kind of work it is, let it at least be unmixed and uniform', line 23). *The Golden Ass* could almost have been written as a direct response to the challenge posed by the *Ars poetica*. Apuleius has attached not only an ass's body to a man's mind, but also a sublime rapture of Isiac revelation to a scabrous collection of Milesian tales.

For much of the twentieth century, opinion concerning *The Golden Ass* was split between 'unitarians' and 'separatists'.[5] At the heart of the debate was the question of whether Book 11 was to be regarded as an 'anchor' to the concerns of the rest of the novel, or merely as 'ballast'.[6] Chief advocate for the latter

[3] See C. Martindale, *Redeeming the Text: Latin Poetry and the Hermeneutics of Reception* (Cambridge: CUP, 1993).

[4] *Humano capiti ceruicem pictor equinam | iungere si uelit...risum teneatis, amici?* (*Ars poetica* 1–5). Horace's own practice as a poet, of course, violates his theory. See A. D. Nuttall, 'Fishes in the Trees', in his *The Stoic in Love* (London: Harvester Wheatsheaf, 1989), 68–81.

[5] C. Schlam, 'The Scholarship on Apuleius since 1938', *CW* 64 (1971), 285–309.

[6] G. N. Sandy, 'Book 11: Ballast or Anchor?', in *Aspects of Apuleius' Golden Ass*, ed. B. L. Hijmans and R. Th. van der Paardt (Groningen: Bouma, 1978), 123–40.

school was Ben Perry whose researches heralded the real beginning of modern Apuleian studies:

Instead of building into the framework of his story-book as a whole an ostensible meaning in terms of satire, philosophical critique, or allegory which would be evident from start to finish, as is the case in Lucian's novels, Apuleius is content merely to tack on at the end a piece of solemn pageantry as ballast to offset the prevailing levity of the [245] preceding ten books.[7]

A flurry of publications in the 1960s and the appearance, in the 1970s, of important studies by P. G. Walsh and James Tatum, revealed, in place of ham-fisted suturing, a complex pattern of intra-textual relations through which the Isiac conclusion was repeatedly prefigured in the first ten books.[8] Thus, the seemingly casual reference to 'Egyptian papyrus' and 'Nilotic reed' in the opening sentence is found to contain a coded allusion to the finale.[9] The mysterious Zatchlas—the linen-clad wise-man who extracts truth from an animated corpse in the tale of Thelyphron (*AA* 2. 28)—is unmasked as a priest of Isis. Even the hilarious scene of the officious market inspector trampling Lucius' costly fish into the ground (*AA* 1. 25) can be interpreted as a cryptic allusion to the rites of Osiris.[10] And in the tale of 'Cupid and Psyche' one can find obvious parallels with Lucius' own situation (fatal curiosity, repeated trials, and ultimate salvation through divine intervention). So persuasive were these arguments for the novel's artistic and thematic coherence that the separatist voice seemed to have been virtually silenced.[11] The debate, however, was by no means over. With its rich and witty blend of traditional scholarship and post-structuralist strategies, John J. Winkler's *Auctor & Actor: A Narratological*

[7] B. E. Perry, *The Ancient Romances: A Literary-Historical Account of their Origins* (Berkeley and Los Angeles: U of California P, 1967), 244–5. Perry was by no means the first to propound a 'separatist' view of the novel: Louis C. Purser makes much the same case in his edition of *The Story of Cupid and Psyche as Related by Apuleius* (London: Bell, 1910), pp. xx–xxi. 'Separatism' only became a significant title when there was a 'unitarian' view to oppose it. Perry's arguments carry particular weight because he continued to maintain them in the face of growing opposition.

[8] P. G. Walsh, *The Roman Novel: The 'Satyricon' of Petronius and the 'Metamorphoses' of Apuleius* (Cambridge: CUP, 1970); J. Tatum, *Apuleius and 'The Golden Ass'* (Ithaca: Cornell UP, 1979).

[9] e.g. Tatum, 28.

[10] e.g. ibid. 37. Plutarch, *De Iside et Osiride* 358b, 363f, describes the fish feeding on Osiris' phallus which his murderer, Seth, had cast into the Nile. On this and other 'crypto-Egyptian elements', see Winkler, *Auctor & Actor: A Narratological Reading of Apuleius's 'The Golden Ass'* (Berkeley and Los Angeles: U of California P, 1985), 318.

[11] Though a kind of halfway house has been posited by critics arguing for a limited unity in the *Metamorphoses*. Thus Sandy, 'Book 11: Ballast or Anchor?', 126: 'The conclusion therefore is that the piquant, self-contained tales of the middle books except, as it appears, that of Cupid and Psyche … are designed purely for comic entertainment rather than to put into relief the moral degradation of which Lucius is supposed to become penitent in Book 11.'

Reading of Apuleius's 'The Golden Ass' transformed, once again, the whole
terrain of Apuleian studies.[12] Rather than attempting, in the unitarian manner,
to gloss over the apparent 'slips and inconsistencies in the narrative', Winkler
subjects them to the full rigour of narratological analysis in order to show
how fundamentally problematic the text remains.[13] While rejecting 'critical
totalitarianism', he follows the deconstructive path of giving 'a position of
privilege to those portions of *The Golden Ass* that are models (whether serious
or ironic) for the process of reading, of interpreting a scene or tale'.[14] The *Ass*
that emerges is a very different animal from that presented by either Perry, at
one extreme, or Reinhold Merkelbach, at the other.[15] Winkler speaks of the
work as 'a modern-seeming narrative about narratives', characterizes Apuleius'
attitude as one of 'salutary insouciance', and contends that 'this novel, more
than most, continuously involves the reader in games of outwitting, a *modus
operandi* that I will call hermeneutic entertainment'.[16] In place of a rag-bag of
Milesian tales or an Isiac aretalogy, we have 'a philosophically sensitive comedy
about religious convictions that enacts in its own reading the thesis that guides
its writing. That thesis, in a phrase, is that all answers to cosmic questions are
non-authorized.'[17]

   Auctor & Actor has won many converts; but a substantial camp of Apuleian
scholars remains unconvinced.[18] In some cases, the reactions seemed to result
from a general scepticism about the relevance of post-structuralist theory to
ancient literature; but specific objections (e.g. 'anachronistic' and 'distorting')
have also been raised.[19] It has been observed, for instance, that Winklerian
narratology yields alarmingly similar results when applied to a very different
text, the *Aethiopica* of Heliodorus.[20] Carl Schlam's *The 'Metamorphoses' of
Apuleius: On Making an Ass of Oneself* serves, in part, as a rejoinder to *Auctor*

   [12] See n. 10, *supra*.
   [13] Tatum, 19: 'Most specialists are now willing to take the eleven books of *The Golden Ass* as a unified work of literature, despite earlier scholarly objections to some slips and inconsistencies in the narrative.'
   [14] Winkler, pp. x, 13.
   [15] According to Merkelbach, *Roman und Mysterium in der Antike* (Munich: Beck, 1962), *The Golden Ass*, like all the ancient novels bar Chariton's, is imbued, from the very outset, with elements of the mystery religions. See also his 'Novel and Aretalogy' in *The Search for the Ancient Novel*, ed. J. Tatum (Baltimore: Johns Hopkins UP, 1994), 283–95.
   [16] Winkler, 10–11.
   [17] Ibid. 125.
   [18] Mary Beard stated in her review of recent readings in the ancient novel ('Greek Love', *TLS*, 15 Apr. 1994, p. 7), that Winkler's book 'has almost achieved the status of orthodoxy', but this claim is belied by the work of E. J. Kenney, Carl Schlam, and many of the founding members of the Groningen school of Ancient Novel studies.
   [19] See e.g. R. Van der Paardt, 'Playing the Game', in *GCN* 1 (1980) 103–12.
   [20] K. Dowden, 'Apuleius Revalued', *CR*, NS 37 (1987): 39–41, at 40, with reference to J. J. Winkler, 'The Mendacity of Kalasiris and the Narrative Strategy of Heliodoros' *Aithiopika*', *YCS* 27 (1982), 93–158.

& Actor.[21] In place of Winkler's concern with 'hermeneutic entertainment', Schlam speaks in more traditional terms of Apuleius' commitment to 'narrative entertainment, blending the comic with the serious', and discerns not 'the self-consciousness of a sophisticated poststructuralist, but that of a Middle Platonist in the second century'.[22] More recent studies have stressed the rhetorical dimensions of *The Golden Ass* and Apuleius' role as a peripatetic sophist.[23]

Schlam's account of Apuleius is admirably level-headed but his *modus operandi* seems to be either to ignore the interpretative difficulties thrown up by the text, or to brush them under the accommodating carpet of jocoseriousness (*serio ludere*).[24] We ought, of course, to be alive to the possibility that the hermeneutic problems which we perceive in *The Golden Ass* are not really problems at all, but merely artefacts of the critical processes to which we subject the text. It is an academic commonplace that ancient authors wrote to be heard, rather than merely read—and the aural experience of a text is very different from the visual. There is a limit to how much even ancient listeners could hold in their head at any one time: the narrative moment is very much foregrounded, and inconsistencies between details in earlier and later episodes are less readily noticed or more easily forgiven.[25] Apuleius exploits to the full the aural dimension of his writing and we impoverish our appreciation of his artistic achievement if we confine ourselves to a silent enactment of the text.[26] Yet the two levels of engagement are in constant play, one with the other. The speaker of the prologue promises to soothe our ears with a 'charming whisper' in the course of this 'Milesian discourse' (*sermone isto Milesio... auresque tuas beniuolas lepido susurro permulceam, AA* 1. 1), but only if we are willing to 'examine' (*inspicere*) his 'Egyptian papyrus'. Even the famous exhortation, *lector intende, laetaberis* ('Reader, pay attention: you will be delighted'), fuses the image of the reader poring over a manuscript with that of an audience composing itself to hear a story.[27] Yet while *lector intende, laetaberis* suggests that one's pleasure will be

---

[21] (London: Duckworth, 1992).

[22] Schlam, *The 'Metamorphoses' of Apuleius*, 3 and 2.

[23] G. Sandy, *The Greek World of Apuleius: Apuleius and the Second Sophistic* (Leiden: Brill, 1997); S. J. Harrison, *Apuleius: A Latin Sophist* (Oxford: OUP, 2000).

[24] Schlam, 1.

[25] Cf. C. M. Bowra on listener/reader response to Homeric 'inconsistencies' in *From Virgil to Milton* (London: Macmillan, 1945), 4.

[26] Augustine (*Confessions* 6. 3. 3) seems surprised to find Ambrose reading so intently to himself, without using voice or tongue. See Peter Brown, *Augustine of Hippo* (London: Faber, 1967; repr. 1979), 82.

[27] Cf. the prologues in New Comedy, e.g. Plautus, *Amphitryon* 94, 151; *Asinaria* 1, 14; and the beginning of *Aeneid* 2 where Aeneas is about to relate the Sack of Troy: *conticuere omnes intentique ora tenebant.*

dependent, in part at least, upon one's attentiveness, the phrase *papyrus Aegyptia* should remind us of an important difference between the reading experience of today's critics and that of Apuleius' contemporaies. Armed with our modern editions (paper and electronic), and assisted by the *Index Apuleianus*, we have immediate—and simultaneous—access to all parts of *The Golden Ass*. Second-century readers, on the other hand, are more in the position of the user of microfilm: confined by their papyrus rolls to the linear movement of a small window of text. It is only with the transference from roll to codex in the fourth century that the reader can jump backwards and forwards, with something like modern ease, between different parts of the work.[28] Nevertheless, *The Golden Ass*, more, perhaps, than any other piece of ancient literature, seems designed to attract precisely the sort of close, non-linear, analysis that critics like Winkler have applied. Apuleius, of course, did not invent literary self-consciousness (Ovid and the whole Callimachean tradition stand as obvious precedents), but the self-referential passages in the novel—in particular, the apostrophe to the *lector scrupulosus*—invite the 'careful reader' to become involved in the text in a manner which seems peculiarly modern.[29] Accepting that invitation entails considering the possibility that Apuleius' apparent carelessness—his seeming indifference to precise causality and narrative 'loose ends'—is a calculated effect, and one pregnant with hermeneutic significance.[30] Such a hypothesis is no mere creature of deconstructionist whimsy: the Platonic (and, more precisely, the Middle Platonic) tradition which informs both Apuleius and his novel provides a conceptual framework for evaluating narrative. Socrates observes in Plato's *Phaedrus* (a work of central importance to *The Golden Ass*) that 'every discourse (λόγος) must be organised, like a living being, with a body of its own, as it were, so as not to be headless or footless, but to have a middle and members, composed in fitting relation to each other and to the whole'.[31] And Apuleius—destined to be remembered as a

---

[28] It would appear that some of the less sophisticated examples of prose fiction circulated in codex form well before this date—as, of course, did Christian writings. But see Jerome's contemptuous reference (Ch. 1 *infra*) to young men 'unrolling Milesian tales'.

[29] *AA* 9. 30; cf. 10. 7, 10. 33, 11. 23, and Winkler, 60 ff. Scrupulosity features frequently in the novel: Milo interrogates Lucius *scrupulosissime* (1. 26); the nightwatchman performs his duties *scrupulosa diligentia* (3. 3); the wicked sisters question Psyche *scrupulose curioseque* (5. 8); the soldiers inspect *scrupulosius* the house where the gardener is hiding (9. 42); Lucius, displaying his appetite for human cuisine, calculates *scrupulose* what an ass would be most likely to contemn (10. 16).

[30] Contrast Walsh, *Roman Novel*, 154: 'These loose ends...demonstrate that Apuleius anticipates from his readers not a sustained and critical analysis, but applause for improvised spontaneity.'

[31] *Phaedrus* 264c (Loeb). Cf. Van der Paardt, *Aspects*, 81.

philosopher and logician—tells us in the *Florida* what he expects of his audience with regard to all of his works: *meum uero unumquodque dictum acriter examinatis, sedulo pensiculatis* ('You closely examine every single word of mine, you weigh it carefully in the mind').[32] We should be willing to do the same.

This is not the place for a detailed, synchronic examination of *The Golden Ass* as a literary text. We can, however, isolate certain aspects of the work that will feature prominently in subsequent receptions. The abrupt shifts between titillation and Platonic allegory, between pornographic love-scenes and epiphanic paeans, placed the work beyond the limits of traditional literary theory. Apuleius generally failed (where a Menippean satirist like Lucian was to pass) the test imposed by the most influential Horatian formulas:

But once againe, least my discourse runne too farre awry, wyll I buckle my selfe more neerer to English Poetry: the vse wherof, because it is nothing different from any other, I thinke best to confirme by the testimony of *Horace*, a man worthy to beare authority in this matter, whose very opinion is this, that the perfect perfection of poetrie is this, to mingle delight with profitt in such wyse that a Reader might by his reading be pertaker of bothe; . . . In his treatise *de arte Poetica,* thus hee sayth:

> *Aut prodesse volunt, aut delectare poetae,*
> *Aut simul et iucunda et idonea dicere vitae.*

As much to saye: All Poets desire either by their works to profitt or delight men, or els to ioyne both profitable and pleasant lessons together for the instruction of life. And againe:

> *Omne tulit punctum qui miscuit utile dulci,*
> *Lectorem delectando pariterque monendo.*

That is, He misseth nothing of his marke which ioyneth profitt with delight, as well delighting his Readers as profiting them with counsell.[33]

These two mottoes (*Ars poetica* 333, 343) are quoted repeatedly in the Renaissance.[34] Critics such as Sir Philip Sidney could invoke the Horatian formula of 'delightful teaching' to explain how Vergil beguiles us with the music of his poetry, while edifying us with exempla of *pietas* in Aeneas; or how a satirist uses his coruscating wit to alert us to moral failings in ourselves and

---

[32] *Florida* 9. 8.

[33] William Webbe, *A Discourse of English Poetry* (1586), in *Elizabethan Critical Essays,* ed. G. Gregory Smith, 2 vols. (London: OUP, 1904; repr. 1950), 250.

[34] e.g. the title page of George Pettie's *A Petite Pallace of Pettie his Pleasure* (1576) which bears the motto, *Omne tulit punctum qui miscuit vtile dulci,* and the prefatory letter by 'R.B.' (?Barnaby Rich) which addresses the 'Gentle Gentlewomen Readers' and speaks of 'your common profit and pleasure'. See *A Petite Pallace of Pettie His Pleasure,* ed. I. Gollancz (London: Chatto & Windus, 1908), 1.

others. But the formula is less successful in its assertion of a divisibility between 'profitt' (*utile*) and 'delight' (*dulce*)—the notion that the text is an *inuolucrum* ('wrapper') or *cortex* ('rind') in which the uncontaminated *nucleus* ('kernel') of meaning is contained.[35] Much of the finest achievement of the Renaissance is attributable, we shall argue, to the spirit of proteanism—the rejection of the rigid Horatian notion of the existence in literary works of discrete components, *dulce* and *utile*, entertainment and edification, medium and message. Ovid, of course, is the protean artist par excellence, but the basic narrative units with which he was working in the *Metamorphoses*—ancient myths—contain such deep structures that no amount of rhetorical sophistication could protect the work against the allegorical exegeses that accreted during the Middle Ages and Renaissance. Apuleius, on the other hand, is using, as building blocks, *Milesiae*—what the canon in *Don Quixote* (1605) defines as 'extravagant tales, whose purpose is to amaze, and not to instruct; quite the opposite of Moral Fables, which delight and instruct at the same time'.[36] One way to track the development of modern literary sensibilities is by the changing status of the Milesian tale—the elevation of what might be termed 'autonomous fictions' to the rank of literature.

THE PROTEAN ASS

The study of ancient prose fiction has grown enormously over the last twenty years as the narrative sophistication and hermeneutic complexity of these texts have become more generally recognized. Important work has been done (in many languages) on various facets of Apuleius' *Nachleben*. For broader accounts of the reception of *The Golden Ass*, however, anglophone readers have had to rely on Elizabeth Haight's ground-breaking (but poorly documented and now very dated) *Apuleius and his Influence* (1927) and J. J. M. Tobin's heroic (if, to some tastes, monomaniac) study, *Shakespeare's Favorite Novel: 'The Golden Asse' as Prime Source* (1984).[37]

---

[35] Heywood's *Loves Maistresse* and Marmion's *Cupid and Psyche* are limited, artistically, because they do precisely this. See Ch. 8, *infra*.

[36] Miguel Cervantes, *The Adventures of Don Quixote*, trans. J. M. Cohen (Harmondsworth: Penguin, 1950; repr. 1985), Pt. I, ch. 47, p. 208. Cf. Walsh, *Roman Novel*, 1, and Ch. 9 *infra*.

[37] P. G. Walsh's seminal study, *The Roman Novel* (1970), contains a helpful (but largely derivative) concluding chapter on the *Nachleben*. Mariantonietta Acocella's *L'Asino d'oro nel Rinascimento: Dai volgarizzamenti alle raffigurazioni pittoriche* (Ravenna: Longo, 2001) furthers our understanding of the role of the the pseudo-Lucianic *Onos* in the Italian Renaissance's reception of Apuleius' *Ass*. Pasquale Accardo's *The Metamorphosis of Apuleius: Cupid and Psyche,*

There is a great deal of interesting material on Apuleius in Margaret Anne Doody's *The True Story of the Novel* (1997), but her central thesis ('Novel and romance are one') is as problematic as it is brilliant, and the pedestrian academic business of investigation, discrimination, and verification is often subordinated to the creative demands of the *vera historia* being told.[38] In what follows, I have not shied away from telling stories myself (even ones which prove, on closer inspection, to be 'mere' fictions) where they help to illuminate possible paths for the scholarly exploration of *The Golden Ass*'s reception. Indeed, given the broad chronological and geographical scope of the subject, one has to be both selective and teleological. The 'end point' for the grand narrative being constructed here is the English Renaissance. I have therefore tended not to pursue the Italian and French receptions of Apuleius much beyond the middle of the sixteenth century when *The Golden Asse* becomes available in English translation.

In the prologue to *The Golden Ass*, Apuleius' speaker apologizes for any offence he may cause as a *rudis locutor* amongst the eloquent and the expert. I should like to crave the same indulgence. Like him, I have often found myself making incursions into intellectual territories in which (*nullo magistro praeeunte*) I have felt myself a stranger (*aduena*). Like him, also, I am conscious of a certain *desultoria scientia* ('art of the switch-back rider') in my approach—a varying of pace, emphasis, depth, and detail of coverage as I explored different ways of dealing with the fortunes of a significant but often controversial text. The opening chapters are essays in relatively 'straight' literary history. In the middle chapters (4–6), I have deliberately 'thickened' the description, providing cultural contexts for the reception of *The Golden Ass*, while also suggesting some of the ways in which those acts of recovery, dissemination, exegesis, criticism, translation, and imitation, can help us to read early modern culture in Italy and Germany. The Italian reception of Apuleius could easily fill many books by itself. I have made the *Hypnerotomachia Poliphili* the centrepiece of this study in the belief that it displays, in miniature, many of our central concerns. In contrast, Chapter 8 is, for large stretches, little more than a preliminary survey or annotated catalogue of English responses to *The Golden Ass*. The monograph concludes with three case studies, showing the resonances of Apuleian material in three canonical (but very different) English writers, Sidney, Spenser, and Shakespeare.

Beauty and the Beast, King Kong (Madison, NJ: Fairleigh Dickinson UP; London: Associated University Presses, 2002) adds little in the way of original scholarship to the field. Julia Haig Gaisser has done much recently to illuminate the reception of Apuleius by Filippo Beroaldo (see Bibliography). We look forward to the appearance of her entry for 'Apuleius' in one of the future volumes of the *Catalogus Translationum et Codicorum*.

[38] (London: HarperCollins, 1997), 1. For a critique, see R. H. F. Carver, ' "True Histories" and "Old Wives' Tales": Renaissance Humanism and the "Rise of the Novel" ', *Ancient Narrative* 1 (2000–1) 322–49, at 323–7.

Note on Texts

The interplay of synchronic and diachronic perspectives in the study of reception is also reflected in our choice of editions. Humanist responses to Apuleius usually involve the assimilation and reinterpretation, rather than the radical rejection, of preceding authorities. Boccaccio, in the fourteenth century, picks out details for his retelling of 'Cupid and Psyche' from the fifth-century writer Martianus Capella; while Beroaldo, at the turn of the sixteenth century, goes back a thousand years to quote from Fulgentius' *Mitologiae*.[1] The medieval veneration of *auctores* is still apparent in the references to Apuleius (culled from Augustine, Fulgentius, and later writers) which appear in the front of many fourteenth- and fifteenth-century manuscripts, and Renaissance editors like Petrus Colvius (1588) and Johann à Wower (1606) continue the practice, prefacing their editions with 'Testimonies of Ancient Writers' relating to Apuleius.[2] Indeed, as late as 1637, we find Shakerley Marmion reproducing Fulgentius' interpretation at the head of *Cupid and Psiche, or an Epick Poeme of Cupid, and his Mistress*. The reactions of Antiquity and the Middle Ages can thus be seen to form an integral part of the Renaissance reception of Apuleius.

I have aimed, wherever possible, to consult the latest critical editions of ancient, medieval, and early modern texts. In reproducing excerpts, however, I have often taken a Renaissance edition (typically, the *editio princeps*) as copy text in order to ground our study of reception in one particular textual *locus*. I have, in almost all cases, expanded contractions and (with the exception of the ampersand) resolved abbreviations, indicating, by underlining, the interpolated matter. I have standardized 'ſ' to 's' (while retaining the given usage of 'i' and 'j', and 'u' and 'v') and in reproducing passages of mixed type, I have taken roman as norm, italic as deviant.

Except where indicated to the contrary, all translations are my own.

---

[1] For Beroaldo, see Ch. 3, *infra*.

[2] The *Veterum Scriptorum de L. Apuleio Platonico & eius scriptis testimonia* prefaced to Wower's *L. Apuleii Madaurensis Platonici opera* ([Basle:] Ex Bibliopolio Frobeniano, 1606), sigs. †2ʀ ff., are appropriated almost verbatim from those given by Colvius in his *L. Apuleii Madaurensis opera omnia quæ exstant* (Leiden: Franciscus Raphelengium, 1588).

1

The *Metamorphoses* of Apuleius: From Antiquity to the Early Middle Ages

varias fabulas conseram...

(*AA* 1. 1)

THE PAGAN *ASS*

On 18 February 197, at Lugdunum (Lyons) in Gaul, the Roman emperor, Lucius Septimius Severus, faced the army of the imperial contender, Clodius Albinus. Like Severus (b. 145/6 at Lepcis Magna), Albinus was a North African Roman, having been born in Hadrumetum (modern-day Sousse in Tunisia), not far from Apuleius' own home town of Madauros. He had been consul in the late 180s and commanded Roman armies on the Rhine and (since about 191) had been governor of Britain. Severus (emp. 193–211) had nominated Albinus as his successor (designating him 'Caesar'), but broke his pledge, leading to Albinus' entry into Gaul and his proclamation as emperor.

The fighting at Lugdunum was fierce and the outcome uncertain, but the second day brought victory to Severus' forces.[1] According to Julius Capitolinus in the *Historia Augusta*, Albinus was dragged, half-dead (*paene seminecis*), into the emperor's presence and decapitated. His body was laid out in front of his house and his head was sent back to Rome.[2] Capitolinus describes Albinus' appetite for elegant clothes and tasteless banquets, his sexual proclivities ('a womanizer amongst the foremost lovers, always unacquainted with sodomy and a persecutor of such things'),[3] and his literary habits—a writer of Georgics, and of Milesian tales 'whose reputation is held to be not undistinguished, although they are not particularly well written'.[4] He also

---

[1] Dio Cassius, 75. 6–7; *OCD3*, 1390–1.   [2] Life of Septimius Severus, 11.

[3] *mulierarius inter primos amatores, aversae Veneris semper ignarus et talium persecutor.*

[4] *Milesias nonnulli eiusdem esse dicunt, quarum fama non ignobilis habetur, quamvis mediocriter scriptae sint.* In *Scriptores Historiae Augustae*, vol. i, ed. E. Hohl (Leipzig: Teubner, 1965), 12. 11, p. 178.

reproduces a letter, purportedly written by Severus to the Roman Senate, besmirching the character of Albinus, and berating the Senate's judgement in preferring him. The letter begins with a list of Severus' own services to Rome, attacks Albinus as an upstart from Africa who has fabricated a noble lineage, and ends (the climax of the attack) with an exposé of the deficiencies of his enemy's taste in literature. Septimius is appalled that so many in the Senate could consider someone 'worthy of praise as a man of learning' (*pro literato laudandus*) who, 'busying himself with some old-womanish nursery-songs, was growing old amongst the Carthaginian Milesian tales and literary trifles of his Apuleius'.[5] 'From this it is apparent', Capitolinus comments in the next line, 'with what severity he punished the faction of Pescennius and Albinus.'[6]

If we could place any reliance at all upon the *Historia Augusta*, this would be powerful testimony to the literary and social standing of Apuleius in his own century: *The Golden Ass* was being read (and imitated) in the far corners of the Roman Empire within a decade or two of its composition.[7] The notion of a Caesar (and would-be Augustus) in Britain, entertaining himself with the Milesian tales of his fellow North African is certainly beguiling. Unfortunately, the ostensible dates and authorship of the *Historia Augusta* are highly suspect.[8] The manuscript tradition ascribes its various sections to the reigns of Diocletian (emp. 284–305), Constantius (emp. 305–6), and Constantine (d. 337), but modern scholars have made attributions as late as the fifth and sixth centuries, and current opinion points to 'a single person working in or very close to the last decade' of the fourth century.[9] 'Julius Capitolinus' and his fellow *scriptores* appear (like many—if not all—of their documents) to be fictions. Indeed, T. D. Barnes locates the *Historia Augusta* between 395 and 399, the very period during which the *Metamorphoses* of Apuleius was being edited at Rome and Constantinople.[10]

---

[5] *Maior fuit dolor, quod illum pro literato laudandus plerique duxistis, cum ille nænijs quibusdam anilibus occupatus inter Milesias Punicas Apuleij sui consenesceret.* Text from the compilation of *Testimonia* in *L. Apuleii Madaurensis Platonici opera*, ed. Jan Wower ([Basle:] Froben, 1606), sig. [): (9]ᵛ. The Teubner text concludes more fully: *Apulei sui et ludicra litteraria consenesceret.*

[6] *hinc apparet, quanta severitate factionem vel Pescennianam vel Clodianam vindicaverit.* *SHA*, ed. Hohl, 12. 12, p. 179.

[7] Griffiths (*Isis-Book*, 12) and Walsh (*Roman Novel*, 249 n. 7) treat the reference in just such a way. I am assuming that *The Golden Ass* was written in the 170s or 180s. The chronology of Apuleius' works is controversial, but (*pace* Rohde and Purser who saw signs of youthful exuberance in *The Golden Ass*) the absence of reference to the novel in either the *Apologia* or the *Florida* suggests a late date. See Griffiths, *Isis-Book*, 8, 13; S. J. Harrison, *Apuleius: A Latin Sophist* (Oxford: OUP, 2000), 9–10. On Apuleius in his own time, see also G. Sandy, *The Greek World of Apuleius: Apuleius and the Second Sophistic* (Leiden: Brill, 1997).

[8] H. Dessau laid the groundwork for modern criticism by positing a single author and a 4th-cent. date for the *Historia Augusta*. See 'Über Zeit und Persönlichkeit der *SHA*', *Hermes* 24 (1889), 337–92.

[9] *OCD3*, 713.

[10] T. D. Barnes, *The Sources of the 'Historia Augusta'* (Brussels: Latomus, 1978), 18.

We owe these dates to a *subscriptio* appearing (at the end of Book 9 of the *Metamorphoses*) in Laur. 68. 2 (known as F), the eleventh-century manuscript which constitutes our oldest witness to the texts of the *Metamorphoses*, *Apologia*, and *Florida*:

Ego sallustius legi & eme̲ndaui rome felix. Olib<r>io & pro̲bino | ui̲ris clari̲ssimis consulibus. In foro martis c̲ontroue̲rsia̲m declamans oratori endelechio.| Rursus co̲nstantinupoli recognoui cesario & attico consu̲libus.[11]

(I, Sallustius, read and emended this happily at Rome during the consulship of the Most Honourable Olibrius and Probinus [i.e. AD 395] in the Forum of Mars [i.e. the Forum of Augustus] while practising disputation under the orator Endelechius. I corrected it again at Constantinople under the consulship of Caesarius and Atticus [i.e. AD 397].)

The *subscriptiones* to Books 2–8 and Book 10 merely declare, *ego Sallustius emendaui Romae felix*, but the end of Book 1 of the *Apologia* makes him the namesake of the famous historian (*c.*86–35 BC): *Ego G. CRISPVS SALVSTIVS EMENDAVI ROME FELIX.*[12] The Sallustii are a prominent family in the fourth century, and while the precise identity of this Sallustius is unclear (in Marrou's words, 'nous en [*sc.* Sallustii] connaissons une dizaine, mais rien ne nous permit de choisir entre eux'), he is almost certainly connected with the circle of pagan reactionaries grouped around Quintus Aurelius Symmachus.[13] Saturnius Sallustius Secundus had been a friend of Julian the Apostate (emp. 361–3) and was possibly the author of a treatise, Περὶ θεῶν καὶ κόσμου (*De deis et mundo*), which has been called 'a manual of Neoplatonic piety'.[14] Another Sallustius (*Praefectus urbis Romae* in 386) invited Symmachus to attend his son's wedding in 398—a date which makes the son a likely candidate for identification with Apuleius' editor.[15]

---

[11] Adapted (contractions expanded) from D. S. Robertson, ed., *Apulée: Les Métamorphoses*, vol. i (Paris: Budé, 1940), 101. Cf. O. Pecere, 'Esemplari con *subscriptiones* e tradizione dei testi latini: L'Apuleio Laur. 68,2', in *Atti del convegno internazionale: Il libro e il testo (Urbino, 20–24 settembre 1982)*, ed. C. Questa and R. Raffaelli (Urbino: Università degli studi di Urbino, 1984), 111–38. I am grateful to Dr Mariateresa Horsfall Scotti for sending me a copy of this paper from Rome.

[12] *Apologia*, ed. P. Vallette (Paris: Budé, 1960), c. 65. The common notion that the *nomen*, Crispus, appears in the *subscriptions* in the *Metamorphoses* is a delusion to which not even H.-I. Marrou is immune. See his 'La Vie intellectuelle au Forum de Trajan et au Forum d'Auguste', *Mélanges d'archéologie et d'histoire de l'École française de Rome* 49 (1932), 93–110, at 93.

[13] Marrou, 'La Vie intellectuelle', 94.

[14] *OCD3*, 1349. See A. D. Nock, trans., *Sallustius: Concerning the Gods and the Universe* (Cambridge: CUP, 1926), p. c for Sallustius' denial of the existence of evil *daemones*, and p. 5 for his views on the function of myths (μῦθοι). Pecere ('Esemplari', 116) favours Flavius Sallustius as the author of the treatise.

[15] Symmachus, *Ep.* 6. 35. Cited by H. Bloch, 'The Pagan Revival in the West at the End of the Fourth Century', in *The Conflict between Paganism and Christianity in the Fourth Century*, ed. A. Momigliano (Oxford: Clarendon, 1963), 193–218, at 206.

The fourth century is a period of religious and cultural transformation in the Roman Empire.[16] Christianity, given official endorsement by Constantine the Great (d. 337), suffered temporary eclipse under Julian (d. 363); but the Apostate's campaign to foster the old religion at the expense of the new was reversed by his successors, Gratian's removal of the Altar of Victory from the Senate House in 382 serving as a prelude to the closing of temples and the banning of pagan sacrifice by Theodosius in February 391.[17] The Altar came to serve as a potent symbol of the struggle between the two factions, the plea for its restoration made in 384 by Symmachus (the Prefect of the City) being defeated largely through the influence of Ambrose, Bishop of Milan. The usurper Eugenius, though nominally a Christian, was a friend of Symmachus, had taught rhetoric at Rome, and was sympathetic to the pagan religion. After being proclaimed Augustus in 392, he restored the Altar of Victory; but the hopes of the pagan aristocracy for a permanent return to the old order were cut short by the defeat of 'the last pagan army of the ancient world' at the hands of Theodosius on 6 September 394.[18]

It is tempting to set the Sallustian *subscriptio* in F against this dramatic backdrop of imperial usurpations and Christian/pagan conflict.[19] We might also note the canonical implications of being copied at the end of the fourth century. This was the period when pagans consciously adopted the superior reading technology of the Christians, abandoning the traditional *volumen* in favour of the *codex*, which enabled simultaneous access to different parts of the same text. Apuleius thus cleared one of the first major hurdles facing any ancient text—the transfer from roll to book-form.[20] Yet we might still ask what he is doing in such company. Livy, with his celebration of the traditional values of the Roman Republic, is an obvious subject for editorial attention

---

[16] See, generally, C. N. Cochrane, *Christianity and Classical Culture* (London: OUP, 1940); A. Alföldi, *A Conflict of Ideas in the Later Roman Empire* (Oxford: Clarendon, 1952); J. Geffcken, *The Last Days of Greco-Roman Paganism*, rev. and trans. S. MacCormack (Amsterdam/Oxford: North-Holland, 1978); R. Lane Fox, *Pagans and Christians* (Harmondsworth: Viking, 1986); R. MacMullen, *Christianity and Paganism in the Fourth to Eighth Centuries* (New Haven: YUP, 1997); J. R. Curran, *Pagan City and Christian Capital: Rome in the Fourth Century* (Oxford: OUP, 2000).

[17] Curran (*Pagan City*, 216) calls the law of 391 'the most significant legal point in the history of fourth-century Rome'.

[18] Bloch, 'Pagan Revival', 201. Eugenius had also been *magister scriniorum*, responsible for the imperial chancery.

[19] Recent scholarship has called attention to what Curran (*Pagan City*, 260) calls 'the many limitations of viewing the period as one of pagan-Christian conflict'. Thus A. Cameron, 'Paganism and Literature in Late Fourth Century Rome', *Christianisme et formes littéraires de l'Antiquité tardive en Occident* (Geneva: Fondation Hardt, 1977), 1–30.

[20] See, generally, C. H. Roberts and T. C. Skeat, *The Birth of the Codex* (London: OUP for the British Academy, 1983). Pecere ('Esemplari', 128 ff.) notes that Sallustius' recension was 'certamente un codice', but that vestiges of the original *volumen* format are preserved even in the earliest surviving MS, F (e.g. in the blank spaces left between books).

during a pagan revival; it is difficult to make the same claim for the author of *The Golden Ass*. The answer may be that the pagan reaction was both defensive *and* offensive: while trying to maintain the public observances due to the gods of the old Roman state religion, the reactionaries also supported the more recently imported mystery cults of Eastern deities such as Isis and (in particular) Mithras which were better able to compete with Christianity in popular and personal appeal.[21] Apuleius is one of only a handful of literary figures to appear on the contorniates—'coin-like monuments' from Rome which circulated 'as pagan propaganda' during this period.[22] It would be wrong, however, to see the production of the text as purely a piece of religious propaganda. The literariness of the *Metamorphoses*, its rich vocabulary—at once archaistic and neologistic—and its ingenious use of parody and pastiche must have appealed to the sophisticated palates of the fourth-century pagan aristocracy; and if the lubricious quality of much of the first ten books squares ill with our sense of the decorum of Symmachus' circle, we ought to be mindful of generic considerations. Apuleius' opening sentence proclaims (we should be careful about taking him entirely at his word) the genre to which his work belongs: *sermone isto Milesio uarias fabulas conseram* ('I shall weave together various tales in this Milesian discourse'). James Tatum has provided an account of the genre in his chapter on 'The Notoriety of the Milesian Tale'.[23] Its invention is attributed to Aristides of Miletus in the

---

[21] An Iseum and Serapeum had been built at Rome by Maximian in 354. See Curran, *Pagan City*, 44. Nock (*Sallustius*, p. xlix) observes that Julian 'was a warm adherent of the cult of [the Egyptian] gods; the latter appear frequently on his coins, and are mentioned with reverence in his writings'. In 'Symmachus and the Oriental Cults', *JRS* 63 (1973), 174–95, J. F. Matthews questions the validity of distinguishing between 'traditionalist' and 'orientalist' factions amongst pagans in Rome.

[22] Bloch, 'Pagan Revival', 200. The others include Homer, Euripides, Terence, Sallust, Horace, and Apollonius of Tyana. See A. Alföldi, *Die Kontorniaten: Ein verkanntes Propagandamittel der stadtrömischen heidnischen Aristokratie in ihrem Kampfe gegen das christliche Kaisertum* (Budapest: Magyar Numizmatikai Társulat; Leipzig: Harrassowitz, 1942–3), 90 and 137, and pl. xviii, nr. 9. Alföldi ascribes the Apuleius contorniate to the years 356–94 and (at 137) identifies the image on the reverse as 'Heros vor Tempelchen' ('hero in front of small temple'). The same period also furnishes Isis festival-coins. See Alföldi's *A Festival of Isis under the Christian Emperors of the IVth Century* (Budapest: Pázmány U, 1937). In his review of *Die Kontorniaten*, *JRS* 35 (1945), 115–21, J. M. C. Toynbee questions Alföldi's 'theory that the contorniates were issued by the Roman aristocracy as a vehicle of pagan propaganda' (118), preferring to associate them with public games and spectacles (*ludi*) which may have included 'recitations from the poets, historians, and orators and . . . readings from the lives of sages and popular philosophers. . . . Apuleius and Apollonius of Tyana were particular favourites in the fourth century. . . . We should suspect that their popularity was due to their intrinsic interest rather than to the use which could be made of them to counteract the Christian faith' (121). See, also, J. O'Donnell, 'The Demise of Paganism', *Traditio* 35 (1979), 45–88.

[23] Tatum, *Apuleius*, 92–104. See, also, S. J. Harrison, 'The Milesian Tales and the Roman Novel', *GCN* 9 (1998), 61–73.

second century BC. Almost nothing of his Μιλησιακά (nor of Cornelius Sisenna's Latin translations from the following century) survives; but Plutarch, in his *Life of Crassus* (32) records the literary criticism of the Parthian general, Surena, at the Battle of Carrhae. Having cut off the triumvir's head and hand, Surena ridiculed the Romans for taking the works of Aristides with them into battle.

The Milesian tales of Petronius and Apuleius, Tatum tells us,

also treat of sexual adventures, with an occasional account of the supernatural, and they are never less than indelicate. The lewdness of these tales is often remarked upon. ... [98] ... As a literary form, then, Milesian tales are no more pretentious than a Greek pantomime or a comedy of Plautus; in view of their typical morals, they are usually a good deal less respectable than either.[24]

The status of *Milesiae* is slightly more complicated, however, than Tatum suggests. Ovid points out from exile in Tomis that neither Aristides nor Sisenna was banished, despite the lascivious content of their writings.[25] Yet the most erotic or pornographic scenes in the *Satyricon* and *The Golden Ass* are found, not in the inset Milesian tales (such as Petronius' 'Widow of Ephesus' or the 'Pergamene Boy'), but in the main narratives (e.g the love-scene with Fotis, the ass's interlude with the Corinthian *matrona*). Apuleius, moreover, goes out of his way to emphasize that 'Cupid and Psyche' (hardly noted for its 'lewdness') is also a Milesian tale (*propter Milesiae conditorem*, 4. 32). Sisenna was a Roman of high rank and a historian noted for his vivid literary style; and 'Julius Capitolinus' finds no incongruity in the fact that Clodius Albinus composes Georgics *and* Milesian tales. The very statement that his *Milesiae* were *mediocriter scriptae* suggests that it was possible for Milesian tales to be written well—they constituted a recognized literary genre. Men of action like the Emperor Severus might ridicule them, but they could be fit subjects for literary criticism. The analogy with 'unpretentious' pantomime is thus an imperfect one. *Milesiae* seem, rather, to represent the refurbishing by a literary elite of a popular genre—the *anilis fabula* (the old wives' tale). Sex, brigandage, and the supernatural may supply the subject matter, but the key feature of *Milesiae* appears to be the 'twist in the tail' which delights the reader by defeating his or her expectations. These are short prose narratives, lacking the moral or religious edification of fable or parable, the cathartic effect of tragedy, or the ennobling exempla of epic, possibly employing satirical elements, but without seeking the corrective power of

---

[24] Tatum, *Apuleius*, 97–8.

[25] *Tristia* 2. 413–14: *iunxit Aristides Milesia crimina secum,* | *pulsus Aristides nec tamen urbe sua est*; and 2. 443–4: *vertit Aristiden Sisenna, nec obfuit illi* | *historiae turpis inseruisse iocos.* Cited in *OCD3*, 161.

satire. *Milesiae* seem, indeed, to be closest to the erotic *novelle* of Boccaccio's *Decameron*—in some sense forerunners of the modern short story.

It may, in fact, be no mere coincidence that the anonymous author of the *Historia Augusta* should choose to refer to Apuleius at the very time that a member of Symmachus' circle was preparing an edition of some of Apuleius' 'Carthaginian Milesian tales'. Surena's rough mix of decapitation and anti-Milesian literary judgements (*Life of Crassus*, 32) may have inspired 'Julius Capitolinus' to fabricate Severus' letter to the Senate (or, at least, the *inter Milesias Punicas Apulei sui et ludicra litteraria consenesceret* section of it); but it is also worth considering the possibility that in Clodius Albinus—the defeated second-century usurper and would-be *littérateur*—the historian may be reflecting a very recent usurper, the rhetorician and friend of Symmachus, Eugenius.[26]

APULEIUS AND THE CHURCH

All the evidence, so far, points to the edition of Apuleius being a product of the so-called 'pagan revival'. What complicates the picture is the fact that Sallustius' teacher has been identified with Severus Sanctus Endelechius—a Gallo-Roman rhetorician, friend of Paulinus of Nola (*c*.352–431), and author (*c*.400) of a poem entitled *De mortibus boum*, 'a dialogue between cow-herds' (based on the first of Vergil's *Eclogues*) which 'recommends Christianity as a protection from cattle-plague'.[27] Endelechius' involvement with Apuleius seems at odds with what Markus calls 'a wide-spread hardening among Christians towards secular learning and letters at the end of the fourth century'.[28] Apuleius, moreover, had hardly endeared himself to the Christian cause. The earliest

---

[26] Eugenius suffered the same fate as Albinus (and Crassus) after his defeat: his head was cut off and paraded around the camp. Alföldi's identification of the 'Eugenius' depicted as a charioteer on one of the contorniates with the usurper is dismissed by Toynbee in his review of *Die Kontorniaten*, 119.

[27] *OCD3*, s.v. 'Endelechius', 525. The setting of the *De mortibus boum* suggests that Endelechius hailed from Aquitania. The poem is reproduced in *Anthologia Latina*, ed. F. Buecheler and A. Riese, 2nd edn., 2 vols. (Leipzig: Teubner, 1894–1906), i/2. 334–9 (no. 893). Cf. W. Schmidt, 'Endelechius', *Reallexikon für Antike und Christentum*, ed. T. Klauser, vol. v (Stuttgart: Hiersemann, 1962), 1; T. Alimonti, *Struttura, ideologia ed imitazione virgiliana nel 'De mortibus boum' di Endelechio* (Turin: Giappichelli, 1976); M. Barton, *Spätantike Bukolik zwischen paganer Tradition und christlicher Verkündigung—Das Carmen 'De mortibus boum' des Endelechius* (Trier: WVT, 2000). On the complex interplay between Christian belief and pagan culture in the Ausonius–Paulinus–Endelechius triangle, see M. Roberts, 'Paulinus Poem 11, Virgil's First *Eclogue*, and the Limits of *Amicitia*', *TAPA* 115 (1985), 271–82, esp. 280–1.

[28] R. A. Markus, 'Paganism, Christianity and the Latin Classics in the Fourth Century', in *Latin Literature of the Fourth Century*, ed. J. W. Binns (London: RKP, 1974), 1–21, at 7.

reliable reference to Apuleius relates not to his literary and philosophical writings but to his reputation as a thaumaturge.[29] The Christian apologist Lactantius (*c.*240–*c.*320) was distressed by Apuleius' fame as a magician, rivalling or surpassing Christ. In Book 5 of the *Institutiones diuinae* (written, according to Monat, between 313 and 315) we find the following mention:

Lactantius Diuin. Instit. lib. V. cap. III.

Cum facta eius mirabiliter destrueret, nec tamen negaret; voluit ostendere Apollonium vel paria vel etiam maiora fecisse. Mirum quod Apuleium prætermiserit, cuius solent multa & mira numerari.[30]

(While he [Hierocles] was refuting [Christ's] miracles (without, however, denying them) he tried to show that Apollonius had done things either equal [to Christ] or even greater. It is a wonder that he overlooked Apuleius whose many and extraordinary doings are usually enumerated.)

Lactantius goes on in the next sentence to relish the prospect of Apollonius and his followers (and, by implication, Apuleius and Apuleians) being punished in eternity by the true God.[31] Later, he returns to the same theme:

'Fecit mirabilia': magum putassemus, ut et uos nunc putatis et Iudaei tunc putauerunt, si non illa ipsa facturum prophetae omnes uno spiritu praedicassent. 20. Itaque deum credimus non magis ex factis operibusque mirandis quam ex illa ipsa cruce, quam uos sicut canes lambitis, quoniam simul et illa praedicta est. 21. Non igitur suo testimonio— cui enim de se dicenti potest credi?—, sed prophetarum testimonio, qui omnia quae fecit ac passus est multo ante cecinerunt, fidem diuinitatis accepit, quod neque Apollonio neque Apuleio neque cuiquam magorum potuit aut potest aliquando contingere.[32]

('He performed miracles.' We would have reckoned him a magician—as you now reckon him and the Jews then reckoned him—if all the prophets had not, in a single breath, foretold that he was going to do those things. And so we believe him to be God not from his deeds or his marvellous works, but from that very Cross, which you lick

---

[29] Curran (*Pagan City*, 217) points to the 'unity of purpose in the war against magic and harmful divination, which links all the emperors of the fourth century, Christian and non-Christian alike'.

[30] Wower, sig. [): (9]ᵛ. The modern text in *Lactance: Institutions Divines Livre V*, vol. i, ed. and trans. P. Monat (Paris: Éditions du Cerf, 1973), 141–2, is substantially the same, except for a change of mood (*praetermisit* for *praetermiserit*) and the substitution of passive infinitives (*memorari* for *numerari*). Monat notes (ii. 52): 'Lactance adresse au pamphlétaire un reproche de maître d'école: il a mal utilisé l'exemple traditionnel des magiciens.' Sossianus Hierocles had been using Porphyry in his attack on Christianity.

[31] *Cur igitur, o delirum caput, nemo Apollonium pro deo colit? nisi forte tu solus, illo scilicet deo dignus, cum quo te in sempiternum uerus deus puniet* ('Why then, O foolish man, does no one worship Apollonius as a god? Except perhaps you alone—clearly worthy of this god, along with whom the true God will punish you in Eternity'). See Monat, vol. i, 5. 3. 19–21, p. 144.

[32] Not given by Wower or by Petrus Colvius, ed., *L. Apulei Madaurensis opera omnia* (Leiden: Ex Officina Plantiniana apud Franciscum Raphelengium, 1588). Text in Monat, vol. i, 5. 3. 19, p. 144.

like dogs, since that, too, was predicted at the same time. For he received proof of his divinity not from his own testimony—for what credence can be given to someone talking about himself?—but from the testimony of the prophets who, long before, foretold everything that he did and suffered. This could not have happened to Apollonius or Apuleius or any of those magicians, and never could.)

Lactantius actively advocated the reading of pagan literature, but Lactantian poetics would have had little truck with the fictive excesses of Apuleius' novel. His remark, *Totum autem quod referas fingere, id est ineptum esse et mendacem potius quam poetam* ('To invent all that you present is to be a fool and a liar, rather than a poet') was taken up by Isidore of Seville and became part of the literary theory of the Middle Ages.[33]

Lactantius' attack on Apuleian thaumaturgy was reiterated by other Early Fathers. In the *Breviarum in Psalmos*, a work attributed (doubtfully) to St Jerome (*c*.348–420), a contrast is drawn between the sort of miracles claimed for Apollonius of Tyana and Apuleius, and the miracles of Christ which inspired men to die for their belief:

Hoc enim dicit Porphyrius: Homines rusticani et pauperes, quoniam nihil habebant, magicis artibus operati sunt quaedam signa. Non est autem grande facere signa. Nam fecere signa in Ægypto magi contra Moysen (Exod. VII). Fecit et Apollonius, fecit et Apuleius. Infiniti signa fecerunt. Concedo tibi, Porphyri, magicis artibus signa fecerunt, ut divitias acciperent a divitibus mulierculis, quas induxerant: hoc enim tu dicis. Quare mortui sunt? Quare crucifixi? Fecerunt et alii signa magicis artibus, sed pro [1067] *homine mortuo non sunt mortui, pro homine crucifixo non sunt crucifixi.*[34]

(For Porphyry says this: 'Rustics and paupers, since they had nothing, performed certain miracles with magic arts.' But it is no great thing to make miracles. For the magicians in Egypt performed miracles against Moses (Exodus 7). Apollonius also did this; so did Apuleius. Countless men have performed miracles. I grant you, Porphyry, they have performed miracles with magic arts to get riches from poor wealthy women whom they have captivated: for this you say. What have they died for? For what were they crucified? Others, too, have performed miracles with magic arts; but they have not died for a dead man; they have not been crucified for a crucified man.)

The allusion to the captivation of wealthy women by magic arts could well relate to the charge brought by Sicinius Aemilianus (and defended in the *Apologia*) that Apuleius had used magic to win the hand of the wealthy (and older) widow Pudentilla.[35] But whether the attribution of the *Breviarum in*

---

[33] Lactantius, *Institutiones* 1. 11. 25. Cf. E. R. Curtius, *European Literature and the Latin Middle Ages*, trans. W. R. Trask (London: RKP, 1953, repr. 1979), 454. I am grateful to Dr Oliver Nicholson for pointing me towards this chapter of the *Institutes*.

[34] Commentary on Psalm 81, in *PL* 26, col. 1066.

[35] Ammianus Marcellinus (28. 1. 14), however, records the case of a public advocate named Marinus who, in the wake of investigations begun during the urban prefecture at Rome of

Psalmos is correct or not, we can certainly extrapolate what Jerome's views of *The Golden Ass* would have been from his contemptuous references to the genre to which it belongs. In the *Apologia aduersus libros Rufini*, he derides the 'troop of curly-locks, reciting the fictions of Milesian tales in the schools' (*Quasi non cirratorum turba Milesiarum in scholis figmenta decantet*), while in the *Commentarii in Isaiam prophetam*, he is even more explicit in his attack on pagan taste:

> *Nullus tam imperitus scriptor est, qui lectorem non inveniat similem sui. multoque pars major est Milesias fabellas revolventium, quam Platonis libros. in altero enim ludus et oblectatio est, in altero difficultas et sudor mixtus labori. denique Timaeum de mundi harmonia astrorumque cursu et numeris disputantem ipse qui interpretatus est Tullius se non intelligere confitetur, testamentum autem Grunnii Corocottae porcelli decantant in scholis puerorum agmina cachinnantium....*[36]

(There is no writer so unskilled that he cannot find a reader like himself; and there is a far greater proportion of readers unrolling Milesian tales than the books of Plato. For, in the one, there is sport and delight, in the other, difficulty and sweat mixed with toil. Indeed, even Cicero—the very man who translated the *Timaeus*—confesses that he did not understand his discourses on the harmony of the universe and the course and numbers of the stars; but, in the schools, masses of laughing boys sing the 'Last Will and Testament of Grunnius Corocotta the Little Pig'.)

Given the hostility expressed towards Apuleius by the Christian apologists, how do we account (if the identification is correct) for Endelechius' involvement with Sallustius' edition? The term 'Christian' covers a broad spectrum of commitment (the usurper, Eugenius, was, as we noted, a nominal Christian) and religious colours were often a function of expediency. Distinguished Christian rhetors were working at Rome throughout the 350s, and Julian's decree of 362 excluding them from teaching in the schools caused bitter

---

Q. Clodius Hermogenianus Olybrius (368–70), was charged with having attempted to gain a wife (Hispanilla) by *artibus prauis* ('forbidden arts'). We should note that pagan emperors during this period were as hostile towards magi (especially those involved in private haruspection) as Christian emperors. See Curran, *Pagan City*, 201, 195, and 172–3. P. G. Walsh's statement (*Roman Novel*, 229) that 'In the fourth century, Lactantius, Jerome, [*sc.* and] Ausonius reveal acquaintance with the novel' is inaccurate. Lactantius and Jerome refer to Apuleius explicitly only in connection with magic. Ausonius mentions only Apuleius' (lost) epigrams.

[36] *Apologia aduersus libros Rufini* 1. 17 (*PL* 23, col. 412); *Commentarii in Isaiam prophetam* 12 (*PL* 24, col. 409). On the *Testamentum porcelli* see *OCD3*, 1488. Robert Burton assumes that Jerome is referring to *The Golden Ass* when he mentions *Milesiae fabellae*: 'A farre greater part had rather read Apuleius then Plato: Tully himselfe confesseth he could not understand *Plato's Timæus*, and therefore cared lesse for it, but every schoole-boy hath that famous testament of *Grunnius Corocotta Porcellus* at his fingers ends.' See *The Anatomy of Melancholy*, ed. T. C. Faulkner et al., 6 vols. (Oxford: Clarendon, 1989–200), iii. 5 (= 3.1.1.1).

resentment.[37] Some preferred to follow Julian into apostasy rather than be excluded from participation in the literary culture they loved. Endelechius, we might think, could have been one such tergiversator. But it is also possible that our account, so far, presupposes a polarization between pagan and Christian views of literature which had little basis in actual practice.

Nothing about the fourth century is simple, least of all the skein of religious, cultural, and political relations between paganism and Christianity. Tertullian's cry at the beginning of the third century, *Quid ergo Athenis et Hierosolymis? quid academiae et ecclesiae?* ('What has Athens to do with Jerusalem? What has the Academy to do with the Church?') represents only one facet of the early Church's response to its secular cultural inheritance.[38]

Many of the leading figures of the late fourth and early fifth centuries exhibit a kind of intellectual doublethink—the ability to maintain two parallel but contradictory sets of values. Moreover, the gossamer web of *amicitia*, with its attendant privileges and responsibilities, unites Christian and pagan alike. The issues at stake were of fundamental importance—the preservation of the cultural and religious heritage that had supposedly made Rome great; and the turning from the City of Man towards the City of God—yet the 'real issues' are often concealed by a veil of etiquette. On the one hand, there is the sense of what Markus calls 'shadow-boxing' in the polemics between Christians and pagans—an antiquarian academicism which refuses to engage with contemporary figures and events.[39] On the other hand, a pagan such as Virius Nicomachus Flavianus—an editor of Livy, a translator of Philostratus (the Life of Apollonius of Tyana), and a close friend of Symmachus—was sufficiently moved to commit suicide after the defeat of the 'pagan reaction' in 394.[40] In the anonymous *Carmen contra paganos* (generally held to be aimed at Virius Nicomachus Flavianus), a Roman *praefectus* is derided for his belief in a variety of deities, including Egyptian ones such as Sarapis, Anubis, Isis, and Osiris.[41] Towards the end of the poem, we are left with an image of the

---

[37] Markus, 'Paganism', 2–3.

[38] *De praescriptione haereticorum ad martyras: ad scapulam,* ed. T. Herbert Bindley (Oxford: Clarendon, 1893), cap. 7, pp. 40–1. In the same chapter, Tertullian (echoing St Paul in 1 Timothy 1: 4) also attacks fables (*illae fabulae et genealogiae interminabiles, et quaestiones infructuosae, et sermones serpentes velut cancer,* p. 40) and intellectual curiosity (*Nobis curiositate opus non est post Christum Iesum, nec inquisitione post evangelium,* p. 41). On the other hand, Tertullian also asks, in *De idololatria* 10, *Quomodo repudiamus saecularia studia, sine quibus divina non possunt?* ('How do we repudiate secular studies without which divine studies cannot exist?'). Quoted by H. Hagendahl, *Latin Fathers and the Classics: A Study on the Apologists, Jerome and other Christian Writers* (Göteburg: [Elanders boktr. aktiebolag; distr.: Almqvist & Wiksell, Stockholm], 1958), 109 n. 1.

[39] Markus, 'Paganism', 8.

[40] Ibid. 8, 11. On Nicomachus, see Bloch, 'Pagan Revival', 210.

[41] See, generally, J. F. Matthews, 'The Historical Setting of the *Carmen contra paganos* (Cod. Par. Lat. 8084)', *Historia* 19 (1970), 464–79.

credulous pagan which resembles the closing shot of Lucius as the shaven-headed and (potentially risible) devotee of Isis (*AA* 11. 30):

> *quis te plangentem non risit, calvus ad aras*
> *sistriferam Phariam supplex cum forte rogares...*[42]

(Who did not laugh at you as you wailed, when, perchance, bald-headed before the altars, you were beseeching the rattle-waving Isis in supplication?)

If we find it curious that a Christian rhetor such as Endelechius should be expounding an author so intimately connected with pagan values in 395—at a time when 'the age-old tensions between paganism and Christianity were once again as sharply crystallised as they were never again to be'[43]—we should bear in mind that paradox is the operative principle of the period and that it was difficult, in any case, for polemicists on either side to gain a detached perspective on the common rhetorical and artistic culture that had produced them.

Symmachus' career is eloquent of such complexities. Despite the imprudence of having addressed a panegyric to the usurper Maximus in 388, he seems to have escaped retribution, rising to the consulship in 391.[44] Nor does his championing of the pagan cause appear to have occluded his friendships with Christian *literati*. He met the poet Ausonius of Bordeaux (*c.*310–95) in 369 during a visit to Gaul. Ausonius became, in about 364, tutor to the young Gratian and, though sufficiently committed a Christian to be fastidious in his Eastertide observances, was well disposed towards pagan culture. His favourite pupil was Paulinus of Nola, the author of a (lost) panegyric (suggested by, and dedicated to Endelechius) commemorating Theodosius' victory over Eugenius in 394.[45] Ausonius defends the explicitness of the *consummatio matrimonii* scene in his *Cento nuptialis* by reference to other writers who have been lascivious in their poetry, but chaste in their personal lives:

meminerint autem, quippe eruditi... esse Apuleium in uita philosophum, in epigrammatis amatorem;[46]

---

[42] *Anthologia latina*, ed. D. R. Shackleton Bailey (Stuttgart: Teubner, 1982), vol. i, fasc. 1, pp. 17–23, at 22 (vv. 98–9).

[43] Markus, 'Paganism', 12.

[44] Bloch, 'Pagan Revival', 197.

[45] H. Isbell, 'Decimus Magnus Ausonius: The Poet and his World', in *Latin Literature of the Fourth Century*, ed. Binns, 22–57, at 34 and 50–3. Paulinus refers to Endelechius' role in the panegyric in a letter (*Ep.* 28. 6) to Sulpicius Severus. Roberts ('Paulinus Poem 11', 281) raises the possibility that 'Paulinus, in turn, proposed to Endelechius the subject for his Christian pastoral', the *De mortibus boum*. Cf. D. E. Trout, *Paulinus of Nola: Life, Letters, and Poems* (Berkeley and Los Angeles: U of California P, 1999), au 110–11.

[46] *Opuscula*, ed. S. Prete (Leipzig: Teubner, 1978), 168–9; *The Works of Ausonius*, ed. R. P. H. Green (Oxford: Clarendon, 1991), 139 and 525. Cf. E. Haight, *Apuleius and his Influence*

(But let them remember, learned as they are, that Apuleius is a philosopher in his life, but a lover in his epigrams.)

Most importantly of all, Symmachus patronized Augustine (354–430) when the latter aspired to become a man of letters. It was Symmachus, indeed, who recommended Augustine to Ambrose, Bishop of Milan, as a teacher of rhetoric in 384.[47] Augustine had been to school in Apuleius' home town of Madauros (366–9) and, like the speaker of Apuleius' prologue, he had experienced in Italy the paradox of being simultaneously an accomplished rhetorician and a *rudis locutor* (*AA* 1. 1).[48] Apuleius' account of Lucius' affair with Fotis may also have had a particular resonance for Augustine who spent some fifteen years (*c.*370–85) in a state of concubinage with a woman who is generally thought to have been a slave or ex-slave.[49]

Can we discern any influence of *The Golden Ass* upon the *Confessions* (written at some point between 397 and 401)?[50] Both depict the fall, suffering, and redemption of a well-born young man; both involve a combination of *curiositas* and sexual indulgence; both comprise an odd number of books. In each case, moreover, the conclusion seems (at first glance, at least) to be out of kilter with the bulk of the work.[51] Whether we see evidence here of deliberate allusion, unconscious echoes, or merely the congruences to be expected in any two conversion narratives, there is no doubt that Augustine knew Apuleius' works. In 412, he and Marcellinus were both cultivating a nobly born pagan,

(London: Harrap, 1927), 95. Ausonius' reference is overlooked by the Renaissance editors, but we need not imply a direct acquaintance with the lost epigrams. He may merely be recalling Apuleius' own statement to this effect in *Apologia* 9–11.

[47] *Confessions* 5. 13. 23; T. D. Barnes, 'Augustine, Symmachus and Ambrose', in *Augustine: From Rhetor to Theologian*, ed. J. McWilliam (Waterloo, Ont.: Wilfrid Laurier UP, 1992), 7–13; N. McLynn, 'Symmachus', in *Augustine through the Ages: An Encyclopedia*, gen. ed. A. D. Fitzgerald (Grand Rapids, Mich.: Eerdmans, 1999), 820–1.

[48] *De ordine* 2. 17. 45; P. Brown, *Augustine of Hippo: A Biography* (London: Faber, 1967), 88 n. 1.

[49] *Confessions* 6. 15. 25; G. Bonner, *St Augustine of Hippo: Life and Controversies*, 3rd edn. (Norwich: Canterbury P, 2002), 56 and 78; K. Power, 'Concubine/Concubinage', in *Augustine through the Ages*, 222–3.

[50] See P. Courcelle, *Les Confessions de Saint Augustin dans la tradition littéraire: Antécédents et postérité* (Paris: Études augustiniennes, 1963), 101–9; R. Martin, 'Apulée, Virgile, Augustin: Réflexions nouvelles sur la structure des *Confessions*', *Revue des études latines* 68 (1990), 136–50; N. Shumate, *Crisis and Conversion in Apuleius' 'Metamorphoses'* (Ann Arbor: U of Michigan P, 1996). H. Hagendahl doubts 'any connection between the two works'. See *Augustine and the Latin Classics*, 2 vols. (Göteborg: Acta Universitatis Cothoburgensis, 1967), ii. 687. For the terminal dates of the *Confessions*, see F. van Fleteren, '*Confessiones*', in *Augustine through the Ages*, 227.

[51] Books 11–13 of the *Confessions* are devoted to an exegesis of Genesis, but the second-time reader will notice that the conclusion has been anticipated in earlier books. The famous episode of the stolen pears (*Confessions* 2. 4. 9 ff.), for example, is typologically linked with the Edenic theft of fruit (Genesis 3).

Volusianus, who was disposed to favour Christianity, but held back because of the conflict he perceived between divine and civic duties.[52] Volusianus becomes the excuse for an orchestrated exchange of questions and answers, objections and refutations, concerning the Faith. The debate over Christian versus pagan thaumaturgy figures yet again:

Marcellinus ad D. Augustinum. [= Ep. 136]

In quibus nihil aliud Dominum, quam alij homines facere potuerunt fecisse vel legisse [PL: gessisse] mentiuntur. Apollonium siquidem suum nobis & Apuleium, aliosque Magicæ artis homines in medium proferunt, quorum maiora contendunt extitisse miracula.[53]

(...in which they falsely declare that our Lord did nothing more than other men could have done or performed. Indeed they bring forward into our midst their Apollonius and Apuleius and the other men of the magic art whose miracles they claim to have been greater.)

Jerome had scoffed that no one was prepared to die on account of Apuleius' miracles. Augustine argues that Apuleius' magical powers cannot have been very great since he was unable, despite the advantages of birth and his manifest ambitions, to rise to high political rank:

D. Augustinus Epist. V [= Ep. 138]

Quis autem vel risu dignum non putet, quod Apollonium & Apuleium, ceterosque artium Magicarum peritissimos conferre Christo, vel etiam præferre conantur?

Apuleius enim, [PL: ut de illo potissimum loquamur] qui nobis Afris Afer est notior, non dico ad regnum, sed nec ad aliquam qui[):(10]ʳ dem iudiciariam potestatem cum omnibus suis Magicis artibus potuit peruenire: honesto patriæ suæ loco natus, & liberaliter educatus, magnaque præditus eloquentia. An forte ista, vt Philosophus, voluntate contemsit, cui cum sacerdos prouinciæ, pro magno fuit: vt munera ederet venatoresque vestiret, & pro statua sibi apud Oeenses locanda, ex qua ciuitate habebat vxorem, aduersus contradictionem quorundam ciuium litigaret? Quod posteros ne lateret eiusdem litis orationem scriptam memoriæ commendauit. Quod ergo ad istam terrenam pertinet felicitatem, fuit magnus quoad potuit. Vnde apparet eum nihil amplius fuisse, non quia non voluit, sed quia non potuit. Quamquam & aduersus quosdam, qui ei Magicarum artium crimen intenderant, eloquentissimè se defendit.[54]

[PL continues: Vnde miror laudatores ejus, qui eum nescio quæ fecisse miracula illis artibus, prædicant, contra ejus defensionem testes esse conari. Sed viderint utrum verum ipsi perhibeant testimonium, et ille falsam defensionem.]

---

[52] I take the dates (but not the English version) from J. G. Cunningham, trans., *Letters of Saint Augustine, Bishop of Hippo* (Edinburgh: T. & T. Clark, 1872–5). Cf. *The Works of Saint Augustine: A Translation for the 21st century. Part 2, Letters. Vol. 2, Letters 100–155*, trans. and annot. R. Teske; ed. B. Ramsey (Hyde Park, NY: New City P, 2003), 210–11.
[53] Wower, sig. [):(9]ᵛ; *PL* 33, col. 514.   [54] Ibid. [):(9]ᵛ–[):(10]ʳ.

(But who would not consider it worthy of laughter that they attempt to compare Apollonius and Apuleius, and those others who are most experienced in magic arts, with Christ, or even prefer them to him? [*A long attack on Apollonius follows*] For Apuleius [to speak most about him] who, as an African is better known to us Africans, was unable with all his magic arts to achieve, I do not say kingship, but even judicial power—though born in a noble part of his homeland, given a liberal education, and gifted with great eloquence. Or did he perhaps, as a philosopher, despise such things—he who, as priest of the province, considered it so important to give games and equip gladiatorial hunters and who took legal action against certain citizens who opposed the erection of a statue of him amongst the people of Oea, the city from which he obtained a wife? Lest this be concealed from those who came after him, he committed to record the speech of this lawsuit.

In terms, therefore, of what pertains to that earthly happiness, he was as great as he could be. Hence it is clear that he was no greater not because he did not want to be but because he was not able to be. Although he also defended himself most eloquently against certain people who brought a charge of magic arts against him.

[Hence I am amazed at his praisers (who preach that he performed I know not what miracles by those arts) trying to be witnesses against his own defence. But let them see whether they themselves provide the true testimony, and he, the false defence.])

Augustine's engagement with Apuleius was deeper than these excerpts might suggest. Indeed, it has been said that 'No post-classical Latin author has such a place in Augustine's writings [681] as Apuleius.'[55] Augustine began the *De ciuitate dei* in 413, three years after the sacking of Rome by Alaric the Goth. In Book 8, having admitted that Platonism, of all pagan philosophies, comes closest to the Truth, he refutes the 'Platonic' theory of *daemones*, using, as the focus of his attack, the *De deo Socratis* of Apuleius.[56] Augustine rejects Apuleius' thesis that *daemones* mediate between men and gods, arguing, instead, that they are evil spirits—'demons' in the modern sense of the word. Apuleius' *daemones*, Plato's expulsion of the Poet (*Rep.* 398a), and the perniciousness of stage-plays are all intertwined in a discussion which will have significant cultural and philosophical resonances over the course of the next twelve centuries or more.[57] One of the *De ciuitate dei*'s more curious progeny is the *Anonymi contra philosophos*, in which Augustine's refutations of pagan philosophy are recast in dialogue form, and Apuleius appears as an interlocutor speaking in the first person.[58]

---

[55] Hagendahl, *Augustine*, ii. 680–1.

[56] *De ciuitate dei* 8. 14–22. See, generally, G. O'Daly, *Augustine's 'City of God': A Reader's Guide* (Oxford: Clarendon, 1999), 115–21; V. Hunink, '*Apuleius, qui nobis afris afer est notior*: Augustine's Polemic against Apuleius in *De Civitate Dei*', *Scholia* NS 12 (2003), 82–95.

[57] The Protestants who turned to Augustine in support of their doctrine of predestination would also find ammunition here for their attacks on the theatre.

[58] ed. D. Aschoff, CCSL 58A (Turnhout: Brepols, 1975).

The *Apologia* and *The Golden Ass* are also introduced into the *De ciuitate dei* as part of Augustine's attack on Apuleian daemonology:

Lib. IIX. cap. XIX.

Ipse Apuleius nunquid apud iudices Christianos de magicis artibus accusatus est? Huius Philosophi Platonici copiosissima & disertissima extat oratio, qua crimen artium magicarum alienum à se esse defendit; seque aliter non vult innocentem videri, nisi ea negando, quæ non possent ab innocente committi.

(Was Apuleius himself accused of witchcraft before Christian judges? There is extant a most eloquent and learned speech of this Platonic philosopher in which he fends off the charge of witchcraft as having nothing to do with him; and he does not wish himself to be seen to be innocent except by denying those things which could not be committed by an innocent man.)

In Book 18, while discussing the 'transformations which seem to happen to men by the craft of demons', Augustine makes a passing reference to *The Golden Ass*—but one crucial to the subsequent reception of the novel:

Lib. XVIII. cap. XVIII

Nam & nos cum essemus in Italia, audiebamus talia de quadam regione illarum partium: vbi [):(11]ᵛ stabularias mulieres imbutas his malis artibus in cæseo dare dicebant, quibus vellent seu possent viatoribus, vnde in iumenta illicò verterentur, & necessaria quæque portarent, postque perfuncta opera iterum ad se redirent nec tamen in eis mentem fieri bestialem, sed rationalem humanamque seruari. sicut Apuleius in libris, quos titulo Asini aurei inscripsit, sibi ipsi accidisse, vt accepto veneno, humano animo permanente, asinus fieret, aut iudicauit, aut finxit.[59]

(For when we were in Italy, we heard such things of a certain region in those parts where (they said) lady innkeepers, steeped in these wicked arts, used to give [substances] in cheese to any travellers they wished to (or were able to), whereby they were changed on the spot into pack-animals and carried whatever was required and, upon completion of the task, returned to their true selves. Their mind, however, did not become bestial, but remained rational and human, just as Apuleius, in those books which he inscribed with the title *The Golden Ass*, either believed or feigned to have happened to himself—that, on taking poison, he became an ass while his mind remained human.)

This passage is the earliest instance of the title *De asino aureo* being used for Apuleius' novel.[60] Sallustius' *subscriptio* gives only the one title, *Metamorphoses*, the result, perhaps, of the attempt to promote the work as an elevated piece of pagan propaganda while dissociating it from the realms of vulgar storytelling implied by the alternative title. Augustine had had strong links with the literary

---

[59] Wower, sig. [):(11]ʳ⁻ᵛ.

[60] Winkler (*Auctor*, 294–5) uses Augustine's testimony to support his thesis that the original title was double. Cf. Colvius on alternative titles; Sandy, *Greek World*, 233–4; Harrison, *Latin Sophist*, 210 n. 1.

circle from which Sallustius' recension had sprung. His use of the alternative title implies that it is by this name that he expects his readers to recognize the work. Sallustius', clearly, was not the only text in circulation during the fifth century.[61]

Augustine's attitude towards such miracles is ambivalent. His immediate response to the Apuleian passage sounds sceptical: *Haec vel falsa sunt vel tam inusitata, ut merito non credantur* ('These things are either false or so unusual that they might deservedly not be believed'). He is willing to concede, however, that demons might be able to change the *appearance* of things created by the true God, so that they seem to be what they are not (*specie tenus, quae a vero Deo sunt creata, commutant, ut videantur quod non sunt*). Neither the soul nor even the body can truly be changed by the power of demons, but a man's phantom (*phantasticum hominis*) may appear to others in the form of some animal and the man himself may imagine that he is such a creature. Augustine cites the case of a certain Praestantius (one of those people 'whom we could never consider to have lied to us', *quos nobis non existimaremus fuisse mentitos*) whose father took the potion in some cheese and fell into a deep, unbreakable sleep. Upon waking, some days later, he told how it had seemed that he was 'transformed into a horse and, along with other pack-animals, carried grain to soldiers' (*caballum se . . . factum annonam inter alia iumenta baiulasse militibus*). It was then discovered that this had happened just as he had said.

Amongst the mass of scholia on Horace which has come down to us under the name of the second-century critic Helenius Acro, is a confusing reference to Apuleius' novel.[62] Prompted by Horace's passing allusion to reincarnation in *Epode* 15. 21 (*nec te Pythagorae fallat arcana renati*, 'neither do the secrets of Pythagoras reborn deceive you'), pseudo-Acro observes:

Vnde etiam Apuleius dicit similiter animam suam fuisse in corpore asini et meminisse deuexisse plurima sagmata et onera in Egiptum. Vnde etiam facit librum quendam, quem appellat de aureo asino . . .

(Whence also Apuleius says similarly that his soul was in the body of an ass and remembered having carried a great many pack-saddles and burdens into Egypt. Whence he also makes a certain book which he calls *Concerning the Golden Ass*.)[63]

---

[61] See M. Horsfall Scotti, 'Apuleio tra magia e filosofia: la riscoperta di Agostino', in *Dicti studiosus: Scritti di filologia offerti a Scevola Mariotti dai suoi allievi* (Urbino: QuattroVenti, 1990), 297–320.

[62] According to R. A. Kaster (*OCD3*, 675), the 'attribution to Acro does not antedate the Renaissance'.

[63] *Pseudacronis scholia in Horatium vetustiora*, ed. O. Keller, 2 vols. (Leipzig: Teubner, 1902–04), ii. 387. Colvius and Wower reproduce the *scholium* in slightly different form. Thus, Wower, sig. [ ]:(11]ᵛ: *Simili modo etiam Apuleius scribit de Asino aureo, animam suam fuisse in corpore asini, meminisseque se deuexisse plurima segmenta & onera in Ægyptum* ('In a similar way Apuleius also writes about *The Golden Ass* that his soul was in the body of an ass and that he remembered that he had carried a great many trimmings and burdens into Egypt').

The earliest of the three recensions of pseudo-Acronic scholia dates from the fifth century, while the reference to Apuleius appears in an eleventh- or twelfth-century manuscript known as the *Codex Franekeranus*.[64] The strange notion of the asinine Apuleius carrying burdens into Egypt suggests a hasty reading (or faded memory) of Augustine—a conflation of the separate references to Praestantius and Apuleius.

Most of the passages from Augustine have dealt with the credence to be accorded to miracles, the debate over poets and fictions imposing itself only indirectly on the subject matter. But a letter written by Augustine in 409 in reply to Deogratias is interesting because it deals directly with *narratives* about miracles. According to Deogratias, one of the principal sources of amusement for the pagan ridiculers of Christianity is the credence given to the absurd story of Jonah surviving three days (with his clothes on!) in the belly of a whale.[65] Augustine had been invited to supply a figurative interpretation of the passage (*Aut si figura est, hanc dignaberis pandere*), but while he points out the symbolic meaning (a foreshadowing of Christ's three days in the tomb), he insists on the literal truth of the story:

Neque enim debent unum aliquid tanquam incredibile proponere, et in quæstionem vocare, sed omnia quæ vel talia, vel etiam mirabiliora narrantur. Et tamen si hoc quod de Jona scriptum est, Apuleius Madaurensis, vel Apollonius Tyaneus fecisse diceretur, quorum multa mira nullo fideli auctore jactitant, quamvis et dæmones nonnulla faciant Angelis sanctis similia, non veritate sed specie, non sapientia sed plane fallacia: tamen, si de istis, ut dixi, quos magos vel philosophos laudabiliter nominant, tale aliquid narraretur, non jam in buccis creparet risus, sed typhus. Ita rideant Scripturas nostras: quantum possunt rideant, dum per singulos rariores paucioresque se videant, vel moriendo vel credendo;[66]

(Nor should they put forward only one thing as being unbelievable and call it into question; but all [stories] that are told, either like this or even more marvellous. But if Apuleius of Madaura or Apollonius of Tyana were said to have done this which is written of Jonah—people (without any reliable authority) keep bringing up their marvellous doings, although demons can also do some things similar to Angels, not in truth but in appearance, not through wisdom but deceit—but if, as I said, such a tale were told concerning those men whom they flatteringly call magicians or philosophers, laughter would no longer rattle in their cheeks, but pride. So, let them

---

[64] Leeuwarden, Provinciale Bibliotheek B.A. Fr. 45. Keller notes (*praefatio* to vol. i, p. ix): 'f est codex Franekeranus, nunc Leeuwardensis 45, olim Cluniacensis, saec. XI–XII'.

[65] On Jerome's response to pagan incredulity at the story of Jonah, see his commentary, *In Ionam* (*PL* 25, cols. 1171–1208), 406 (on Daphne and Phaethon in Ovid's *Met.*), and Hagendahl, *Latin Fathers and the Classics*, 211.

[66] *Ep.* 102 (*PL* 33, col. 383). Colvius (sig. [*7]ᵛ) and Wower (sig. [):(10]ʳ) also note the allusion.

laugh at our Scriptures; let them laugh as much as they can, while, day by day, they see themselves thinner and fewer, either through death or conversion.)

Even as Augustine glories in the demise of his pagan opponents, we see the atrophy (or perhaps, more actively, the forced starvation) of the critical faculties necessary to deal with literary fictions. This is, on Augustine's part, of course, disingenuous. He had been steeped in pagan literature and rhetoric from an early age—Vergil had been his first and chiefest love—yet he rejects, in the *Confessions*, the 'poetic fictions' that had so enticed him as a boy.[67] There is no place, in the scheme presented here in the *De ciuitate dei*, for what the nineteenth century, groping towards an expression of what occurs when we read fiction, called the 'suspension of disbelief'. The first question that Augustine asks when confronted by a narrative is, 'Did this happen?' In the case of a biblical narrative, the answer is 'yes', though the incident is *recorded*, he says, because of the symbolic meaning it carries. His response to Apuleius' narrative is to say that the incident is probably too incredible to have taken place, but if it did, it was the work of demons who may alter the appearance (but not the substance) of the material world.

The debate over the veridical status of the Jonah-narrative is of profound and lasting significance for the development of fiction. In *Lectures upon Ionas, Deliuered at Yorke in the Yeare of our Lord 1594*, a future bishop of London, John King, refurbishes patristic polemic in his attack upon the contemporary vogue for 'frivolous stories'.[68] The Psalms of David, he says, contain all the poetry one could wish to find in the pagan poets, while the account of Jonah's travails and adventures satisfies the human appetite for narrative, without straying into the unnecessary waters of fiction:

I haue hearde the descriptions both of auncient Poets, and of those in our latter daies, Tassus, Ariostus, and the like so highly extolled, as if wisedome had lived and died with them alone. And it may be *the sinne of Samaria,* the sin of this lande and age of ours (perhappes the mother of our atheisme) to commit idolatry with such bookes, that insteed of the writings of Moses and the prophets, and Evangelists, which were wont to lie in our windowes as the principall ornaments, & to sit in the vppermost roumes as the best guests in our houses, now we haue Arcadia, & the Faëry Queene, and

---

[67] e.g. *Confessions*, 1. 13: *dulcissimum spectaculum vanitatis equus ligneus plenus armatis, et Troiae incendium, atque ipsius umbra Creusae* ('the Wooden Horse filled with armed men, and the burning of Troy, and the ghost of Creusa herself [provided] the most delightful show of unreality').

[68] (Oxford: Joseph Barnes, 1597). King (*c*.1559–1621) became bishop of London in 1611, having also been dean of Christ Church, Oxford (1605), and vice-chancellor of the University of Oxford (1607–10). He was happy to cite Apuleius when it suited him. In *A sermon preached at White-Hall the 5. day of November. ann. 1608* (Oxford: Joseph Barnes, 1608), he quotes from Isis' speech (*AA* 11. 5): 'And let those … *trilingues Siculi,* as [28] *Apuleius* called the *Sicilians,* togither with all their companions, craftesmasters for fraud and forgerie, resigne to the Jesuits' (27–8).

Orlando Furioso, with such like frivolous stories: when if the wanton students of our time (for all are students, both [356] men and women in this idle learning) would as carefully read and as studiously obserue the eloquent narrations and discourses contained in the Psalmes of David and other sacred bookes, they would finde them to be such, as best deserued the name & commendation of the best Poets. So rightly did Ierome pronounce of David to Paulinus, that he is our *Simonides, Pindarus, Alceus, Flaccus, Catullus, Serenus,* & in steed of al others. For the warrant of my sayings, consider but this scripture now in hand.[69]

ON THE BRINK OF THE MIDDLE AGES: APULEIUS IN TRANSITION

Ambrosius Theodosius Macrobius (*fl. c.*430)

The main conduits linking classical and early medieval thought are the encyclopaedists of late antiquity. The commentaries, compilations, and condensations of learning (usually given at several removes from the sources they claim to be quoting) of Calcidius, Macrobius, Martianus Capella, Boethius, Cassiodorus, and Isidore of Seville supplied the early Middle Ages with most of their knowledge of the ancient world and much of what they thought they needed to know about their own.

Ambrosius Theodosius Macrobius was possibly Augustine's contemporary.[70] His *Saturnalia*—'perhaps the most outstanding document of the pagan revival'—is a compendium of learning (ostensibly designed as a source of instruction for his son) presented in the dialogue-form of a symposium held sometime before 385 and attended by the leading pagans of the day—Symmachus, Praetextatus, Nicomachus Flavianus, and many others.[71] One chapter is devoted to the nature of gibes or jests (*scommata*), the varied responses to be expected to them, and the contexts in which they might be used or should be avoided. Macrobius' character Eustathius (a Greek) ends the discussion by warning the young Avienus (a fellow-guest) to refrain from

[69] *Lectures upon Ionas*, 355–6.

[70] For the problem of dating, see L. Scarpa, ed., *Macrobii Ambrosii Theodosii commentariorum in Somnium Scipionis libri duo* (Padua: Liviana, 1981), 3–16. The *Saturnalia*, says Scarpa (4), was clearly composed at some time between 383/4 and 485 but 'una soluzione certa non si raggiunga' (16). A. Cameron gives what Markus ('Paganism', 14) calls a 'wholly convincing' date of 'soon after 431' for the *Saturnalia*. Cf. *OCD3*, 906–7. See 'The Date and Identity of Macrobius', *JRS* 56 (1966), 25–38.

[71] Bloch, 'Pagan Revival', 207. The setting is, of course, fictitious and anachronistic, many of the participants being too young in 385 to have taken part in such a symposium.

scommata at dinner parties and to stick, instead, to proposing or opposing motions for debate (*quaestiones conuiuiales*). Such dinner-party debates are sanctioned by eminent authority: Aristotle, Plutarch, and 'your own Apuleius' (*uester Apuleius*) had all written them and 'what has earned the attention of so many philosophers should not be despised'.[72] This excerpt is interesting mainly for the heady company in which Apuleius is placed. *Vester Apuleius*, as spoken by a Greek, may mean no more than 'Apuleius, like you, a Roman'; yet we should remember that Apuleius was an African by birth, claimed to write equally in Greek and Latin, and was closer, in many ways, to the Greek writers of the Second Sophistic than to his Roman contemporaries. *Vester Apuleius* may well mean 'your beloved Apuleius', reflecting the special place he held in the affections of the *littérateurs* of the pagan aristocracy.

A still more significant reference occurs in 'that second Bible of medieval men', Macrobius' Neoplatonist commentary on Cicero's *The Dream of Scipio*, where Macrobius attempts to establish the proper position of fiction in relation to philosophy—a relationship which is of central importance to the status of fiction in the Middle Ages and beyond.[73] *The Dream of Scipio* ('one of the most precious compositions in Cicero's entire collection') comes at the end of Book 6 of the *De republica*.[74] From late antiquity until the discovery of a palimpsest in 1820, this was the only portion of the complete work extant, its survival during the Middle Ages and Renaissance being due to its inclusion in Macrobius' commentary. Cicero's *Republic* owes much to Plato's treatise of the same name, and Cicero, like Plato, employs a visionary fiction at the end of his philosophical work. Plato closes his *Republic* (Book 10) with the Vision of Er, a soldier who revives on the funeral pyre ten days after being slain in battle and gives an account, from his experience in the world beyond, of the transmigration of souls. Cicero chooses as a mouthpiece, not a common soldier, but a famous general, Scipio Africanus Maior, making him appear in a dream to his adoptive

[72] *Saturnalia* 7. 3: *Quod genus ueteres ita ludicrum non putarunt: ut & Aristoteles de ipsis aliqua conscripserit & Plutarchus & uester Apuleius. Nec contemnendum si: quod tot philosophantium curam meruit* ('So far were the ancients from considering this category as sport that Aristotle wrote some things about these, as did Plutarch and your Apuleius; and what has earned the attention of so many philosophers should not be despised'). Text from *ed. princ.* of Macrobius' works (Venice: N. Jensen, 1472) (no signatures or folio numbers). The passage is quoted by John of Salisbury in *Policraticus: Of the Frivolities of Courtiers and the Footprints of Philosophers*, Book VIII (290).
[73] The biblical accolade is from D. C. Allen, *Mysteriously Meant: The Rediscovery of Pagan Symbolism and Allegorical Interpretation in the Renaissance* (Baltimore: Johns Hopkins P, 1970), 209. See, generally, T. Whittaker, *Macrobius, or Philosophy, Science and Letters in the Year 400* (Cambridge: CUP, 1923).
[74] The appraisal is that of W. H. Stahl, trans. and introd., *Macrobius: Commentary on the Dream of Scipio* (New York: Columbia UP, 1952), 10. Short passages from the *De republica* had also been preserved by Augustine in the *De ciuitate dei*.

grandson, Scipio Africanus Minor, who razed Carthage in 146 BC. Cicero (following the example of Plato) had certainly made use of the devices of fiction in setting his philosophical dialogues and delineating the characters of his speakers, but the *Dream of Scipio* exhibits a special creative and imaginative richness, a fictive bounty exceptional in the Ciceronian canon.

Fiction and Truth have long shared an uneasy relationship. At the beginning of the *Commentarii in Somnium Scipionis*, Macrobius responds to Epicurus' disciple Colotes (who had attacked Plato's use of fiction in the Vision of Er) by categorizing the types of fiction which are admissible and inadmissible in philosophical discourse:

Nec omnibus fabulis repugnat philosophia nec omnibus acquiescit: & ut facile secerni possit: quæ ex his ab se abdicet: ac uelut profana ab ipso uestibulo sacræ disputationis excludat: quæue etiam sæpe ac libenter admittat diuisionum gradibus explicandum. Fabulæ quarum nomen indicat falsi professionem: aut tantum conciliandæ auribus uoluptatis: aut adhortationis quoque in bonam frugem gratia repertæ sunt: auditum mulcent uelut comœdiæ quales Menander eiusue imitatores agendas dederunt: uel argumenta fictis casibus amatorum referta. Quibus uel multum se Arbiter exercuit: uel Apuleium nonnumquam lusisse miramur. Hoc totum fabularum genus quod solas aurium delicias profitetur e sacrario suo in nutricum cunas sapientiæ tractatus eliminat.[75]

(Philosophy is not opposed to all stories; nor does it assent to them all. And so that it might easily be discerned which of these it disowns and excludes, as profane, from the very entrance of sacred disputation, and which it frequently and even gladly admits, the degrees of differences need to be explained. Fables (their name indicates the acknowledgement of falsity) are devised either for the sake merely of procuring pleasure for the ears or, also, for the sake of an encouragement towards virtue. They delight the ear as do the comedies which Menander or his imitators gave for performance, or the writings crammed with the fictitious mishaps of lovers in which Petronius busied himself greatly or in which Apuleius (to our amazement) amused himself on occasion. The whole class of stories which promises only the delighting of ears, the discourse of Philosophy removes from its own shrine to the cradles of wet-nurses.)

Macrobius expresses his surprise that a serious philosopher like Apuleius should have wasted time in frivolous amusements. The *Satyricon* and *The Golden Ass* are banished at a single stroke to the nursery, along with all other forms of fiction which seek only to entertain.

This suspicion of fictions has, of course, a distinguished pedigree.[76] But Macrobius goes on to characterize two superior species of fiction, the Aesopic

[75] *Ed. princ.* [= fol. 4ᵛ]. The standard modern edn., *Ambrosii Theodosii Macrobii commentarii in somnium Scipionis*, ed. J. Willis (Leipzig: Teubner, 1970), has, in this passage (1. 2.16–8, p. 5), few significant divergences from the *ed. princ.*

[76] Plato's arguments for the Expulsion of the Poet (*Republic* 3 and 10) provide the *locus classicus*. Cicero has similarly critical comments to make in the *De republica* (4. 9. 9), comments endorsed (with some irony) by Augustine, *De ciuitate dei* 2. 13.

fable which has an edifying force but is unsuitable for philosophical discourse because it is fictitious in both its conception and its narration;[77] and the *narratio fabulosa* which uses fiction allegorically in order to convey truths about the gods or philosophical mysteries. Provided certain requirements of subject matter and propriety are satisfied, the *narratio fabulosa* may be used by 'the philosopher who is prudent in handling sacred matters' (*hoc est solum figmenti genus quod cautio de divinis rebus philosophantis admittit*).[78] We might note, in passing, that it does not occur to Macrobius to include even 'Cupid and Psyche' in this third category of fictions, despite his appreciation of Apuleius' eminence as a Platonist.

Macrobius' influence on the Middle Ages was enormous. Stahl calls the *Commentary* 'one of the basic source books of the scholastic movement and of medieval science'.[79] Boccaccio bases much of his defence of fiction in the *De genealogia deorum* on Macrobius' account, though we shall see that he subtly alters it to provide a place for Apuleius' fictions.

Apuleius in Roman Gaul

The Gallo-Roman bishop, aristocrat, and *littérateur* Sidonius Apollinaris (*c*.430–*c*.480) exemplifies the extent to which the literary values of Symmachus' circle had, by the middle of the fifth century, been assimilated into Christian culture.[80] Though Sidonius makes explicit reference only to Apuleius' *Quaestiones conuiuiales* and a translation of Plato's *Phaedo* (both lost), his naming of Pudentilla suggests familiarity with the *Apologia,* and he holds Apuleius in high esteem, praising the 'lightning power of Apuleian authority' (*ponderis Apuleiani fulmen*).[81] The reference comes in a reply to his friend

[77] *quae concepta de falso per falsum narratur* (*Commentary,* ed. Willis, 1. 2. 10, p. 6). Note the slightly ambiguous status of Aesopic fables. Macrobius (*Comm.* 1. 2. 9) says that Aesop's fables are 'distinguished by the elegance of their fiction' (*elegantia fictionis illustres*). We know, also, that Avianus dedicated his own collection of fables to our 'Theodosius' (*OCD3*, 226).

[78] Stahl, trans., 85; ed. Willis, 1. 2. 11, p. 6.

[79] Stahl, *Macrobius*, 10.

[80] See, generally, R. W. Mathisen, 'Epistolography, Literary Circles and Family Ties in Late Roman Gaul', *TAPA* 111 (1981), 95–109, and 'The Theme of Literary Decline in Late Roman Gaul', *CP* 83 (1988), 45–52; R. E. Colton, *Some Literary Influences on Sidonius Apollinaris* (Amsterdam: Hakkert, 2000); J. Harries, *Sidonius Apollinaris and the Fall of Rome, AD 407–485* (Oxford: Clarendon, 1994). Sidonius became bishop of Clermont after holding the prefecture of Rome in 468.

[81] *Ep.* 4. 3. 1 in *C. Sollius Apollinaris Sidonius,* ed. P. Mohr (Leipzig: Teubner, 1895), 73. Cf. *Ep.* 2. 9. 5 (to Donadius, setting Apuleius' translation of the *Phaedo* as a benchmark); 2. 10. 1 (to Hesperius, on Pudentilla); 9. 13. 3 (to Tonantius, mentioning the *Quaestiones conuiuiales*). On the subsequent reception of the Pudentilla reference, see Ch. 2, *infra.* Sidonius' reference to *Quaestiones conuiuiales* may be indebted to Macrobius, *Saturnalia, 7. 3.*

Claudianus Mamertus (d. *c*.473), who had reproached him for failing to acknowledge the dedication of Claudianus' treatise *De animae statu*:

Committi, domine maior, in necessitudinis iura pronuntias, cur quod ad salve tibi debitum spectat a stilo et pugillaribus diu temperem quodque deinceps nullas viantum volas mea papyrus oneraverit, quae vos cultu sedulae sospitatis impertiat. praeter aequum ista coniectas, si reare mortalium quempiam, cui tamen sermocinari Latialiter cordi est, non pavere, cum in examen aurium tuarum quippe scriptus adducitur; tuarum, inquam, aurium, quarum peritiae, si me decursorum ad hoc aevi temporum praerogativa non obruat, nec Frontonianae gravitatis aut ponderis Apuleiani fulmen aequiperem, cui Varrones, vel Atacinus vel Terentius, Plinii, vel avunculus vel Secundus, compositi in praesentiarum rusticabuntur.

(You declare, most honoured master, that I have offended against the laws of friendship: you allege that though it is my turn to give you epistolary greeting, I have let my tablets and stylus lie, and no traveller's hand has been burdened with papyrus of mine inscribed with my assiduous wishes for your welfare. The suggestion is unfair; you cannot really suppose that any man on earth, with the least devotion to Latin letters, would lightly submit his compositions to the ordeal of being read to you; you, with whose accomplishments, but for the overwhelming privilege of antiquity, I should never rank either Fronto's gravity, or the fulminating force of Apuleius; for compared with you the Varros, both he of the Atax and he of Reate [Reatinus], and the Plinies, uncle and nephew, will always seem provincial.)[82]

Sidonius' self-conscious references to writing-materials have some (vague) analogues in *The Golden Ass*, but there is no persuasive evidence of his acquaintance with the novel.[83] Sidonius does, however, conclude his letter to Claudianus with an Apuleian adverb, *ambifariam* ('in two ways'):

nam te, cui, seu liberum seu ligatum placeat alternare sermonem, intonare ambifariam suppetit, pauci, quos aequus amavit, imitabuntur. Vale.

(But as for you, who can ring the changes on verse and prose and write in metre or without it exactly when you please, your emulators will be few, and those only whom Apollo loves. Farewell.)[84]

Claudianus' *De animae statu* shows even clearer signs of being indebted to Apuleius' *Apologia*. The influence is seen not only in diction but in the depiction of adversaries: the obloquy poured upon Apuleius' accusers supplies some of the most vivid imagery in Claudianus' attacks on proponents of

---

[82] *Ep.* 4. 3. 1; *The Letters of Sidonius*, trans. O. M. Dalton (Oxford: Clarendon, 1915), ii. 7–10, at 7. Dalton dates the letter to AD 472.

[83] Cf. *AA* 1. 1 (*si papyrum Aegyptia argutia Nilotici calami inscriptam non spreueris inspicere*) and 6. 25 (*dolebam me Hercules quod pugillares et stilum non habebam*).

[84] With *ambifariam* cf. *Apologia* 4 and *Florida* 18.

a corporalist view of the soul.[85] Alimonti characterizes Claudianus' approach as 'un arcaismo creativo' rather than merely 'una passiva imitazione'.[86] According to Sidonius:

nova ibi verba, quia vetusta, quibusque conlatus merito etiam antiquarum litterarum stilus antiquaretur...

(You have found ancient words which by their very age regain the charm of novelty; compared with these even a classic vocabulary seems obsolete)[87]

The cultivation of archaic (and archaizing) authors by members of Sidonius' circle is part of a wider aggressive-defensive strategy to preserve classical culture in the face of barbarian settlement and the collapse of Roman rule. In another letter (dated by Owen to AD 478), Sidonius congratulates his friend Johannes on 'deferring the decease of Literature' (*quod aboleri tu litteras distulisti*). Thanks to the latter's achievements, 'Our contemporaries and our successors' (*aequaevi vel posteri nostri*) 'shall preserve in the very midst of an invincible but alien race this evidence of their ancient birthright' (*iam sinu in medio sic gentis invictae, quod tamen alienae, natalium vetustorum signa retinebunt*). But the hunting out and displaying of rare words is also a means for an increasingly marginalized and disenfranchised Gallo-Roman aristocracy to redefine its status as an elite:

nam iam remotis gradibus dignitatum, per quas solebat ultimo a quoque summus quisque discerni, solum erit posthac nobilitatis indicium litteras nosse

(Since old grades of rank are now abolished which once distinguished the high from the low, in future culture must afford the sole criterion of nobility.)[88]

We might note, finally, the parallel drawn by Massimo Oldoni between the punishment proposed by some of the bystanders for the *uxor egregia* who has murdered her husband in Thelyphron's tale (*hii pessimam feminam uiuentem statim cum corpore mariti sepeliendam, AA* 2. 29) and the two live burials described in the *Historiarum libri* by Gregory of Tours (538

---

[85] T. Alimonti, 'Apuleio e l'arcaismo in Claudiano Mamerto', in *Forma futuri: Studi in onore del Cardinale Michele Pellegrino* (Turin: Bottega d'Erasmo, 1975), 189–228; cf. Harrison, *Latin Sophist*, 27. To take only one example, Claudianus (*De statu animae* 137. 1–13) writes: *Cernas hic alium situ* fetidinarum *turpium ex* olenticetis suis *ac tenebris cloacam ventris et oris inhalare sentinam interque ructandum quasdam suggillantiunculas* fringultientem *ab alio, qui stipem suam variis* conlurcinationibus dilapidavit, *parasitico more laudari.* Text from *Claudiani Mamerti opera*, ed. A. Engelbrecht (Vienna: Geroldi Fil., 1885) (emphasis added). Alimonti (209) directs us towards *Apologia* 8. 3 (*fetutinis et olenticetis suis*); 98. 9 (*singulas syllabas fringultientem*); and 75. 9 (*omnimodis collurchinationibus dilapidavit*).

[86] 'Apuleio e l'arcaismo', 202.

[87] *Ep.* 4. 3. 3.   [88] *Ep.* 8. 2. 1–2. Cf. Mathisen, 'Literary Decline', 51.

or 539 to 593 or 594).[89] These parallels (like most of those adduced by Oldoni) seem very tenuous in themselves, but we can discern possible lines of transmission: Gregory (born Georgius Florentius at Arverni, i.e. Clermont-Ferrand) belonged to a distinguished Gallo-Roman family and was brought up by his uncle Gallus, the Bishop of Clermont (an episcopal throne formerly occupied by Sidonius Apollinaris whose works Gregory quotes).[90]

However dormant Apuleius' novel, itself, may have been during the Middle Ages, the continued circulation of at least a shadow and a splinter of the original was ensured by the popularity of two works, also of North African origin, Martianus Capella's *De nuptiis Mercurii et Philologiae* (composed in the fifth century) and the *Mitologiarum libri tres* of Fabius Planciades Fulgentius (late fifth or early sixth century).[91]

Martianus Capella

Martianus draws extensively on 'Cupid and Psyche' in the narrative structure of the *De nuptiis* which opens with Mercury's frustrated attempts to find a wife. He considers the potential candidates, but finds them either unsuitable or unavailable:

Voluit saltem Endelechiæ [Entelechiae] *ac Solis filiam postulare: quod speciosa quam maxime: magnaque deorum sit educata cura. Nam ipsi ψυχΗ natali die Dii ad conuiuium corrogati multa contulerant. Iupiter quippe Diadema: quod æternitati filiæ honoratiori detraxerat: capiti eius apposuit. Iuno quoque expurgatioris auri splendente uena addiderat crinibus sociale uinculum. Tritonia etiam interula: resoluto ricinio: trophioque instar flammarum cocco: atque ipso sacri pectoris ac prudentis amiculo uirginemque Virgo contexit. Delius quoque: ut ramalem Laurum gestitit: diuinatrice eadem coniecturalique Virga uolucres illi: ac fulgurum iactus: ac ipsius meatus cæli syderumque monstrabat. Aniæ autem prænitens speculum: quod inter donaria eius Adytis Sophia defixerat | quo se recognoscens etiam originem uellet exquirere: clæmenti benignitate largita est. Lemnius quoque faber insopibilis illi perennitatis igniculos: ne*

---

[89] 'Streghe medievali e intersezioni da Apuleio', in *Semiotica della novella latina* (Rome: Herder, 1986), 267–79, at 269–70; *Historiarum Libri* 4. 12 (the priest, Anastasius, placed in a tomb by Cautinus, the rapacious bishop of Tours) and 5. 3 (the newly married pair of slaves buried alive by their master, Rauchingus).

[90] *NCE2*, s.v. 'Gregory of Tours St.' Oldoni makes no mention of these Gallo-Roman connections.

[91] *OCD2* dated *De nuptiis* between AD 410 and 439, but Danuta Shanzer argues in *A Philosophical and Literary Commentary on Martianus Capella's 'De Nuptiis Philologiae et Mercurii' Book I* (Berkeley and Los Angeles: U of California P, 1986), 5–28, for the seventh or eighth decades of the 5th cent (cf. her article in *OCD3*, 932–3). H. D. Jocelyn (*OCD3*, 613–14) describes Fulgentius as 'a late 5th-cent. writer of Christian persuasion'.

caligantibus tenebris nocteque cæca opprimeretur accendit. Omnes uero illecebras circa sensus cunctos apposuit Aphrodite. Nam & unguentis oblitam: floribusque redimitam halatus pasci fouerique docuerat: & melle permulserat: & auro atque monilibus inhiare: membraque uinciri honorationis cælsæ affectatione persuaserat. Tunc crepitacula: tinnitusque quis infanti somnum adduceret: adhibebat quiescenti. Prætereaque ne ullum tempus sine illecebris oblectamentisque decurreret: pruritu sub scalpente: circa ima corporis apposuerat uoluptatem. Sed uehiculum ei atque uolatiles rotas quis posset mira uelocitate discurrere: tradiderat ipse Cyllenius licet eam auri compedibus illigatam memoria prægraueret. His igitur superis ψυχΗν opimam ditemque muneribus atque mluta [sc. multa] cælestium collatione decoratam in connubium Archas superiorum cassus optabat. Sed eam Virtus: ut adhærebat forte Cyllenio: pene lachrimans nunciauit impotentiam pharetrati: uolantisque superi de sua societate correptam: captiuamque Adamantinis nexibus a Cupidine detineri.[92]

(He wanted to ask the daughter of Endelechia [Entelechia] and the Sun, because she was as beautiful as could be and had been brought up under the careful eye of the Gods.[93] For on the day of Psyche's birth, the Gods themselves were invited to a banquet to which they brought many things. Jupiter placed on her head a diadem which he had taken from his well-honoured daughter, Eternity. Juno, too, had placed in her hair a nuptial band with a gleaming vein of very pure gold. The Tritonian [*sc.* Minerva] removed from her tunic the flowing, flame-red veil and—a virgin herself— covered the virgin with the very mantle of her sacred and wise breast. And the Delian [*sc.* Apollo], since he carried the laurel-bough, showed her with that same wand of divination and conjecture, the birds, the lightning-bolts, and the courses of heaven itself and of the stars. But, by the kind bounty of Ania [*sc.* Urania], there was bestowed a shining mirror which, amongst her gifts, Sophia had fastened in the inmost parts— wherein, recognizing herself, she [*sc.* Psyche] could even attempt to seek her origin. Also, the craftsman of Lemnos [*sc.* Vulcan] kindled for her little fires of inextinguishable eternity, lest she should be oppressed by dark shadows and blind night. But Aphrodite placed about all her senses, all manner of enticements. For she had taught Psyche (bedaubed in ointments and wreathed in flowers) to cherish and feast herself on fragrances and had rubbed her gently with honey; and she had persuaded her to gaze with longing on gold and necklaces and to gird her limbs in a high-falutin' fashion.[94] Then she bestowed on her as she rested, rattles and bells with which to bring sleep to the infant. Moreover, lest any time should go by without allurements and pleasures, subject to the titillating itch of sensual desire, she placed Pleasure in the vicinity of her private parts. But the Cyllenian himself [*sc.* Mercury] had handed over

---

[92] *De nuptiis Philologiæ et Mercurii* (Vicenza: Henricus de Sancto Vrso, 1499), *Liber Primus*, sig. aiiiʳ (my trans). Square brackets are used to indicate my glosses (preceded by '*sc.*') and the readings of the most recent text, *Martianus Capella*, ed. J. Willis (Leipzig: Teubner, 1983), i. 7, pp. 4–5, where they differ significantly from the *ed. princ.*

[93] According to Shanzer (*Commentary*, 68), '*endelichiae*, which appears in all the MSS ... is, in fact, correct'. See *infra*, 135, n. 104.

[94] Cf. Shanzer, *Commentary*, 204: 'had persuaded her to gape at gold bracelets, and to put them round her arms in her striving for high esteem'.

to her a swift-wheeled vehicle on which she could move at marvellous speed; although he weighed her down, bound in shackles of gold by Memory. Mercury, therefore, sought in marriage Psyche, rich and splendid in these heavenly gifts and adorned with the abundant contribution of celestial things. But Virtue, as she clung hard to Mercury, announced (almost weeping) that Psyche had been snatched from her company into the power of the quivered and flying god and that she was being held captive by Cupid in adamantine fetters.)[95]

This version of 'Cupid and Psyche' is obviously very different from Apuleius'. There are no obscure oracles, unseen husbands, or jealous mothers-in-law: Aphrodite, far from persecuting Psyche, provides her with sexual gratification in the form of Voluptas—in Apuleius' tale, Psyche's daughter.[96] And in place of the complex narrative sequence which enables the lovers' final union in Apuleius, Martianus (reverting to the more traditional iconography of Soul constrained by Desire) simply reports that Psyche has been seized by Cupid and bound 'in adamantine fetters'. According to Shanzer, '*De Nuptiis* takes the form of an epic redemption myth, where the fall of the individual soul into generation deprives Mercury of a bride and initiates the rise of Philologia and her deathless apotheosis through theurgical rites.'[97]

But however divergent these two accounts may seem, the *De nuptiis* as a whole represents an extraordinary rewriting of Apuleius. The work begins with Mercury's frustrated suit to Psyche; it ends with Martianus' farewell to his son—a self-depreciatory gesture in which the author, describing his work as 'an old (wo)man's tale' (*Habes anilem, Martiane, fabulam*, 9. 997), invites comparisons with the aged narratrix of Apuleius' *bella fabella* (*AA* 6. 25).[98]

---

[95] According to C. Moreschini, Psyche is not mentioned again after this passage. See 'Towards a History of the Exegesis of Apuleius: The Case of the "Tale of Cupid and Psyche" ', in *Latin Fiction: The Latin Novel in Context,* ed. H. Hofmann (London: Routledge, 1999), 215–28, at 217. In fact, at 1. 23 (ed. Willis, 11), we find: *nam Ψυχὴν incultam ac ferino more versantem apud hanc asserit expolitam, ita ut, si quid pulchritudinis ornatusque gestaret, ex Philologiae sibi cultibus arrogarit, quae ei tantum affectionis impenderit, ut eam semper immortalem facere laborarit* ('In addition, said Virtue, Psyche, who at first lived a primitive sort of existence, has been so refined by Philology that whatever beauty and embellishment Psyche had she acquired from the polish Philology gave her; for the maiden had shown Psyche so much affection that she strove constantly to make her immortal'). Trans. from W. H. Stahl and R. Johnson with E. L. Burge, *Martianus Capella and the Seven Liberal Arts,* 2 vols. (New York: Columbia UP, 1971–7), ii. 14.

[96] In the opening frame to Book 9 ('Harmony'), Martianus describes how Venus, 'lying backward, leaned into the embrace of Pleasure, who was standing by her' (*resupina paululum reclinisque pone consistentis sese permisit amplexibus voluptatis,* Stahl and Johnson, ii. 345; ed. Willis, s. 889, p. 338). Voluptas also appears (whispering in Mercury's ear) at the beginning of Book 7 ('Arithmetic') and during an interlude (Stahl and Johnson, ii. 263; ed. Willis, s. 704, p. 250) in Book 6 ('Geometry').

[97] *Commentary,* 57.

[98] Martianus' final two lines (Book 9, ed. Willis, s. 1000, p. 386) also emphasize his old age (*veternum*).

And in between (particularly in the first two books), we find a stream of verbal echoes and structural parallels.[99]

Martianus deprives Psyche of a nuptial union with Cupid in order to redeploy the Apuleian material in his description of Philology's marriage to Mercury. But these are no simple borrowings—Martianus combines (what would seem to be) the most incongruous materials from Apuleius. To take one example: the drinking of the cup of immortality (2. 139–40) which will allow Philology to ascend to heaven in a palanquin, recalls not just the climactic draught in 'Cupid and Psyche' (*AA* 6. 23), but also (through its diction) Psyche's disastrous glimpse of Cupid as well as the first love-scene between Lucius and Fotis (*AA* 2. 16 ff.).[100] Moreover, aspects of the Isiac theophany (*AA* 11. 5) are incorporated into the description of Philology's celestial ascent: she enters 'the circle of the moon' which contains 'the sistra of Egypt, the lamp of Eleusis, Diana's bow, and the tambours of Cybele'.[101]

Martianus' debt to Apuleius is immense and (though he never mentions him by name) he evidently held him in high esteem. But the freedom that Martianus permits himself in transforming the lineaments of his Apuleian material is an important witness to the reception of 'Cupid and Psyche' in Late Antiquity. It brings us somewhat closer to the 'horizon of expectations' (*Erwartungshorizont*) that may have prevailed amongst Apuleius' own readers two and a half centuries earlier, and suggests that Apuleius was not seen as establishing fixed mythic norms, but as giving a Platonic overlay to a narrative structure that was as adaptable as any other *anilis fabula*.[102]

Martianus' mixing of fictional and philosophical ingredients is by no means unique. It has been observed that 'Myths are the characteristic form of speech for a deviant Platonism that flourished in the second and third centuries A.D.'[103] In *De anima* 23, Tertullian characterizes the cosmological systems elaborated by the second-century Gnostic Valentinus as *historiae atque Milesiae*:

---

[99] See Stahl and Johnson, i. 27, 32, 42, 84–5.

[100] As noted by Willis, 43; Stahl and Johnson, ii. 48 n. 75. Compare *exhausto pallore confecta* (*De nuptiis* 2. 139: Philology has just vomited forth 'a stream of writings of all kinds' in 'great volumes' and 'many languages', 2. 136) with *marcido pallore defecta* (*AA* 5. 22: Psyche's collapse after seeing Cupid by the light of the lamp).

[101] Stahl and Johnson, ii. 55; Willis, 49: *in eo sistra Niliaca Eleusinaque lampas arcusque Dictynnae tympanaque Cybeleia videbantur* (2. 170).

[102] On *Erwartungshorizont*, see H. R. Jauss, 'Literaturgeschichte als Provokation der Literaturwissenschaft', in his *Literaturgeschichte als Provokation* (Frankfurt am Main: Suhrkamp, 1970), 144–207; trans. into English as 'Literary History as a Challenge to Literary Theory', in *New Directions in Literary History*, ed. R. Cohen (Baltimore: Johns Hopkins UP, 1974), 11–41.

[103] M. J. Edwards, 'The Tale of Cupid and Psyche', *ZPE* 94 (1992), 77–94, at 87.

Examen Valentini semen Sophiae infulcit animae, per quod historias atque milesias aeonum suorum ex imaginibus uisibilium recognoscunt. Doleo bona fide Platonem omnium haereticorum condimentarium factum.

(The hive of Valentinus fortifies the soul with the germ of *Sophia*, or Wisdom; by means of which germ they recognise, in the images of visible objects, the stories and Milesian fables of their own Æons. I am sorry from my heart that Plato has been the caterer to all these heretics.)[104]

In the *Adversus Valentinianos*, Tertullian writes:

Iam si et in totam fabulam initietur, nonne tale aliquid <recor>dabitur se in infantia inter somni difficultates a nutricula audisse, Lamiae turres et pectines Solis? 4. Sed qui ex aliqua conscientia uenerit fidei, si statim inueniat tot nomina Aeonum, tot coniugia, tot genimina, tot exitus, tot euentus felicitates infelicitates dispersae atque concisae diuinitatis, dubitabitne ibidem pronuntiare has esse fabulas et genealogias indeterminatas, quas apostoli spiritus, his iam tunc pullulantibus seminibus haereticis, damnare praeuenit?

(Now, even suppose that you are initiated into the entire fable, will it not occur to you that you have heard something very like it from your fond nurse when you were a baby, amongst the lullabies she sang to you about the towers of Lamia, and the horns of the sun? Let, however, any man approach the subject from a knowledge of the faith which he has otherwise learned, as soon as he finds so many names of Æons, so many marriages, so many offsprings, so many exits, so many issues, felicities [and] infelicities of a dispersed and mutilated Deity, will that man hesitate at once to pronounce [123] that these are 'the fables and endless genealogies' [1 Tim. 1: 4] which the inspired apostle by anticipation condemned, whilst these seeds of heresy were even then shooting forth?)[105]

Tertullian is using nursery images in order to disparage Gnostic 'scriptures' as 'old wives' tales', but the very seriousness of his attack acknowledges the seductive power of such fictions. Moreover, his application of the term *Milesiae* to theological narratives involving the Fall and suffering of an allegorical figure (Sophia), followed by her 'marriage' to the 'Son of God' and her production of a female offspring, casts an oblique light upon Apuleius' introduction of 'Cupid and Psyche' as a 'Milesian tale' (*AA* 4. 32). The Gnostic material also provides a context for the exegesis of 'Cupid and Psyche' given by Fulgentius the Mythographer.

---

[104] *De anima*, ed. J. H. Waszink (Amsterdam: North-Holland, 1947), 31; *Ante-Nicene Christian Library*, xv, trans. P. Holmes (Edinburgh: Clark, 1870), 463. Cf. S. Costanza, *La fortuna di L. Apuleio nell'età di mezzo* (Palermo: Scuola Salesiana del libro, 1937), 50.

[105] *Adversus Valentinianos* 3. 3–4, ed. E. Kroymann, in *Quinti Septimi Florentis Tertulliani opera, Pars II: Opera Montanistica*, CCSL 2 (Turnhout: Brepols, 1954), 755; *Ante-Nicene Christian Library*, xv, trans. P. Holmes, 123–4.

Fabius Planciades Fulgentius (late fifth or mid-sixth century)[106]

Fulgentius has been subjected to a good deal of abuse over the past five centuries: his Latin is wretched; his thinking cloudy; his motives obscure. Traces of such 'Golden Age' and Enlightenment bias persist even in the latest edition of the *Oxford Classical Dictionary* where his works are characterized as being 'marked by considerable foolishness of thought and by an extremely mannered style'.[107] In the Middle Ages, however, Fulgentius was much admired and he was championed in the Renaissance by a small though vocal minority (chiefly, Johannes Baptista Pius). More recent scholarship has drawn attention to his role in the transmission of Classical culture and to his place within the specific context of the so-called 'Vandal Renaissance' in North Africa.[108] We should remember, also, that had *The Golden Ass* itself not survived (and it seems to have hung through most of the Middle Ages by the slenderest of threads), Fulgentius would be our only witness to the Apuleian plot of 'Cupid and Psyche'. In Book 3 of his *Mitologiae*, Fulgentius provides a detailed précis of the story:

Fabula psiches & cupidinis

Apuleius in libris metamorphoseon hanc fabulam planissime designauit: dicens esse in quadam ciuitate regem & reginam: habere tres filias: duas natu maiores esse temperata specie: Iuniorem non [uero] tam magnificæ esse figuræ qui [quae] crederetur uenus esse terrestris. Denique duabus maioribus quæ erant temperata [temperata erant] specie connubio uenere [conubia euenere]: illam uero ueluti deam non quisquam amare ausus: quam uenerari pronus: atque hostiis sibimet deprecari [deplacare]. Contaminata ergo honoris maiestate Venus succensa inuidia cupidinem petit: ut in contumacem formam seueriter uindicaret. Ille ad matris ultionem aduentans uisam puellam adamauit. pœna enim in affectu [affectum] conuersa est: & ut magnificus iaculator ipse se suo telo percussit. Itaque apollinis denunciatione iubetur puella in montis cacumine sola dimitti <et> uelut feralibus deducta exequiis pennato [pinnato] serpenti sponso destinari. perfecto nanque [iamque] choragio [coragio] puella per montis decliuia zephiri flantis leni uectura delapsa in quandam domum auream rapitur: quæ pretiosa sine pretio: sola consideratione laude deficiente poterat existimari [aestimare]. Ibique uocibus <sibi>

[106] In 'The Date and Identity of the Mythographer Fulgentius', *JML* 13 (2003), 163–252, G. Hays argues firmly against the identification of the Mythographer with the Bishop of Ruspe, and (at 244) suggests a tentative date for the *Mitologiae* of 'soon after 550'. Fulgentius cites Martianus Capella. See Shanzer, *Commentary*, 12–13. See also C. Moreschini, *Il mito di Amore e Psiche in Apuleio* (Naples: M. D'Auria, 1994), 27–30; and S. Mattiacci, 'Apuleio in Fulgenzio', *SIFC* 4th ser. 1 (2003): 229–56.

[107] H. D. Jocelyn, *OCD3*, 613–14.

[108] Most notably, G. Hays, '*Romuleis Libicisque Litteris*: Fulgentius and the "Vandal Renaissance"', in *Vandals, Romans and Berbers: New Perspectives on Late Antique North Africa*, ed. A. H. Merrills (Aldershot: Ashgate, 2004), 101–32.

tantummodo seruientibus ignota [ignoto] *atque mansionario utebatur coniugio. Nocte enim adueniens maritus ueneris præliis obscure peractis: ut* [fol. xxxiii^v] *inuise uespertinus aduenerat: ita crepusculo incognitus etiam discedebat. habuit ergo uocale seruitium: uentosum dominium nocturnum commentum* [commercium]: *ignotum coniugium. Sed ad huius mortem deflendam sorores adueniunt: montisque conscenso cacumine germanum lugubri uoce flagitabant uocabulum: & quamuis ille coniunx lucifuga sororios ei comminando uetaret aspectus: tamen consanguineæ charitatis inuincibilis ardor maritale obumbrauit imperium. Zephyri ergo flagrantis* [flabrantis] *auræ anhelante uectura ad semet sororios perducit affectus: earumque uenenosis consiliis de mariti forma quærenda consentiens curiositatem suæ salutis nouercam arripuit: & facillimam credulitatem: quæ semper deceptionum mater est. postposito cautelæ suffragio arripuit* [arripit] *denique credens sororibus se marito serpenti coniunctam: uelut bestiam interfectura nouaculam sub puluinari* [puluinal] *abscondit: lucernamque modio contegit. Cunque altum soporem maritus extenderet: illa ferro armata lucernaque modio* [modii] *custodia eruta: cupidine cognito dum immodesto amoris torretur affectu scintillantis olei desputamento maritum succendit Fugiensque cupido multa super curiositate puellæ increpitans domo extorem* [extorrem] *ac profugam dereliquit* [derelinquit]. *Tandem multis iactata* [iactatam] *uenenis* [Ueneris] *persecutionibus postea ioue petente in coniugio cupidinem accepit.*[109]

The Tale of Cupid and Psyche

Apuleius set out this tale most clearly in the books of *Metamorphoses*, saying that in a certain city there were a king and queen. They had three daughters—the elder two were of moderate beauty; the youngest of such splendid form that she was believed to be an earthly Venus. In due course, marriage came to the elder two who were of moderate beauty, but the youngest, as though she were a goddess, no one dared to love.

Venus therefore, incensed with envy at the defilement of the grandeur of her reputation, sought Cupid, so that he might savagely avenge this insolent beauty. He, hastening to avenge his mother, fell in love at the sight of the girl. For punishment was converted into desire so that the mighty archer struck himself with his own weapon. And so, by decree of Apollo, it was ordered that the girl should be left alone on the peak of the mountain, having been led, as though in a funeral procession, and chosen

---

[109] The Latin text is reproduced from the *ed. princ.*, edited (with commentary) by Giovanni Battista Pio, *Enarrationes allegoricæ fabularum* (Milan: V. Scinzenzeler, 1498). I have collated this with the text of *Fabii Planciadis Fulgentii V. C. opera*, ed. R. Helm (Leipzig: Teubner, 1898), 66–70, indicating Helm's readings in square brackets whenever they differ substantially from Pio's. The English translation is my own. The introduction to Leslie Whitbread's translation of the Helm text, *Fulgentius the Mythographer* ([Columbus]: Ohio State UP, 1971), is a pioneering contribution to the study of an obscure and neglected author, but the translation itself (at least of 'Cupid and Psyche') is extremely deficient. He translates the Latin, *perfecto iamque coragio puella per montis decliuia zephiri flantis leni uectura delapsa*, as 'Full of courage, the maiden was borne across the mountain slopes in a carriage and, when left alone, floated downwards, gently wafted by the breath of Zephyr'. For *germanum ... flagitabant uocabulum*, he gives, 'were entreating in sisterly words'. He even misunderstands the function of the ablative absolute: *Cupidine cognito, dum inmodesto amoris torretur affectu* is rendered by 'as she recognized Cupid, he was burned by the dire results of her love'.

for a winged serpent as a spouse. And now, with the funeral complete, the girl, having glided down the slopes of the mountain on the gentle carriage of the blowing Zephyrus, is taken into a certain golden house which, precious beyond price, could only be valued by bankrupting praise. And there, with only voices for servants, she enjoyed her unknown marriage in the house. For her husband, in the same way that he came to her unseen in the evening and waged the warfare of Venus in the dark, so too, at dawn, he went away, unknown. She had, therefore, voices for servants, rule over the wind, falsehood [intercourse] by night, a marriage with the unknown.

But the sisters arrive to bewail her death and having climbed to the top of the mountain, they call their sister's name over and over in mournful voice. And although that photophobic husband, by threatening her, forbade her the sight of her sisters, the invincible ardour of sisterly love still overshadowed her husband's command. So, by the breathing carriage of Zephyrus' ardent air, she conducted to herself the sisters she loved; and agreeing with their poisonous plans to seek to learn the appearance of her husband, she laid hold of curiosity, the stepmother of her safety, and that all-too-easy credulity, which is always the mother of deceptions. And laying aside the voice of caution and believing her sisters that she was wedded to a serpent for a husband, intending to kill him as a beast, she hid a razor underneath a cushion and concealed a lamp in a peck. And when her husband was drawing out a deep sleep, armed with the blade and lamp, she threw off the the the peck that served as a cover and recognized Cupid. While she was being scorched by an immoderate desire for Love, she burnt her husband with the spittle of the flashing oil. Cupid, flying away and casting down reproaches on the girl's curiosity, deserted her, banished from her home and an exile. At last, after being tormented by Venus' many acts of persecution, at Jove's behest, she received Cupid in matrimony.)

Fulgentius now embarks on an exegesis designed, it seems, to demonstrate the foolishness of the tale itself, while rescuing its deeper meanings:

Poteram quidem totius fabulæ ordinem hoc libello percurrere: qualiter & ad infernum descenderit: & ex stygiis aquis urnulam delibauerit: & solis armenta uellere spoliauerit: & seminum germina confusa discreuerit: & de proserpinæ pulcritudine particulam moritura præsumpserit. Sed quia hæc saturantius & apuleius pene duorum continentia libro~rum~ tantam falsitatum congeriem ennarauit: & aristophantes [Aristofontes] athe~neus~ in libris: qui diserestia [disarestia] nuncupantur hanc fabulam enormi [inormi] uerbor~um~ circuitu discere cupientibus prodit [prodidit]: ob hanc [xxxiiii ͬ] rem super-uacuum duximus ab aliis digesta nostris inserere libris [libris inserere]: ne nostra opera aut <a> propriis exularemus officiis: aut alienis adiceremus [addiceremus] negociis. Sed dum his: qui fabulam legent [is qui hanc fabulam legerit] in nostra hæc transeat sciturus quod [quid] sibi illorum falsitas sentire uoluerit. Ciuitatem posueru~nt~ quasi in modum mundi: in qua regem & regiam [reginam] uelut deu~m~ & materiam posuerunt: quibus tres <filias> addunt <id est> carnem: ultromntantem [ultronietatem]: quam liberta-tem arbitrii dicimus: & animam. ΨυχH [Psice] enim græce anima dicitur: quam ideo iuniorem uoluerunt: quod corpori iam facto postea inclitam [inditam] esse <animam> dicebant. hanc igitur ideo pulcriorem: quod & a libertate superior: & a carne nobilior.

huic inuidet uenus quasi libido: ad quam perdendam cupidinem [cupiditatem] *mittit.*
Sed quia cupiditas est boni & [est] *mali cupiditas animam diligit: & ei uelut in*
coniunctionem [coniunctione] *miscetur quam persuadet ne suam faciem uideat idest*
cupiditatis delectamenta discat: unde & adam quamuis uideat nudum se non uidet donec
de concupiscentiæ arbore comedat: Ne ue suis sororibus id est carni et libertati de suæ
formæ curiositate perdiscenda consentiat: Sed illarum conpulsamento percita [perter-
rita] *lucernam desubmodio eiecit* [eicit] *idest desiderii flammam in pectore absconsam*
depallat [depalat]: *uisamque taliter dulcem amat: ac diligit* [xxxiiii^v] *quam ideo*
lucernæ ebullitione dicitur intendisse [incendisse]: *quia omnis cupiditas quantum*
diligitur tantum ardescit: & peccatricem suæ carni confingit [configit] *maculam. ergo*
quasi cupiditate nudata ex [et] *potenti fortuna eruitur* [priuatur]: *& periculis: iactatur*
& regia domo expellitur. Sed nos quia longum est ut dixi omnia persequi tenorem
dedimus sentiendi. Si quis uero in apuleio ipsam fabulam legerit: nostra expositionis
materia quæ non diximus ipse reliqua cognoscat [recognoscit]. (Fulgentius, = Helm, 3.
6. 116–18)

(I could, indeed, run through, in this little book, the course of the whole story—how
she descended into Hell and took away a small urnful of the waters of the Styx; how
she spoiled the Sun's flocks of their fleece; how she separated the mixed up types of
seeds; and how, in the face of death, she took in advance a little bit of Proserpine's
beauty. But because Apuleius related these things to satiety as well as a great mass of
falsities in the contents of almost two books and Aristophontes of Athens, in books
which are called *Disarestia*,[110] set forth this tale in an enormous compass of words for
those eager to learn, we have deemed it superfluous, on account of this fact, to include
in our books things digested from others, lest we should either banish our works from
their proper duties, or devote them to the business of others [i.e. distract them from
their appointed tasks or devote them to what are other people's concerns].

But let whomever has read this tale switch now to our words to find out what
meaning these men's falsehood intended for him: They have placed the City as if in the
manner of the World, in which they have placed the King and the Queen as God and
Matter. To these, they add three daughters, that is the Flesh, Voluntariness (which we
call Free Will), and the Soul. For the Soul, in Greek, is called Psyche. They wanted her
to be younger because they said that when the body had already been made, the Soul
was imparted to it. For that reason, therefore, she is the more beautiful, because she is
superior to Free Will and more noble than Flesh. Venus (that is, Lust) envies her and
sends Cupid [Desire] to destroy her, but because Desire is both for good and evil, it
loves the Soul and is joined, as it were, in union with her. Desire persuades Soul that
she should not see his face, that is, she should not learn the delights of desire (whence,
also Adam, although he has sight, does not see that he is naked until he eats of the Tree
of Concupiscence) and that she should not accord with her sisters (that is, with Flesh
and Free Will) in their curiosity to know fully about his appearance.[111] But, roused

[110] Plasberg's suggestion of Διὸς ἀριστεία ('The Deeds of Zeus') is cited by B. Baldwin,
'Fulgentius and his Sources', *Traditio* 44 (1988), 37–57, at 41.
[111] See Thomas Heywood's use of this section in Ch. 8, *infra*.

[terrified] by their exhortation, she takes out an oil-lamp from beneath a peck (that is, she reveals the flame of lust hidden in her breast) and, having seen it, she loves and values it. For that reason, she is said to have kindled it with the spluttering of the lamp, because all desire is inflamed as much as it loves and joins a sinful mark to its flesh. Therefore, stripped, as it were, of desire, she is both deprived of her powerful fortune and tossed about by dangers and expelled from her royal home. But because, as I have said, it is tedious to follow up everything, we have given a sense of how it is to be interpreted. If anyone, indeed, should read the tale itself in Apuleius, he may recognize for himself the remaining things that we have not mentioned in the substance of our exposition.)

Fulgentius claims to have no interest in the details of the narrative qua narrative. He is more a philosophical and philological archaeologist, trying to uncover (often by means of curious etymologies) the eternal verities buried beneath the 'mass of falsehoods' (*falsitatum congeries*) heaped up by the 'lying Greeks'—his generic term (2. 5) for fabulists like Apuleius and (the otherwise unknown) Aristophontes of Athens.[112] It may seem paradoxical that a man who took such pains to reduce ancient stories to narrative nullities, should have provided posterity with a compact compendium of classical mythology. This, of course, is often the irony of polemics—in rebutting the opposition one preserves its teaching (indeed, *The Golden Ass* may well owe its very survival to Augustine's reference to it in *De ciuitate dei* 18. 18, in the course of his confutation of the daemonoloy of the *De deo Socratis*).

The prologue to the *Mitologiae*, however, reveals Fulgentius' relationship with fiction (and with Apuleius) to be profoundly dialectical.[113] Calliope (Muse of epic), juxtaposing Nero and Plato, tells Fulgentius to expect fame, not for his poetry, but for his philosophy. But by calling his own work a 'tale wrinkled with an old woman's furrows' (*rugosam sulcis anilibus ordior fabulam*), Fulgentius evokes the despised genre of *aniles fabulae* (compare the exordium to 'Cupid and Psyche': *sed ego te narrationibus lepidis anilibusque fabulis protinus auocabo*, *AA* 4. 27), and by introducing it with almost the same formula (*tuarum aurium sedes lepido quolibet susurro permulceam*) that Apuleius had used at the beginning of *The Golden Ass* (*auresque tuas beniuolas lepido susurro permulceam*, *AA* 1. 1), he gives it a specifically Milesian gloss. He then stresses, however, that the reader will not find in his books the 'presiding lamps by which either the shamelessness of little Sulpicia or the

---

[112] The entry (s.v. 'Aristophon' 8) in *Paulys Real-Encyclopädie* (1896), ii. 1008, declares that he is 'offenbar später als Apuleius' ('manifestly later than Apuleius').

[113] On the prologue, see J. C. Relihan, *Ancient Menippean Satire* (Baltimore: Johns Hopkins UP, 1993), 152–63, and app. B (203–10) for trans. Having noted that 'Apuleius is often cited as a major (even the primary) influence on Fulgentius' extravagant prose style', Hays observes ('Fulgentius and the "Vandal Renaissance" ', 108) that 'he also anticipates important aspects of Fulgentius' literary persona: his ostentatious bilingualism, pretensions to encyclopaedic culture, and flirtation with demonology and other occult matters'.

curiosity of Psyche was revealed' but, rather, something akin to Cicero's *Somnium Scipionis*.[114] He informs Calliope that she has been deceived by the *Mitologiae*'s title (*Index te libelli fefellit*). He is not concerned with the usual run of tales of adultery and illicit passion (Europa, Danae, Adonis, Ganymede, Leda):

nec lignides puellas inquirimus, Ero atque Psicen, poeticas garrulantes ineptias, dum haec lumen queritur extinctum, illa deflet incensum, ut Psice uidendo perderet et Ero non uidendo perisset

(Nor do we seek after those shrieking girls, Hero and Psyche, babbling poetic trifles while one bemoans the extinction of a lamp, the other mourns the lighting of one, since Psyche lost utterly through seeing, and Hero perished through not seeing)

Yet, in the third book, of course, Fulgentius does reveal Psyche's curiosity, and his *praeteritio* (*Poteram quidem totius fabulæ ordinem hoc libello percurrere...*) suggests a desire to advertise not just his knowledge of the narrative details but the details themselves, even those 'falsehoods' which have no apparent exegetical value. That seemingly casual allusion to *The Dream of Scipio* is pregnant with significance. It suggests that Fulgentius is here attempting to accommodate his compilation of fabulous narratives to the Macrobian rule. From a Macrobian perspective, Fulgentius' prologue can be seen to be setting up the *Mitologiae* as a field of creative play between the poles of *anilis fabula* and *narratio fabulosa*, thus bringing it closer than one might expect to Martianus Capella's *De nuptiis*.[115]

Martianus' exposition of the Seven Liberal Arts helped to shape the pedagogy of the whole Middle Ages. Manuscripts and commentaries abound from the Carolingian period onwards, and as late as the 1380s and 1390s, Chaucer will give him an honourable mention in his *House of Fame* (985) and invoke him for ironic effect in *The Merchant's Tale* (1722–41). And while modern critics may number Fulgentius' works among the most 'pretentious yet essentially trivial' 'remnants of an effete and expiring classicism', it is clear that he played an important role in the mythographical and allegorical tradition.[116] The Fulgentian allusions and echoes that Laistner detects in such authors as John

---

[114] *Neque enim illas Eroidarum arbitreris lucernas meis prae-*[4]*sules libris, quibus aut Sulpicillae procacitas aut Psices curiositas declarata est. ...* (Helm, 3–4). In a poem celebrating the fifteenth wedding anniversary of the 1st-cent. poet Sulpicia and her husband Calenus, Martial (10. 38, vv. 6–8) refers to the 'lucky bed' (*felix lectulus*) and the 'lamp, drunk on the perfumer's clouds' (*lucerna ... / nimbis ebria Nicerotianis*), witnessing their 'battles' (*proelia*) and 'reciprocal bouts' (*utrimque pugnas*).

[115] See also V. Lev Kenaan, '*Fabula anilis*: The Literal as a Feminine Sense', in C. Deroux, ed., *Studies in Latin Literature and Roman History*, vol. x (Brussels: Latomus, 2000), 370–91, at 384–7.

[116] M. L. W. Laistner, 'Fulgentius in the Carolingian Age', in his *The Intellectual Heritage of the Early Middle Ages* (Ithaca, NY: Cornell UP, 1957), 202–15, at 204. See, generally, J. Whitman, *Allegory: The Dynamics of an Ancient and Medieval Technique* (Oxford: Clarendon, 1987), 104–11.

Scottus Erigena, Martin of Laon, Remigius of Auxerre, Sedulius Scotus, Paschasius Radbertus, Ermenrich of Ellwangen, and Gunzo of Novara (*fl. c.*960), enable him to conclude that the Mythographer 'was a favourite author' during the Carolingian period.[117]

But if the Carolingians and their successors were making such good use of Apuleius' legacies to Fulgentius and Martianus Capella, what was happening to *The Golden Ass* itself during this period?

THE INVISIBLE ASS

With Fulgentius, *The Golden Ass* seems to fade from view. Apuleius' exotic Latinity was, potentially, a rich quarry for the grammarians of Late Antiquity; but *The Golden Ass* features only in Fulgentius' *Expositio sermonum antiquorum*.[118] Sergius, a commentator (of unknown date) on the *Ars* of Aelius Donatus (fourth century), provides a dim echo in his explanation, *De metaplasmis: nam dictio, quae transformatione componitur, metamorfoseos dicitur, quod Obidius scripsit uel Apuleius*.[119] At the beginning of the sixth century, Priscian is able to quote from what appears to be another example of Apuleian prose fiction, the *Hermagoras*; but the only extant work to which he refers is the *De deo Socratis*.[120] The *Hermagoras* fragments are particularly tantalizing:

Aspera hiems erat, omnia ningue canebant

(It was a harsh winter: everything was white with snow)

et cibatum, quem iucundum esse nobis animadverterant, eum adposiverunt

(and, having noticed that we found him agreeable, they set him down to eat)

---

[117] Laistner, 'Fulgentius', 211. R. Edwards cites the case of Sigebert of Gembloux (*c.*1030–1112) who observes that 'every reader can be in awe of the keenness of [Fulgentius'] genius' (*omnis lector expavescere potest acumen ingenii ejus*) as an interpreter of the whole system (*series*) of *fabulae*. See 'The Heritage of Fulgentius', in *The Classics in the Middle Ages*, ed. A. S. Bernardo and S. Levin (Binghamton, NY: CMERS, 1990), 141–51, at 141; and *De scriptoribus ecclesiasticis* 28 (*PL* 160, col. 554). Note that Lucius (*AA* 1. 26) describes himself as being 'tired out by [Milo's] series of stories' (*fabularum . . . serie fatigatum*).

[118] The African grammarian Flavius Sosipater Charisius (late 4th cent.) can quote from Apuleius' *De prouerbiis*. See *Grammatici Latini*, ed. H. Keil, 7 vols. (Leipzig: Teubner, 1857–80), i. 240. The fragments are given by J. Beaujeu, ed., *Apulée: Opuscules philosophiques* (Paris: Budé, 1973) and discussed by Harrison, *Latin Sophist*, 16–36.

[119] Keil, *Grammatici Latini*, iv. 565.

[120] Priscian's references to *Hermagoras* are given by Keil at *Grammatici Latini*, ii. 279, 528, 111, 85 (the four fragments reproduced below), and 135 (a brief observation of Apuleius' use of *scius* ['knowing, having knowledge'] in place of *sciens*); and to *De deo Socratis* at ii. 509. Cf. B. E. Perry, 'On Apuleius' *Hermagoras*', *AJP* 48 (1927), 263–6.

verum infirma scamillorum obice fultae fores

(but the doors were secured by the flimsy obstacle of *scamilli*)[121]

Visus est et [or *ei*] *adulescens honesta forma quasi ad nuptias exornatus trahere <se> in penitiorem partem domus*

(it seemed that a young man of handsome appearance, dressed up as though for a wedding, was dragging her into the inner part of the house)[122]

pollincto eius funere domuitionem paramus

(his corpse having been made ready for the funeral, we prepare to return home)[123]

Any attempt to reconstruct a plot from such tiny shards is bound to be highly speculative, but we may recognize some of the topoi of the ancient romances: it would appear that banquets, dreams, and domestic space (barred doors, inner rooms, etc.) are being used to convey erotic attraction (as well, perhaps, as maidenly anxiety) among young people of good birth. The allusion to a funeral need not necessarily imply a tragic catastrophe. The recurrence of the participle *pollinctus* in *Florida* 19. 4—where Asclepiades carefully examines a supposed 'corpse' which is 'already washed and almost prepared for burial' (*iam eum pollinctum, iam paene paratum contemplatus*)—should remind us of Apuleius' penchant for *Scheintod* (cf. the physician and the 'dead' boy in *AA* 10. 12).[124] Nor should we be surprised by the combination of a strong narrative drive (as evinced by the fragments) with the rhetorical associations of the title.[125] Many other questions remain. Did Priscian encounter the *Hermagoras* in his (presumed) homeland of North Africa?[126] Was a

[121] Lit. 'little benches or stools'; perhaps, here, 'ridges', 'projections', or 'beading'.

[122] Perry (who translates only this single fragment) suggests (266): 'In her (his?) dream a young man of seemly appearance and dressed up as for a wedding seemed to be dragging her (him?) into the inner part of the house' (parentheses are Perry's).

[123] This final fragment is preserved by Fulgentius, *Expositio sermonum antiquorum*, 3 (*Opera*, ed. Helm, 112).

[124] The use of the vivid 'historic present' tense in *domuitionem paramus* prepares the ground for just such a reversal.

[125] Perry (264): 'The name Hermagoras ... was presumably that of the leading character; and since this name was well known in antiquity as belonging to several rhetoricians, it may be reasonably inferred that Apuleius chose this name because he thought it appropriate to a protagonist whom he was representing as a professional rhetorician.' We might compare the ability of Apuleius (whose commitment to philosophy, religion, and rhetoric is well attested by his other writings) to play comically (indeed, satirically) with all three in *The Golden Ass*. Cf. Harrison who also observes (*Latin Sophist*, 22) that 'attempts to interpret some of the fragments ... as metrical, thus matching the prosimetric format of the *Satyrica*, are unpersuasive'.

[126] *Subscriptiones* indicate that the *Institutio grammatica* was complete before 526/7 and that Priscian was *Caesariensis* ('of Caesarea'). See Pauly-Wissowa, xxii/2, col. 2329. In 'Some Latin Authors from the Greek East', *CQ* 49 (1999), 606–17, J. Geiger explores the possibility that Priscian's birthplace may have been 'Caesarea' in Palestine rather than 'Caesarea' in Mauretania (now Cherchell in Algeria).

manuscript available to him while he was teaching in Constantinople?[127] Or should we associate his knowledge of a range of (now lost) Apuleian works with the final incarnation of the Symmachi's cultural circle in Rome?[128] It is difficult to say.

Priscian's contemporary, Cassiodorus Senator (*c*.490–*c*.583), was also acquainted with a number of Apuleius' works, but in the second book of his *Institutiones diuinarum et saecularium litterarum*—intended to provide his monks at Vivarium (in Squillace in Calabria) with a 'compendium of such secular knowledge as was indispensable to the study of Holy Writ'[129]—the only extant work of Apuleius mentioned is the *Peri hermeneias*, recommended for its full explanation of 'the rules of categorical syllogisms'.[130]

St Isidore of Seville (*c*.570–636), the last of the encyclopaedists of Late Antiquity, was born, like Apuleius, in the region of Carthage. His bishopric in Spain placed him, one would have thought, in a strategic position for the transmission of literature from North Africa to Europe.[131] Yet, though he refers to Apuleius several times (drawing at least once upon Cassiodorus), he makes no mention of *The Golden Ass*.[132] His account of the pagan gods

---

[127] Cassiodorus (*De orthographia* 1. 13; = Keil, vii. 207) refers to Priscian being a *doctor* ('teacher') at Constantinople *nostro tempore* ('in our day').

[128] Priscian dedicated three of his minor treatises to Q. Aurelius Memmius Symmachus (great-grandson of Q. Aurelius Symmachus, father-in-law of Boethius, and editor of Macrobius' *Commentary on the Dream of Scipio*). For a discussion of Priscian's quotations from Apuleius' *Epitoma historiarum*, his *Libri medicinales* (or *Medicinalia*), and his translation of Plato's *Phaedo*, see Harrison, *Latin Sophist*, 16–36.

[129] R. A. B. Mynors, ed., *Cassiodori Senatoris institutiones* (Oxford: Clarendon, 1937; repr. 1963), p. ix.

[130] Ibid. 118: *has formulas categoricorum syllogismorum qui plene nosse desiderat, librum legat qui inscribitur* Perihermenias Apulei, *et quae subtilius sunt tractata cognoscit.* Cf. *PL* 70, *De artibus ac disciplinis liberalium litterarum*, col. 1173A. See L. D. Reynolds and N. G. Wilson, *Scribes and Scholars: A Guide to the Transmission of Greek and Latin Literature*, 3rd edn. (Oxford: Clarendon, 1991), 83. Cassiodorus mentions the *Peri hermeneias* again (p. 28) and refers to a translation by Apuleius of Nicomachus' *De arithmetica* (p. 140) and a work, *De musica*, which he has heard of but not seen (*fertur etiam Latino sermone et Apuleium Madaurensem instituta huius operis effecisse*, p. 149).

[131] See, generally, E. Brehaut, *An Encyclopedist of the Dark Ages: Isidore of Seville* (New York: Columbia UP, 1912; repr. New York: B. Franklin, 1964); J. Fontaine, *Isidore de Séville et la culture classique dans l'Espagne wisigothique*, 3 vols. (Paris: Études augustiniennes, 1959–83); Curtius, *ELLMA*, 450; *S&S3*, 84.

[132] *The 'Etymologies' of Isidore of Seville*, ed. and trans. S. A. Barney et al. (Cambridge: CUP, 2006), 84 (2. 28: *Perihermenias*), 89 (3. 2: Apuleius as translator of mathematical works), and 190 (8. 11. 100: attributing to Apuleius a gloss on *Manes* or 'spirits of the dead'). The gloss is appropriated (verbatim) by Rabanus Maurus (AD 776 [or 784]–856) in *De universo* 15. 6 (*PL* 111, col. 434C): *Apuleius autem ait eos cata antiphrasin dici manes, hoc est, mites ac modestos, cum sint terribiles et immanes, ut Parcas et Eumenides* ('But Apuleius says that they are called *Manes*—that is, mild and gentle—by antiphrasis, since they are dreadful and frightful, [being named in the same way] as the Parcae and Eumenides'). Cf. *De deo Socratis* 153.

(*De diis gentium*) in his twenty-book compendium, *Origines siue etymologiae*, provides a brief description of Cupid, but he ignores Psyche completely.[133]

Earlier in the same work, Isidore mentions the transformations by Circe (of Ulysses' men into swine), by the Arcadians (men into wolves), and refers to those who 'affirm, not in some fabulous fiction but in an historical confirmation, that Diomedes' companions were changed into birds'.[134] Isidore has digested this straight from Augustine, *De ciuitate dei* 18. 16, 17. In the next chapter of Augustine's work, Isidore would have found the reference to the *De asino aureo*, but he makes no mention of Apuleius' asinine transformation in the very place one would have expected it.

Isidore, it appears, had no knowledge of *The Golden Ass*. If he had, he might have considered it a ripe subject for his disquisitions on the proper limits of human enquiry. In his *Synonima, siue soliloquia*, Isidore expresses the orthodox view of *curiositas*:

De curiositate, cap. xv.

NVlla sit tibi curiositas sciendi latentia: caue indagare quæ sunt à sensibus remota. Nihil vltra quàm scriptum est, quæras, nihil amplius perquiras quàm diuinæ literæ, prædi [320] cant. Scire non cupias, quod scire non licet. Curiositas periculosa præsumptio est, curiositas damnosa peritia est. In hæreses enim prouocat, in fabulas sacrilegas mentem præcipitat.[135]

(Let there be in you no curiosity for knowing hidden things: beware of investigating those things which are disconnected from the senses. Seek nothing beyond what is written; examine nothing more than the Divine Writings declare. Do not desire to know what it is not permitted to know. Curiosity is dangerous presumption; curiosity is pernicious knowledge. For it incites the mind towards heresies; it hurls it into sacrilegious stories.)

Fulgentius could find, in the fable of Psyche, a moral depiction of the consequences of *curiositas*. Isidore's thinking seems to go in the opposite direction: one of the worst aspects of 'curiosity' is that it can propel us towards

---

[133] *Etymologiae* 8. 11. 80, in *Opera omnia*, ed. Frater Iacobus du Breul (Paris: Michael Sonnius, 1601), 113: *Cupidinem vocatum ferunt propter amorem. Est enim dæmon fornicationis. Qui deo* [sc. *ideo*] *alatus pingitur: quia nihil amantibus leuius, nihil mutabilius inuenitur. Puer pingitur, quia stultus est & irrationabilis amor. Sagittam & facem tenere fingitur. Sagittam, quia amor cor vulnerat: facem, quia inflammat* ('They say that he is called Cupid on account of Love. For he is the *daemon* of fornication. He is represented as winged, because nothing flightier than lovers is found, nothing more changeable. He is represented as a boy, because love is foolish and irrational. He is feigned to hold an arrow and a torch; an arrow, because love wounds the heart; a torch, because it inflames it'). Cf. the characterization of Love (*Amor*) as a *daemon* in *De deo Socratis* 154–5.

[134] *Etymologiae*, 9. 4 (*De transformatione*), in *Opera omnia*, 157: *Nam & Diomedis socios in volucres fuisse conuersos, non fabuloso mendacio, sed historica affirmatione confirmant.*

[135] *Opera omnia*, 319.

'sacrilegious stories'. The hostility of the Early Church was directed particularly towards the seductive myth-making of heretics, but St Paul's exhortation to 'refuse profane and old wives' fables' (*Ineptas autem et aniles fabulas deuita*) could easily be read by subsequent ages as a general prohibition on fictions designed to entertain.[136] To compound such hostility, the subject of metamorphosis itself seems to have been considered suspect.[137] Augustine was probably attacking the doctrine of metempsychosis when he decried 'that ridiculous and noxious notion of the recycling of souls, either of men into beasts, or of beasts into men', but his criticism of the one extends easily to the other.[138]

Late Antiquity and the early Middle Ages evolved a variety of strategies in accommodating, within a Christian culture, the pagan pantheon of classical Greece and Rome.[139] Pre-Christian writers like Cicero and Vergil could be adopted as virtuous pagans, denied, by time of birth, a view of Christian revelation, but gifted, nonetheless, with a foretaste of the Truth. Apuleius, however, was not only born into the Christian era and, as an educated philosopher, in a position to embrace or reject Christian Truth;[140] he could actually be seen to be advocating, in the *Metamorphoses*, an Egyptian cult which, at the beginning of the first millenium, was one of Christianity's strongest rivals. Zacharias Scholasticus gives us an amusing anecdote (in his life of his friend Severus, Patriarch of Antioch, AD 512–18) of the conflict between the two cults.[141] Moreover, the apparent jibe against Christianity in Apuleius' description of the Baker's adulterous and murderous wife in Book 9 as one who spurned all the gods of the righteous and affirmed one God only as her own can hardly have endeared the work to the Christian apologists.[142]

---

[136] 1 Tim. 4: 7. KJV and *Nouum Testamentum Latine secundum editionem Sancti Hieronymi*, ed. J. Wordsworth and H. White (Oxford: Clarendon, 1920; repr. 1953).

[137] As late as the 14th cent., Chaucer takes pains to remove the avine metamorphosis in his retelling of Ovid's tale of Ceyx and Alcyone in *The Book of the Duchess*.

[138] Augustine, *Commentary on Genesis*, ch. 29 (*PL* 34, col. 445); L. Thorndike, *A History of Magic and Experimental Science*, 8 vols. (New York: Columbia UP, 1923–58), i. 509.

[139] See Curtius, *ELLMA*, esp. 442; and J. J. Seznec, *The Survival of the Pagan Gods: The Mythological Tradition and its Place in Renaissance Humanism and Art*, trans. B. F. Sessions (New York: Pantheon, 1953).

[140] Being a pagan in the Christian era was not necessarily incompatible with being acceptable in the Middle Ages. Macrobius, who 'became a philosophic and scientific authority for the entire Middle Ages', is generally considered to have been a pagan Neoplatonist. See Curtius, *ELLMA*, 443.

[141] *Vita Severi*, in *Sévère Patriarche d'Antioche 512–518: Textes syriaques*, ed. and trans. M.-A. Kugener, 2 vols. (Paris: Firmin-Didot, 1907), i. 23. Cf. Shanzer, *Commentary*, 26.

[142] For possible relations to a real report of a trial at Rome, see B. Baldwin, 'Apuleius and the Christians', *LCM* 14/4 (Apr. 1989), 55. In the introd. (pp. xxxvi–xxxix) to his translation of *The Golden Ass* (Oxford: Clarendon, 1994), P. G. Walsh speculates that 'this fervid recommendation of the religion of Isis may represent a counterblast to the [xxxviii] meteoric spread of Christianity in Africa in the later second century'.

The *De deo Socratis* had provided Augustine with a useful précis of Middle Platonic daemonology—a convenient object of attack. Controversy, in this instance, was probably favourable to the survival of Apuleius' philosophical works which were helped, also, by being suffused in the reflected glow of Plato.[143] It would have been less easy, however, to detach works so steeped in necromancy as the *Metamorphoses* and the *Apologia* from the persona of Apuleius the Thaumaturge—a persona which had attracted the attacks of such Church Fathers as Augustine, Lactantius, and Jerome.

The possibility of active suppression should not be ruled out. St Paul's bibliocaustic efforts at Ephesus (Acts 19: 19) may have provided the scriptural authority for an imperial edict of 409 which encouraged the burning of many books of magic.[144] The simpler explanations are those of accident and neglect. Apuleius' Latin in *The Golden Ass* can be difficult enough in a clearly punctuated modern edition; it would have been particularly challenging to an ill-equipped potential reader in the sixth or seventh centuries. It is worth noting that the works of Apuleius which were known in the Middle Ages were philosophical in content and (relatively) straightforward in style, while the *Florida* and the *Apologia*, both works of an epideictic nature, vanished along with *The Golden Ass*. Taking as approximate termini the dates 550 and 750, L. D. Reynolds gives us an image of textual transmission during this period:

The copying of classical texts tapered off to such an extent during the Dark Ages that the continuity of pagan culture was nearly severed; our model has the waist of a wasp.[145]

The *Abolita* Glossary

Most of our evidence suggests that *The Golden Ass* disappeared into the maw of (what we used to call) the 'Dark Ages' sometime during the latter part of the sixth century, taking with it the *Apologia* and the *Florida*. The one piece of counter-evidence is the so-called '*Abolita* glossary' preserved in the margins of another glossary (*Abstrusa*) in a manuscript (MS Vat. Lat. 3321) copied in Italy (perhaps at Rome) *circa* AD 750.[146]

---

[143] This is perhaps why the philosophical works have descended in separate traditions.

[144] L. Fargo Brown, 'On the Burning of Books', *Vassar Mediæval Studies*, ed. C. Forsyth Fiske (New Haven: YUP, 1923), 249–71, at 267. Shanzer (*Commentary*, 25) refers us to Ammianus Marcellinus' account (29. 1. 41) of 'the burning of books in the *liberales disciplinae* along with magical books'.

[145] *Texts and Transmission: A Survey of the Latin Classics* (Oxford: Clarendon, 1983), p. xvii.

[146] The glossaries are named after their first lemma.

W. M. Lindsay has hypothesized the following scenario for the creation of the *Abolita* glossary in its original form:

> In the seventh century (towards its close?), some monastery-teacher in Spain took from the shelves of the monastery-library a copy of Festus and decided to make a glossary out of it. He found however that it did not provide enough of suitable material and, after he had filled a number of pages with excerpts from its lemmas, looked about for a means of completing his design. He ordered some (young and ignorant) monk to copy out the brief marginal notes in the library text of Virgil, of Terence, of Apuleius and of at least two (unknown) Christian authors, and to set them (each in the order of its occurrence) in the glossary. ... The Apuleius volume (possibly including some works now lost) did not provide so many marginalia as the Terence; but any scraps from a 7th century Spanish MS of Apuleius (or of Terence) are welcome. For example, 'concipulassent' (not 'compilassent') [351] seems to have been its reading in Met. 9, 2; 'satagentes' (not 'satis agentes') in Met. 8, 17.[147]

Lindsay attributes the (lost) archetype of Vat. Lat. 3321 to Spain on the basis of Hispanic orthographical preferences (*v* for *f*), 'the occasional survival of the Spanish abbreviation-symbols', and transcriptional errors caused by an Italian scribe's difficulty in distinguishing 'Spanish miniscule *t*' from 'Italian *a*'.[148]

At first glance, the material seems very unpromising and should certainly be treated with caution. The lemmata are unattributed, consisting of single words or (at best) two-word phrases; the text is often corrupt; and the process of alphabeticization has done much to break up the original sequences. However, whereas most of the *Abstrusa* glossary has already reached the third stage of alphabeticization (ABC-), *Abolita* is at a more primitive stage (AB-) and several scholars have felt able to identify Apuleian 'batches'—short 'runs' of glosses relating to the *Metamorphoses*, the *Apologia*, and (occasionally) the *Florida*.[149] Thus we find, *inter alia*:

Gloss. Lat. iii. 108: *Crapula* (*AA* 7. 12; 8. 13); *Caperratum supercilium* (*AA* 9. 10); *Carc<h>es[s]ium* (*AA* 11. 16)

Gloss. Lat. iii. 151: *Nubilum* (*AA* 10. 28?); *Nundinat* (*AA* 10. 33?); *Nugonem* (*AA* 5. 30); *Nullo pacto* (*AA* 6. 17 etc.?); *Nutu* (*AA* 11. 25 etc.?)

Gloss. Lat. iii. 152: *Obtutus* (*AA* 2. 20); *Obsistit* (*AA* 3. 28); *Obsepta* (*AA* 3. 28); *Obtionem* (*AA* 4. 15)

---

[147] W. M. Lindsay, 'The St. Gall Glossary', *AJP* 38 (1917), 349–69, at 350–1.

[148] 'The "Abolita" Glossary (Vat. Lat. 3321)', *Journal of Philology* 34 (1918), 267–82, at 268–9.

[149] G. Loewe, *Prodromus corporis glossariorum Latinorum: Quaestiones de glossariorum Latinorum fontibus et usu* (Leipzig: Teubner, 1876), 144; R. Weir, 'Apuleius Glosses in the Abolita Glossary', *CQ* 15/1 (Jan. 1921), 41–3, and 'Addendum on Apuleius Glosses in the "Abolita" Glossary', *CQ* 15/2 (Apr. 1921), 107.

Because of its position in such a 'batch', Lindsay suggests that the gloss, *Conlutiones (-lud-) studiis intentas : studentes famalas nominavit* (*Gloss. Lat.* iii. 113), may preserve a fragment of a lost Apuleian work. Equally tantalizing is *Abolita*'s gloss, *Onos Graece asinus dicitur* ('The ass is called *Onos* in Greek').[150] It is tempting to infer that the gloss came from a manuscript of Apuleius in which a marginal (or prefatory) note pointed to the similarities between the *De asino aureo/Metamorphoses* and the extant *Onos* of pseudo-Lucian. And in the *Abstrusa* glossary (which hosts the *Abolita* glossary in the oldest surviving manuscripts) we find a gloss on *Milesiae* (*amatoria gesta*) and on *Ludicra* (*quae in ludis geruntur, turpis vel inania*).[151]

In the Appendix to the present volume, the (putative) Apuleian glosses for the *Metamorphoses* have been regrouped on narrative rather than alphabetical lines. The integrity of any remaining 'batches' is thereby destroyed, but the process may reunite separated glosses. For example, Apuleius describes the music accompanying Psyche's funereal wedding procession to the rock: *sonus tibiae zygiae mutatur in querulum Ludii modum* (*AA* 4. 33). *Abolita* provides two glosses (on *Tibia zigia* and on *Modus Lydius*) which may have been created in response to the one passage. The baker's wife is described as *saeva scaeva, virosa ebriosa, pervicax pertinax* (*AA* 9. 14). At least three of these terms (*virosa, ebriosus,* and *pervicax*) are glossed by *Abolita*.

The regrouping also makes it easier to see where the original glossator's attentions may have been focused. The average number of 'likely candidates' for each book is between ten and eleven, but Book 9 (adultery tales) has about twenty-two, most of them relating to the story of the baker and his wife.

Apuleius in the East

As a self-respecting second-century sophist, Apuleius claimed equal proficiency in Greek and Latin; and one might expect him to have left some traces in the eastern part of the Empire.[152] One might even hope for a Byzantine connection in the transmission of the novel, given the well-attested links between Monte Cassino and the eastern capital, and Sallustius' statement that he had revised his emended version of the *Metamorphoses* at Constantinople in 397.[153]

[150] *Glossaria Latina* ... vol. iii (*Abstrusa, Abolita*), ed. W. M. Lindsay and H. J. Thomson (Paris: Société anonyme d'édition 'Les belles lettres', 1926), 153 (*ON* 2).

[151] Ibid. 56 (*MI* 4) and 55 (*LU* 16–17).

[152] *Florida* 9. 29. On the (likely) limits of Apuleius' professed bilingualism, see Harrison, *Latin Sophist*, 15.

[153] Desiderius, Abbot of Monte Cassino (AD 1058–87), had ordered the great doors for the Basilica from Byzantium.

Yet one has to search hard for evidence of the survival of Latin literature in the East.[154] Ioannes Laurentius Lydus (b. 490), a Greek writer and teacher of Latin philology at Constantinople, refers several times to Apuleius' *Astronomica*, and once to an (otherwise unknown) 'work entitled *Eroticus*' ('Ἐρωτικός) by 'Apuleius, the Roman philosopher'.[155] Photius had composed his famous *Bibliotheca* (a series of reviews of 280 prose works compiled for the benefit of his absent brother Tarasius) sometime before becoming Patriarch of Constantinople for the first time in 858. At Cod. 129 of the *Bibliotheca*, Photius makes his much-debated comparison between the *Metamorphoses* of one 'Lucius of Patrae' and the *Lucius, or the Ass* of pseudo-Lucian; but, though he refers in chapter 163 to a (now lost) work of Apuleius, *De re rustica*, he shows no knowledge of his *Metamorphoses*.[156] Another Byzantine work, the *Geoponica* (compiled in the tenth century from a range of agricultural sources), names Apuleius in its prologue and refers to him another twenty times in the course of its twenty books.[157]

Greek culture also preserved the tradition of Apuleius as sage and magus. The *Greek Anthology* includes a 'Description of the statues in the public gymnasium called Zeuxippos' by Christodorus of Thebes (*fl.* 497).[158] The 'gymnasium' (actually a bath-complex) had originally been built in the centre of Byzantium by Septimius Severus (whose contempt for 'Punic' Milesian tales is 'recorded' in the *Historia Augusta*). It was refurbished by Constantine who established the statue gallery as part of his consecration of Constantinople

---

[154] Cf. B. Baldwin, 'Vergilius Graecus', *AJP* 97 (1976), 361–8.

[155] For the *Astronomica*, see *De mensibus* (4. 73) and *De ostentis* ('On Celestial Signs', 3, 4, 7, 10, 44, 54). Cited by H. E. Butler and A. S. Owen, eds., *Apulei Apologia sive Pro se de Magia Liber* (Oxford: Clarendon, 1914), p. xxviii. For the *Eroticus*, see Lydus, *De magistratibus* (3. 64). According to Harrison (*Latin Sophist*, 28–9), this was probably a dialogue debating the relative merits of homosexual and heterosexual love.

[156] *PG* 330, Cod. 129. The *De re rustica* reference is given by Butler, *Apologia*, p. xxviii.

[157] R. Martin, 'Apulée dans les *Géoponiques*', *Revue de philologie* 46 (1972), 246–55; R. H. Rodgers, 'The Apuleius of the *Geoponica*', *CSCA* 11 (1978), 197–207; Harrison, *Latin Sophist*, 27. Martin explores possible links between the *Geoponica* and Apuleius' surviving works: e.g. Apuleius' recommendation of the leaves of laurel roses as a poison for mice (*Geoponica* 13. 5) and Lucius' disquisition on the toxicity of *rosae laureae* in *AA* 4. 2 (*cuncto pecori cibus letalis est*; cf. Martin, 253). Rodgers takes a more cautious view: 'we are on safer ground if we overcome the temptation to identify "the Apuleius of the *Geoponica*" with the philomath of Madaura' (203). He does point, however, to the occurrence of Apuleius' name nine times in an Arabic work, the *Kitāb al-Filāha* of Balīnās al-Hakīm, or pseudo-Apollonius of Tyana. Many of the references (e.g. 'Apuleus [*sic*] the wise of the Romans') correspond to passages in the *Geoponica* (Rodgers, 206–7 n. 44). Apuleius' name does not appear in the 12th-cent. Latin translation (*Liber de vindemiis*) made by Burgundio of Pisa of part of the wine-making section of the *Geoponica*. See *Liber de vindemiis a Domino Burgundione Pisano de Graeco in Latinum fideliter translatus*, ed. F. Buonamici, in *Annali delle Università Toscane* 28 (1908), 1–29.

[158] The 'Ἔκφρασις appears in both versions of the *Greek Anthology*: the *Anthologia Palatina* (assembled in the 10th cent.) and the *Anthologia Planudea* (12th or 13th cent.).

in AD 330.[159] The eighty-one statues described in Christodorus' Ἔκφρασις include a large number of Greek literary figures (Homer, Hesiod, Euripides, Sappho, Plato, Aristotle, and Demosthenes among them), and a very small number of Romans: Julius Caesar, Vergil ('the clear-voiced swan dear to the Italians... another Homer'), and Apuleius:

> Καὶ νοερῆς ἄφθεγκτα Λατινίδος ὄργια Μούσης
> ἄζετο παπταίνων Ἀπολήϊος ὅντινα μύστην
> Αὐσονὶς ἀρρήτου σοφίης ἐθρεψατο Σειρήν.

(APULEIUS was seated considering the unuttered secrets of the Latin intellectual Muse. Him the Italian Siren nourished, a devotee of ineffable wisdom.)[160]

Apuleius' statue is preceded by Apollo, Aphrodite, Achilles, and Hermes, and followed by Artemis, Homer, Pherecydes, and Heraclitus. Various attempts have been made to discern a cultural or ideological programme in the choice and positioning of the statues. For Reinhold Stupperich, the predominance of Homeric figures reflects Constantine's concern to establish his capital as a 'New Troy'.[161] Sarah Guberti Bassett rejects Stupperich's reading as overdetermined, preferring to see the arrangement of statues as a traditional mix of mythological, literary-philosophical, and contemporary figures, appropriate to a building devoted to physical well-being, entertainment, and public debate. Bassett observes that the healing-god Aesculapius is 'Noticeably absent' from Christodorus' description and suggests that he may have been 'mentioned in the missing verses of the *Ekphrasis*'.[162] One could argue, however (on the basis of the immediate proximity of Hermes' statue and the references to 'unuttered secrets' and 'ineffable wisdom'), that Aesculapius may be present by proxy in the person of Apuleius. We know, from references in his extant writings, that Apuleius was the author of several lost works with an Aesculapian theme: a speech, *de Aesculapii maiestate* ('on the majesty of

---

[159] S. G. Bassett, '*Historiae Custos*: Sculpture and Tradition in the Baths of Zeuxippos', *AJA* 100 (1996), 491–506. Archaeological excavations in the 1920s uncovered two round statue bases with inscriptions matching the names given by Christodorus. The statues would appear to have been at least life-size and to have been made of bronze or marble. They were destroyed by fire during the *Nika* riots of AD 532.

[160] Text and translation from W. R. Paton's Loeb edn., *The Greek Anthology*, 5 vols. (London: Heinemann, 1917–18), i. 82–3. Cf. Costanza, 39–40; and C. Moreschini, 'Sulla fama di Apuleio nel medioevo e nel rinascimento', in *Studi filologici letterari e storici in memoria di Guido Favati*, ed. G. Varanini and P. Pinagli, 2 vols. (Padua: Antenore, 1977), ii. 457–76, at 461. We must, of course, consider the possibility that the 'Apuleius' referred to is not our friend from Madauros. The reference to the Siren, for example, would be more appropriate to Apuleius Celsus, the 1st-cent. physician from Centuripe (now Centorbi) in Sicily than to a North African.

[161] 'Das Statuenprogramm in den Zeuxippos-Thermen: Überlegungen zur Beschreibung des Christodoros von Koptos', *Istanbuler Mitteilungen* 32 (1982), 210–35.

[162] '*Historiae Custos*', 502.

Aesculapius'), a hymn (in Greek and Latin), and a dialogue (also bilingual) in his honour.[163] These references to lost works may account for the inclusion of the Latin *Asclepius* (a dialogue between Hermes Trismegistus and Asclepius) in the same manuscript tradition as Apuleius' philosophical *opera*.[164] The current critical consensus is against Apuleian authorship of the *Asclepius*, but (as the most accessible specimen of Hermetic writing) it made a significant contribution to Apuleius' reputation in the West during the Middle Ages and Renaissance.

The themes of healing and *magia* converge in the *Quaestiones et responsiones* of St Anastasius Sinaita (*fl.* 640–700), where Apuleius figures (anachronistically) as one of three magi summoned by Domitian to help deliver Rome from plague:

Φησὶ δὲ Ἀπολέϊος.«ἐγὼ τὴν ἐν τῷ τρίτῳ μέρει τῆς πόλεως ἐνδημήσασαν λοιμίκην φθορὰν καταπαύσω ιέ ἡμερῶν »[165]
(Apuleius said: 'Within fifteen days, I will put an end to this pestilential corruption which has spread through a third part of the city.')

Apollonius of Tyana offers to end the plague in another third of the city in ten days; but Julianus is able to save the whole of Rome in almost no time at all. The contest of the magi follows on immediately from an account of Simon Magus who made a habit of 'turning himself into a serpent and metamorphosing into other animals' (ὄφις ἐγίνετο, καὶ εἰς ἕτερα ζῷα μετεμορφοῦτο).[166] These stories form part of Anastasius' answer to a wider question (*Quaestio* 20) about why those who are strangers to the Truth (of Christian Revelation) are often able to prophesy and to perform miracles.[167]

In the eleventh century, Michael Psellos (1018–*c*.1078) compares Apuleius with the reputed author of the *Chaldean Oracles*:

---

[163] *Apologia* 55. 10; *Florida* 18. 37; *De deo Socratis* 154; Harrison, *Latin Sophist*, 34–5.

[164] *Hermès Trismégiste: Corpus Hermeticum*, ed. A. D. Nock, trans. A.-J. Festugière, 4 vols. (Paris: Société d'édition 'Les belles lettres', 1945–54), ii. 259–355; *Hermetica: The Greek 'Corpus Hermeticum' and the Latin 'Asclepius' in a New English Translation*, trans. B. P. Copenhaver (Cambridge: CUP, 1992). The case for Apuleian authorship (previously made by G. F. Hildebrand and B. L. Hijmans) has recently been restated by V. Hunink, 'Apuleius and the *Asclepius*', *Vigiliae Christianae* 50 (1996), 288–308, and rebutted by M. Horsfall Scotti, 'The *Asclepius*: Thoughts on a Re-opened Debate', *Vigiliae Christianae* 54 (2000), 396–416. Cf. Harrison, *Latin Sophist*, 12–13. Horsfall Scotti suggests (407) that it was Augustine's 'polemic juxtaposition' in the *De ciuitate dei* of the *Asclepius* and the *De deo Socratis* which led to the inclusion of the *Asclepius* in the ms. tradition of Apuleius' *philosophica*.

[165] *PG* 89, cols. 524D–525B; Costanza, 41. R. J. Penella compares the story to Philostratus' account (*Vita Apollonii* 5. 27–38) of Vespasian's meeting 'with three philosophers, Apollonius, the Stoic Euphrates, and Dio Chrysostum, at Alexandria in A.D. 69'. See 'An Overlooked Story about Apollonius of Tyana in Anastasius Sinaita', *Traditio* 34 (1978), 414–15, at 414. Anastasius' *Quaestiones* are thought to contain interpolations from a later editor.

[166] *PG* 89, col. 524C.   [167] *PG* 89, cols. 518C–532B.

Ἰουλιανὸς ὁ Χαλδαῖος καὶ ὁ Λίβυς Ἀπουλήϊος· ἦν δ' ἄρα οὗτος μὲν ὑλικώτερος, ἅτερος δὲ νοερώτερος καὶ θειότερος.[168]

(Julianus the Chaldean and Apuleius the Libyan: the latter more worldly, the former more intellectual and divine....)

Apuleius is being considered in the context of theurgy, the practice (which originated among Egyptian Platonists) of communicating with beneficent spirits in order to produce miraculous effects:

κατάγουσί τε τοὺς παρ' ἑαυτοῖς θεοὺς θελκτηρίοις ᾠδαῖς καὶ δεσμοῦσι καὶ λύουσιν, ὥσπερ τὸν Ἑπτάκτιν ὁ Ἀπουλήϊος ὅρκοις καταναγκάσας μὴ προσομιλῆσαι τῷ θεουργῷ.[169]

(They draw the gods down beside them by means of enchanting spells, and they bind and they loose [them], just as Apuleius, by means of oaths, constrained the Seven-Rayed One not to converse with the theurgist.)

The collocation of Apuleius and 'Heptaktis' ('the Seven-Rayed One') is especially interesting, given Julian the Apostate's desire to promote the Sun-God, and the solar concerns of Heliodorus' *Aethiopica*.[170]

We might also note an obscure (but tantalizing) trace of Apuleius the storyteller within the Sindbad-complex (the eastern manifestation of the Seven Sages tradition). The Hebrew version (*Mischle Sindbad*) identifies the

---

[168] ed. C. N. Sathas, 'Fragments inédits des historiens grecs', *Bulletin de correspondance hellénique* 1 (1877), 121–33 and 309–20, at 309; Costanza, 40. The only source given by Sathas for the passage is 'Allatius, *de quorundam Græcorum opinionibus*, p. 177'. See Leone Allacci (1586–1669), *De templis Græcorum recentioribus ... necnon de græcorum hodie quorundam opiniationibus ad Paullum Zacchiam* (Cologne: Jodocus Kalcovius, 1645), 177. The adjective ὑλικώτερος ('more material/worldly/secular') derives from ὕλη ('Hyle' or 'matter') which is traditionally opposed to νοῦς (the intelligent principle). On the status of ὕλη, see (e.g.) *Asclepius*, 14. Michael Psellos played a role in the transmission of the (now fragmentary) *Chaldean Oracles*. See Julianus the Theurgist, *The Chaldean Oracles: Text, Translation, and Commentary*, ed. R. Majercik (Leiden: Brill, 1989); H. Lewy, *Chaldaean Oracles and Theurgy: Mysticism, Magic and Platonism in the Later Roman Empire* (2nd edn.), rev. M. Tardieu (Paris: Études augustiniennes, 1978).

[169] *Michaelis Pselli philosophica minora*, ed. J. M. Duffy and D. J. O'Meara, 2 vols. (Stuttgart: Teubner, 1989–92), i. 9; Costanza, 40. I am grateful to Dr Augustine Casiday for commenting on my translations of Byzantine Greek in this section. Regarding the final extract, he notes: 'προσομιλῆσαι ("to converse") is a word with religious overtones; Evagrius uses it to describe prayer as a "conversation" with God. It tends to suggest a long-term interaction, rather than a casual conversation as we might use the term.'

[170] On Heptaktis, see Julian the Apostate, *Oratio V* ('Hymn to Cybele'), 172D–173A; Lydus (*De mensibus* 4. 53: Iao and Sabaoth). Cf. H. P. Blavatsky, *Isis Unveiled: A Master-key to the Mysteries of Ancient and Modern Science and Theology*, 2 vols. (London: J. W. Bouton, 1877), ii. 417: ' "And were I to touch upon the initiation into our sacred Mysteries," says Emperor Julian, the kabalist, "which the Chaldean bacchised respecting the *seven-rayed God, lifting up the souls through Him,* I should say things unknown, and *very unknown to the rabble,* but well known to the *blessed Theurgists.*" '

third Sage as Apuleius (the others being Sindibad, Hippocrates, Lucian, Aristotle, Pindar, and Homer).[171]

Apuleius in the Carolingian Renaissance

The survival of most of the pagan literature extant today is due to the copying of texts (many of which had survived, uncopied, from Late Antiquity) during the Carolingian Revival of the eighth and ninth centuries. *The Golden Ass* is a happy exception. Charlemagne's court was certainly receptive to Apuleius. Amongst the writings composed in the emperor's name, we have a work, *De imaginibus* ('On Images'), in which Apuleius is praised for disputing 'most subtly' (*subtilissime*) in the *Peri hermeneias* on the function of syllogism.[172] Leighton Reynolds observes that our oldest manuscript of Apuleius' *opera philosophica* (Brussels 10054–6) dates from 'the third decade of the ninth century' and that 'the α family to which it belongs must have sprung from the heart of the Carolingian revival'.[173] But what of the *Apologia*, the *Metamorphoses*, and the *Florida*? The general assumption is that these texts 'had survived at Montecassino' while the *opera philosophica* 'emerged and initially circulated in northern Europe'.[174] There are, however, several problems with this thesis.

The Carolingian scholars who peppered their own writings with 'echoes of the tortured and artificial periods of Fulgentius' as 'marks of a high style'[175] would have taken no less delight in the rhetorical excesses of such works as the *Metamorphoses* and the *Florida*. And the title, at least, of Apuleius' *De asino aureo* may have been heard in Charlemagne's halls, if we can credit Einhard's

---

[171] See K. Campbell, 'A Study of the Romance of the Seven Sages with Special Reference to the Middle English Versions', *PMLA* 14 (1899), 1–107, at 16. Campbell contends that the Hebrew version cannot 'be dated later than the eleventh century' (15), and may be the oldest 'of any text which has been preserved', though he acknowledges 'traces of a Greek influence' (6) in the names given to the sages, and notes the assumption of Comparetti that 'the Hebrew text stands for a late and very free version of the romance' (8).

[172] *PL* 98, col. 1238B: *dicente Apuleio philosopho Platonico Madaurensi qui de hujusmodi syllogistici industria in libro qui inscribitur, De perihermeniis Apulei, subtilissime disputavit* ('So says Apuleius the Platonic Philosopher of Madaura who, on the subject of the use of syllogism of this kind, disputed most subtly in the book which is entitled *Apuleius' Concerning Interpretation*'). This picks up the *subtilius* in Cassiodorus' recommendation (*Institutiones* 118) discussed *supra*. Text also given in *PL* 70, *De artibus ac disciplinis liberalium litterarum* 1173A. On the *Peri hermeneias*, cf. J. Marenbon, 'Carolingian Thought', in *Carolingian Culture: Emulation and Innovation*, ed. R. McKitterick (Cambridge: CUP, 1994), 171–92, at 173.

[173] *Texts and Transmission*, 17.

[174] Ibid. 16.

[175] Laistner, 'Fulgentius', 204.

report that the emperor liked to be read to at table, being 'fond of Saint Augustine's books, especially the one entitled *The City of God*.[176]

Moreover, if such works were preserved at Monte Cassino (and that is a very big 'if'), there were open channels for their transmission to Carolingian scholars in northern Europe. Charlemagne's uncle, Carloman, had retired to Monte Cassino before his death in 755;[177] and Charlemagne himself had visited the abbey and in 787 ordered an accurate copy to be made of the Rule of St Benedict. One of Monte Cassino's greatest men of letters, Paul the Deacon, spent several years in Charlemagne's court circle, joining it some time after May 782 and returning to the abbey before 787.[178] Peter of Pisa welcomed him with a somewhat ironic encomium, crediting him with know-ledge of Greek, Latin, and Hebrew, and calling him 'A Virgil in Latin, a Horace in metre, and a Tibullus in eloquence'.

Yet with all these opportunities, what we might call the 'epideictic trio' (*Apologia, Metamorphoses, Florida*) seems to have escaped notice in the north. When one considers how the Carolingians dismembered their text of Petro-nius, one may feel grateful that *The Golden Ass* reached us by another route;[179] but the Carolingian failure to access these desirable writings makes us wonder how and where *The Golden Ass* managed to survive.

[176] *Vita Caroli Magni*, ch. 24, trans. in *Carolingian Civilization: A Reader*, ed. P. E. Dutton (Peterborough, Ont.: Broadview P, 1993), 36–7. D. A. Bullough observes, however: 'I very much doubt whether the court had a complete *De civitate Dei*: there is no pre-tenth-century manu-script of all twenty-two [355] books … while Einhard's *libris* … *his qui de civitate Dei* PRAETITULATI *sunt* suggests to me a collection of extracts.' See 'Charlemagne's Court Library Revisited', *Early Medieval Europe*, 12/4 (2003), 339–63, at 354–5.

[177] Einhard, *Vita Caroli Magni*, 2.

[178] P. Godman, ed., *Poetry of the Carolingian Renaissance* (London: Duckworth, 1985), 8 and 82; 84–5.

[179] See R. H. F. Carver, 'The Rediscovery of the Latin Novels', in *Latin Fiction: The Latin Novel in Context*, ed. H. Hofmann (London: Routledge, 1999), 253–68. Perceived incongruities and discontinuities in the opening (ss. 103–13) of the *De deo Socratis* in the *textus receptus* have led scholars (from as early as Pierre Pithou in 1565 and Justus Lipsius in 1585) to identify all (or most) of it as a 'False Preface' made up of material rightfully belonging to the *Florida*. The argument implies that, at some point in Late Antiquity or the (very) early Middle Ages, a codex existed in which the *Opera philosophica* (*De deo Socratis, Asclepius, De Platone,* and *De mundo*) were joined to the *Metamorphoses, Apologia,* and *Florida*. When the manuscript tradition bifurcated, material from the end of the fourth book of the *Florida* (which lacks Sallustius' *subscriptio* in F) became detached, five fragments going to form the 'False Preface' to the *De deo Socratis* (which had evidently already lost its authentic opening). For the majority view (in favour of reascribing the material to the *Florida*), see Harrison, *Latin Sophist*, 91–2, and *Apuleius: Rhetorical Works* (Oxford: OUP, 2001), 77–80. For a survey of the problem (and a defence of the unity of the *De deo Socratis*), see V. Hunink, 'The Prologue of Apuleius' *De Deo Socratis*', *Mnemosyne* 48 (1995), 292–312.

2

Apuleius in the High Middle Ages

MONTE CASSINO

In February 1944, the Allied conquest of Italy—a prerequisite for the liberation of Europe as a whole—depended upon control of the Liri valley, halfway between Naples and Rome. Dominating the valley, from its height of 1,700 feet, was the abbey of Monte Cassino, an acropolis perched on a natural fortress. The Germans had taken up strong positions around the valley, but as the fountain-head of Western monasticism, the preserver of much that is best in the Classical heritage,[1] and the temporary repository of the ashes of Percy Bysshe Shelley, the abbey had been excluded from the Gustav Line by Marshall Kesselring, and a 300-metre-wide cordon had been drawn around it.[2]

The Allies' destruction of the undefended abbey—subjected to the most concentrated bombardment of the entire war—can be read as a twisted parable for the twentieth century.[3] But the enduring strategic importance of the Liri valley also reminds us that it was the happy conjunction of topography with the line of spiritual devotion inspired by St Benedict and his Rule, that allowed Monte Cassino to exert such a powerful influence on the course of European culture.[4]

---

[1] The texts which are thought to depend for their survival on a Cassinese transmission include the later *Annals* and the *Histories* of Tacitus, Seneca's *Dialogues*, Varro's *De lingua latina*, Frontinus' *De aquis*, and the *Apologia*, *Metamorphoses*, and *Florida* of Apuleius. See Reynolds and Wilson, *S&S3*, 109.

[2] Shelley's ashes were amongst the items stored in the abbey which Lt.-Col. Julius Schlegel had 'rescued' from the Keats-Shelley Memorial House in Rome. See T. Leccisotti, *Monte Cassino*, ed. and trans. A. O. Citarella (Abbey of Monte Cassino, 1987), 134. H. Bloch, 'The Bombardment of Monte Cassino (February 14–16, 1944): A New Appraisal', *Benedictina* 20 (1973), 383–424, at 390, points us to 'War-Time Rescue by Panzer Colonel', *The Times*, 8 Nov. 1951; and Rudolf Böhmler, *Monte Cassino*, trans. R. H. Stevens (London: Cassell, 1964), 110–14.

[3] The principal instigator of the destruction was the commander of the New Zealand forces, General Sir Bernard (later Baron) Freyberg (1889–1963), who, as one of the 'Argonauts', had helped to carry the coffin at the midnight burial of Rupert Brooke on Skyros in April 1915. He also became a friend of J. M. Barrie. See I. Wards, 'Freyberg, Bernard Cyril', *ODNB*. The local German commander, Fridolin von Senger (1891–1963)—an Old Etonian and former Rhodes Scholar (1912–14)—had given personal assurances that the abbey itself would not be used for military purposes.

[4] Within little more than a week of the capture of Monte Cassino, General Clark had taken Rome (Marshal Kesselring having gained permission from Berlin to withdraw without a fight), the D-Day landings at Normandy had begun (2 June 1944), and the war had entered its final phase.

Tradition ascribes Benedict's arrival at Monte Cassino to the year 529, the same year in which Justinian closed the philosophy schools in Athens and promulgated his codex of Roman Law.[5] The chronicles of Monte Cassino draw repeated parallels between the abbey's foundation and biblical figures, places, and events: the mountain itself is linked to Sinai, while Benedict is a new Moses who also imitates Christ in his mission of twelve disciples.

Monte Cassino was for centuries a vital point of exchange between east and west. It was able to exploit its position at the centre of the competing claims of the papacy, the western emperors, and Byzantium (which continued to control much of southern Italy); and it served as an intermediary between the papacy and the Normans in the southern states. By the latter part of the eleventh century it had become 'the most notable centre of learning of its age in all Christendom'.[6] 'Monte Cassino' was an entity extending far beyond the physical confines of the mountain. The panels of the bronze doors which Maurus of Amalfi gave to Monte Cassino in 1066 record that the 'land of St Benedict' (*terra sancti Benedicti*) comprised some 560 churches and forty-seven castles.[7] Indeed, in the eleventh and twelfth centuries, it was virtually a principality in its own right, enjoying the status of an *abbatia nullius*, answerable only to the Holy See.

Palaeographical evidence indicates that it was here that our oldest surviving copy of the *Metamorphoses*, the *Apologia*, and the *Florida* was written, in Beneventan (i.e. southern Italian or 'Lombardic') script, in the eleventh century. This manuscript, now held in the Laurentian Library in Florence (Laur. 68.2), is generally designated F. It is usually associated with the 'great efflorescence of artistic and intellectual activity that reached its peak under abbot Desiderius (1058–87)'.[8] The orthodox view, propounded most cogently by D. S. Robertson in 1924 and 1940, is that all the surviving manuscripts of the *Metamorphoses*, the *Apologia*, and the *Florida* descend from this one copy.[9]

---

[5] Leccisotti, 15.

[6] H. E. J. Cowdrey, *The Age of Abbot Desiderius: Monte Cassino, the Papacy, and the Normans in the Eleventh and Early Twelfth Centuries* (Oxford: Clarendon, 1983), 45.

[7] Ibid. 4, 10.

[8] *S&S3*, 97. For reasons to associate Laur. 68.2 with Monte Cassino, see E. A. Lowe, 'The Unique Manuscript of Tacitus' *Histories* (Florence Laur. 68.2)', in *Casinensia: Miscellanea di studi Cassinesi* (Monte Cassino: Monte Cassino, 1929), 257–72; repr. in his *Palaeographical Papers 1907–1965*, ed. L. Bieler, 2 vols. (Oxford: Clarendon, 1972), i. 289–302, at 295. See generally, F. Newton, 'The Desiderian Scriptorium at Monte Cassino: The Chronicle and Some Surviving Manuscripts', *Dumbarton Oaks Papers* 30 (1976), 37–54, and *The Scriptorium and Library at Monte Cassino, 1058–1105* (Cambridge: CUP, 1999). Newton (*Scriptorium*, 126) notes that it was rare for Classical texts to be written (as F is) in two columns and that we have no surviving examples after 'about the mid 1070s'.

[9] D. S. Robertson, 'The Manuscripts of the *Metamorphoses* of Apuleius, Parts I & II', *CQ* 18 (1924), 27–42, 85–99; and introd. to *Apulée: Les Métamorphoses*, vol. i (Paris: Budé, 1940).

The study of the manuscript tradition of Apuleius has traditionally been the preserve of the textual critic concerned with establishing a text as close as possible to that actually written by the author. Yet the cross-fertilization of textual criticism and literary history can be fruitful. Desiderius' 'beloved friend', Alfanus of Salerno (*c.*1015–85), went in 1056 to Monte Cassino where he became 'the Cassinese Vergil'.[10] Lowe observes that he was 'noted as physician, poet, and theologian, was an intimate friend of the abbot, and is supposed to have had great influence with him'.[11] In the *Vita et passio s. Christianae*, Alfanus speaks of Apuleius in glowing terms:

In illo namque libello Apuleii, qui De Deo Sacratis [sic] titulatur, in quo propter incredibilem copiam suavitatemque dicendi sæpe et multum studere solebamus... [12]

(For in that book entitled, *On the God of Socrates*, with which we are wont to busy ourselves often and much because of the unbelievable copiousness and sweetness of expression...)

Francis Newton uses Alfanus in his hypothetical 'sketch to explain the intellectual and political background for the copying of the Mediceus'—the manuscript of Tacitus (*Annales* 11–16 and *Historiae* 1–5) which is now bound together with F.[13] He notes that the style of script in the Tacitus 'is precisely that of the first period of the Desiderian scriptorium, when Grimoald's presence and example was inspiring monks trained in the cassinese tradition to greater clarity of presentation of the text.'[14] The Mediceus was clearly a deluxe production: 'The initials and headings in the Apuleius give a cruder look to its page, as compared to that of the Tacitus. The modern student, however, should not be misled; it is clear that the Apuleius text was regarded as a treasure, as was the other.'[15]

Further light may be cast on the date of F (or its exemplar) by Guaiferius, Monk of Monte Cassino, who died, according to Herbert Bloch, between 1069 and 1086.[16] In 1018, during the construction of the town of Troia on the ruins of Aecae in Apulia, a sarcophagus was discovered containing the remains of San Secondino, the ancient city's bishop. In his *Vita S. Secundini*, Guaiferius observes:

[10] Leccisotti, 217.

[11] *The Beneventan Script* (Oxford: Clarendon, 1914), 12. Newton (*Scriptorium*, 12) provides text and translation of the relevant passage in the *Chronica Monasterii Casinensis* (3. 7).

[12] *PL* 147, col. 1272B. Alfanus goes on to quote a passage from the *De deo Socratis* unknown to us today. See M. Manitius, *Geschichte der lateinische Literatur des Mittelalters*, 3 vols. (Munich: Beck, 1911–31), ii. 635; O. Pecere, 'Qualche riflessione sulla tradizione di Apuleio a Montecassino', in *Le strade del testo*, ed. G. Cavallo (Bari: Adriatica, 1987), 99–124, at 119 n. 34.

[13] *Scriptorium*, 106–7.

[14] Ibid. 100.

[15] Ibid. 108.

[16] *Monte Cassino in the Middle Ages*, 3 vols. (Cambridge, Mass.: HUP, 1986), i. 554.

64   *Apuleius in the High Middle Ages*

Hec vero civitas, si nominis significationem advertimus (Ecana etiam dicta est), anti-
quissima fuit, cum et monumentorum marmoratio, scenarum columnatio, eminentia
culminum id designent.[17]

(But this city, if we take note of the significance of the name—for it was called
'Ecana'—was most ancient, as the marble-lining of the monuments, the use of pillars
to support stages, the loftiness of the gables indicate.)

The description of Aecae clearly draws on Apuleius' praise of Carthage and its
citizens in *Florida* 18:

praeterea in auditorio hoc genus spectari debet non pauimenti marmoratio nec proscaenii
contabulatio nec scaenae columnatio, sed nec culminum eminentia nec lacunarium
refulgentia nec sedilium circumferentia … nihil amplius spectari debet quam conuenien-
tium ratio et dicentis oratio. (ed. Helm)

(Moreover, in an auditorium of this kind, what ought to be looked at is not the
marbling of the paving, nor the flooring of the proscenium, nor the pillaring of
the stage, nor the eminence of the roof, nor the brilliance of the panelled ceiling, nor
the expanse of the seating … nothing else ought to be looked at more closely than the
enthusiasm of the audience and the vocalism of the speaker.)[18]

Guaiferius' philological archaeology—unearthing rare words (such as *mar-*
moratio) from an extremely rare author—mimics the activity of the builders
of Troia (who are salvaging classical materials for their new cathedral) and
anticipates the (highly creative) antiquarianism that we will see (Chapter 6,
infra) to be such a feature of quattrocento humanism.[19]

In his catalogue of miracles at the end of the *Vita S. Secundini*, Guaiferius
seems to extract from Lucius' vision of Isis' mantle (*palla … nodulis*
fimbriarum, AA 11. 3), the 'threads of the mantle' which, despite being
'surrounded by ashes' have somehow remained 'intact' (*palle fimbrie cineribus*
involute sed integre).[20] In *Florida* 23, Apuleius had employed the metaphor of
a well-built and 'elegantly painted' ship which, for all its accoutrements, is
easily lost if 'the helmsman fails to steer her, or a storm drives her':

[17] *Vita S. Secundini*, 2. Text from O. Limone, 'L'opera agiografica di Guaiferio di Montecassino', in *Monastica III: Scritti raccolti in memoria del XV centenario della nascita di S. Benedetto*
(480–1980) (Monte Cassino: Pubblicazioni cassinesi, 1983), 77–130, at 96. Cf. *PL* 147, 1295C.
The parallel is noted by Manitius (*Geschichte*, ii. 486) and Newton (*Scriptorium*, 288 n. 235)
who explains Guaiferius' pun as a play on *Aecanus* ('of Aecae') and *ecanus* ('very grey').

[18] Trans. J. Hilton, in *Apuleius: Rhetorical Works*, ed. Harrison, 167. Hilton's rendering of
ratio/oratio ('judgement'/'rhetorical power') as 'enthusiasm'/'vocalism' concludes his brave
attempt to mimic Apuleius' linguistic play throughout the passage. The same effect might be
achieved more accurately by 'good sense'/'eloquence'.

[19] Cf. Newton (*Scriptorium*, 288): 'it is clear that the hagiographer was handling "spolia" as
rare as any that the builders around him were using'. Newton suggests (288 n. 237) that 'The
theme of ruins was perhaps invoked in Guaiferius' artistic consciousness by the earlier reference
(*Florida* 15) to half-overthrown walls at Samos.'

[20] Parallel noted by Limone, 104.

Sicuti navem bonam, fabre factam, bene intrinsecus compactam, extrinsecus eleganter depictam, mobili clavo, firmis rudentibus, procero malo, insigni carchesio, splendentibus velis, postremo omnibus armamentis idoneis ad usum et honestis ad contemplationem, eam navem si aut gubernator non agat aut tempestas agat, ut facile cum illis egregiis instrumentis aut profunda hauserint aut scopuli comminuerint!

In his account of Pope Lucius I (reputedly martyred in AD 254), Guaiferius appropriates the Apuleian passage in order to illustrate how vulnerable human beings would be to the forces of damnation had the early martyrs not struggled on their behalf:

ne velut navem solida et durabili materia fabre factam, tenaci compage solidatam, variis coloribus auroque distinctam, mobili clavo, firmis rudentibus, malo excelso, [117] *carchesio insigni, velis splendentibus, postremo omnibus armamentis et ad usum idoneis et ad contemplandum honestis, si eam nulli gubernatores, nulli remiges agant, facile cum huiusmodi instrumentis aut in pelagus merget aut in scopulos tempestas allidet.*[21]

(... like a ship, built of solid and durable material, fastened together with tight joints, decorated in gold and various colours, with a nimble helm, stout rigging, tall mast, a notable mast-head, gleaming sails—in short, with all her tackle fit for use and decent to behold: if no helmsmen steer her or oarsmen drive her, in spite of all the equipment of this kind, a storm will easily plunge her into the sea or drive her onto the rocks.)

Because of the method used to prepare the parchment, the ink quickly began to flake off the flesh side of manuscripts written at Monte Cassino in the eleventh century.[22] Many were retouched during the thirteenth century, and some were copied. The second oldest MS of the *Metamorphoses, Apologia,* and *Florida* (Laur. 29.2) was written in Beneventan 'about the year 1200' and is designated ϕ.[23] In Lowe's opinion, ϕ, like its exemplar, F, was written at Monte Cassino and remained there until both MSS were removed in the fourteenth century, finally finding its way into the Laurentian Library in Florence.

Because ϕ is an apograph (a direct and uncontaminated copy) of F, it has usually been used purely as a means of restoring the reading of the exemplar where F has become illegible. The correspondence between a 'destructive rent' in fol. 160 of F and 'a series of intentional gaps in ϕ, filled up by a later hand in the fourteenth century' indicates that F was already torn when ϕ was made.[24]

---

[21] Noted by Limone, 116–17; my trans.

[22] Newton (*Scriptorium*, 61) notes that flaking was 'endemic at Monte Cassino in our period', but 'not restricted to that scriptorium'.

[23] Lowe, 'The Unique Manuscript of Apuleius' *Metamorphoses* (Laurentian. 68.2) and its Oldest Transcript (Laurentian. 29.2)', *CQ* 14 (1920), 150–5, at 155. Scholars prior to Lowe generally dated ϕ to the 12th cent. Robertson ('Manuscripts', 27) notes that 'Rostagno and Schiaparelli adhere to the old dating'.

[24] Robertson, 'Manuscripts', 27. The rent affects the description of Thrasyllus' courtship of Charite following his murder of Tlepolemus (*AA* 8. 7–9).

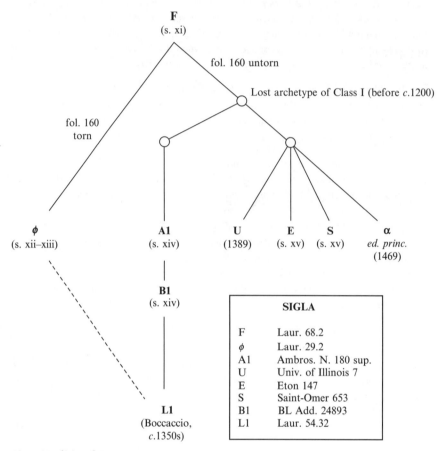

Fig.1 Traditional Stemma

Earlier scholars had held that the *supplementa* to the gap found in ϕ and later MSS were the result of conjecture, a thesis rejected by Robertson as improbable. Robertson argued, instead, that a group of existing MSS ('Class I') descends, not from F (torn) or ϕ, but from an older copy (now lost) of F made before fol. 160 was torn. It was from this class that a later hand had copied the *supplementa* now appearing in ϕ (see Fig. 1).

The last century has seen various attempts to prove the existence of a manuscript tradition independent of F. Concetto Marchesi staked such a claim for Boccaccio's autograph (Laur. 54.32 or L1), a claim dismissed by D. S. Robertson with the laconic remark that Marchesi had merely established that L1 was 'not a *direct* copy' of F.[25] Hopes were raised in the 1940s by the discovery at Assisi of ten leaves (Assisi 706, usually designated C) of the *Apologia* which seemed as old as F, if not older. Robertson, returning to the field he had dominated thirty years before, argued for C's dependence on F, as well as scotching the notion that C represented a fragment of the lost archetype of Class I.[26]

Oronzo Pecere, however, has revived the debate by pointing out the difficulties in Robertson's model.[27] Pecere hypothesizes that Class I descends, not from a lost apograph of F (untorn), but from the lost archetype of F and C. He exploits the discrepancy between Lowe's two dates for F (middle and end of eleventh century) and the fact that Lowe felt, on his initial observation in 1956, that C, if anything, seemed older than F. The MSS in Class I, moreover, show a marked preference for the marginal variants in F, suggesting descent not from F but from its ancestor.[28]

THE *SPURCUM ADDITAMENTUM*

There is, finally, the enduring enigma of the so-called *spurcum additamentum*, the 'obscene interpolation' added to the margins of ϕ (fol. 66^r) and of Boccaccio's

---

[25] C. Marchesi, 'Giovanni Boccaccio e i codici di Apuleio', *Rassegna bibliografica della letteratura italiana* 20 (1912), 232–4, repr. in C. Marchesi, *Scritti minori di filologia e di letteratura*, 3 vols. (Florence: Olschki, 1978), iii. 1010–11; Robertson, 'Manuscripts', 28.

[26] 'The Assisi Fragments of the *Apologia* of Apuleius', *CQ*, NS 6 (1956), 68–80.

[27] Pecere, 'Qualche riflessione'.

[28] Robertson ('Manuscripts', 32) himself averts to such an explanation when, having stated that all the MSS are 'closely connected with F, and almost certainly derived from it alone', he adds, in a footnote (n. 2), 'The only alternative possibility is that some are derived from F's immediate ancestor.' For an estimation of the scholarly impact of Pecere's challenge, see L. Graverini's bibliographical updating to the reprint of the article in O. Pecere and A. Stramaglia, *Studi apuleiani* (Cassino: Edizioni dell' Università degli Studi di Cassino, 2003), 183–4; for criticism, see G. Magnaldi in *Apuleio: Storia del testo e interpretazioni*, ed. G. Magnaldi and G. F. Gianotti (Alessandria: Edizioni dell'Orso, 2000), 31.

autograph copy, L1 (Laur. 54.32), next to the description of the asinine Lucius' love-making with the *matrona* at Corinth (*AA* 10. 21).[29] Robertson noted that 'It . . . has been added to φ's margin in a hand which Professor Rostagno confidently assigns to the thirteenth century', but G. Billanovich assigned the interpolation in φ to the hand of the fourteenth-century humanist Zanobi da Strada (1312–61).[30] It appears, however, that Boccaccio did not derive his *additamentum* from φ, but that he and Zanobi (if Billanovich's identification is correct) copied from another (no longer extant) manuscript:

et hercle orcium pigam [H: *bigam*] *perteretem hyaci fragrantis et chie rosacee lotionibus expurgauit* [M: *expiauit*]. *At dein digitis, ypate, lichanos, mese, paramese et nete hastam inguinis niuei mei spurciciei pluscule excorias* [φ and M: *excorians*] *emundauit. Et cum ad inguinis cephalum formosa mulier concitim* [H: *confestim*] *ueniebat ab orcibus ganniens ego et dentes ad Iouem eleuans priapo* [H: *Priapum;* M: *Priapon*] *frequenti frictura porrixabam ipsoque pando et repando uentrem sepiuscule tractabam* [φ and M: *tactabam*]. *Ipsa quoque inspiciens quod genius* [H: *genitus*] *inter anthteneras* [H: *anteas teneras;* M: *antheras*] *excreuerat modicum illud morule qua lustrum sterni mandauerat anni sibi reuolutionem autumabat.*[31]

(And, by Hercules, she cleansed my round scrotum, my balls, with perfumed wine and rosewater of Chios. And then with her fingers, thumb, forefinger, middle finger, ring finger and little finger, she withdrew the foreskin, and cleared the shaft of my penis of the plentiful whitish dirt. And when the beautiful woman arrived very soon at the top of my penis from my testicles, braying and lifting my teeth toward the sky, I got, through the regular friction, an erection of the penis, and while it moved up and down I often touched her belly with it. She as well, when she saw what came out of my penis among her perfumes, declared that that small delay, during which she had ordered our love-nest to be prepared, had been to her the orbit of a year.)[32]

---

[29] The passage also appears in the margins of L2 (Laur. 54.12), and L4 (Laur. 54.24), and has been incorporated into the text of V5 (Urb. Vat. 199), but L2's version copies φ, L4's copies L1, and V5's copies L4. See M. Zimmerman, *Apuleius Madaurensis Metamorphoses Book X* (GCA; Groningen: Forsten, 2000), 433 (following Mariotti); and, most recently, V. Hunink, 'The *spurcum additamentum* (Apul. *Met.* 10,21) once again', in *Lectiones Scrupulosae: Essays on the Text and Interpretation of Apuleius' 'Metamorphoses' in Honour of Maaike Zimmerman*, ed. W. H. Keulen, R. R. Nauta, and S. Panayotakis (Groningen: Barkhuis/Groningen UL, 2006), 266–79.

[30] Robertson, 'Manuscripts', 31; Billanovich, *I primi umanisti e le tradizioni dei classici latini* (Fribourg: Edizioni universitarie, 1953), 29–33, 40–1.

[31] Text based on L4 (Laur. 54. 24), as presented by J. Van der Vliet, ed., *Lucii Apulei Metamorphoseon libri XI* (Leipzig: Teubner, 1897), 238–9, with emendations ('H' and 'M') in square brackets proposed by L. Herrmann, 'Le Fragment obscène de l'*Âne d'or* (x, 21)', *Latomus* 10 (1951), 329–32, and S. Mariotti, 'Lo *Spurcum Additamentum* ad Apul. *Met.* 10, 21', *SIFC* 27–8 (1956), 229–50.

[32] Translation from M. Zimmerman (GCA x. 434) based on Mariotti's text. For a 'tentative' (but even racier) English version, see Lytle (*infra*), 357–8. Hunink ('The *spurcum additamentum*', 278–9) offers some attractive refinements to Zimmerman's translation, e.g.: 'the fine round pouch of my balls' (1); 'she lightly skinned the shaft of my organ and cleaned it of its snow-white dirt' (2); 'observing what kind of genital had grown among her mixtures' (4).

In 1914, H. E. Butler declared that the *spurcum additamentum* was 'clearly not by Apuleius' but that it nonetheless 'must raise the suspicion that there was in existence in the fourteenth century at least a fragment of the *Metamorphoses*, representing a tradition other than that contained by Laur. 68. 2'.[33] Robertson was also intrigued: 'I agree with [Butler] that it can scarcely be a medieval or early Renaissance forgery.'[34] If the passage is genuine, it implies the survival into the thirteenth or fourteenth century of a manuscript tradition that is independent, certainly of F, and possibly even of Sallustius' fourth-century recension.[35]

An alternative explanation for the passage has also been proposed. In a monograph (1950) and article (1952), Antonio Mazzarino and Reinhold Merkelbach claimed (separately) that the *spurcum additamentum* was actually a portion of the long-lost *Milesiae* of L. Cornelius Sisenna.[36] They argued that the passage did not fit the context of Apuleius' love-scene, but that it had been placed in the margin of an early manuscript as a *locus similis* by someone with access to a text of Sisenna.[37] In 1953, Eduard Fraenkel demolished the Sisenna argument with lexical cannon balls (*excorians, revolutio*, etc.), dismissing the ithyphallic passage as a late forgery.[38] The Apuleianness of the passage has been urged, however, by Léon Herrmann who argued that the *additamentum* belonged not in *AA* 10. 21 (between *tura* [*cura* in F] *etiam nares perfundit meas* and *tunc exosculata pressule*) but at the junction of 10. 21 and 10. 22 (between *prolubium libidinis suscitarem* and *sed angebar plane*).[39] John J. Winkler declared (without providing much argument) that the *additamentum* had been 'banished by most scholars as non-Apuleian for inadequate critical reasons'—a view reinforced most recently by Ephraim Lytle who argues, on narratological lines (and by reference to the mating preparations

---

[33] Butler, *Apulei Apologia*, p. xxix.

[34] Robertson, 'Manuscripts', 31.

[35] Some of the quotations from Apuleius in Fulgentius' *Expositio sermonum antiquorum* appear to suggest that he was following a non-Sallustian manuscript tradition. Psyche's sister complains about her husband: *At ego misera primum patre meo seniorem maritum sortita sum, dein cucurbita calviorem et quouis puero pusilliorem ...* (*AA* 5. 9). Cf. *Expositio* 17: [*Quid sit pumilior, quid sit glabrior.*] *Apuleius in asino aureo inducit sorores Psicae maritis detrahentis; dicit: 'quovis puero pumiliorem et cucurbita glabriorem'; pumilios enim dicunt molles atque enerues, glabrum uero lenem et inberbem.*

[36] A. Mazzarino, *La Milesia e Apuleio* (Turin: Chiantore, 1950); R. Merkelbach, 'La nuova pagina di Sisenna ed Apuleio', *Maia* 5 (1952), 234–41.

[37] It has been suggested that Fragment 10 of Sisenna (*ut eum penitus utero suo recepit*) derives from an account of a woman making love to an ass (cf. *AA* 10. 22: *totum me, sed prorsus totum recepit*). See *Petronii Saturae*, ed. F. Buecheler, rev. W. Heraeus (Berlin: Wiedmann, 1958), 264.

[38] E. Fraenkel, 'A Sham Sisenna', *Eranos* 51 (1953), 151–4.

[39] 'Le Fragment obscène', 331.

recommended in ancient manuals of animal husbandry), for the passage's genuineness.[40]

Maaike Zimmerman's survey of the debate endorses Scevola Mariotti's argument from 1956, concluding that 'there is no doubt about the medieval origin of the *spurcum additamentum*'.[41] In rejecting claims for Sisenna's authorship, Fraenkel had pointed to the 'catalogue of the names of the fingers' which correspond to the names of musical strings: 'it smells of the school-master's lamp rather than the famous roses of Miletus'.[42] This objection does not, in itself, of course, dispose of Apuleius' claims on the passage: his lost works include a *De musica*, and he was perfectly capable of combining neo-Pythagorean harmonies with extreme eroticism. Fraenkel, however, is able to point to the presence of a description of the strings (*hypate... mese... paramese... nete*) in a surviving text, Boethius' *De institutione musica* (1. 20).[43] We should also note that Book 9 ('Harmony') of Martianus Capella's erotic-didactic *De nuptiis* includes all the notational names used by 'Spurcus' (scattered, in the order, *hypate, meson, nete, paramese,* and *lichanos,* across sections 941–6), as well as an indication (9. 946) of the relation of strings to fingers. Moreover, when one looks at medieval manuscripts of Martianus Capella, one is immediately struck (as 'Spurcus' may have been) by the phallic appearance of the diagrams illustrating the strings.[44]

On this reading, the *spurcum additamentum* is either a calculated forgery, or a *jeu d'esprit*, a piece of creative embroidery or *aemulatio,* which found its way (long after its creator's death) into the margins of φ and Boccaccio's L1. A plausible candidate in either case would be Peter the Deacon (Petrus Diaconus), the twelfth-century librarian at Monte Cassino who has been called 'one of the most prolific and brazen forgers in history'.[45] Peter (b. *c.*1107, d. after 1153) is by far the most interesting figure in the Cassinese community at this time, and we know, from the accounts which he fabricated of the rape of a young noblewoman leading to the destruction of Atina, that

[40] *Auctor & Actor,* 193; E. Lytle, 'Apuleius' *Metamorphoses* and the *Spurcum Additamentum* (10. 21)', *CP* 98 (2003), 349–65. Lytle's thesis is contested by Hunink who finds ('The *spurcum additamentum*', 270) 'a deplorable lack of attention for the philological side of the matter, not only concerning the manuscript tradition, but also in the field of Latin idiom'.

[41] Zimmerman, GCA x. 433–9, at 439; S. Mariotti, 'Lo *Spurcum Additamentum* ad Apul. *Met.* 10, 21', *SIFC* 27–8 (1956), 229–50.

[42] 'A Sham Sisenna', 152.

[43] ed. G. Friedlein (Leipzig: Teubner, 1867), 206, 18; Fraenkel, 'A Sham Sisenna', 153.

[44] See the illustrations in M. Teeuwen, *Harmony and the Music of the Spheres: The 'Ars Musica' in Ninth-Century Commentaries on Martianus Capella* (Leiden: Brill, 2002), 187–9. Fraenkel (153) mentions a diagram (*descriptio*) in Boethius.

[45] H. Bloch, 'Peter the Deacon of Monte Cassino', *NCE2* xi. 206. Cf. E. L. E. Caspar, *Petrus Diaconus und die Monte Cassineser Fälschungen: ein Beitrag zur Geschichte des italienischen Geisteslebens im Mittelalter* (Berlin: Springer, 1909), esp. 88.

he had an interest in fictional narrative.[46] On the basis of a small number of entries in the *Abolita* glossary (*Remillo : repando et pronulo*; and *Recellit : retro agit*), W. M. Lindsay floated the possibility that the *spurcum additamentum* might be 'quite ancient or even genuine'.[47] An alternative possibility is that some medieval reader of Apuleius ('Spurcus'), having recourse to the *Abolita* glossary for *recellit*, spotted *repando* in the preceding gloss and worked it into the design of the *spurcum additamentum*.

QUALIFICATIONS TO MONTE CASSINO'S ROLE

All that we have so far seen emphasizes the importance of Monte Cassino in preserving (and providing early responses to) Apuleius' works. We must be careful, however, not to overstate the abbey's significance. One of the obstacles to an unprejudiced assessment of the claims for Apuleian influence in the Middle Ages is a tendency among scholars to fetishize F (Laur. 68.2) and its Cassinese context when considering the survival and diffusion of the *Apologia*, *Metamorphoses*, and *Florida*. It seems highly unlikely, in fact, that these works reached Monte Cassino before the eleventh century when F was produced. The abbey suffered a number of sackings and severe depredations between the sixth and tenth centuries. It was overwhelmed by the Lombards in the period 577–89, looted and burned by the Arabs in 883, and not reoccupied until 950, the monks having spent the interim at Teano (where a fire during the period 889–99 destroyed their quarters and their most precious possession, the original manuscript of St Benedict's Rule). Its literary wealth is mainly a product of the eleventh century.[48]

Transcriptional errors in F indicate that the manuscript from which it was copied had itself been written in Beneventan, the southern Italian script (known to Renaissance humanists as 'Lombardic') which emerged in the eighth century.[49] It is therefore possible that the text of the *Florida* used by Guaiferius was either F itself or its immediate ancestor. We can thus be certain

---

[46] H. Bloch (ed.), *The Atina Dossier of Peter the Deacon of Monte Cassino: A Hagiographical Romance of the Twelfth Century* (Vatican City: Biblioteca Apostolica Vaticana, 1998), 288–9. Bloch (113) calls it 'perhaps the strangest of all of Peter the Deacon's inventions'. According to Cowdrey (*Age of Abbot Desiderius*, 227), Peter 'never mastered the Beneventan script'.

[47] *Gloss Lat.* iii. 164, app. crit.: *Si revera nostri sunt glossarii et ad Met. 10, 21–2 spectant, testantur hunc locum Apuleianum satis antiquum (vel etiam genuinum) fuisse.*

[48] See Leccisotti (*Monte Cassino*, 20 and 44) on the sackings, Bloch (*Monte Cassino*, i. 10) on the date of the return, and Newton ('Desiderian Scriptorium') on the dearth (*paupertas*) of books at Monte Cassino before the 11th cent.

[49] Butler and Owen, eds., *Apulei Apologia*, p. xxxii.

that at some point between the outer limits of AD 700 and, say, 1050, someone
in the south of Italy—perhaps at a major cultural node such as Salerno (the
great centre for medical learning) or Benevento (the old Lombard capital and
the birthplace of Desiderius who assumed the abbacy of Monte Cassino in
1058)—had access to a text of the recension which Sallustius had made at
Rome in 395 and at Constantinople in 397 and was motivated (or commissioned) to produce a copy which became, in turn, the exemplar for F.[50]
Within the Sallustian tradition alone, therefore, there were at least two
manuscripts—the grandparent and parent of F—which could have generated
additional descendants before (and after) the production of F. We should also
recall the long-standing connections between late antique Gaul and Apuleius.
Some of his works (most significantly, the *Apologia*) were known to such
figures as Ausonius of Bordeaux (*c.*310–95) whose favourite pupil, Paulinus of
Nola, was a correspondent of Severus Sanctus Endelechius (a native, apparently, of Aquitania, and probably identical with the 'Endelechius' who supervised Sallustius' recension at Rome in 395).[51] An interest in Apuleius
continued in the circle of Sidonius Apollinaris which dominated Romano-
Gallic literature in the third quarter of the fifth century. It is not inconceivable
that a copy of the *Metamorphoses, Apologia,* and *Florida* survived in Gaul after
Sidonius' death (post-489). We have, moreover, seen in the *Abolita* glossary
some evidence for the existence in Spain in the seventh century of a manuscript of *The Golden Ass* which may have belonged to the (arguably independent) tradition known to Augustine and Fulgentius and which may have
infiltrated Europe from North Africa.

The lines of transmission are also complicated by the influence of Fulgentius. Helped, no doubt, by the frequent identification of the Mythographer
with the Christian apologist Bishop Fulgentius of Ruspe, the *Mitologiae* (and
various dilutions or embellishments thereof) achieved wide circulation during the Middle Ages, appearing in German and French catalogues from the
ninth century onwards, Italian catalogues from the tenth century, and in
English catalogues from the middle of the thirteenth.[52] We should therefore

---

[50] Highlighting the importance of southern Italian sites outside Monte Cassino, Newton
notes (*Scriptorium,* 11) that Benevento was 'one of the major centers of book copying in Italy'.
Without discussing issues of textual transmission, M. Oldoni observes a parallel between
Thelyphron's tale of the murderous *uxor egregia* (*AA* 2. 29) and a story in the anonymous
Salerno Chronicle (second half of 10th cent.) in which a man who has helped to strangle his
lover's husband is condemned to be buried alive, 'face to face on top of the corpse' (*super
mortuum facie ad faciem*). See 'Streghe medievali e intersezioni da Apuleio', in *Semiotica della
novella latina* (Rome: Herder, 1986), 267–79, at 270–1; and *Chronicon Salernitanum,* ed. U.
Westerbergh (Stockholm: Almquist & Wiksell, 1956), cap. 15, pp. 20–1.

[51] See Ch. 1, *supra.*

[52] M. Manitius records entries for the work at Glastonbury as early as 1247 (*Fulgencias super
fabulas philosophice expositas*), at Peterborough in the 14th cent., and at Canterbury in 1483 and

look carefully for medieval echoes of Fulgentius' 'Cupid and Psyche' while being alert to the possibility that the fable may also have have been absorbed into, and transformed by, traditions of oral storytelling.

Conscious of this complex web, we can turn to the question of the wider influence of *The Golden Ass* in the High Middle Ages. This may seem like a superfluous labour, given the recent essays by Carl Schlam and Claudio Moreschini.[53] Moreschini does much to illuminate the reception of 'Cupid and Psyche' in Late Antiquity and the Renaissance, but in leaping from Fulgentius to Boccaccio, he passes over the main substance of the present discussion. And while Schlam's study is a miracle of compression and general good sense, his robust dismissal of claims for the direct influence of *The Golden Ass* in the Middle Ages is based, like so much work in this area, on a codicological model that is flawed.

EVIDENCE IN FAVOUR OF DIFFUSION
FROM MONTE CASSINO

Guaiferius' echo of the *Florida* is the first demonstrated use of material from the epideictic trinity posterior to the *Abolita* glossary; and a conservative approach would see it as an isolated occurrence. One factor militating against the diffusion of Cassinese texts beyond the confines of southern Italy was the difficulty of the Beneventan script compared with the more widespread Caroline miniscule. It is clear, nonetheless, that twelfth-century France did have access to some of the literary productions of Monte Cassino. The works of the Saracen convert Constantinus Africanus (a 'Carthaginian'-turned-Cassinese polymath of the eleventh century whose career has remarkable parallels with that of Apuleius himself)[54] had diffused rapidly enough for

1484. See M. Manitius, *Handschriften antiker Autoren in mittelalterlichen Bibliothekskatalogen* (Leipzig: Harrassowitz, 1935), 303. One entry missed by Manitius is in 'The Catalogue of the Library of the Augustinian Friars at York', ed. M. R. James, in *Fasciculus Ioanni Willis Clark dicatus* (Cambridge: CUP, 1909), 2–96. Entry 490 (written in a hand 'not much later' than 1372) records the presence of the *mithologie fulgenc* along with a *Genealogia deorum*.

[53] C. Schlam, 'Apuleius in the Middle Ages', in *The Classics in the Middle Ages*, ed. A. S. Bernardo and S. Levin (Binghamton, NY: CMERS, 1990), 363–69; C. Moreschini, 'Towards a History of the Exegesis of Apuleius', and *Il mito di Amore e Psiche in Apuleio: saggio, testo di Apuleio, traduzione e commento* (Naples: d'Auria, 1994).

[54] On Constantinus, see Bloch, *Monte Cassino*, i. 98–110. E. A. Lowe's unconscious sense of the parallels with Apuleius' *Apologia* seems to be behind his statement (*Beneventan Script*, 13) that Constantinus Africanus 'came to Italy as a fugitive from Carthage, where his enemies had accused him of being a magician'. Peter the Deacon's biography of Constantinus merely states that the Africans decided to kill him after his return from Egypt and other eastern parts because

William of Conches to make use of them 'in his two main works, the *De philosophia* of about 1122–7 and the *Dragmaticon* of 1146–9',⁵⁵ and for Bernardus Silvestris (if we allow the attribution) to refer explicitly to him in his twelfth-century commentary on Martianus Capella.⁵⁶ Seneca's *Dialogi* were not far behind, making their way over the Alps to the schools of Paris in time for John of Garland to use them 'as early as 1220'.⁵⁷ We know, also, that leading twelfth-century humanists travelled in southern Italy. Adelard of Bath (1075?–1160) had visited Salerno and Magna Graecia before studying at Tours (which would become intellectual home to Bernardus Silvestris) 'in the early years of the twelfth century';⁵⁸ and it was at Benevento that John of Salisbury (an enthusiast for Apuleius' philosophy and rhetoric) gained from his friend, Pope Hadrian IV, the papal bull (*Laudabiliter...*) granting Ireland to Henry II in 1155.⁵⁹

Moreover, the monastery of Glanfeuil (or Saint-Maur-sur-Loire) which is 'situated on the left bank of the Loire between Saumur and Angers, in the neighborhood of Gennes' (a mere 40 miles from Tours) laid claim to a long association with Monte Cassino, its founder, St Maur, having been identified since AD 845 with 'the favorite pupil of St. Benedict'.⁶⁰ In 1096, the Council of Tours (which had been called to adjudicate competing claims for control of Glanfeuil) resulted in a bull issued by Pope Urban II which 'gave papal

they were jealous of his learning. The text of the *De viris illustribus Casinensibus* (ch. 22: *De Constantino*) given in Bloch (*Monte Cassino*, i. 127–34) supersedes that of Migne (*PL* 173, cols. 1034 ff.). Constantinus found refuge first at Salerno and was then received, through the mediation of Alfanus, into Desiderius' community at Monte Cassino.

⁵⁵ Bloch (*Monte Cassino*, i. 108), citing B. Lawn, *The Salernitan Questions: An Introduction to the History of Medieval and Renaissance Problem Literature* (Oxford: Clarendon, 1963), 51–6. It is likely that Constantinus' works reached France via Salerno, the renowned medical centre. According to R. M. Thomson, the Bury library contained three copies of Constantinus' *Pantegni*, 'of which one, a scriptorium copy dated before c. 1150, survives'. See 'The Library of Bury St Edmunds Abbey in the Eleventh and Twelfth Centuries', *Speculum* 47 (1972), 617–45, at 634. Moreover, 'The Wellcome Museum has a MS from the abbey library, part of which is in a 12th-century Beneventan script associated with Montecassino (formerly Bury St Edmunds Cathedral MS4)'. On the circulation of other Cassinese texts beyond southern Italy, see Newton, *Scriptorium*, 326–7.

⁵⁶ *The Commentary on Martianus Capella's 'De nuptiis Philologiae et Mercurii' Attributed to Bernardus Silvestris*, ed. H. J. Westra (Toronto: PIMS, 1986), 62. 'Bernardus' (iii. 384 ff.) quotes from the *Pantegni*.

⁵⁷ Reynolds and Wilson, *S&S3*, 117. According to Newton (*Scriptorium*, 291 and 327), the *Dialogi* 'spread across Europe in the twelfth and thirteenth centuries'. The *Dialogi* and Apuleius' *Florida* are connected by the fact that it is Guaiferius who makes the earliest recorded use of each work.

⁵⁸ P. Dronke, ed., *Bernardus Silvestris: Cosmographia* (Leiden: Brill, 1978), 8.

⁵⁹ D. Knowles, *The Evolution of Medieval Thought* (2nd edn.), ed. D. E. Luscombe and C. N. L. Brooke (London: Longman, 1988), 125.

⁶⁰ Bloch, *Monte Cassino*, ii. 969, 971.

sanction to the Maurus legend ... and exalted in no uncertain terms the vital part which Monte Cassino had played in the origin of Glanfeuil'.[61] The archives of Monte Cassino record (in the *Registrum Petri Diaconi*) a twelfth-century attempt to consolidate these links. 'On March 10, 1133 Abbot Drogo of Glanfeuil appeared in Monte Cassino with relics of St. Maur and a portion of the Rule, which St. Benedict "had written with his own hand" as gifts. He declared in the Chapter that he had come on account of the in-[979]timate connections which bound the two monasteries to each other and which he hoped would last forever.'[62]

Drogo and his entourage spent several months in Monte Cassino and took back to Glanfeuil 'copies of the documents which had been "discovered" by Peter the Deacon in the archives of Monte Cassino'.[63] The links were re-inforced in the summer of 1147 at Auxerre when 'Pope Eugene III under the influence of his subdeacon Simon, a monk of Monte Cassino, and in fact a relative of the abbot, the cardinal priest Raynald, reconfirmed the dependence of Glanfeuil on Monte Cassino and commissioned the same Simon accord-ingly to supervise the election and introduction of the new abbot in Glanfeuil itself'.[64] There is also a tradition that Bernardus Silvestris' *Cosmographia* was recited in the presence of Pope Eugene III (1145–53) during this visit to Gaul (1147–8) and 'won his benevolent approval'.[65] And in 1153, Abbot William II of Glanfeuil came to Monte Cassino in fulfilment of the stipulation of quinquennial visits.[66]

According to the traditional stemmatic model established by D. S. Robert-son, Class 1 manuscripts descend from a (lost) copy of F made before fol. 160 was torn (i.e. prior to the copying of ϕ in about 1200). There is no reason in principle, therefore, why this copy (or copies of it) should not have travelled over the Alps into France, especially if Peter the Deacon did have an interest in *The Golden Ass*.[67] It is also noteworthy that many of the texts which we will be examining as possible *loci* of Apuleian influence are the work of writers who

[61] Ibid. 976.

[62] Ibid. 978–9.

[63] Ibid. 994.

[64] Ibid. 995.

[65] Dronke (*Cosmographia*, 2) notes that the tradition is preserved in a marginal gloss to a passage praising Pope 'Eugenius'. Eugene was a Cistercian and a former pupil of Bernard of Clairvaux. In *Myth and Science in the Twelfth Century: A Study of Bernard Silvester* (Princeton: PUP, 1972), 11 n. 1, B. Stock questions the reliability of the gloss, though he acknowledges (228 etc.) Bernardus' use of Constantinus Africanus' works.

[66] Bloch, *Monte Cassino*, ii. 997.

[67] Bloch (*Atina Dossier*, 289 n. 1) discusses Peter the Deacon's account (*Epitome Chronicorum Casinensium*) of the wife of the emperor, Louis II, who (in imitation of Potiphar's wife in Genesis 39: 7–20) tried to seduce Tucbald, the emperor's *comes palatii*. One merely notes the presence of a not-dissimilar tale in Apuleius (*AA* 10. 2–12).

come from the same area of France: Blois, Meung-sur-Loire, and Vendôme form a cluster halfway between Tours (closely associated with Bernardus Silvestris and Glanfeuil) and Chartres.

Twelfth-Century Attitudes towards Fiction

As well as these potential conduits, there was also a profound change in the intellectual climate which rendered it much more amenable to fiction. Martianus Capella begins Book 2 of the *De nuptiis* by voicing Philology's anxiety that 'this grand marriage' with Mercury might not be 'in her own interest. She [35] had a fear, not without substance, that after she had ascended to the sky, she would forgo altogether the myths and legends of mankind, those charming diversities of the Milesian tales'.[68] Book 2 concludes with an address to the Reader: 'So now the mythical part is ended; the books which follow set forth the arts. With true intellectual nourishment they put aside all fable and for the most part explain serious studies, without however avoiding entertainment.'[69] Different ages have responded in different ways to the dynamic interplay expressed in the *De nuptiis* between fictional entertainment and intellectual edification. During the Carolingian age, manuscripts containing the complete text are the norm. But a change of sensibility seems to set in during the High Middle Ages, for, from the twelfth to the fourteenth centuries, manuscripts containing only Books 1–2 (the most 'fabulous'—and, incidentally, the most Apuleian—portions of the work) abound.[70]

These trends in the domain of textual production and consumption are matched by developments in the theorization of fiction. Macrobius' influence on the Middle Ages was enormous. The *Commentary on the Dream of Scipio*

---

[68] Trans. Stahl and Johnson, ii. 34–5. Willis, ed., 29 (2. 100): *quod utrum sibi haec nuptialis conduceret amplitudo anxia dubitabat? nam certe mythos, poeticae etiam diversitatis delicias Milesias historiasque mortalium, postquam supera conscenderit, se penitus amissuram non cassa opinatione formidat.* In *The Berlin Commentary on Martianus Capella's 'De nuptiis Philologiae et Mercurii'. Book II*, ed. H. J. Westra and T. Kupke (Leiden: Brill, 1998), tentatively dated to 'possibly the late twelfth or early thirteenth century' (vol. i, p. xxxvii), the commentator (11–12) glosses *Milesias delicias poetice diversitatis* as *fabulas delectantes, quas lirica pagina contineat* ('pleasing tales which the lyric page contains'). He bases his explanation on the figure of Thales of Miletus, one of the Seven Sages 'who was the first inventor of fables which have a tendency to give pleasure' (*qui primus fuit inventor fabularum, que ad delectationem pertinent*). However, while he displays his knowledge of Fulgentius in his gloss on *se penitus amissuram mithos* by observing, *id est fabulas (unde Fulgencii liber Mithologiarum dicitur)*, he reveals no awareness of Apuleius' *sermone isto Milesio varias fabulas conseram (AA 1. 1).*

[69] Trans. Stahl and Johnson, ii. 63. Willis, ed., 57–8 (2. 220): *nunc ergo mythos terminatur; infiunt | [58] artes libelli qui sequentes asserent. | nam fruge vera omne fictum dimovent | et disciplinas annotabunt sobrias | pro parte multa nec vetabunt ludicra.*

[70] See Stahl and Johnson, i. 73.

served as 'one of the basic source books of the scholastic movement and of medieval science'.[71] In the course of the High Middle Ages (and well into the Renaissance), we see successive attempts at redefining Macrobius' terms to meet the fictive appetites of each period.

In the first half of the twelfth century, William of Conches (*c.*1080–1154) cleverly adapts Macrobius' allusion to fictions suitable only for the nursery:

Nutricum cunas *vocat auctores, quia ut a nutrice puer in cunis nutritur levioribus cibis, ita discipulus, scilicet in levioribus* [69] *autoribus sententiis, et causa exercicii, ut levius graviores possit intelligere.*

(He calls the literary authors 'children's nurseries': for as the nurse nurtures the infant in the cradle on lighter foods, so is the student nurtured on matter from the lighter authors; this is also for the sake of practice, so that he may more easily understand the heavier ones.)[72]

As Dronke points out, William disregards Macrobius' distinction between the mere *fabula* and the (philosophically acceptable) *narratio fabulosa* because 'he is determined to re-admit the philosopher to every kind of *fabula*, to envisage the possibility of metaphorical reading in a far wider range of fictional material than Macrobius allowed'.[73] 'Bernardus Silvestris' adopts the same line in his commentary on the *Aeneid*: *Sunt namque poete ad philosophiam introductorii, unde uolumina eorum 'cunas nutricum' uocat Macrobius* ('For poets serve as an introduction to philosophy, whence Macrobius calls them "wet-nurses' cradles"').[74] Alanus de Insulis seems to revert to a less generous interpretation of Macrobius' cradles in the *De planctu Naturae* (his Menippean satire on sexual deviation) when he makes Nature turn on her mortal interlocutor (who has dared to suggest that the Classical gods are as wayward in their proclivities as humans):

an umbratilibus poetarum figmentis quae artis poeticae depinxit industria, fidem adhibere conaris? Nonne ea quae in puerilibus [0451C] *cunis poeticae disciplinae discutiuntur, altiori distinctionis lima, senior philosophiae tractatus eliminat?*

---

[71] Stahl, *Macrobius: Commentary*, 10.

[72] Latin text from P. Dronke, *Fabula: Explorations into the Use of Myth in Medieval Platonism* (Leiden: Brill, 1974), 17 (English) and 68 (Latin). Dronke (57) observes that 'We cannot assign a precise date to William's commentary on Macrobius.' William also produced a commentary on Priscian (who mentions Apuleius) and promised a commentary on Martianus Capella which has not survived (though Dronke detects substantial traces of William's teaching in a 14th-cent. Florentine manuscript containing a commentary on the opening portion of the *De nuptiis*).

[73] Dronke, *Fabula*, 21. Cf. *The Berlin Commentary on Martianus Capella ... Book II*, 12: *Per Millesium autem accipies quemlibet qui philosophiam fabulose tractavit* ('By "The Milesian" you will understand anyone who has handled Philosophy using fictions').

[74] *The Commentary on the First Six Books of the 'Aeneid' of Virgil Commonly Attributed to Bernardus Silvestris*, ed. J. W. Jones and E. F. Jones (Lincoln, Nebr.: U of Nebraska P, 1977), 36. The attribution to Bernardus is disputed.

(Are you trying to give credence to the poets' shadowy figments which the efforts of the poetic art have painted? Do not a reappraisal from more profound discernment and a more advanced treatment by philosophy erase what has been learned in the childhood cradles of poetic teaching?)[75]

Within a dozen lines, however, Nature admits that 'the poetic lyre gives a false note on the outer bark of the composition but within tells the listeners a secret of deeper significance so that when the outer shell of falsehood has been discarded the reader finds the sweeter kernal of truth hidden within'.[76]

Given such favourable conditions, can we find any compelling evidence for the resurrection of *The Golden Ass* during the twelfth century? Manitius (and his dependants) saw Apuleius' tale of the incestuous stepmother in Book 10 as the source of a poem, *De illa quae impudenter filium suum adamavit*, written by Petrus Pictor in about 1100.[77] The connection between the two passages is not particularly strong. Apuleius (*AA* 10. 2–12) relates the story of a stepmother whose unrequited passion for her stepson turns to vengeance. When her own child drinks the poison intended for his half-brother, she accuses her stepson of fratricide and attempted incest. He is saved from punishment by a wise physician's disclosure that the poison was merely a sleeping-potion; and all ends happily. In Petrus Pictor's poem, a mother is in love with her own son. Rebuffed, she denounces him for attempted rape. He refuses to incriminate her and is condemned to be thrown into the river, whereupon the town is blasted by divine thunderbolts. The only elements in common are incest, passion-turned-to-vengeance, and wrongful accusation—elements that could easily be derived from Apuleius' own source, Seneca's *Hippolytus*, or from a combination, say, of the account of Joseph and Potiphar's wife (Genesis 39) with aspects of the incest stories in Ovid (e.g. Myrrha, *Met.* 10. 312 ff.). It is interesting, however, that Petrus Pictor is associated with Saint-Omer (in northern France) which would become home to an important Class-I manuscript of *The Golden Ass* (Saint-Omer 653).[78]

[75] *PL* 210, col. 0451B–C; *Alan of Lille: The Plaint of Nature*, trans. J. J. Sheridan (Toronto: PIMS, 1980), 139–40. For a superior Latin text, see N. M. Häring, ed., in *Studi medievali*, 3rd ser. 19/2 (1978), 797–879.

[76] Trans. Sheridan, 140. *PL* 210, col. 0451C: *At, in superficiali litterae cortice falsum resonat lyra poetica, sed interius, auditoribus secretum intelligentiae altioris eloquitur, ut exteriore falsitatis abjecto putamine, dulciorem nucleum veritatis secrete intus lector inveniat.*

[77] Manitius, *Geschichte*, iii. 880; Walsh, *Roman Novel*, 230; L. van Acker, ed., *Petri Pictoris carmina nec non Petri de Sancto Audemaro librum de coloribus faciendis* (Turnhout: Brepols, 1972), 108–12. Orlandi ('Classical Latin Satire', 112 n. 50) is not 'convinced that Apuleius was read by Petrus Pictor'.

[78] The MS is ascribed by Marshall (*Texts and Transmission*, 16) to the first part of the 15th cent., but if its parent was also at Saint-Omer this would strengthen the Petrus Pictor claim. Note too that a Stefano Colonna (d. 1379) was provost of the chapter of Saint-Omer and a correspondent of Petrarch (e.g. *Epistolae seniles* 15. 1). On the interest shown in Apuleius by various generations of the Colonna family, see Ch. 3 and 5, *infra*.

Met(h)amorphosis Golye episcopi (*c.*1142)

A more fruitful place to look is the *Met(h)amorphosis Golye episcopi* ('The Metamorphosis of Bishop Golias'), an anonymous poem of 236 lines written in about 1142 in response to the condemnation of Peter Abelard at the Council of Sens in 1140. The *Met(h)amorphosis* contains what, on the face of it, seems to be evidence of familiarity with both *The Golden Ass* and the *Apologia*. One may be tempted to find, in the description of the palace at the beginning of the poem, a memory of Apuleius' *domus regia* in 'Cupid and Psyche'; but divine palaces adorn many poems from Late Antiquity and the Middle Ages and it would be rash to posit Apuleian influence on this basis alone.[79] Inside the palace, however, we meet Psyche herself:

> *Vel sunt dotes, opifex quas Sychi largitur,*
> *quibus circumcingitur, quibus investitur*
> *et quibus per circulos labens insignitur*
> *cum carnis hospicium fragile aditur.*[80]

(Or they are the gifts which the maker bestows on Psyche, | by which she is surrounded, in which she is covered, | and by which she is distinguished, gliding along through her orbits, | when the frail chamber of the flesh is approached.) (lines 125–8)

> *Nexibus Cupidinis Syche detinetur*

(Psyche is being held in Cupid's bonds) (line 161)

> *Syche per illecebras carnis captivatur*

(Psyche is taken captive through the allurements of the flesh) (line 165)

The poem's nineteenth-century editor, Thomas Wright, comments, in a casual note to line 161, 'An allusion to the story in Apuleius'. Ludwig Traube tells us that the author of this poem (which he assigns to the thirteenth century) knew both the *Apologia* of Apuleius and the tale of 'Cupid

---

[79] In *Platonism and Poetry in the Twelfth Century: The Literary Influence of the School of Chartres* (Princeton: PUP, 1972), 128, W. Wetherbee divines the influence of Ovid's *regia solis* (*Met.* 2. 1–18); but we might find several other possible sources (including Claudian, Sidonius Apollinaris, and Andreas Capellanus) in the survey of the 'various palaces of the Love divinities' given by W. O. Sypherd in *Studies in Chaucer's 'Hous of Fame'* (London: Chaucer Soc., 1909), 132–8.

[80] Latin text from R. B. G. Huygens, 'Mitteilungen aus Handschriften', *Studi medievali* 3 (1962), 747–72, at 769, based on a collation of BM Harley 978 (saec. XIII) with Saint-Omer 710 (saec. XIV). According to R. L. Poole, the earlier of these MSS was 'transcribed about 1240 by a monk, as is supposed, of Reading Abbey'. See 'The Masters of the Schools at Paris and Chartres in John of Salisbury's Time', *EHR* 35 (1920), 336–42, at 336. The Harleian text used in T. Wright's earlier edn., *Latin Poems Commonly Attributed to Walter Mapes* (London: Camden Soc., 1841), 21–30, reads *per titulos habens insignitur* in line 127. Cf. Wetherbee, *Platonism*, 128.

and Psyche'.[81] And Edward A. Synan confidently asserts that 'there can be no doubt but that Goliath's verses depend heavily upon the long account of Cupid and Psychē by Apuleius'.[82]

A backward glance at *The Marriage of Mercury and Philology*, however, will show us that Golias' Psyche owes her fetters (*Nexibus Cupidinis Syche detinetur*) not to Apuleius, nor to Fulgentius, but to Martianus Capella (*captiuamque Adamantinis nexibus a Cupidine detineri*).[83] Yet within twenty lines, we have Apuleius being mentioned by name—and in connection with his wife:

> *Secum suam duxerat Cetam Ysopullus,*
> *Cynthiam Propercius, Delyam Tibullus,*
> *Tullius Terenciam, Lesbiam Catullus,*
> *vates huc convenerant, sine sua nullus.*
>
> *Queque suo suus est ardor et favilla,*
> *Plinium Calpurnie succendit scintilla,*
> *urit Apuleium sua Prudentilla,*
> *hunc et hunc amplexibus tenet hec et illa.*[84]

(Ysopullus had brought with him his Ceta,[85] Propertius his Cynthia, Tibullus his Delia; Cicero his Terentia, Catullus his Lesbia; no poet had assembled here without his woman: each is his flame and spark. Calpurnia's spark sets Pliny on fire; Pudentilla burns her Apuleius: this woman and that woman holds this man and this man in their embraces.)

On the face of it, a reference to Pudentilla seems to suggest access to the *Apologia* in the twelfth century, thus demanding a radical revision of our understanding of the availability of Apuleian texts in northern Europe during

---

[81] L. Traube, 'O Roma nobilis. Philologische Untersuchungen aus dem Mittelalter', *Abhandlungen der philosophisch-philologischen Classe der königlich Bayerischen Akademie der Wissenschaften* 19 (1891), 299–395, at 308.

[82] 'The Classics: Episcopal Malice and Papal Piety', in *The Classics in the Middle Ages*, ed. Bernardo and Levin, 379–402, at 383. Father Synan gives no real evidence to support the claim beyond observing that the title must be an allusion to Apuleius' work since it is so inappropriate to what actually happens in the poem. J. R. Clarke argues, in contrast, that the Golias poet drew his inspiration from Martianus Capella's reference (1. 30) to Apollo and Mercury's metamorphosis into planets as they approached the palace of Jupiter. See his 'Metamorphosis in the Twelfth-Century *Metamorphosis Golye Episcopi*', in *Classical Texts and their Traditions*, ed. D. F. Bright and E. S. Ramage (Chico, Calif.: Scholars P, 1984), 7–12, at 10. Cf. his 'Love and Learning in the *Metamorphosis Golye Episcopi*', *Mittellateinisches Jahrbuch* 21 (1986), 156–71.

[83] See E. A. Synan, 'A Goliard Witness: The *De nuptiis Philologiae et Mercurii* of Martianus Capella in the *Metamorphosis golye episcopi*', *Florilegium* 2 (1980), 121–45. Cf. Schlam, 'Apuleius in the Middle Ages', 365. Shanzer (*Commentary*, 69) confuses the poem with the *Apocalypsis Goliae*.

[84] vv. 177–84, ed. Huygens, 770. Cf. Wright, *Latin Poems*, 27–8.

[85] No satisfactory identification of these characters has been made. In 'Who was Ysopullus?', *Speculum* 23 (1948), 112, S. T. Collins suggests the emendation, *secum suam duxerat Getam Naso pullus* ('Ovid, all mournful [because in exile] brought his Gothic lady').

the Middle Ages. Claudio Moreschini, indeed, describes the list of poets and their lovers as 'un elenco derivato, come ben vide il Manitius dal *De magia*, cap. 10', that chapter of the *Apologia* being well known as a source of the 'real identities' of the women celebrated pseudonymously by the Latin love elegists.[86]

If we turn, however, to Sidonius Apollinaris, the immediate source of the names becomes clear.[87] In a letter (*c.*470) to Hesperius, he urges his friend not to be distracted from his studies by his impending marriage. He should remember the examples of old, of wives who 'held candles and candlesticks' for their husbands, while the latter were 'reading and meditating': Marcia for Hortensius; Terentia for Cicero; Calpurnia for Pliny; Pudentilla for Apuleius; Rusticiana for Symmachus.[88] Nor should he neglect his poetry, being mindful that 'Corinna often completed a line with her Ovid, Lesbia with Catullus, Caesennia with Gaetulico, Argentaria with Lucan, Cynthia with Propertius, Delia with Tibullus.'

The coincidence of Psyche and Apuleius in a poem entitled '*Met(h)amorphosis...*' is nevertheless intriguing and reflects, I suggest, the intermediate influence of Fulgentius. The clue is the detail of Pudentilla 'burning' (*urit*) Apuleius. Sidonius merely numbers Pudentilla among those who 'held candles and candlesticks' for their husbands, but the Golias poet seems to have conflated in his own mind the dutiful Sidonian candle with the ejaculatory Psychic lamp, for his preceding line, *Plinium Calpurnie succendit scintilla* ('Calpurnia's spark sets Pliny on fire'), was surely inspired by Fulgentius' description of the climax of the anagnorisis, *affectu scintillantis olei desputamento maritum succendit* ('she scorched her husband with the spittle of the flashing oil'). At the very least, this is a delightful piece of intertextual play which would have given pleasure to its creator; at best, it is an extremely learned joke, aimed at a select circle of twelfth-century humanists whose interests included Apuleius.[89] Most importantly for our purposes, it indicates that at least one twelfth-century writer was able to appropriate Martianus' delineation of Psyche while maintaining (through Fulgentius) an awareness of Apuleius' alternative narrative.

---

[86] Moreschini, 'Sulla fama di Apuleio nel medioevo e nel rinascimento', 467; Manitius, *Geschichte*, iii. 269. Cf. Oldoni, 'Streghe medievali', 276.

[87] Noted also by Schlam, 'Apuleius in the Middle Ages', 365.

[88] *legentibus meditantibusque candelas et candelabra tenuerunt* (*Epistola* 2. 10. 5). Text in *C. Sollius Apollinaris Sidonius,* ed. P. Mohr (Leipzig: Teubner, 1895). On Sidonius' familiarity with the *Apologia,* see Ch. 1, *supra.*

[89] It is an interesting coincidence that MSS belonging to the δ branch of Apuleius' *Opera philosophica* (which appears to have its origins in France) also preserve the Ten-Book tradition of Pliny's *Letters.* See Reynolds, *Texts and Transmission,* 17.

Berengar of Poitiers, *Apologia* (*c.*1140)

It is interesting to note that another product of the feud between Abelard and Bernard of Clairvaux also features an apparent echo of Apuleius' *Apologia*, and from the same chapter (no. 10). Berengar of Poitiers' *Apologia* includes, in its attack on Bernard, the sentence: *Plato Alexim puerum, cui amatorias cantiunculas composuerat, insigni titulo ducit ad tumulum* ('Plato takes to the grave by means of a famous inscription/epitaph, the boy Alexis, for whom he had composed amatory songs'). The editor notes, 'The only source known to me for this story is Apul., *Apol.* 10, a very rare text, although not unknown, in the twelfth century'.[90] Berengar's apparent echo of Apuleius requires further investigation (one would need, for example, to eliminate the possibility of 'leakage' from other sources, such as the *Greek Anthology* and its derivatives, or the commentary tradition on the second of Vergil's *Eclogues*).[91] But if we provisionally allow the claim (and couple Berengar with the *Golias* poet), we may wish to impute to Abelard's circle a particular interest in Apuleius (which would complement Abelard's known admiration for Macrobius).[92] We should certainly note the presence of ass-allusions in Berengar's *Apologia*.[93]

[90] R. M. Thomson, 'The Satirical Works of Berengar of Poitiers: An Edition with Introduction', *Mediaeval Studies* 42 (1980), 89–138, at 124. Repr. in his *England and the 12th-Century Renaissance* (Aldershot: Ashgate, 1998), no. xiii.

[91] Cf. *Anthologia Palatina*, vii. 100 (one of the epigraphs on Alexis ascribed to 'Plato'), and *Eclogues* 2 (*Formosum pastor Corydon ardebat Alexim* ...). Apuleius' failure to mention a funeral mound or epitaph in *Apologia* 10 makes me doubt his influence on Berengar in this passage. Diogenes Laertius' account (*Lives of the Philosophers* 3. 29–33) of (pseudo-)Plato's poem on Alexis follows immediately on from a discussion of how his lament on the death of Dion was inscribed on his tomb in Syracuse. Such an account may well have filtered through to a Latin commentary tradition. See, generally, J. Hutton, *The Greek Anthology in France and in the Latin Writers of the Netherlands to the Year 1800* (Ithaca, NY: Cornell UP, 1946), and A. Cameron, *The Greek Anthology: From Meleager to Planudes* (Oxford: Clarendon, 1993).

[92] In his *Expositio in Hexaemeron* (*PL* 178, col. 752), Abelard makes use of Augustine's account (*De ciuitate dei*) of Apuleian demonology (*De deo Socratis*). Stahl (*Macrobius*, 44) records Abelard's praise of Macrobius, while Dronke (*Fabula*, 58–9) adumbrates the possibility that Macrobius held a special place in the studies of the so-called 'School of Chartres'.

[93] 115–16: *Hanc certe* [116] *caudam non vult hic asinus* ('Certainly, this ass does not want this tail'). 116: *Petrus, inquit, semper turbat Ecclesiam, semper excogitat novitatem. O tempora! o mores! Sic judicat de sole caecus. Sic pingit in ebore mancus. Sic urbem appretiatur asinus* (' "Peter", he says, "is always disrupting the Church; he is always contriving some novelty." What times! What customs! This is a blind man's judgement of the sun. This is how a maimed man paints on ivory. This is the value that an ass places on a city'). 121: *Solemus ridere picturas incipientes ab homine et in asinum desinentes* ('It is our custom to laugh at pictures which begin with a man and end with an ass').

Peter of Blois

The *Carmina Burana* have also been posited as possible recipients of Apuleian input. Peter Dronke believes that 'the ardent drinking of kisses from the girl's weeping eyes' in *Grates ago Veneri* (*c*.1160)—a poem attributed to Peter of Blois—'may well be inspired ... by the eroticism (and the rhythmic prose) of Apuleius, rare author though he was at this time'.[94] The parallels with the description of Fotis' eyes (*AA* 3. 14) are (at least superficially) impressive, especially using Dronke's lineation:

> *flentis bibo lacrimas*
> *dulcissimas ...*
> *plus haurio   fervoris*
>
> *et subridens tremulis*
> *semiclausis oculis ... sopita*
>
> (Peter of Blois)
>
> *oculos   Photidis meae*
> *udos   ac tremulos*
> *et prona libidine marcidos*
> *iamiamque semiadopertulos*
> *adnixis   et sorbillantibus sauiis*
> *sitienter hauriebam*
>
> (*AA* 3. 14)

Fotis' eyes, however, are wet, not with tears, but with desire; and the drinking of tears is a familiar motif in amatory poetry.[95] Ovid is a far more obvious source than Apuleius for Peter of Blois' poem:

> *et sicco lacrimas conbibat ore tuas*
>
> (Let her drink your tears with parched mouth)
>
> (*Ars amatoria* 2. 326)
>
> *adspicies oculos tremulo fulgore micantes*
>
> (You will see her eyes glittering with a trembling brightness.)
>
> (*Ars amatoria* 2. 721)

---

[94] 'Profane Elements in Literature', in *Renaissance and Renewal in the Twelfth Century*, ed. R. L. Benson and G. Constable (Oxford: Clarendon, 1982), 569–612, at 579. For full text and translation of the poem (*Carmen Buranum* 72), see P. Godman, 'Literary Classicism and Latin Erotic Poetry of the Twelfth Century and the Renaissance', in *Latin Poetry and the Classical Tradition: Essays in Medieval and Renaissance Literature*, ed. P. Godman and O. Murray (Oxford: Clarendon, 1990), 149–82, at 163–5. In *Petri Blesensis Carmina*, ed. C. Wollin (Turnhout: Brepols, 1998), 456 and 653, Dronke's claims for an Apuleian echo are cited with approval, though *Ars amatoria* 2. 721 is also quoted.

[95] e.g. Ovid, *Fasti* 3. 509: *lacrimasque per oscula siccat*; and *Tristia* 3. 5. 14: *et lacrimas cernens in singula verba cadentes | ore meo lacrimas, auribus illa bibi*.

The similarity probably stems from the fact that Apuleius is also echoing Ovid.[96] It is interesting, however, that Peter of Blois was a student of Bernardus Silvestris and had travelled as far as Sicily where he 'served betwen 1167 and 1168 as the praeceptor of William II of Palermo'.[97]

Echoes of the Myrmex and Philesitherus story (*AA* 9. 17–21) have been detected in *Milo*, a Latin verse comedy by another of Bernardus Silvestris' students, Matthew of Vendôme (b. *c.*1130), which features a cuckolded husband having to break into his own house causing the king to flee, leaving his sandals behind in the bedroom.[98] According to Giovanni Orlandi, 'a cluster of such details might well be found in any story of adultery then current. There is no need, therefore, to postulate for Matthew a direct knowledge of the *Metamorphoses*'.[99]

The Romance Tradition

Other claims for the influence of *The Golden Ass* in the Middle Ages are less easy to dismiss. The most sustained of these relate to the French romances of the twelfth century. Nor is this a sterile academic debate. The medieval French romances have a seminal role in the development of European literature: they

[96] Apuleius' Ovidian debt is noted by R. T. Van der Paardt, ed., *The Metamorphoses: A Commentary on Book III* (Amsterdam: Hakkert, 1971), *ad loc.* The detail of the half-closed eyes remains an interesting correspondence between Peter of Blois and Apuleius. Dronke (*Cosmographia*, 9) remarks on Peter's use of Bernardus Silvestris. We should also note Peter's intimate knowledge of John of Salisbury's works. In a letter (*Epistola* 12), Peter refers to the *versus et ludicra* that he had written at Tours. According to R. W. Southern, however, the additions to the corpus of Peter's poems 'suggested by various eminent scholars and finally and most lavishly of all by Peter Dronke are either certainly or probably not by the letter writer'. See 'Blois, Peter of (1125×30–1212)', *ODNB*.

[97] Godman, 'Literary Classicism', 158. Godman (160) points to the 'crude chronology that places Peter's erotic poetry in the 1150s and his religious verse thirty years later'. Some of his erotic lyrics can be dated to *c.*1190.

[98] For a text, see *Mathei Vindocinensis Opera*, ed. F. Munari, 3 vols. (Rome: Storia e letteratura, 1977–88), vol. ii (*Piramus et Tisbe, Milo, Epistule, Tobias*).

[99] 'Classical Latin Satire and Medieval Elegiac Comedy', in *Latin Poetry and the Classical Tradition*, ed. Godman and Murray, 97–114, at 112 n. 50. Orlandi (108 ff.) prefers to source the main plot in 'the story of the farmer and the lion's footprints' ('one of the *Tales of Sindbad* or *The Seven Wise Masters*') found in the *Syntipas* of Michael Andreopulos (11th cent.), and to derive the slippers-episode from Horace (*Satires* 1. 2. 127–33, where the adulterer flees *pede nudo*, 'bare-footed'), with a cross-reference to the *Geta* (463 ff.) of Vitalis of Blois (*fl.* 1160–75). Orlandi observes (112 n. 15) that 'The detail of the sandals, apparently the most impressive of all, is to be found also in the Spanish version of the Sindbad, the *Libro de los engaños*...', translated from the Arabic in the thirteenth century.' For a text of *Geta*, see *Three Latin Comedies*, ed. K. Bate (Toronto: Centre for Medieval Studies, 1976). Cf. S. Pittaluga, 'Narrativa e oralità nella commedia mediolatina (e il fantasma di Apuleio)', in *Der antike Roman und seine mittelalterliche Rezeption*, ed. M. Picone and B. Zimmermann (Basle: Birkhäuser, 1997), 307–20.

were the most accomplished specimens of narrative fiction to have been produced since Late Antiquity (indeed, they are often seen as poetic pre-cursors of the modern novel);[100] they document (and, arguably, help to construct) an emergent sense of individual consciousness;[101] and they serve to define the cultural values which we associate most readily with the High Middle Ages—chivalry and *fin'amor* ('refined love').

If any twelfth-century writer is going to make use of *The Golden Ass* for literary purposes, it is likely to be Chrétien de Troyes. Chrétien is a man proud of his book-learning: at the beginning of *Cligés,* he tells us that his first literary undertakings were translations from Ovid (a poem entitled *Philomena* is attributed to him) and he adapts the *translatio studii* topos, boasting that 'learning' (*la clergie*), having passed from Greece to Rome, 'has now come to France' (*Qui ore est an France venue*).[102] In the prologue to *Erec and Enide* (often hailed as 'the first Arthurian romance'), he emphasizes his distance from the common hawkers of tales; at the end of the poem, he portrays himself as a disciple of Macrobius (ll. 6736 ff);[103] and in the whole course of the work, he reveals his debt to Martianus Capella.[104]

The most extreme claim for Apuleian influence relates to Chrétien's final romance, *Perceval ou il Conte du Graal* (left unfinished at his death in *c.*1185). According to Henry and Renee Kahane and Angelina Pietrangeli, 'Chrétien's story of Perceval and Apuleius' story of Lucius are essentially the same. Both narrate a salvation or rebirth.'[105] One might make the preliminary objection that if you compare *any* two soteriological narratives you are bound to find parallel structures. In any event, the 'parallelisms' adduced between Perceval's repentance and Lucius' Isiac initiation are simply insufficient to justify the authors' conclusion that 'Chrétien must have known ... Apuleius' *Metamorphoses*'. The flaws in their methodology are evident in their assertion

---

[100] An extreme statement of this position is given by F. E. Guyer, *Chrétien de Troyes: Inventor of the Modern Novel* (London: Vision, 1960). Guyer eschews footnotes in favour of wild claims: Lancelot's long journey, we are told (79), 'recalls the search of Cupid for Psyche [*sic*!] as related in Apuleius' *Golden Ass* which was known and imitated elsewhere in Old French literature'. See, more generally, G. T. Shepherd, 'The Emancipation of Story in the Twelfth Century', in *Medieval Narrative: A Symposium*, ed. H. Bekker-Nielson et al. (Odense: Odense UP, 1979), 44–57.

[101] See R. W. Hanning, *The Individual in Twelfth-Century Romance* (New Haven: YUP, 1977).

[102] *Kristian von Troyes: Cligés*, ed. W. Foerster (Halle: Niemeyer, 1921), 1–2 (vv. 30–5).

[103] See A. Hunt, 'Chrétien and Macrobius', *Classica et Mediaevalia* 33 (1981), 211–27.

[104] J. A. Nightingale, 'Chrétien de Troyes and the Mythographical Tradition: The Couple's Journey in *Erec et Enide* and Martianus' *De Nuptiis*', in *King Arthur through the Middle Ages*, ed. V. M. Lagorio and M. Leake Day, 2 vols. (New York: Garland, 1990), i. 56–79; K. D. Uitti, 'Vernacularization and Old French Romance Mythopoesis with Emphasis on Chrétien's *Erec et Enide*', in *The Sower and his Seed: Essays on Chrétien de Troyes,* ed. R. T. Pickens (Lexington, Ky.: French Forum, 1983), 81–115, at 95–101.

[105] 'On the Sources of Chrétien's Grail Story', in *Festschrift Walther von Wartburg zum 80. Geburstag*, ed. K. Baldinger (Tübingen: Niemeyer, 1968), 191–233, at 201.

that 'Any search today for independent corroborative proof of such know-ledge is futile; too little documentation has survived. All we can do is to show that it would not have been impossible for Chrétien to have known them'.[106]

Such an approach is not merely defeatist—it verges on the disingenuous.[107] In support of his claim that Chrétien de Troyes's earliest romance, *Eric et Enide* (*c.*1170), derives directly from Apuleius, David Rollo legitimately deplores what he calls 'an often belligerent skepticism toward the possibility of a twelfth-century [348] Francophone readership' for *The Golden Ass*.[108] He points out rightly that 'to confuse what has not survived with what was not known is historically jejune' (348); and he is understandably resistant to the reductive tendencies of the folklorists, dismissing them as 'anachronistic statisticians' (365). He seriously weakens his case, however, when he declares: 'Because the argument demanding material [349] proof is really no argument at all if assessed in the context of a scribal culture, the only cogent evidence that can exist must be derived from the eloquent testimony of contemporaneous literary production'.

In fact, the 'exhuming quest for material evidence' which he ridicules as 'an ever-frustrated form of cultural archeology' (348) can yield rich fruits. The more we strive to discern potential lines of transmission from antiquity to the Middle Ages—the more we learn about medieval intellectual net-works—the better. It is interesting to note, for instance, that John of Salisbury (who was Bishop of Chartres from 1176 until his death in 1180 and who is fulsome in his praise of the *De deo Socratis* and the *De dogmate Platonis*) draws on Apuleius in a letter to Henry, Count of Champagne, whose wife, Marie of Champagne (daughter of Eleanor of Aquitaine and Louis VII), was Chrétien de Troyes's patron:

Nam ut ait Apuleius in libro de deo Socratis, laudem celeritatis simul et diligentiae nullus assequitur, sed ad grandum librorum graues materiae in eandem scedulam nulla umquam diligentia compinguntur.

---

[106] 'On the Sources of Chrétien's Grail Story', 228. The claims made for the influence of the Latin *Asclepius* (a work frequently attributed to Apuleius during the Middle Ages) are infinitely more plausible.

[107] e.g., the authors base part of their case on the (supposedly confirmed) Apuleian content of *Partonopeu de Blois* (concerning which, see *infra*).

[108] 'From Apuleius' Psyche to Chrétien's Erec and Enide', in *The Search for the Ancient Novel*, ed. J. Tatum (Baltimore: Johns Hopkins UP, 1994), 347–69, at 347–8. Rollo (despite his claim at 349) is not the first to consider *Erec et Enide* 'with reference to the Apuleian paradigm'. See M. Kawczynski, 'Ist Apuleius im Mittelalter bekannt gewesen?', in *Bausteine zur Romanischen Philologie: Festgabe für Adolfo Mussafia* (Halle: Niemeyer, 1905), 193–210, at 207, and C. Luttrell, *The Creation of the First Arthurian Romance: A Quest* (London: Edward Arnold, 1974), 232–3.

(For, as Apuleius says in his book *On The God of Socrates* [Prologue, c. 3], no one attains praise simultaneously for speed and diligence; nor can the weighty matters of great books be compacted into the same little sheet.)[109]

Chrétien tells us at the beginning of *Le Chevalier de la charrete* that it was Marie (whose great-grandfather has been called 'the first known troubadour') who had supplied him with the 'subject-matter and the treatment' (*matiere et san*) for his poem about Lancelot.[110] So we have a possible conduit for the intercourse of ideas between the humanists of Chartres and the *littérateurs* of Troyes.

We know, too, that in 1179, Walter Map (for a long time considered to be the author of the prose *Lancelot* as well as Goliardic verse which included the *Metamorphosis Golye Episcopi*)[111] attended the Third Lateran Council and, en route to Italy from England, was entertained by Count Henry.[112] Map's *De nugis curialium* contains a passage which, in the opinion of M. R. James and C. N. L. Brooke, 'seems clearly to refer to Apuleius' *Metamorphoses*'.[113] In one story, *De fantastica decepcione Gerberti*, the future Pope Sylvester II (AD 999–1003) is utterly transformed by the sight of a beautiful girl, 'the mirror and marvel of the city' (*speculum et admiracio ciuitatis*):

Egreditur, uidet, admiratur, cupit et alloquitur; audit et allicitur; haurit ab apotheca Scille furorem, et a matre Morphoseos edoctus obliuisci morem suo non abnegat ueneno, cuius uirtute degenerat in asinum, ad onera fortis, ad uerbera durus, ad opera deses, ad operas ineptus, in omni semper miseria petulcus.

(He went forth, saw, wondered, desired, and addressed her: listened and was entranced: he imbibed madness from the laboratory of Scylla, and taught by Morpheus' mother to forget, did not refuse obedience to her poison, and by its power sank to be

---

[109] *The Letters of John of Salisbury*, ed. W. J. Millor, H. E. Butler, and C. N. L. Brooke, rev. edn., 2 vols. (Oxford: Clarendon, 1979–86), ii. 318, Letter 209 (my trans.). On Marie as patron, see, generally, J. F. Benton, 'The Court of Mary of Champagne as a Literary Centre', *Speculum* 36 (1961), 551–91, esp. 553–4 and 573–5.

[110] *Arthurian Romances*, trans. D. D. R. Owen (London: Dent, 1987), pp. xii and 185; *Les Romans de Chrétien de Troyes*, ed. M. Roques, 6 vols. (Paris: H. Champion, 1952–75), iii. 2 (vv. 26–7).

[111] M. R. James notes that 'the prose cycle of Lancelot' emerged from 'France, perhaps from Champagne, in the period *c.*1215–30' and that the final two parts of the cycle (the *Queste del Saint Graal* and the *Mort Artu*) 'claim to be translations from a Latin original preserved at the abbey of Salisbury, made by "Walter Map at the request of King Henry his Lord" '. See *Walter Map: De nugis curialium. Courtly Trifles*, ed. and trans. M. R. James, rev. C. N. L. Brooke and R. A. B. Mynors (Oxford: Clarendon, 1983), p. xx. The only romance currently ascribed to Map is the story of 'Sadius and Galo' (*De nugis* 3. 2). The attribution to Map of the *Metamorphosis Golye Episcopi* may be a product of the poem's evident Abelardian bias.

[112] Benton, 'Mary of Champagne', 576: 'This visit may have been the occasion for an exchange of anecdotes with a local raconteur, since both Walter and Henry's clerk, Maître Etienne, related scurrilous stories about Saint Bernard [another Abelardian link!] which seem to be versions of the same tale.' See *De nugis curialium*, 225–6.

[113] *De nugis curialium*, 351. S. Costanza (*La fortuna di L. Apuleio nell'età di mezzo*, 73) talks of Map's 'allusioni evidenti alle *Metamorfosi*'.

an ass, strong to bear burdens, impervious to blows, sluggish to toil, stupid in skilled labour, ever prone to kick at any hardship.)[114]

According to Massimo Oldoni, the girl is a 'nouva Fotide medio-latina' who 'rides' ('cavalca') Gerbert just as Fotis 'rode' Lucius (as a *pendula Venus, AA* 2. 17) before she changed him into an ass.[115] We should note, however, that Gerbert's metamorphosis is merely figurative,[116] and that the description of the meta-morphic agent (*uenenum*) and its effects associates the tale with the tradition of quadrupedic transformation preserved by Augustine (*De ciuitate dei* 18. 18) and such writers as William of Malmesbury (*Gesta regum anglorum* 2. 171).[117] But

[114] Text and translation from *De nugis curialium*, 350–1. Cf. Dist. 4. 3, pp. 288–9: 'A Dissuasion of Valerius to Rufinus that he should not take a wife': *Ne sus fias aut asinus, tacere non possum* ('Lest you be turned into a hog or ass, I cannot keep silent'). It may well be that Walter, striving to convey an erotic loss of self-possession, has conflated Scylla with the nearby whirlpool of Charybdis, just as Alanus de Insulis does in the *De planctu Naturae* (Metre 8, ll. 1–2; trans. Sheridan, 194) where he advises how 'To prevent Scylla with her greedy whirlpool from plunging you into the deep night of lust' (*Ne te gulosae Scylla voraginis* [0471A] | *Mergat profunda nocte libidinum*).

[115] 'Streghe medievali', 276. Oldoni's case is weakened by his belief (276) in Map's authorship of the *Metamorphosis Goliae* and by his failure to consider the intermediate influence (detailed *supra*) of Martianus Capella and Sidonius Apollinaris which explains the presence of apparently Apuleian material in the poem.

[116] This would be in keeping with the view (espoused by John Chrysostom, among others), that Homer intended us to believe in a figurative, rather than a literal, transformation of Ulysses' companions into swine—a reminder that lustful appetites reduce men to the semblance of beasts.

[117] *Gesta regum anglorum*, ed. and trans. R. A. B. Mynors, R. M. Thomson, and M. Winterbottom, 2 vols. (Oxford: Clarendon, 1998–9), i. 292–3. William's editors (ii. 158–9) discuss the 'tantalizing resemblances to the *Golden Ass*' of his story (related by an Aquitanian monk) of the young acrobat transformed into a donkey by two 'old crones' (*aniculae*) at an inn on the road to Rome. They ignore, however, the likely influence of Augustine whose account of the Italian landladies changing their guests into swine comes in the same chapter (*De ciuitate dei* 18. 18) as his mention of *The Golden Ass*. The acrobat's tale is situated within a series of stories (2. 167–72) illustrating the magical arts of the same Gerbert who features in Walter Map's anecdote. The account ends with a tantalizing reference to Peter Damian (*literaturae peritus*, 'a man of great literary learning'). Damian, William tells us, assured a sceptical Pope Leo that such things were possible, adducing the example of Simon Magus who caused his own visage to appear in the face of Clement's father, Faustianus (see *The Clementine Recognitions*, ed. A. Roberts and J. Donaldson, trans. T. Smith, in *Ante-Nicene Christian Library*, iii (Edinburgh: T. & T. Clark, 1867), 459–60). William certainly knew the *De ciuitate dei* (and should therefore have been familiar with Augustine's reference to *The Golden Ass* in his account of bestial transformations) and there is evidence to suggest that he actually annotated a manuscript of the philosophical writings of Apuleius (see R. Thomson, *William of Malmesbury* (Woodbridge: Boydell, 1987)). Yet he makes no mention of him. More tantalizing still, Peter Damian (1007–72) was in correspondence with Desiderius, who was Abbot of Monte Cassino in or around the time that the oldest surviving manuscript of *The Golden Ass* was copied there. Damian actually addresses to Desiderius a treatise, *De variis miraculosis narrationibus* (*PL* 145, col. 571 ff), though, disappointingly, he makes no mention of Apuleius, either here or, it would appear, anywhere else. The debate may, however, furnish additional context for the copying of *The Golden Ass* in the eleventh century.

if there is nothing in the story that is directly Apuleian,[118] *a matre Morphoseos* remains a fascinating crux: the emendation *metamorphoseos* (suggested by Webb and adopted by James in the 1923 edition of his translation) might indeed suggest an allusion to the title of Apuleius' work.[119]

Interesting, also, is the fact that Gerald of Wales ('Giraldus Cambrensis', 1147–1223), who associates himself closely with Walter Map, should provide us with one of the earliest medieval mentions of *The Golden Ass*.[120] In the *Topographia Hibernica* (2. 19), Gerald begins his catalogue of the recent marvels of Ireland with the story of a priest's encounter (datable to 1183 or 1184) with a man and woman who have been turned into wolves while retaining human minds and human speech. Gerald validates the story by claiming to have met the priest personally, and provides patristic authority for such transformations by quoting Augustine's comments on Apuleius' asinine metamorphosis in *De ciuitate dei* 18. 18.[121]

One might note, finally, that Map also seems to share the Abelardian bias of the men of the previous generation such as Berengar and the Golias poet. Map recalls a discussion (in the presence of Thomas à Becket) of Bernard of Clairvaux's condemnation of Abelard. One of the interlocutors deflated the Cistercians' praise of Bernard's miracles by relating the story of how the venerable abbot, 'seated on a great she-ass' (*super asinam magnam sedens*), tried to cast the 'unclean spirit' out of a man possessed (*demoniacus*) and was stoned for his pains.[122]

All of this evidence of literary networks and Apuleian (and asinine) interests could usefully be marshalled in support of Rollo's claims for French writers'

[118] See Stahl, *Martianus Capella*, i. 65, for Gerbert's reference (Letter 161) to Martianus Capella.

[119] The latest editor, Brooke, regards the emendation as 'improbable' (351), but concedes the possibility of a play between the two concepts. Cf. Oldoni, 'Streghe medievali', 274–5. Of course, an allusion to the title need not imply knowledge of the work. Augustine uses only the title *De asino aureo* and Fulgentius' exegesis of 'Cupid and Psyche' gives no hint of an asinine dimension to the work (entitled *Metamorphoses*) which contains it. However, Fulgentius' indiscriminate use of the two titles in the *Expositio sermonum antiqorum* (including a reference to Psyche which he attributes to the *De asino aureo*) would have made it possible for a medieval scholar without access to manuscripts of the Apuleian text to have divined something of the work's contents.

[120] On the relations between the two men, see K. A. Bate, 'Walter Map and Giraldus Cambrensis', *Latomus* 31 (1972), 860–75.

[121] *Giraldi Cambrensis opera*, 8 vols. (London: Longmans, 1861–91), v, ed. J. F. Dimock, 105–6. Rollo (365) cites the passage but makes no attempt to discern any networks. See also C. W. Bynum, 'Metamorphosis, or Gerald and the Werewolf', *Speculum* 73 (1998), 987–1013, at 1011, and *Metamorphosis and Identity* (New York: Zone Books, 2001), 77–111, at 107. Gerald quotes from the *De dogmate Platonis* (2. 7 [602]) in cap. 10 (*De principis justitia*) of his *De principis instructione* (written, according to the Rolls Series editor G. F. Warner) in about 1216). See *Giraldi Cambrensis opera*, viii. 38: *Quia, ut ait Apulegius, 'vera justitia est, utilitatis ut suæ, sic fida speculatrix alienæ'.*

[122] *De nugis curialium*, 78–9. See A. R. Rigg, *A History of Anglo-Latin Literature, 1066–1422* (Cambridge: CUP, 1992), 88–93, esp. 89.

direct access to *The Golden Ass* during the twelfth century. Unfortunately, the specific correspondences adduced by Rollo seem to me too tenuous. One can certainly find a structural congruence between the lamplit anagnorisis in 'Cupid and Psyche' and the bedroom scene in *Erec et Enide* in which the young wife incurs the wrath of her husband when she laments that he has been dishonoured through uxoriousness:

> *Son seignor a mont et a val*
> *comanca tant a regarder,*
> *le cors bien fet et le vis cler;*
> *et plore de si grant ravine*
> *que plorant dessor la peitrine*
> *an chieent les lermes sor lui,*
> *et dist: «Lasse, con mar m'esmui*
> *de mon pais que ving ca querre?*
> *Bien me devroit essorbir la terre,*
> *quant toz li miaudres chevaliers,*
> *li plus hardiz et li plus fiers,*
> *qui onques fust ne cuens ne rois,*
> *li plus leax, li plus cortois,*
> *a del tot an tot relanquie*
> *por moi tote chevalerie.*

(lines 2486–500)

(She began to look her husband up and down, gazing at his shapely body and clear features. Then she weeps so abundantly that her tears fall on her husband's breast; and she says: 'Alas, what a misfortune that I ever left my country! What did I come here to find? The earth ought to swallow me up when the very best knight, the boldest, most resolute, noblest and most courtly ever to be numbered among counts and kings has on my account utterly given up the whole practice of chivalry.')[123]

When he wakes, Erec forces Enide to repeat what she has said, and then orders her brusquely: 'Get ready at once, and prepare yourself to go riding' (*Aparelliez vos or androit, | Por chevauchier vos aprestez!*).[124] Enide assumes that she is being banished for her bold speech, but Erec confounds expectations by travelling with her, subjecting her to trials and dangers which he shares until, honour restored, the pair return to the castle for their coronation.

The absence of key Apuleian/Fulgentian motifs in the climactic bedroom scene is explained by what Rollo calls Chrétien's 'procedures of romance realignment'. Thus the element of Psyche's threatened violence to her husband is deployed in subsequent episodes which feature 'a recurrent and remarkably Apuleian stress

---

[123] *Les Romans de Chrétien*, i. 76 (vv. 2486–500); *Arthurian Romances*, trans. Owen, 33.
[124] *Les Romans de Chrétien*, i. 79 (vv. 2574–5); Owen, 35.

on decapitation, which is proposed once by Enide (3386) and twice by the count (3525, 3528) as an appropriate means of killing Erec'.[125] And the injunction on sight imposed prior to the lamp scene in 'Cupid and Psyche' is replaced by a prohibition on Enide speaking to Erec *after* her unfortunate bedroom lament.

Many of Rollo's 'parallels' are so nebulous (and his treatment of them so tendentious) that one is tempted to dismiss his argument out of hand. For example, in support of his thesis that Chrétien must have been following Apuleius directly rather than Fulgentius, Rollo claims that Fulgentius makes no mention of 'the nuptial and funereal journey Psyche undertakes as the living corpse' (*AA* 4. 33) which is paralleled in *Erec et Enide* in the description of the journey towards the amorous count's palace (4696–705).[126] How does he explain, then, Fulgentius' reference to Psyche 'having been led, as though in a funeral procession, and chosen for a winged serpent as a spouse'? And while Chrétien is often praised for his interest in interiority, Rollo credits him with a level of psychological sophistication that belongs more to our own post-Freudian world than to the twelfth century.

Yet, amid all his excesses, Rollo raises some significant issues.[127] Why, he asks, in a provocative peroration,

should Chrétien's *Erec et Enide* and *Chevalier de la Charrete*, Marie de France's *Yonec*, Renaut de Beaujeu's *Bel Inconnu*, and the anonymous *Partonopeu de Blois* all exploit a narrative structure similar to the classical model in order to explore questions of power and gender...? If this is to be explained in terms of folklore, why should all these authors not only know the same folk tale but also set out to transform it into the literary text by exploiting a common nexus of symbols, do so with a similar effect, and [365] in all cases show analogies to Apuleius's treatment of these issues?'[128]

---

[125] Rollo, 357. As parallels go, these are utterly *un*remarkable. Chrétien makes it clear that Enide's inner thoughts are different from her speech when she tries to outwit the amorous count by suggesting that he have Erec beaten up or killed (*Arthurian Romances*, trans. Owen, 45). Moreover, decapitation is hardly an unusual occurrence in chivalric romance.

[126] Rollo, 364. Rollo may have been misled by Whitbread's translation of Fulgentius' *Perfecto... choragio* (ed. Helm, 121) as 'Full of courage' rather than 'with the funeral having been completed'.

[127] In his concluding remarks, Rollo (369 n. 36) adumbrates a correspondence between Apuleius' notion of *mutuus nexus* (*AA* 1. 1) and Chrétien's much-discussed reference to *conjointure* (on which, see generally, D. Kelly, 'The Source and Meaning of *Conjointure* in Chrétien's *Erec* 14', *Viator* 1 (1970), 179–200; and Nightingale, 68–9). In response to Rollo, one might equally note the incidence of the word *coniunctio* towards the end of the Fulgentius passage (*Mitologiae* 3.6) and the collocation of both terms in *De deo Socratis*, s. 15 (*coniunctionem nostram nexumque*), but the coincidence of concepts is certainly suggestive. Rollo also notes the similarity in the reception afforded Erec and Lucius on their respective visits to the houses of the impoverished vavasor and the miserly Milo (Fotis and Enide both tend to the well-born visitor's horse). We might add to Rollo's list the fact that our last glimpse of Enide before the calamitous bedroom scene is of her 'seated in a room on a coverlet of brocade imported from Thessaly' (ll. 2406 ff.; *Arthurian Romances*, trans. Owen, 32).

[128] Rollo, 364–5.

Let us take first the case of Marie de France (late twelfth century) and the narrative poems which she composed in emulation of the Breton *lais*.[129] It does appear that twelfth-century French writers had access to a rich array of Celtic story 'matter'—lines of transmission are often traced (perhaps a little too neatly) from Ireland, through Wales, to Brittany. But given the propensity of twelfth-century authors to disguise or invent their 'sources', we should be wary of taking Marie entirely at her word when she declares, in the prologue to *Guigemar* (the first *lai* in her collection): 'I shall relate briefly to you stories which I know to be true and from which the Bretons have composed their lays.'[130]

In Marie's *Yonec*, a knight assumes the form of a hawk in order to visit a beautiful matron sequestered in her tower, imposing upon her the simple condition that she not request his presence too often. She disregards the injunction of moderation; her husband, grown suspicious, has 'large iron spikes forged' (the tips of which are 'more shaply pointed than any razor', 89), and places them around the narrow window, so that the lover is mortally wounded. At the climax of the *lai*, the product of this adulterous union (now grown to manhood) cuts off his stepfather's head with his natural father's sword.

One might note the resemblance between the hawk-lover and Pamphile's erotically induced avine metamophosis (*AA* 3. 21), though Rollo's interest lies in the motifs of 'emasculating razors' (364) and decapitation which he also discerns in Chrétien's *Erec et Enide* (noted above) and *Chevalier de la Charrete* (e.g. the Sword Bridge and the Perilous Bed). Tracing lines of filiation in such texts is enormously difficult, and even if we accept a Celtic provenance for all these stories, it is still perfectly possible that, as oral material was absorbed into the sophisticated literary culture, it was shaped, or coloured by the Apuleian/Fulgentian paradigm.

Moreover, an Apuleian dimension can legitimately be invoked whenever one encounters a mysterious lover in the literature of this period—though its source is not *The Golden Ass* but one of the most important philosophical

---

[129] According to M. A. Doody, *The True Story of the Novel* (London: HarperCollins, 1997), 187, 'The fiercely comic adultery story in [Marie de France's] *Equitan*, with its climax in the mixup of the murderous boiling bath, is reminiscent of the adultery stories in Apuleius. The great European stockpot of stories is now fully available.' As a scholarly argument, this is alarmingly casual. The treatment of adultery in *Equitan* is conventionally moralistic and distinctly unApuleian—the adulterers are 'hoist by their own petard'. For a critique of Doody, see R. H. F. Carver, ' "True Histories" and "Old Wives' Tales": Renaissance Humanism and the "Rise of the Novel" ', *Ancient Narrative*, 1 (2001), 322–49.

[130] *les contes ke jo sai verrais,* | *dunt li Bretun unt fait les lais,* | *vos conterai assez briefment* (19–21); *The Lais of Marie de France*, trans. G. S. Burgess and K. Busby (London: Penguin, 1986), 43.

works of the Middle Ages, the *De deo Socratis*, which furnished a hugely influential theory of demonology.

Geoffrey of Monmouth (c.1138)

Indeed, one of the foundation texts for the whole tradition of Arthurian romance—Geoffrey of Monmouth's *Historiae regum Britanniae* (usually dated to 1138)—contains an account of the birth of Merlin which is frequently linked to 'Cupid and Psyche'.[131] Merlin and his mother are brought before the King who asks how 'the boy who has no father' came to be conceived. Merlin's mother explains the virgin conception:

> ... *neminem agnoui qui illum in me generauit. Vnum autem scio. quod cum essem inter consocias meas in thalamis nostris.' apparebat mihi quidem in specie pulcherrimi iuuenis. & sepissime amplectens me strictis brachiis.' deosculabatur. Et cum aliquantulum mecum moram fecisset.' subito euanescebat. ita ut nichil ex eo uiderem. Multociens quoque me alloquebatur dum secreto sederem.' nec usquam comparebat. Cumque me in hunc modum frenquasset.' coiuit mecum in specie hominis sepius. atque grauidam in aluo deseruit.*[132]

(I do not know who engendered him in me. But one thing I do know—that when I was with my companions in our chambers, someone appeared to me in the form of a most beautiful young man and, embracing me most often in his tight arms, began to kiss me warmly. And when he had dallied a little while with me, he suddenly vanished so that I saw nothing of him. Many times, too, he would address me when I was sitting in private, nor would he ever be visible. And when he had visited me frequently in this way, he had intercourse with me in the form of a man many times and deserted me, laden in womb.)

The King listens amazed and then asks his sage whether what the woman said could have happened. Maugantius replies:

> *In libris philosophorum nostrorum. & in plurimis hystoriis reperi multos homines huiusmodi procreationem habuisse. Nam ut apulegius de deo socratis perhibet. inter lunam & terram habitant spiritus quos incubos demones appellamus.* [382] *Hii partim habent naturam hominum. partim uero angelorum. & cum mulieribus coeunt. Forsitan unus ex eis huic mulieri apparuit & iuuenem istum ex ipsa generauit.*

---

[131] Manitius, *Geschichte*, iii. 479; Haight, *Apuleius*, 102; Walsh, *Roman Novel*, 231; J. J. M. Tobin, *Shakespeare's Favorite Novel: A Study of 'The Golden Asse' as Prime Source* (Lanham: UP of America, 1984), p. xii. Costanza (*La fortuna*, 73) cites Geoffrey in support of his claim that '[u]na importante tradizione del romanzo si affermava, larga e più decisa che in altre nazioni, nelle scuola di Inghilterra'.

[132] *The Historiae Regum Britanniae*, ed. A. Griscom (London: Longmans, Green, 1929), 381–2 (= 6. 18).

(In the books of our philosophers and in a great many (hi)stories, I have found that many men have been begotten in this way. For, as Apuleius says in the *De deo Socratis*, between the moon and earth live spirits whom we call *incubi* or demons. These have the nature partly of men but partly of angels and they have intercourse with women. Perhaps one of these appeared to this woman and produced from her that young man.)

Superficially, the resemblance between the two stories seems strong—a virgin is visited by an unknown but apparently beautiful lover who dallies with her and departs unseen, ultimately deserting her when she is pregnant with his child. But, as Maugantius says, similar occurrences may be found in 'a great many (hi)stories' and the correspondences are insufficient to credit Geoffrey with knowledge of *The Golden Ass* or even of Fulgentius' account of 'Cupid and Psyche'.[133]

The passage should remind us, however, that Apuleius actually characterizes Love (*Amor*) as a daemon in *De deo Socratis* 16; thus the erudite literary community which produced the twelfth-century chivalric romances and shorter works such as Marie de France's *lais* would have been preconditioned to discern a daemonic dimension in all accounts of mysterious lovers, whether they found them in Celtic stories or some version of 'Cupid and Psyche'.[134]

Partonopeu de Blois

The richest field in which to fossick for Apuleian nuggets remains the anonymous *Partonopeu de Blois*. Composed at some time between the early 1170s and 1196, the poem contains resemblances to 'Cupid and Psyche' which do merit the epithet 'remarkable'.[135] Partonopeu, the young nephew of Clovis, King of France (himself a descendant of Priam of Troy), becomes lost during a hunt in the Ardennes and is taken on an enchanted ship to a strange country

[133] See e.g. J. Ö. Swahn, *The Tale of Cupid and Psyche (Aarne-Thompson 425 & 428)* (Lund: Gleerup, 1955).

[134] One notices an almost comic concern on the parts of the magical paramours to reassure the hero or heroine that their powers are compatible with Christianity. In *Partonopeu de Blois*, when Melior finds a man in her bed, she calls upon the Virgin Mary, which comforts Partonopeu, 'for now he knew that she was not a demon'. See F. Fisher, *Narrative Art in Medieval Romances* (Cleveland, Ohio: n.pub., 1938), 105. Compare the hawk-knight who proves his humanity in Marie de France's *Yonec* by assuming the lady's form in order to receive communion from a priest. See D. Fehling, *Amor und Psyche: Die Schöpfung des Apuleius und ihre Einwirkung auf das Märchen, eine Kritik der romantischen Märchentheorie* (Mainz: Akademie der Wissenschaften und der Literatur, 1977), 38.

[135] A. Fourrier, *Le Courant réaliste dans le roman courtois en France au moyen-âge* (Paris: Nizet, 1960), i. 384, provides termini of 1182 and 1196 and favours 1182–5 as the likely date of composition. P. Simons and P. Eley suggest 'the early 1170s'. See 'Male Beauty and Sexual Orientation in *Partonopeus de Blois*', *Romance Studies* 17 (1999), 41–56, at 54 n. 4. A useful summary and a translation of excerpts are given by Fisher (*Narrative Art*, 21–30).

where he finds an unbarred palace filled with riches and a table already laid. He is waited on by invisible (and inaudible) servants, retiring to bed to be joined by a young woman (later identified as Melior, Empress of Byzantium) who says that she has brought him thither by magic after hearing of his prowess and seeing him in person. She promises to marry him in two and a half years' time when he comes of age but forbids him to look at her in the interim. He enjoys the pleasures of palace and bed for a year, but then begins to pine for friends and family and is twice permitted to return home. His mother, convinced that he has been ensnared by a devil, consults (on her son's first visit) the King (who tries to distract Partonopeu by betrothing him to his own niece, line 3976) and then (on the second visit) the Archbishop of Paris (who supplies a magic lamp). Prompted by his mother's urgings, Partonopeu decides to countermand his lover's injunction:

> Le covertoir a trait amont;
> La traïson desos repont.
> Aprés s'estoit fais descauchier
> Et tos nus el lit despoillier,   4516
> Puis s'est covers del covertor;
> Li cierge estagnent tot entor.
> Parmi la cambre vient la bloie,
> De son ami a molt grant joie;   4520
> De son mantel est deffublee,
> Les son ami est avalee.
> Quant Parthonopeus l'a sentue
> Et set qu'ele est trestote nue,   4524
> Le covertoir a loing jeté,
> Si l'a veüe o la clarté
> De la lanterne qu'il tenoit.
> A descovert nue le voit;   4528
> Mirer le puet et veïr bien
> C'onques ne vit si bele rien.
> Cele est pasmee et cil l'entent
> Qu'il a ovré trop folement;[136]   4532

(He lifted up the blanket;
He conceals beneath it the treachery.
After this, he had taken off his shoes
and all his clothes until quite naked in the bed;
then he covered himself in the blanket;

---

[136] *Partonopeu de Blois: A French Romance of the Twelfth Century*, ed. J. Gildea, 2 vols. (Villanova: Villanova UP, 1967–70), i. 184.

all around, the candles go out.
Through the middle of the chamber comes the Fair One,
to the very great joy of her beloved.[137]
She divested herself of her robe;
and lay down by the side of her beloved.
When Partonopeu felt her there
and knew that she was completely naked,
he threw the coverlet right off,
and then viewed her in the light
of the lamp he was holding.
Quite openly he looked at her in her nakedness;
he was able to gaze upon her and fully recognize
that he had never seen anything so beautiful.
She fainted and he realized
that he had behaved very foolishly.)

It is interesting to note that in the Middle English translation, the description
of Melior's beauty is even closer to Apuleius' account of the revealed Cupid:

His lantren he put vp wyth his lyght.
Alle naked there had he the syght
Of the fayrest shapen creature
That euer was foordened thorow nature...[138]

Partonopeu is banished from his lover's presence; seeks death; endures hardships; and is only reunited with Melior (through the agency of her sister,
Urake) after performing valorous deeds in a three-day tournament.

To critics like Kawczynski, the similarities between the two narratives seemed
sufficient to indicate direct Apuleian input in the *Partonopeu de Blois*.[139] These
claims were challenged by Huet (who pointed out that library catalogues before

---

[137] Or, possibly, 'of her beloved she has great joy'. I am grateful to Dr Geoffrey Bromiley for
clarifying several aspects of the Old French.

[138] The translation is quoted (with a slight simplification of orthography) from the text of
Univ. College, Oxford MS. C.18 given by A. Trampe Bödtker, ed., *The Middle-English Versions of
'Partonope of Blois'* (London: OUP, 1912), 222 (vv. 5863–6). Bödtker ascribes all the English
MSS. to the 15th cent. On the *Partonope* translator's debts to Chaucer, see B. Windeatt, 'Chaucer
and Fifteenth-Century Romance: *Partonope of Blois*', in *Chaucer Traditions*, ed. R. Morse and
B. Windeatt (Cambridge: CUP, 1990), 62–80.

[139] 'Ist Apuleius im Mittelalter bekannt gewesen?', 199–200. Kawczynski also considered the
claims of *Huon of Bordeaux, Floire et Blancheflor*, and *Erec et Enide*. In 'Quelques remarques sur
les sources de *Floire et Blancheflor*', *Revue de philologie française* 19 (1905), 153–75, J. Reinhold
argued (157) that the author of *Floire et Blancheflor* 'a emprunté à l'*Amour et Psyché* d'Apulée le
motif du mariage inégal' (quoted by M. M. Pelan, ed., *Floire et Blancheflor*, 2nd edn. (Paris: Les
Belles Lettres, 1956), p. xxv). One might note Martianus Capella's *De nuptiis* as a possible
intermediate source for this theme.

1300 mention Apuleius' philosophical works, but say nothing of his novel),[140] and dismissed by Swahn (as being 'entirely incorrect').[141] For morphologists of the folk tale such as Swahn, what appear to be impressive parallels with Apuleius' story are merely structural motifs (the Mysterious Lover, the Injunction on Sight, the Revealing Lamp, the Punishment of the Violation, and so on) which are common to a vast range of world literatures.[142]

The main weakness in the folk-tale model, as Detlev Fehling's revolutionary (if somewhat reductive) critique has demonstrated, is that it relies on extrapolating backwards from written accounts to an oral tradition; and hard (i.e. written) evidence for the existence of these folk tales is generally posterior to the dates by which we know manuscripts (or even printed editions) of Fulgentius and/or Apuleius to have been in circulation.[143]

Nonetheless, glittering palaces, invisible servants, and imposed taboos are found in many narratives (including Celtic ones) and we cannot establish the influence of the Apuleian/Fulgentian paradigm on the basis of a few, disconnected parallels. *Yonec*, and stories like it, should only be used in detecting a wider pattern, or as supporting evidence where the influence of the paradigm is readily demonstrable.

Such a case is provided by *Partonopeu de Blois*. The narrative parallels are so close in both sequence and detail that the poet's acquaintance with at least some version of 'Cupid and Psyche' is surely beyond doubt.[144] Fulgentius is the obvious source, though it is also possible that the *Partonopeu* poet used a Fulgentian derivative such as the abridged account of 'Cupid and Psyche' given by the first of the so-called 'Vatican Mythographers'.[145] Fulgentian

[140] G. Huet, 'Le Roman d'Apulée était-il connu au moyen âge?', *Le Moyen Âge*, 2ᵉ série, 13 (1909), 23–8, at 23–4. Huet's claim that 'the story of Psyche has only reached us via this novel' is, as we saw from Fulgentius and his epitomists, patently untrue. But see his follow-up to the original article, *Le Moyen Âge* 19 (1918), 45–6. Cf. Schlam, 'Apuleius in the Middle Ages', 366.

[141] Swahn, *Cupid and Psyche*, 383 n. 27.

[142] For the motif of a lamp being used to reveal the identity of an unknown lover, one need only look to Ovid's account of Cinyras discovering his daughter, Myrrha (*Met.* 10. 473–4: *post tot concubitus, inlato lumine vidit | et scelus et natam*). Cf. Hyginus, *Fab.* 58.

[143] *Amor und Psyche*. For reviews, see K. Dowden, *CR* NS 29 (1979), 314 (sympathetic); J. Tatum, *AJP* 101 (1980), 109–11 (mixed); C. Schlam, *CP* 76/2 (Apr. 1981), 164–6 (cautiously welcoming); and A. Scobie, *Apuleius and Folklore* (London: Folklore Soc., 1983), 38–9 (negative).

[144] Thus T. H. Brown, 'The Relationship between *Partonopeus de Blois* and the Cupid and Psyche Tradition', *Brigham Young University Studies*, 5/3–4 (Spring–Summer 1964), 193–202, at 201–2; Fehling, *Amor und Psyche*, 40–3.

[145] It is interesting that both *Primus Mythographus* and the French poet begin with genealogies which include the names Priam and Parthonopeus/Partonopeu. *Primus* (falsely identified in the manuscript tradition as *C. Hyginus*) concludes his account with the marriage (*postea Jove petente in conjugium accepit*) and omits the whole of the exegesis. The difficult portions of Fulgentius are either removed or glossed in the body of the text. Thus *Perfecto igitur choragio* (Helm, 121) is explained with a gloss (*id est virginali funere*) taken from Fulgentius' *Expositio*

influence would thus explain the 'use of a lantern at night to break the taboo' (an incident unique to the *Partonopeu*) which has been identified as a specifically Apuleian element.[146]

One might add that in *Partalope*, the Old Norse version of the romance, the hero is concerned, not that he might be sleeping with a demon, but that his mistress may be ugly.[147] He sees the woman, not by the light of a lantern, but by means of a magic stone; and then wakes her deliberately in order to pay the compliment, 'Never before did I see that face which seemed equally good to me'.[148]

In both *Partonopeu* and 'Cupid and Psyche', the liaison has to be clandestine because it is opposed by the older generation (Venus in Apuleius/Fulgentius; the empress's advisers in *Partonopeu*)—the final marriage serves to validate a previously consummated union. The magic ship which 'bore you off so gently' (*Qui ci vos amena soëf*, line 1390) is perhaps merely taking the place of 'the gentle carriage of the blowing Zephyrus' in Fulgentius (*zephiri flantis leni uectura*).[149] And one could excuse the absence of a 'razor' in the poem by an appeal to chivalric values—the notion of Partonopeu drawing a blade on a sleeping woman might have seemed incongruous.

There remain, however, in *Partonopeu de Blois* certain resemblances to the Apuleian account which cannot be attributed to Fulgentius. Psyche and Partonopeu follow a similar sequence of activities on entering the palace: Psyche sleeps, bathes, eats, and goes to bed; Partonopeu washes, eats, and goes

---

sermonum antiquorum 36 (*Quid sit Coragium*). For texts, see *Mythographi Vaticani I et II*, ed. P. Kulcsár (Turnhout: Brepols, 1987), 89–90; and *Le Premier Mythographe du Vatican*, ed. N. Zorzetti, trans. J. Berlioz (Paris: Les Belles Lettres, 1995), 126–7. Cf. Fehling, 41–2. See, generally, R. M. Krill, 'The "Vatican Mythographers": Their Place in Ancient Mythography', *Manuscripta* 23 (1979), 173–7.

[146] H. Newstead, 'The Traditional Background of *Partonopeus de Blois*', *PMLA* 61 (1946), 916–46, at 945. Newstead fails, however, to consider the possibility of Fulgentius as a mediator.

[147] *Partalope* should be considered in the context of the 'Norwegian and Icelandic translations commissioned by Hákon Hákonarson and his thirteenth-century successors of the Old French *romans* and of certain Latin works, like Walter of Châtillon's *Alexandreis*'. See F. Amory, 'Things Greek and the *Riddarasögur*', *Speculum* 59 (1984), 509–23, at 509.

[148] *Partalopa Saga*, ed. L. Præstgaard Andersen (Copenhagen: Reitzels, 1983), 167. In other versions (P & K) it is a gold ring containing a stone (Andersen, p. xix). Some scholars (though not Præstgaard Andersen who discusses the claims at p. xv) have argued that the Z-class of versions to which *Partalope* belongs is older than the Y-class which includes the French and Middle English versions. On the differences between the French and Scandinavian versions, see Amory, 'Things Greek', 517. Cf. L. Præstgaard Andersen, '*Partalopa saga*, homologue scandinave d'*Eros et Psyché*', *Revue des langues romanes* 102 (1998), 57–64.

[149] Fisher, *Narrative Art*, 108; Gildea, ed., 56. Fehling (*Amor und Psyche*, 42) suggests that the French poet may have misunderstood the description in Fulgentius.

to bed.[150] Both characters have two separate meetings with the family members who ultimately persuade them to violate the prohibition (collapsed into one in Fulgentius). The French poet (like Apuleius) emphasizes the surpassing beauty of the unknown lover at the moment of the anagnorisis (a detail omitted by Fulgentius). And both Cupid and Melior are incapacitated by the violation—Cupid (scorched by the oil) retiring to his mother's house to nurse his wounds (*AA* 5. 28; 6. 21; Fulgentius merely tells us that Cupid has been burned), Melior no longer able to exercise her power to conceal, and rendered vulnerable to her nobles. Like Psyche (*AA* 5. 25; 6. 17—but not in Fulgentius), Partonopeu seeks death after his violation of the vow (ll. 5061–834).

There are also some notable (and un-Fulgentian) parallels in the descriptions of the residences of the unknown lovers. Describing the palaces in Melior's magical city, the poet tells us:

> *Sor les pomiaus sont li lion*
> *Et li aiglet et li dragon,*
> *Et ymages d'autre figure*
> *Qui sanblent vives par nature,*
> *Totes covertes de fin or;*
> *Par grant savoir le fisent Mor.*
>
> (841–6; ed. Gildea, 34–5)

(On the summits were lions, eagles, and dragons, and images in other shapes which seemed to be naturally alive—and all covered with fine gold. Moors made them with great art.)[151]

In Cupid's palace, we are told:

> *... parietes omnes argenteo caelamine conteguntur bestiis et id genus pecudibus occur-entibus ob os introeuntium. mirus prorsum homo immo semideus uel certe deus, qui magnae artis suptilitate tantum efferauit argentum.* (*AA* 5. 1)

(... all the walls were covered with embossed silver, with wild beasts and other animals confronting the visitor on entering. Truly it was a wonderful man or demigod or indeed god, who with such art had given wild life to all that silver!)[152]

---

[150] T. H. Brown ('Relationship', 201–2) declares: 'I am inclined to believe that the unknown poet of *Partonopeus de Blois* had the original by Apuleius in his possession when writing his romance. Some details appear in Apu-[202]leius' "Cupid and Psyche" and *Partonopeus*, but not in Fulgentius' résumé.' Brown points (correctly) to the 'sumptuous banquet prepared for Psyche upon her arrival at Cupid's palace' and the careful account of a dinner prepared for Partonopeus at Chief d'Oire', but his claim for a unique parallel of 'invisible servants' in Apuleius and Partonopeus ignores the clear references in Fulgentius (*Mitologiae* 3): *Ibique uocibus <sibi> tantummodo seruientibus... habuit ergo uocale seruitium* ('And there, with only voices for servants... She had, therefore, voices for servants'). See Ch. 1, *supra*.

[151] Trans. Fisher (*Narrative Art*, 101). Dr Geoffrey Bromiley has suggested to me that *pomiaus* refer to 'some kind of decoration—a decorative knob or finial—at the apex of a roof'.

[152] Trans. Kenney.

If one were to accept the hypothesis of a direct link between the two texts, one would explain the conversion of (semi-)divine into merely Moorish artistry as being consistent with the French poet's policy of containing fantastic and supernatural subject matter within the bounds of reason and Christian theology.[153] Partonopeu may appear to have entered an enchanted palace taken straight from the realms of fairy tale, but he is actually in a real city with real people who have been rendered invisible only by Melior's proficiency in necromancy—a skill which has merely been added (as the poem emphasizes) to the solid base provided by her training in the Seven Liberal Arts.

At the structural level, one might also note that in both *The Golden Ass* and *Partonopeu de Blois*, the revelation scene comes near the midpoint of the work and acts as the narrative hinge. Most interesting of all is the fact that the *Partonopeu* poet chooses to reverse the sexes in his adaptation of the 'Cupid and Psyche' story.[154] This generates a certain amount of comedy in the initial nocturnal encounter between Melior and Partonopeu. Melior has orchestrated the whole scene, having chosen Partonopeu to be her spouse and having drawn him to her city by magic. But when she finds a young man in her bed, she expresses outrage and resists the loss of her virginity. This restructuring of gender is, at the very least, a creative manipulation of the Fulgentian paradigm; but the presence in the Apuleian text of Psyche's change of sex at the moment of seizing the lamp and razor (*et prolata lucerna et adrepta nouacula sexum audacia mutatur*, AA 5. 22—a detail not in Fulgentius) raises the delicious possibility that the *Partonopeu* poet may have consciously transformed Apuleius' figurative gender-reversal into a literal one.[155] One might also notice the 'unusually explicit' nature of the bedroom scene. It has been observed that 'in no other romance text of the period does the relationship between hero and heroine *begin* with a sexual encounter'.[156]

---

[153] The French account is closer to Apuleius than to Ovid's description of the carved doors in the *regia solis* (*Met.* 2. 1–18) which provided Apuleius with his immediate model.

[154] M. Tomaryn Bruckner addressed this issue at ICAN 2 in 1989 in 'When the Empress of Byzantium Plays Cupid to a French Knight's Psyche in the Upside Down World of *Partonopeu de Blois*', abstracted in *The Ancient Novel: Classical Paradigms and Modern Perspectives*, ed. J. Tatum and G. Vernazza (Hanover, NH: Dartmouth/NEH, 1990), 125–8. Bruckner's study is marred by a failure to consider the contemporary availability of manuscripts of *The Golden Ass* (and the possible contributions of folklore or Fulgentius) and by an alarming insouciance in her indiscriminate use of the term 'Cupid and Psyche' to denote two quite different things: the actual story told by Apuleius and the narrative sequence common to a group of stories from all over the world which folklorists have grouped, for convenience, under the Apuleian title.

[155] On gender play generally in the poem, see Simons and Eley, 'Male Beauty and Sexual Orientation in *Partonopeus de Blois*'.

[156] Ibid. 41 and 42. Apuleius is not mentioned as a possible source.

According to Keith Busby, this was, 'inside romance at least, probably the most lascivious of seduction scenes .... one feels the proximity of the world of the *fabliaux* and a certain sense of incongruity'.[157]

Whatever the merits of the claims for direct Apuleian input, it is clear that *Partonopeu de Blois* was both popular and influential, and that the Apuleian/ Fulgentian paradigm thereby became a significant component in the romance tradition of medieval Europe. Translations and imitations abound. *Partonopeu*'s 'famous scene—the nocturnal encounter—is enshrined nearly verbatim' in another romance, *Cristal et Clarie*.[158] And as late as the seventeenth century, one sees, in Lope de Vega's drama *La viuda valenciana* (*c.*1606), an acknowledgement of the affinity between Apuleius and *Partonopeu*. Lope appears to owe much to the Spanish version, *Partinuplés de Bles,* in his plot of a rich widow who becomes enamoured of Camilo, summons him to assignations, but forbids him to see her. When a servant suggests that he take along a lantern, however, Camilo invokes the example of Psyche ('Que si Psíques vió al Amor...').[159]

COUNTER-EVIDENCE

We have seen that, from a codicological point of view, there can be no objection, in principle, to the notion of one or more manuscripts of *The Golden Ass* being available in twelfth-century France. We have also considered several pieces of ambiguous (but nonetheless suggestive) evidence for the work's direct influence. Against these claims, however, we must weigh a powerful *argumentum ex silentio*. The failure of poets and satirists to mention Apuleius' novel in their own works is not in itself decisive: medieval authors are notoriously reluctant to acknowledge their sources. But the leading scholars, philosophers, and philologists of the twelfth century—those whom we would most expect to show acquaintance with *The Golden Ass*—appear to know little or nothing of the work.

---

[157] '*Cristal et Clarie*: A Novel Romance?', in *Convention and Innovation in Literature*, ed. T. D'haen et al. (Amsterdam: Benjamins, 1989), 77–103, at 94.

[158] Fisher, *Narrative Art*, 96. See *Cristal und Clarie: Altfranzösischer Abenteuerroman des XIIIe Jahrhunderts*, ed. H. Breuer (Dresden: Gesellschaft für romanische Literatur, 1915), vv. 8221 ff. On the reception of *Partonopeu*, see Denis Piramus' comments, cited in *The Lais of Marie de France*, trans. G. S. Burgess and K. Busby (London: Penguin, 1986), 11.

[159] M. A. Buchanan, '*Partinuplés de Bles*: An Episode in Tirso's *Amor por Señas*. Lope's *La viuda valenciana*', *MLN* 21/1 (Jan. 1906), 3–8, at 7–8. See also A. Trampe Bødtker, '*Parténopeus* in Catalonia and Spain', *MLN* 21/8 (Dec. 1906), 234–5.

Commentaries on Martianus Capella

The best known of the medieval commentators on the *De nuptiis*—Johannes
Scotus Eriugena and Remigius of Auxerre in the ninth century, 'Bernardus
Silvestris' in the twelfth—all discuss Martianus' account of Psyche;[160] and they
make use of Fulgentius' *Mitologiae* in other sections of their commentaries; but
'Bernardus' stands out for his attempt to synthesize the two Psyche traditions.[161] One of the works undisputedly by Bernardus, the prosimetric *Cosmographia*, is partly based on the *Asclepius* (the hermetic treatise attached in the
manuscript tradition to Apuleius' *philosophica*) and contains not only echoes of
the *De deo Socratis*, the *De dogmate Platonis*, and the *De mundo*, but also a
description of the Sun (Apollo) with his daughter (Psyche) 'taking up from her
father's lamp the little fires which he would scatter over heaven and earth'
(*Psyche de paterna lampade quos in caelum terramque diffunderet igniculos
insumebat*).[162] Yet, in his commentary on the *De nuptiis*, 'Bernardus' begins
his gloss on Martianus' *eam detineri a Cupidine* with the words *Hanc Siches
captivitatem Fulgentius latius pertractat* ('Fulgentius deals in greater detail with
this captivity of Psyche') and makes no reference to Apuleius.[163] The narrative
itself is reduced to the merest outline, shorn of its oracle, the golden house, the
prohibition against sight, the transgression, the trials, and the ultimate reunion:

*Scribit enim regem cuiusdam civitatis tres habuisse filias, quarum unam tante pulcritu-
dinis dicit fuisse, quod dea reputata est. Unde timebant proci eius matrimonium inire.
Suasu autem Veneris rapuit eam Cupido et detulit in montem, nocte adveniens, mane
recedens. Illa vero habebat humile servitium et vocale eloquium. Post vero, monitu
sororum, posuit in lecto novaculam. Cognovit Cupido, nec amplius accessit.*

(For he writes that the king of a certain city had three daughters, one of whom, he
says, was of such beauty that she was reputed to be a goddess. Suitors, consequently,

---

[160] Dronke (*Fabula*, 109) says: 'Throughout the Middle Ages it was one of the most
frequently discussed points in Martianus' text.'

[161] For the commentators, see Wetherbee, *Poetry and Platonism*, 115; C. E. Lutz, ed., *Iohannis
Scotti annotationes in Marcianum* (Cambridge, Mass.: Mediaeval Academy of America, 1939),
10; Lutz, ed., *Remigii Autissiodorensis commentum in Martianum Capellam*, 2 vols. (Leiden: Brill,
1962–5), i. 76–8, 80–1, 97–8. None of the glosses on Martianus attributed to 'Dunchad'
(perhaps composed, in fact, by Martin of Laon) survives for Book 1. See Lutz, ed., *Dunchad
glossae in Martianum* (Lancaster, Pa.: APA, 1944).

[162] *Cosmographia*, ed. Dronke, 131 (= 2. 5). For a full English translation and important
introduction, see *The 'Cosmographia' of Bernardus Silvestris*, trans. W. Wetherbee (New York:
Columbia UP, 1973), esp. 31–3 (*Asclepius*), 39–45 (*Endelechia*), 24–5, 40–2, 52–3, 102, 140, 159,
162 (Psyche). Curtius (*ELLMA*, 109) dates the work to between 1145 and 1153. Stock suggests
(*Myth and Science*, 126) that Bernard may have taken the subtitle of the *Cosmographia* (*De
mundi universitate*) from the phrase, *mundi universitas* (cap. 36), found in the *De mundo*
attributed to Apuleius (cap. 36; Thomas' edn., p. 172).

[163] *Commentary*, ed. Westra, 171–2. The commentary is tentatively dated by Dronke (*Fabula*,
160) to *c*.1135–40.

were afraid to enter into marriage with her. But, at the behest of Venus, Cupid seized her and took her to a mountain, where he visited her by night, departing in the morning. She indeed experienced lowly servitude and communication by voice. Afterwards, however, on the advice of her sisters, she hid a razor in the bed. Cupid found out and came no more.)

The accommodation of Fulgentius to Martianus Capella hinges upon the words *habebat humile servitium et vocale eloquium*. The *uocale seruitium*—the invisible body of servants composed of voices which Psyche enjoys in the *Mitologiae*—becomes, in 'Bernardus', a 'lowly servitude' to which Psyche is subjected during her imprisonment:

Dum a Cupidine tenetur, habet Siche humile servitium quia appetitu irretita anima divina subditur contagio viciorum.

(While she is being held by Cupid, Psyche experiences lowly servitude because the divine Mind, trapped by appetite, is subdued by a plague of vices.)

And whereas Fulgentius is clear that Psyche's tribulations result directly from her surrender to *curiositas* in violating her husband's injunction, Bernardus makes the razor an instrument for good:

Novacula est ratio quia utile ab inutili, honestum ab inhonesto, iustum ab iniusto, verum a falso secernit. Hac Cupido expellitur quia ratio et temporalium appetitus in eodem simul non morantur.

(The razor is Reason because it separates the useful from the useless, the honest from the dishonest, the just from the unjust, the true from the false. Cupid is driven away by it because Reason and the appetite for temporal things do not tarry at the same time in the one being.)

It is possible that Bernardus was using an abridged redaction of Fulgentius (e.g. Primus Mythographus), but, whatever his source, the erasure of the Apuleian narrative adumbrated in the *Mitologiae* is almost complete.

Fabliaux

Nor does the situation show any obvious amelioration in the thirteenth century. Perhaps the most telling evidence is the lack of any obvious Apuleian influence on the French fabliaux of the thirteenth century. While their subject matter is often obscene and their expression coarse, these are sophisticated works, composed in the octosyllabic metre of the courtly romances and perhaps catering to the same audience. In many cases, the fabliaux (despite being in verse) achieve the effects that we would expect in a Milesian tale, although the 'moral' appended to many of them brings them (ostensibly) closer to the fable (*apologus*) familiar to us from the collections of Aesop, Babrius, Phaedrus, et al. The narrative dynamics are often very similar to Milesian tales: *De la Damoiselle qui sonjoit* resembles Petronius' 'The Pergamene Boy' (*Satyricon*, 85–7) in its motif of erotic prey-turned-predator.[164] Asses appear in such satires as Rutebeuf's *Testament de l'asne* where a donkey has been buried in consecrated ground,[165] but while the collections abound in tales of adultery and hoodwinked cuckolds, no one, to my knowledge, has detected any exclusively Apuleian elements in the surviving fabliaux.

Library Catalogues and Encyclopaedias

The library of Richard de Fournival—a man famed for his knowledge of the classics—can boast the presence of the *De deo Socratis*, the *De dogmate Platonis*, the *De mundo*, and the *Asclepius*, but the catalogue of 1250 contains no trace of the novel.[166] P. G. Walsh tells us that 'there is no evidence for a knowledge of the *Metamorphoses* in France before the mention by Vincent of Beauvais in the thirteenth century'.[167] Walsh's unsourced reference to Vincent (who died in about 1264) belongs to a scholarly stemma that includes Haight and Huet and leads ultimately back to Manitius' statement that 'Vincenz v. Beauvais . . . kennt von Apuleius: *libri asini aurei, de deo Socratis* und *de vita et moribus Platonis*'.[168] Manitius provides a string of references to the *Speculum maior*, all but one of which prove to be to the *De deo Socratis*. The exception is Book 2, chapter 105 of the first volume of the *Speculum* where Vincent discusses the phenomenon of men being transformed into animals. Vincent's supposed 'knowledge' of *The Golden Ass* consists merely in his having quoted (in a tiny chapter, *De falsis transmutationibus*) the extract from Augustine (*De ciuitate dei* 18. 18) which contains the sentence, *Sic Apuleius in libris asini aurei sibi accedisse scripsit, ut accepto veneno, humano animo permanente*

---

[164] See, generally, *Cuckolds, Clerics, and Countrymen: Medieval French Fabliaux*, trans. J. DuVal, ed. E. Eichmann (Fayetteville: U of Arkansas P, 1982), 8–9.

[165] See *The Humor of the Fabliaux: A Collection of Critical Essays*, ed. T. D. Cooke and B. L. Honeycutt (Columbia: U of Missouri P, 1974), 47.

[166] *La Biblionomia de Richard de Fournival du Manuscrit 636 de la Bibliothèque de la Sorbonne: Texte en facsimilé avec la transcription de Léopold Delisle*, ed. H. J. Vleeschauwer, Mousaion 62 (Pretoria: n.pub., 1965), 525, 527, 530; cf. Manitius, *Handschriften*, 149. R. H. Rouse identifies the MS containing these works as Vatican, Reg. lat., MS. 1572 (= *Biblionomia* 85). Its provenance is French and it was 'Probably written for Fournival.' See 'Manuscripts belonging to Richard de Fournival', *Revue d'histoire des textes* 3 (1973), 253–69, at 266.

[167] *Roman Novel*, 231.

[168] Huet, 'Le Roman d'Apulée', 24; M. Manitius, *Philologisches aus alten Bibliothekskatalogen (bis 1300)* (Frankfurt: Sauerländer, 1892), 73.

asinus fieret.[169] In a section of the *Speculum historiale* not cited by Manitius, Vincent makes it clear, in fact, that he knows only two of Apuleius' works, the *De deo Socratis* and the *De dogmate Platonis*:

> *De Apuleio platonico & dictis eius.*
> *Cap. VII.*

De apuleio multa loquitur Augu. in lib. de ci. Dei. huius repperi duos libros, vnum scilicet de vita & moribus Platonis de quo iam aliqua superius posui vbi dictum est de ortu Platonis, alium vero qui intitulatur de Deo Socratis de quo hæc pauca quæ sequuntur excerpsi.[170]

(Augustine says many things about Apuleius in *The City of God*. I have found two of his books—namely, one about the life and character of Plato, about whom I have already given some details in my earlier discussion of the birth of Plato [Book 2, *De ortu Platonis*. cap. 60]; the other, indeed, which is entitled the *De deo Socratis*, from which I have selected these few bits that follow.)

Alanus de Insulis and Jean de Meun

Alanus de Insulis is a nicely equivocal case. Peter Dronke locates Alanus in 'an intellectual milieu which valued verbal virtuosity and did not shy away from risqué themes, especially if they had a halo of the ancient world about them'.[171] Alanus shows, however, no knowledge of Apuleius or Psyche in his detailed account of Desire (Cupid, son of Venus and Hymenaeus) in *De planctu Naturae*.[172] Yet the *De planctu Naturae* has many features which remind one of *The Golden Ass*. The account of Generosity (*Largitas*), for example, reveals an almost Apuleian obsession with hair (which may alert us to a Platonic dimension in Lucius' trichomanic descriptions of Fotis and Isis).[173] And Alanus' extravagant descriptions are often reminiscent of those found in the Isis book. In Alanus' *blason* of Nature, we read: 'A linen tunic, with pictures from the embroiderer's art, concealed the maiden's body

---

[169] *Speculi maioris ... tomus primus* (Venice: Dominicus Nicolinus, 1591), ii. 105. In the preceding chapter (*De Obitu Platonis & de discipulis eius. cap. VI*), Vincent quotes from Hugh of Fleury: *Hugo floriacensis in historia ecclesiastica lib. I. Platoni successit Apuleius, & Apuleio Hermes ægyptius, quem Trismegistum vocant.* In ch. 10 (*De Mercurio Trismegisto, & dictis eius*), Vincent quotes from the *Asclepius* but does not link it with Apuleius.

[170] *Speculum historiale* 4. 7, in *Speculi maioris ... tomus quartus*, fol. 41ᵛ.

[171] Dronke, ed., *Cosmographia*, 1.12.

[172] Prose IV– Metre 5.

[173] [0474C] *Aureus tamen crinis gratiori igne flammantior, aureo diademati indignando videbatur praestare subsellia: qui nec forficis apocopatus industria, nec in tricaturae manipulos colligatus, sed pigressiori excursione luxurians, limites humerorum transgrediens, terrae videbatur condescendere paupertati.* Sheridan (74) observes: 'Alan seems preoccupied with hair in his description of both men and women. This derives from the *Timaeus* 76C–D. The brain is all-important. The skull protects it and for safety's sake the hair serves "as a light roofing for the part around the brain." ' Cf. *AA* 2. 8–9 and 11. 3.

beneath its folds. The tunic, bestarred with many a colour, gathered into folds to make the material heavier, sought to approximate the element, earth.'[174] This garment includes pictures of a host of animals, among them 'the ass' who, 'offending our ears with his idle braying, as though a musician by antiphrasis, introduced barbarisms into his music'.[175]

In Prose 2, Nature, 'coming from the confines of the heavenly court, was borne to the hut of the passable world by a car of glass. This was drawn by Juno's birds, which were held in check by no jurisdiction of yoke but joined together of their own free choice.'[176] The obvious inspiration for Nature's transport is Ovid's description of Venus returning from heaven where she has asked Jupiter to favour Aeneas (*Met.* 14. 597): *perque leues auras iunctis inuecta columbis* ('drawn through the easy air by yoked doves'). But we should also look at Apuleius' description of Venus' golden chariot:

at Venus terrenis remediis inquisitionis abnuens caelum petit. iubet construi currum quem ei Vulcanus aurifex subtili fabrica studiose poliuerat et ante thalami rudimentum nuptiale munus obtulerat limae tenuantis detrimento conspicuum et ipsius auri damno pretiosum. de multis quae circa cubiculum dominae stabulant procedunt quattuor candidae columbae et hilaris incessibus picta colla torquentes iugum gemmeum subeunt susceptaque domina laetae subuolant...cedunt nubes et Caelum filiae panditur et summus aether cum gaudio suscipit deam...

(Venus, however, discarded earthbound expedients in her search and set off for heaven. She ordered to be prepared the car that Vulcan the goldsmith had lovingly perfected with cunning workmanship and given her as a betrothal present—a work of art made notable by what his refining tools had pared away, valuable through the very loss of gold. Of the many doves quartered round their mistress's chamber there came forth four all white; stepping joyfully and twisting their coloured necks around they submitted to the jewelled yoke, then with their mistress on board they gaily took off...The clouds part, Heaven opens for his daughter and highest Aether joyfully welcomes the goddess...)[177]

---

[174] Sheridan, 98. Prose 1: *Tunica vero polymita opere picturata plumario, infra se corpus claudebat virgineum. Quae multis stellata coloribus, in grossiorem materiam conglobata,* [0437D] *in terrestris elementi speciem aspirabat. In hujus vestis parte primaria, homo sensualitatis deponens segnitiem, ducta ratiocinationis aurigatione, coeli penetrabat arcana.* Cf. AA 11. 3–4: *Tunica multicolor...Per intextam extremitatem et in ipsa eius planitie stellae dispersae coruscabant, earumque media semenstris luna flammeos spirabat ignes.* With *conglobata,* cf. *conglobatos* at AA 2. 9 (the gathering of Fotis' tresses). *Polymitus* means 'wrought with many threads' (πολύμιτος) but the KJV translation of Joseph's *tunicam polymitam* (Genesis 37: 3, Vulgate) as 'coat of many colours' brings Alanus' *tunica* closer to Apuleius'.

[175] Sheridan, 100. Prose 1: *Illic asinus clamoribus horridis aures fastidiens, quasi per antiphrasim organizans, barbarismum faciebat in musica.* Cf. [0438B]: *Illic onager, asini exuens servitutem, naturae manumissus imperio, montium incolebat audaciam.*

[176] Sheridan, 108. Prose 2: [0439D]: *Virgo igitur ... a coelestis regionis emergens confinio, in mundi passibilis tugurium, curru vitreo ferebatur, qui Junonis alitibus, nullius jugi ministerio disciplinatis, sed sibi spontanea voluntate conjunctis, trahebatur.*

[177] AA 6. 6; trans. Kenney, *Cupid & Psyche*, 94–5.

The stress in each passage on the design of the chariot and the attitude of the doves is noteworthy. But Alanus' immediate inspiration for the theme of willing subjugation may have been Martianus Capella's description of Apollo's conveyance in Book 1 of the *De nuptiis: augurales vero alites ante currum Delio constiterunt, uti quis vellet vectus ascenderet* ('the Delian's augural birds halted for him in front of his chariot, in order that he might ascend and be carried up by them if he wished').[178]

Alanus in turn exerted a heavy influence on Jean de Meun's part of the *Roman de la Rose* (*c*.1275) where we find:

Then she had her household called. She ordered them to harness her chariot since she did not want to walk through the mud. The chariot was beautiful; it was a four-wheeled one, starred with gold and pearls. Instead of horses, there were six doves hitched in the shafts; she kept them in her beautiful dovecote. Everything was made ready, and Venus, who makes war on Chastity, mounted into her chariot. None of the birds flew out of place; they beat their wings and flew off. The air in front of them broke and parted, and they came to the army.[179]

Neither of these examples constitutes 'proof' of access to *The Golden Ass*, but they indicate, at the very least, the ways in which the most educated minds of the period could (re-)create Apuleian effects through their imitation of narrative and descriptive sources (such as the *De nuptiis*) which were themselves suffused with Apuleian themes and diction.

---

[178] ed. Willis, s. 26, p. 12; Stahl and Johnson, ii. 15.

[179] C. Dahlberg, trans., *The Romance of the Rose by Guillaume de Lorris and Jean de Meun* (Hanover: UP of New England, 1983), 267. Cf. *Le Roman de la Rose*, ed. F. Lecoy, vol. ii (Paris: Librairie Honoré Champion, 1985), 229, vv. 15749–63: *Lors fist sa mesnie apeler, | son char conmande a esteler, | qu'el ne veust pas marchier les boes. | Biau fu li chars, a .iiii. roes, | d'or et de pelles estelez. | En leu de chevaus estelez | ot au limons .VI. columbiaus | pris en son columbier, mout biaus. | Toute leur chose ont aprestee. | Adonc est en son char montee | Venus, qui Chasteé guerroie; | Nus des oisiaus ne se derroie; | batent les eles, si s'an partent. | L'air devant eus rompent et partent, | vienent en l'ost.* At vv. 10535 f. (trans. Dahlberg, 187), the author identifies himself as 'Johans Chopinel', born at Meung-sur-Loire. Jean shows off his learning in the God of Love's complaint (vv. 10477–95) that 'I am undone, for I lack Tibullus, who knew my characteristics so well ... [187] ... We would have needed Gallus, Catullus, and Ovid, who knew well how to treat of love; but each of them is dead and decayed.'

3

Asinus Redivivus: The Recovery
of *The Golden Ass*

MONTE CASSINO AND THE FLORENTINE HUMANISTS

In Canto XXII of the *Paradiso*, Dante encounters 'the largest and most lustrous' of the hundred 'pearls'—the contemplatives who inhabit the Eighth Sphere.[1] St Benedict speaks of the order that he had founded on the ancient pagan site of Monte Cassino, and his success in drawing away 'the neighbouring towns from the impious worship that led the world astray'.[2] Dante asks for 'a great favour' (*tanta grazia*)—that he might see the saint with his face unveiled (*ch' io | ti veggia con imagine scoverta*, 59–60). Benedict promises that all Dante's desires will be fulfilled in 'the last sphere' (*l'ultima spera*), a region beyond space (*non è in loco*) reached by the same ladder (*scala*) which Jacob (Genesis 28: 12) once saw 'laden with angels' (*quando li apparve d'angeli sì carca*):

> Ma, per salirla, mo nessun diparte
> da terra i piedi, e la regola mia
> rimasa è per danno delle carte.
> Le mura che solìeno esser badia
> fatte sono spelonche, e le cocolle
> sacca son piene di farina ria.

(But now none lifts his foot from the earth to climb it, and my Rule is left to waste the paper; the walls that were once an abbey have become dens and the cowls are sacks full of rotten meal.)[3]

In his commentary on the passage, Benvenuto da Imola (*c*.1330–*c*.1387) attempts to mitigate Dante's disparaging remarks by explaining that he is castigating not the whole of the Benedictine Order but only the depraved monks of Monte Cassino.[4] By way of explication, he recalls an account given

---

[1] *la maggiore e la più luculenta | di quelle margherite* (*Parad.* xxii. 28–9).
[2] *ch' io ritrassi le ville circunstanti | dall'empio colto che 'l mondo sedusse* (*Parad.* xxii. 44–5).
[3] *Parad.* xxii. 73–8, in *The Divine Comedy*, trans. J. D. Sinclair, 3 vols. (London: Bodley Head, 1939), i. 320–1.
[4] Latin text from C. C. Coulter, 'Boccaccio and the Cassinese Manuscripts of the Laurentian Library', *CP* 43 (1948), 217–30, at 218. For Benvenuto, see *DBI* viii. 691–4.

to him 'jocosely' by his 'venerable teacher, Boccaccio' of a visit to the abbey.[5] Drawn by the fame of the place and the books it was fabled to hold, Boccaccio had arrived at the monastery and humbly (*humiliter*) asked a monk if he would open up the library for him (*quod deberet ex gratia aperire sibi bibliothecam*).[6] The monk motioned him rudely towards a high staircase: 'Go on up. It's open' (*At ille rigide respondit, ostendens sibi altam scalam: ascende quia aperta est*). Climbing eagerly (*laetus ascendens*), he entered to find a doorless ruin—grass on the windows, priceless books in the dust, spoiled and mutilated. He retreated, weeping (*dolens et illacrymans recessit*), and, on meeting a monk in the cloister, asked how such a terrible thing could have happened. He was told that some monks, for the sake of a few *soldi,* cut up the parchment to make psalters for schoolboys and breviaries for ladies.

Boccaccio's narration serves as a kind of *midrash* on Dante's text, the key elements of the celestial episode being reconfigured in resolutely humanistic terms: the library (with its treasury of pagan learning) on the upper floor at Monte Cassino takes the place of the *ultima spera* (Empyrean) anticipated by Benedict (xxii. 62); whereas Beatrice 'impels' Dante up Jacob's *scala* in spite of his own nature,[7] Benvenuto's rude monk leaves Boccaccio to ascend the *altam scalam* unaided; and the Benedictines' spiritual neglect of their founder's *Rule* (xxii. 74–5) is transmuted into the mercenary misuse of ancient parchments as palimpsests for Christian texts.

If Boccaccio left the library with tears running from his eyes, he has also been supposed by later scholars to have left with some of the manuscript treasures tucked under his cloak, one of them being the codex (Florence, Laur. 68.2) containing Apuleius and Tacitus (Mediceus II). It is a dramatic scenario—the great humanist rescuing, from the dust and decay of medieval avarice and ignorance, one of the seminal texts of the Renaissance.[8] The facts, sadly, do not quite measure up to the legend.

[5] *quod narrabat mihi josose venerabilis praeceptor meus Boccaccius de Certaldo.* According to Coulter (218 n. 6), '*jocose*... must connote not lighthearted jest but... bitter amusement'.

[6] Cf. Dante's request that Benedict 'open' his face to him (*Parad.* xxii. 59–60), and Benedict's stipulation that 'if we wish to attain the summit of humility... we must set up that ladder which appeared to Jacob in a dream' (*si summae humilitatis volumus culmen attingere... scala illa erigenda est quae in somnio Iacob apparuit*). See *Regula Benedicti*, ed. R. Hanslik, 2nd edn., CSEL 75 (Vienna: Hoelder-Pichler-Tempsky, 1977), 7. 5–6 (*De humilitate*).

[7] *La dolce donna dietro a lor mi pinse | con un sol cenno su per quella scala, | sì sua virtù la mia natura vinse* (*Parad.* xxii. 100–2).

[8] See e.g. Enrico Rostagno's introd. to his facsimile edn. of Tacitus, *Codex laurentianus Mediceus, 68-I & 68-II* (Leiden: Sijthoff, 1902). In *Le scoperte dei codici latini e greci ne' secoli xiv e xv*, 2 vols. (Florence: Sansoni, 1905–14); repr. with corr., ed. E. Garin (Florence: Sansoni, 1967), ii. 202, Remigio Sabbadini stated that 'Il Boccaccio scoprí e asportò il cod. Cassinese (ora Laur. 68.2), archetipi di tutti gli altri.' Sabbadini gives a more cautious view at ii. 29, but Boccaccio's supposed agency remains embedded in anglophone discourse on the reception of Apuleius. Thus Walsh (*Roman Novel,* 232) tells us that Apuleius became 'well known in Italy during the

Like Boccaccio, Benvenuto possessed a copy of Apuleius' works.[9] And there is certainly something suspicious about Benvenuto's account of his master's visit to Monte Cassino. As E. A. Lowe says:

It all sounds uncommonly like an apology. He seems to be anxious to show that it was only an act of simple piety to remove the precious classics to a place of safety, say to Florence. The letter which he wrote in 1371 to the Calabrian abbot Niccolò di Montefalcone requesting the return of a quire from the Tacitus, suggests that he probably had accomplices. But no one can doubt that the Tacitus manuscript was dishonestly obtained after reading Poggio's letter of 27 September 1427 to Niccolò Niccoli: 'Cornelium Tacitum cum venerit, observabo penes me occulte. Scio enim omnem illam cantilenam, et unde exierit et per quem, et quis eum sibi vendicet: sed nil dubites, non exibit a me ne verbo quidem.'[10] The manuscript which was written at Monte Cassino left its original home [297] sometime before 1370, and its home has been Florence since the end of the fourteenth century.[11]

The great earthquake of 1349 which destroyed most of the abbey left the library unharmed, yet in the following decades, it suffered heavy depredations, prompting Pope Urban V, in a bull of 1367, to lament, as Leccisotti tells us, 'the ruin of the books among the other sacrilegious devastations'.[12]

Boccaccio may well have been involved in removing some of the books from Monte Cassino, but it now seems clear that Laur. 68.2 was not one of them. Cornelia Coulter, in 1948, pointed out some of the chronological and codicological problems in attributing to Boccaccio the removal of Laur. 68.2 and suggested that 'The person mainly responsible for the removal of classical texts from Monte Cassino may have been Niccolò Acciaiuoli', the Grand Seneschal of the Kingdom of Naples.[13]

fourteenth century through the enthusiasm of Boccaccio, who in 1355 discovered a manuscript of *The Golden Ass* at Monte Cassino and transcribed it with his own hand'. Cf. J. F. D'Amico, 'The Progress of Renaissance Latin Prose: The Case of Apuleianism', *RQ* 37 (1984), 351–92, at 364–5: 'Apuleius... was discov[365]ered anew by Boccaccio'; and Doody, *True Story*, 204.

[9] Vatican City, Biblioteca Apostolica Vaticana, MS. Vat. Lat. 3384. See P. de Nolhac, *La Bibliothèque de Fulvio Orsino* (Paris: F. Vieweg, 1887). D'Amico ('Progress', 365 n. 46) refers to this as a 'commentary on Apuleius' works'. A visit to the Biblioteca Apostolica reveals that Bevenuto's work is not so much a 'commentary' on Apuleius as a manuscript of the text with marginal annotations.

[10] 'When Cornelius Tacitus comes to me, I shall look at him secretly, by myself. For I know all that gossip—both where he came from and through whom and who lays claim to him for himself: but have no doubt—he will not get away from me, not even in conversation.'

[11] 'The Unique Manuscript of Tacitus' *Histories* (Florence, Laur. 68.2)'; repr. in *Palaeographical Papers,* i. 289–302, at 296.

[12] Leccisotti, 247. Leccisotti continues: 'Gregory XI, a decade later, also reported and deplored the removal and theft of volumes.' Leccisotti includes amongst these depradations, Laur. 68.2, resting the blame squarely on Boccaccio: 'He certainly removed the Tacitus and Apuleius codex, now in the Laurenziana library in Florence.'

[13] Coulter, 229.

In 1953, Giuseppe Billanovich credited Zanobi da Strada with 'liberating' the famous codex.[14] Zanobi (1315–61 or 1312–64) met Petrarch personally in Florence in 1350 and was also a friend of Boccaccio.[15] In 1352, he became secretary to Niccolò Acciaiuoli and lived at Monte Cassino from 1355 until 1357; in 1359, the Bishop of Monte Cassino, Angelo Acciaiuolo, appointed him vicar general; and shortly afterwards, he was appointed protonotary and papal secretary of briefs by Innocent VI at Avignon.[16] Billanovich makes no mention of Coulter, but the two theories are not really so incompatible as Ullman's dismissal of Coulter's argument would suggest.[17] After Zanobi's death, his manuscripts passed to Niccolò Acciaiuoli who, on his own death a few years later (1365 or 1366), bequeathed his thus-augmented library to the Certosa of San Lorenzo at Florence.

Billanovich identified, as the hand of Zanobi, annotations to F, ϕ, and C (the ten surviving leaves of the *Apologia* found at Assisi) as well as the infamous *spurcum additamentum* ('obscene interpolation') added to ϕ's description of the asinine Lucius' love-making with the Corinthian *matrona* (*AA* 10. 21). Billanovich gave little evidence to support his identification, yet his view of Zanobi da Strada's role has now become received wisdom.[18] Worse still, even distinguished scholars have continued to confuse the removal from Monte Cassino of the oldest manuscript of *The Golden Ass* with the discovery of the novel itself.[19] Roberto Weiss tells us that Boccaccio 'was able to profit from the discoveries of ancient texts made at Montecassino by Zanobi da Strada, which included Tacitus and much of what was then unknown of Apuleius'.[20] Reynolds and Wilson note that 'within a few years' of the discovery of Monte Cassino's treasures (Tacitus, Apuleius, and Varro), 'the manuscripts themselves had been spirited away from their medieval home and were in the hands of the Florentine humanists'.[21]

---

[14] *I primi umanisti e le tradizioni dei classici latini* (Fribourg: Edizioni universitarie, 1953), 30–3, esp. 31.

[15] For Zanobi, see *S&S3*, 133, 273.

[16] M. E. Cosenza, *BBDIH* v. 492.

[17] B. L. Ullman and P. A. Stadter, *The Public Library of Renaissance Florence* (Padua: Antenore, 1972), 100.

[18] For challenges to (as well as partial confirmation of) Billanovich's identifications, see M. Fiorilla, 'La lettura apuleiana del Boccaccio e le note ai manoscritti Laurenziani 29,2 e 54,32', *Aevum* 73/3 (1999), 635–68, esp. 654–9.

[19] L. Vertova, 'Cupid and Psyche in Renaissance Painting before Raphael', *JWCI* 42 (1979), 104–21, at 105; E. J. Kenney, ed., *Apuleius: Cupid and Psyche* (Cambridge: CUP, 1990), 8, refers to 'the rediscovery of the *Met.* by Zanobi da Strada'. On the confusion, see M. D. Reeve, 'The Rediscovery of Classical Texts in the Renaissance', in *Itinerari dei testi antichi*, ed. O. Pecere (Rome: 'L'Erma' di Bretschneider, 1991), 115–57, at 145–7.

[20] R. Weiss, *The Spread of Italian Humanism* (London: Hutchinson UP, 1964), 30.

[21] *S&S3*, 133.

If Zanobi was the 'discoverer' of *The Golden Ass*, then the earliest that he could have conveyed the manuscript to the 'Florentine humanists' was, presumably, some time in the 1350s when he had privileged access to Monte Cassino.[22] There are clear Apuleian traces, however, in works by Boccaccio from the late 1330s and early 1340s. It looks as though the young Boccaccio had access to at least one of the Cassinese manuscripts during his time in Naples (1327–41), for φ contains annotations that appear to be in his hand.[23] Amongst the surviving manuscripts of Apuleius, moreover, are several that appear to date from the early fourteenth century. Robertson identifies (*inter alia*) L6 (Laur. 54.14), V4 (Bib. Vat., Ottob. Vat. 2091), and V6 (Vat. Lat. 2194)—V6 being an illuminated manuscript copied at Bologna in 1345 by Bartolomeo de'Bartoli (fl. 1330–84) for Bruzio Visconti, illegitimate son of Luchino Visconti, a friend of Petrarch, and a poet in his own right.[24]

THE PREHUMANISTS

Responsibility for the 'rediscovery' of *The Golden Ass* may, in fact, rest with scholars consigned to that somewhat unsatisfactory category of 'Prehumanists'. It is possible that the first extant medieval claim to familiarity with *The Golden Ass* was made by Benzo d'Alessandria (Bentius Alexandrinus), who was born in about 1260 and died, in Verona, in about 1330.[25] He may have studied at Bologna before taking up successive positions in Milan, Como, and Verona (where he was in the service of the Scaligers from 1325 to 1329). Benzo, as Cosenza tells us, 'collected and searched for manuscripts (thus anticipating Petrarch and Poggius), and travelled very extensively in Northern and Central Italy to gather materials for his great work'.[26] Benzo's 'great work' was the *Cronica a mundi principio*, composed in three parts between 1312 and 1322. Only the first part survives and, with it, a passage in which he trumps Vincent of Beauvais's catalogue of Apuleius' works:

[22] In his more recent studies, Billanovich has pushed the date of Zanobi's access to Monte Cassino back to 1332. See 'Zanobi da Strada tra i tesori di Montecassino', *RANL*, 9th ser. 7/3 [=393] (1996), 653–63, and 'Biografia e opere del Petrarca tra miti e realtà da Sennuccio del Bene a Laura', *RANL*, 9th ser. 8/4 [=394] (1997), 627–31, at 628: '...nel 1332 Niccolò Acciaioli...cominciò da Napoli a depredare la biblioteca del decaduto Montecassino: ricavandone per l'amico Zanobi un vecchio codice con le opere narrative di Apuleio'. Cf. Fiorilla, 'La lettura apuleiana del Boccaccio', at 659.

[23] Ibid.

[24] Robertson, 'Manuscripts', 30. On the scribe, see S. De Laude, 'La *spola* di Bartolomeo de'Bartoli: Sull'esperimento metrico di una canzone illustrata del Trecento', *Anticomoderno* 2 (1996), 201–18.

[25] Sabbadini, *Le scoperte*, ii. 202.

[26] Cosenza, *BBDIH* v. 68 (card 250); *DBI* viii. 723–6. See, generally, J. R. Berrigan, 'The Prehumanism of Benzo d'Alessandria', *Traditio* 25 (1969), 249–64.

Huius Apulei *duos se repperisse libros dicit Vincencius, unum scilicet* De vita et moribus Platonis, *alium qui intitulatur* De deo Socratis. *Ego vero alium eiusdem Apulei librum legi qui intitulatur sic:* Apulei platonici floridorum; *alium quoque librum eiusdem comperi qui intitulatur* Asini aurei *vel secundum alios sic:* Lucii Apulei platonici Madaurensis Methamorfoseos liber.[27]

(Vincent says that he has found two books of this Apuleius—namely, one *Concerning the Life and Character of Plato*; the other entitled *On the God of Socrates.* But I have read another book of this same Apuleius entitled *The Florida of Apuleius the Platonist.* I have also learnt of another book of this same man which is entitled, *The Golden Ass;* or, according to others, *The Book of the Metamorphoses of Lucius Apuleius the Platonist of Madaura.*)

The choice of verbs is important: *legi* proclaims that he has actually *read* the *Florida*; but *comperi* could either mean that he has merely 'obtained knowledge' of the existence of *The Golden Ass,* or that he has actually 'discovered' a copy of the work itself.[28] The double title is also significant. Augustine uses the title *De asino aureo* (and does not mention 'Cupid and Psyche'), while Fulgentius, in the *Mitologiae*, calls the work *Metamorphoses*, but deals only with 'Cupid and Psyche', without giving any hint of the tale's asinine frame. In the *Expositio sermonum antiquorum*, however, he uses the two titles indiscriminately, but never together. The manuscript tradition of F makes no mention of an *asinus aureus* and the only external reference to suggest that *The Golden Ass* and the *Metamorphoses* of Apuleius are one and the same work is in the *Expositio sermonum antiquorum,* where Fulgentius writes: *Apuleius ASINO AUREO introducit sororem Psyches marito detrahentem dicere* etc. Benzo's comprehensive title suggests that he himself has seen the manuscript or at least had contact with someone who has.

Liber de vita ac moribus philosophorum poetarumque veterum

Another significant treatment of Apuleius is found in the *Liber de vita ac moribus philosophorum poetarumque veterum* attributed to the scholastic

---

[27] Sabbadini (*Le scoperte*, ii. 202) reproduces the passage from fol. 280 of Milan, MS Ambrosiano B. 24. Cf. W. G. Hale, 'Benzo of Alexandria and Catullus', *CP* 5 (1910), 56–65, at 56.
[28] Butler (*Apologia*, p. xl) gives a description of a 14th-cent. MS. (Naples Biblioteca Nazionale Cod. IV. D. 11) containing only the *Metamorphoses* and (in a different hand) the first part of the *Florida* (down to ch. 7, *perfacile est*). Robertson, however, dates it to the end of the century ('Manuscripts', 29). See, also, M. Petoletti, 'Montecassino e gli umanisti, III: I *Florida* di Apuleio in Benzo d'Alessandria', in *Libro, scrittura, documento della cività monastica e conventuale nel basso medioevo (secoli XIII–XV),* ed. G. Avarucci et al. (Spoleto: Centro italiano di studi sull'alto medioevo, 1997), 224–38. See Fiorilla, 'La lettura apuleiana', 659.

philosopher Walter Burley, which enjoyed an enormous vogue during the late
Middle Ages and Renaissance: over 270 manuscripts survive and there were at
least twelve printed editions in the fifteenth century alone.[29] Born, probably
in England, in 1274 or 1275, Burley studied at Merton College, Oxford, and
then at Paris (c.1309–27). He visited the papal court at Avignon in 1327 and
1330, and was a member of the household of Richard Bury, Bishop of
Durham, from 1334 to 1340.[30] The years 1341–3 were spent in southern
France and Italy (he disputed at Bologna in 1341 and was back in Avignon
in November 1343), and the *De vita* has been 'assigned to this period, in the
light of solid evidence for the work's inception in southern Europe'.[31] The
trend in recent scholarship, however, has been to deny Burley authorship on
stylistic and chronological grounds.[32] As M. C. Sommers observes:

large sections from the *De vita et moribus* are found in a manuscript dated 1326, when
Burley was in Paris, and this, together with the claim that no attribution of the work to
him is recorded before the fifteenth century, has led to a presumption against Burley's
authorship. Nevertheless this evidence is not conclusive, and given his habits of
appropriating large amounts of text from other authors and frequently reworking
his own writings, it may yet be found that the *De vita et moribus* passed through
Burley's hands at some point in its history.[33]

The table of contents of the earliest printed edition of the *De vita* refers to
Apuleus [*sic*] *Atheniensis*; and the text contains a description of his philosophical treatises followed by this account:

[29] M. C. Sommers, *ODNB*, s.v. 'Walter Burley'; J. O. Stigall, 'The Manuscript Tradition of the
De vita et moribus philosophorum of Walter Burley', *M&H* 11 (1957), 44–57; J. Prelog, 'Die
Handschriften und Drucke von Walter Burleys *Liber de vita et moribus philosophorum*', *Codices
manuscripti* 9 (1983), 1–18. See also C. E. Lutz, 'Walter Burley's *De vita et moribus philo-
sophorum*', in her *Essays on Manuscripts and Rare Books* (Hamden, Conn.: Archon, 1975), 51–6.
Burley's work includes studies of Aristotle's logic which could have stimulated an interest in
Apuleius. See 'Walter Burley's *Quaestiones in librum Perihermenias*', ed. S. F. Brown, *Franciscan
Studies* 34 (1974), 200–95. See *Quaest.* 2. 29 (p. 223) and 2. 49 (p. 234) for logic-chopping
discussions of the perception of an ass (*Tantum ab istis videtur asinus* etc.)

[30] Sommers, *ODNB*, s.v. 'Walter Burley'. Richard Bury had met Petrarch at Avignon. See K.
W. Humphreys, 'The Library of John Erghome and Personal Libraries of the Fourteenth
Century in England', *PLPLS* 18 (1982), 106–23, at 110.

[31] Sommers, *ODNB*, s.v. 'Walter Burley'.

[32] M. Grignaschi, 'Lo Pseudo Walter Burley e il *Liber de vita et moribus philosophorum*',
and '*Corrigenda et addenda* sulla questione dello Ps. Burleo', *Medioevo* 16 (1990), 131–90 and
325–54. See also A. Vidmanová, 'La Formation de la second rédaction des *Vite philosophorum* et
sa relation à l'œuvre originale', *Medioevo* 16 (1990), 253–72.

[33] *ODNB*, s.v. 'Walter Burley'. J. Ottman and R. Wood acknowledge that 'it is now generally
accepted that the modern philologists who have taken away from Burley his most popular work
are correct', but contend that 'the evidence for this conclusion is not yet wholly compelling'. See
'Walter of Burley: His Life and Works', *Vivarium* 37 (1999), 1–23, at 22.

Item alium quem in duodecim libros distinxit quem asinum aureum intitulauit. vbi scripsit sibi accidisse quod accepto veneno a quadam muliere sibi dato: humano animo permanente visum illi fuit quod in asinum fuisset mutatus a qua illusione postmodum est curatus.[34]

(Also another which he divided into twelve books which he entitled *The Golden Ass* where he wrote that it happened to him that on taking poison given to him by a certain woman, it seemed to him that—though his mind remained human—he had been transformed into an ass. He was afterwards cured of this illusion.)

The most striking aspect of this passage is its reference to twelve books.[35] Is this a simple slip? The result of indirect reporting? Or evidence of an abnormal book division or the incorporation of other material (say, the *Florida*) as additional books at the end of the novel? Danielle van Mal-Maeder has dared to think the unthinkable: extrapolating from Oronzo Pecere's observation that Book 11 appears to be incomplete (since it lacks a *subscriptio* and the scribe of F seems to have indicated a hiatus after 11. 30), she tentatively suggests that, in Burley's day, a manuscript may have been circulating which contained a whole extra book of *The Golden Ass*.[36] It is a beguiling thesis, but rather spoiled by the fact that 'Burley' gives no clear evidence of having read the novel: his account depends heavily upon Augustine, particularly in its reference to the transformation being an 'illusion' caused by 'poison'.[37] But the entry for Apuleius remains intriguing, particularly in its inclusion of an extended quotation from chapter 18 of the *Apologia*, where Apuleius answers Pudens' charge that he is poor (and so, by implication, married Pudentilla for her money) with an encomium on Poverty:

Scripsit insuper Apuleus librum oratorium contra Emilianum. vbi inter cetera paupertatem commendans ait. non est erubescenda exprobratio paupertatis. Est enim paupertas acceptum philosophis crimen et vltro profitendum...

'Burley' speaks of the work only as an 'Oratorical book against Aemilianus' and gives no sense of its central purpose as a rebuttal of a charge of witchcraft. One would be tempted to suggest that 'Burley' was quoting from some sort of

---

[34] *Liber de vita ac moribus philosophorum poetarumque veterum* ([Cologne: U. Zell, after 1469]), fol. 61ʳ.

[35] Cf. Edward Leigh, *A Treatise of Religion and Learning* (London: A[braham]. M[iller]. for Charles Adams, 1656), 117 (Lib. III, cap. 2): 'There are twelve books of his *De aureo asino*'.

[36] '*Lector, intende: laetaberis*: The Enigma of the Last Book of Apuleius' *Metamorphoses*', *GCN* 8 (1997), 87–118, at 114 n. 85. Cf. R. H. F. Carver, 'The Rediscovery of the Latin Novels', in *Latin Fiction: The Latin Novel in Context*, ed. H. Hofmann (London: Routledge, 1999), 253–68, at 261.

[37] *De ciuitate dei* 18. 18: *sicut Apuleius in libris, quos titulo Asini aurei inscripsit, sibi ipsi accidisse, accepto veneno, humano animo permanente, asinus fieret, aut iudicauit, aut finxit.* See Ch. 1, *supra*.

florilegium, were it not for the awareness of context displayed in the phrase *inter cetera* and the naming of the prime accuser (Aemilianus).

We should also note that Giovanni Colonna's *De viris illustribus* (wr. *c.*1340) is partly modelled on the *De vita* and reproduces the passage describing Apuleius' works, omitting only the *Respublica* and the pseudo-Apuleian *De herbis* (i.e. *Herbarius*).[38]

Nicholas Trevet and Thomas Waleys

The Dominican friar Nicholas Trevet has been called 'one of the first English scholars since the twelfth century to develop an extensive knowledge of classical authors, and certainly the earliest northern European writer to absorb the new Italian currents in classical scholarship'.[39] He travelled in Italy (perhaps visiting Florence, Padua, and Pisa), settled in Paris (*c.*1307), was in Avignon in 1308, and produced commentaries on Seneca's *Tragedies* (completed *c.*1315), Boethius' *Consolatio,* and Augustine's *De ciuitate dei.* In his commentary on *De ciuitate dei* 4. 2, Trevet informs us that Apuleius wrote three works, the *De moribus et vita Platonis,* the *De deo Socratis,* and the *De mundo.* Of these, he has seen only the first.[40]

A younger Dominican, Thomas Waleys (*fl.* 1318–49)—student of Oxford, lector to San Domenico, Bologna (from 1326), and chaplain to Cardinal Matteo Rosso Orsini in Avignon (from 1331)—was more successful. In his commentary on the first ten books of the *De ciuitate dei* (completed, according to manuscript tradition, in 1332), Waleys claims to have seen five:

De apuleio scribit hugo floriacensis in primo libro ecclesiasticæ historiæ suæ | quod Apuleius succesit platoni.

Scripsit autem libros quinque quos vidi | scilicet de domate [sic] *platonis | de deo socratis | de mundo, qui vocatur cosmographia Apuleij. Item de magia, in quo defendit se contra accusatores qui eum vti arte magica dicebant: De quo libro facit augustinus mentionem infra libro octauo | capitulo decionono. Item librum de asino aureo | qui et metamorphoseos appellatur: in quo narrat mirabiles transmutationes factas arte magica, et de seipso quomodo in asinum conuersus erat: de quo libro facit Augustinus mentionem infra libro decimooctauo | capitulo decimooctauo. Macrobius vero super somnium*

---

[38] Grignaschi ('*Corrigenda et addenda*', 326), citing Venice, Cod. Marc. Lat., cl. X, 58, fol. 20ʳ. On the debt to Burley, see R. Sabbadini, 'Giovanni Colonna biografo e bibliografo del sec. XIV', *ARAST* 46 (1911), 830–60, at 833. See also, W. Braxton Ross, Jr., 'Giovanni Colonna, Historian at Avignon', *Speculum* 45 (1970), 533–63; G. M. Gianola, 'La raccolta di biografie come problema storiografico nel *De viris* di Giovanni Colonna', *Bullettino dell'Istituto storico italiano per il medio evo e Archivio Muratoriano* 89 (1982), 509–40.

[39] J. G. Clark, *ODNB,* s.v. 'Trevet'.   [40] Smalley, 90.

scipionis sentit quod fuerunt ficta: vnde dicit loquens de fabulis sic Quibus apuleium nonnunquam lusisse miramur.[41]

(As for Apuleius, Hugh of Fleury writes in Book 1 of his *Ecclesiastical History* that Apuleius followed Plato.[42] But he wrote five books which I have seen, namely the *De dogmate Platonis*, the *De deo Socratis*, the *De mundo* (which is called the *Cosmography* of Apuleius); also, the *De magia*, in which he defends himself against his accusers who said that he used the art of magic (Augustine makes mention of this book below, Book 8, ch. 19); also, the book of *The Golden Ass*, which is also called the *Metamorphoses*, in which he relates the marvellous transformations made by the art of magic and tells, with reference to his own self, how he was changed into an ass. Augustine makes mention of this book below at Book 18, ch. 18. But Macrobius, in his *Commentary on the Dream of Scipio*, believes that these things were made up: whence he says, talking of tales: 'We marvel that Apuleius amused himself on occasion in such things.')

In his gloss on *De ciuitate dei* 8. 19 (*Postremo ipse apuleius numquid apud iudices christianos de magicis artibus accusatus est*), Waleys discusses the *De magia* (quoting from it the opening words, *certus quidem eram*):

Postremo ipse etc. *Tertio probat idem per factum apulei qui scripsit librum quendam qui intitulatur de magia & incipit sic: certus quidem eram proque vero obtinebam etc. qui continet orationem agitatam sub claudio maximo, proconsule qua defendit se contra emilianum æmulum suum: qui accusauit eum de arte magica: nitensque pluribus argumentis probare intentum suum: scilicet apuleius sibi obiecta negauit: & omnia tam euidenter quam eloquenter repulit: vt omnes astantes in iudicio mirarent | & etiam in nullius corde de eius innocentia scrupulus remaneret. Constat tamen quod augustinus epistola prima ad marcellinum dicit eum magicis artibus fuisse intentum vbi etiam loquens de oratione sua & defensione | innuit ipsum de falso defendisse.*

(Thirdly, Augustine demonstrates through the case of Apuleius who wrote a certain book which is entitled *On Magic* and begins thus: 'I was indeed certain and held it as truth etc.' in which he defended himself against his rival, Aemilianus, who accused him of the practice of magic, striving with a great many arguments to prove his intention; that is to say, Apuleius denied the charges against him and rebutted everything as clearly as he does eloquently, so that all those standing in judgement were amazed and not a shred of doubt remained in anyone's heart as to his innocence. It is well known, however, that Augustine, in his first letter to Marcellinus, says that

---

[41] *Diui Aurelij Augustini...de Ciuitate dei contra paganos...Cum commentarijs Thomæ Valois et Nicolai Triueth* (Basle: Adam Petri, 1515), sig. i4ᵛ. Smalley (90) reproduces the middle portion of the quotation, omitting references to Hugo and Macrobius.

[42] The 12th-cent. monk (aka Hugues de Sainte Marie) provides a marginal note listing *Viri doctrina illustres* in the order: Plato, Apuleius, Hermes Trismegistus (*proinde Platoni successit Apuleius, & Apuleio Hermes Ægyptius, quem Trismegistum vocant*), and Pythagoras. See *Hugonis Floriacensis monachi Benedictini Chronicon*, ed. B. Rottendorf (Monasterium Westphaliae: Bernard Raesfeld, 1638), 24–5. Waleys may have derived the Fleury reference from Vincent of Beauvais (see Ch. 2, *supra*).

Apuleius was bent on magic arts; also, when speaking about his oration and defence, he intimated that he defended himself falsely.)

Waleys then considers the necromantic content of *The Golden Ass*:

Apuleius etiam in libro quem fecit de asino aureo | dicit de seipso quod artem illam libentissime didicerit | scilicet male sibi cessit ex hoc vt narrat. quia dum artem illam volebat discere | in asinum vt sibi videbatur conuersus est: & de hoc loquitur augustinus infra lib. xviiij. ca. xvij.

(Apuleius also says of himself, in the book which he made about the *Golden Ass*, that he learned that art most willingly, that is to say, he wickedly gave in to himself on this count, as he tells us: because while he was trying to learn that art, he was changed, as it seemed to him, into an ass. And Augustine speaks about this below in Book 18, ch. 17 [*sc.* 18].)

Waleys's description of the contents and his use (like Benzo) of alternative titles suggest at least some direct contact with a manuscript of the novel, though the information he supplies is insufficient to posit a close reading of the work. His account of the *De magia* is much more detailed: he can quote the opening line; and he gives the name of the governor of the province who is hearing the case and the cognomen of the principal accuser, Sicinius Aemilianus.[43] But his reference to the effect of the speech on the jury is surprising. Apuleius seems to be so successful in ridiculing his accusers that his acquittal has always been assumed—but the surviving manuscripts of the *Apologia* make no mention of such a result. No one, to my knowledge, has ever suggested that the text of the *Apologia* was incomplete (F and φ end with *Dixi*, 'I have spoken', followed by the subscription of Sallustius, *DE MAGIA LIB. II. Explicit*), but Waleys is sufficiently confident to point out an incongruity between his assertion of Apuleius' acquittal and the famed Church Father's intimations that Apuleius was guilty anyway. However tempting it might be to posit from such evidence the erstwhile existence of a longer text of the *Apologia* or a postscript to it containing the verdict of the case, the most likely explanation is that Waleys is extrapolating from an imperfectly read text, or interpolating Augustine's own critique.

The importance of Waleys's testimony was recognized by his successors. He appears in the list of authorities which prefaces Benvenuto da Imola's copy of Apuleius' works: *de Isto Apuleio | thomas Wayleys Anglicus . . . sic scribit. . . .*[44]

---

[43] Butler's text (based on a collation of F and an examination of all the surviving manuscripts then known) gives *equidem* in place of Waley's *quidem*—though I quote only from the 1515 printed edition without verification from the Cambridge MS.

[44] Biblioteca Apostolica Vaticana, MS Vat. Lat. 3384, fol. ɪvʳ (quoting Waleys on the *De magia*). The passage, *De Apuleio | scribit hugo floriacensis . . .*, is given at fol. ɪvᵛ.

Avignon

Apuleius' reception at Avignon has left some traces in the surviving catalogues of the papal library. An inventory (datable to 1405–7) of the books which had formerly been in the 'Chamber of the Flying Deer' (next to the Pope's bedroom and containing his personal library), but were 'now' in the 'Great Library', contains the following entry: *Item libellus Luci Apuleyi Madaurensisse de asino aureo*.[45] It would be tempting to presume that this was the very manuscript that Waleys consulted when he was studying at Avignon; but there are problems with such an inference, the first being that the Avignon catalogue describes only a manuscript of *The Golden Ass* (and thus does not account for the knowledge of the *De magia* shown by Waleys or 'Burley'); the second, that the manuscript does not feature in earlier catalogues (e.g. those from 1369 and 1375) of the Avignon libraries.[46] We know, from the correspondence between Stefano Colonna and Simone da Brossano, that there was a copy of the novel at Avignon by 1375.[47] Petrarch, Boccaccio, Acciaiuoli, and Zanobi da Strada were all associated with Avignon, and any one of them might have provided the copy catalogued here.[48]

The catalogue of the Library at Peñiscola in Catalonia (to which the papal collection was moved) records, in 1409, a more complete copy of Apuleius' works: *Item Asinus aureus Apulei, et liber de deo Socratis, et liber quartus ejusdem qui dicitur floritor[i]um et liber ejusdem de magia Apulei*.[49] This may, in fact, merely be a fuller catalogue record of the same work, but the ignorance of the *Florida* shown by 'Burley' and Waleys militates against such an explanation.

The testimonies of Benzo, 'Burley', and Waleys do point, however, to a significant (and usually unremarked) aspect of the textual tradition of Apuleius. Most of the surviving manuscripts share the trinitarian aspect of F: the

---

[45] *Inventarium librorum qui solebant esse in camera Cervi Volantis, nunc vero sunt in magna libraria turris.* See M. Faucon, *La Librairie des Papes d'Avignon: Sa formation, sa composition, ses catalogues (1316–1420)*, 2 vols. (Paris: Thorin, 1886–7), ii. 31; Manitius, *Handschriften*, 149. For the dating, and on the location of the *camera Cervi Volantis*, see M.-H. Jullien de Pomerol and J. Monfrin, *La Bibliothèque pontificale à Avignon et à Peñiscola pendant le grand schisme d'occident et sa dispersion*, 2 vols. (Rome: École française de Rome, 1991), i. 26–7.

[46] According to Smalley (75–6), Waleys was at Avignon in 1318 and from late 1331 to the New Year of 1333.

[47] See *infra*, 141–4.

[48] Petrarch was living at Avignon from his father's death in 1326 until 1337, and at Vaucluse and Avignon in the years 1337–41, 1345–7, and 1351–3. See E. H. Wilkins, 'Petrarch's Ecclesiastical Career', *Speculum* 28 (1953), 754–75.

[49] Faucon, ii. 129, no. 927. Faucon is puzzled by the reference to Apuleius' *Florida* and confuses it with the pseudo-Apuleian *Herbarius*.

Apologia, the *Metamorphoses*, and the *Florida* have descended as a unit.[50] Benzo, however, has read the *Florida* and knows about the *De asino aureo/ Metamorphoses* but not the *De magia*.[51] 'Burley' and Waleys know the *De magia* (in some detail) and (at least the name of) the *De asino aureo/ Metamorphoses*, without having heard of the *Florida*. In some fourteenth-century manuscripts, the *Metamorphoses* and the *Florida* are fused into a single work, so that the declamations seem to form a continuation of the novel; but this cannot account for all the discrepancies, and it is clear that, towards the beginning of the fourteenth century, the *De magia*, the *De asino aureo/Metamorphoses*, and the *Florida* were circulating in Italy individually or in pairs, rather than as a tripartite unit.[52] What is not clear is whether these manuscripts represent the breaking up of the trinitarian tradition of F, or the survival of a distinct tradition (now lost), possibly going back to Fulgentius or even Augustine. The use of alternative titles in Benzo's and Waleys's accounts generates three possible explanations: (1) manuscripts of the *Metamorphoses* from the F family were found to correspond with the descriptions of the *De asino aureo* given by Augustine and Fulgentius, and the latter title became current; (2) a manuscript (or manuscripts) from the textual tradition known to Augustine and Fulgentius survived into the fourteenth century bearing the title *De asino aureo*, but later perished); (3) a manuscript tradition which preserved both titles together survived until the early Renaissance, but no later. The third hypothesis must remain idle speculation. Support for the second might seem to be indicated by the Fulgentian variants found in manuscripts from as early as 1345 (e.g. *glabriorem* for F's *caluiorem* in *AA* 5. 9), but Robertson demonstrates that these are interpolations from Fulgentius' *Expositio sermonum antiquorum*, rather than survivals from a common tradition.[53]

Nevertheless, the cumulative evidence lends weight to the recent attacks on the primacy of F discussed above.[54] And whichever stemmatic model we follow, our conclusions on at least one point must be the same: while F may constitute our best surviving witness to Sallustius' fourth-century recension, it was not, in itself, the manuscript that intitiated the revival of the novel's fortunes at the beginning of the fourteenth century. We need to replace the

[50] There are a few exceptions: e.g. V6 (Vat. Lat. 2194, copied at Bologna in 1345) contains only the *Met.*; N2 (Naples, Cod. IV. D. 11) lacks the *Apol.* and runs the *Met.* and the *Flor.* together to form 13 books. See Robertson, 'Manuscripts', 29–30; Butler, *Apologia*, p. xl.

[51] Robertson ('Manuscripts', 29 n. 1) notes that D (Dresden, Sächs. Landesbibliothek DC 178, copied in 1356) lacks the *Apol.*

[52] See Butler, *Apologia*, pp. xxxix and xxxvii.

[53] Robertson, 'Manuscripts', 31.

[54] On the challenge to F, see Griffiths, *The Isis-Book*, 66; for a reaffirmation of its primacy, see K. Dowden, 'Eleven Notes on the Text of Apuleius' *Metamorphoses*', *CQ* 30 (1980), 218–26.

romanticized Cassinese scenario of a single, discrete discovery with a more complex (if prosaic) picture. Lowe imagined that, after the copying of ϕ, both manuscripts remained in Monte Cassino until their removal to Florence in the fourteenth century. But, even if this is true, the Cassinese manuscripts were not entirely lost to view. Robertson's model presupposes the escape of at least one manuscript (the lost archetype of Class I) before 1200; and Class II (which includes both Petrarch's manuscript and a manuscript copied in 1345) derive 'd'une seule source, aujourd'hui perdue, séparée de F par plusieurs intermédiares'.[55] To this skein we must add (if we admit Pecere's contentions and the hypotheses tentatively presented above) the possible influence, either of an ancestor (or collateral relative) of F or even of manuscripts independent of the Sallustian tradition represented by F.

Albertino Mussato (1261–1329)

A good example of the dangers of fetishizing F is furnished by Albertino Mussato, the Paduan poet laureate, best known as the author of the Latin tragedy *Ecerinis* (1314?), a Senecan study of tyranny based on the life of Ezzelino III da Romano (1194–1259).[56] Mussato's *Somnium in egritudine apud Florentiam* ('Dream during an illness at Florence') is a poem of 314 hexameters belonging to the Platonic and Ciceronian tradition of dream-visions preserved by Macrobius in his *Commentarium in Somnium Scipionis*. Mussato tells us that he fell ill during a visit to Florence in September 1319. He was taken to the bishop's palace where the doctors 'made him drink a potion of violets imported from abroad, undressed him, and massaged his body with ointments.' A bizarre metamorphosis ensues:

> *In caput evolvor suppressaque lumina condo;*
> *tuncque meum video subito plumescere pectus*
> *brachiaque extensas se se convertere in alas*
> *astrictosque pedes unam coniungere caudam,*
> *os quoque mutatum rostro se extendit acuto:*
> *iam sum avis et facto gaudens nova tegmina quasso.*[57]

(My head spins and my sight is dimmed; I see my breast growing feathers, my arms becoming extended wings, and my feet joining together in a tail; while my mouth is transformed and elongated into a sharp beak. I have become a bird and, delighting in the fact, I flutter my new plumage.)

---

[55] Introd. to Budé edn., p. xlvi.
[56] ed. L. Padrin et al., introd. and trans. J. R. Berrigan (Munich: Fink, 1975).
[57] M. Pastore Stocchi, 'Il *Somnium* di Albertino Mussato', in *Studi in onore di Vittorio Zaccaria*, ed. M. Pecoraro (Milan: Unicopli, 1987), 41–63, at 57 (vv. 86–91).

Michele Feo comments: 'Strangely enough, this passage recalls the description of the witch Pamphile in Apuleius' *Golden Ass* (3. 21), though Mussato could not have known this text, if the only extant manuscript in the early Trecento (Laurentianus LXVIII. 2, 11th c.) was indeed not brought from Montecassino to Florence until many years later.'[58] With this (reluctant) dismissal of Pamphile, Feo concentrates, instead, on 'more plausible' sources (most notably, Horace, *Odes* 2. 20, ll. 9–12)—a perfectly proper procedure given the general rule that the literary genealogist should privilege the accessible over the recondite. In this case, however, the Cassinese premiss which impels such privileging is flawed: Mussato did not necessarily require access to F or ϕ in order to read *The Golden Ass*.[59] Furthermore, Mussato was sufficiently close to Benzo d'Alessandria to call him *Bencium carissimum amicorum* in his dedication of the *De gestis italicorum post mortem Henrici VII* (1313–29).[60] While his 'dearest of friends' was reading the *Florida*, Mussato could have been reading *The Golden Ass*.

In the light of this revelation, we can develop Feo's initial suggestion of Apuleian significance. Mussato's 'head spins and [his] sight is dimmed'; he 'flutters' (*quasso*) his 'new plumage', and flies out through a slit (*rima*). Lucius watches through a crack (*rima*) as Pamphile smears herself with ointment, shakes (*quatit*) her limbs, and is transformed, while he, in turn, is pushed beyond the limits of his own mind and rubs his eyes repeatedly (*Sic exterminatus animi, attonitus in amentiam vigilans somniabar. Defrictis adeo diu pupilis...*, AA 3. 22). In the course of his flight, Mussato arrives *ad medios celi terreque meatus* ('at the middle turning-points of heaven and earth'). This may put us in mind of Lucius' spiritual flight to heaven and hell in *AA* 11. 23 (itself picking up Psyche's catabasis in 6. 16–20), though Dante, of course, presents a more immediate model (even though he himself, it seems, was influenced by Martianus Capella).[61]

Dante Alighieri (1265–1321)

The case for Mussato's use of Apuleius in 1320 looks strong. Aldo Manetti has claimed an even earlier Apuleian echo in Dante's *Divine Comedy* (written

---

[58] 'The "Pagan Beyond" of Albertino Mussato', in *Latin Poetry and the Classical Tradition*, ed. Godman and Murray, 115–47, at 123.

[59] Implicit in Marshall's account in *Texts and Transmission* is the notion that these works survived at Monte Cassino until they were discovered by Zanobi da Strada and brought to Florence. Cf. Carver, 'The Rediscovery of the Latin Novels', 258.

[60] Berrigan, 'Prehumanism', 255.

[61] According to Stahl (*Martianus Capella*, i. 71), 'The heavenly journey of Philology served as a model and inspiration for other similar literary journeys, including that of Dante through the celestial spheres.'

between 1306 and 1321).[62] In Canto VIII of the *Inferno*, Dante encounters the shade of Filippo Argenti:

> *Mentre noi corravam la morta gora,*
> *dinanzi mi si fece un pien di fango...*
> *...Allora stese al legno ambo le mani;*
> *per che 'l maestro accorto lo sospinse,*
> *dicendo: 'Via costà con li altri cani!'*

(While we were running through the stagnant channel there rose up in front of me one covered with mud... Then he reached out to the boat with both hands; on which the wary Master thrust him off, saying: 'Away there with the other dogs!')[63]

Manetti notes the resemblance of this episode to the passage in which the Tower advises Psyche how to conduct herself on her journey to the Underworld:

nec setius tibi pigrum fluentum transmeanti quidam supernatans senex mortuus putris adtollens manus orabit ut eum intra nauigium trahas, nec tu tamen inlicita adflectare pietate. (*AA* 6. 18)

(Likewise, as you traverse the sluggish stream, a dead old man, raising his rotting hands, will beseech you to drag him into the boat. But, once again, do not be swayed by unlawful pity.)

Such parallels are by no means conclusive—the 'stagnant channel' (*la morta gora*) and 'sluggish stream' (*pigrum fluentum*) may be derived independently from *Aeneid* 6;[64] and Dante may simply be responding to Vergil's general image of the dead 'holding forth their hands in their desire for the further bank' (*tendebantque manus ripae ulterioris amore, Aeneid* 6. 314) as they beg Charon to ferry them to the Other Side.[65] But Manetti's attempt to link the Tower's warning against showing 'forbidden pity' (*inlicita... pietas*) with Virgilio's words in *Inferno* xx. 28 (*Qui vive la pietà quand'è ben morta*, 'Here pity lives when it is quite dead') is thought-provoking. The injunction to suppress natural pity is unsettling enough in Apuleius; in the *Inferno*, we are given something much more extreme: not only do Dante and Virgilio fail to show any pity towards Argenti; they actually gloat at the sight of his torments being redoubled (viii. 52–66). We should also note that Dante had a potential

---

[62] 'Nota su Dante e Apuleio', *L'Alighieri* 22/2 (July–Dec. 1981), 61–2.

[63] *Inferno* viii. 31–2, 40–2; trans. Sinclair.

[64] Kenney (*C&P*, 215) notes the Vergilian precedents for Apuleius' 'sluggish stream': *turbidus... caeno... gurges* (*Aen.* 6. 296); *tenebrosa palus* (6. 323); *Stygiam... paludem* (6. 323).

[65] Note that Kenney suggests, as Apuleius' own model, Aeneas' encounter with Palinurus (*Aen.* 6. 337–83).

conduit to Apuleian texts in the person of Benzo who served as *cancellarius* to
Can Grande della Scala, the dedicatee of Dante's *Paradiso*.[66]

FRANCESCO PETRARCA (1304–74)

The absence of Apuleius' name from Petrarch's list of favourite books (*libri
mei peculiares*) has tended to blind scholars to the importance of *The Golden
Ass* to the man traditionally regarded as the fountain-head of the Renaissance.
B. L. Ullman states that Apuleius never figures in Petrarch's published works,
but that in the margins of Petrarch's books, he is quoted in Petrarch's hand
seventeen times.[67] A letter of 1359 seems to confirm Petrarch's merely cursory
interest in Apuleius:

*Legi semel apud Ennium, apud Plautum, apud Felicem Capellam, apud Apuleium, et legi
raptim, propere, nullam nisi ut alienis in finibus moram trahens. Sic praetereunti multa
contigit ut viderem, pauca decerperem, pauciora reponerem eaque ut communia in
aperto et in ipso, ut ita dixerim, memorie uestibulo.*[68]

(I read once amongst the works of Ennius, of Felix Capella, of Apuleius, and I read
snatchingly, hastily, making no delay except, as it were, for other ends. As I passed over
them in this way, it happened that I saw many things: I gathered a few; an even smaller
number, I placed in the open and in the very forecourt—as I called it—of the
memory.)

Petrarch's *Legi semel* is contradicted by the evidence of his own manuscript
copy (MS Vat. Lat. 2193) which unites the two groups of Apuleius' writings,
the philosophical and the epideictic. The text of the *Metamorphoses* has notes
in Petrarch's hand bearing the dates 1348, 1349, 1350, 1353, 1359, and 1369,
suggesting prolonged and repeated exposure to the novel.[69] Nolhac established a *terminus ante quem* of 1348 for Petrarch's gaining possession of the
Metamorphoses. Caterina Tristano demonstrates that this date can, in fact, be
pushed back to 1343–5 or even 1341–3.[70]

Moreover, Ullman's contention that Apuleius never figures in Petrarch's
published works is contradicted by the frequent use of Apuleius in such works
as the *Familiarum rerum libri*.[71] Apuleius is prominent in the very first letter

[66] Berrigan, 'Prehumanism', 254.

[67] *Studies in the Italian Renaissance* (Rome: Edizioni di storia e letteratura, 1973), 127.

[68] *Familiarum rerum libri* 22. 2, 11; cf. Ullman, *Studies*, 115.

[69] Nolhac, *La Bibliothèque*, 300–1; Ullman, *Studies*, 130.

[70] C. Tristano, 'Le postille del Petrarca nel Vaticano Lat. 2193 (Apuleio, Frontino, Vegezio,
Palladio)', *IMU* 17 (1974), 365–468.

[71] *Fam.* 1. 1. 12; 1. 4. 4; 1. 10. 3; 9. 10. 4; 9. 13. 27. Apuleius also appears in the dialogue *De
remediis utriusque Fortunae* (11. 17). See A. Scobie, 'The Influence of Apuleius' *Metamorphoses*

of this carefully constructed collection. Addressing 'Socrates' (Ludwig van Kempen), he says:

Non audeo illud Apuleii Madaurensis in comune iactare: 'Lector, intende: letaberis'; unde enim michi id fiducie, ut lectori delectationem letitiam ve pollicear?

(I do not dare to make public that boast of Apuleius of Madaura, 'Reader, pay attention: you will be delighted.' For how could I be confident of offering pleasure or delight to my reader?)[72]

Petrarch begins a letter to Cardinal Giovanni Colonna (d. 1348), by relating how he recently 'travelled through France, not on business … but simply from a youthful ardour and zeal for sight-seeing'.[73] Lucius' exploration of Hypata (*AA* 2. 1) becomes an ironic paradigm for the proto-humanist's attempt to disentangle fact from fable in his first encounter with Paris:

Introii non aliter animo affectus quam olim Thesalie civitatem Ypatham dum lustrat, Apuleius. Ita enim solicito stupore suspensus et cuncta circumspiciens, videndi cupidus explorandique vera ne ad ficta essent que de illa civitate audieram, non parvum in ea tempus absumpsi, et quotiens operi lux defuit, noctem superaddidi. Demum ambiendo et inhiando, magna ex parte didicisse videor quis in eadem veritati, quis fabulis locus sit …

(I must have felt much the same upon entering the town as did Apuleius when he wandered about Hypata in Thessaly. I spent no little time there, in open-mouthed wonder; and I was so full of interest and eagerness to know the truth about what I had heard of the place that when daylight failed me I even prolonged my investigations into the night. After loitering about for a long time, gaping at the sights, I at last satisfied myself that I had discovered the point where truth left off and fiction began.)[74]

Milo's miserly hospitality (*AA* 1. 21 and 26) is invoked in *Familiarum* 1. 10. 3 (*Hospitem Apuleii Milonem prodigalitatis arguet quisquis …*; 'Whoever will

in Renaissance Italy and Spain', in *Aspects*, ed. Hijmans and van der Paardt, 211–25, at 211–12. Scobie does not date any of the references, nor does he mention the *Invectivae contra quendam medicum*.

[72] *Fam.* 1. 1. 12. Petrarch's proemic first letter also resembles Apuleius' prologue in its discussion of Petrarch's conception, birth, and early travels. Like Petrarch, Ludwig had been a member of Cardinal Giovanni Colonna's household. See *Petrarch's Book without a Name*, trans. N. P. Zacour (Toronto: PIMS, 1973), 19.

[73] *Fam.* 1. 4. 1: *Gallias ego nuper nullo quidem negotio … sed visendi tantum studio et iuvenili quodam ardore peragravi.* Cf. *AA* 1. 2: *Thessaliam … ex negotio petebam.* The letter is signed, *Aquis, XI Kal. Iulias* ('Lyons, August 9'). Petrarch's trip to France, Germany, and the Netherlands has been dated to 1333, but Petrarch's habit of revising his correspondence make it unsafe to use this letter as hard evidence of his very early acquaintance with *The Golden Ass*. In *Petrarca letterato*, i (Rome: Edizioni di storia e letteratura, 1947), 48, G. Billanovich dates the letter to 1350–1 (two or three years after its supposed recipient's death).

[74] *Fam.* 1. 4. 4; *Petrarch, the First Modern Scholar and Man of Letters: A Selection from his Correspondence*, trans. J. H. Robinson (New York: Putnam, 1898), 300.

accuse Apuleius' host Milo of extravagance...') and (by way of contrast) in *Familiarum* 9. 10. 4 (*evasi in cubiculum non quidem solis fabulis, ut apud Milonem Ypathe olim Apuleius, sed lautissimis cenatus cibis*; 'I made my way to my bedchamber, having dined, not on tales alone—as Apuleius once did at Milo's house in Hypata—but on most sumptuous dishes'). Apuleius provides a bridge to Homer in Petrarch's use (*Fam.* 9. 13. 27) of the discussion of Odysseus (*non immerito... virtutes cecinit, AA* 9. 13). And in *Familiarum* 20. 1. 21, Petrarch quotes the description of Philesitherus' confidence in his ability to gain access to Barbarus' wife, Arete (*certusque fragilitatis humanae fidei et quod pecuniae cunctae sint difficultates perviae auroque soleant adamantinae etiam perfringi fores, AA* 9. 18).

In his *Invectives against a Physician* (1352–5), Petrarch gives his most sustained defence of poetry, and uses Apuleius as part of his artillery. He calls him a 'celebrated Platonist' (*præclarus Platonicus Apuleius*) as he plays upon the theme of the 'philosophizing ass' (*AA* 10. 33).[75]

The campaign to persuade the papal court to return to Rome from its self-imposed exile in the 'French Babylon' of Avignon occupied Petrarch's mind for much of his life. In the penultimate letter of the *Liber sine nomine*, he surprises us with a lurid tale about a high-ranking ecclesiastic who employs a 'bird-catcher' (*auceps*) to satisfy his sexual appetites.[76] The 'bird-catcher' procures a 'wretched little maid or, rather, a wretched little tart' (*misella uirguncula an meretricula*) who, 'just like that Psyche of Lucius Apuleius—worthy to be honoured with a happy marriage—enters the bed-chamber of an unknown husband' (*uelut Psyche illa Lucij Apulei, fœlicibus nuptijs honestanda, ignoti uiri thalamum subit*).[77] The 'old man flies towards her' (*senex aduolat*), 'kissing her with his trembling lips, nibbling her with his toothless mouth as he pants to consummate the latest nuptials' (*pendulis labiis exosculans, atque inermi ore commorsitans consummare nouas nuptias anhelabat*).[78] The girl is so disgusted by his appearance that she refuses his embrace, but she is mollified when he returns with his red hat on his 'shiny, bald head' (*albo caluoque uertici*) and declares: 'Do not be afraid, daughter: I'm a cardinal!' (*Cardinalis sum, ne timeas, filia*).

Petrarch's method here is quite different from the *Liber*'s general discourse of denunication: the account is carefully set off as one of the 'thousand funny

---

[75] *Opera omnia*, 1209, 1213; *Invectives*, ed. and trans. D. Marsh (Cambridge, Mass.: HUP, 2003), 51 and 75.

[76] *Liber sine nomine*, 18. Cf. *Petrarch's Book without a Name*, 115–17.

[77] *Opera... omnia* (Basle: Henrichus Petrus, 1554), ii. 808. Cf. Scobie, 'Influence', 212.

[78] On the rare word *commorsitans*, cf. *AA* 7. 16, and 10. 22. For Petrarch's characterization of the cardinal as a *seniculus* ('little old man'), cf. *AA* 1. 25; for his reference to the girl as *amasiola* ('lovelette'), cf. *amasio* (*AA* 3. 22 and 7. 21).

stories' that Avignon contains.[79] The greater freedom of the narrative voice may be accounted for by the fact that the *Liber sine nomine* was not intended for wide circulation; but it may also reflect the influence of his younger friend Boccaccio.

GIOVANNI BOCCACCIO (1313–75)

Petrarch has been identified as the recipient of Boccaccio's letter beginning *Mavortis miles extrenue*...(dated 1339), although more recent research has preferred to view the text as a stylistic exercise, rather than an autobiographical document.[80] Boccaccio's use of Apuleian phrases gives a *cento*-like effect to the piece, anticipating the technique of the *Hypnerotomachia Poliphili* (1499). Boccaccio draws on the story of Socrates and Aristomenes in describing how he once rose just before daybreak (*antelucio*), feeling 'languid and half-asleep' (*marcidus et semisopitus*), left his 'hut' (*gurgustiolum*), and walked along the seashore in the Bay of Naples.[81] Suddenly, a 'shining woman, or descending lightning-flash' (*subito suda mulier, ceu fulgur descendens*) appeared, leaving him stupefied (*obstupui*) and so changed that he knew himself to be 'an image of a ghost' (*larvale simulacrum*).[82] His response is identical to Lucius' in the face of Pamphile's transformation (*AA* 3. 22):

[79] *Mille locus hic ridiculosas historias capit, unam accipe.* Petrarch concludes with *Plaude, fabula acta est* ('Applaud! The tale is finished'). Dr Elizabeth Archibald has kindly alerted me to an Apuleian allusion (*caeca et prorsus exoculata fortuna*; cf. *AA* 7. 2) in the (perhaps contemporaneous) *Comedia sine nomine*, VII. vi. See *Études sur le théâtre français du XIVe et du XVe siècle*, ed. E. Roy (Paris: E. Bouillon, 1902), 152.

[80] Boccaccio, *Opere latine minori*, ed. A. F. Massèra (Bari: Laterza, 1928), 111–14. Cf. G. Billanovich, *Restauri boccacceschi* (Rome: Edizioni di storia e letteratura, 1947), 65–76; V. Branca, *Boccaccio medievale* (Florence: Sansoni, 1956), 146; T. Nurmela, 'La Misogynie chez Boccacce', in *Boccaccio in Europe*, ed. G. Tournoy (Leuven: Leuven UP, 1977), 191–6, at 194; E. Mass, 'Tradition, und Innovation im Romanschaffen Boccaccios: Die Bedeutung des *Goldenen Esel* für die Erneuerung des Prosaromans durch die *Elegia di Madonna Fiammetta* (1343/4)', *GCN* 2 (1989), 87–107, at 94. See, generally, C. Caballlot, 'La *Mavortis miles*: Petrarca in Boccaccio?', in *Gli Zibaldoni di Boccaccio*, ed. M. Picone and C. Cazalé Bérard (Florence: Cesati, 1998), 129–39.

[81] Cf. *AA* 1. 15: Aristomenes wanting to leave the inn before daybreak (*antelucio*); Socrates feeling tired after having his heart cut out in the night by a former lover (*marcidus et semisopitus*). Milo (*AA* 1. 23) disparages his own house as a 'hovel' (*gurgustiolum*). Cf. *AA* 4. 10. Coluccio Salutati uses *gurgustiolio* in one of his letters (*Epistolario* 1. 10, line 1). See R. May, 'The Prologue to Apuleius' *Metamorphoses* and Coluccio Salutati: MS Harley 4838 (With an Appendix on Sozomeno of Pistoia and the Nonius Marginalia)', in *Lectiones Scrupulosae*, ed. Keulen et al., 280–312, at 286.

[82] The vision shares some aspects with the theophanies in the *Aeneid* (1. 314–417) and Boccaccio's *Ameto* (xli–xliv), but we note, also, Lucius' littoral vision of Isis (*AA* 11. 1–3) and his response to Fotis in the kitchen (*obstupui, AA* 2. 7). Boccaccio's observation that the vision 'conformed to my auspices in character and appearance' (*meis auspitiis...moribus et forma conformis*) borrows two elements from Lucius' description of Fotis as being *forma scitula et moribus ludicra* (*AA* 2. 6).

sic exterminatus animi actonitus in amentia vigilans sonniabar, destrictis adeo diu pupulis an vigilarem scire querebam.

(Driven in this way beyond the limits of my mind, astonished to the point of madness, dreaming while fully alert, I kept rubbing my eyes as I tried to work out whether I really was awake.)

Boccaccio is possessed by a 'fearsome and tyrannical love' (*amor terribilis et imperiosus me tenuit*). Like Aristomenes (*AA* 1. 6), he is ignorant of the slippery ways of Fortune (*fortunarum lubricas ambages et instabiles incursiones ac reciprocas vicissitudines ignorarem*), and, like Socrates (*AA* 1. 6), he covers his face with his cloak (*multotiens centuculo dudum faciem punicantem obtectam lacrimis insistebam*). Charite's prayer as she flees the robbers' cave on Lucius' back (*AA* 6. 28) serves to articulate his amatory suffering:

suspirans altius celumque sollicito nutu petens incepi:—0 superi! tandem meis supremis suppliciis [A.A. periculis] opem facite et tu fortuna durior iam sevire desiste: sat tibi miseria istis cruciatibus meis litatum est!

(Sighing more deeply, and entreating heaven with an anxious inclination of the head, I began: 'O Gods above! Grant me succour at last in my extreme distress. And you, cruel, cruel Fortune, put an end now to your raging: I have made sufficient atonement to you through the wretched torments that I have suffered!')

The friend (*amicus etate scitulus et prorsus argutulus*) who arrives to comfort him is configured as a male version of Fotis (*forma scitula... et prorsus argutula, AA* 2. 6), but rather than offering sex or magic (or even Isiac roses), he calls upon the 'most sacred name' of the letter's recipient, promising an end to Boccaccio's miseries if he tastes the 'riches' of the recipient's words (*perorans in sacratissimum nomen vestrum incidit, asserens me meis miseriis finem dare, si vestrorum verborum copiam de-gustarem*). At the end of the letter, Boccaccio imitates Apuleius' prologue (*haec... vocis immutatio desultoriae scientiae stilo... respondet, AA* 1. 1), apologizing for 'blathering on' in a 'desultory manner' (*Scio me stilo desultorio nimia inepte ac exotica blacterando narrasse*), and declares that he deserves 'to be transformed into a marble statue' (*in marmoream statuam merui transformari*).[83] In the letter as a whole, we see how the erotic, necromantic, and theophanic elements in Apuleius have been redirected towards humanistic concerns with *amicitia*, linguistic *copia*, and the pursuit of knowledge.

The *Mavortis miles* is a remarkable piece of (re-)writing and it may supply a clue to the real nature of Boccaccio's relationship with Monte Cassino and its manuscripts. Maurizio Fiorilla has provided a detailed examination of the correspondences between the Apuleian diction displayed in the *Mavortis miles*

---

[83] Cf. *AA* 1. 1 (*exotici... sermonis rudis locutor*) and 4. 24 (*his et his similis blateratis*).

and marginal and interlineal annotations in ϕ, many of which appear to be in Boccaccio's, rather than Zanobi da Strada's hand.[84]

Boccaccio's *Ameto* or *Comedia delle ninfe fiorentini* (1341–2) displays some of the same Apuleian elements as the penultimate letter of Petrarch's *Liber sine nomine* and a similar blending of disparate discourses. In Agapes' tale (*Ameto* xxxii. 7–28), the description of the ancient husband looks like an elaboration of the complaints of Psyche's sisters (*AA* 5. 9–10). The catalogue of *il vecchio*'s defects includes the following:

Le labbra sue sono come quelle dell'orecciuto asino pendule e sanza alcuno colore, palide, danti luogo alla vista de'male composti e logori e gialli, anzi pitosto rugginosi . . .

(His lips were colorless, pale and drooping, like those of the long-eared ass, and they offered the sight of his teeth, which were badly placed and yellow, in fact rather rusty and rotten, and their number was deficient in many points.)[85]

We note, in the same chapter of the *Ameto*, Agapes' reaction to Cupid, whom Venus reveals in all his beauty, 'hidden away among dense foliage':

Oh quante volte ricordandomi di Psice, la reputai felice e infelice; felice di tale marito e infelice d'averlo perduto, felicissima poi d'averlo riavuto da Giove.

(Oh, how many times, recalling Psyche, I judged her [93] happy and unhappy: happy for such a husband and unhappy for having lost him, and then exceedingly happy for having him returned by Jove.)[86]

Earlier in the work (*Ameto* xxvi), we find a reference to Lucius' transformation in the description of Pomona's garden which is filled with *rose bianci e vermiglie, molto già disiate da Lucio allora che, asini divenendo, perdè l'umana forma* ('white and red roses once so desired by Lucius when he became an ass and lost his human form').[87] And in chapter XII, Boccaccio draws extensively on Lucius' rapturous account of Fotis' hair (*AA* 2. 8–10) for his description of one of the ladies encountered by Ameto in the company of Lia:

Ma Ameto, il quale non meno l'occhio che l'audito diletta d'essercitare, quello che puote prende della canzone, sanza dalle nuovamente venute levare la vista. Egli rimira la prima, la quale, e non immerito, pensava Diana nel suo avvento; e di quella i biondi capelli, a qualunque chiarezza degni d'assomigliare, sanza niuno maesterio, lunghissimi,

[84] Fiorilla (638) also mentions two other letters (i: *Crepor celsitudinis* and iii: *Nereus amphytrutibus*) contained in Laur. 29.8 (and dated 1339) which display Apuleian diction. Cf. G. Vio, 'Chiose e riscritture apuleiane di Giovanni Boccaccio', *Studi sul Boccaccio* 20 (1992), 139–65.

[85] *Comedia delle ninfe fiorentini (Ameto)*, ed. A. E. Quaglio, in *Tutte le opere di Giovanni Boccaccio*, gen. ed. V. Branca (Verona: Mondadori, 1964), ii. 99; *L'Ameto*, trans. J. Serafini-Sauli (New York: Garland, 1985), 89.

[86] *Ameto* xxxii. 43 (= *Tutte le opere*, ed. Branca, ii. 778); and *L'Ameto*, trans. Serafini-Sauli, 92–3.

[87] *L'Ameto*, trans. Serafini-Sauli, 64. Cf. Mass, 'Tradition, und Innovation', 95.

parte ravolti alla testa nella sommità di quella, con nodo piacevole d'essi stessi, vede raccolti; e altri più corti, o in quello non compressi, fra le verdi frondi della laura ghirlanda più belli sparta vede e raggirati; a altri dati all'aure, ventilati da quelle, quali sopra le candide tempie e quali sopra il dilicato collo ricadendo, più la fanno cianciosa. A quelli con intero animo Ameto pensando, conosce i lunghi, biondi e copiosi capelli essere della donna speziale bellezza; de' quali se essa Citerea, amata nel cielo, nata nell'onde e nutricata in quelle, bene che d'ogni altra grazia piena, si vegga di quelli nudata, appena potrà al suo Marte piacere. Adunque tanta estima la degnità de' capelli alle femine quanta se, qualunque si sia, di preziose veste, di ricche pietre, di rilucenti gemme e di caro oro circundata proceda, sanza quelli in dovuto ordine posti, non possa ornata parere; ma in costei essi, disordinati, più graziosa la rendono negli occhi d'Ameto.[88]

(But Ameto, who took pleasure in exercising the eye as well as the ear, culled what he could of the song, without taking his glance from the newcomers. He admired the first maiden, whom [*sic*] he thought was Diana at her arrival—and not undeservedly. He observed her very long blond hair, worthy of comparison to any splendor, which was gathered in part on top of her head without any artifice, and bound with a lovely knot of her same hair; and other locks, either shorter or not bound in the knot, were still more beautifully dispersed and twisted in a laurel wreath, while still others were blown by the wind around her temples and around her delicate neck, making her even more delightful.

Completely absorbed in her, Ameto recognized that the long abundant blond hair was the special beauty of this maiden; and if Venus, born and nourished in the waves and loved in heaven, were divested of such hair, though perfect in all other graces, she would scarcely appeal to her Mars. Therefore he deems the beauty of her hair so [28] important for a woman that anyone, whoever she may be, though she go covered in precious garments, in rich stones, in glimmering gems and bright gold, without her hair tressed in due order, she cannot seem properly adorned; yet in this maiden the disorder thereof renders her still more charming to Ameto's eyes.)[89]

Through passages such as this, Apuleius' Fotis helps to define Renaissance ideals of feminine pulchritude: the hair as the chief glory of women's beauty; the tresses gathered up 'without any artifice' (*sanza niuno maesterio*); the seeming paradox of graceful 'disorder'.[90] In the sixteenth century, Fotis' *inordinatus ornatus* (*AA* 2. 9) will be easily absorbed into the notion of *sprezzatura* ('artful artlessness', or 'studied nonchalance') that Castiglione establishes as one of the chief marks of the successful courtier. But her 'presence' at such an epiphanic moment in the *Ameto* has a further significance. As we will see again in our discussion of the *Hypnerotomachia Poliphili*, the Fotis-figure is a *mediatrix*, mediating between the carnal and

---

[88] *Ameto* xii. 6–9 in *Tutte le opere*, ed. Branca, ii. 706–7.

[89] *L'Ameto*, trans. Serafini-Sauli, 27–8. Cf. *AA* 2. 9: *Sed in mea Photide non operosus sed inordinatus ornatus addebat gratiam.*

[90] See the accounts of Coluccio Salutati, Francesco Colonna, and Agnolo Firenzuola, *infra.*

the spiritual, the Milesian and the allegorical dimensions of these three works. Almost all of Boccaccio's fictions pose hermeneutic challenges in their blending of high and low elements. Apuleius may have provided a model for combining the two, not only in Fotis but, more generally, in the Platonic theory of *Venus vulgaris* and *Venus caelestis* which he transmitted most famously in the *Apologia* (12. 1–5). In the *De genealogia deorum gentilium* (1.15), Boccaccio draws on the *De dogmate Platonis* (2.14) where Apuleius describes Plato's tripartite division of love:

Quorum primum dixit esse divinum.... Alterum degeneris animi corrupteque voluntatis passionem. Tertium ex utroque permixtum.[91]

(He has said that the first of these is divine... The second is a passion of a degenerate mind and a corrupted will. The third is a mixture of both.)

In the *Amorosa visione* (*c.*1342–3; revised *c.*1355–60), Boccaccio reworks Dante's litany of pagan poets in Limbo (*Inferno* iv. 82–105) in order to display his enhanced knowledge of Classical literature.[92] Painted on the walls of 'a spacious chamber' representing worldly glory, the dreamer sees Lady Wisdom flanked by *sette donne* (the Seven Liberal Arts), upon whom 'fervently' gaze 'the ancient wise men' (*li savii antichi*). Virgil, Homer, Horace, Lucan, Ovid, Juvenal, Terence, Pamphilus, Pindar, and Statius are followed, in eleventh place, by Apuleius:

> *Bell'uom tornato d'asino, soletto*
> *sedevasi il buon Lucio, cui seguiva*
> *quel greco da cui tolle il bel suggetto.*

> (Turned back into a handsome man from ass,
> alone sat good Lucius, followed by
> that Greek from whom he took the pleasing matter.)[93]

Boccaccio's use of Apuleius in the *Decameron* (1349–52, revised 1370–1) has been so well documented that it need not detain us long.[94] In Novella v. 10, Apuleius' baker (*AA* 9. 22–8), is refashioned as a wealthy Perugian, Pietro

---

[91] Quoted by R. Hollander, *Boccaccio's Two Venuses* (New York: Columbia UP, 1977), 154. Hollander has built an entire reading of Boccaccio's vernacular works upon the play between a 'Heavenly' and an 'Earthly Venus'. Note the replacement of *voluptas* by *voluntas* in Boccaccio's version.

[92] For the dates, see V. Branca, introd. to *Amorosa Visione*, trans. R. Hollander et al. (Hanover, NH: UP of New England, 1986), pp. xii and xxii. Apuleius comes ahead of such authors as Euripides, Sallust, Cato, Livy, and Tacitus.

[93] *Amorosa visione* v. 37–9, trans. Hollander et al., 22–3.

[94] E. H. Haight, 'Apuleius and Boccaccio', in her *More Essays on Greek Romances* (New York: Longmans, Green, 1945), 113–41; Scobie, 'Influence', 212–13; L. Sanguineti White, *Boccaccio e Apuleio: Caratteri differenziali nella struttura narrativa del 'Decameron'* (Bologna: Edizioni italiane moderne, 1977).

di Vinciolo. Boccaccio preserves the inner tale (*AA* 9. 25) of the fuller's wife
(and her lover betrayed by sulphur fumes), but he boosts consistency of
characterization by revealing Pietro's pederastic tendencies at the outset,
thereby foregoing the 'twist in the tail of the tale' which is such a feature of
sermo milesius. Apuleius' baker surprises readers by exercising the ancient
right of cuckolded husbands to humiliate their cuckolders sexually. After
enjoying his 'most gratifying revenge' (*gratissima ... vindicata perfruebatur,
AA* 9. 28), he has the boy beaten and thrown out of the house. His victory,
however, is short-lived: his divorced wife hires a witch to cause his death.
Boccaccio ignores these darker aspects, turning the baker's ironic promise of a
harmonious *ménage à trois* (*AA* 9. 27) into a comic reality: when a stray
donkey treads, by chance, on the fingers of the lover hidden underneath the
hen-coop, Pietro is delighted to recognize the boy whom he had long been
pursuing himself (*per la sua cattività*).[95]

Novella vii. 2 comes straight from Apuleius' account of the crafty wife who
leans over a storage-jar (*dolium*) while her husband services it from the inside
and her lover attends to her from behind (*AA* 9. 5–7). Boccaccio gives the
adulteress a 'local habitation' (Avorio Street in Naples) and a name (Pero-
nella), but otherwise follows the original very closely.[96] Novella viii. 8 (Zeppo
and Spinelloccio) is far more original, but it adapts elements from both of the
former tales. When Zeppo discovers that he has been cuckolded by his best
friend, he squares the account by making love to Spinelloccio's wife on top of
a chest in which Spinelloccio himself is concealed. At the end of the novella, all
four parties resolve to share everything and live together 'without any dispute
or contention' (*senza alcuna quistione o zuffa*).[97]

If Boccaccio was drawing on φ for the Apuleian content of many of his early
to middle works, he turned elsewhere when he decided (probably in the

---

[95] The theme of an unsatisfied wife with a pederastic husband is also found in the short
theatrical *scena* in Latin elegiac couplets entitled *De Cavichiolo* or *Conquestio uxoris Cavichioli
papiensis.* The piece survives in a number of 15th-cent. manuscripts from Italy and Germany
and has been variously claimed as a 12th- or 13th-cent. comedy inspired by Apuleius, as a source
for the *Decameron*, or as a derivative of it. For a text, see *Teatro goliardico dell'Umanesimo*, ed.
V. Pandolfi and E. Artese (Milan: Lerici, 1965), 31–45. For discussion, see D. Radcliff-Umstead,
The Birth of Modern Comedy in Renaissance Italy (Chicago: U of Chicago P, 1969), 261–2;
I. Gualandri and G. Orlandi, 'Commedia elegiaca o commedia umanistica? Il problema del *De
Cavichiolo*', in *Filologia e forme letterarie: Studi offerti a Francesco Della Corte*, ed. S. Boldrini
et al., 5 vols. (Urbino: Università degli Studi di Urbino, 1987), v. 335–56. According to Scobie
('Influence', 213), *De Cavichiolo* is 'indebted' to Apuleius. However, Gualandri and Orlandi
(337) find no direct correspondences between the two texts.

[96] Cf. M. G. Bajoni, 'La novella del *Dolium* in Apuleio *Metamorfosi* IX, 5–7 e in Boccaccio,
Decameron VII, 2', *Giornale storico della letteratura italiana* 171 [111: 554] (1994), 217–25.

[97] Cf. the baker's words to the boy: *sine ulla controversia vel dissensione tribus nobis in uno
conveniat lectulo* (*AA* 9. 27).

1350s) to make his own copy of *The Golden Ass, Apologia,* and *Florida.*[98] Boccaccio's autograph (Florence Laur. 54.32)—labelled L1 by Robertson—is a copy neither of F (the oldest extant manuscript), nor of φ (the oldest surviving copy of F). Robertson, as we saw in our last chapter, allots it to a group of manuscripts designated as Class I—manuscripts descended (he conjectures) from a copy (now lost) of F made before fol. 160 in F was torn (i.e. before the copying of φ in about 1200). Robertson concludes that B1 (a fourteenth-century MS now held in the British Library as Add. MS 24893 and a direct copy of A1—i.e. Bibl. Ambros. N. 180 sup.) is an ancestor of L1, though between B1 and L1 lies another lost manuscript and there is evidence of contamination from φ. A1 belongs, by Robertson's dating, 'au début du XIVe siècle'.[99] It is clear that, by the time Boccaccio made his own copy (which abounds, as Marchesi puts it, in 'distorted words and disordered and incomprehensible phrases'), a complex textual stemma had already evolved.[100]

Boccaccio the Encyclopaedist

Apuleius clearly had a formative and enduring influence on Boccaccio's vernacular works. Indeed, the influence of these reworked Apuleian elements on Renaissance dream-visions, prose fiction, and comic drama would require a volume by itself. It was on his encyclopaedic treatises, however, that Boccaccio rested his hopes of immortality. In the *De genealogia deorum gentilium* (1360, revised up to 1374), Boccaccio purposed to represent the whole pagan pantheon within a framework of relationships, beginning with Demogorgon, the god created by a misreading of Plato's term, Demiourgos.[101] Boccaccio calls Apuleius a 'philosopher of no mean authority' (*non mediocris auctoritatis*)[102] and, in Book 5, ch. 22, he affords Psyche ample space in the pantheon:

De Psyche .xv. Apollinis filia. c. xxii.

Psyches (ut dicit Martialis [sic] *Capella in libro quem de nuptiis Mercurii & Philologiæ scripsit) filia fuit Apollinis & Eudelichiæ* [sic]. *Ex qua Lutius Apuleus* [sic] *in libro*

---

[98] Marchesi ('Giovanni Boccaccio e i codici di Apuleio', 1010) posited a date of *c*.1338, doubtless in response to the date of the *Mavortis miles* (1339), but the critical consensus points to a date 'dopo la metà del Trecento'. Thus Fiorilla (635 n. 1). Coulter ('Boccaccio and the Cassinese Manuscripts', 223) suggested *c*.1350; A. C. de la Mare thought that it 'probably' belonged to the 'later 1350s'. See *The Handwriting of Italian Humanists*, vol. i, fasc. i. (Oxford: OUP for Association Internationale de Bibliophilie, 1973), 26–7.

[99] Introd. to Budé text, p. lxiv.

[100] Marchesi, 1010.

[101] For Demiourgos, see Plato, *Republic* 530a.

[102] *De genealogia deorum* 1. 5.

metamorphoseon: qui uulgariori uocabulo asinus aureus appellatur: longiusculam recitat fabulam talem. Regem scilicet fuisse & reginam: quibus tres fuere filiæ: quarum duæ maiores natu: & si forma spectabiles essent: iunior: cui Psyches nomen erat: in tantum pulchritudine cæteras excedebat mortales: ut non solum admiratione teneret spectantes: sed infigeret animis ignaris rei miraculo credulitatem: ut Venus esset: quæ descendisset in terris: & fama longe latequæ uulgata inuisæ formositatis egit: ut non solum ciues: sed exteri ad uisendam Venerem: ac sacram honorandam accederent: templis uerae Veneris neglectis. Quod ægre Venus ferens in Psychem accensa Cupidini filio suo iussit: ut eam amore seruentissimo hominis extremae sortis incenderet. Interim pater de nuptiis uirginis Milesium Apollinem consuluit. Qui respondit: ut illam in uertice montis deduceret: ibique diuina stirpe creatum: esto pessimum & uipereum nanciscere tur uirgo maritum. Quo responso parentes affecti cum lacrimis & moerore totius ciuitatis uirginem in praedestinatum deduxere culmen: ibique solam liquere. Quæ & si solitudine & incerto timore futuri coniugis anxiaretur: non tamen diu perstitit: et uenit Zephyrus mitis & suaui spiritu eam assumens: in floridam detulit uallem: in qua cum aliquali somno lenisset ærumnam: surgens uidit gratum oculis nemus: & argenteis undis manantem fontem: atque palatium non solum regium: sed diuinum miris ornatum diuitiis. Quod cum intrasset: & ingentes inuenisset thesauros absque custode: & [new page] *miraretur plurimum obsequentium uocibus absque corporibus auditis intrauit lauacrum: inuisis sibi assistentibus obsequiosis. Inde coena diuinis conferta dapibus sumpta: cubiculum intrans: conscendit genialem torum & soporatae maritus affuit. Qui cum eam sibi fecisset coniugem ueniente luce inuisus abiit: & sic sæpius magna Psychis consolatione continuans factum est: ut sorores eiusdem: audito Psychis infortunio: e domibus maritorum ad lugubres parentes accederent: & cum eis sororis infoelices nuptias deflerent. At cupido præsentiens quid inuidia sororum pararetur Psychi eam præmonuit: ut earum omnino floccifaceret lachrymas nec in suam perniciem pia atque credula esset. Quod cum spopondisset Psyches: se caepit deplorare captiuam: & quod sorores uidere: & alloqui non posset: & uenientem atque redarguentem Cupidinem præcibus in eam sententiam traxit: ut cum eis loqui posset: Zephiroque iuberat: ut eas ad se leni deferret flatu. Qui cum fecisset concessit etiam ut ex thesauris: quos liberet asportare permitteret: sed earum suasionibus nullo modo crederet nec suam uidere formam alicuius consilio exoptaret. Tandem complorata domi Psyche a sororibus: scopulum conscendere: & ululatu foemineo redintegrato: a Psyche autitæ sunt: atque paucis consolatae uerbis: & postremo illas Zephirus Psychis imperio in uallem detulit amoenam. Ibi a Psyche festiua congratula- tione susceptæ sunt: eisque omnes ostensæ ditiæ: ex quibus inuidiæ factæ sorores. ei totis suasere uisibus* [sc. uiribus] *: ut uiri formam conaretur uidere: quæ credula eis cum donis remissis: nouaculam parauit: nocte sequenti uisura: quisnam esset is cuius uteretur concubitu: occisura eum: si esset illi forma uerbis sororum conformis. Intrat igitur more solito lectum cupido & in somnum soluitur: Psyches uero aperto lumine uidet illum mira formositate conspicuum iuuenem: alis prenicibus insignitum: & ad eius pedes arcum & pharetram sagittis confertam: ex quibus cum unam mirabundam eduxisset expertura aciem adeo digito impressit suo: ut aliqualis scaturiret euulnere sanguis Quo facto miro dormientis adhuc amore flagrauit. Dumque illum stupescens inspiceret: fauillula ex lucerna prosiluit: dexterum dormientis humerum. Quamobrem expergefactus Cupido* *repente fugam arripuit. Verum Psyches: cum illum cœpisset crure atque fortiter teneret: tandiu ab eo per aerem delata est: donec fessa: eo dimisso caderet. Cupido autem in uicinam cupressum euolans longa quærela eam redarguit: se ipsum ob eius pulcritudine uulnerasset: & inde euolauit. Psyches anxia perditi uiri mori uoluit: fraude tandem sorores ambas: quarum consiliis in ærumnam uenerat: in præcipicium deduxit. Inde a Venere obiurgata acriter: & pedissequis eius lacessita uerberibus: in labores mortali inexplicabiles iussu Veneris implicita: opere uiri adiuta perfecit inuicta: cuius postremo ad Iouem præcibus actum est: ut in ueneris deuenerit gratiam: & in cælis assumpta Cupidinis perpetuo frueretur coniugio: cui peperit uoluptatem.*[103]

(Psyche—as Martianus Capella says in the book he wrote concerning the *Marriage of Mercury and Philology*—was the daughter of Apollo and Endelechia.[104] Lucius Apuleius relates (at considerable length) the following story about her in his book *The Metamorphoses*, which is known by the more common title of *The Golden Ass*: There were once a king and a queen who had three daughters. The elder two were remarkable in their appearance, but the younger, whose name was Psyche, so much surpassed other mortals in her beauty that she not only bound onlookers in wonder, but planted in their ignorant minds a readiness to believe in something miraculous—that she was Venus who had come down to earth. And the fame of this unseen beauty spread far and wide with the result that not only citizens, but foreigners too, came to see this Venus and reverence her with sacrifices, while the temples of the true Venus were neglected. Venus, bearing this badly against Psyche, ordered her son, Cupid, to burn Psyche with a most slavish love for a man of the basest condition.

Her father, meanwhile, consulted Apollo at Miletus about the maiden's marriage. Apollo replied that he should lead her to the top of the mountain and there the maiden would obtain a husband, born of divine stock, but most wicked and serpent-like. Moved by this reply, her parents, to the tears and grief of the whole state, led her to the appointed ridge and left her there alone. And although she was troubled by being alone and by the uncertain fear of her husband-to-be, she did not stay long. For Zephyrus, the gentle West Wind, lifted her up and brought her down to a valley filled with flowers where she soothed her distress with a little sleep. Getting up, she saw an eye-pleasing wood and a fountain flowing with silver waters, and a palace adorned with marvellous riches, fit not just for a king but for a god. She entered it and found huge stores of treasure without a guard, and she marvelled most of all at hearing the voices of those who waited upon her but had no bodies. She went into the bath where unseen attendants assisted her. Then, after enjoying a meal stuffed with divine banquets, she entered the bedroom and climbed into the marriage-bed. Her husband

---

[103] The extract is taken from the *editio princeps, Genealogiæ deorum gentilium* (Venice: Wendelm of Speier, 1472) (no signatures or folio numbers). To my knowledge, Boccaccio's version of 'Cupid and Psyche', has never, hitherto, been translated into English. The only parts of the *Genealogia* available in English are Books 14 and 15.

[104] On the confusion (which dates back to Cicero, *Tusculan Disputations* 1. 10) of Aristotelian ἐντέλεχεια ('absoluteness, actuality') with ἐνδελέχεια ('continuance, constancy'), see the discussion of Martianus Capella in Ch. 1 (*supra*) esp. 37 n.93.

joined her once she was asleep. When he had made her his wife, he went away at the approach of dawn, unseen.

As this went on in this way with increased frequency—to the great consolation of Psyche—it happened that her sisters, having heard of Psyche's misfortune, came from their husbands' homes to their mourning parents, and wept with them for the unhappy marriage of their sister. But Cupid, anticipating what the sisters' envy would contrive for Psyche, forewarned her that she should take no account at all of their tears and that she should not—to her own destruction—be dutiful and trusting. When she had promised this solemnly, Psyche began to bemoan her captivity and her inability to see her sisters and speak with them. And although Cupid took issue with her and contradicted her, by her entreaties she dragged him to the decision that she should be able to see her sisters and that he would order Zephyrus to carry them down to her on a gentle breeze. Having done this, he also conceded that he would allow them to take away whatever they wanted from the treasure-stores, but she should not in any way give credence to their exhortations, nor, by either sister's advice, should she long to see what he looked like.

At last, when Psyche had been mourned at home by her sisters, they climbed the rock and, having renewed their womanly wailing, they were heard by Psyche and found comfort in a few words. And finally, at Psyche's command, Zephyrus brought them down into the pleasant valley. There they were received by Psyche with joyful thanksgiving and shown all the riches, at which the sisters became envious. They urged her, with all their powers, to try and see what her husband looked like. The credulous Psyche, after sending them home with gifts, procured a razor and hid a lamp underneath a peck, intending to see, the following night, just who this man was who enjoyed her company in bed and to kill him, if his appearance accorded with the sisters' description.

Cupid therefore gets into bed in his ususal manner and slips into sleep. But Psyche, with the lamp uncovered, beheld him: a young man remarkable for his extraordinary beauty, distinguished by his shining wings. At his feet she saw the bow and quiver crammed with arrows, one of which, full of wonder, she drew forth to test the point. But she pushed it so hard against her finger that some blood gushed out, at which she burned with an astonishing love for him while he still slept. And while she was gazing at him, dumbfounded, a tiny spark leapt forth from the lamp onto his right shoulder as he slept. Awakened by this, Cupid suddenly took flight. But Psyche seized him by the leg and held on tight and was carried by him through the air until, exhausted, she let go of him and fell. But Cupid, flying up to a nearby cypress, reproved her in a long accusation, censuring himself because, having been sent by his mother to burn Psyche with love for the meanest man, he had wounded his very own self because of her beauty. Then he flew away.

Distressed by the loss of her husband, Psyche wanted to die. Finally, by means of deceit, she brought to a precipitous end the two sisters, by whose counsel she had come to grief. Then, harshly punished by Venus, struck with blows by her attendants, and entangled, by Venus' command, in tasks inexplicable to a mortal, she made it through to the end, unvanquished, helped by the efforts of her husband, by whose entreaties to Jupiter it was finally settled that she should come into Venus' favour and, assumed into heaven, enjoy the eternal wedlock of Cupid to whom she bore Pleasure.)

Boccaccio, we see, gives a very full précis of the first part of the story, describing the effects of Psyche's beauty, the jealousy of Venus, the terms of Apollo's oracle, the enchantments of the palace, and the intrigues of the wicked sisters. Yet the account is truncated at the point where Cupid deserts Psyche after being scorched by the lamp. Only the baldest mention is made of Psyche's wish to die, her revenge upon the sisters, and her harsh treatment at the hands of Venus; and the long sequence of trials is conveyed in a mere phrase, 'tasks inexplicable to a mortal' (*labores mortali inexplicabiles*). After mentioning the birth of Pleasure, Boccaccio turns to exegesis:

Serenissime rex: si huius tam grandis fabulæ adunguem sensum: enucleare uoluerimus: in ingens profecto uolumen euaderet: & ideo cur Apollinis & Endelechiæ filia dicatur Psyches: quæ eius sorores: & cur Cupidinis dicatur coniunx: cum paucis ex contingentibus dixisse satis sit. Psyches ergo anima interpretatur. Hæc autem Apollinis id est solis filia dicitur: eius scilicet qui mundi uera lux est deus: cum nullius alterius potentiæ sit rationalem creare animam: nisi dei. Endelichia autem (ut dicit Calcidius super Thymeo Platonis) perfecta aetas interpretatur: cuius omnino rationalis anima dicitur filia: quia &si in utero matris illam a patre luminum suscipiamus: non tamen eius apparent opera: nisi in ætate perfecta: cum potius naturali quodam instinctu usque ad ætatem perfectam formamur: quam iudicio rationis. Aetate uero perfecta agere incipimus ratione. Ergo bene Apollinis & Endelichiæ filia dicitur. Sunt huic duæ sorores maiores natu: non quia primo natae sint: sed quoniam primo potentia utuntur sua: quarum una uegetatiua dicitur: altera uero sensitiua: quæ non animæ sunt: ut quidam uoluerunt: sed huius animæ sunt potentiæ: quarum ideo Psyches dicitur iunior: quia longe ante eam uegetatiua potentia conceditur foetui: & inde tractu temporis sensitiua. Postremo autem huic Psychi conceditur ratio: & quia primo in actu sunt: ideo primæ dicuntur iunctae coniugio: quod huic rationali diuinæ stirpi seruatur: id est amori honesto: seu ipsi deo: cuius inter delitias a zephyro id est a uitali spiritu: qui sanctus est: defertur: & matrimonio iungitur. Hic coniugi prohibet: ne eum uidere cupiat: ni perdere uelit: hoc est nolit de æternitate sua: de principiis rerum: de omnipotentia uidere per causas: quæ sibi soli nota sunt. nam quotiens talia mortales perquirimus: illum: immo nosmetipsos deuiando perdimus. Sorores autem nonnumquam ad methas usque primas delitiarum Psychis deueniunt: & ex thesauris eius reportant, in quantum penes rationem uiuentes melius opus suum uegetatio peragit: & sensitiuæ uirtutes clariores sunt: & longius perseuerant. Sane inuident sorori: quod minime nouum est: sensualitatem cum ratione discordem: & dum illi blandis uerbis suadere non possunt: ut uirum uideat id est uelit naturali ratione uidere quod amat: & non per fidem cognoscere: eam terroribus conantur inducere: asserentes eum immanem esse serpentem: seque eam deuoraturum. Quod quidem totiens fit: quotiens sensualitas conatur rationem sopire: & ostendere animæ contemplationem: & cognitarum rerum per causam non solum delectationes sensitiuas auferre: sed labores maximos: & angores minime opportunos ingerere: & nil demum placidæ retributionis affere. Anima autem: dum minus prudens: talibus demonstrationibus [new page] *fidem adhibet & quod negatur uidere desyderat, occisura si uoto non correspondeat forma. Videt effigiem uiri pulcherrimam id est extrinseca dei opera. Formam id est diuinitatem uidere non potest: quia deum nemo uidit unquam: & cum fauillula lædit: & uulnerat id est superbo desyderio: per quod inobediens facta: & sensualitati credula: bonum contemplationis admittit: & sic a diuino separatur coniugio. Tandem poenitens & amans perniciem sororum curat astutia: easque adeo opprimit: ut aduersus rationem nullæ sint illis uires: & ærumnis et miseriis purgata, præsumptuosa superbia atque inobedientia: bonum diuinæ dilectionis atque contemplationis iterum reassumit: eique se iniungit perpetuo: dum perituris dimissis rebus in æternam defertur gloriam: & ibi ex amore parturit uoluptatem id est delectationem & lætitiam sempiternam.*

(Most serene Majesty, if we wanted to explain, to a nicety, the meaning of so grand a tale as this, it would extend at once to a huge volume.[105] Let it therefore suffice to say—along with a few related matters—why Psyche is called the daughter of Apollo and Endelechia, who her sisters were, and why she is called the wife of Cupid. Psyche, then, is interpreted as the Soul. She is the daughter of Apollo, that is, of the Sun, who obviously is God, the true light of the world, since it is within no one's power but God's to create the rational soul. Endelechia—as Calcidius[106] says in his commentary on Plato's *Timaeus*—is interpreted as being mature age. Her completely rational soul is said to be her daughter because, although we receive her in our mother's womb from the Father of Lights, her works only become apparent in mature age since, until mature age, we are directed rather by a certain natural instinct, than by the judgement of reason. But in mature age we begin to act with reason. Therefore, she is aptly called the daughter of Apollo and Endelechia. She has two elder sisters, not because they were born first but because they use their power first, one of which is called the vegetative, the other, indeed, the sensitive. These are not souls as some would have it, but are powers of this soul. For this reason, Psyche is said to be younger than they, since, long before her, the vegetative—and thereafter, in the course of time, the sensitive—power is granted to the foetus. But, at last, reason is granted to this Psyche and because they [i.e. the elder sisters] are first to act, for that reason, they are said to be joined first in marriage. In the case of this rational sister, marriage is preserved for divine stock—that is, for honourable Love, or God himself. She is brought down into the midst of his pleasures by Zephyrus, that is, by the life-giving Spirit, which is holy, and is joined in matrimony. He forbids his wife to attempt to see him, unless she wants to lose him; that is, she should not try to investigate the causes of his own eternity, the principles of things, his omnipotence, things which are known to him alone. For whenever we mortals seek such things, we lose him, nay, our very selves, by turning from the straight road. But the sisters, on several occasions, come to the first limits of Psyche's delights and take from her treasury, in so far as—living things being possessed of reason—the vegetative principle completes her work better and the powers of the

---

[105] Boccaccio dedicates the work to Hugo, King of Cyprus and (titular) King of Jerusalem (reg. 1324–59).

[106] See *Platonis Timaeus interprete Chalcidio cum eiusdem commentario*, ed. J. Wrobel (Leipzig: Teubner, 1876), 258.

senses are brighter and endure longer. The sisters are indeed envious, which is nothing strange given the discord between reason and sensuality; and while they are unable, with their inticing words, to persuade her to see her husband—that is, to try to see with the natural reason what she loves, rather than knowing through faith—they attempt to force her through fear, claiming that he is a huge serpent and is going to eat her. Indeed, as often as this happens, so often does sensuality attempt to lull reason to sleep and to reveal contemplation to the Soul and, for the sake of knowing things, not only carry off delights for the senses, but also inflict the greatest toils and torments—by no means advantageous—and finally impose retribution of a most ungentle kind. But the Soul, while she is less on her guard, gives credence to such descriptions and desires to see what is denied, planning to kill if the appearance does not correspond to the thing wished for. She sees the gorgeous image of a man, that is, the external works of God. That is, she is not able to see divinity, because no one ever sees God. And when she hurts and wounds him with the embers—that is, with arrogant desire, through which she is made disobedient, and trusting to the capacity for sensation—she loses the gift of contemplation and thus is separated from her divine spouse. Finally, penitent and loving, she sees adroitly to the destruction of her sisters, and so subdues them that they have no power against reason. And, purged by her tribulations and misfortunes, her presumptuous pride and disobedience, she again receives the gift of divine love and contemplation. And so she joins herself to him for ever, and, having renounced mortal things, she is brought into eternal glory and there, out of Love, she gives birth to Pleasure, that is, everlasting happiness and delight.)

In the ninth book, Boccaccio returns, briefly, to the same story. In chapter 4 of the autograph, he quotes extensively from Apuleius' account (*AA* 5. 22) of Cupid as revealed by Psyche (*Apuleius autem, ubi De asino aureo, eum describit formosissimum dormientem sic: Cum videlicet capitis aurei genialem cesariem . . . et quale peperisse venerem non peniteret etc.*).[107] And in chapter 5 of the *editio vulgata*, we find:

De Voluptate filia Cupidinis. Cap. V.

Voluptas ut dicit Apuleius Cupidinis atque Psyches filia fuit. cuius generationis fabula supra, ubi de Psyche latissime dicta est. Cuius figmenti ratio aperietur facile cum enim contingit nos aliquid optare, & optato potiri, proculdubio obtinuisse delectamur. hanc delectationem prisci uoluptatem uocauere.[108]

(Pleasure, as Apuleius says, was the daughter of Cupid and Psyche. The story of her begetting [is given] above where [the story] of Psyche is told in great detail. The reason for this fiction is readily apparent; for when we happen to desire something and obtain the thing desired, we are delighted, doubtless, to have obtained it. This delight, the ancients called Pleasure.)

---

[107] *Genealogie deorum gentilium libri*, ed. V. Romano, 2 vols. (Bari: Laterza, 1951), ii. 451–2.
[108] *Ioannis Bocatii peri genealogias deorum, libri quindecim, cum annotationibus Iacobi Micylli* (Basle: Io. Hervagius, 1532), 223.

Boccaccio seems to embody, in one person, the two conflicting reactions to *The Golden Ass*—able, in the *Decameron*, to respond to the wit, the irony, the ludic quality, of the tales; yet reverting, here, to a mode of exegesis which would not be out of place in the pages of Bernardus Silvestris.[109] His capacity for exegetical ingenuity is often coupled with a kind of critical myopia. He seems quite untroubled, for instance, by the inconsistency of making Psyche the daughter of Apollo (following Martianus Capella) and then sending her father to consult Apollo's oracle.[110] This apparently schizoid quality may be the result of critical interventions. The text given above is that of the *editio vulgata*. Boccaccio's autograph manuscript (Biblioteca Laurenziana, Pluteo 52.9) provides a much fuller account of the Apuleian narrative.[111] Luisa Vertova observes that '[t]he nature of the changes, and the correspondence between Boccaccio and Pietro Piccolo da Monteforte *c.*1372, make it clear that Boccaccio's critics imposed on him the cuts in the narrative and the more orthodox, Aristotelian exegesis.'[112]

Yet even this 'more orthodox' version preserves Boccaccio's awareness that the tale does not function on the allegorical level alone. The *Genealogia* is not merely a compendium of mythology: the preface and the last two books serve as a defence of fiction.[113] Particularly interesting is Boccaccio's adaptation in Book 14 of Macrobius' distinction between different types of fiction. The fourth kind of fiction, he tells us, contains 'no truth at all, neither on the surface, nor hidden within, since it is merely the invention of rambling old women'.[114] Such fictions have nothing to do with the works of poets. Boccaccio brings his argument under the rein of Horace when he says that (the valuable sort of) fictions 'please the unlearned on first contact and exercise the wits of the learned with their hidden truths, thus giving profit and delight in one and the same reading'.[115] Nonetheless, he also cites the tale of 'Cupid

---

[109] Boccaccio's analysis seems, in fact, to owe much, if not to Bernardus himself, then certainly to the tradition in which he was writing.

[110] To be fair, Boccaccio does disclaim, in his dedicatory epistle, any intention of harmonizing contradictory sources: *satis erit mihi comperta rescribere, et disputationes philosophantibus linquere* ('It will be enough for me to reproduce what I have ascertained and leave disputes to philosophers'); but his confusion of paternity takes this principle to an absurd degree.

[111] *Genealogie deorum gentilium libri*, ed. V. Romano, 2 vols. (Bari: Laterza, 1951), i. 255–61.

[112] 'Cupid and Psyche', 106 n. 10. See G. Martellotti, *Le due redazione delle 'Genealogie' del Boccaccio* (Rome: Edizioni di storia e letteratura, 1951).

[113] See O. Hecker, ed., *Boccaccio-Funde* (Brunswick: Westermann, 1902) for a Latin text (*editio vulgata*). For an English translation, see C. G. Osgood, *Boccaccio on Poetry: Being the Preface and the Fourteenth and Fifteenth Books of Boccaccio's 'Genealogia Deorum Gentilium'* (Princeton: PUP, 1930). The translations that follow, however, are my own.

[114] *De genealogia deorum* 1.4. 9 (Hecker, 217): *Quarta quidem species nil penitus in superficie nec in abscondito ueritatis habet, cum sit delirantium uetularum inuentio.*

[115] Hecker, 219: *tanti quidem sunt fabulae, ut earum primo contextu oblectentur indocti, et circa abscondita doctorum exerceantur ingenia, et sic una et eadem lectione proficiunt et delectant.* Cf. Horace, *Ars poetica* 333: *aut prodesse volunt aut delectare poetae* ('Poets desire either to benefit or to delight').

and Psyche' (told by one of those 'little old women' he has lately disparaged) amongst his examples of fictions that can provide refreshment (to the minds of great men worn out by cares of state) and consolation (to Charite grieving at her captivity).[116] The most remarkable shift, however, comes at the end when he says that 'there was never a little old woman so rambling . . . that she did not sense some meaning beneath the guise of the things she told' (*nullam esse usquam tam delirantem aniculam . . . que sub pretextu relatorum non sentiat aliquem . . . sensum*).[117] Boccaccio is groping towards a theory that will finally incorporate 'pure fictions' (*aniles fabulae*) into the canon of 'respectable' literature. The cracks are widening in the Horatian edifice.

Stefano Colonna and Simone da Brossano

A vivid dramatization of the confrontation between scholastic and humanist tastes is given in an exchange of letters (written at some time after 1371 and before 1375) between a cleric, Stefano Colonna, and Simone da Brossano, Archbishop of Milan.[118] Colonna had written to the archbishop at Avignon, asking him 'to supply the book which one delights to entitle *On the Monarchy of the Present Time*' (*De monarchia moderni temporis*) which Brossano had said was held there.[119] Colonna may have been asking for a pseudo-Apuleian work, the *De monarchia* (probably composed between the late twelfth and early fourteenth centuries), or he may have been making a coded comment on the 'asinine' state of contemporary political or ecclesiastic leadership by playing between the titles of this work and the *De asino aureo* (the work that he really wanted). In any case, the book had not been received and when Colonna repeated his request, he received only a rebuke, emphatic, though not devoid of irony:

It pleases you to entitle this book, *On the Monarchy of the Present Time;* but it would have pleased more if you had said simply, *On Monarchy.* . . . For it is [known] amongst certain men as *Concerning the Ass* and just so is the web [*textura*] of the book. How,

---

[116] Hecker, 219.   [117] Ibid. 218.

[118] The terminal dates are provided by A. Coville, 'Une correspondence à propos d'Apulée, 1371–1375', *Humanisme et Renaissance* 2 (1935), 203–15. The letters are printed in Petrarch, *Opera omnia*, ii. 1233–6. See Costanza, 68. On Brossano, see *DBI* 14 (1972), 470–4. There were many Stefanos in the Colonna family (see *DBI*). Petrarch addresses at least two of them in his *Epist. Fam.* (3. 3, 4; 8. 1; 15. 7; and 20. 11).

[119] See B. G. Kohl and N. G. Siraisi, 'The *De Monarchia* attributed to Apuleius', *Mediaevalia* 7 (1984 for 1981), 1–39. Kohl and Siraisi (3 and 13) identify the Apuleian enthusiast with the Stefano Colonna (d. 1379) who was provost of the chapter of Saint-Omer (diocese of Thérouanne, near Calais), grandson of Sciarra Colonna, brother of Agapito, and uncle of Odone Colonna (subsequently Pope Martin V). Agapito and Stefano were both made cardinals in 1378.

therefore, will you associate with the others? For it is written: 'Thou shalt not plough with an ox and an ass together.'[120]... Don't become an ass, nor 'like a horse or mule in which there is no power of intellect'.[121]

'I do not cherish', the archbishop remarks, 'the adulation expressed in your letter for the book of Apuleius'.[122] The desire for such a work threatens not merely 'ignorance' (*ignorantia*), but 'mental aberration' (*alienatio mentis*), 'crippling of the faculties' (*sensuum debilitas*), and 'weakness of reason' (*infirmitas rationis*). He asks Colonna how he can strive 'for the fabulous and the feigned which the Holy Spirit shuns' (*quomodo ergo fabulosum & fictum ambis, quem spiritus sanctus effugit?*), reminding him of St Paul's prohibition on the reading of old wives' tales (*saltem addere debeas, ut secundum Apostolum ad fabulas non fiat conuersio*). Colonna, Brossano warns, has crossed that fine line between the acceptable and the reprehensible use of pagan authors: 'I believed that you were going to this book as a scout; now, it appears, as a deserter'.[123] There is, however, in Master Nicholas of Sicily—a reliable theologian of the old school—some 'hope of a remedy, of an expiation of this vice'.[124] It will be Colonna's 'safest defence and wholesome refuge, to drink from his fount and to eat crumbs beneath his table'.[125]

Colonna opens his reply with a consideration of the competing merits of the Stoic and Peripatetic teachings on the regulation of the passions. He goes on to invoke the allegorical metaphors of 'the sweet kernel which the dry casing conceals' (*dulcis nucleus, quem arida testa celat*) and the 'sweet fruits lying hidden beneath bitter leaves' (*subtus amara folia dulcia latent poma*) in order to justify his reading of Apuleius:

Haud aliter de Apuleij libro dicere uelim. Curiosam fortè & fabulosam continet & lasciuam, sub qua, ueluti sub uirentium & luxuriantium foliorum umbraculis, gratissimus fructus absconditur, profunda & altissima iacet sententia, quam summo studio, meliori ingenio, toto conatu, maximo ocio, multoqúe sudandi tempore haurienda foret.[126]

---

[120] *Opera omnia*, ii. 1234. Cf. Deuter. 22: 10 (KJV).

[121] Cf. Psalms 32: 9: *Nolite fieri sicut equus & mulus, in quibus non est intellectus* (Vulgate); 'Be ye not as the horse, or as the mule, which have no understanding' (KJV).

[122] *Opera omnia*, ii. 1233: *Ambitionem tamen libri Apuleij literis tuis impressam, non amplector.*

[123] Ibid. 1234: *sed credebam te ad hunc librum, ut exploratorem transire, nunc apparet quasi transfugam.* Cf. Seneca, *Epistolae ad Lucilium* 1. 2. 5 (introducing a quotation from Epicurus): *soleo enim et in aliena castra transire, non tamquam transfuga, sed tamquam explorator* ('For it is my custom to cross over into the enemy's camp, not as a deserter but as a scout'). Ben Jonson inscribed the motto *Tamquam explorator* in many of the books in his possession.

[124] *Opera Omnia*, ii. 1234: *huius tamen uitij expiationis est remedij spes.*

[125] Ibid.: *tutamen tuum tutissimum erit, & salubre profugium, de fonte eius haurire, et sub mensa micas edere.*

[126] Ibid. 1235.

(I should like to speak about Apuleius' book in the same way. It contains, perhaps, curious, fabulous, and lascivious [material], under which, as though beneath the shady bowers of flourishing and luxuriant leaves, most welcome fruit is concealed, profound and most lofty meaning lies which would have to be drunk with the greatest exertion, a good deal of talent, with the greatest leisure and a great period of sweating.)

Brossano had criticized Colonna for squandering the brief but precious span allotted to us on 'pernicious curiosity' (*noxia curiositas*) and 'superfluous vacuity' (*superuacua uanitas*) of this kind;[127] but Colonna disagrees:

Sanè hoc in studio non tempus perditur, sed colligitur & seruatur. Nam fictum haud ambigo, nec fucum amplector, sed philosophantium ueras cum ratione insector senten- tias, & uarijs cuniculis usque penè ad centrum terræ descendens, cupidus sub mundi machina, auri uenas exquiro. Quod cum in parte fecisse rebar, cum à te de aureo asino Apuleij librum, quem sic apud quosdam intitulatum asseris, obtinere potuissem, non equidem perscrutaturus fabulas, sed illius antiqui Poëtæ adepturus philosophiam, haud aliter, quam sub sterquilinio margaritas.[128]

(Indeed time is not lost in this study, but is collected and preserved. For I do not debate what is feigned; nor do I embrace drossy dissimulation; but I pursue with reason the true meanings of the philosophers and in diverse mines, descending almost as far as the centre of the earth, eager beneath the fabric of the world, I search out veins of gold. I thought that I had accomplished this in part when I was in a position to have from you that book of Apuleius *On the Golden Ass*, which you claim is so-called amongst certain people, not, indeed, planning to examine fables, but to obtain the philosophy of that ancient poet, in the very same way as pearls under a dung-heap.)

And while 'the curious fables of the poets delight a great many people in this age', they hold no attraction for Colonna—except in so far as they constitute 'that reward and welcome respite from studying which must, by order of Quintilian, be given to all'.[129]

It is significant that Colonna identifies his own age as one in which 'a great many people' are attracted to stories. One wonders how sincere he is in his expressed disdain for such things—seeking only the kernel of Truth contained in the ugly husk of fabulation. There is a tendency to view the allegorical mode of interpreting myth as an exclusively medieval phenomenon; but it belongs as much to the Renaissance as to the Middle Ages. The *Ovide moralisé* only appears at the beginning of the fourteenth century at a time when humanism is just getting under way in Italy.[130] It is easy, from the perspective

---

[127] Ibid. 1233.   [128] Ibid. 1235.

[129] Ibid.: *Et quanquam plurimos huius æui delectent, me autem non alliciunt curiosæ Poëtarum fabulæ præter illa, quandoque mercede & accepta studendi remissione, quæ omnibus danda est iubente Quintiliano...*

[130] The tradition is continued through the Ovidian moralizations of Pierre Bersuire (*c.*1340), Arthur Golding (1565/7), and George Sandys (1626).

of the twenty-first century, to be amused at the convoluted attempts of humanists to justify the enjoyment of something that we take for granted— entertaining fiction. But ours is an age in which the novel is the pre-eminent literary form. The triumph of fiction has taken place in two stages: the first task was to justify the value of fiction in the face of powerful detractors— philosophers and the Church—and allegory was a valuable ally in this campaign. The second stage occurs relatively late in the Renaissance: the final escape from allegory and the proclamation of the autonomous value of fiction. In both these campaigns, Apuleius' novel figures prominently.

COLUCCIO SALUTATI AND HIS CIRCLE

Lucius' trichophiliac musings in reponse to Fotis (*AA* 2. 8–9) are cited with approval in the *De laboribus Herculis* by Coluccio Salutati (1331–1406), chancellor of Florence, and successor to Petrarch and Boccaccio as the leading exponent of quattrocento humanism. In Book 3, ch. 42, Salutati uses Fulgentius' reading (*Mitologiae* 1. 21) of Medusa as 'forgetfulfulness' (*oblivio*) in order to gloss the third gorgon as a personification of Rhetoric (which causes former concepts to be forgotten):

Hec ultima pulcrior est reliquis, decore presertim in crinibus, quoniam ornamentis (que per crines significantur, qui sunt, ut demonstrat Apulegius, precipuum mulierum decus. Nam si tollantur, nulla fuerit adeo pulcra quin turpissima videatur) et circumstantiis rhetorica florescat oratio... [131]

(The last of these [*sc.* Medusa] is more beautiful than the others, especially in respect of her hair, since it is in its ornaments (which are signified by the hair, which is, as Apuleius demonstrates, the chief glory of woman. For, should her hair be removed, there is no woman so fair that she would not seem most foul) and in its incidental details that rhetorical speech flourishes...)

Salutati was acquainted with Zanobi da Strada and possessed a copy of the *Metamorphoses*, *Apologia*, and *Florida* (B3) which he seems to have annotated in his 'middle period (from 1370 onwards)'.[132] Regine May has done much to illuminate the significance of this manuscript, drawing particular attention to Salutati's innovation in rewriting the prologue (*AA* 1. 1) as verse—a reflection of his awareness of its affinities with Plautine comedy.[133] Salutati's decision

---

[131] *De laboribus Herculis*, 2 vols., ed. B. L. Ullman (Zurich: Thesaurus Mundi, 1951), i. 417. Cf. May, 'Prologue', 286–7.

[132] May, 'Prologue', 282 and 285. For the identification of Salutati's hand, see de la Mare, *Handwriting*, 42 and 34 n. 2.

[133] May, 'Prologue', esp. 298–300.

influenced a number of manuscripts and sparked a long-running debate about the metrical status of Apuleius' opening.[134] His legacy is still visible in Renaissance translators such as Louveau, Adlington, and Pomponio Vizani (who translate some or all of the prologue into verse) and it raised important questions about the genre of *The Golden Ass*, leading Lodovico Castelvetro— in his *Poetica d'Aristotele vulgarizzata et sposta* (1570/1576)—to place Apuleius (along with Petronius, Boethius, Martianus Capella, and Iacopo Sannazaro) in the class of works which 'are to be considered monstrous' for combining verse and prose 'into a single body'.[135]

After his death, Coluccio Salutati's manuscript of Apuleius (B3) was acquired by Sozomeno da Pistoia (aka Zomino di Ser Bonifazio, 1387–1458), 'one of the Poggio group of humanists at Florence, where he had the chair of Poetry and Rhetoric'.[136] Poggio Bracciolini (1380–1459), the book-hunter responsible for the recovery and preservation of a significant fraction of the ancient literature now extant, had been a student of Salutati's and he draws on Apuleius' *Florida* 22. 3 in a speech to the Council of Constance in 1417.[137] Poggio was also the first to make the pseudo-Lucianic *Ass* available in Latin. In the preface (*ad Cosmam de Medicis*), Poggio discusses the circumstances of his discovery of the text and his view of its relation to Apuleius' work.[138] He is concerned to relate his own perception of Apuleius to received authority (the judgement of St Augustine) even as he indicates how his own knowledge supersedes that received opinion. At first, he tells us, he believed (with Augustine) that what Apuleius described 'had either happened to him himself or was his own invention and fabrication' (*existimabam, aut sibi ipsi*

---

[134] R. H. F. Carver, '*Quis ille?* The Role of the Prologue in Apuleius' *Nachleben*', in *A Companion to the Prologue*, ed. Kahane and Laird, 165–7; May, 'Prologue', 298–308.

[135] *Castelvetro on the Art of Poetry*, trans. A. Bongiorno (Binghamton: MRTS, 1984), 12. Cf. Carver, '*Quis ille?*', 166–7.

[136] BL, MS Harley 4838. The description in *A Catalogue of the Harleian Manuscripts in the British Museum* (London: British Museum, 1808), iii. 210, ends with the note, *Sequuntur quaedam de auctore, ex Macrobio et Augustino* ('Extracts from Macrobius and Augustine, concerning the author, follow'). Zomino bequeathed his books to the library of the Sapienza at Pistoia where they remained until the dispersal of the collection in the early 18th cent. The MS was obtained on 22 June 1726 by John Gibson, a Scottish book-buyer who 'dealt in MSS. and early printed books acquired in Italy through agents apparently operating from Florence from 1720 onwards.' See C. Wright, *Fontes Harleiani* (London: British Museum, 1972), 162. May ('Prologue', 287 n. 34) notes the presence of marginalia (*de Fotide* and *de capillis*) to *AA* 2. 8 f. on fol. 141ʳ, though 'The hand could be Sozomeno's rather than Salutati's.'

[137] *Oratio ad padres reverendissimos*, in R. Fubini, *Umanesimo e secolarizzazione da Petrarca a Valla* (Rome: Bulzoni, 1990), 329. Quoted by D. Marsh, 'Alberti and Apuleius: Comic Violence and Vehemence in the *Intercenales* and *Momus*', in *Leon Battista Alberti: Actes du Congrès International de Paris*, ed. F. Furlan et al., 2 vols. (Paris: Librairie Philosophique J. Vrin; Turin: Nino Aragno, 2000), i. 405–26, at 405. On Poggio's links with Salutati, see May, 'Prologue', 282–3.

[138] *Poggii . . . Facetiarum liber // accessit Lucii Philosophi Syri comoedia lepidissima, quæ asinus intitulatur* (Cracow: n.pub., 1592), 169–70.

quod scripserat accidisse, aut extitisse id inuentum). The discovery of the *Ass*, however, makes him see that this 'renovated comedy by Apuleius was in no way to be accepted as real' (*ab Apuleio, veluti innouatum comœdiam nequaquam esse pro vero accipiendam*).

There is some evidence that Apuleius' own *Ass* had been translated by the middle of the fifteenth century. In Book 1, chapter 6 of *De politia litteraria* ('On literary polish'), the Ferrarese humanist Angelo Camillo Decembrio (1415–67?) depicts the Prince of Ferrara, Leonello d'Este (1407–50), discussing the merits of vernacular literature with Feltrino Boiardo (d. 1456):

Feltrinus intercepit: Quid autem de Apuleio et Asino nostro aureo? De quo ut abundantius cum meis ridere possem, eum ego ipse in uernaculum sermonem transtuli: an non ea fabula ut plautina delectat? At Leonellus: Equidem inter fabulosa recipiendum arbitror. Cuius stilus ideo uarius incompositus rigidusque, [Witten: *quod*] *auctori graeco minor fuerit nostri sermonis familiaritas.*

(Feltrino interrupted: 'But what about Apuleius and our *Golden Ass*? In order to spread my amusement more widely among my friends, I myself translated him into the vernacular tongue. Or does that tale not delight like a Plautine play?' But Leonello: 'I certainly think that it should be counted amongst fictitious works. His style is varied, disordered, unpolished, owing to the fact that, as a Greek author, he was less familiar with our language.')[139]

The *De politia litteraria* is set in the 1440s, but Decembrio's intention of dedicating an early version (comprising Books 1, 2, and 5) to Leonello was thwarted by the prince's death in 1450. The seven-book version (completed by the early 1460s) was dedicated to Pope Pius II (pont. 1458–64).[140] If Feltrino did indeed produce a translation of *The Golden Ass* before his death in 1456, it has left no apparent trace in contemporary manuscripts. We do, however, have the Italian translation (pr. 1518) attributed to Feltrino's grandson, Matteo Mario Boiardo, which will be discussed in the next chapter.

---

[139] Biblioteca Apostolica Vaticana, Vat. Lat. 1794, fol. 17. I am grateful to Dr Danielle Mal-Maeder for sending me her transcription of this passage in 2000. The text in N. Witten's critical edn. of *De politia litteraria* (Munich: Saur, 2002) is identical at this point (1. 6. 1, p. 163) except in minor details of punctuation and the substitution of *rigidus quod* (which I have followed in my translation) for *rigidusque*. The reference to Apuleius as a 'Greek author' doubtless stems from a failure to set the Greek identity assumed by the prologue (*AA* 1. 1) against the evidence for North African origins provided by the *Apologia*, *Florida*, etc. C. S. Celenza's translation ('Apuleius's style was so varied, ill-arranged, and rigid, that, as an author, he had less familiarity with our speech than a Greek') avoids the problem by distorting the natural sense of the Latin. See 'Creating Canons in Fifteenth-Century Ferrara: Angelo Decembrio's *De politia litteraria*, 1.10', *RQ* 57 (2004), 43–98, at 60.

[140] Celenza, 56.

APULEIUS IN ENGLAND

Our researches have shown that copies of the *Apologia*, *Metamorphoses*, and *Florida* were available in Italy (singly, in pairs, or triplets), to those able to look hard enough, in the first three decades of the fourteenth century. The evidence of Petrarch, Boccaccio, and Benvenuto indicates that the work was becoming important in Italy in the latter part of that century. At what stage did it reach England?

Medieval Catalogues

The *Registrum Angliae de libris doctorum et auctorum veterum*—a catalogue of the 'works of the Fathers and a few other authors in English libraries, compiled by the Franciscans in the mid thirteenth century'—contains very few pagan writings (the tragedies of Seneca and the *De senectute* of Cicero are among the exceptions) and makes no mention of Apuleius.[141] But a later compilation, the *Catalogus scriptorum ecclesiae* (which absorbed most of the *Registrum*), is rich in information. This 'comparative Catalogue of Monastic Libraries' was formerly attributed to a certain 'John Boston of Bury' who was thought to have flourished about 1410.[142] His plan (never fully realized) was to

list in alphabetical order all the authors, pagan and secular, of whom any knowledge was to be had, with their dates, the titles of their works, and for each work the number of books contained in it, its first and last words, and references as far as possible to libraries in Great Britain where it might be consulted.[143]

More recent scholarship, however, has identified the compiler as Henry Kirkestede (b. *c.*1314, d. in or after 1378), monk and (from 1361) prior of Bury St Edmunds.[144] The *Catalogus*' entry for Apuleius would seem to give us

---

[141] R. A. B. Mynors, 'The Latin Classics Known to Boston of Bury', in *Fritz Saxl: 1890–1948*, ed. D. J. Gordan (London: Nelson, 1957), 199–217, at 200 n. 1. See *Registrum Anglie de libris doctorum et auctorum veterum,* ed. R. H. Rouse, M. A. Rouse, and R. A. B. Mynors (London: British Library, 1991), R83 and R84, pp. 220–4.

[142] M. R. James, *On the Abbey of S. Edmund at Bury* (Cambridge: Cambridge Antiquarian Soc., 1895), 34.

[143] Mynors, 'Latin Classics', 199.

[144] R. H. Rouse, 'Bostonus Buriensis and the Author of the *Catalogus Scriptorum Ecclesiae*', *Speculum* 41 (1966), 471–99; R. Sharpe, 'Reconstructing the Medieval Library of Bury St Edmunds: The Lost Catalogue of Henry of Kirkstead', in *Bury St Edmunds: Medieval Art, Architecture, Archaeology and Economy,* ed. A. Gransden (Leeds: British Archaeological Assoc., 1998), 204–18. Rouse (*ODNB,* s.v. 'Kirkestede') ascribes the bulk of Kirkestede's work on the *Catalogus* to the period 1338–61.

our most comprehensive overview of the state of access to Apuleius' works in England in the third quarter of the fourteenth century:

APULEIUS Platonicus philosophus Madaurensis floruit ante Incarnationem et scripsit secundum Augustinum libro de ciuitate Dei De deo Socratis *lib. I: 'Quoniam me... nec accessit.'* De uita et moribus Platonis *lib. I.* Cosmographiam *(quidam tamen* [212] *dicunt quod hii tres libri sunt unum uolumen intitulatum* De deo Socratis; *quod puto uerum.) Edidit etiam librum* Peryermenias, *cuius libri commentator Apuleii annumerat librum* Mercurii Trismegisti de Divinitate *etc. Forte Apuleius hunc librum transtulit de Graeco in Latinum et scribitur ei). item composuit* Phedronem. *item* De republica, *secundum Fulgentium libro* De rebus signatis (?) *ad Calcidium. item librum qui dicitur* Hermogoras [sic]. *item librum* Medicinalem. *item* Ephitomen sanctorum Patrum *in 6. item* De asino aureo, *secundum Fulgentium ubi supra. item* De ponderibus et numeris. *item librum* Ludicrorum.[145]

(Apuleius the Platonic Philosopher of Madaura flourished before the Incarnation[146] and wrote, according to Augustine in his book *On the City of God*, one book *On the God of Socrates* (*Quoniam me... nec accessit.*); one book *On the Life and Character of Plato*; the *Cosmographia* (some people, however, say that these three books are a single volume entitled *On the God of Socrates*—and I think that is true). He also produced a book *Peri hermeneias*—the commentator on this book of Apuleius lists a book of Hermes Trismegistus *On Divination* etc. Perhaps Apuleius translated this from Greek into Latin and it is ascribed to him). He also composed a *Phaedo*. According to Fulgentius in his book, *On Guarded Things*, dedicated to Calcidius, he also composed *On the State*. Also a book called *Hermagoras*. Also a *Medical Book*. Also an *Epitome of the Sacred Fathers* in six books. Also, according to Fulgentius (see above), *On the Golden Ass*. Also, *On Weights and Numbers*. Also a book of *Jests*.)

Mynors notes:

Apuleius (with the aid of Vincent of Beauvais V, 6 and 7) makes a brave show of which much might be said; but evidently Boston has had direct access to none of these works except the *De deo Socratis*, for he gives a reference to St John's, Colchester,... this limited knowledge not unfairly represents the impression to be derived of Apuleius from the English catalogues until Duke Humphrey's gifts to Oxford University in 1439 introduce a new world with the *De asino aureo*.

The *Catalogus scriptorum ecclesiae* was undoubtedly an ambitious undertaking, but we should be wary of viewing it as a complete 'Union Catalogue'. M. R. James portrayed 'Boston' as a peripatetic bibliophile, going from library

---

[145] Mynors, 'Latin Classics', 211. Mynors notes, after the curious reference to the *Epitome of the Holy Fathers*, 'The transcriber of our Boston MS (whose spelling I follow) seems to have been puzzled here.'

[146] It is interesting that the *Catalogus* should place Apuleius before Christ since Augustine's reference (*De ciuitate dei* 8. 19) to Apuleius being charged 'before Christian judges' (though wrong in fact) makes the chronology clear.

to library across Britain in search of manuscripts. Mynors anchored him much more firmly in the cloisters of Bury, gathering his information at many removes: 'a monk-librarian...not an itinerant investigator'.[147] Rouse takes an intermediate position, observing Kirkestede's use of Vincent of Beauvais and earlier examples of the *De viris illustribus* tradition (Jerome, Gennadius, Isidore), while noting his visits to at least eleven libraries in East Anglia.[148] The *Catalogus*' use of Augustine's title (*De asino aureo*) and the citation of Fulgentius as the source confirm the impression that Apuleius' novel was *known about* but not *known* in England at this time; but the list is more surprising in its account of the philosophical works. P. G. Walsh expresses a general view when he calls the *De dogmate Platonis* 'one of the best-known accounts of Plato's thought known to the Middle Ages'; but to judge from the the the *Catalogus*, Apuleius would seem to have become less well known as a philosopher since the high point of the twelfth-century renaissance when John of Salisbury quoted him extensively.[149]

The references to lost or spurious works require some clarification. Beryl Smalley tells us that 'Boston' has confused Apuleius with Plato by attributing to one the other's *Republic*.[150] Fulgentius, however, refers in the *Expositio sermonum antiquorum* (Boston's *De rebus signatis*) to a work by Apuleius entitled *De republica*; and Sidonius Apollinaris and Priscian mention his Latin translation of Plato's *Phaedo*.[151] Boston's attribution to Apuleius of a 'Phaedro' is either a scribal error or Boston's own conflation of the *Phaedo* and the *Phaedrus*. Fulgentius and the grammarian Priscian are also the source for a few fragments of the lost novel of Apuleius, *Hermagoras*, and Priscian refers to his *Medicinalia*.[152] The reference to a work, *De ponderibus et numeris* ('On Weights and Numbers'), probably derives from Priscian's quotation from a work of Apuleius entitled *Epitome historiarum*: *Apuleius in epitome: sed tum sestertius dipondium semissem, quinquessis, denarius decussis ualebat*.[153] The bizarre attribution to Apuleius of an *Epitome of the Holy Fathers* may be a dim echo of this same work or, alternatively, a garbled reference to some work which mentions an earlier Apuleius, the disciple of Peter, whose martyrdom at Rome is commemorated on 7 October.[154] Apuleius quotes a poem from his

[147] Mynors ('Latin Classics', 200 n. 1), citing James, *Abbey of S. Edmund*, 34–40.
[148] *ODNB*, s.v. 'Kirkestede'.
[149] P. G. Walsh, ed. and trans., *Andreas Capellanus on Love* (London: Duckworth, 1982), 21.
[150] *English Friars*, 232 n. 2.
[151] Fulgentius' *Expositio* is dedicated to Calcidius.
[152] The references to these and other lost works of Apuleius are given by Butler, *Apologia*, pp. xxvi–xxviii. For Priscian, see Keil, ed., *Grammatici Latini*, ii. 203. 14.
[153] See Butler, *Apologia*, p. xxvii.
[154] W. Smith and S. Cheetham, *A Dictionary of Christian Antiquities*, 2 vols. (London: Murray, 1875), i. 134.

Ludicra in chapter 6 of the *Apologia*, but it would be rash to attribute to Boston knowledge of the *Apologia* on such a basis, since Nonius Marcellus—the fourth-century lexicographer and grammarian from North Africa—quotes a line from the *Ludicra* in his illustration of the word *abstemius*.[155]

Surviving Manuscripts

P. G. Walsh's casual reference to manuscripts of *The Golden Ass* surviving from Britain is unfounded.[156] They are all Italian in origin, but the date of their arrival in England is relevant to their possible influence. Five early manuscripts containing Apuleius' novel are currently held in English libraries. The provenance of E (Eton College 147), O (Bodley, MS Laud. Lat. 55), and B3 (BL, MS Harley 4838) is discussed elsewhere.[157] The British Library contains another two copies of *The Golden Ass*.[158]

B1 (Add. MS 24893) is a fourteenth-century vellum manuscript containing the *De magia apologia* followed by the *Metamorphoses* and the *Florida*, the latter two works being run together to form fourteen books of *Metamorphoses*.[159] The manuscript was acquired by the BM in 1862 and formerly belonged to M. de Bure and the Reverend John Mitford.[160]

B2 (MS Burn. 128) belonged to the collection bequeathed to the British Museum in 1818 by the Reverend Charles Burney (1757–1817). The manuscript has an interesting double title and an intriguing addition (*Hercules*) to the author's name: *Lutii Apulegii Herculis Madaurensis de asino aureo methamorfoseos*.[161] At the front of the manuscript is the inscription *Hunc librum emi… magistro Bartholomeo Cartolario, anno Domini millessimo quadrigentesimo…* ('I bought this book for Master Bartolomeo Cartolari in 1400').[162]

We might note the contents of three other manuscripts in the British Library. MS Egerton 2516 contains only two works by Apuleius, the *De deo*

---

[155] *Nonii Marcelli de compendiosa doctrina libros XX*, ed. W. M. Lindsay, 3 vols. (Leipzig: Teubner, 1903), i. 96. Cited in Pauly-Wissowa (1895), ii, col. 249.

[156] Walsh, *Roman Novel*, 231: 'copies proliferate in the fourteenth and fifteenth centuries, and manuscripts survive from Italy, France and Britain'.

[157] See Ch. 3 (B3), *supra*, and Chs. 6 (*F*) and 8 (0), *infra*.

[158] For a conspectus of Apuleian holdings, see *Index of Manuscripts in the British Library*, vol. 1 (Cambridge: Chadwyck-Healey, 1984), 133.

[159] As we have seen, B1 is, by Robertson's reckoning, a copy of A1 (Milan, Biblioteca Ambrosiana, N.180) and an ancestor of L1 (Laur. 54. 32), Boccaccio's autograph. Butler (*Apologia*, p. xliii) dates it to the 'close of the fourteenth century'. If Robertson's thesis is correct, B1 must have been written before the middle of the century.

[160] *Catalogue of Additions to Manuscripts of the British Museum 1864–1875*, 116.

[161] This is the result, I hazard, of a misinterpretation of Byrrhena's companion's cry at *AA* 2. 2: *Est, inquit, hercules Lucius* ('By Hercules, it's Lucius!').

[162] *Catalogue of… The Burney Manuscripts* (London: British Museum, 1840).

Socratis and *De habitudine doctrinarum et natiuitate Platonis phylosophi.* Written in Italy in the early fourteenth century, it contains (at fol. 162), the inscription *Liber Magistri Leonardi [Mansueti] de Perusio, ordinis predicatorum [ob.* 1480]. It belonged to William Henry Black in 1827.[163] Add. MS 25104 (acquired by the BM in 1863) is a collection of excerpts from authors, including Apuleius, written in an Italian hand and dating from the fifteenth or sixteenth century.[164] Sloane 2586 contains the *Apologia,* the *Florida,* the *De deo Socratis,* and the *De philosophia.*[165] It dates from the sixteenth century.[166]

The apparent promise of the manuscript evidence is thus seen to be illusory: all the medieval manuscripts of the *Metamorphoses* now in England seem to have been acquired since the seventeenth century. Such evidence, obviously, is by no means conclusive. The loss of manuscripts through natural decay and the vicissitudes of Chance has been augmented by sources of more systematic destruction. The dispersal of the monastic libraries during the dissolution of the monasteries under Henry VIII and the despoliation of ecclesiastical and collegiate collections at the hands of Edward VI's Commissioners in 1550 ensured the destruction or dislocation of a large percentage of the medieval and early Renaissance manuscripts then extant. These losses, coupled with the paucity of surviving pre-Reformation library catalogues, make it difficult to determine, accurately, the nature of manuscript holdings before the sixteenth century.[167] My researches to date, however, have failed to find any reference by an Englishman to Apuleius' novel prior to Thomas Waleys and Walter Burley, or any evidence of the presence in England of actual manuscripts before Duke Humphrey of Gloucester's gift to the University of Oxford in 1439.

Chaucer

One is conscious of the paradoxes of taxonomy when one considers that Chaucer is usually assigned to the close of the Middle Ages and Petrarch, forty years his senior, to the beginning of the Renaissance. England, it is true, was considered as the end of the world and was a byword for literary

---

[163] *Catalogue of Additions to the Manuscripts in the British Museum in the Years MDCCCLXXVI–MDCCCLXXXI* (London: British Museum, 1882; repr. 1968), 305.

[164] *Catalogue of Additions to Manuscripts of the British Museum 1864–1875,* 155.

[165] S. Ayscough, *A Catalogue of…the Collection of Sir Hans Sloane* (London: Ayscough, 1782), 411, 710, 871.

[166] Butler, *Apologia,* p. xliv.

[167] See C. E. Wright, 'The Dispersal of the Libraries in the Sixteenth Century', in *The English Library before 1700: Studies in its History,* ed. F. Wormald and C. E. Wright (London: U of London, 1958), 148–75.

backwardness; but there were at least potential conduits for the intercourse of ideas between Italy and England.

We have already discussed the case of the English Friars like Thomas Waleys, theologians with an interest in the recovery of pagan literature. Another conduit (this time, a literary rather than a scholarly or theological one) is Geoffey Chaucer. Chaucer travelled to Italy in 1372/3, and the fact that he visited Florence tempted earlier scholars to believe that he may have met Petrarch and, perhaps, also, Petrarch's friend, Boccaccio—an attractive notion, but one unsupported by hard evidence.[168] Had such a meeting taken place, Petrarch might well have shown Chaucer his own manuscript of Apuleius and referred him to Boccaccio's discussion of 'Cupid and Psyche' in the *De genealogia deorum*. In any event, Chaucer was certainly familiar with many of Boccaccio's works, since he drew the story of *Troilus and Criseyde* (1372–8) from Boccaccio's *Il filostrato* and adapted the *Teseida* in 'The Knight's Tale'.[169]

Several claims have been made for Apuleian influence in *The Canterbury Tales*. According to J. J. M. Tobin,

Chaucer . . . is now increasingly thought to have known *The Golden Ass* as part of the Menippean satiric tradition he himself belonged to and as an analogue to his *Canterbury Tales* 'which exhibits the same diverse collocations of styles and stories.'[170]

During a discussion of Spenser's use of Apuleius, A. C. Hamilton asserts (without any critical support) the probability of Apuleian influence in 'The Franklin's Tale':

> For o thyng, sires, saufly dar I seye,
> That freendes everych oother moot obeye,
> If they wol longen holden compaignye.
> Love wol nat been constreyned by maistrye.
> Whan maistrie cometh, the God of Love anon
> Beteth his wynges, and farewel, he is gon!

---

[168] See J. J. Jusserand, 'Did Chaucer Meet Petrarch?', *Nineteenth Century* 39 (1896), 993–1005. F. J. Mather argues against the meeting. See 'On the Asserted Meeting of Chaucer and Petrarch', *MLN* 12 (1897), cols. 1–18. For Chaucer's use of Petrarch and Boccaccio, see *Chaucer and the Italian Trecento*, ed. P. Boitani (Cambridge: CUP, 1983).

[169] See H. G. Wright, *Boccaccio in England from Chaucer to Tennyson* (London: U of London, Athlone P, 1957); P. Boitani, *Chaucer and Boccaccio* (Oxford: SSMLL, 1977); *Chaucer's Boccaccio: Sources of 'Troilus' and the Knight's and Franklin's Tales: Translations from the 'Filostrato', 'Teseida' and 'Filocolo'*, ed. and trans. N. R. Havely (Cambridge: Brewer; Totowa: Rowman & Littlefield, 1980); D. Wallace, *Chaucer and the Early Writings of Boccaccio* (Woodbridge: Brewer, 1985). As Douglas Gray notes, 'He seems also to have drawn on the Latin *De mulieribus claris* and *De casibus virorum illustrium* and on the *Filocolo*' (*ODNB*, s.v. 'Chaucer').

[170] Tobin (*SFN*, p. xii) quoting F. A. Payne, *Chaucer and Menippean Satire* (Madison: U of Wisconsin P, 1981), 25.

Love is a thyng as any spirit free.
Wommen of kynde, desiren libertee,
And nat to been constreyned as a thral;
And so doon men, if I sooth seyen shal.[171]

Hamilton comments:

Chaucer's source is probably Apuleius's legend: when Psyche sought the 'maisterie',
the God of Love flew from her; and Spenser certainly would recognize this source.[172]

One might make the preliminary observation that Psyche is not punished for
attempting 'maisterie' over Cupid, but for disobeying him. She has come to
his side, lamp and razor in hand, intending to cut off his head, but the crime
which precipitates the God of Love's departure (*AA* 5. 23) is Psyche's breach of
promise in attempting to see her husband's face.

   There remains, nevertheless, a general resemblance between the two episodes, and it is certainly possible that Chaucer was acquainted with 'Cupid
and Psyche', either directly, through manuscripts available in Italy, or indirectly, through Fulgentius or Boccaccio. Herbert Wright tells us that 'John of
Whethamstede, elected abbot of St. Alban's in 1420, quotes *De genealogia
deorum* and his protector, Humphrey, duke of Gloucester', possessed a copy of
the work.[173] We can probably go half a century better than Wright's
Whethamstede. The catalogue of the library of the Austin Friars at York
records, in a hand 'not much later' than 1372, the gift of books by John
Erghome which include the *Genealogia deorum* and the *mithologie fulgencii*.[174]
If the date is correct, it suggests either an earlier 'publication' date for the
Genealogia than the year 1372 given by Haight, or an extremely fast rate of
transmission from Italy to England. Chaucer's contemporary, John
Gower, may have known the *De genealogia*,[175] and his 'disciple', John Lydgate

[171] 'The Franklin's Tale', Fragment V (Group F) lines 761–7, in *The Works of Geoffrey Chaucer*,
ed. F. N. Robinson, 2nd edn. (London: OUP, 1957).
[172] *The Structure of Allegory in the 'Faerie Queene'* (Oxford: Clarendon, 1961), 181. On
medieval representations of Cupid, see, generally, 'Blind Cupid' in Erwin Panofsky, *Renaissance
and Renascences in Western Art* (London: Paladin, 1960; repr. 1970), 95–128.
[173] *Boccaccio*, 3.
[174] M. R. James, 'The Catalogue of the Library of the Augustinian Friars at York', in *Fasciculus
Ioanni Willis Clark dicatus* (Cambridge: CUP, 1909), 2–96, Entry 490. Cf. Humphreys, 'The
Library of John Erghome'. According to M. J. Curley (*ODNB*, s.v. 'John of Bridlington'), Ergome
'became both master regent and prior of the York convent in 1385.... [He] was probably the
Johannes de Anglia who was admitted to the faculty of theology in Bologna in 1380. He became
master of the studium of the Roman curia in 1386, and in the same year served as *magister
antiquus* ('senior master') in the Naples convent.... Ergome's library, which numbered over 220
books, was one of the largest personal collections in England during the middle ages, and
included a wide range of classical and medieval authors.'
[175] D. A. Dilts, 'John Gower and the *De Genealogia Deorum*', MLN 57/1 (Jan. 1942), 23–5.

(*c*.1370–1451?), certainly knew the work, for he 'alludes to it and borrows from it in *The Fall of Princes* and *The Siege of Thebes*.'[176]

The immediate source for Chaucer's passage, however, may be Agapes' 'discovery' of Cupid in Boccaccio's *Ameto* (xxxii):

Oh, how many times, recalling Psyche, I judged her [93] happy and unhappy: happy for such a husband and unhappy for having lost him, and then exceedingly happy for having him returned by Jove.... But while I remained suspended above this fountain and admired my reflection, the young son of the goddess, fluttering his holy wings, which glittered with the brightest gold [*ventilando le sante penne lucenti d'oro chiarissimo*], went forth from that spot with the forged arrows. And in less time than it takes the sun, when touching our horizon, to leave one hemisphere and to pass to the other, he had flown over our house.[177]

Perhaps the most compelling argument against the attribution to *The Golden Ass* of direct influence upon Chaucer is also the most obvious: the stories in Apuleius (as Boccaccio's *Decameron* shows) are eminently amenable to being separated and reworked in other narrative structures, and *The Canterbury Tales* is the very place where one would expect to find evidence of an English poet exploiting those resources. The fact that Apuleius' witty tales of cuckoldry and clever reversals were not used by Chaucer suggests that they were not known to him. Nor can we safely posit the *Decameron* as a conduit for Apuleian influence upon Chaucer. According to Wright, 'there is no convincing internal evidence that Chaucer had read any of the tales or that the framework for his *Canterbury Tales* was suggested by that of the *Decameron*'.[178] Claims for direct influence have been made by more recent critics, but the general trend is to leave questions of filiation unresolved while concentrating on comparative studies of analogous structures and themes.[179] Chaucer's apparent ignorance of the *Decameron* is less surprising, however, than it might appear. We think of Boccaccio and Petrarch as intimate friends, but

---

[176] Wright, *Boccaccio*, 36. *The Fall of Princes* was begun about 1430 under the patronage of Humphrey. Lydgate refers to the *Mitologiae* ('Methologies') of Fulgentius ('Fulgence') in Book 2 of his *Troy Book* (vv. 2486–7). The first book printed in English—the *Recuyell of the Historyes of Troye* (*c*.1474), translated by William Caxton from the French of Raoul Lefevre—draws heavily on the *Genealogia*. Erasmus recommended the *Genealogia* for study in his *De ratione studii* (1511). See *CWE* xxiv. 674.

[177] *L'Ameto*, trans. Serafina-Sauli, 92–3. The influence of the *Ameto* may also be found in 'The Merchant's Tale' where Chaucer's depiction of the hideous husband, Januarie, parallels Agapes' account of her own husband. See J. S. P. Tatlock, 'Chaucer's "Merchant's Tale" ', *MP* 33/4 (May 1936), 367–81, at 378–80.

[178] *Boccaccio*, 114.

[179] See, generally, N. S. Thompson, *Chaucer, Boccaccio, and the Debate of Love: A Comparative Study of the 'Decameron' and the 'Canterbury Tales'* (Oxford: Clarendon, 1996); L. M. Koff, and B. Deen Schildgen, eds., *The 'Decameron' and the 'Canterbury Tales': New Essays on an Old Question* (Madison, NJ: Fairleigh Dickinson UP; London: Associated University Presses, 2000).

Petrarch claims that he knew nothing of the *Decameron* until shortly before 1373, when he sent Boccaccio his Latin version of the Griselda tale (*Decameron* x. 10) which he had translated from the (inevitably mutable) vernacular in order to preserve it for posterity.[180]

According to A. C. Hamilton, 'Chaucer treats Psyche's labours in his tale of the patient Griselda'.[181] 'The Clerk's Tale' derives, as the Prologue tells us (lines 31–3), from 'Fraunceys Petrak, the lauriat poete', 'whos rhetoricke sweete| Enlumyned al Ytaille of poetrie'.[182] Hamilton does not cite any evidence from 'The Clerk's Tale', but examination reveals details which may appear, superficially, to be Apuleian. Both stories concern beautiful young girls who are chosen, unbeknownst to them, by lordly spouses, separated from them, exposed to severe trials, and finally reunited with their husbands.

The literary versions of Griselda's story have been linked 'with a special class of folk tale which have [*sic*] been denominated the Patience Group of the Cupid and Psyche genre'.[183] This does not necessarily mean that the Griselda story is *derived* from Apuleius' tale of 'Cupid and Psyche', merely that the motif of patient suffering found in each marks them out as members of the same class of folk tale—one designated 'Cupid and Psyche' because of its most famous exemplar. According to the folklorists' model, the 'Griselda' figure is a distant cousin of Apuleius' Psyche, not a lineal descendant.

We have already considered the challenge posed by Detlev Fehling to the folklorists' notion of a pre-Apuleian 'Cupid and Psyche' surviving in the oral tradition. Moreover, in Petrarch's version (and, by descent, in Chaucer's) we find evidence of a kind of textual incest—a contamination of sources. When Petrarch 'discovered' the final novella of the *Decameron*, he seems to have recognized its affinities with 'Cupid and Psyche' and to have introduced into his own version elements from Apuleius not present in Boccaccio. Thus, Chaucer's description of Griselde's fame derives (through Petrarch) from Apuleius' account of Psyche:

Sic immensum procedit in dies opinio, sic insulas iam proxumas et terrae plusculum provinciasque plurimas fama porrecta pervagatur: iam multi mortalium longis itineribus atque altissimis maris meatibus ad saeculi specimen gloriosum confluebant . . . (AA 4. 29)

---

[180] *Ep. Seniles* 17. 3.

[181] 'Spenser's Treatment of Myth', *ELH* 26 (1959), 335–54, at 348.

[182] Chaucer depended on both a Latin manuscript of Petrarch's tale and an anonymous French prose translation. See J. B. Severs, *The Literary Relationships of Chaucer's 'Clerkes Tale'* (New Haven: YUP, 1942), 4. Chaucer's ignorance of Boccaccio's version (which in many ways is closer in spirit to Chaucer's version than Petrarch's) is further evidence that Chaucer did not know the *Decameron*.

[183] Severs, *Literary Relationships*, 4. See also, Robinson, ed., *The Works of Geoffrey Chaucer*, 709–10.

(Thus her reputation advances day by day, without end; thus her fame, stretched forth, ranges over the nearest islands and rather more of the earth and most of the provinces: now many mortals, by long journeys and the greatest courses over the sea, were flocking towards this glorious ornament of the age...)

Iamque non solum intra patrios fines sed per finitimas quasque provincias suum nomen celebri preconio fama vulgabat, ita ut multi ad illam visendam viri ac matrone studio fervente concurrerent. (Petrarch, *Epistolae seniles* 17. 3)

(And now fame was spreading her name by frequent proclamation not just within the borders of her homeland but throughout the furthest provinces, so that men and women with burning zeal were flocking *en masse* to see her.)

> Noght oonly of Saluces in the toun
> Publiced was the bountee of hir name,
> But eek biside in many a regioun,
> If oon seide wel, another seyde the same;
> So spradde of hire heighe bountee the fame
> That men and wommen, as wel yonge as olde,
> Goon to Saluce, upon hire to biholde.[184]

We notice, however, a shift in moral emphasis. So great is Psyche's beauty that she is worshipped as a new Venus (*Puellae supplicatur*, 4. 19). The 'worshipful' Griselde, by contrast, gains such esteem for her 'wise and rype wordes' and 'juggementz of so greet equitee, | That she from hevene sent was, as men wende' (lines 401, 438–40).[185]

There remains a promising-looking passage in Chaucer's *Parliament of Fowls* (211–17) where Cupid's daughter, Will, tempers the heads of her father's arrows:

> Under a tre, besyde a welle, I say
> Cupide, oure lord, his arwes forge and file;
> And at his fet his bowe al redy lay;
> And Wille, his doughter, temprede al this while
> The hevedes in the welle, and with hire file
> She touchede hem, after they shulde serve
> Some for to sle, and some to wounde and kerve.

There is no disputing the ultimate influence of Apuleius on this passage, but the immediate source appears to be the 'Temple of Venus' episode (7. 50–66) in Boccaccio's *Teseida* (AD 1339–41?). In the glosses which Boccaccio supplied to his own poem, we find:

---

[184] *The Canterbury Tales*, Fragment IV (Group E), lines 414–20.
[185] On the subsequent reception of the 'Patient Grissel' figure, see A. Baldwin, 'From the *Clerk's Tale* to *The Winter's Tale*', in *Chaucer Traditions*, ed. R. Morse and B. Windeatt (Cambridge: CUP, 1990), 199–212.

Volutà dice que le tempera in una fonte; ove è da sapere che Amore prese per moglie una
giovane, la quale fu chiamaa Psice, e ebbe di le' una figliuola, cioè questa Volutà; per la
quale Psice intende qui l'autore la speranza, la quale quante volte viene o dimora con
amore nella mente dello innamorato, cotanto volte generano questa figliuola, cioè
Volutà; la quale s'intende qui per uno diletto singulare che l'anima sente dentro a sè,
sperando d'ottenere la cosa amata; e questa cotale dilettazione è quell ache tempera le
[465] saette d'Amore, cioè che le fa forti a potere bene passionare il cuore...

(He [the author] says that Pleasure tempers them [Cupid's arrows] in a spring. Here it
should be understood that Love took as his wife a girl called Psyche and had by her a
daughter, namely Pleasure herself. By this Psyche the author here means Hope—and
whenever she, together with Love, enters or remains in the mind of the lover they
beget between them this daughter Pleasure, who here stands for the particular delight
the mind feels within itself because of its hopes of gaining the object of its love. This
kind of gratification is what tempers the arrows of love, making them powerful
enough to inflame the heart throughout...)[186]

Humphrey, Duke of Gloucester

Chaucer, we have argued, was precisely the kind of writer who would have
exulted in the narrative riches provided by Apuleius; but he was born, it
would seem, just a generation too soon to have direct contact with *The Golden
Ass*. The earliest testimony to the physical presence of the novel in England is
provided by Humphrey, Duke of Gloucester—the figurehead of English
Renaissance humanism. A younger son of Henry IV, and brother of Henry
V, he was a bibliophile, patron of the new learning, and founder of the main
collection in the University of Oxford's Library. A letter of appreciation
written by the university in 1441 reflects the high regard in which the duke
was held by Continental as well as English scholars:

Quod si Latini omnes gracias abundantissimas sublimitati vestre justissime pro tanto
munere debeant, maximi nos Anglici, qui in angulo mundi constituti sumus: quos
quanquam pelagus spaciosissimaque terrarum loca a prospectu rerum mundialium
impediant, per hos tamen libros et volumina vestra liber et propatulus omnium rerum
datur intuitus. [204] Nihil Africa, nihil Asia secretum continet, quod non in hiis
voluminibus aperte legamus.[187]

(But if all the Latin peoples so justly owe most abundant thanks to your sublimity for
so great a gift, most of all do we, the English, who are set in the corner of the world.

---

[186] *Tutte le opere*, ed. Branca, ii. 464–5; trans. in Havely, *Chaucer's Boccaccio*, 131. Cf.
G. Morgan, 'Chaucer's Adaptation of Boccaccio's Temple of Venus in *The Parliament of Fowls*',
RES NS 56 (2005), 1–36.

[187] *Epistolae Academicae Oxon. (Registrum F)*, ed. H. Anstey (Oxford: Oxford Historical Soc.,
1898), i. 203–4.

Although the sea and the vastest tracts of land shackle us from the sight of the things of the world, nevertheless, through these books and volumes of yours, a free and open view of all things is being given. Africa and Asia keep nothing hidden which we cannot openly read in these volumes.)

Apuleius may well have been one of the African treasures that Oxford had in mind. In 1439, Humphrey had donated to the university a consignment of 120 volumes which included, amongst such works as Lactantius' *Diuinae institutiones* and Macrobius' *Saturnalia,* two manuscripts of especial importance. The indenture acknowledging receipt of Humphrey's gift contains (at fol. 53a) the following entries:

Item, Boccasius '*De genealogie Deorum gentilis*' secundo folio *humeris*

[One intervening entry]

Item, Apulius '*De asino aureo*' secundo folio *proclivis.*[188]

The duke obtained most of his humanist texts from Italy, through agents like Pier Candido Decembrio (elder brother of Angelo Camillo Decembrio); but it is by no means certain that Decembrio was the source of this particular manuscript. Writing to Decembrio in 1440, Humphrey numbers *ille Apuleius* among those 'praiseworthy' authors (*qui sint digni laude*) whom he is eagerly seeking in his attempt to build up a collection of works which have learning as their particular object (*cum ea maxime effectamus quae ad eruditionem maxime pertinent*).[189] A letter of July 1441 indicates that the duke was waiting for Decembrio to send him copies of Apuleius' *De magia* and *Florida* two years after his donation of the *De asino aureo*; and Decembrio, writing on 1 July 1444, informs Gloucester that he has *omnia Apulegii opera . . . parata.*[190] The chronology remains confusing.[191]

As a result of Humphrey's donation, the university passed a decree requiring all books to be kept in lockable chests from which they might 'be borrowed by masters of arts, actually lecturing in those subjects . . . and under certain circumstances by Principals of halls'.[192] This might seem to

---

[188] *Epistolae Academicae*, i. 183, 236. The first word of the second leaf (*secundum folium*) is quoted as a means of identifying the manuscript. Anstey corrects the careless scribe's entry for Boccaccio so that it reads, *De genealogia Deorum gentilium.* See R. Weiss, *Humanism in England during the Fifteenth Century*, 3rd edn. (Oxford: Blackwell, 1967), 63.

[189] M. Borsa, 'The Correspondence of Humphrey Duke of Gloucester and Pier Candido Decembrio', *EHR* 19 (1904), 509–26, at 517.

[190] Ibid. 521; cf. Weiss, *Humanism in England*, 59.

[191] W. L. Newman calls attention to some of the problems with the dates given in the MSS. See 'The Correspondence of Humphrey, Duke of Gloucester, and Pier Candido Decembrio', *EHR* 20 (1905), 484–98.

[192] Anstey's précis, *Epistolae Academicae*, i. 189.

suggest that *The Golden Ass* would only have seen the light of day if it formed part of a university curriculum or caught the fancy of a passing head of house. In practice, however, the regulation of access to the manuscripts was far less stringent than the decree prescribed. The university showed little interest in acquiring printed books (it was left to the individual colleges to take advantage of the new technology) and by 1550, when the Library was despoiled by Edward VI's commisioners, it is believed that many of the volumes had already disappeared.[193] The manuscript of *The Golden Ass* is still listed, a century after its donation, in the catalogue made by the antiquarian John Leland (1506?–52), though the last word of the entry, *de asino aureo, sublatus*, indicates that the manuscript had already been removed or destroyed.[194] Humphrey donated about 300 books to the Oxford library and his whole collection has been estimated at around 500 volumes.[195] Of these, a mere thirty-four have been identified, some of them surviving only as fragments in sixteenth-century book-bindings. Apuleius is not among them.[196] Did Humphrey's *Ass* exert any influence during its brief sojourn in the Library of Oxford? Two members of Gloucester's circle allude to Apuleius' philosophical works, John Doget quoting Apuleius' *De deo Socratis*,[197] and John Hardynge, in his *Chronicle* (*c.*1436), drawing upon Geoffrey of Monmouth's invocation of Apuleius in his discussion of the birth of Merlin:

> ¶[Notwithstanding that philosophiers wise,]
> Affirme well that sprites suche there beene,
> Betweene the moone and therth, called Incubice,
> That haue gotten chyldren of wemen vnseene,

---

[193] I am grateful to the late Prof. Albinia de la Mare for illuminating this aspect of the history of Duke Humfrey's Library in conversation.

[194] Leland's catalogue is reproduced from Hearne's edn. (1715) by A. Sammut, *Unfredo duca di Gloucester e gli umanisti italiani* (Padua: Antenore, 1980), 95 ff.

[195] Ullman, *Studies in the Italian Renaissance*, 349, 351.

[196] R. Weiss, 'The Private Collector and the Revival of Greek Learning', in Wormald and Wright, eds., *The English Library before 1700*, 112–35, at 119. Humphrey also employed scholars who copied manuscripts in his own household and Ullman suggests that he probably donated to Oxford manuscripts for which he had limited use or of which he possessed a second copy. One might, therefore, have expected another copy of the *De asino aureo* to have turned up after the Duke's death in 1447. A. L. N. Munby tells us, in 'Notes on King's College Library in the Fifteenth Century', *Transactions of the Cambridge Bibliographical Society* 1 (1949–53), 280–4, that Humphrey had intended his whole collection to be left to the University of Oxford, but after his death, the residue of his books was obtained by King's College, Cambridge. The Inventory of the Library of King's College made in 1452 and reprod. by M. R. James as an appendix to *A Descriptive Catalogue of the Manuscripts other than Oriental in the Library of King's College, Cambridge* (Cambridge: CUP, 1895) does not mention any Apuleian manuscripts.

[197] For Doget, Weiss (*Humanism in England*, 166) cites BL, MS Add. no. 10344, fol. 85ᵛ.

As in stories diuerse I haue so seene:
Howe the philosophier, wise Magancius,
Affirmeth it also, and Apuleyus.[198]

In 1446, at Ferrara, a very youthful Niccolò Perotti copied, for William Grey, 'a fragment of Apuleius concerning the Diphthongs, which was found in the oldest codex' (*Apuleii fragmentum de diphthongis quod in uetustissimo codice repertum est*).[199] The work on diphthongs is spurious, but its copying suggests a demand for things Apuleian. I have not yet, however, encountered any reference, within this coterie, to *The Golden Ass*.

CONCLUSIONS

Evidence of first-hand acquaintance with *The Golden Ass* exists from the beginning of the trecento. By the middle of the century, copies are in the hands of the leading humanists Petrarch and Boccaccio. By the end of the century, Psyche has been re-enthroned in the *Genealogia*, and *The Golden Ass* is on its way to becoming part of the common property of the Italian Renaissance.

Yet it is still a predominantly Italian preserve. Manitius' first record of the *Ass* in Spain is in 1409—the result of the transfer of the Curial collection from Avignon—and there is no mention in Germany or France (if we exclude Avignon) until well into the fifteenth century.[200] The (precocious) scholarly interest in matters Apuleian shown by Waleys and 'Burley' seems to have had no literary ramifications, and we can say, with confidence, that the direct influence of *The Golden Ass* in England before 1400 was, if not non-existent, then at least negligible. It is significant, however, that Chaucer, whom we think of as the most forward-looking English writer of the late Middle Ages, should have been guided by Italian masters who were themselves much influenced by *The Golden Ass*.

---

[198] *The Chronicle of John Hardynge*, ed. H. Ellis (London: F. C. & J. Rivington, 1812), 115 (I am grateful to Dr Marcella McCarthy for pointing this out to me). Hardynge was connected with the Italian humanists by Giuliano Cesarini, who had been sent to England in 1426 by Pope Martin V. According to Weiss (*Humanism in England*, 23), Cesarini 'spent part of his spare time explaining Justin to the chronicler'.

[199] Weiss, *Humanism in England*, 89. Cf. *De nota aspirationis et de diphthongis* (Milan: J. A. de Honato, c.1480); L. Biondi, 'Apuleius, *De nota aspirationis* e *De diphthongis*: Ricognizioni su modelli strutturali e teorici in due testi medievali sull'ortografia latina', *ACME* 54/3 (2001), 73–111.

[200] Manitius, *Handschriften*, 151.

4

The Inky Ass: Apuleius in the Age of Print (1469–1500)

EDITIO PRINCEPS, 1469

In 1464, two German clerics, Konrad Sweynheim and Arnold Pannartz, arrived at the Benedictine monastery of Santa Scolastica in Subiaco, 47 miles to the east of Rome.[1] They had travelled a long way—from Mainz to Augsburg, following the old Benedictine route across the Alps into Italy, and then down the peninsula to the papal states. The final stretch of their journey took them along the *Via dei monasteri*, shaded by the ancient holm-oaks that were said to have bowed at the sight of St Benedict and remained stooped ever since. Their Teutonic looks and 'rough' voices, however, would not have caused much of a stir in Subiaco—ten of the eighteen monks at S. Scolastica's (including the prior) were fellow countrymen.[2] What made these new arrivals exceptional was their baggage. For they brought with them items that had never been used before in Italy: cases of movable type, that marvel of fifteenth-century German ingenuity which had transformed the familiar technology of agricultural extraction (the screw-press) into an engine of reproduction.

Italy's prototypographers were self-styled 'disciples' (*alumni*) of Johann Fust, the lawyer who had financed the production at Mainz of the Forty-two-line Bible and then taken control of Gutenberg's printing works in 1455

[1] According to J. V. Schloderer et al., eds., *Catalogue of Books Printed in the Fifteenth Century Now in the British Museum. Part IV: Subiaco and Rome* (London: British Museum, 1916), 1: 'They were clerks respectively of the dioceses of Mainz and Cologne'. See their Petition to Pope Sixtus IV (attached to vol. V of their edn. of Nicolaus de Lyra's *Postilla super totam Bibliam*, 20 Mar. 1472), reprod. in *G. A. Bussi: Prefazioni alle edizione di Sweynheym e Pannartz prototipografi*, ed. M. Miglio (Milan: Polifilo, 1978), 83–4. Pannartz died in 1476; Sweynheim was dead by 1478.

[2] H. Barolini, *Aldus and his Dream Book* (New York: Italica, 1992), 11. On the legend of the holm-oaks, see A. Sagramora, *Travelling in the Province: Itineraries in the Province of Rome* (Rome: Fratelli Palombi, 2000), 114. The printers identify themselves as being German (*gente theotonica*) in the colophon to the 1467 edn. of Cicero's *Epistolae ad familiares* (Schloderer, *Catalogue... British Museum. Part IV*, p. vii). On the printers' defence of their 'rough German names', see Barolini, 28.

following legal action for recovery of debt.[3] The sack of Mainz on 27 October 1462 (the result of an episcopal power struggle) had led to economic disruption and the dispersal of many of its printers, and Santa Scolastica (the sister-house of Monte Cassino) must have seemed a welcome haven—close enough to Rome (the centre of curial humanism) to ensure a healthy demand for books, but sufficiently removed to provide some insulation against pontifical caprice.[4] Sweynheim and Pannartz managed to produce four volumes during their time at the monastery: an edition of Aelius Donatus' ever-popular grammar, the *Ars minor* (probably chosen to advertise their presence in Italy and no longer extant), Cicero's *De oratore* (before September 1465), Lactantius' *Opera* (29 October 1465), and Augustine's *De ciuitate dei* (12 June 1467).[5] According to Maury Feld, 'printing was originally summoned to Italy by curial humanists as a means of enhancing the status of their favored classical texts' and the three extant productions of Subiaco constitute a 'tonic triad' designed 'to display the harmonious relationship between the major elements of humanist scholarship', a 'pagan-patristic synthesis, in which Cicero, through the agency of Greek wisdom, had been reconciled with St. Augustine'.[6] Leon Battista Alberti (an enthusiast for Apuleius as well as for Lucian) seems to have visited Subiaco during Sweynheim and Pannartz's residency, for in his preface to *De componendis cifris* (*c.*1466), he reminds Leonardo Dati of how they had witnessed 'the new German invention that enables three men to produce two hundred volumes in one hundred days'.[7]

---

[3] Sweynheim and Pannartz style themselves thus in the preface to their Lactantius volume.

[4] As M. D. Feld observes, the reality was more complicated. Subiaco was under the governance of the (admittedly, elderly) Spanish cardinal Juan de Torquemada (Johannes Turrecremata (1388–1468)), and was subject to 'direct curial supervision'. See 'A Theory of the Early Italian Printing Firm, Part I: Variants of Humanism', *HLB* 33 (1985), 341–77, at 360. Venice and Florence might seem more obvious targets for aspirant printers, but their very proximity to northern Europe (and the relative ease of colportage) may have made them vulnerable to competition. It is likely that the pair stopped at Rome before reaching Subiaco.

[5] Schloderer (*Catalogue...British Museum. Part IV*, 1) suggests 'the end of 1464 or the beginning of 1465' for the printing of the *De oratore*.

[6] 'The First Roman Printers and the Idioms of Humanism', *HLB* 36/1 (1988) (special issue), 10–11.

[7] Feld, 'First Roman Printers', 18. See L. B. Alberti, *Dello scrivere in cifra*, ed. D. Kahn (Turin: Galimberti, 1994), 27–8. Feld notes (39) that, in 1466, Dati was 'confidential secretary (*primo segretario*) to Pope Paul II' and finds an 'incongruity' between 'Dati's official duties and his covert activities' in sponsoring humanist enterprises. Feld observes (19) that Alberti dedicated his *De statua* (*c.*1464) to Bussi. See *On Painting and On Sculpture: The Latin Texts of 'De pictura' and 'De statua'*, ed. and trans. C. Grayson (London: Phaidon, 1972), 118–19. Cf. D. Marsh, 'Alberti and Apuleius: Comic Violence and Vehemence in the *Intercenales* and *Momus*', in *Leon Battista Alberti: Actes du Congrès International de Paris*, 2 vols. (Paris: Librairie Philosophique J. Vrin; Turin: Nino Aragno, 2000), i. 405–26.

Even before the printing of the Augustine was complete, however, Sweynheim and Pannartz had already begun to transfer operations to Rome, for by November 1467 they were established in the house of Petrus Maximus (the Palazzo Massimo), very near to the *Studium Urbis* (the university now known as *La Sapienza*). It was here that the *editio princeps* of Apuleius' works appeared (without commentary) in 1469, the colophon being dated 28 February.[8] The folio was edited by Sweynheim and Pannartz's *corrector*, the Bishop of Aleria (in Corsica), Giovanni Andrea de Bussi (Johannes Andreas de Buxis), and dedicated to no less a personage than Pope Paul II (1464–71) who had appointed him papal librarian in 1467.[9] Paul II (born Pietro Barbo in 1418) is a contradictory figure in the history of the Renaissance. Ingrid D. Rowland describes him as 'a dourly practical Venetian', but this is a little one-sided. He was an avid collector of antiquities (especially coins and gems), one of the first pontiffs to issue decrees designed to protect the material fabric of ancient Rome, and (albeit on his own terms) a significant patron of humanism (it was, after all, by his licence that Sweynheim and Pannartz brought their printing press into Rome, to be followed shortly by Ulrich Hans and Sixtus Reissinger).[10]

It is certainly true, however, that relations between humanists and the papacy were rather fraught during this period. Paul's immediate predecessor, Enea Silvio Piccolomini (Pius II, 1458–64), had enjoyed considerable success as a man of letters before his ordination in 1446, having been crowned poet laureate by the emperor, Frederick III, during his years in Germany, and having produced the *De duobus amantibus* (a Latin prose-romance charting

---

[8] *Lucii Apuleii platonici madaurensis philosophi metamorphoseos liber: ac nonnulla alia opuscula eiusdem: necnon epitoma Alcinoi in disciplinarum Platonis desinunt* (Rome: [C. Sweynheim & A. Pannartz], 28 Feb. 1469). The *ed. princ.* measured 12½ " by 9" (321 mm by 230 mm) and in the *Registorum librorum impressorum Romae* (Munich, Bayerische Staatsbibliothek, MS. Einbl. VIII, 1ᵗ) compiled by Hartmann Schedel in 1470, is priced at 'three papal ducats'. See Miglio, *Prefazioni*, p. lvi. In the list of Sweynheim and Pannartz's publications provided in their Petition to Pope Sixtus IV (1472), Bussi gives the number of copies of the Apuleius as 275. This is the same print run as for Aulus Gellius and compares with 300 copies of Pliny, 550 of Vergil, 825 of Augustine's *De ciuitate dei*, 825 of Lactantius, and 1100 of Jerome's *Epistles*. See Miglio, *Prefazioni*, 83–4, and M. D. Feld, 'Sweynheym and Pannartz, Cardinal Bessarion, Neoplatonism: Renaissance Humanism and Two Early Printers' Choice of Text', *HLB* 30 (1982), 282–335, at 284–8.

[9] E. Lee, *Sixtus IV and Men of Letters* (Rome: Edizioni di storia e letteratura, 1978), 109.

[10] I. D. Rowland, *The Culture of the High Renaissance: Ancients and Moderns in Sixteenth-Century Rome* (Cambridge: CUP, 1998), 14. For a more sympathetic portrait, see R. Weiss, *Un umanista veneziano: Papa Paolo II* (Venice: Istituto per la collaborazione culturale, 1958). One might note that, in Sept. 1469, Francesco Filelfo 'received a sum of 400 ducats from the papal treasurers as the reward' for the Latin translation of Xenophon's *Cyropaedia* that he had completed two years earlier. See L. A. Sheppard, 'A Fifteenth-Century Humanist, Francesco Filelfo', *The Library*, 4th ser. 16 (1936), 1–26, at 11.

the adulterous and interracial love between a Roman matron, Lucretia, and
Eurialus, a member of the entourage of Sigismund, Duke of Austria), an erotic
comedy (*Chrysis*, dated 1444), and several illegitimate children.[11] In November 1463 and May 1464, Pius reorganized the College of the Abbreviators of
the Chancery, to the advantage of the humanist party. Pope Paul II's attitude
towards literature was altogether less sympathetic and he seems to have made
a conscious effort to limit the influence of his predecessor.[12] One of Paul's first
acts, after assuming the papal throne on 30 August 1464, was to reduce the
autonomy of the College of the Abbreviators and dismiss many of Pius II's
appointees, thus cutting off a major source of the humanists' economic
support.[13] He antagonized them further in February 1468 by persecuting
the Academia Romana, the antiquarian sodality founded by Guilio Sansever-
ino (1427–98), a colourful rhetorician who taught to great acclaim at the
Studium Urbis (where he succeeded his teacher, Lorenzo Valla) and who had
adopted the names Julius Pomponius Laetus in his drive to reconfigure
himself as a fully 'antique Roman'.[14] 'Pomponio Leto' (as he is better known
to us today) had decamped to Venice the previous year (1467), but many of
the Academicians were arrested (on charges of paganism, sodomy, and
mounting a conspiracy against the Pope) and imprisoned in the Castel
Sant'Angelo (the remodelled mausoleum of Hadrian).[15] However, despite

---

[11] Amongst his other writings were an *Historia Bohemica* and a *Somnium* (which includes a
'dream visit' by Pietro da Noceto to 'the libraries of Subiaco and Montecassino'). See M. Davies,
'Juan de Carvajal and Early Printing: The 42-line Bible and the Sweynheym and Pannartz
Aquinas', *The Library* 18 (1996), 193–215, at 202 n. 29. Davies (201) comments upon 'the
popularity of Pius II among the Germans'.

[12] According to Platina (an understandably hostile witness), Paul II 'had such a hatred and
contempt for humanistic studies that he applied the collective label of "Heretics" to those who
followed that course' (*Humanitatis . . . studia ita oderat & contemnabat: ut eius studiosus uno
nomine hæreticos appellaret*). See *De uita Christi: ac Pontificum omnium* (Venice, 1479), fol.
[238]ʳ.

[13] L. Pastor, *The History of the Popes*, ed. [and trans.] F. I. Antrobus, 4th edn. (London: Kegan
Paul, Trench, Trubner, 1923), iv. 37–41. Pastor (iv. 38) gives the official date of the decree as
3 Dec. 1464, but considers Oct. as the more likely month. The uncertainties of these opening
years of Paul II's pontificate may have made Sweynheim and Pannartz's sponsors reluctant to
bring them to Rome immediately. According to Feld ('First Roman Printers', 20), Leon Battista
Alberti was one of the humanists purged from the Curia at this time.

[14] According to Lee (*Sixtus IV*, 177), Leto was 'Without question the most important of the
professors of Latin literature in Sixtus' Rome'. The fullest account remains V. Zabughin, *Giulio
Pomponio Leto: Saggio critico*, 3 vols. (Rome: La vita letteraria, 1909–12).

[15] See A. J. Dunston, 'Pope Paul II and the Humanists', *Journal of Religious History* 7 (1973),
287–306; R. J. Palermino, 'The Roman Academy, the Catacombs and the Conspiracy of 1468',
Archivum historiae pontificiae 18 (1980), 117–55; J. F. D'Amico, *Renaissance Humanism in Papal
Rome: Humanists and Churchmen on the Eve of the Reformation* (Baltimore: Johns Hopkins UP,
1983), 92–7. In *Pagan Mysteries* (1968), 8 n. 26, Wind suggests (citing Zabughin vol. i), that the
'mystifying effect' of the 'ritual initiations' and acquisition of 'cryptic names' may have contributed to Paul II's suspicions of the Roman Academy, which he mistook for a conspiratorial
society'. See Valeriano, *DLI* 2. 62 (ed. Gaisser, 225).

the use of torture (most notably on Bartolomeo Platina, author of an Epi-curean cookbook, *De honesta voluptate*, and future Vatican Librarian and papal biographer), there was insufficient evidence to support a conviction and Leto's *fratres* were released over the course of the following year.[16]

Leto's documented association with Bussi leads Feld to conjecture that he 'had had a hand in the move' from Subiaco to Rome.[17] The ill fortune of the Pomponians in 1468 certainly seems to have affected Sweynheim and Pan-nartz's publishing strategy. According to one of the Milanese ambassadors, the day after the arrest of the Academicians, the Pope began 'to damn greatly' (*damnare molto*) the humanists' pursuits and declared his intention of en-suring 'that it would not be permissible' (*que non fosse licito*) to study 'these senseless histories and poems, which are full of heresies and blasphemies' (*queste vane historie et poesie perche sono piene de heresie et maledictione*).[18] In Pope Paul's eyes, Platina suggests, Platonism was suspect, and by even uttering the word 'academy' in jest one ran the risk of being condemned of heresy.[19] It can hardly be coincidental that Sweynheim and Pannartz interrupted their series of patristic and Ciceronian texts to print their only non-humanist work, a treatise by Roderigo Sánchez de Arévalo, Bishop of Zamora and castellan of Sant'Angelo where the Academicians were incarcerated.[20] Appearing in the following year, the *editio princeps* of Apuleius thus belongs to a delicate period of rapprochement between the papacy and the humanists.

---

[16] Rowland, 14–16. Platina (1421–81) succeeded Bussi as papal librarian in Feb. 1475 and became *custos* of the Vatican Library in June of the same year. See Lee, *Sixtus IV*, 111. His account of the events of Feb. 1468 is given in his *Hystoria de vitis pontificum periucunda* (Venice: Philippus Pincius Mantuanus, 1504). Cf. B. Platina, *The Lives of the Popes*, ed. Rev. W. Benham, 2 vols. (London: Griffith, Farran, Okeden & Welsh, 1888), 275–96, at 288. Pincius had repub-lished Bussi's Apuleius in Venice in 1493.

[17] Feld, 'First Roman Printers', 20. Leto played a part in the appearance of several of Sweynheim and Pannartz's edns. Bussi addresses Leto as *Pomponius Infortunatus* in the dedica-tory epistle to his second edn. of Vergil (which appeared in 1471, immediately following the death of Paul II) and closes with the apostrophe *Pomponi amantissime*. See Miglio, *Prefazioni*, 41, 43; Davies, 'Juan de Carvajal', 206; Kenney, *Classical Text*, 13. Cf. Zabughin, ii. 72.

[18] Johannes Blanchus (Giovanni Bianchi) to Galeazzo Maria Forza, Duke of Milan (29 Feb. 1468, Rome). Italian text and translated excerpts in Pastor, *History of the Popes*, iv. 59 and 491. Cited by Palermino, 129. Pastor (iv. 492) notes: 'Original in the State Archives of Milan, Cart. Gen. *Wrongly placed under February*, 1463'.

[19] Platina, *Liber de vita Christi ac omnium pontificum*, ed. G. Gaida, RIS 3/1 (Città di Castello: Lapi, 1913–32), 389: *Paulus . . . haereticos eos pronunciavit, qui nomen Academiae vel serio, vel ioco deinceps commemorarent. Iusta est haec ignominia Platoni, ipse se tueatur.* Quoted by Palermino, 139 n. 66.

[20] Rodericus Zamorensis, *Speculum vitae humanae* (Rome: Sweynheim & Pannartz, [after 28 Feb.] 1468). Feld ('First Roman Printers', 41) argues that the work was 'published under duress'. On Rodericus' relations with Bessarion, see J. Monfasani, '*Bessarion Latinus*', *Rinascimento*, NS 21 (1981), 165–209, at 177.

Its editor, Bussi (1417–75), had studied at Mantua under Vittorino da Feltre in the early 1440s (Theodore Gaza being a fellow pupil) and had taught at Genoa before becoming secretary, in 1458, to Nikolaus Krebs von Kues, better known to us as Cardinal Nicholas of Cusa or Nicolaus Cusanus.[21] Cusanus (1401–64) was the author of the *De docta ignorantia* ('On learned ignorance') as well as notable studies of Proclus. Bussi tells us, in his preface to the *Letters* of St Jerome (13 December 1468), that Cusanus was also an early enthusiast for printing: 'he greatly desired that this sacred art, which then seemed to be arising in Germany, should be brought to Rome' (*peroptabat, ut haec sancta ars, quae oriri tunc videbatur in Germania, Romam deduceretur*).[22] From August 1466 to September 1467, Bussi had been in Venice, in the entourage of Juan de Carvajal, Cardinal of Sant'Angelo. Carvajal had been 'perhaps the first person' outside Germany to hear of the new technology of printing, thanks to a letter (12 March 1455) sent to him in Rome by Aeneas Silvius Piccolomini regarding 'that marvellous man' (*De viro illo mirabili*), seen at Frankfurt in October 1454, who was able to produce 158 or 180 copies of the Bible.[23]

Apuleius' appearance in the very cradle of Italian printing clearly results from an attempt to exploit the overlap between his patristic reputation as a Platonic philosopher and his humanist appeal as an eloquent and erudite writer whose name was also attached to the *Asclepius*, the Latin translation of the work of Hermes Trismegistus which formed a central part of the Renaissance's efforts to reconstruct the *prisca theologia*.[24] Feld calls the naming of Paul II in Bussi's preface 'a transparent formality', the 'real subject' of the dedication being revealed in the opening sentence as Cardinal Johannes Bessarion (*c.*1403–72), Metropolitan of Nicaea, Patriarch of Constantinople, Bishop of Sabina, and author of the *In calumniatorem Platonis* ('Against the

---

[21] *The World of Aldus Manutius: Business and Scholarship in Renaissance Venice* (Oxford: Blackwell, 1979), 24–6. On Theodore Gaza, see Lee, *Sixtus IV*, 107 n. 96. On Cusanus, see F. E. Cranz, *Nicholas of Cusa and the Renaissance*, ed. T. M. Izbicki and G. Christianson (Aldershot: Ashgate, 2000). R. Levao analyses the relationship between Cusanus' philosophy and the use of fictional narrative in *Renaissance Minds and their Fictions: Cusanus, Sidney, Shakespeare* (Berkeley and Los Angeles: U of California P, 1985).

[22] Miglio, *Prefazioni*, 4. See also Lowry, *World of Aldus*, 25. The *ed. princ.* of Apuleius (1469) includes a brief encomium of Cusanus (Miglio, 17–18). Bussi arranged 'for his own burial next to the cardinal's tomb' (Lee, *Sixtus IV*, 108 n. 104).

[23] Davies, 203. The man was Gutenberg, Fust, or Schöffer.

[24] Feld goes too far, however, when he claims ('First Roman Printers', 26) that 'Apuleius is the sole pagan neo-Platonist [*sic*] mentioned by Augustine in non-adversarial and even benevolent terms'. The appearance of Apuleius coincides with the first Italian printing of a book outside Subiaco or Rome: Johannes de Spira (Speier) completed his edn. of Cicero's *Epistolae ad familiares* in Venice probably by the 'middle of February 1469'. See *BM Part V* (Venice) (London: British Museum, 1924), p. ix.

Detractor of Plato') and the *De præstantia Platonis præ Aristotele* ('On the Superiority of Plato over Aristotle').[25]

Bessarion is himself both a metamorphic and a syncretistic figure.[26] He had been instrumental in the attempt to reunite the Eastern Orthodox and Roman Catholic churches in the face of Ottoman aggression, but had settled permanently in Rome in 1440 after the people of Constantinople rejected the concordance achieved by the Council of Ferrara-Florence (1438–9).[27] In the eyes of the West, the cardinal retained the dignity of his Orthodox office while also being a loyal servant of the papacy; and he played a vital role as both promoter and protector of humanism in Rome where his household became an informal Platonic academy.[28] Bessarion's concern to foster Greek studies in Italy made him an energetic collector of manuscripts from all genres, but his accumulation of three copies of Heliodorus' *Aethiopica* indicates that he was, at least, not dismissive of ancient prose fiction.[29] And even the cardinal, evidently, was not entirely secure in the face of Paul II's hostility towards the humanists: as a former (and still devoted) pupil of the radically paganizing Neoplatonist Gemistos Plethon, he may have felt vulnerable.[30] In the wake of the 'conspiracy' crisis of 1468, Bessarion arranged for his entire library (including over 800 manuscripts) to be bequeathed to St Mark's in Venice, where it would come eventually into the custody of one of Leto's former pupils, Marcantonio Sabellico.[31]

In the preface to his second volume of Jerome's *Epistolae* (dated 13 December 1468), Bussi provides a list of forthcoming titles: the works of Apuleius, Aulus Gellius, and Macrobius will serve as 'background reading' for Bessarion's Platonic writings.[32] In the *In calumniatorem Platonis* (which

[25] 'First Roman Printers', 42.

[26] See N. G. Wilson, *From Byzantium to Italy: Greek Studies in the Italian Renaissance* (London: Duckworth, 1992), 57–67.

[27] Feld, 'First Roman Printers', 15.

[28] For Feld (ibid. 23), the litany of titles proclaims Bessarion as 'the personification of the universality of the Christian religion' (Nicaea), 'guarantor of the essential unity of Christianity's various creeds' (Constantinople), and 'visible proof of the primacy of the See of Rome' (Sabina). It should be noted, however, that 'Patriarch of Constantinople' was a title conferred by Pope Pius II in 1463. See *NCE2*, s.v. 'Bessarion', ii. 341.

[29] Doody, *True Story*, 179. Cf. L. Labowsky, *Bessarion's Library and the Biblioteca Marciana: Six Early Inventories* (Rome: Edizioni di storia e letteratura, 1979), entries B 32, B 629, B 995 (Heliodorus); and B 828 and B 840 (Apuleius).

[30] C. M. Woodhouse, *George Gemisthos Plethon: The Last of the Hellenes* (Oxford: OUP, 1986); J. Monfasani, 'Platonic Paganism in the 15th Century', in *Reconsidering the Renaissance*, ed. M. A. di Cesare (Binghamton, NY: CMERS, 1992), 45–61; repr. in Monfasani, *Byzantine Scholars in Renaissance Italy: Cardinal Bessarion and Other Emigrés* (Aldershot: Ashgate, 1995), no. x.

[31] Lowry, *World of Aldus*, 229–30. Monfasani ('*Bessarion Latinus*', 182) argues that the transfer happened much later.

[32] Feld, 'First Roman Printers', 26. Miglio, *Prefazioni*, 10–11. Feld ('First Roman Printers', 26–7) argues that the printing of Macrobius was abandoned in the climate of papal disapproval

appeared within six months of the *editio princeps* of Apuleius), Bessarion
responds to the attacks of George of Trebizond (Trapezuntius, 1396?–1484) by
adducing, *inter alia*, the testimony of Apuleius and Pliny (*qui multis in locis
non modo uitam & mores et sapientiam Platonis laudant: extollunt: admiran-
tur*) as evidence of the high esteem in which Plato was held by the Romans
(*Ex quibus constat quale latinorum de Platone iudicium fuerit*).[33] Bussi reinforces the rebuttal, with Apuleius pressed into service on the side of the
(neo-)Platonizing humanists in the battle against the neo-Aristotelians.[34] As
part of his programme of making known those Platonists who 'excel above all
in their gravity and learning' (*grauitate & doctrina in primis excellentes*), the
bishop has brought together the scattered writings of Apuleius, 'in whom an
outstanding copiousness and gracefulness of speech is joined to the greatest
erudition' (*in quo uno: summe eruditioni precipua lingue copia: & gratia
coniuncta est*).[35]

The *editio princeps* contains the expected run of Apuleian *philosophica* (*De
deo Socratis, De dogmate Platonis, De mundo*), but it also includes the *Asclepius* and the *Epitome disciplinarum Platonis* of Alcinous.[36] It is a mark,
perhaps, of the popular appeal of *The Golden Ass* (or *Metamorphoses* as it is
entitled here) that Bussi uses it to open the *Opera omnia*, 'as though it were a
pamphlet in a greater work'.[37] Lucian, who wrote 'more in sport than out of

of pagan philosophy. Pastor records (*History of the Popes*, iv. 56) that, while incarcerated in the
Castel Sant'Angelo, Pomponio Leto asked his gaoler for copies of Lactantius and Macrobius, but
was sent a copy of Bishop Rodericus' 'treatise on the errors of the Council of Basle' instead. Cf.
M. Creighton, *A History of the Papacy during the Period of the Reformation*, 5 vols. (London:
Longmans, Green, 1882–94), iii. 44–5, 276–84.

[33] *Bessarionis. . . libri aduersus calumniatorem Platonis* (Rome: Sweynheym & Pannartz [be-
fore 28 Aug. 1469]), 1. 3, fol. 20ᵛ.

[34] See, generally, J. Monfasani, *George of Trebizond: A Biography and a Study of his Rhetoric
and Logic* (Leiden: Brill, 1976), ch. 7: 'The Plato-Aristotle Controversy', 201–29; and his
'*Bessarion Latinus*' etc. It should be noted that Bessarion had translated Aristotle's *Metaphysics*
and was actually concerned to reconcile the thought of the two philosophers rather than to
denigrate Aristotle.

[35] Bussi's praise of the combination of eloquence and erudition is typical of quattrocento
humanist taste (Wind, *Pagan Mysteries*, 10, records Pico's love of Proclus' 'Asiatic richness'), but
the issue of Apuleian style will become increasingly controversial in the decades that follow.

[36] On the contents, see A. Coates et al., *A Catalogue of Books Printed in the Fifteenth Century
now in the Bodleian Library, Oxford*, 6 vols. (Oxford: OUP, 2005), i. 211–12. The *Epitome*
(translated into Latin by Petrus Balbus) has long been thought to be by Albinus. See R. E.
Witt, *Albinus and the History of Middle Platonism* (Cambridge: CUP, 1937). More recent
scholarship favours the attribution to Alcinous. See Harrison, *a Latin Sophist*, 197 n. 87.

[37] *Ab ea ego: uti a maioris opere libello: initium feci*. The *Florida* and *Apologia* follow next. For
this, and all subsequent extracts, I have used, as copy text, the 1469 edn. (*GW* 2301) in the
Bodleian Library (which does not provide signatures, folio, or page numbers), indicating (in
square brackets) any significant divergences from it in the edns. of 1488 (*GW* 2302) and 1493
(*GW* 2303). I have not noted minor discrepancies in orthography or punctuation (such as the
use in the later edns. of *æui* for *eui* and *puellæ* for *puelle*); nor have I consulted the edn. of 1497

spite' (*lusu uerius: quam calumnia*), had 'made play with this Golden Ass' (*Lucianus asinum... aureum lusit*) and Apuleius—'a man of abundant and (as an African) most shrewd talent and the finest philosopher of all in his age'—attempted to rival his achievement, relating 'in a humorous tone' (*festiua dictione*) the 'wearisome and manifold disasters' into which he falls (*in erumnosas: ac multifarias incidit calamitates*).[38] Bussi continues:

Quo in toto sermone: si quis recte intendat: mores humanos effictos: liquido perspiciet explicari: et impremeditatas fallaciarum argutias discet: quibus etiam cauti sepissime capiantur: cum non homo homini: sed lupus sit potius homo: ut scite plautus inquit: dum qualis sit homo: non noscitur. Inspergit tamen [1493: tum] ubique res eiusmodi noster Lucius: ex quibus omnium eruditissimus ut predixi illius temporis mortalium: facile fuisse uideatur. quod ex ea potissimum cernere est fabula: quam obiter anum [1488: annum] quandam consolatricem puelle captiue referentem inducit: quam quidem rem: qui certius cupiunt nosse: fulgentii de ea ipsa fictione interpretamenta perquirant. Is enim uir doctus in primis commentatus est illam. Tandem exanclatis multis erumnosisque laboribus: ut ipse ait: id est cum summa animi anxietate: et corporis molestia superatis: ac uictis transcursisque multiplicibus uite huius fallacium hominum machinamentis: atque exercitiis. lune auxiliatricis ope: rosis de manu egyptii sacerdotis acceptis: ac deuoratis: homini est priori suo restitutus: & religionibus magnis initiatus. hic est asinus ille aureus: tanto dicendi lepore ac sale et lingue gratia compositus: ut quisquis illum studiosus lectitarit: in dictione latina fieri tersior queat atque cumulatior. Nam quod res sunt diuersissime omnes secretiores lingue thesauros in eo lutius effundit ac quantum in dicendo ualuerit reserat: uerbis adeo propriis et accommodatis ut non scribere: sed pingere plane historiam uideatur. perpauca sane uti ego arbitror in media uita homini possunt accidere: que latine proferre aut scribere cupienti. hinc depromi sufficienter non ualeant: ubique enim est lepidus castigatus uenustus aptus uarius copiosus concinnus presto: ut nasci ibidem non extra adscisci uideatur oratio: dixerit fortassis aliquis: minus tritam esse: atque usurpatam Apuleii nostri dictionem. Idipsum est: quod ego demiror: quod laudo: quod extollo. quia non detrita quadam: non succida: non rustica: non squalenti et laciniosa oratione: non proculcata: non uulgatissima denique res cotidianas ex media uita sumptas edisserit: quippe qui non popinis: aut meritoriis tabernis: aut nugalibus triuiis: aut misticorum compitis scribit: sed elegantie ac cultioris doctrine urbanis hominibus atque studiosis.

(In the whole of this discourse, should anyone attend rightly, he will perceive human manners represented clearly and the unforeseen subtleties of deceits in which even the wary are very often caught; since (as Plautus shrewdly says) man is not a man, but a

---

(*GW* 2304) which is described (*Catalogue of Books Printed in the* XV[th.] *Century now in the British Museum*, vi. Italy [London: British Museum 1930], 782) as a 'page for page reprint' of the 1493 edn. For a modernized text, see Miglio, *Prefazioni*, 12–13.

[38] *hunc asinum noster Lucius emulaturus ingenii alioqui exuberantis: et ut Afer acerrimi: philosophus omnium illius eui subtilissimus...*

wolf to a man, so long as it is not known what kind of man he is.[39] However, this Lucius of ours sprinkles things of this kind everywhere, from which he can easily be seen to have been (as I said before) the most learned of all mortals of his time.

This can be most easily seen from that tale told, in passing, by a certain old woman whom he introduces as a consoler of a captive girl. Those, indeed, who desire to be more certain of this matter may examine Fulgentius' explanations of this very fiction. For that learned man, particularly, wrote upon it. Finally, having endured, as he himself says, many and wearisome toils, that is, having overcome and conquered them with extreme mental anguish and bodily discomfort, and having traversed the manifold stratagems and exercises of deceitful men in his life, with the assistance of the helpful moon, after receiving roses from the hand of the Egyptian priest and eating them, he was restored to his former humanity and initiated into great religious rites.

This is that Golden Ass, composed with such charm of style and wit and grace of tongue that any student who reads him often can become purer in his Latin speech and more copious. For, because his subjects are so diverse, Lucius pours out in his work the more secret treasures of the language, and reveals his own capacity in speech with words so characteristic and appropriate, that he seems not to write but, clearly, to paint his narrative. Very few things, in my judgement, can happen to a man in the course of his life which, if he wishes to mention or describe them in Latin, cannot be drawn sufficiently from this source.

For everywhere, he is to hand: elegant, restrained, charming, appropriate, varied, copious, polished, so that the style seems to be born in that very place, not adopted from outside. Someone perhaps might say that Apuleius' diction is less familiar and well used. It is that very thing which I wonder at, which I praise, which I extol, because he does not relate everyday things taken from the midst of life in some worn-out, sappy, rustic, rough and jagged style of speech, not in a trite, nor (finally) in a grossly common one. For he does not write for the eating-houses or for the brothel-shops, or for the trifling public streets, or for the crossroads of the secret rites, but for the refined and studious men of more cultivated learning.)

We might note, in the penultimate paragraph of this section, the implicit construction of *The Golden Ass* as a *thesaurus* ('treasure house') or cornucopia of words and *exempla*; the bestowal on Apuleius of those two most Catullan of accolades, *lepidus* and *venustus*; and the stress on the 'painterly' quality of his narrative (*pingere...historiam uideatur*) which evokes both the Horatian-Plutarchan notion of an affinity between word and image (*ut pictura poesis*) and a particularly Renaissance concern with *enargeia* ('vividness').[40] Some

[39] In Plautus' *Asinaria* (495), a merchant refuses to give the slave, Leonida, any money since he is a stranger: *lupus est homo homini, non homo, quom qualis sit non nouit* ('A man is a wolf to a man, not a man, when the latter does not know what kind of man he is'). Cited by Miglio, *ad loc.*

[40] Horace, *Ars poetica* 361: *Ut pictura poesis.* Plutarch's comments in *De gloria Atheniensium* 3. 347a (quoting Simonides of Keos) produced the popular Latin tag, *poema pictura loquens, pictura poema silens.* On *enargeia*, see Quintilian, *Instit. Orat.* 6. 2. 32 and 8. 3. 62.

concessions are made to religious orthodoxy: the authority of Augustine (*De ciuitate dei* 18. 18) is invoked in the discussion of the transformation; the lubricious content of the work is glossed over; and the restoration is seen as the result, not of Isiac intervention, but of the 'assistance of the helpful moon' (*lune auxiliatricis ope*). Yet, for the most part, the *Ass* is sent into the world unfettered. The asinine metamorphosis is merely 'an unwished-for occurrence' (*haud optabili occasione*), rather than a consequence of carnal involvement or irreligious *curiositas*, the description of Lucius going to Thessaly 'inflamed with desire for knowledge and experience' (*sciendi: atque experiendi incensum cupiditate*) smacking more of humanist delight in intellectual enquiry than of patristic condemnation. Apuleius, in the bishop's eyes, is not only the 'finest philosopher of his age', but an excellent model for fifteenth-century writers wishing to develop the purity and copiousness of their Latin prose-style. Bussi, significantly, picks out the tale of Cupid and Psyche for special mention, but rather than essaying his own explication of the myth, he is content to rely on the exegesis provided by Fulgentius.[41] Indeed, his peroration shows him trying to neutralize Paul's inveterate dislike of pagan poets and storytellers: *Da veniam pater beatissime, contra fabulosos et lucifugas hosce, fabulis utenti* ('Bestow forgiveness, Most Blessed Father, on one using fables against these fablers and shunners of the light').[42] Even here, however, Bussi appears to be drawing on Apuleius, employing Psyche's description of her husband as *lucifuga* (*AA* 5. 19). The curious Psyche's sacrilegious lamp revealed her 'monstrous' husband to be a god; so too, the bishop seems to be implying, divine truths may be perceived beneath the bestial surface of Apuleius' narrative.

According to E. J. Kenney, 'Bussi was one of the entourage of (it should be said) the second rank collected by Pope Nicholas V; his own scholarly and critical gifts were certainly not of a very high order'.[43] Bussi admits in his preface to Apuleius that he has assembled the volume with only 'moderate care, as far as was permitted by the paucity of manuscripts' (*mediocri uigilantia: ut in exemplariorum penuria licuit*).[44] The *editio princeps* provided no

[41] Earlier bibliographical studies (e.g. Copinger, *Supplement to Hain*, 533) contain a ghost entry for a quarto volume printed in the Netherlands entitled *Fabulosa narratio de nuptiis Psyche* [Deventer: Richard Paffraet, 1495]. The *Gesamtkatalog* (ii. 533) describes it as being *Nicht nachweisbar* ('not traceable').

[42] Miglio, *Prefazioni*, 19.

[43] *Classical Text*, 12. See also his 'The Character of Humanist Philology', in *Classical Influences on European Culture, 500–1500*, ed. R. R. Bolgar (Cambridge: CUP, 1971), 123–4; and Lowry, *World of Aldus*, 24–6. On Theodore Gaza helping Bussi to edit Aulus Gellius (1469) and Pliny's *Historia naturalis*, see D. J. Geanakoplos, *Constantinople and the West* (Madison: U of Wisconsin P, 1989), 87.

[44] = Miglio, *Prefazioni*, 13. Cf. Kenney, *Classical Text*, 13. Robertson ('Manuscripts', 30) notes that the *ed. princ.* (*a*) is itself 'an important witness'. Miglio (103) points to a Vatican City

assistance to the reader trying to find a way through the strange diction (at once archaistic and neologistic) and often convoluted syntax of Apuleius' more flamboyant writings; but in making the collected works available in this form, Bussi was evidently both meeting and creating a demand, as the appearance of new editions in 1488 (Vicenza: Rigo di Ca'zeno), 1493 (Venice: Philippus Pincius), and 1497 (Milan: Leonardus Pachel) indicates.[45]

One of the fruits of Bussi's edition seems to have been the translation of the *Asino d'oro* attributed to the Count of Scandiano, Matteo Maria Boiardo (*c*.1434–94).[46] Angelo Decembrio's reference to an (otherwise unattested) translation by Feltrino Boiardo led E. G. Gardner to ask, more than a century ago: 'Is Matteo Maria's version, perhaps merely a revision of his grandfather's work?'[47] This passing suggestion proved very attractive to subsequent scholars, but Edoardo Fumagalli has produced considerable evidence in support of his view that the major basis of Matteo Maria's translation was a copy of the *editio princeps*.[48] The translation was not printed until 1518, but letters survive from 1479, 1481, and 1512 referring to manuscript copies of the work.[49] There were at least eight further editions between 1519 and 1549.[50]

Niccolò da Correggio's verse paraphrase, *Psiche* (1491), is another manifestation of the widespread interest in Apuleius in the north of Italy at the end of the quattrocento.[51] Further south, appreciation of his works can hardly have

---

MS (Bibl. Ap. Vat. Inc. Rossiano 1078 C. b 1r) as a source for the *ed. princ.* According to Feld ('Sweynheim and Pannartz', 312), Bussi's edn. was 'almost certainly derived' from one of Bessarion's mss. now in the Biblioteca Marciana in Venice (Lat Z 476) 'which from the evidence of the calligraphy' had been produced sometime in the 1460s.

[45] As a native of Ingolstadt, Leonhard Pachel provides another link between Italy and German humanists such as Conrad Celtis who show an interest in Apuleius. Ludwig Hain's *Repertorium Bibliographicum* includes a ghost entry (+1315) for a folio edn. of Apuleius' *opera* published in Venice in 1472 by Nicolas Jenson. The *Gesamtkatalog* (ii. 530) describes it as being *Nicht nachweisbar* ('not traceable').

[46] *Apulegio volgare* (Venice: Nicolò d'Aristotele da Ferrara and Vincenzo de Polo da Venetia, 1518).

[47] *Dukes and Poets in Ferrara: A Study in the Poetry, Religion, and Politics of the Fifteenth and Early Sixteenth Centuries* (London: Constable, 1904), 268, 1. Discussed by E. Fumagalli, *Matteo Maria Boiardo volgarizzatore dell' 'Asino d'Oro': Contributo allo studio della fortuna di Apuleio nell'umanesimo* (Padua: Antenore 1988), 16.

[48] Fumagalli's approach to this complex problem involves minute examination of a variety of manuscript and printed sources, above all, an annotated copy of Bussi's *ed. princ.* now in the Huntington Library at San Marino, California. See esp. *Boiardo*, 39 and 206.

[49] Fumagalli, *Boiardo*, 4–5, 11, 13.

[50] For these (and the 'ghost edition' of 1516), see Fumagalli, 94, 163–4.

[51] Haight, *Apuleius*, 120. There were several Venetian edns. (e.g. 1507, 1515, 1521, and 1553). See, also, Niccolò da Correggio, *Opere: Cefalo, Psiche, Silva, Rime*, ed. A. Tissoni Benvenuti (Bari: Laterza, 1969). Correggio (1450–1508) was the son of Beatrice d'Este and was educated in the Court at Ferrara, serving on several occasions as an ambassador to Rome. Between 1490 and 1498, he was in the service of the Duke of Milan. See A. Arata, *Niccolò da Correggio nella vita letteraria e politica del tempo suo, 1450–1508* (Bologna: Zanichelli, 1934).

been harmed by the translation to St Peter's Seat of Cardinal Rodrigo Borgia in 1492. Paolo Cortesi may have considered him a 'barbarian', but as Alexander VI (1492–1503), the Spanish-born pontiff presided over a Rome that has been called the 'New Alexandria'.[52] The 'Borgia Apartments' in the Vatican were decorated by Bernardino Pinturicchio (*c*.1454–1513) with frescoes which featured Egyptian themes, above all, the repeated motif of the bull— taken from the Borgia coat of arms but metamorphosed into the form of the sacred Apis.[53] The Sala dei Santi ('Hall of the Saints') displays the most elaborate examples of pagan–Christian syncretism, with Christian scenes (such as St Catherine of Alexandria) being depicted on the walls, while 'a whole Egyptian pageant plays out on the stuccoed ceiling' with episodes from the lives (and deaths) of Isis, Osiris, Typhon, Horus, and Anubis, culminating in Osiris' resurrection as Apis, the golden bull.[54] Mediating between these figures, unifying walls and ceiling, is the figure of Hermes Trismegistus (the hero of the Hermetic corpus with which Apuleius' name was closely associated) who not only links Egyptian mythology with Greek philosophy, but also anticipates the truths of Christian revelation. A cultural milieu such as this was likely to be hospitable to a book so steeped in Egyptian lore as *The Golden Ass*.[55] Indeed, the Borgia papacy witnessed the erection of the Italian Renaissance's two greatest literary monuments to Apuleius, the anonymous *Hypnerotomachia Poliphili* (1499) and Filippo Beroaldo's massive folio edition (with commentary) of *The Golden Ass* (1500).[56] One was published at Venice, the other at Bologna, but whatever direct connection may exist between them in

---

[52] Rowland, *Culture*, 48, 46.

[53] Ibid. 48. In 'Pinturicchio and the Revival of Antiquity', *JWCI* 25 (1962), 35–55, J. Schulz suggests that Pinturicchio participated in some of the same subterranean adventures as the Roman Academicians, inspecting the vaults of Nero's Domus Aurea. M. Calvesi argues that Pinturicchio derived his images from the mosaic of the Nile in the Temple of Fortuna belonging to the Roman prince, Francesco Colonna of Palestrina—the real author, in Calvesi's view, of the *Hypnerotomachia Poliphili*. See 'Il gaio classicismo Pinturicchio e Francesco Colonna nella Roma di Alessandro VI', in *Roma, centro ideale della cultura dell'antico*, ed. S. D. Squarzina (Milan: Electa, 1989), 71–101. Calvesi's claims are opposed by P. F. Brown, *Venice & Antiquity: The Venetian Sense of the Past* (New Haven: YUP, 1996), 289.

[54] Rowland, *Culture*, 51.

[55] Rowland observes (ibid. 48) that '*The Golden Ass* succeeds brilliantly at doing what the Roman Academy also aimed to do so many centuries later: it still brings the ancient world palpably alive as it amuses, titillates, instructs, and bears witness to the author's enduring religious faith.' I would endorse most of this, reserving judgement only on the final four words.

[56] One might also note an extremely rare work by one of Beroaldo's disciples, Giovanni Battista Pio's *Praelectio in Plautum et Apuleium* (Bologna: Johannes Antonius de Benedictis, *c*.1500). A copy is held by the Bayerische Staatsbibliothek in Munich. Cf. J. F. D'Amico, 'The Progress of Renaissance Latin Prose: The Case of Apuleianism', *RQ* 37 (1984), 351–92, at 368, who takes the title from Hain (13026), *Praelectio in Plautum, Accium, et Apuleium*.

terms of authorship, they certainly seem to flow from a common intellectual and imaginative source.[57]

FILIPPO BEROALDO (BOLOGNA, 1453–1505)

Bologna had long been a centre of learning, boasting the 'oldest university in the world' (*alma mater studiorum*). Its fame traditionally rested on its legal studies, but at the time of Beroaldo's birth, Cardinal Bessarion was effectively governing the factious city as papal legate and was deeply involved in recruiting humanists to the university.[58] Beroaldo took up his chair at the Studium in 1479 and was, as Julia Gaisser reminds us, 'one of the most popular and influential teachers in Italy', attracting daily audiences of 300 students—many of them foreigners, 'from Spain and France, but above all from Germany and eastern Europe'.[59] Indeed, the Bodleian's copy of the *Commentarii... conditi in asinum aureum* from which we shall be quoting was originally bought in 1503 (as its garish bookplate tells us) by Christoph Scheurl of Nuremberg (1481–1542) at Bologna (where his studies for the Doctorate in Jurisprudence spanned the period 1498–1506).[60] After his death in 1505, Beroaldo was lamented as 'the universal teacher of almost all nations' (*communis pene omnium gentium praeceptor*).[61]

[57] G. Pozzi doubts a Bolognese connection. See *Francesco Colonna: Hypnerotomachia Poliphili. Edizione critica e commento*, ed. G. Pozzi and L. A. Ciapponi, 2 vols., 2nd edn. (Padua: Antenore, 1980), ii. 11. Simon Bevilaqua printed an edn. of Beroaldo's commentary in Venice in 1501.

[58] *NCE2*, s.v. 'Bessarion' ii. 340–1; *DBI* S. V. 'Bessarione', ix. 686–96 at 689.

[59] 'Teaching Classics in the Renaissance: Two Case Histories', *TAPA* 131 (2001), 1–21, at 2. See also her 'Reading Apuleius with Filippo Beroaldo', in *Being there Together: Essays in Honor of Michael C. J. Putnam*, ed. P. Thibodeau and H. Haskell (Afton, Minn.: Afton Historical Soc. P, 2003), 24–42; her 'Filippo Beroaldo on Apuleius: Bringing Antiquity to Life', in *On Renaissance Commentaries*, ed. M. Pade (Hildesheim: Olms, 2005), 87–109; and K. Krautter, *Philologische Methode und humanistische Existenz: Filippo Beroaldo und sein Kommentar zum Goldenen Esel des Apuleius* (Munich: Fink, 1971). M. Grossmann calls Beroaldo 'the most beloved teacher of the *humaniora* in Bologna'. See *Humanism in Wittenberg 1485–1517* (Nieuwkoop: De Graaf, 1975), 51.

[60] *Commentarii a Philippo Beroaldo conditi in asinum aureum Lucii Apulei* (Bologna: Benedictus Hectoris, 1500). The copy (Auct. N inf. 2.20) was obtained for the Bodleian Library in 1826. See Coates et al., *A Catalogue of Books Printed in the Fifteenth Century now in the Bodleian Library*, i. 213–14. On Scheurl, see P. N. Bebb, 'The Lawyers, Dr. Christoph Scheurl, and the Reformers in Nürnberg', in *The Social History of the Reformation*, ed. L. P. Buck and J. W. Zophy (Columbus: Ohio State UP, 1972), 52–72; *Deutsche biographische Enzyklopädie*, vol. viii (Munich: Saur, 1998), 619–20; S. Ozment, *Flesh and Spirit: Private Life in Early Modern Germany* (New York: Viking, 1999), *passim*.

[61] Jean de Pins, *Vita Philippi Beroaldi Bononiensis*, in *Vitae summorum dignitate et eruditione virorum*, ed. J. G. Meuschen, 4 vols. (Coburg: Jo. Georgius Steinmarck, 1735–41), i. 123–51, at 125. Quoted by J. B. Wadsworth, 'Filippo Beroaldo the Elder and the Early Renaissance in Lyons', *M&H* 11 (1957), 78–89.

Beroaldo's edition appeared on 1 August 1500, some months later than scheduled, having been held up in the press by a paper shortage. It announces itself, almost immediately, as a very different project from the *editio princeps*. Its scope is simultaneously local and international: Beroaldo dedicates the commentary to one of his former students at Bologna, Peter Vàradi (Petrus de Varda, c.1450–1502), erstwhile chancellor at the court of the Hungarian king, Matthias Corvinus (d. 1490), and now archbishop of Colocza (Kalocsa).[62] The appearance of the work was evidently a major publishing event. The contract which Beroaldo signed with his printer, Benedetto d'Ettore, on 22 May 1499 stipulated a print run of 1,200 copies.[63] Beroaldo himself refers, in the dedication, to 'around two thousand volumes' being 'printed off from the formes' (*voluminia … circiter duo millia formis excussa*, sig. a1ᵛ), and either sum is extremely impressive, especially given the expense of the folio format.[64]

In the *editio princeps*, Bussi had made *The Golden Ass* his starting point for the *Opera omnia*—an elegant (and, perhaps, commercially astute) way to introduce the writings of a learned and distinguished Platonist. The title page of Beroaldo's folio promises 'annotations on the remaining works' of Apuleius (*Mox in reliqua Opuscula eiusdem Annotationes imprimentur*) but such a volume never materialized, and one inevitably sees, in the amount of critical attention devoted entirely to *The Golden Ass*, the beginning of the shift away from the medieval notion of Apuleius as pre-eminently a philosopher, towards the modern view of him as a literary artist and shaper of fictions.[65]

Beroaldo's preface opens, however, not with literary analysis, but with a counterblast to the patristic attacks on magic:

[Iᵛ] *Ecclesiastici conditores magicas præstigias uocitant tamquam fallacia quadam præstringentes hominum mentes rerum ueritatem ementiantur: Et ita curiositati mortalium callenter illudant: Ceterum non parum multi credulitatem suam addixerunt magicæ doctrinæ: perinde ac rerum cunctarum potentissimæ: Inter quos | ut cæteros preteream Lucius Lucianus patrensis Diuinationis gnarus nec minus Elegans sophista:*

(The ecclesiastical authors are wont to call the magic arts 'sleights of hand' as though, by some stratagem binding fast men's minds, they fabricate the true nature of things

---

[62] For Petrus de Varda, see Cosenza, *BBDIH* v. 1383. See, more generally, R. Feuer-Toth, *Art and Humanism in Hungary in the Age of Matthias Corvinus* (Budapest: Akademiai Kiado, 1990).

[63] Gaisser, 'Teaching Classics', 10.

[64] Ibid. 11 n. 30. Cf. C. F. Bühler, *The University and the Press in Fifteenth-Century Bologna* (Notre Dame, Ind.: Mediaeval Institute, U of Notre Dame, 1958).

[65] Beroaldo was responsible for translating into Latin prose two *novelle* (IV. 1—the story of Guiscardo and Ghismonda—and x. 8—Titus and Gisippus) from Boccaccio's *Decameron*. They were published in 1491, were included (as *quaedam mythicae historiae*) in *Varia Philippi Beroaldi opuscula* (Basle: J. Froben, 1513), and were translated ('from the Laten') into English by William Walter: *Tytus & Gesyppus* (London: Wynkyn de Worde, 1525); *Guystarde and Sygysmonde* (London: Wynkyn de Worde, 1532).

and thus cunningly make sport with mortals' curiosity. But a good many men have given their credence to the Art of Magic and thus to the most powerful of all things—amongst them (to overlook the rest) Lucius Lucian of Patrae, expert in divination and a no less elegant sophist.)

Lucian's acquaintance with magic was superficial, however, compared with that of Apuleius:

Græcus ille magiam primoribus labris gustasse uideri potest quamuis de se scripserit μαντισ αγαθοσ [sic]. *Vaticinus bonus Hic uero noster plenis haustibus hausisse: In tantum ut Magorum maximus crederetur. Et ut auctor est Augustinus. Apuleium & Apollonium dixere non minorem quam Christum fecisse miracula. Et ut Lactantius refert solent Apuleii & multa & mira memorari. Ipse tamen magi nomen respuens aduersus calumniatores: qui ei magicarum artium Crimen intenderant | eloquentissime se defendit:*

(That Greek can be seen to have tasted magic with the edge of his lips although he describes himself as μάντις ἀγαθός ('a good seer'); but this Apuleius of ours seems to have drunk it in great draughts—so much so that he was believed to be the greatest of magicians. And as Augustine says—'They say that Apuleius and Apollonius performed miracles no less than Christ.' And as Lactantius relates—'The many and marvellous doings of Apuleius are usually recounted.' Apuleius, however, spitting the name of magician back in their faces, defended himself with great eloquence against his detractors who had brought the charge of witchcraft.)

In talking of 'Lucius Lucian of Patrae', Beroaldo conflates the second-century sophist and satirist Lucian of Samosata with the shadowy figure of Lucius of Patrae—the name both of the hero in the surviving epitome and (*teste* Photius) of the author of the lost *Metamorphoses* (which modern scholars regard as the common source of the two extant ass-stories).[66] Lucian, Beroaldo tells us, had 'toyed with this Golden Ass in a very elegant style' (*stilo pereleganti lusit Asinum aureum*); but even he is surpassed by Apuleius:

quem noster Apuleius Emulatus Et ipse apud latinos Consimili argumento stiloque nitidissimo condidit undecim uolumina de Asino aureo. siue metamorphoseon: In quibus Elegans est. Eruditus. Emunctus. Et cum haud dubie ex racemis Luciani sibi fecerit uindemiam: Eoque uno archetypo prope peculiariter sit usus: Magna tamen inter græcum Latinumque Asinum differentia: Ille breuis. Hic copiosus. Ille uniformis & summatim ex homine in Asinum ex Asino in hominem transformationem reformationemque perscribens. Noster uero multiplex & fabellis tempestiuiter intersertis omnem aurium fastidium penitus absterget. (Beroaldo, fol. 1ᵛ)

(Our friend Apuleius rivalled him and produced, among Latin-speakers, eleven volumes about *The Golden Ass* or *Metamorphoses*, with a similar plot and in a truly dazzling style. In these volumes he is elegant, erudite, acute. And since he undoubtedly

---

[66] Beroaldo, fol. 1ᵛ. For bibliography on Lucius of Patrae, see S. J. Harrison, ed., *Oxford Readings in the Roman Novel* (Oxford: OUP, 1999), p. xxx.

made a vintage for himself from Lucian's clusters of grapes, he used that one original almost as his own property. The difference between the Greek and Latin *Ass,* however, is great. The former is concise, the latter copious. Lucian is uniform, describing, briefly, his transformation from man into ass and his retransformation from ass into man. Our Apuleius, on the other hand, is multiplex and, by interweaving tales at appropriate moments, keeps his listeners completely rapt.)

Beroaldo is here perpetuating the mistaken belief that the *De asino aureo* derived from the pseudo-Lucianic *Loukios or the Ass.* And he surpasses even Bussi in his advocacy of the Apuleian style:

Sunt præterea in Lucio nostro uerba non parum multa interseminata: quibus magis delecter quam utar. plurima uero quibus perinde utar. ac delecter. Et sane nouator plerumque uerborum est elegantissimus tantoque cum decore & uenere. ut nihil decentius: nihil uenustius fieri possit: Denique hic noster Asinus sicut uerbo dicitur ita re ipsa aureus conspicitur: tanto dicendi lepore tanto cultu: tanta uerborum minime triuialium elegantia concinnatus compositusque: ut de eo id dici meritissimo possit: Musas Apuleiano sermone loquuturas fuisse si latine loqui uellent: & ut dicam quod sentio plurimum conferre Apuleii frequens lectio ad excolendam linguam potest: & ad eam eloquentiæ partem quam sermonatricem appellant maxime est accommodata: Cuius Eloquentiam Sidonius Apollinaris uelut fulminantem præconio uirtutis extollit: & Diuus Augustinus in epistolis Apuleium eloqnentissimum [sic] *esse testatur: de quo sic scribit: Apuleius Afer honesto patriæ suæ loco natus & liberaliter educatus: magnaque præditus eloquentia: Eundem in libris de ciuitate Dei Platoni cum græca & Latina lingua nobilem appellat. Quamobrem te lector. oro. moneo. Hortor: ut familiaris tibi fiat hic scriptor: sitque tuum quasi manuale & Enchiridion: In quo si quid durum uidebitur id nostrorum commentariorum expolitione emollietur: ac leuigabitur: quorum Ianuam* [2ʳ] *repandet precursoria hæc & ueluti prodromos enarratio compendiaria de Lucii Apuleii patria ingenio. & libris. Solet enim & hæc quoque studiosis esse non iniucunda cognitio.*

(There is, besides, interspersed in Apuleius, no small multitude of words, which I should rather delight in than use, but a great many which, equally, I should delight in *and* use. He is, indeed, the most elegant coiner of a great many words, and with such grace and charm that nothing could be done more gracefully, nothing more charmingly. In short, this Ass of ours is seen to be as golden in fact as he is said to be in the word, being arranged and composed with such charm and polish in speech, with such elegance in words (which are by no means commonplace) that of him it could most deservedly be said that if the Muses wanted to speak Latin, they would speak in the style of Apuleius. And (to say what I believe) the frequent reading of Apuleius can contribute most to the refinement of speech and is adapted most of all to that part of Eloquence which they call Conversational. Sidonius Apollinaris extols his eloquence [as being] like a thunderbolt in his commendation of virtue; and the divine Augustine bears witness in his letters to his being most eloquent. He writes about him thus in his letters: 'Apuleius the African was born in a distinguished part of his country, given a liberal education, and gifted with great eloquence.' In his books about *The City of God,* he calls the same man 'excelling in both the Greek and Latin tongue'.[67]

For this reason, Reader, I beg you, I advise you, I exhort you: that this writer should become familiar to you; that he should be, as it were, your guide and manual. If anything in him seems hard, it will be softened and made smooth by the polishing of our commentaries. These preliminaries will open the door to them as will (in the manner of the North-North-East wind) this compendious account of the country, character, and books of Lucius Apuleius. For this knowledge too is usually not displeasing to those devoted to study.)

In the *Scriptoris intentio atque consilium* that follows, Beroaldo attempts to explain the whole of the novel as an allegory of the life of Man and the progress of the Soul:

In exponendis auctoribus id quoque spectari querique solet: quæ fuerit scribentis intentio atque consilium: Ego Apuleium quidem nostrum confirmo Lucianum græcum scriptorem argumento consimili imitari. Verum sub hoc transmutationis inuolucro | naturam mortalium & mores humanos quasi transeunter designare uoluisse. ut admoneremur ex hominibus Asinos fieri: quando uoluptatibus belluinis immersi Asinali stoliditate brutescimus | nec ulla rationis virtutisque scintilla in nobis elucescit: sic enim homo ut docet origines in libris periarchon | fit equus & mullus | sic transmutatur humanum corpus in corpora pecuina: Rursus ex Asino in hominem reformatio significat calcatis uoluptatibus exutisque corporalibus deliciis rationem resipiscere: & hominem interiorem | qui uerus est homo ex ergastulo illo cenoso | ad lucidum habitaculum | Virtute & religione ducibus remigrasse: Ita ut dicere possimus iuuenes illicio uoluptatum possessos | in Asinos transmutari | mox senescentes | oculo mentis uigente | maturescentibusque uirtutibus exuta bruti effigie humanam resumere | Scribit enim Plato in symposio quod tunc mentis oculus acute incipit cernere cum primum corporis oculus deflorescit. Quin etiam proclus nobilis Platonicus monet multos esse in uita lupos multos porcos: plurimos alia quadam bruti spetie circumfusos | Quod minime mirari nos oportet cum terrenus locus circes ipsius sit diuersorium: cum animæ aut unguentis delibutæ | aut pharmacis epotis inebriatæ transfigurentur in brutas animantes. Pharmaca autem sunt obliuio error | inscitia: Quibus anima consopita brutescit. donec gustatis rosis hoc est scientia | quæ mentis illustratio est | cuiusque odor suauissimus | auide hausta in humanam formam hoc est rationalem intelligentiam reuertatur exuto asinali corio | idest deposito inscitiæ & rerum terrenarum crassiore uelamento. & sane reperiunter animæ quam paucissimæ: quæ corporeis pedicis inuolutæ | & brutalibus uoluptatibus irretitæ. existant sobriæ puræ imperturbatæ nulla in Asinum aliasque brutas animantes facta transfiguratione. Potest & metamorphoseos causa referri ad multiiugos humanæ uitæ labores multiformesque uarietates: quibus homo pene quotidie transmutatur: illa uero eruditioribus principalis huiusce transmutationis causa ualdeque probabilis uideri potest. Vt uidelicet sub hoc mystico praetextu Apuleius noster pythagoricæ platonicæque philosophiæ consultissimus

---

[67] *Ep.* 138 (see Ch. 1, *supra*); *De ciu. dei* 8. 12: *in utraque autem lingua, id est et graeca et latina, Apuleius Afer extitit Platonicus nobilis.*

dogmata utriusque doctoris ostenderet & sub hac ludicra narratione palingenesiam atque metempsychosim idest regenerationem transmutationemque dissimulanter assereret. (Beroaldo, fol. 2ᵛ)

(In expounding authors, it is usual for this to be examined and asked: 'What was the intention and plan of the writer?' I do indeed affirm that our Apuleius imitates the Greek writer Lucian with a similar subject matter. Truly, under the wrapper of this transformation he wanted (as it were, in passing) to represent the nature of mortal men and human customs, so that we might be warned against changing from men into asses; when, having been sunk in beastly pleasures, we become brutish with the stupidity of an ass and no spark of reason and virtue shows itself in us: for in this way (as Origen shows in his books Περί ἀρχῶν) man becomes a horse or a mule; thus the human body is changed into the bodies of beasts.[68] The restitution from ass back into a man signifies the recovery of reason when pleasures are trampled underfoot and corporeal delights cast off and the return of the inner man (who is the true man) from that foul penitentiary, with virtue and religion as his guides, to the dwelling-place full of light. Thus we can say that young men, possessed by the allurement of pleasures, are transformed into asses. Soon, growing old, as the eye of the mind flourishes and their virtues mature, they shed their brutish form and resume their human <form>. For Plato writes in the *Symposium*: 'The eye of the mind begins to discern clearly as soon as the eye of the body withers.'[69] But Proclus, the renowned Platonist, warns that, in life, many men are wolves, many are swine; most are enclosed within some other form of beast. We should not wonder at this since the dwelling-house of Circe herself is a place on earth; when souls, either besmeared with ointments, or intoxicated by the drinking of drugs, are transformed into brutish beasts. But <these> drugs are Forgetfulness, Error, Ignorance. The soul, stupefied by these things, becomes brutish until, with the tasting of the roses, that is, with knowledge (which is the illumination of the mind and whose smell is most sweet) having been avidly drunk, he returns to human form (that is the rational intelligence), having shed his asinine hide, that is, having laid aside the heavier covering of ignorance and earthly things. And indeed there are found the very fewest souls which, enwrapped in corporeal shackles and enmeshed in brutish pleasures, emerge prudent, pure, untroubled, without any transformation into an ass or other brutish animals being made. And the cause of metamorphosis may be attributed to the manifold labours and multiform varieties of human life by which man is almost daily transformed. That indeed, to the more learned, may be seen as the principal and very probable cause of this transformation. So it is easy to see that, under this mystical pretence, our Apuleius, steeped in Pythagorean and Platonic philosophy, was displaying the doctrines of each teacher,

---

[68] *Origen On First Principles: Being Koetschau's Text of the 'De Principiis'*, trans. G. W. Butterworth (London: SPCK, 1936), 1. 4, p. 41 (fragment omitted in Rufinus' Latin trans. but preserved by Jerome in his *Ep. ad Avitum* 3): 'It is a mark of extreme negligence and sloth for any soul to descend and lose its own nature so completely as to be bound, in consequence of its vices, to the gross body of one of the irrational animals'.

[69] *Symposium* 219a. On the literary topos of the *oculus mentis* see Curtius, ELLMA, 136, and Wind, 'Orpheus in Praise of Blind Love', in his *Pagan Mysteries*, 55–80, esp. 58–9.

and beneath this sportive narrative, he was secretly declaring *palingenesia* and met-empsychosis, that is, being born again, and transmigration.)[70]

Beroaldo's exegesis is subtle in its shifts of reference. He presents the novel, at one level, as an admonitory fable (*ut admoneremur*), the text being an *inuolucrum* ('wrapper'), containing and concealing the moral content. Lucius' metamorphosis is interpreted tropologically, as a mirror reflecting 'the nature of mortal men and human customs', but Beroaldo also sees it anagogically, as an allegory of the progress of the Soul. He invokes, first, a theologian, the Alexandrian Origen (*c*.185–254), whose attempts to reconcile Christian and Platonic thinking have, over the centuries, attracted admiration and condemnation in almost equal measure.[71] Origen was a speculative theologian, anxious to uphold orthodoxy where doctrine had been settled, but willing to propel his mind deep into uncharted realms. In the Περί ἀρχῶν, he appears to endorse such notions as the pre-formation of souls (and the attendant theory of metempsychosis), the ultimate salvation of all rational creatures (including the devil), and a relationship between the human, the angelic, and the d(a)emonic that is fundamentally metamorphic (and, by the later lights of the Church, heterodox): 'angels may become daemons and daemons angels or men, or...men may become daemons and any being may become any other'.[72] For Origen, such transformations are the result, not of accident or divine caprice, but of the exercise of free will.[73]

With the introduction of the pagan Neoplatonist Proclus (*c*.410–85), Beroaldo's emphasis shifts even more decidedly towards the metaphysical. The asinine transformation can be seen by 'the more learned' (*eruditiores*) to be a 'mystical pretence' (*mysticum praetextum*) beneath which Apuleius secretly (*dissimulanter*) declares Platonic and Pythagorean truths about the passage of the Soul. Beneath the 'sportive narrative' (*ludicra narratio*) there lies an exclusive reading, awaiting the privileged reader.[74]

Unlike those Renaissance translators (such as Boiardo and de la Bouthière) who were so disappointed (or offended) by the Isiac theophany that they

---

[70] See 'Bessarion's Letter on Palingenesis', in Wind, *Pagan Myseries*, 256–8.

[71] Several of the propositions that Origen appears to have expounded in the Περί ἀρχῶν were anathematized at the Second Council of Constantinople in 553 (Butterworth, *On First Principles*, 125 n. 7).

[72] Jerome's version (*Ep. ad Avitum* 10) of the argument of Περί ἀρχῶν, 3. 6. See *On First Principles*, 249 n. 1. Jerome had been an enthusiastic reader of Origen in his youth but became increasingly hostile as he grew older. On Satan, see *On First Principles* 1. 5, pp. 45 ff.

[73] Ibid. 1. 6, p. 57. Cf. 1. 5, p. 51.

[74] Note how this reconfigures previous attacks. We saw, in Ch. 1 (*supra*), the *Historia Augusta*'s account of Septimius Severus ridiculing Clodius Albinus for indulging in Apuleian *ludicra*. See Harrison, *Latin Sophist*, 19.

replaced Apuleius' final book with an ending drawn from the pseudo-Lucianic *Onos*, Beroaldo views Book 11 as the acme of *The Golden Ass*:

<T>otus quidem Apuleius elegantia & eruditione plenus est | hic uero nouissimus liber inter omnis excellit. in quo dicuntur quædam simpliciter | multa ex fide historica plurima ex secretariis philosophiæ & religionis egyptiæ: in principio eloquenter explicatur oratio non asinalis sed theologica ad lunam: (Beroaldo, fol. 251ᵛ)

(The whole of Apuleius is, indeed, full of elegance and erudition, but this last book excels amongst the rest. In it, some things are said simply; many things are said from historical truth, and a great many things from the secret places of philosophy and Egyptian religion. At the beginning is set out eloquently an oration to the moon, not asinine but theological.)

In his epilogue to the work, Beroaldo reaffirms the centrality of magic to the work:

Lectio Asini Apuleiani nimirum speculum est rerum humanarum | istoque inuolucro effecti nostri mores | expressaque mago uitæ quotidianæ conspicitur. Cuius finis & summa beatitas est religio cultusque diuinæ maiestatis una cum eruditione copulata connexaque. Iam uale Decus antistitum & commentarios hosce una cum asino aureo consertos perlege. quo plane opere Lucius noster magiam asserere | eamque rerum omnium potentissimam ostendere pro uirile parte contenditt (Beroaldo, fol. 280ᵛ)

(The reading of Apuleius' *Ass* is truly a mirror of human affairs and in that wrapper our morals are depicted and (expressed in it) the image of our daily life is seen—the end and greatest blessing of which is religion and the worship of divine majesty, joined and connected with learning. Now farewell, gracious Bishop, and read through these commentaries, entwined together with *The Golden Ass;* in which work our Apuleius plainly strove for the manly part, to declare magic and show that it is the most powerful of things.)

'Magic' (*magia*), of course, is to be understood here, not in the modern sense of conjuring or sorcery, but in the esoteric sense of the 'science of the Magi', the *prisca theologia* which so fascinated Pico, Ficino, Henricus Cornelius Agrippa, and other Renaissance Neoplatonists.[75]

   Given this esoteric interest, it may seem curious that (in contrast to Bussi), Beroaldo makes no mention, in his introductory matter, of the tale of Cupid and Psyche and no attempt to use the apparently Platonic content of that myth in support of his claim that Apuleius was displaying Platonic philosophy beneath the veil of the narrative. In the text itself, he gives no indication of the beginning or end of the tale, marking the event only by a paraphrase, in the surrounding commentary, of Fulgentius' exegesis (Beroaldo, fol. 95ʳ⁻ᵛ). Indeed, he remarks: *Non tam allegorias in explicatione huiusce fabulae sectabimur quam historicum sensum et rerum reconditarum verborumque interpretationem explicabimus, ne*

---

[75] See, generally, F. Yates, *Giordano Bruno and the Hermetic Tradition* (London: RKP, 1964); Wind, *Pagan Mysteries*, 6 ff.

philosophaster magis videar quam commentator ('In the explication of this fable we will not hunt down allegories so much as explain the interpretation of recondite matters and words, lest I seem to be a *philosophaster* rather than a commentator').[76]

Beroaldo is able, however, to combine the esoteric with the anecdotal and the deeply personal. Julia Gaisser has pointed to some of Beroaldo's delight-fully intimate digressions, in particular to his celebration of his own wedding:

Condentibus haec nobis et has psyches ac cupidinis nuptias commentantibus siderali opinor decreto factum est, ut ego... uxorem ducerem.... Dii faxint, ut hoc connubium sit nobis foelix faustum ac fortunatum, utque ex eo voluptas gignatur (Beroaldo, fol. 134[r–v])[77]

(While I was producing these [words] and commenting on this marriage of Cupid and Psyche, it happened—by decree of the stars, I fancy—that I took a wife. May the gods grant that this union be happy, favourable, and fortunate for us, and that from it, pleasure may be born)

This is not some aberrant eruption of uxoriousness, but it does indicate divergent tendencies within humanist thinking. In 1470 (in the course of a letter to Francesco Guarneri exposing the errors in Bussi's edition of Pliny's *Natural History*), Niccolò Perotti (Archbishop of Siponto and closely con-nected with members of the Roman Academy) had described the use of editorial prefaces as 'joining a sewer to the altar' (*are cloacam iungere*).[78] Perotti had a keen interest in the *recherché* vocabulary of authors such as Apuleius, but he belongs to the (still honoured) philological tradition which believes that the sacred Classical text should speak in its own voice, untainted by editorial 'presence'.[79] Beroaldo's gloss, in contrast, is symptomatic of his powers of intellectual projection and the intensity of his imaginative iden-tification with Apuleius and his creation.[80] It is the same antiquarian process of cognitive realignment that was such a feature of Leto's sodality, and we see it again in the work published only nine months before Beroaldo's commentary, the *Hypnerotomachia Poliphili*.

---

[76] Cited by Krautter, 149 n. 1, and M. Acocella, *L'Asino d'oro nel Rinascimento: Dai volgar-izzamenti alle raffigurazioni pittoriche* (Ravenna: Longo, 2001), 57.

[77] Gaisser, 'Teaching Classics', 8.

[78] J. Monfasani, 'The First Call for Press Censorship: Niccolò Perotti, Giovanni Andrea Bussi, Antonio Moreto and the Editing of Pliny's *Natural History*', *RQ* 41 (1988), 1–31, at 5 and 26.

[79] *Quis autem eorum qui in presentia vivunt tam temerarius sit aut scripta sua etiam cum infimis conferre?* ('But who of those alive today would be so rash as to dare to compare his own writings to even the worse things of the ancients?'). See Monfasani, 'First Call', 26.

[80] Gaisser, 'Teaching Classics', 6: 'Sometimes... it is hard to decide whether Beroaldo has brought Apuleius to Renaissance Bologna or placed himself in the world of the *Golden Ass.*' Wadsworth ('Filippo Beroaldo', 82) calls attention to Beroaldo's digression (in a gloss on Apuleius' description of Cupid's palace, *AA* 5. 1) celebrating the *voluptas* experienced during holidays spent on his friend Mino Rossi's country estate.

5

The Antiquarian Ass: Apuleius and the *Hypnerotomachia Poliphili* (1499)

The *Hypnerotomachia Poliphili* ('The Strife of Love in a Dream of Poliphilo')—first published in Venice in December 1499—has long been regarded (particularly by art critics and bibliophiles) as one of the great glories (and curiosities) of Western civilization. For George Painter,

> Gutenberg's *Forty-Two-Line Bible* of 1455 and the *Hypnerotomachia* of 1499 confront one another from opposite ends of the incunable period with equal and contrasting pre-eminence. The Gutenberg *Bible* is sombrely and sternly German, Gothic, Christian and mediaeval; the *Hypnerotomachia* is radiantly and graciously Italian, classic, pagan and renascent. These are the two supreme masterpieces of the art of printing, and stand at the two poles of human endeavour and desire.[1]

We shall argue below that this is actually a facile polarization; but Rabelais's parody in *Le Quart Livre* (1548, 1552) conveys (with remarkably little exaggeration) the general impression that a reader is likely to gain by dipping casually into the *Hypnerotomachia*. When the Pantagruelists visit the Island of the Macreons, they are given a tour of the sights by the 'eldest Elderman' named Macrobius (*Macrobe* in the original):

> in the desert and dark Forest, We discover'd several old ruined Temples, Obeliscs, Pyramids, Monuments, and ancient Tombs, with diverse Inscriptions, and Epitaphs, some of them in hieroglyphic Characters, others in the Gothic Dialect, some in the Arabic, Agarenian, [105] Sclavonian, and other Tongues: Of which *Epistemon* took an exact Account (*Desquelz Epistémon feist extraict curieusement*)[2]

The combination of lavish woodcuts and 'exact Accounts' of the ruins that Poliphilo encounters in his dream during his search for Polia has often led to

---

[1] G. D. Painter, *The 'Hypnerotomachia Poliphili' of 1499* (London: Eugrammia, 1963), 3. Cf. Barolini, *Aldus and his Dream Book*, 6.

[2] *Pantagruel's Voyage to the Oracle of the Bottle, Being the Fourth and Fifth Books of the Works of Francis Rabelais, M.D.*, trans. Peter le Motteux (London: Richard Baldwin, 1694), IV. xxv, pp. 104–5. Cf. A. Blunt, 'The *Hypnerotomachia Poliphili* in 17th Century France', *JWI* 1 (1937–8), 117–37; M. Françon, 'Francesco Colonna's *Poliphili Hypnerotomachia* and Rabelais', *MLR* 50 (1955), 52–5; A. K. Hieatt and A. L. Prescott, 'Contemporizing Antiquity: The *Hypnerotomachia* and its Afterlife in France', *Word & Image* 8 (1992), 291–321.

the misnomer, 'architectural treatise', being applied to the *Hypnerotomachia*. Much of Book 1, it is true, seems to be an extended exercise in *effictio*: a series of *ecphrases* of curious buildings and monuments, an architectural extravaganza inspired by Vitruvius' *De architectura*, Leon Battista Alberti's *De re aedificatoria* (wr. *c*.1450, pr. 1482), and the physical traces of Classical antiquity that surrounded the author.[3]

The pictorial, however, is merely one facet of the *Hypnerotomachia*'s achievement. For while it was the only illustrated book to issue from Aldus Manutius' press, it was also 'the first vernacular work' and 'the first modern work of a purely literary nature'.[4] And although it is almost completely ignored by literary historians, the *Hypnerotomachia* is probably the most remarkable piece of prose fiction to emerge in the fifteenth century and deserves (with all its bizarreries) an honoured place in the Western Canon between the *Decameron* and *Gargantua and Pantagruel*.[5] It is certainly the work of Renaissance literature that displays most exuberantly its debts to Apuleius.[6] Indeed, it provides a conspectus of ancient, medieval, and Renaissance fiction. This is where *Le Roman de la Rose*, the *Divine Comedy*, Petrarch's *Trionfi*, and Boccaccio's *Ameto* and *Amorosa visione* meet *The Golden Ass*.

The *Hypnerotomachia* is divided into two books of unequal length and distinct emphases, and both its date and authorship are subjects of lively debate. Though published anonymously in December 1499, the closing chapter of the second (and shorter) book is dated 1 May 1467, while the initial letters of the thirty-eight chapters in the work as a whole form an acrostic: *POLIAM FRATER FRANCISCVS COLVMNA PERAMAVIT* ('Brother Francesco Colonna loved Polia exceedingly'). This *frater* is traditionally identified as a friar (b. 1433/4, d. 1527) of SS. Giovanni e Paolo, an unreformed Dominican monastery in Venice, though another contender is the Francesco Colonna who was a prince of Palestrina (the site of ancient Praeneste, 20 miles to the east of Rome) and, reputedly, a member (*frater*) of Pomponio Leto's Roman Academy.[7] Some scholars, however, have dismissed the acrostic as a

---

[3] L. Lefaivre notes that 200 of the book's 370 pages 'are exclusively devoted to architectural description'. See *Leon Battista Alberti's 'Hypnerotomachia Poliphili': Re-cognizing the Architectural Body in the Early Italian Renaissance* (Cambridge, Mass.: MIT, 1997), 9.

[4] P. Dronke, introd. to facs. edn., *Francesco Colonna: Hypnerotomachia Poliphili (Venetiis, Aldo Manuzio, 1499)* (Saragossa: Ediciones de Pórtico, 1981), 16.

[5] Pozzi's description of the work as a 'romanzo... senza narrato' is justly demolished by Dronke, *Francesco Colonna*, 10–11. See M. T. Casella and G. Pozzi, *Francesco Colonna: Biografia e opera*, 2 vols. (Padua: Antenore, 1959), ii. 124.

[6] P. Emison calls the work a 'memorable spin-off on Apuleius' *Golden Ass*'. See 'Asleep in the Grass of Arcady: Giulio Campagnola's Dreamer', *RQ* 45 (1992), 271–92, at 279.

[7] M. Calvesi, *Il Sogno di Polifilo prenestino* (Rome: Officina, 1980). Feld ('First Roman Printers', 66) cites Calvesi as authority for the 'compelling evidence... that *Hypnerotomachia* was of Roman provenance and that its inspiration came from the humanist circles associated

literary feint, championing, as the real author, a wide range of figures, including Felice Feliciano, Lorenzo de' Medici, Fra Eliseo da Treviso, and Leon Battista Alberti.[8]

The question is too complex for detailed discussion here and, for the sake of convenience, I will retain the traditional attribution, 'Colonna', while noting my instinctive feeling that the acrostic is part of an elaborate game over authorial identity and that the work is not only a 'Romano-Venetian hybrid', as Rowland calls it, but a collaborative venture.[9] The *Hypnerotomachia* published in 1499 seems to be based on a shorter work, quite possibly drafted by the Dominican Francesco Colonna in 1467. The printed edition may well have involved additional input from Francesco, but it also appears to owe much to its sponsor, the Veronese lawyer Leonardo Grassi, and his associates (who include, I suspect, Pierio Valeriano's uncle, Fra Urbano Bolzanio).[10] One aspect of authorship, however, is beyond dispute: whoever

with Sweynheim and Pannartz'. Calvesi's thesis has been strenuously opposed by Pozzi and others, but he has, more recently, established links between Grassi and Rome. See his '*Hypnerotomachia Poliphili*. Nuovi riscontri e nuove evidenze documentarie per Francesco Colonna signore di Praeneste', *Storia dell'arte* 60 (1987), 85–136. Cf. Brown, *Venice & Antiquity*, 287–90. Leonardo Grassi was 'a Venetian humanist with a position in the Roman curial court'. See Rowland, *The Culture of the High Renaissance*, 66. As an example of the use of *frater* in the Pomponian Academy, one might note the title of a poem from 1468 by Paolo Marsi da Pescina, *Ad fratres Academicos Romae captivos* ('To the Brothers of the Academy imprisoned at Rome'). See Palermino, 'The Roman Academy', 124 n. 27.

[8] For overviews, see Rowland, *Culture*, 272–3, and Brown, *Venice & Antiquity*, 287–90.

[9] Rowland, *Culture*, 273 n. 37. A copy of the *Hypnerotomachia* now in Strasbourg (Bibliothèque Nationale et Universitaire) contains a tantalizing anonymous annotation: *Fertur operis huius auctor reverendus magister Boninus de Ligniaco seu Lignago, magister in sacra pagina, frater ordinis predicatorum, qui mihi dixit habuisse duos socios et fecisse cum iuvenilem etatem ageret* ('The author of this work is said to be the Reverend Master Bonino of Ligniaco or Lignago, a master of scripture, a friar of the Order of Preachers, who told me that he had two accomplices, and that he did it when he was a young man'). The authorship of the *Hypnerotomachia* is the subject of Ian Caldwell and Dustin Thomason's thriller *The Rule of Four* (New York: Dial P, 2004) and Joscelyn Godwin's *The Real Rule of Four: The Unauthorized Guide to the 'New York Times' Bestseller* (New York: Disinformation Company, 2005).

[10] In the liminary verses, Giovanni Battista Scita describes the work as the child of 'two fathers' (*bis genitum*), Poliphilo and Crasso (fol. 2ʳ; G 3). For further discussion, see Ch. 6, ('Sodalities'), *infra*. Fra Urbano Bolzanio (1442–1524) studied at both Treviso and Venice, was a noted enthusiast of hieroglyphs, a teacher of Sabellico (Pomponio Leto's first biographer), and an editor of Greek texts for Aldus Manutius. I am grateful to Dr Paolo Pellegrini for sending me a copy of G. Biasuz, 'Le probabili relazioni di Pierio Valeriano e Gio. Battista Scita con l'autore del *Polifilo*', *Archivo storico de Belluno, Feltro e Cadore* 31 (1960), 148–9, as well as for pointing out its defects. Painter seems to make the same mistake as Biasuz in confusing Valeriano with his uncle when he claims (19) that Valeriano 'studied theology at Treviso in 1466–72 when the *Hypnerotomachia* was in its first gestation there'. Valeriano's *Hieroglyphica* (Basle: [Michael Isengrin], 1556; Basil: Thomas Guarin, 1567) draws at several points on the *Hypnerotomachia*.

wrote (or polished) the *Hypnerotomachia* was (or were) saturated in the works of Apuleius.[11]

LANGUAGE AND ALLUSION IN THE *HYPNEROTOMACHIA*

Humanism in the latter part of the quattrocento tended to endorse two models for prose composition: 'Classical' (increasingly taken to be synonymous with 'Ciceronian') Latin and the Tuscan dialect which had been promoted since the time of Petrarch and Boccaccio as the national standard for the (literary) vernacular. Colonna opted for neither model, fashioning the *Hypnerotomachia* from an almost macaronic melange of Italian and Latin, pervaded by Apuleian diction.[12] For Painter, 'The *Hypnerotomachia* is the *Finnegan's Wake* of the fifteenth century'.[13] More typical is the response of Martin Lowry who calls it 'a linguistic and literary debauch, choked with recondite imagery, erudite periphrases, and exotic verbiage: a work so bizarre that many critics have felt a certain uneasiness at Aldus' agreeing to print it'.[14] Colonna's hybrid style may have offended linguistic purists, but Baldassare Castiglione's Giuliano dei Medici suggests that it appealed to a particular class of amorous courtier, even if the ladies were more bemused than allured by Poliphilian discourse:

ché già ho io conosciuti alcuni che, scrivendo e parlando a donne, usan sempre parole di Polifilo e tanto stanno in su la sottilità della retorica, che quelle si diffidano di se stesse e si tengon per ignorantissime, e par loro un'ora mill'anni finir quel ragionamento e levarsegli davanti; [435] *altri si vantano senza modo;*

For in times past I have knowen some that in writinge and speakinge to women used evermore the woordes of Poliphilus, and ruffled so in their subtill pointes of Rhetoricke, that the women were oute of conceit with their owne selves, and reckened

---

[11] It is possible to construct a network linking interests in Apuleius, architecture, print technology, and art. We have mentioned (Ch. 4, *supra*) Alberti's use of *The Golden Ass* in his satirical fictions; his visit to Sweynheim and Pannartz's printing press at Subiaco; and his dedication to Bussi of the *De statua* (*c*.1464). Lefaivre overlooks much of this evidence, but does observe (157) that Poliphilo is dressed like a papal abbreviator (Alberti was one of the abbreviators purged in 1464). We might also note that during the period 1466–7 (1467 being a key date in the genesis of the *Hypnerotomachia*, as well as the year in which Leto left Rome and the printing press arrived), Bussi was 'in the retinue of cardinal Juan de Carvajal, then on legation in Venice'. See Lee, *Sixtus IV*, 105.

[12] P. Dronke, introd., *Francesco Colonna*, 21.

[13] *The 'Hypnerotomachia Poliphili'*, 6.

[14] *World of Aldus*, 120.

themselves most ignoraunt, and an houre seemed a thousand yeere to them, to ende
that talke and to be rid of them . . . [15]

   But however perplexing or ridiculous Poliphilian words may have appeared to
subsequent ears, a serious purpose lay behind them. While the upper-case type
of the *Hypnerotomachia* mimics the finest Classical inscriptions,[16] its language
functions more diachronically, making manifest both the pastness and presence
of the ancient world. Renaissance Ciceronians strove to refine (and confine)
their Latin style, to imitate as closely as possible the purity attained in a
particular place (Rome) at a particular time (the last days of the Republic).
Colonna, in contrast, is an eclectic of an extreme kind, choosing his diction from
archaic, classical, and decadent sources, but mixing these Latin 'finds' with
dialect words from the Veneto.[17] The result is a language that works triadically,
carrying within itself the splendours of the past, the 'ruins of Time' (in all their
pathos and attractiveness), and the attempt to repair the effects of that decay
while creating something new (and, potentially, superior).[18]
   Edoardo Fumagalli's investigations into Apuleian borrowings in the *Hypnerotomachia* support the view of a two-stage production of the text:
'Colonna' draws, throughout Book 1 (printed in 1499), on the 1488 Vicenza
edition of Apuleius' works, but depends, for most of Book 2 (dated 1467), on
one or more manuscripts.[19] Colonna's engagements with *The Golden Ass* over
the course of these two or three decades take many forms. At the most
obvious level, Apuleian allusions are drawn into the pattern of mythological
parallels that Colonna provides for his two main characters, Poliphilo and
Polia. For example, while fleeing the dragon that he imagines to be pursuing
him through a labyrinth, Poliphilo describes himself as being:

*in maiore spauento & exitio, delursato Thrasileo latrone, & in maiore angustie di Psyche
& in piu laboriosi periculi dil asinato Lucio. Et quando egli sentiua il consilio degli latroni
dil suo interito . . .* (F.C. d4ʳ)[20]

---

   [15] *Il cortegiano* (1528), III. lxx. See *Il libro del cortegiano con una scelta delle opere minori*, ed.
B. Maier, 2nd edn. (Turin: UTET, 1964), 434–5; *The Book of the Courtier*, trans. Sir Thomas
Hoby, introd. W. H. D. Rouse (London: Dent, 1928; repr. 1959), 250. *Il cortegiano* is set in
Urbino in 1507, but Castiglione also spent many years in Rome where he was a member of the
second Roman Academy (Rowland, *Culture*, 252).
   [16] See Lowry, *World of Aldus*, 137; Brown, *Venice & Antiquity*, 272; Painter, 18.
   [17] Brown, *Venice & Antiquity*, 290.
   [18] Cf. D'Amico's discussion of *aemulatio* ('Progress', 358).
   [19] E. Fumagalli, 'Francesco Colonna lettore di Apuleio e il problema della datazione dell'
Hypnerotomachia Poliphili', *IMU* 27 (1984), 233–66.
   [20] Thrasyleon provides an ironic contrast to Poliphilo: despite being surrounded by dogs and
armed men, he maintains his pretence to the end in a magnificent display of doomed heroism
(*AA* 4. 15–21). At *AA* 6. 31–2, the thieves resolve to kill and gut the ass and sew Charite naked
inside his belly, with only her head sticking out. Her projected fate—exposed on the top of some
'jagged rock' (*super aliquod saxum scruposum*) where she is to be devoured by animals—
parodies Psyche's exposure at *AA* 4. 35.

...more trembling then the theefe Thrasilius in his beares skinne. In sorrowe more abounding then poor *Pscyphes*. And in more laboursome daunger then *Lucius Apuleus*, when hee heard the theeues consulting to knocke him on the head and kyll him (R.D. I1ʳ; = G 63)[21]

Apuleian allusions of this kind are, as we shall see, repeated throughout the work. Moreover, in the latter part of Book 1, Psyche appears (with her husband, Cupid) as a direct participant in the action on the island of Cytherea. But besides such explicit references to *The Golden Ass*, we can also trace a steady stream of more covert Apuleian influence. At least 131 of the 459 pages of Pozzi and Ciapponi's edition contain significant allusions to, or echoes of, *The Golden Ass*; and this tally does not take account of the copious borrowings from Apuleius' other works which these editors have noticed, particularly from the *Apologia*, *Florida*, and *De deo Socratis*.[22]

The academic pursuit of 'echoes' and 'allusions' raises, of course, both theoretical and historical questions.[23] It is one thing to identify the primary materials that went into the composition of a particular work; it is quite another to prove that such 'sources' determine the way that the work is, or ought to be, read. We should therefore be cautious about endowing lexical parallels with particular interpretive significance. It would be sensible to assume, as the starting point for our investigations, that the primary motivation behind Colonna's Apuleian diction was antiquarian or epideictic. Indeed, the glossematic impulse has much in common with the numismatic: in the milieu of the eclectic or archaizing humanists, rare old words are just as likely as ancient coins to be dug up and put on display.[24] Erasmus may have

[21] *Hypnerotomachia. The Strife of Loue in a Dreame* (London: Simon Waterstone, 1592), facs. edn., introd. L. Gent (Delmar, NY: Scholars' Facsimiles & Reprints, 1973). Other issues were printed for William Holme and John Busbie. The translator, 'R.D.', is generally identified with (Sir) Robert Dallington (1561–1637), a Cambridge-educated schoolmaster who rose to be master of Charterhouse (1624–37). See K. J. Höltgen, 'Sir Robert Dallington (1561–1637): Author, Traveler, and Pioneer of Taste', *HLQ* 47 (1984), 147–77. Since R.D. translates only about 40 per cent of the *Hypnerotomachia*, I have moved freely between his version and the complete translation by Joscelyn Godwin (London: Thames & Hudson, 1999), references to the latter being indicated by the abbreviation 'G' followed by the page number. The folio numbers of the 1592 translation are so erratic that I have cited by signatures throughout. R.D.'s rendering of *asinato Lucio* ('Lucius-turned-ass') as '*Lucius Apuleus*' obscures the fact that Apuleius is never named in the course of the work.

[22] *Hypnerotomachia Poliphili. Edizione critica e commento*, ed. Pozzi and Ciapponi. No fewer than 445 passages in the *Hypnerotomachia* have been traced to Apuleius (Lefaivre, 58, citing Pozzi and Ciapponi's *Commento*)—a tally twice that for Ovid (223) and surpassed only by Pliny the Elder (500). Fumagalli ('Francesco Colonna lettore di Apuleio') adds many Apuleian borrowings overlooked by Pozzi and Ciapponi.

[23] See e.g. S. Hinds, *Allusion and Intertext: Dynamics of Appropriation in Roman Poetry* (Cambridge: CUP, 1998).

[24] Feld points out ('First Roman Printers', 16) that 'The method of [Valla's] *Elegantiae* was archaeological.' The same might be said of Perotti's *Cornu Copiae*.

had the *Hypnerotomachia* in mind in the *Moriae encomium* when he made Folly ridicule the excavation of such Apuleianisms as *bu(b)sequa* ('cowherd'):

Iam adde et hoc voluptatis genus, quoties istorum aliquis Anchisae matrem aut voculam vulgo incognitam in putri quapiam charta deprehenderit, puta bubsequam, bouinatorem aut manticulatorem, aut si quis vetusti saxi fragmentum, mutilis notatum literis alicubi effoderit: O Iupiter, quae tum exultatio, qui triumphi, quae encomia, perinde quasi vel Africam deuicerint vel Babylonas ceperint![25]

(Then there's this further type of pleasure. Whenever one of them digs out of some mouldy manuscript the name of Anchises' mother or some trivial word the ordinary man doesn't know, such as neatherd, tergiversator, cutpurse, or if anyone unearths a scrap of old stone with a fragmentary inscription, O Jupiter, what a triumph! What rejoicing, what eulogies! They might have conquered Africa or captured Babylon.)[26]

We know, from the researches of Pozzi and others, that Colonna sought out recondite terms in the works of many authors besides Apuleius—most prominently, Pliny the Elder, Aulus Gellius, Martianus Capella, and Nonius Marcellus. He also appears to have depended on contemporary glossematic works such as Niccolò Perotti's *Cornu Copiae* (first printed in 1489, but republished by Aldus just six months before the *Hypnerotomachia*) which, though ostensibly concerned with Martial, makes frequent reference to 'Apuleius'.[27] We know, too, that humanists such as Angelo Colocci (who took over Pomponio Leto's house on the Quirinal after his death and headed the revived Academia

---

[25] *Opera omnia*, iv–3 (Amsterdam: North Holland, 1979), 138. Erasmus includes *bu(b)sequa* (from *AA* 8. 1) in *De copia*, Book I, *Opera omnia* i-6 (Amsterdam: North-Holland, 1988), 50. Notice that Erasmus (however ironically) applies the term *voluptas* to this pursuit of philological archaeology.

[26] *Praise of Folly*, trans. B. Radice, introd. A. H. T. Levi (London: Penguin, 1971), 145 [= ch. 49]. Cf. *CWE* xxvii. 123.

[27] Perotti's citations raise interesting problems since only 26 of the 181 quotations ascribed to 'Apuleius' come from Apuleian texts known to us today. See R. P. Oliver, ' "New Fragments" of Latin Authors in Perotti's *Cornucopiae*', *TAPA* 78 (1947), 376–424; S. Prete, 'La questione della lingua latina nel Quattrocento e l'importanza dell'opera di Apuleio', *GCN* 1 (1988), 123–40, at 128–38; F. Brancaleone, 'Considerazioni sulle citazioni apuleiane e pseudo-apuleiane nel *Cornu Copiae* di Perotti', *SUP* 14 (1994), 49–54; A. Stramaglia, 'Apuleio come *auctor*: Premesse tardoantiche di un uso umanistico', *SUP* 16 (1996), 137–61. For Perotti's use of the pseudo-Apuleian *De nota aspirationis*, see L. Biondi, '*Hara*. Nuove considerazione sul problema', *ACME* 54/1 (2001), 59–84. The likelihood is that the otherwise unattested 'Apuleian' quotations are Renaissance forgeries, but that in itself indicates the status of 'Apuleius' as a site of linguistic play amongst quattrocento humanists. The Aldine edn. of the *Cornu Copiae* (July 1499) is the first to employ the type-face (described by Painter, 18, as 'improved Bembo') made famous by the *Hypnerotomachia*. Perotti had been secretary to Cardinal Bessarion and took over the position of *corrector* (in-house editor) to Sweynheim and Pannartz when Bussi became Vatican Librarian in Apr. 1472 (Feld, 'First Roman Printers', 29). His edn. of Pliny's *Historia naturalis* is dated 7 May 1473. As Palermino notes (121 n. 11), Perotti 'was an associate of Pomponio and a collaborator with him in scholarly enterprises'. These associations may constitute additional circumstantial evidence for a Roman provenance for the *Hypnerotomachia*.

Romana) were in the habit of 'tabulating' books as they read them, drawing up (often in the margins) lists of words as an aide-memoire.[28] The *Tabula Apulei* that opens Beroaldo's commentary reflects the same interest: *Habes Lector humanissimæ. L. Apulei de Asino aureo tabulam uocabulorum & historiarum*... In the dedicatory epistle to the *Hypnerotomachia*, 'Poliphilo' makes the tantalizing claim that he abandoned the original style of the work and 'translated' it into the present one at Polia's behest (*lasciando il principiato stilo, & in questo ad tua instantia traducto*, F.C. a1ᵛ). Very frequently, the words that Colonna appropriates are *hapax legomena* (forms that appear only once in the whole corpus of Classical literature) or they are exclusive to Apuleius. One can readily imagine 'Colonna' embellishing original drafts with such words or phrases drawn from 'tables' or commonplace books that he had compiled himself; and in such a process the borrowings might be completely stripped of their Apuleian context.[29]

Colonna, for example, borrows diction (including one of the rare words—*bu(b)sequa*—to which Folly objects) from the opening of the slave's account of Charite's death—*Equisones, opilionesque, etiam busequae* ('Grooms and shepherds, neatherds too', *AA* 8. 1)—for the very different purpose of evoking the solitude of the landscape in which Poliphilo finds himself at the beginning of the dream: *non uideua Opilione alcuno,... ne Busequa, ne Equisio* ('one could see no shepherd... herdsman or groom', F.C. a3ʳ; G 13).[30] Similarly, he redeploys a phrase from Lucius' description of the statuary of Diana and Actaeon (*mustulentus autumnus*, 'Autumn abounding in new wine', *AA* 2. 4) in his picture of Poliphilo in the wood, 'trembling like the loose leaves shaken by furious Aquilon in the vinous autumn' (*mustulento autumno*, G 15; F.C. a4ʳ).

In case after case, however, an awareness of Apuleian diction in the *Hypnerotomachia* has interpretive significance. Peter Dronke has provided a brief but brilliant account of the 'imaginative penetration' with which Colonna read Apuleius: 'it is the particular *conjointure* of eroticism and gnosis in Apuleius' romance that was a decisive influence on Francesco's thought, and hence also a wellspring for his diction'.[31]

Attempts to reconstruct early reading communities or original 'horizons of expectations' (to use Jauss's term) are bound to be fraught, but there is sufficient documentary and material evidence to indicate that the *Hypnerotomachia*

[28] Rowland (*Culture*, fig. 4) reproduces a page from Pliny's *Historia naturalis* 8 which has been tabulated in this way by Marco Fabio Calvo and Colocci.

[29] *Mutatis mutandis* if we accept the theory of collaborative authorship, or of an earlier work being revised by members of Grassi's circle.

[30] Even here, it is possible (at a pinch) to impute hermeneutic significance to the borrowing. If one accepts the theory (posited below) of a hierophantic use of Apuleian diction, one might read the passage as a coded allusion to the fact that, beyond the framework of the dream, Polia—typologically linked with Charite—is actually dead.

[31] *Francesco Colonna*, 66 and 18.

was not, in commercial terms, at least, an immediate success.[32] In 1509, many copies of the original edition (priced at 1 ducat each) were still unsold; and many of those that had been purchased remained (to judge from their almost pristine state today) unread: there were clearly plenty of non-buyers and non-readers who simply declined Colonna's invitation to participate in the linguistic and literary games that he provided in the *Hypnerotomachia*.[33] Yet annotated copies of the *Hypnerotomachia* do exist, providing indisputable evidence that the generous margins of the Aldine edition attracted glossematic attention of the precise kind that I have been suggesting. The sixteenth-century marginalia to a copy now held at Modena identify some sixty authors, including Apuleius, Francesco Filelfo, Pomponio Leto, and Niccolò Perotti.[34] Dorothea Stichel observes that the reader 'very often records the author, and sometimes also the title of the work', but also 'occasionally book, chapter, column etcetera'. But while he 'deals with the form, meaning and use of individual words' and does much, '[b]y means of paraphrases', to elucidate 'the cryptic allusions so dear to the author of the *Hypnerotomachia*', he seems to treat it 'more or less as a non-fictional work.... There are no stylistic observations at all, no allegorical interpretations'.[35] The copies discussed by Edoardo Fumagalli, however, do include interpretive marginalia of a more allegorical kind.[36] The copy now in the Biblioteca Comunale in Siena contains annotations by two hands 'contemporaneous with the printing of the *Hypnerotomachia*'.[37] Hand C responds to Poliphilo's wandering in the forest (sig. a3$^\mathrm{v}$) with a note that begins: *Poliphilus, indulgens voluptati et delascivo amori, deperdit viam virtutis sequebaturque ignorantiam fomitem errorum...* ('Poliphilo, indulging in pleasure and lascivious

---

[32] See Rowland, *Culture*, 273 n. 37, and 276 n. 52. It may be that the *Hypnerotomachia* is only now finding the wider readership that it deserves. While an undistinguished copy of the first edn. was available on the internet in Sept. 2006 for US$185,000, Thames & Hudson recently (2005) brought out a reduced-size paperback version (£8.54) of Joscelyn Godwin's translation (first published in 1999).

[33] The 'Anonymous Elegy to the Reader' ends with the warning: 'Behold a useful and profitable book. If you think otherwise, | Do not lay the blame on the book, but on yourself' (G 5). Cf. Rowland (*Culture*, 66) for comments on the unreadability of the *Hypnerotomachia*. In his *De rerum varietate* (the section entitled *Cura morborum superstitiosa*), Girolamo Cardano (1501–76) claims that 'Whenever I hear the story of Poliphilo I fall asleep immediately' (*Ego cum audio Poliphili historiam statim dormio*). See his *Opera omnia*, ed. Charles Spon (Lyons: Jean-Antoine Huguetan & Marc-Antoine Rauaud, 1663), iii. 169; and D. Stichel, 'Reading the *Hypnerotomachia Poliphili* in the *Cinquecento*: Marginal Notes in a Copy at Modena', in *Aldus Manutius and Renaissance Culture*, ed. D. S. Zeidberg and F. G. Superbi (Florence: Olschki, 1998), 217–36, at 217.

[34] Stichel, 223–4.

[35] Ibid. 222 and 234.

[36] 'Due esemplari dell' *Hypnerotomachia Poliphili* di Francesco Colonna', *Aevum* 66/ 2 (1992), 419–32. Cf. Brown, *Venice & Antiquity*, 290.

[37] Fumagalli, 'Due esemplari', 423.

love, loses the way of virtue and began to follow ignorance, the kindling-wood of errors...'). Hand A complements C with what Fumagalli calls 'un parallelo non ovvia':

Apuleius platonicae disciplinae imitator multa varia et nephanda se vidisse scribit, dum corium asininum indutum fingat, profecto ne insimularetur, comodo ea vidisset quae nepharium est coram hominibus perpetrare et palam narare. Scimus enim iumenta homines in agendis sceleribus nequaquam vereri, verentur vero hominum aspectus: iccirco finxit se asinum ad tot delatus (sic) erumnas, cui non erat respectus: igitur ubicumque ut asinus assistebat, ea in eius aspectu fiebat (sic), quae nequaquam in praesentia hominum agerentur. Poliphilus, imitator Apulegii, volens igitur narare multa et varia, quae homini realiter apparere non possunt, igitur non forma beluina tectus voluit manifestare se vidisse quae naraturus est, sed in somno et non realiter. Nihilominus cuncta quae in somno se vidisse recitat, narat tamquam si cuncta realiter et sensibus vidisset descenditque ad particulas, quod factum ab aliquo non habetur observatum, nisi a Luciano in quibusdam picturis.[38]

(Apuleius, an imitator of Platonic teaching, writes that he saw many diverse and unmentionable things while clad, as he feigns, in the hide of an ass, assuredly to avoid being interrogated as to how he managed to see things which it is a crime to commit and narrate openly in the presence of men. For we know that men, when they are committing crimes, do not fear beasts of burden at all; but they do fear the gaze of humans. For that reason, he feigned himself an ass, subjected to so many hardships—an ass to which no regard was paid. Therefore, wherever he was an asinine bystander, things went on beneath his gaze which would never have been done in the presence of humans. Poliphilus, an imitator of Apuleius, wanting therefore to relate diverse and varied things which could not appear to a man in reality, therefore wanted to make clear that he had seen what he was about to relate, not hidden in the shape of a beast, but in a dream and not in real life. Nonetheless, everything that he tells us that he saw in a dream, he relates as if he had seen it in real life and with his senses, and he comes down to small details, which has not been observed being done by anyone, except by Lucian in some of his sketches.)

The comparison is certainly an arresting one. The *somnium*, or dream-vision, was as much a feature of Renaissance humanist culture as it was of medieval literature, and its use by Colonna hardly demands a reference to *The Golden Ass*. Nor is there anything obviously Apuleian about the passage being glossed. The willingness to provide a totalizing Apuleian reading of the *Hypnerotomachia* at such an early stage in the book suggests that 'A' has recognized (or is privy to) the author's intention of mapping Poliphilo's adventures onto those of Lucius.

The annotations by Hand A evidently carried some weight, for the State Library of New South Wales' copy of the 1499 *Hypnerotomachia* (Z/LQ2/C) contains (sig. a2[r]) a modified version of them:

Poliphilus imitator L. Apul. volens narrare multa et varia quae homini realiter aparere non possunt, non forma beluina tectus, sed somno oppressus, multa se vidisse commemorat

[38] Fumagalli, 'Due esemplari', 430.

tanquam si cuncta sensibus subiecta vidisset descenditque ad minima et particularia describenda, Lucium ac Lucianum in suis fictis narrationibus imitatus, ut humana omnia quae sensibiliter seu ymaginarie comprehenduntur non nisi somnium esse demonstrat, etc.[39]

(Poliphilus, an imitator of Apuleius, wanting to relate many and varied things which could not appear to a man in reality, recalls that he saw many things—not hidden in the shape of a beast, but overcome by a dream—as if all the things that he had seen had been comprehended by the senses; and he comes down to the smallest details and particulars, having imitated Lucius and Lucian in their fictional narratives, so that he proves that all mortal things which are comprehended by the senses or the imagination are nothing but a dream. . . .)

Taken together, these annotated copies suggest that at least some sixteenth-century readers were prepared to treat the *Hypnerotomachia* in the same way that its author(s) had treated the classical texts. Given such evidence of contemporary readers' ability to recognize Colonna's extensive pattern of explicit allusions and tacit borrowings, we may feel more confident about drawing the whole of *The Golden Ass* into the hermeneutic field of the *Hypnerotomachia*. The result is a two-way exchange: a knowledge of Apuleius helps to illuminate and enrich our reading of the *Hypnerotomachia* and the intellectual culture from which it emerged; but Colonna's reworkings can also serve as a gloss or commentary on *The Golden Ass*.[40]

At the same time, we need to remember that, for humanists like Colonna, *renovatio* involves not merely *imitatio*, but *aemulatio*. While drawing his inspiration from the past, Colonna repeatedly insists that the buildings which Poliphilo encounters surpass anything that existed in Antiquity. He seems to take a similar approach to the texts (such as *The Golden Ass*) which he transforms. As he sits with Polia 'among the sweete flowers and redolent roses', Poliphilo declares: 'The flouds and fields of Thessalie must giue place to this' (*Ceda quiqui dunque il thessalico fiume & agro*, R.D. Cc3^r; F.C. p4^r; = G 239). And the nymphs and youths attending the *trionfi* are dressed, 'not in Milesian wool' (*non di Milesia lana*), but in materials of an unparalleled

---

[39] Ibid. 430 n. 18.

[40] We might compare the role of Colonna's other major quarry, Pliny's *Historia naturalis*: it may be used to solve certain local problems in the *Hypnerotomachia* (the meaning of a recondite term, the identity of a particular gem or plant), but it also serves, in the words of Leonard Barkan, as 'the central grounding text of the rediscovery of ancient art' in the Renaissance. See *Unearthing the Past: Architecture and Aesthetics in the Making of Renaissance Culture* (New Haven: YUP, 1999), 66. As we have seen, Bessarion and Bussi both mention Pliny in the context of Apuleius (Miglio, 10–11). Note the edns. of Pliny by Bussi (1470), Perotti (1473), and Beroaldo (1476, with many reprints, including one from Treviso, 1479: Goff P-0791); Sabellico's *Emendationes seu annotationes in Plinium* (Venice: n.p., *c.*1497); and the tabulating of a copy by Angelo Colocci. See Monfasani, 'First Call for Press Censorship', *passim*.

delicacy, including 'linen finer than any produced in Egypt' (*tali di Lino subtilissimo quale nello Aegypto non e producto*, G 156; F.C. k2ᵛ).[41] Given the association of Isiac priests with white linen (e.g. Zatchlas in *AA* 2. 28), it is tempting to see this as a coded reference to Colonna's claim for a higher significance in the fabric of 'mere' tales.[42]

GELOIASTOS AND THE FIVE SENSES

We find, for instance, frequent instances of Colonna dismembering Apuleius' story but then recombining elements in his own narrative to systematic effect. Early on in the *Hypnerotomachia*, Poliphilo encounters a group of extremely hospitable nymphs (allegorically, the Five Senses) who invite him to join them as they bathe naked in an ornamental fountain which sports the inscription ΓΕΛΟΙΑΣΤΟΣ.[43] Overcoming his initial reluctance, he enjoys himself immensely with the nymphs until Achoe ('Hearing') asks him to fetch cold water from the statue of a 'pissing Boye':

And I had no sooner set my foote vpon the steppe, to receiue the water, as it fell, but the pissing Boye lift vp his pricke, and cast sodeinlye so colde water vppon my face, that I lyke at that instant to haue fallen backward. Whereat they so laughed, and it made [M3ʳ] such a sounde in the roundnes and closeness of the bathe, that I also beganne (when I was come to my selfe) to laugh that I was almost dead. (R.D. M2ᵛ–M3ʳ; = G 85; = F.C. e7ʳ)

Colonna's fountain partakes of a long tradition of seductive but destructive waters (one recalls the fates of Narcissus, Hylas, Actaeon, Leucippus et al.). It has an immediate counterpart in the 'clear fountain that, laughing, kills' (*chiaro fonte, che, ridendo, occide*) described by Matteo Maria Boiardo in poem 82 of his *Amorum libri*, and in the 'stream which has the name of Laughter but in truth is a source of Lamentation' (*una riviera, | Qual nome ha Riso, e veramente è un pianto*) which figures in the *Orlando innamorato* (III. vi. 55);[44] and it looks

---

[41] R.D. ignores the 'Milesian' reference, but gives 'some in white curled Sendall, such as Ægipt neuer affoorded' (Y4ʳ). Cf. Colonna's description of the arrangement of flowers just before the Isis-inspired Venereal theophany: 'there was nothing like it in Memphis' (G 357). In some Egyptian texts, Memphis was the place in which Osiris' penis was buried after his dismemberment by Seth.

[42] For Pliny on *aemulatio*, see Barkan, *Unearthing the Past*, 74.

[43] From γέλως ('laughter', 'matter for laughter'). Note the form ὁ γελοιαστής ('jester', 'buffoon'). Lefaivre (156) points to the appearance of a character named Gelastos in Alberti's *Momus*.

[44] See J. A. Cavallo, *Boiardo's Orlando innamorato: An Ethics of Desire* (Rutherford: Fairleigh Dickinson UP, 1993), 123. On the reception of Colonna's fountain episode in the English

forward to Tasso's *fonte del riso*, the deadly fountain of laughter near Armida's palace (*GL* xiv. 74).[45]

However, the specific combination of laughter, total sensory indulgence, and (mock) punishment in the fountain is the result of Colonna's conflation of the Ficinian tradition of the Banquet of the Senses with three elements from the early books of *The Golden Ass*: the Festival of Risus (3. 1–11), the affair with Fotis, and the voiding of the witches' bladders over Aristomenes' face (1. 13).[46] After the bath, the nymphs anoint themselves with soothing unguents and hand Poliphilo a jar so that he can follow their example (a clear parody of Pamphile's anointings in *AA* 3. 21 and Lucius' in 3. 24). They open 'vases of delicate confections' (*delicatissimi confecti*) 'which they and I enjoyed tasting, and afterwards came precious drink' (*il pretioso poto*), perhaps reflecting the 'arrangements for a banquet' (*epularum dispositiones*) that Fotis has made for Lucius in the form of 'appetizers for the gladiatorial games of Venus' (*gladiatoriae Veneris antecenia, AA* 2. 15). And then:

Dunque sufficientemente refecte & reiterabonde ad gli speculi cum scrupuloso examine del decoramento delle diue praesentie et della luculente fronte, ombrata di globuli degli flaui crinuli antependuli. Et cum limpico tegmine gli madidi crini obuoluti (F.C. e7ᵛ)

(When they had eaten enough they returned to their mirrors for a minute examination of the ornaments on their divine bodies and radiant brows, shaded with hanging ringlets of yellow hair, and rolled their wet hair in diaphanous veils) (G 86)

When they had eaten sufficiently, they returned againe to their looking Glasses, with a scrupulous examination, about their bodies, and the attire of their heades, and dressing of their yealow curling haires depending, and hemicirculately instrophiated about their diuine faces. (R.D. M4ʳ)

The 'hanging ringlets of yellow hair' (*globuli degli flaui crinuli antependuli*, F.C. e7ᵛ; = G 86) belonging to the Five Senses have been borrowed from

---

Renaissance, see R. H. F. Carver, '"Transformed in Show": The Rhetoric of Transvestism in Sidney's *Arcadia*', *ELR* 28 (1998), 323–52, at 342–4.

[45] We might contrast the suppressed laughter of Lia's companions in Boccaccio's *Ameto* v (trans. Serafini-Sauli, 10).

[46] Dronke (*Francesco Colonna*, 35 n. 45) notes the correspondence of urination in Colonna and Apuleius. In his *Commentarii in Convivium*, Marsilio Ficino pits *Ratio, Visus*, and *Auditus* against *Olfactus, Gustus, and Tactus*. See *Commentary on Plato's Symposium on Love*, trans. S. Jayne, 2nd edn. (Dallas: Spring Publications, 1985), 41 (Speech I, ch. 4) and 84–6 (Speech V, ch. 2); and J. F. Kermode, 'The Banquet of Sense', *BJRL* 44 (1961–2), 68–99. Chapman's *Ovid's Banquet of Sence* (1595) seems to be indebted to Ficino for its Neoplatonism and to the *Hypnerotomachia* for its description of Corinna's fountain, 'So cunningly to optick reason wrought' and replete with 'curious imagrie' (vv. 24, 30). See M. MacLure, *George Chapman: A Critical Study* (Toronto: U of Toronto P, 1966), 51, and R. M. Ribner, 'The Compasse of This Curious Frame: Chapman's *Ovids Banquet of Sence* and the Emblematic Tradition', *SR* 17 (1970), 233–58, at 244.

Apuleius' account of Psyche's first glimpse of the sleeping Cupid (*crinium globos… antependulos, AA* 5. 22). The radiance of his body (*corpus… luculentum*) may have lent an added lustre to the 'radiant brows' (*luculente fronte*) of Colonna's nymphs; yet, if we continue to play this glossematic game, we find an even closer parallel (*luculentam… faciem*) in Thelyphron's account of the weeping widow who employs him to guard the body of the husband she has poisoned: *At illa, crinibus antependulis hinc inde dimotis etiam in maiore luculentam proferens faciem* ('But she drew back the forward-hanging tresses from this side and from that, revealing a face radiant even in grief', *AA* 2. 23).[47] The collocation of passages helps us to see that the murderess, kissing her husband's corpse as she inspects every detail by the light of a lamp, anticipates Psyche's kissing of the body of the husband she had intended to kill (*AA* 5. 23). But once we are aware that both of the Apuleian vignettes (Psyche's erotic epiphany and the false radiance of the widow) are being echoed, we may feel bound to take a more critical view of the bathing-scene (and the attendant pleasures of the Five Senses). Indeed, the final detail of the nymphs' damp hair and transparent covering (*cum limpico tegmine gli madidi crini obvoluti*) recalls the appearance (*illae limpido tegmine crines madidos obuolutae*) of the women who had been 'initiated into the divine mysteries' (*sacris diuinis initiatae, AA* 11. 10).[48] The way in which the nymphs use their mirrors for a 'minute examination' of their own perfections, however, forms a marked contrast to the attitude of the women in the 'special procession of the saviour goddess' (*sospitatricis deae peculiaris pompa*) who carry 'shining mirrors reversed behind their backs, to show homage to the goddess as she passed' (*AA* 11. 9; trans. Hanson). The implication seems to be that the senses have a necessary part to play in enlightenment, but not a sufficient one.

According to Ingrid D. Rowland, 'the *Hypnerotomachia* made no attempt to hide its real identity as a steamy novel'.[49] Joscelyn Godwin speaks (in similarly modern terms) of the 'unapologetic paganism' of the work: 'The *Hypnerotomachia* is like a bible of this heretic religion, which used the prestige of classical learning to excuse its indulgence in eroticism and the celebration of an unfallen nature' (G, p. xvii). And in the view of Martin Lowry, 'the bulk of steady and orthodox opinion, which Aldus needed to conciliate, will have found the work an obscene, heathen carnival', the Priapus tableau (F.C. m6[r]; G 195), in particular, being regarded as 'a sensuous wallowing in the revived

---

[47] The falsely radiant widow is merely another manifestation of Apuleius' continual play with notions of light in *The Golden Ass*, e.g. the ambiguous 'illumination' suggested by the names Lucius (*lux*) and Fotis (φῶς).

[48] See Fumagalli, 'Francesco Colonna', 251.

[49] Rowland, *Culture*, 61.

glories of the pagan past, stripped by the force of its illustration of any real pretence to moral symbolism'.[50]

Such appraisals, however, fail to do justice to the complex relationship between *dulce* and *utile* in the *Hypnerotomachia*. The (half-apologetic) reference in the liminary verses to the work as *el nouo inuito erotico* ('the new erotic guest') may be read as an acknowledgement of the author's innovation in introducing to humanistic discourse the overt sexuality associated with the Milesian tale, the medieval fabliau, and the Boccaccian *novella* (a departure from the more refined eroticism of *Stilnovisti* works such as Dante's *Vita nuova*, Petrarch's *Rime sparse,* and Boccaccio's *Amorosa visione*). Indeed, it is this combination of the idealizing tropes of the Platonic-Petrarchan traditions with the openly sensual, or even Priapic, tendencies of Milesian discourse that makes the *Hypnerotomachia* such a penetrating exploration of the nature of desire.[51]

Osfressia ('Smell') tells Poliphilo to 'be of good cheer and give yourself to pleasure, for you shall find your beloved Polia' (*Ma sta cum laeto animo & da opera a piacere, che la tua dilecta Polia la ritrouerai,* G 84; F.C. e6ᵛ). The scrupulous reader, however, will find in the *Hypnerotomachia* not merely a 'sensuous wallowing', but an extensive critique of pleasure (*Voluptas*) and its uses and abuses.

Indeed, far from being a simple 'celebration of an unfallen nature', Colonna's work is suffused with an awareness of his hero's fluctuating position within the Neoplatonic triad constituted by the bestial, the human, and the divine. Apuleius' narrative of asinine transformation becomes a key means of articulating this philosophical programme. As they set off to see Queen Eleuterylida ('Free Will'), the nymphs

incominciorono di cantilare in phrygio tono rithmiticamente, una faceta metamorphosi. Conciosia cosa che uolendose uno inamorato cum unctione in auicula tramutarse, il bussolo fallite, & transformosi in rude asino. Concludendo che alcuni credeno essere le uncture ad uno effecto, & daposcia e ad uno altro. (F.C. e7ᵛ)

. . . beganne to sing verses in a Phrygial tune, of a pleasaunt metamorphosing of one, who with an oyntment thought to haue transfourmed himselfe into a Byrd, and by mistakyng of the Boxe, was turned into a rude Asse. Concludyng, that manye tooke Oyntmentes to one purpose, and founde the effecte to contrarie their expectations. (R.D. M4ʳ)

---

[50] *World of Aldus*, 124. Lowry points to the 'disastrous timing' whereby the *Hypnerotomachia* appeared just as 'Venice was embarking on a moral, as well as a military crusade' in response to the Turkish success in capturing the Venetian fortress in the Gulf of Lepanto. Compare Painter's reference (10) to 'this impiously pagan work'.

[51] We note the similarly rich (and problematic) fusion of the sensual and the sublime in Apuleius' depiction of Fotis, a character whose influence pervades the *Hypnerotomachia*.

Despite their mocking glances, Poliphilo pays little attention to the song, but he soon finds himself transformed:

Ecco que io repente incomincio tanto in lasciua prurigine & in stimulosa libidine incitarme, che tutto me riuoluea torquentime. Et quelle uersute licentemente rideano, sapendo il mio tale accidente. . . . Et tanto incitamento omni hora incrementare sentendo, Salace & pruriente me cruciaua. Et tanto piu oltra mensura di uenerea libidine pronofl-agraua, quanto che si opportuni & accommodati obiecti uiolentissimi se offeriuano, incremento di una quasi perniciosissima peste & di inexperta urigine percito (F.C. e7ᵛ)

Vpon a sodaine I founde my selfe so lasciuiously bent, and in such a prurient lust, that which way so euer I turned, I could not forbeare, and they as they sung laughed the more, knowing what had happened vnto mee. . . . I was with such a violent desire prickt forwarde, which I felt more and more to increase in a faulte burning. And the more I was to that venerious desire by the violent offers of so oportune and sweete obiects. A foode for suche a pernitious plague, and vnexperienced burning . . . (R.D. M4ᵛ; = G 86–7)

Aphea ('Touch') teases him gently—*hora io te uedo alterato & mutitato* ('now I see you altered and changed', F.C. e7ᵛ; G 87)—and they all frolic and tumble together with great hilarity 'as I spurned virtue and threw myself into a flood of desire,[52] impatient from the excessive tension of the bowstring' (*prosternate le uirtute, & tutto in proluuio de libidine ruente pernimietate del neruico rigore impatiente*, G 87; F.C. e8ʳ).

Colonna is drawing here on three passages in *The Golden Ass*. The 'vnex-perienced burning' which excites Poliphilo (*inexperta urigine percito*, F.C. e7ᵛ) echoes the initial arousal of Meroe's lust (*mox urigine percita*, *AA* 1. 7) which proves so disastrous for Socrates. The archery image derives from the first love-scene in Apuleius, where Lucius strips 'to the groin' and shows Fotis his 'impatience for Venus' (*impatientiam Veneris Photidi meae monstrans*), ex-pressing his fear that his 'bowstring may be snapped by excessive tension' (*nervus rigoris nimietate rumpatur, AA* 2. 16).[53] But the description of Poli-philo's desire (*proluuio de libidine*) echoes the account of how the assified Lucius, on the point of making love to the wealthy *matrona*, 'had aroused [his] sexual appetite with the most fragrant ointment' (*unguento fraglantis-simo prolubium libidinis suscitarem, AA* 10. 21).

The convergence of these Apuleian passages in the one scene suggests a reading of *The Golden Ass* that is not merely glossematic, but collocative or typological. Colonna (like many since) has evidently read Aristomenes' story of Socrates-Meroe as a monitory tale, a warning to Lucius of the dangers of

---

[52] Godwin appears to be deriving *proluuio* from *proluuies* or *proluuium*, rather than from *prolubium*.

[53] R.D. (sig. N1ʳ) completely misses the point about the bowstring.

venereal entanglements.[54] More interestingly, Colonna also seems to have recognized a structural and thematic congruence between Lucius' bestial congress with the libidinous *matrona* and his involvement with Fotis.[55]

Indeed, when we review the sequence (laughing, feasting, romping) in this particular section of Poliphilo's dream, we may recall the opinion of the Diotima-like narratrix of 'Cupid and Psyche': dreams of 'laughing and filling the belly with little honeyed-cakes or engaging in Venereal pleasure will foretell one's being vexed by sadness of the mind, weakness of the body, and all other kinds of loss' (*ridere et mellitis dulciolis ventrem saginare vel in voluptatem Veneriam convenire tristitie animi, languore corporis, damnisque ceteris vexatum iri praedicabunt, AA* 4. 27).

THE CHARACTER OF POLIPHILO

Although Geussia ('Taste') removes the immediate cause of his discomfort by administering a herb (star-wort), and he is later able to sublimate much of his desire in his rapturous encounters with monuments, the effects of this initial metamorphosis are felt throughout much of the work. Poliphilo, in fact, owes many of his principal characteristics to Lucius. He shares the latter's insatiable curiosity and neophilia, his obsession with female hair, his tendency to confuse categories of desire, and his chronic failure to synthesize discrete phenomena into a coherent experience of the world.

Poliphilo's description of himself as being 'eager for novelty' (*auido di nouitate,* F.C. b7^r) and 'strongly impelled by curiosity' (*di curiosa auiditate grandemente incitato,* G 39; F.C. b8^r) as he climbs inside the colossal elephant is echoed in his response to almost everything that he meets, whether it be an approaching troop of nymphs or a fresh vista of ruins.[56] As in *The Golden Ass,* it is this active element—curiosity—which provides the narrative impetus for these engagements.[57] Colonna, of course, is by no means the first to depict a

---

[54] R.D.'s 'metamorphosing of one' (sig. M4^r) obscures the clear link that Colonna makes between Lucius' infatuation with Fotis (as *uno inamorato*) and his transformation.

[55] We might note that both affairs emphasize breast-bands, intense and mutual pleasure, and anointing with unguents; and each provides the trigger, or, at the very least, proves to be a liminary event, for the subsequent (re-)transformation.

[56] Nymphs: 'Curious about such a novelty' (*Per laquale nouitate explorabondo inclinato,* G 75; F.C. e2^r). Ruins: 'my soul again felt an insatiable desire to wander on and investigate fresh novelties' (*ancora sencia dubio mi accreseua lanimo insaciabilmente piu lustrabondo altre nouitate inuestigare*: G 262; F.C. q7^r). Cf. Lucius' description of himself as *sititor… nouitatis* ('a thirster after novelty', *AA* 1. 2).

[57] Poliphilo's neophilia has an ambiguous status in Renaissance thinking. On good and bad curiosity, see N. Kenny, *The Palace of Secrets: Béroalde de Verville and Renaissance Conceptions of Knowledge* (Oxford: Clarendon, 1991), 210–14.

character's encounters with ancient buildings and triumphs.[58] But in late medieval and early modern ecphrastic literature, the protagonist frequently functions as little more than an enabler—a speaking 'eye'—for the description. What distinguishes the *Hypnerotomachia* is the level of Poliphilo's emotional and imaginative involvement with the things that he describes.

Apuleius' hero is often unable to discriminate between erotic, necromantic, and spiritual desire. In Poliphilo we find a similar fluidity, with the place of magic being taken by architecture and inscriptions. Faced with the pyramid and obelisk, for example, he examines 'carefully every part of the beautiful complex' (*curiosamente tutte le parte al uenusto composito*). He is 'warmly aroused' (*excitato caldamente*) by the 'virginal' (*uirginale*) stone and utters 'amorous sighs' (*amorosi... suspiri*) which remind him of the 'amorous and celestial ideal' (*amorosa & celeste Idea*) of Polia (G 30–1; F.C. b3ᵛ).[59] While this interflux of desire is analogous to Lucius' thought-processes at *AA* 2. 6 (melding Fotis and magic; cf. *AA* 3. 19: *magiae noscendae ardentissimus cupitor*), on other occasions his rapturous response to stonework echoes the 'inexpressible pleasure' (*inexplicabilis voluptas, AA* 11. 24) that Lucius experiences when contemplating the statue (*simulacrum*) of Isis. Poliphilo is 'rauished and taken vp with vnspeakable delight and pleasure' (*rapto & prehenso de dilecto & inexcogitabile solatio essendo*, R.D. H1ᵛ; F.C. d1ʳ; = G 57) as he contemplates the work of 'holy and venerable Antiquity' (*dalla sancta & ueneranda antiquitate*); and the *hylaritudine* induced by his examination of the ruined monuments (G 268; F.C. r2ᵛ) matches the shared joy which Lucius experiences in the Isiac procession (*tanta... hilaritudine, AA* 11. 7).[60]

Sometimes a single Apuleian borrowing can open a window on Colonna's whole project. In the cemetery (*Polyandrion*) of unfortunate lovers, Poliphilo finds a *ciborium* (a canopied shrine) raised over an underground chamber covered by a metal grille:

per laqualcosa accenso di curiosa cupidine di potere ad questa parte descendere rimabondo tra quelle fracture, & minutie & ruine perquirendo qualche meato. (F.C. p8ʳ)

(Possessed by an inquisitive desire to go down there, I rummaged through the debris and ruined fragments, searching for some passage.) (G 247)

---

[58] For a mid-14th-cent. example, see Fazio degli Uberti's *Il Dittamondo*, ed. G. Corsi (Bari: Laterza, 1952).

[59] Cf. 'I was much excited by so many comely monuments' (*Excitato summopere da tanto uenustate di monumenti quaeritabondo*, G 255; F.C. q4ʳ).

[60] Note, also, how the 'fertile trees with their fruitful offspring' (*arbores... pomifera subole fecundae*) which seem to Lucius to be joining in the celebrations of Isis (*AA* 11. 7) find their way into the gardens on the longed-for island of Cytherea (*Arbore quivi di pomifera sobole foecunde*, F.C. t3ᵛ; = G 302).

One can readily imagine the pleasure that Colonna took in his neologism *rimabondo*.[61] Its source, *rimabundus*, is another *hapax legomenon*—Apuleius uses it to describe Lucius' minute examination of the statuary of Diana and Actaeon at the centre of Byrrhena's atrium: *Dum haec identidem rimabundus eximie delector* ('while I derive uncommon delight from examining these things again and again', *AA* 2. 5).[62] *Rimor* can mean to 'lay open', to 'rummage', to 'pry into', but *rima* ('cleft', 'crack', or 'chink') seems to give *rimabundus* the sense of 'looking into every nook and cranny'.[63] *Rimabondo* is hence the perfect term to describe both the ocular and the physical activity as Poliphilo rummages amongst the ruins on the surface in search of some 'chink' which will afford him access to the treasures below. But the resonances extend still further. The irony of *rimabundus* is that while Lucius revels in the 'sheen' (*nitore*) of the Parian marble and the verisimilitude of the 'most skilfully polished grapes' (*uuae faberrime politae*), he is unable to assemble the delightful details into any overall meaning and hence fails to see that Actaeon, leaning towards Diana 'with an inquisitive gaze' (*curioso optutu*, *AA* 2. 4) is a warning to himself.[64] Poliphilo is in a similar state of cognitive impairment, condemned (along with his readers) to a seemingly endless iteration of the rhetorical tropes of *effictio*, with every temple, statue, or frieze occasioning an ecphrasis, every nymph being anatomized in a *blason*.[65]

Beroaldo used Lucius' description of 'art rivalling Nature' (*ars aemula naturae*) in the Diana and Actaeon sculpture (*AA* 2. 4) as the occasion for an extended digression extolling the arresting verisimilitude of a contemporary artist, Francesco Francia.[66] Apuleius' statuary also seems to have had a seminal effect on Colonna's imagination.[67] Indeed, *rimabondo* is eloquent of the

---

[61] Cf. *rimirare* ('to look at intently', 'to contemplate') in modern Italian.

[62] Cf. Beroaldo (*Commentarii . . . in asinum aureum*, fol. 35ʳ): *Rimabundus: Speculabundus: uehementerque contemplans: nomina enim in bundus definentia: non tam significant similitudinem ut grammatici hallucinantur: quam uim & copiam: & quasi habundantiam rei* ('*Rimabundus:* "on the look-out" and "observing with great intensity". For words ending in *-bundus* do not signify likeness, as grammarians wrongly imagine, so much as force and *copia*, and, as it were, abundance of material').

[63] Note the description of the transgressive (and soon-to-be-punished) Psyche as she gazes upon Cupid for the first time: *insatiabili animo Psyche satis curiosa rimatur . . .* (*AA* 5. 23).

[64] Hence Byrrhena's laconic remark, *Tua sunt . . . cuncta quae uides* ('Everything you see is yours', *AA* 2. 5). Note that Lucius will be transformed into an ass after peering at the naked Pamphile through a 'crack' in the door (*per . . . rimam ostiorum*, *AA* 3. 21).

[65] Cf. Lucius' reification of Fotis (*AA* 2. 8): *Nec . . . ego prius inde discessi quam diligenter omnem eius explorassem habitudinem* ('Nor . . . did I depart from there until I had carefully explored every aspect of her').

[66] M. Baxandall and E. H. Gombrich, 'Beroaldus on Francia', *JWCI* 25 (1962), 113–15. Cf. J. Gaisser, 'Teaching Classics in the Renaissance: Two Case Histories', *TAPA* 131 (2001), 1–21, at 7.

[67] We will note (*infra*) the role of Actaeon and Diana in the climax of the *Hypnerotomachia* (G 367).

complex topologies of the *Hypnerotomachia*: Colonna is constantly playing with notions of outer and inner, surface and subface, accessibility and penetrability. The *Hypnerotomachia* marks one advance on the usual conventions of ecphrasis: Poliphilo is actually able to enter some of the monuments that he describes (e.g. the Colossus (G 36) and the Elephant (G 39)). At the historical level, he seems to be re-enacting the forays of quattrocento humanists such as Cyriaco d'Ancona (d. *c.*1455), a colleague of Gemistos Plethon, an associate of Cardinal Bessarion, and 'the archetype of the peripatetic early Renaissance antiquary'.[68] But there may also be a more contemporary reference to Pomponio Leto who, we are told, 'explored every nook and corner of old Rome, and stood gazing with rapt attention on every relic of a bygone age'.[69] Pomponio and his *fratres* in the Academia Romana are credited with burrowing their way into subterranean Rome, uncovering friezes in the ruins of Nero's Domus Aurea, filling countless notebooks (*syllogai*) with drawings and transcriptions, and holding quasi-religious ceremonies in the catacombs where they scratched (or daubed) their names on the walls, with Leto figuring as the *Pontifex Maximus* of their sodality.[70]

---

[68] C. Mitchell, 'Archaeology and Romance in Renaissance Italy', in *Italian Renaissance Studies*, ed. E. F. Jacobs (London: Faber, 1960), 455–83, at 468. Mitchell (469) likens the *barathrum* episode in the *Hypnerotomachia* to Cyriaco's account of his descent into a cave, and (without mentioning Apuleius, *AA* 11. 7) sees in *hylaritudine* (G 268; F.C. r2ᵛ) an encapsulation of Cyriaco's approach to antiquities (468–9). In a letter datable to 1423, Cyriaco employs the form of a dream-debate in defence of his interest in pagan literature. See F. Scalamonti, *Vita viri clarissimi et famosissimi Kyriaci Anconitani*, ed. and trans. C. Mitchell and E. W. Bodnar (Philadelphia: American Philosophical Soc., 1996). One of Cyriaco's followers, Felice Feliciano (b. Verona, 1433?; d. Rome, 1479), has been championed as the author of the *Hypnerotomachia*. On Colonna's (ultimate) debt to Cyriaco (and the intermediate influence of the Paduan humanist Giovanni Marcanova), see T. Griggs, 'Promoting the Past: The *Hypnerotomachia* as Antiquarian Enterprise', in M. Leslie and J. D. Hunt, eds., *Garden and Architectural Dreamscapes in the 'Hypnerotomachia Poliphili'*, *Word & Image* 1 & 2 (1998), 17–39.

[69] Creighton, *History of the Papacy*, i. 41–2. Palermino observes (122) that Creighton drew much of his information from Sabellico who provided a biographical sketch for the posthumous edn. of Pomponio's book. One might compare the zeal with which Lucius explores Hypata the morning after his arrival: *curiose singula considerabam* (*AA* 2. 1).

[70] Palermino notes (135) that the most 'incriminating' of the inscriptions associated with the Pomponians appear to post-date the (alleged) conspiracy of 1468. Rowland (*Culture*, 273) records the (privately communicated) opinions of Piero Meogrossi who notes that in 1467 (the date appended to Book 2 of the *Hypnerotomachia*), 'Pomponio Leto had left Rome for the Veneto, bringing all his enthusiasm about Roman antiquities with him'. Meogrossi 'connects the book's environment with the Roman Academy, both the first generation of Platina and his colleagues and the second generation of Paolo Cortesi, Tommaso Inghirami, and Angelo Colocci'. On the discovery (during the 1470s) of the painted vaults in the Domus Aurea, see Rowland, *Culture*, 46, and J. Schulz, 'Pinturicchio and the Revival of Antiquity', *JWCI* 25 (1962), 35–55. We should remember, however, that the practice of compiling *syllogai* (personal collections of ancient inscriptions) was widespread, and flourished particularly in the Veneto in Aldus' day. See Lowry, *World of Aldus*, 140, and Brown, *Venice & Antiquity*, esp. 81–91, 120–26. In *Inscriptiones sacrosanctae vetustatis*, 'the first world-corpus of classical inscriptions to appear

In the humanists' Rome, language and architecture, archaeology and the erotic are intimately connected. Raffaele Maffei describes Niccolò Perotti as 'a most assiduous investigator (*perscrutator*) of words: if he heard something unfamiliar in any place whatsoever, he would not go to sleep or attend to any business until he had investigated it' (*diligentissimus vocabulorum perscrutator: si quod undecunque incognitum audiisset, neque dormitare neque rerum aliquid gerere solebat, priusquam id investigasset*).[71] The graffiti in the catacombs left by Pomponio Leto and his *sodales* include such slogans as *unanimes perscrutatores antiquitatis regnante Pom. Pont. Max.* ('single-minded investigators of antiquity under the rule of Pomponius, the Chief Priest'), *unanimes antiquitatis amatores* ('single-minded lovers of antiquity'),[72] and the rather more ambiguous *Rom pup delitie*, which could be a celebration of 'the pleasures' (*deliciae*) of 'Roman girls'(*Rom[anarum] pup[arum]*) or of 'Roman boys' (*Rom[anorum] pup[orum]*).[73]

Another *graffito* (*Antonius Mar*) bears faint witness to the participation of Venice's future historian, Marcantonio Coccio Sabellico, in these subterranean explorations.[74] Indeed, Sabellico uses Apuleius' coinage in his *Annotationes veteres et recentes*, a work published in the same volume as annotations by Beroaldo, Battista Pio, and Egnazio: *Ego haec rimabundus antea saepius ad disquisitionem vocabam.*[75]

At the level of literary influence, Colonna is appropriating the eroticized architectural spaces of the thirteenth-century *Roman de la Rose*, at the conclusion of which Jean de Meung had daringly used the dreamer's passage through a narrow aperture as an allegory of defloration (see below). We are not merely indulging, however, in post-structuralist platitudes about the inevitable self-referentiality of textual discourse when we say that penetration in the *Hypnerotomachia* is intimately linked with interpretation.

Having found a way inside the giant elephant, Poliphilo admires a tomb, topped by a nude statue of a queen and bearing the epigram:

in print' (Ingolstadt: Petrus Apianus, 1534), Apianus (Peter Bienewitz, 1495–1552) includes, among his sources, Cyriaco, Leto, and the *Hypnerotomachia* (Mitchell, 'Archaeology and Romance', 460).

[71] *Commentariorum vrbanorum Raphaelis Volterrani octo et triginti libri* (Basle: Froben and Episcopius, 1559), 491. Quoted by Oliver, ' "New Fragments" ', 383, and Prete, 'La questione', 128. There are many earlier edns., including one from Rome (per Joannem Besicken, 1506).

[72] Palermino, 143. Platina records Paul's charge against the academicians that 'we were too much in love with paganism' (*quod nimium gentilitatis amatores essemus*) (*Liber*, p. 388, quoted by Palermino, 129 n. 46).

[73] Palermino, 119.

[74] The graffito was transcribed (*c.*1864) by G. B. De Rossi. Palermino (146) describes the identification of Sabellico as the 'most plausible choice'.

[75] *Marci Antonii Sabellici Annotationes veteres et recentes…Joannis Baptiste pii Bononiensis Annotationes* (Venice: Ioa[n]. Tacuinus de Tridino, 1508), sig. A2ᵛ. Cited by Pozzi, *Commento*, 181.

QVISQVIS ES, QVANTVNCVNQVE LIBVERIT HVIVS THESAVRI SVME AT MONEO. AVFER CAPVT. CORPVS NE TANGITO. (F.C. b8ᵛ)

(Whoever you are, take as much of this treasure as you want. But I warn you: Carry off the head. Do not touch the body.) (trans. RHFC; = G 40)

Like Apuleius' statuary of Diana and Actaeon, Colonna's tableau contains a message, I would suggest, for both its immediate observer and for the reader of the work as a whole. It warns Poliphilo against indulging his sensual appetites (*corpus*) at the expense of the intellectual and spiritual pursuits (*caput*) that can lift him to a higher 'pleasure'. But it also offers us a model for reading the *Hypnerotomachia*. Poliphilo's willingness to provide 'translations' of the hieroglyphs that he frequently encounters marks him out as an initiate of the new cult of Egyptology that had taken root in Italy following the arrival, in 1419, of a manuscript of the *Hieroglyphica* of Horapollo Niliacus (brought from Greece by a Florentine priest, Cristoforo de Buondelmonti).[76] Leon Battista Alberti, Fra Urbano Bolzanio (along with his nephew, Pierio Valeriano), and Beroaldo all display an interest in Egyptian symbolism.[77] In response to Lucius' account of Mithras producing 'certain books written in unknown letters' so that their meaning was 'protected from the curiosity of the uninitiated' (*quosdam libros litteris ignorabilibus praenotatos... a curiositate profanorum lectione munita*, AA 11. 22), Beroaldo's disciple, Battista Pio, comments: *Ieroglyphicis litteras his pene uerbis delinauit Appuleius & descripsit* ('With these words Apuleius has virtually sketched and represented hieroglyphic letters').[78]

Yet, in spite of his initiation into these higher hermeneutics, Poliphilo is unable to discern the (comparatively) straightforward admonition supplied by the epigram in the tomb:

Di tanta nouitate digna di relato mirabondo, & degli ænigmati prælegendoli sæpicule, dil tutto io restai ignaro, & dilla interpretatione & sophismo significato molto ambiguo (F.C. b8ᵛ)

(This novelty was worthy of a marvellous tale, but I was left in utter ignorance about it and its riddles, which I reread several times, and in much doubt about their interpretation and deceptive significance) (G 40)

---

[76] Seznec, 99.

[77] Seznec notes (100) that the *Hieroglyphica* of Horapollo Niliacus inspired a chapter of Alberti's *De re aedificatoria* (8. 4) and also influenced the illustrations in the *Hypnerotomachia*. Note the appearance of *Symbola Pythagoræ a Philippo Beroaldo moraliter explicata* (Bologna: Benedictus Hectoris, 1503). See, generally, B. A. Curran, 'The *Hypnerotomachia Poliphili* and Renaissance Egyptology', in *Garden and Architectural Dreamscapes*, ed. Leslie and Hunt, 156–85.

[78] *Marci Antonii Sabellici Annotationes veteres et recentes... Joannis Baptiste pii Bononiensis Annotationes*, fol. xxxvʳ.

There is, in fact, a marked congruence between the erotic and the hermeneutic in Poliphilo's frustrations and ecstasies, and these are mimicked in the
experience of the readers attempting to convert the masses of sensory data with
which they are bombarded into coherent structures of meaning. Colonna's is an
aesthetic of excess and the *Hypnerotomachia* requires (from the modern reader,
at least) a high tolerance of the rhetoric of repetition.[79] It is perhaps significant
that when Poliphilo wants to praise the architect of a particularly cornucopian
complex, he employs an Apuleian borrowing, *multiscio*:

Per lequale tutte cose rectamente se iudicaua, quanto copioso praestauasi il cogitamento
dil multiscio Architecto (F.C. d1ʳ)

(From all this I could well judge how fertile the learned architect's mind must have
been) (G 56)

Apuleius applies the term *multiscius* to Apollo (*Florida* 3) and to Homer
(*Apologia* 31);[80] but Lucius' retrospective gratitude that his asinine state had
rendered him 'much-knowing, albeit less wise' (*etsi minus prudentem, multi-*
scium reddidit, AA 9. 14) may introduce an ironic inflexion to the Colonna
passage.[81] Indeed, it is interesting to note that in the preface to his *Rudimenta*
grammatices (1501), Aldus 'upbraids...the dangerous errors of certain
"*multa scientes*".[82]

At the very least, *multiscio* expresses, in miniature, one of the central
concerns, not merely of the *Hypnerotomachia*, but of the High Renaissance
generally: *copia*. From the sixteenth century onwards, *copia* is associated
specifically with the exploitation of linguistic 'riches' made possible by hand-
books such as Erasmus' *De copia*. But the pursuit of 'plenitude' takes place in a
much wider field, and the cornucopia is one of the dominant emblems of the
Hypnerotomachia.[83]

---

[79] Godwin (p. ix) speaks of a 'theme of excess and superabundance'.
[80] Pozzi, *Commento*, 85.
[81] On the relationship between *sapientia* and *scientia*, see Kenny, *Palace of Secrets*, 168 ff.
[82] Painter, 10. Aldus also condemns 'the neglect of learned men to foster the innocence of the
young'. Painter makes no mention of Apuleius, but does say that '*multiscius*, or polymath, is a
word which was then and long after accepted as one of the meanings of the hero's name,
Poliphilo!' Painter takes such comments (together with the appearance of 'the most edifying of
all his productions, the Saint Catherine of Siena, *Epistole*, of 19th September 1500') as evidence
that Aldus 'was forced to recant' for his publication of the *Hypnerotomachia*.
[83] The work of the *multiscio* architect includes 'cornucopiae with the remains of leaves,
apples, stems, pods and other fruits swelling their bodies, with putti playfully riding on them'
(*Et dagli corni reste di fronde cum pomi scapi, & teche, & altri fructi nella corpulentia pandante,*
Cum pueruli equitanti ludibondi, G 56; F.C. d1ʳ). The liminary texts twice refer to the *Hypner-*
otomachia as a *cornucopia* and stress the variety and plenitude of this 'wonderful work' which
'abounds in such different things' (*Tam uariis mirum rebus abundat opus*). Cf. F.C. y2ᵛ–y3ʳ
(G 348–9) where cornucopiae are clearly indicated in text and image.

Of course, plenitude can be as problematic as it is enriching. Pliny's *Historia naturalis* (the other 'master-text' of the *Hypnerotomachia*) displays a tension between its copious, encyclopaedic tendencies and its claim that the increasing abundance (*copia*) of primary resources has reduced the quality of artistic output (*omnia ergo meliora tunc fuere, cum minor copia*).[84] The first monument encountered (and rapturously admired) by Poliphilo is, from a neoclassical point of view, a monstrosity: a statue, atop an obelisk, atop a pyramid, the whole complex (replete with cornucopia) some 1 mile square and 3 miles high.[85] And according to the ghost of Francesco Filelfo, who arrived in the Elysian Fields in 1481 to find 'a throng of philosophers, poets, and orators' debating the merits of the art of printing, one of the arguments against the new technology was that 'abundance of books makes men less studious'.[86] Indeed, despite his involvement (with Bussi, Perotti, and others) in the earliest printings of the Latin classics, we are told that Pomponio Leto 'read almost nothing unless it was in his own handwriting' (*Nihil fere legit vnquam nisi ex suo chirographo*).[87]

When Pope Paul II, at the height of the conspiracy crisis of 1468, attacked the *poeti* (i.e. the humanists) for using circumlocutions, he was espousing a theory of language—a (prescriptively) precise relationship between *res* and *verba*—which he considered to be imperilled by the rhetorical *copia* favoured by the humanists: *le meglio dire una cosa per li proprii vocabuli cha per queste circuitione che usano poeti*.[88] We shall see, in our next chapter, how controversial linguistic *copia* could be in our discussion of Ciceronianism and the War of Imitation. And we might note the anxiety that redescriptive rhetorical figures such as *paradiastole* would induce in philosophers of the seventeenth and eighteenth centuries.[89] At a more practical level, the cornucopia offers an apt emblem of the antiquary's experience during the Italian Renaissance: the rate of destruction could be terrifying as ancient artefacts disappeared into

---

[84] *Historia naturalis* 35. 50. The passage is quoted (to different effect) by Barkan, *Unearthing the Past*, 69. Cf. Narcissus' complaint in Ovid's *Met.* 3. 466: *inopem me copia fecit* ('abundance has made me poor').

[85] F.C. a7ᵛ–b2ʳ; G 22–7.

[86] The account is nested (Chinese-box like) in 'a sealed letter' that Hieronimo Squarciafico claims to have found after waking from a vision in which Filelfo's ghost had appeared to him. This letter is included in a larger letter (dated 23 Nov. 1481) which was 'appended to de Blavis' edition of Poggio's translation of Diodorus Siculus.' See Sheppard, 'Francesco Filelfo', 25. Cited by Lowry, *World of Aldus*, 29 and 31.

[87] Sabellico, *Pomponij vita*, in *Opera Pomponii Laeti* (Strasbourg: Matthias Schürer, 1515), sig. n[vii]ʳ. The effects of printing are also discussed in Sabellico's *De reparatione linguae latinae*.

[88] Pastor, *History of the Popes*, iv. 491. The word *poeta* in Renaissance discourse is often synonymous with *umanista*.

[89] See Q. Skinner, 'Moral Ambiguity and the Renaissance Art of Eloquence', *EC* 44 (1994), 267–92.

lime-kilns or were swallowed up by papal building projects, yet the amount that remained (and continued to be unearthed) was more than could be processed.[90] Bussi had a vision of printed texts 'stream[ing] forth and spread[-ing] through the world in an abundant flood' (*scaturire et per omnem orbem uberrimo fonte diffluere*), but his efforts to make texts available quickly and cheaply (even when they were inferior to the best manuscripts) exposed him to the hostility of critics, and within ten years of the *editio princeps* of Apuleius, the Italian printing industry was in crisis and Bussi was drafting Sweynheim and Pannartz's petition to Sixtus IV with its famously pathetic complaint that 'our house . . . is full of unsold books but empty of the necessities of life'.[91] We see evidence, here, of two different strains of humanism. While Bussi could be regarded as a popularizer, others were concerned to maintain the hieratic status of classical texts—accessible only to the initiated few.

In the midst of Queen Eleuterylida's lavish banquet, Poliphilo feels overwhelmed by marvels: 'The more I thought over these excellent spectacles, the more ignorant and stupefied I was' (*tanto piu inscio staua et stupefacto*, G 103; F.C. g4ʳ). Poliphilo—like his reader, and like Renaissance humanists in general—is faced with *un embarras de richesse*:

De fora le molte miraueglie, di praecellentia inaudite di diuersitate, cose insuete & dissimile, inextimabile & non humane, Impero allucinato & tutto aequalmente oppresso per omni mio senso (F.C. g7ʳ)

(The many surpassing and unheard-of wonders, the endless parade of priceless and superhuman novelties confused my mind and left all my senses equally distracted) (G 117)

Quale homo da fame exarcebato & tra multiplici & uarii eduli fremente, de tutti cupido di niuno integramente rimane di lardente appetito contento, Ma de Bulimia infecto. (F.C. i6ʳ)

(I vacillated like a starving man faced with an abundance of various foods, desiring them all but not fully satisfied with any of them, and thus left a prey to his hunger.) (G 146)

The word *integramente* (F.C. i6ʳ) may say something about Poliphilo's inability to 'integrate' individual phenomena,[92] but we can also read his bewilderment

---

[90] Only a fraction of the *syllogai* assembled by men like Cyriaco d'Ancona or Pomponio Leto remains. Cardinal Bessarion's collection of 800 manuscripts lay mouldering in crates in Venice for over forty years before a library was built to house them. See Brown, *Venice & Antiquity*, 273.

[91] Preface to the *Letters* of St Jerome (1468) in Miglio, *Prefazioni*. Cf. Lowry, *World of Aldus*, 25 and 67 n. 7. Note that *scaturire* (which Lewis and Short describe as 'very rare') is used by Apuleius to describe the torrent flowing from the top of the mountain in which the robbers' cave is situated (*De summo uertice fons affluens . . . scaturribat, AA* 4. 6). On Perotti, see Feld, 'A Theory', 347. Feld provides an abridged translation of the petition at 358.

[92] At the end of the *Ameto*, Boccaccio's humanized hero is glad 'to have wholly known Lia' (*ad avere interamente saputa Lia*, xlvi. 4; trans. Serafini-Sauli, 139).

as a form of *aporia*, the perplexity induced by the coexistence of individually tenable but mutually incompatible propositions.[93] Polia provides a possible solution to these difficulties, a way of transforming multiplicity into unity, and Poliphilo's declaration that 'I setled my selfe to followe her' (*sectario suo me exposi*, R.D. Y1ʳ; F.C. i7ʳ; = G149) suggests that the work is to be read, in part, at least, as a *paideia*, an account of the education (indeed, the initiation) of the hero.[94]

That is certainly the thrust of Colonna's immediate model, Boccaccio's *Ameto*, in which the eponymous hero is a boorish shepherd who is transformed, by his desire for Lia and her six companion nymphs (allegorically, the Seven Virtues), from 'brute animal' into 'man' (*d'animale bruto, uomo divenuto essere li pare*, xlvi. 5, p. 139).[95] At the end of the *Ameto*, Boccaccio declares that 'there is desire that moves man to salvation' (*quivi disio movente omo a saluto*, xlix. 70, p. 144): Lia is clearly seen as a salvific agent.

THE SIGNIFICANCE OF 'POLIA'

But the simple expansion of 'Lia' to 'Polia' multiplies the interpretive possibilities of the heroine's name.[96] Indeed, 'Polia' can be taken as a version of the Greek, πολλά ('many things') (from πολύς).[97] The gift of multiplicity, of course, also imposes (on Poliphilo and on Renaissance humanists in general) the burden of discrimination. The liminary verses, harking back to the amatory-religious tradition of Dante, Petrarch, Boccaccio, and their followers, hint at a divine dimension to the name when they refer to the work as 'dreams sent by highest heaven' (*summo somnia missa Polo*).[98] Renaissance readers will also

---

[93] Such propositions might be generated (say) by the subject of desire ('Desire reduces us to the level of beasts'; 'Desire draws us closer to the Divine') or Antiquity ('Pagan culture is superseded by Christian revelation'; 'The Wisdom of the Ancients foreshadows the truth of Christian revelation'). Note that *aporia* literally means 'having no way in', 'difficulty of passage'.

[94] See Palermino (141 n. 70) on *sectatores*.

[95] Cf. Dante's notion (*Parad.* i. 67–71) of being 'transhumanized' (*Trasumanar*) by the vision of Beatrice in the same way that the fisherman Glaucus ate a certain herb 'which made him a consort of the other gods in the sea' (*che 'l fè consorte in mar delli altri Dei*).

[96] Note that in Book 2, Polia reveals her original name to be Lucretia (F.C. A3ᵛ; G 386).

[97] The nymph's meditations on the significance of Poliphilo's name provide textual support for this etymology: 'it will please me well . . . if the effect of your conditions be aunswerable to yonr [*sic*] name. . . . Aha I thought your name should signifie that you were a great louer, but now I perceiue that you are a louer of *Polia*' (R.D. M2ʳ; F.C. e6ʳ; G 84). See, generally, Rowland, *Culture*, 62. Biographical gossip has also linked Polia to a Hippolita, reputedly beloved by Fra Francesco Colonna (Dronke, *Francesco Colonna*, 15).

[98] Dronke bypasses the liminary verses but relies on the same etymology to suggest (*Francesco Colonna*, 15) that 'Polia' may be indebted to Alanus de Insulis' *puella poli* ('girl of heaven'),

have been familiar with the idealization (typically in female form) of the city (πόλις) as the embodiment of civilization and (in many cases and more dangerously) of republican values.[99] Dronke dismisses as 'inept' the attempt by 'earlier commentators' to derive 'Polia' from πολιός ('hoary', 'grey'), but the identification of Polia with Antiquity dates back to 1550 or earlier.[100]

Scholars (such as Virginia Brown) may quarrel with the claim for a specifically Roman provenance, but Ingrid D. Rowland is surely right to express an affinity between the erotic pursuit of Polia and the antiquarian pursuit of the true form of ancient culture: 'The object of endless longing, [Polia] slips away every time Poliphilo comes close to embracing her, just as ancient Rome both tempted and eluded Pomponio Leto and his fellow Academics'.[101]

Poliphilo's assertion that Polia's speech would have restored life 'to the dust and ashes of the dead' (*puluereo & cineroso morto*, G 235; F.C. p2ʳ) draws its diction from the coffins inhabited by 'the dusty and now ashy dead' (*puluerei et iam cinerosi mortui*) in which Thrasyleon and his bandits intend to store their loot (*AA* 4. 18). Apuleius may seem, in the new context, to be doing little more than providing the rhetorical climax to a long series of *impossibilia*, but Colonna's expression chimes nicely with Cyriaco d'Ancona's declared intention to 'wake the dead', to use his 'potent and divine art to revive the glorious things which had become buried and defunct through the lapse of ages and persistent injury at the hands of the half-dead; to bring them from the dark tomb to light, to live once more among living men'.[102]

---

the anonymous guide in the *Anticlaudianus*. Polia is sometimes identified with 'Divine Wisdom' (Sophia). See R. Stewering, 'The Relationship between World, Landscape, and Polia in the *Hypnerotomachia Poliphili*', in *Garden and Architectural Dreamscapes*, ed. Leslie and Hunt, 2–10, at 2. One also notes the number of allusions to *polus* ('heaven') as well as to *columna* ('column' or 'Colonna') in the *Coryciana*, a specimen of sodality literature with strong links to the *Hypnerotomachia*.

[99] Stephen Harrison has drawn my attention to the cult image in the Parthenon of Athena Polìas, guardian 'of the city' and goddess of learning. J. Serafini-Sauli notes (*L'Ameto*, p. xviii) that the city (*polis*) is 'a dominant theme in the *Ameto*'. See, more generally, A. J. Rabil, 'The Significance of "Civic Humanism" in the Interpretation of the Italian Renaissance', in *Renaissance Humanism: Foundations, Forms and Legacy*, ed. Rabil, 3 vols. (Philadelphia: U of Pennsylvania P, 1988), i. 141–79, at 142; and L. Bek, 'The Changing Architectonic Aspect of the Ideal City in the Early Renaissance', in *Acta Conventus Neo-Latini Hafniensis*, ed. R. Schnur et al. (Binghamton, NY: MRTS, 1994), 143–53. Note the stress on *urbanitas* in Bussi's preface to the *ed. princ.* of Apuleius.

[100] Dronke, *Francesco Colonna*, 15. The annotator of the Modenese copy glosses 'Polia' as *anus etate, dignitateque ceteris antestans* ('an old woman in age and superior in dignity to the rest', sig. A2ʳ). The Sienese copy offers: *Polion, canities. Polia pro ipsa prudentia, quae in canis est, et pro ipsa virtute* ('Πολιόν, "hoariness". "Polia" on account of the very sagacity that is found in grey hairs, and virtue itself', sig. A2ᵛ). See Stichel, 218.

[101] Rowland, *Culture*, 62.

[102] Mitchell ('Archaeology and Romance', 470), translating from the edn. by Lorenzo Mehus, *Kyriaci Anconitani itinerarium* (Florence: Giovanni Paolo Giovannelli, 1742), 54–5.

One could go further with the theory of a Pomponian provenance. I cannot help wondering, for instance, whether the name 'Polia' might serve (amongst its many functions) as a (vaguely) anagrammatic tribute to the spirit of 'POmponIus LAetus'.[103] We might even detect a coded reference to the Academy in Osfressia's reassuring words which we considered earlier: *Ma sta cum laeto animo & da opera a piacere, che la tua dilecta Polia la ritrouerai* (F.C. e6ᵛ). Godwin translates *ritrouerai* as 'you shall find' (G 84), but its more literal meaning ('recover' or 'rediscover') makes the passage an apt figure for the antiquarian quest. This could be read in an affirmative sense—the only way to embrace Antiquity is in the Pomponian spirit (*cum [L]aeto animo*) of unalloyed pleasure in the past and its remains. But if we take full account of the Apuleian contexts that we have been discussing, then we should also appreciate the work's inbuilt critique of the Pomponian mode: an acknowledgement of the potential excesses of antiquarianism; an awareness that while *laetitia* may take the form of divinely inspired *hylaritudine*, it can easily degenerate into mere ridiculousness.

In considering the significance of 'Polia', we should also add the associations with *polio* and *polita*. As we saw in Chapter 3, Angelo Camillo Decembrio (1415–67?) had devoted an entire work to the subject of 'literary polish' and had placed in Leonello d'Este's mouth the claim that Apuleius' style was 'varied, disordered, unpolished' (*uarius incompositus rigidus*).[104] During the later quattrocento, we find a constant interplay between the verbal and the marmoreal in the notion of 'polish'. Beroaldo (fol. 1ᵛ) describes his commentaries on Apuleius as metamorphic tools which can, by their polishing, soften the hard text (*commentariorum expolitione emollietur*). Grassi refers to the content of the *Hypnerotomachia* as being *perpolitae quadam dicendi nouitate.*

---

[103] The fact that Leto died in 1498, just a year before the publication of the *Hypnerotomachia*, would also account for the discrepancy between Poliphilo's dedicatory epistle (F.C. a1ᵛ) in which 'Polia' is clearly alive (and able to influence the style) and the concluding epitaph in which (the dead) Polia speaks (F.C. F3ᵛ). Such a tribute would be in keeping with the Platonic spirit of the Academy in which *fratres* 'delivered orations and recited poems whose professions of ardent friendship sometimes became openly erotic' (Rowland, *Culture*, 13). It is also interesting to note that Aldus (who was born at Bassiano, just to the south-east of Rome and liked to style himself *Aldus Romanus* in his colophons) was a former student of Leto's, though according to D'Amico ('Humanism in Rome', 285), he 'did not approve of the type of commentary his teacher wrote'. One might, alternatively, pursue the beguiling fact that the Roman Academy had at least one female member, Leto's own daughter, Nigella (mentioned, *en passant*, by Rowland, *Culture*, 10, and by Zabughin). It might also be significant that Ficino died in 1498. One would not wish, however, to press the point: in anagrammatic terms, an even better candidate would be Paolo Pompilio, one of those who wrote in response to the discovery of the 'Roman Girl' in 1485, and described by Barkan (*Unearthing the Past*, 58) as 'connected with some particularly radical notions of paganizing Christian culture'.

[104] *De politia litteraria* 1. 6. 1.

We have already seen Lucius fall victim to the *nitor* ('sheen') of the highly polished grapes (*uuae faberrime politae, AA* 2. 4); Poliphilo is soon to follow.[105] Indeed, Colonna carries Lucius' tendency to confuse life and art to extremes—Poliphilo is a case study in the pathology of reification. His description of Polia's cleavage as 'a delicious little cleft that was the delicate tomb of my soul, such as Mausolus could not have built, for all his wealth' (*una deliciosa uallecula, oue era la delicata sepultura dilalma mia,* G 240; F.C. p4ᵛ) may suggest to us that while the antiquarian spirit can breathe new life into the dead, it can also suffocate the living.

LOGISTICA AND THELEMIA

Informed of his quest for Polia, Queen Eleuterylida entrusts Poliphilo (G 121–2) to the care of two opposing guides, Logistica ('Reason') and Thelemia ('Desire') who lead him to the abode of Queen Telosia ('end' or 'goal'). In a variation on the themes of the 'Choice of Hercules' and the 'Judgement of Paris', he is shown a set of three portals hacked into the side of a mountain, bearing the inscriptions, *Gloria Dei, Mater Amoris,* and *Gloria Mundi* (G 135; F.C. h8ʳ).[106] Logistica realizes that the path demanded by the religious life (*Gloria Dei*) is too stony and thorny for Poliphilo, but she almost persuades him to lodge with Euclelia ('Glorious') and her six companions, symbols of 'Worldly Glory' (*Gloria Mundi*).[107] Thelemia, however, urges Poliphilo to try the middle portal (*Mater Amoris*) first, and he is immediately captivated by the 'wanton and capricious' looks (*risguardi petulci & inconstanti*) of Philtronia and her six serving-maids in what Dallington calls 'the Mansion-house of Voluptuousnes' (*uno loco uoluptuoso,* R.D. V3ᵛ; F.C. i1ᵛ; = G 138). Logistica's response contains a crucial Apuleian borrowing which Pozzi misses. Her alarm at 'seeing mee disposing my selfe abruptlie to the servile loue of them'

---

[105] We might also note Fotis' impersonation of the Venus statue (*AA* 2. 17); Lucius' anxiety about being memorialized in a statue (*AA* 3. 11); Psyche's problem of being universally admired, 'but as a statue, polished by a craftsman' (*sed ut simulacrum fabre politum, AA* 4. 32); and the Isiac initiation in which Lucius is dressed up 'in the manner of a statue' (*in vicem simulacri constitutus*) and put on display (*AA* 11. 24). Cf. Poliphilo's response to the nymphs: *tra che la uoce inseme cum il spirito interdicti, semiuiuo, & quale statua io rimansi* ('with my voice and mind both paralysed, I remained half-dead, like a statue', F.C. e3ʳ; G 7̄7̄).

[106] For the intellectual background to this scene (Macrobius and Fulgentius), see Wind, *Pagan Mysteries,* 81–96, esp. 82.

[107] Is there a vague echo of *AA* 2. 17 (Fotis' playful challenge to Lucius to engage battle: *Comminus in aspectum, si uir es, derige, et grassare nauiter et occide moriturus*) in Logistica's exhortation: *O Poliphile non ti rencresca in questo loco uirilmente agonizare* (F.C. i1ʳ)?

(*gia abruptamente deflexo allamore di essa in seruile modo addicto dixe*, R.D. V4ʳ; F.C. i1ᵛ; = G 138) echoes Lucius' claim that Fotis holds him 'willingly made over and delivered up in the manner of a slave' (*in seruilem modum addictum atque mancipatum teneas uolentem*, *AA* 3. 19).[108] Traditional readings of Apuleius regard this voluntary enslavement as the beginning of Lucius' troubles. Logistica attacks Poliphilo's choice:

... *fucosa & simulata bellecia di costei e mendace, insipida & insulsa, Imperoche si le sue spalle discussamente mirare le uolesti nauseabondo comprenderesti forsa quanta indecentia subiace, & quanto aspernabile sono, & di fetulento stomachose & abhominabile, eminente sopra una alta congerie di sorde.* (F.C. i1ᵛ)

... the alluring and inticing beauties of these, are vaine, deceiuable, and counterfeited, vnsauorie and displeasant, and therfore if thou wouldest with aduisement looke vppon their backes, thou wouldest then hate, contemne, and abhorre theyr lothsome filthinesse and shame, abounding in stinke and noysome sauour aboue any dunghill, which no stomacke can abide. (R.D. V4ʳ; = G 138)[109]

When Logistica perceives that her words are having no effect, she runs away in disgust and we are left with only Poliphilo's perspective as he rhapsodizes about Philtronia[110] and her six serving-maids: 'nothing about them was false, but all was perfect and exquisitely finished by nature' (*Niuna parte simulata, ma tutto dalla natura perfecto, cum exquisita politione*, G 141; F.C. i3ʳ). Poliphilo's appreciation of the nymphs remains (literally) superficial, seduced, as he is, by their 'exquisite polish'. But even apparently trivial correspondences between Colonna and Apuleius may provide some coded endorsement of Logistica's warning. For while the nymphs' *Risguardi mordenti* ('theyr regards biting', F.C. i3ʳ; R.D. x1ʳ; = G 140) resemble Fotis' 'nibbling eyes' (*morsicantibus oculis*, *AA* 2. 10), their tresses, held in place 'with hair pins' (*cum achi crinali detente*, G 141), conceal a debt to the pin (*acu crinali*, *AA* 8. 13) with which Charite gouges out Thrasyllus' eyes when she discovers that, in his desire for her, he has murdered her husband, Tlepolemus.[111]

---

[108] Cf. Ficino, *Commentary*, Speech II, ch. 9: *Tangendi vero cupido non amoris pars est nec amantis affectus, sed petulantie speties et servilis hominis perturbatio* ('the desire to touch is not part of love, nor is it a passion of the lover, but rather a kind of lust and perturbation of a man who is servile', trans. S. Jayne, 58). Latin text from *Marsile Ficin: Commentaire sur le Banquet de Platon*, ed. R. Marcel (Paris: Société d'édition "Les Belles Lettres", 1956, repr. 1978), 159.

[109] Logistica's description anticipates Una's stripping of Duessa's finery to reveal her foul nether parts (Spenser, *FQ* I. viii. 45–9).

[110] From φίλτρον ('love-charm', 'spell to produce love'). In Speech VII, ch. 4 (*Amoris vulgaris est fascinatio quedam*, 'Earthly Love is a Form of Bewitchment') of his *Commentary* (ed. Marcel, 248; trans. S. Jayne, 161), Ficino quotes the infatuated stepmother's words to her stepson (*AA* 10. 3): *Causa omnis et origo praesentis doloris ... Ergo miserere tua causa pereuntis* ('You are the entire cause and source of this present anguish ... Therefore take pity on someone dying because of you').

[111] Even Poliphilo recognizes the nymphs' ability 'to lead the holiest into depravity' (*di prauare omni sanctimonia*, G 141; F.C. i3ʳ).

Almost immediately, Poliphilo meets a 'sun-like nymph' (*questa Elioida Nympha*), so elegant that perhaps 'beautiful Psyche' did not appear thus to 'ardent Cupid' (*Nella bellissima Psyche allardente Cupidine*, G 143; F.C. i4ʳ). He suspects that it is Polia, but is confused by her clothing and unfamiliar context, and her identity remains unresolved for the next seventy-five pages.[112] If 'almighty Jupiter had appointed me as judge, like the Phrygian shepherd', Poliphilo tells us (G 143), he would have awarded the apple to her above the three goddesses. Her dress is described in detail:

Ilquale ingrummato subleuamento & circunsinuato & elegantemente composito intorniaua supra el pudico aluo, cum grato tumento, Et di sopra alle resistente & tremule nate, & al rotundo & piccolo uentre, il residuo del uestire demesso uelaua cum minutissime rugature al reflato delle suaue aure instabillule, & per il moto corporeo, fina alle lactee suffragine cadente. Alcuna fiata dagli temperati spirari di uentuli, il leue indumento impulso, accusaua la pudica & scitula formula, laquale ad quella faceua prompto contempto. (F.C. i4ʳ)

(. . . it was raised in bunches and sinuous folds that made an elegant surround to the chaste womb, and swelled charmingly over the firm and tremulous buttocks and the small, round belly. The rest of the clothing hung loosely in minute wrinkles down to the milk-white heels, wafting in the breath of the suave, mutable breezes and with the motions of her body. Sometimes the gentle puffs of wind lifted the garments to reveal the trim and modest figure, which did not trouble her in the least.) (G 143)[113]

Polia, as Peter Dronke has observed, 're-enacts all the parts of the Apuleian heroines'. She is 'Photis, Charite, Psyche and Venus together'.[114] But her presentation here—flimsily clad, the plaything of breezes—associates her not with Venus herself, but with the actress who impersonates that goddess in Apuleius' pantomime of the Judgement of Paris:

. . . nudo et intecto corpore perfectam formositatem professa, nisi quod tenui pallio bombycino inumbrabat spectabilem pubem. Quam quidem laciniam curiosulus ventus satis amanter nunc lasciviens reflabat, ut dimota pateret flos aetatulae, nunc luxurians aspirabat, ut adhaerens pressule membrorum voluptatem graphice liniaret. (AA 10. 31)

(She displayed a perfect figure, her body naked and uncovered except for a piece of sheer silk with which she veiled her comely charms. An inquisitive little breeze would at one moment blow this veil aside in wanton playfulness so that it lifted to reveal the

---

[112] Note that Poliphilo chooses to describe his uncertainty in philosophical terms as a commendably Sceptical 'suspension of judgement': *cum ueneranda suspensione me conseruai* (G 143; F.C. i4ʳ). Cf. Socrates' commendation of Scepticism (*Phaedrus* 229c).

[113] Dallington takes *laquale . . . contempto* in the opposite way: 'which shee seemed with a prompt readinesse to resist and hynder' (R.D. X2ʳ). For the wind and clothes, see Casella and Pozzi, *Colonna*, ii. 129–30. Compare Fotis' 'milk-white skin' (*lacteam . . . cutem, AA* 3. 14).

[114] Dronke, *Francesco Colonna*, 67, 70. We should compare the description of the nymph (*scitula formula*) with that of Fotis at *AA* 2. 6 (*forma scitula*).

flower of her youth, and at another moment it would gust exuberantly against it so that it clung tightly and graphically delineated her body's voluptuousness.)[115]

The Judgement of Paris serves, of course, as a mythological reprise of the choice that Poliphilo made at the three portals of Queen Telosia; but it may seem a peculiar authorial strategy to burden Polia, on her first public appearance, with the potentially negative connotations of Apuleius' pantomime.[116] On the one hand, the *mimus* can be read as a congeries of meretricious artifice which elicits the most overt moralizing in *The Golden Ass* (Lucius' denunciation of corrupt judgements, *AA* 10. 33) while also serving as a prelude to the main event in the amphitheatre—the grotesque parody of the marriage-ceremony in which the condemned murderess is to be publicly mated with the asinified Lucius and then devoured by wild beasts.[117] On the other hand, the entertainment not only rehearses (albeit in imperfect human terms) the theophany of Book 11, but actually precipitates it by provoking in Lucius the moral and emotional crisis that leads him to break away (*AA* 10. 34–5).

To some extent these moral-aesthetic difficulties had already been negotiated in the preceding century and a half. Boccaccio makes clear use of the Apuleian episode in his accounts of wind-puffed nymphs in the *Ameto*, though the elements usually limit themselves to revealing hair beneath a veil,[118] or, at most, a portion of 'round leg...free of stockings' (*la tonda gambada niuno calzamento coperta*, xv. 19). And a fusion of Apuleius' account of the *mimus* with Ficinian Neoplatonism has been seen (controversially) as informing Botticelli's *Primavera*, the picture (from the late 1470s) which Gombrich calls 'a turning-point in the history of European art':

The 'paganism' of Apuleius' description had undergone a complete transmutation through Ficino's moral enthusiasm and exegetic wizardry. A description of a show, little better than a Montmartre *Revue*, had been translated in all good faith into a vision of the bliss that comes with *Humanitas*.[119]

---

[115] Trans. Hanson. Note that *bombycinus* ('silken') occurs later in the description of the nymph.

[116] The motif of ventilated nymphs is used again in the description of the rowers taking the lovers to the island of Cytherea being subjected to 'The fresh and wanton breeze' (G 277). See Casella and Pozzi, *Colonna*, ii. 129.

[117] *AA* 10. 34–5. Note the parallel with the 'funereal marriage' of Psyche who is exposed on a rock, awaiting (as she thinks) the arrival of her beast of a husband (*saeuum atque ferum uipereumque malum, AA* 4. 33).

[118] e.g. the 'very thin veil' which is 'blown with graceful motion by the gentle breezes' (*ventilato dalle sottili aure con piacevole moto*, xii. 20; trans. Serafini-Sauli, 29). The Judgement of Paris is alluded to in *Ameto* xxxi.

[119] *Symbolic Images: Studies in the Art of the Renaissance* (London: Phaidon, 1972), 45, 64. On Apuleius, see, generally, 45–64, esp. 56. Gombrich (41) sees here the influence of Ficino's identification (expressed in a letter datable to 1477–8) of Venus with *Humanitas*: Love serves as a guide to the Liberal Arts. Gombrich's study of 'Botticelli's Mythologies' appeared initially in

Even allowing for such mediations, the meretricious associations may be deliberate. Thelemia has promised Poliphilo that 'this is the place where... thou shalt finde the deerest thing which thou louest in the world, & which thou hast in thy hart, without intermission determined to seeke and desire' (R.D. V4ᵛ; = G 139; = F.C. i2ʳ), and it is possible that the 'sunlike nymph' whom we see here is a projection of Poliphilo's still immature desires. Ameto discovers, at the end of Boccaccio's work, that 'whereas the nymphs had pleased more his eye than his intellect, they now delighted his intellect more than his eye'.[120] It may be that the 'real' Polia will reveal herself to Poliphilo only after he has shown some comparable indication of inner development.

THE TRIUMPHS

We need to bear Poliphilo's state of cognitive impairment in mind when we approach the series of triumphs that he witnesses in the company of (the as-yet-unrecognized) Polia (F.C. k1ʳ—17ʳ, m3ᵛ—m6ʳ; G 153–81, 190–5). These *trionfi* cover the full gamut of sexual desire, from Jupiter's adulterous affairs, through Vertumnus and Pomona (symbols of natural fruitfulness), to the animal pleasures represented by the cult of Priapus which features, not only an ithyphallic god, but also the sacrifice of a garlanded ass.[121] One Apuleian

---

JWCI 8 (1945), 7–60. The Apuleian thesis has been criticized by E. Panofsky, *Renaissance and Renascences in Western Art* (London: Paladin, 1960; repr. London: Harper & Row, 1970), 194–5 n. 3. Cf. C. Dempsey, '*Mercurius Ver:* The Sources of Botticelli's *Primavera*', *JWCI* 31 (1968), 251–73.

[120] *vede che sieno le ninfe, le quali più all'occhio che allo 'ntelletto erano piaciute, e ora allo 'ntelletto piacciono più che all'occhio* (*Ameto*, ch. xlvi, p. 139).

[121] The devotees are described as 'spattering the foaming blood of the sacrificed ass' (G 194). Note the stress in the liminary verses (G 7; F.C. fol. 4ʳ) on 'the sacrifice to Priapus | with the ass and his monstrous phallus' (*de Priapo el sacrificio | cum asinello, e mentula monstrosa*). Ovid relates (*Fasti* 1. 391 ff.) how 'a young ass is slaughtered for the stiff guardian of the countryside' (*caeditur et rigido custodi ruris asellus*), in annual commemoration of the occasion of the banquet at which Priapus' plan to rape the sleeping nymph, Lotis, was thwarted by the sudden braying of Silenus' ass (*Fasti* 1. 433–4: *ecce rudens rauco Sileni vector asellus | intempestivos edidit ore sonos*). Pseudo-Hyginus records (*De astronomia* 2. 23) the story that Bacchus gave an ass 'a human voice' as a reward for carrying him across a marsh (*Nonnulli etiam dixerunt asino illi quo fuerit vectus vocem humanam dedisse*). Later, however, he had a contest with Priapus, *de natura*, and was defeated and killed by the god (... *eum postea cum Priapo contendisse de natura et victum ab eo interfectum*). *Natura* is usually taken as a euphemism for genital endowment, but it is interesting, in the context of both the *Hypnerotomachia* and *The Golden Ass,* to note the (emulous) collocation of the erotic and the linguistic, the bestial, the human, and the divine. In the woodcut, the ass dominates the foreground while Priapus' phallus occupies the centre of the picture. The ass's organ is not visible, but other items in the composition (the erect tail being gripped—or stroked—by the nymph; the trumpet being raised and blown to the right; the knife

parallel not picked up by Pozzi and Ciaponni occurs in the Second Triumph, where a swan on the top of the carriage is coupling with Theseus' [*sic*] daughter:

Et cum diuini & uoluptici oblectamenti istauano delectabilmente iucundissimi ambi connexi, Et el diuino Olore tra le delicate & niuee coxe collocato. Laquale commodamente sedeua sopra dui Puluini di panno doro, exquisitamente di mollicula lanugine tomentati ... (F.C. k7ᵛ)

(... with divine and voluptuous pleasure the two of them united in their delectable sport, with the god-like swan positioned between her delicate, snow-white thighs. She was lying comfortably on two cushions of cloth of gold, softly filled with finest wool...) (G 166)

The West has, of course, a long tradition of aestheticizing zoophilia through poetry and art. But the presentation of Leda and the swan in the *Hypnerotomachia* still has the power to shock, or, at least, to unsettle. The problem is not simply that Colonna chooses to depict swan and nymph in the very act of coupling, nor that rape is transformed into a mutually pleasurable act of love; disturbing also is the way in which the representation collapses the distinction between art and reality. Rather than being contained in a sculptural frieze on one of the side-panels of the pageant wagon, the unnamed female and the unidentified (and thereby undeified) animal appear as a kind of *tableau vivant* on the top.[122] Some of these tonal complexities are explained by the fact that Colonna seems to be drawing here on Apuleius' account of Lucius' congress with the wealthy *matrona*. Their union takes place on small cushions (*pulvilli*) overlaid by 'coverlets coloured with cloth of gold and Tyrian purple' (*stragula veste auro ac murice Tyrio depicta*). She is a *delicata matrona* (*AA* 10. 22) and Lucius wonders how he will be able to embrace 'such shining and tender limbs composed of milk and honey with his hard hooves' (*tam lucida tamque tenera et lacte ac melle confecta membra duris ungulis*). This Apuleian borrowing achieves a kind of defamiliarization effect, bringing to the fore the naked reality of the encounter.

---

and what looks like a mallet lined up underneath the bowl) seem to be arranged for phallic effect. It may be significant that the ass suffers the fate (having its throat cut) with which Lucius is threatened at *AA* 6. 31. Pseudo-Hyginus was widely available in the Renaissance, though in the edn. compiled by Jacobus Micyllus (Jakob Möltzer) the text reads: *cum Priapo deo naturae contendisse* ('competed with Priapus, the God of Nature'). See *Hyginus: Fabularum Liber, Basel 1535*, facs. (New York: Garland, 1976), sig. g3ᵛ.

[122] Lefaivre (68 and 71) reproduces plates from a Vatican copy of the *Hypnerotomachia* in which the images of Priapus' phallus and of the copulating swan have been blacked out. Lowry suggests (*World of Aldus*, 125) that the inking over was done in Manutius' workshop. In Boccaccio's *Amorosa visione* (xvii. 76), Leda and the swan appear as the last tableau in an extended ecphrasis, but while Leda is shown to be desirous of the swan before Jove changes himself back into his natural form, there is nothing to match the vividness or explicitness of the depiction here.

In the Fourth Triumph, Cupid features with Psyche (an unnamed but 'most beautiful Nymph') on the front and back panels of the carriage:

Allincontro retro el maximo Iupiter uedeuasi in uno tribunale sedente iudice, Et cupidine claudicante, contra la sua benigna matre in iudicio uocata, dolente querimonie [sig. 12ᵛ] *faceua, Conciosia cosa che per sua cagione dellamore duna speciosissima damigella extremamente se medesimo uulnerasse. Et che da una lucernale scintilla gli fusse stata la diuina gambula causticata. Praesente ancora la bellissima Nympha cum la lucerna nelle mano accusata. Et a Cupidine ridibondo gli diceua Iupiter. Perfer scintillam, qui caelum accendis & omnes* (F.C. 12ʳ⁻ᵛ)

In the hinder end was *Iupiter* sitting in a tribunall seate as iudge, and *Cupide* appeering limping before him, and making grieuous complaints against his louing mother, bicause that by hir means he had wounded himselfe extreemly with a drop of a lampe,[123] presenting also the yoong Nymph and the lampe in her hand. And Iupiter with a smiling countenance speaking to Cupid,

    Perfer scintillam qui coelum accendis & omnes,[124] (R.D. Aa1ʳ; = G 172)

Watching 'the delightfull duties of reciprocall loue' (*delecteuoli officii dello aequato & reciprico amore*) of the host of nymphs and beardless youths attending the procession, Poliphilo seems to be on the verge of erotic ecstasy,[125] but instead of tracing the full trajectory of (Neo-)Platonic *ekstasis*, Colonna-Poliphilo changes tack, reducing desire to a form of necromantically induced obstupefaction:

… my minde still fixed vpon delightfull pleasures and their smacking kisses [*gli folposi basii*], and regarding with a curious eie [*cum curioso aspectuo*] the abounding guerdons of the fethered god, me thought at that instant, that I did behold the extreeme perfection of pleasure.[126] And by this meanes I stood wauering and out of measure amazed, and as one which had droonke an amorous potion [*obstupefacto, che quasi philtrato*], calling into remembrance the ointments of the mischeeuous *Circes*, the forcible hearbs of *Medea*, the hurtfull songs of *Byrrena*, and the deadly verses of *Pamphile* [*gli noxii canti de Byrrena et gli sepulchrali canti di Pamphile*],[127] I stood

---

[123] R. D. conflates the two separate events—the self-inflicted wound which Cupid recalls (*AA* 5. 24) in his reproach to Psyche and the accidental burning of the god's shoulder as she gazes at him in the light of her lamp (*AA* 5. 23).

[124] 'Put up with a spark, you who set fire to heaven and everyone.'

[125] Cf. *Ameto* xv. 15: *gli pare gli ultimi termini della beatitudine somma toccare, credendo appena che altroue che in quelli paradiso si truoui.*

[126] Godwin's translation makes the ecstatic element more obvious: 'I seemed truly to feel my enflamed soul making its transition and gently migrating to the extreme limits of bliss' (G 184).

[127] The reference to the 'harmful incantations of Byrrhena' seems like a simple slip, but Poliphilo's negative characterization of Lucius' kindly 'aunt' may be another instance of Colonna's deep reading of Apuleius. Byrrhena (like Fotis) is one of the medial figures in *The Golden Ass*: many of her qualities as benefactress and protectress link her typologically with Isis; but her mysteriousness can also be interpreted less charitably and she is in some way implicated

doubtfull that my eies had seene somthing more than humane, and that a base, dishonorable, and fraile bodie should not be where immortall creatures did abide [*Il perche iuridicamente dubitaua, che gli corporali ochii potesseron ultra la humanitate cernere, & non poterui essere humillimo, ignobile, & graue corpo, oue gli immortali beati conquescono*] (R.D. Bb2^v; F.C. m1^r; = G 184)

He is brought back, however, to a more positive view of these sights by the recognition of his 'imperfect comprehension':

After that I was brought from these long and doubtfull thoughts and phantasticall imaginations, and remembering all those maruellous diuine shapes and bodies which I had persoonally seene with mine eies, I then knew that they were not deceitfull shadowes, nor magicall illusions, but that I had not rightly conceiued of them [*Ma ueramente imperfecte compraehense*] (R.D. Bb2^v; F.C. m1^r; = G 184)

THE TEMPLE OF VENUS PHYSIZOA

At the conclusion of the *trionfi*, the nymph leads Poliphilo towards the shore, where he discovers an ancient temple, 'consecrated to Venus Physizoa' (G 197; F.C. m7^r). The temple is described in great detail (more than a little of which, I suspect, found its way into Marlowe's description of '*Venus* temple' in *Hero and Leander*, 132 ff.).[128] After fourteen pages of architectural rhapsody, they are welcomed by the High Priestess (*la Diva Antiste*) and seven 'holy virgins' (*sacre uirgine*, G 211; F.C. n6^v). A series of religious ceremonies follows, beginning with a Venereal version of the baptismal rite in which Poliphilo plunges the nymph's 'blazing torch into the cold cistern' (*la ardente facola nella frigida cisterna*, G 216; F.C. n8^v). The nymph finally confirms her identity as Polia (G 217–18; F.C. o1^v), the three Graces are invoked (G 224; F.C. o4^v), and the ceremony moves towards its conclusion. The High Priestess scatters 'fragrant roses' 'around the firebox on the altar' (G 231; F.C. o8^r), and after a sacrifice of two swans and a ritual which seems to owe something to the liturgy of the Mass, an explosion is heard: 'I saw a verdant rose-bush miraculously issue out of the pure smoke, grow and multiply' (G 233). The rose-bush bears 'rounded fruits of marvellous fragrance' which 'tempted the taste'.

---

in Lucius' humiliation at the Festival of Laughter, in the aftermath of which he is 'terrified of her house and has a horror of it even at a distance' (*formidans et procul perhorrescens etiam ipsam domum eius*, AA 3. 12).

[128] As L. Gent points out (introd. to *The Strife of Loue*, p. vii), Thomas Nashe (whose name is appended to Marlowe's on the title page of the 1594 quarto edn. of *Dido, Queene of Carthage*), refers explicitly to '*The strife of Love in a Dreame*' in the mock 'Epistle Dedicatory' of his *Lenten Stuff* (1599).

The Priestess plucks three of these, one for herself and two for Polia and Poliphilo. After eating the fruit, 'I felt my crude intellect renewed . . . and I seemed to be transmuted with the sweeter torment of novel qualities of love' (*rinouare il rude & crasso intellecto . . . & cum piu suaue cruciato di nouelle qualitate damore transmutarme mi apparue*, G 234; F.C. p1ᵛ).

We might note the Apuleian inflections of the terms *rude & crasso* and *cruciato*. Lucius' return to human form is marked by the loss of his 'rough hair' (*squalens pilus defluit*), the thinning of his 'thick skin' (*cutis crassa tenuatur*), and the disappearance of his tail (*cauda*)—the thing which 'previously had been crucifying me most of all (*quae me potissimum cruciebat ante*, *AA* 11. 13).[129] We know from Horace (*Satires* 1. 2. 45; 2. 7. 49) that *cauda* can be a euphemism for the *membrum virile*, and the loss of Lucius' 'tail' can be seen as signifying the rejection of the embraces of both Fotis and the *matrona* (who featured, respectively, at the beginning and end of his asinine adventures) and a resolution to the anxieties over castration that had dogged him in between.[130] Poliphilo's transformation, in contrast, is intellectual rather than physical, and it involves not a renunciation of the erotic, but an enhancement, or at least a reconfiguration, of it. All this reflects the nexus of corporeal, spiritual, and intellectual elements which is such a feature of humanist thinking about appetite and *voluptas*. Colonna's *rude* may remind us that *erudition* (literally, 'out of roughness') can itself be a quasi-religious process, a form of illumination, indeed transformation. We saw Bussi's praise of Apuleius' work as being devoid of any 'rough and jagged speech' (*non squalenti et laciniosa oratione*).[131] We should recall, too, Beroaldo's identification of *inscitia* ('ignorance', 'inexperience') as one of the drugs inducing bestiality, and of *scientia* as the 'roses' which retransform one from asinine to human form.[132] The Apuleian transformation from 'rough beast' to Isiac acolyte can thus be read, at one level, as a figure for the 'polishing' (*expolitio*) accorded by philological studies.

The Venus Physizoa episode proves, in fact, to be only one of a series of false climaxes in the *Hypnerotomachia*. This seemingly ludic approach to the

---

[129] There may also be a pun, I suspect, on *Crassus*, the Latin form of Leonardo Grassi's name.

[130] The size of Lucius' asinine member is emphasized at *AA* 3. 24 (Fotis) and 10. 22 (*matrona*). Cf. the Pseudo-Lucianic *Onos* (56), in which the newly humanized Loukios is thrown out of the house when the *matrona* figure he decided to revisit discovers that his equipment has been reduced to simian proportions.

[131] Preface to the *ed. princ.* (ch. 4, *supra*).

[132] Valeriano (*Hieroglyphica*, Book 12, fols. 87ʳ–91ᵛ) presents the ass as a symbol not merely of lasciviousness and stupidity, but also of inexperience (*imperitia*). At fol. 87ᵛ, he quotes what 'that Apuleian ass says about himself' (*Hinc Apuleianus asinus de se ait*) on the auditory compensations of having enormous ears: *Recreabar quòd auribus grandissimis præditus cuncta longulè etiam dissita sentiebam* (cf. *AA* 9. 15).

problem of closure may be more than merely a hermeneutic game: the imitation of Apuleius' trick in Book 11 (trumping the Isiac epiphany with the Osirian) may suggest the nature of intellectual endeavour, with its ever expanding horizons, its end points in continual retreat. It could also reflect the emphasis placed by Christianity (especially within the Benedictine tradition) on the need for continual conversion of the self. In fact, Polia identifies the ceremony as a means of purification, so that 'we may be worthy to behold the divine presences' (G 236).

POLYANDRION

Emerging from Venus' temple, Polia leads Poliphilo to an extensive array of ruins near the shore, which she identifies as a cemetery (*polyandrion*) 'in which were buried the mouldering corpses of those who yielded to a dark and miserable death through base, unfortunate and unhappy love' (G 236).

While they are waiting here for the arrival of Lord Cupid who is to ferry them to the island of Cytherea, Poliphilo becomes so inflamed with desire that he even contemplates rape (G 240; F.C. p4^v), and Polia distracts him by persuading him to indulge once more in his passion for 'the works of antiquity' (G 242). We have already seen, in our discussion of *rimabondo*, Poliphilo's descent into the subterranean depths of the ciborium (G 247; F.C. p8^r). When he returns to the surface, he finds a magnificent mosaic depicting an erotic *Inferno*, a place where 'the souls who had killed themselves because of overheated love' are condemned to 'burning flames', while 'those who had shown themselves frigid and unyielding toward love' are 'plunged in the horrible ice' (G 250, F.C. q1^v). But in this ecphrastic katabasis, the Dantean has been blended with the Apuleian. The doors to this cavern are guarded by Cerberus who, 'capped with frightful snakes', 'kept watch...spying with sleepless vigilance, his eyes open in perpetual sight' (*explorabondo cum inconniua uigilia, in perpetua luce le pupule excubante*, G 249, F.C. q1^r). Colonna has taken the last detail straight from Apuleius' description of the 'savage snakes' (*saeui dracones*) which guard the spring on the top of the jagged precipice from which Psyche is meant to draw a flask of dark water for Venus (*inconiuae uigiliae luminibus addictis et in perpetuam lucem pupulis excubantibus*, AA 6. 14)

The cemetery of unfortunate lovers also provides ecphrastic opportunities of a different kind, a means of intercalating short but complete tales into the main narrative. A succession of Latin funereal inscriptions are reproduced, among them that of P. Cornelia Anna (an incorruptible contrast to Petronius'

Widow of Ephesus) who surrendered herself 'to be condemned, living, to this tomb with my dead husband' (F.C. sig. q7^r; G 261, 470). These 'tragedies of love' serve to balance the *trionfi* that were seen immediately before the Temple of Venus episode.

Having completed his perusal of the epitaphs, Poliphilo marvels at a mosaic depicting the Rape of Proserpina. The mosaic has been damaged by the roots of a fig-tree, 'springing up everywhere like serpents' (*che per tuto le radice oborte serpendo*, G 272; F.C. r4^v), but as he admires what is left, he is frightened by the sound of falling tesserae: 'I quickly turned round and saw a gecko or wall-lizard which had caused this accident' (*retro uoluentime mirando, uidi uno ascalabote, ouero murilego, che era stato causa di tale ruina*, G 272; F.C. r4^v). In mimetic terms, this incident provides a marked contrast to such precursors as Boccaccio's *Amorosa visione*. The gecko—an unexpected eruption from the living world—disturbs the set programme of ecphrastic narrative in a manner which is almost naturalistic. The disintegrating mosaic jerks Poliphilo's thoughts back to Polia, who, he fears, may have been abducted like Proserpina, and it causes him to reflect on his own predilections and priorities: 'Oh, how importunate is my research and unbridled curiosity about things of the past' (*O importuna indagine, & effrena curiositate dille cose praeterite*, G 272).[133] This brief moment of self-knowledge (as rare for Poliphilo as it was for Lucius) leads him to think of someone else (albeit only in terms of the impact upon himself). Indeed, Poliphilo tells us that his concern that Polia has been lost exceeds the trepidation that he felt earlier 'when I saw myself about to suffer the final ruin of being swallowed and digested by the dreadful, gaping jaws of the venomous dragon' (*Che quando me uidi quasi absorbiculo putrescibile tra le hiante & horrende fauce dil uenefico dracone al finitimo interito*, G 273; F.C. r5^r). The chain of imagery here is richly associative: the serpentine roots of the fig-tree 'beget' a seemingly innocuous reptile (the gecko) which generates, in turn, the 'venomous dragon' in Poliphilo's mind. But we should also note how the winged and firespewing dragon which had pursued Poliphilo at the beginning of his dream (F.C. d3^r–d4^r; G 61–3) has been retrospectively configured as an Apuleian snake-monster. The description of Poliphilo's pallid complexion (*il buxante pallore*, F.C. r5^v; G 274;) as he is reunited with Polia recalls the description of the messenger in *The Golden Ass*, 'trembling with a boxwood pallor' (*buxanti pallore trepidus*, 8. 21) as he tells how he found his fellow slave, 'for the most part already consumed by an immense snake which was pressing upon him as it chewed him up' (*iam ex maxima parte consumpto immanem draconem*

---

[133] Cf. Pseudo-Lucian's *Onos*, ch. 15.

mandentem insistere, AA 8. 21).[134] This is the most haunting of the dark narratives of Book 8 which follow in the wake of the death of Charite, and it is peculiarly appropriate that Colonna should draw it into play here. In both Apuleius' account and Poliphilo's mind there is a terrifying stress on death as a form of protracted, digestive processing. Colonna (at whatever level of consciousness) seems to have read the decrepit old man who metamorphoses into a youth-devouring snake in Apuleius as a figure for the all-consuming power of Time. Hastening back to Polia, Poliphilo fears 'that trident-bearing Neptune might have done her violence' (G 273). His emotional reaction—'no longer alive but half dead . . . dashing up to her in a spasm of incredible pain and anguish'—seems quite disproportionate to the specific danger posed; but the Apuleian echoes help us to see that it is not the sea-god, but Time himself, who (as Shakespeare is to put it in his meditation on 'Ruin' in Sonnet 64), 'will come and take my love away'.

Tempus and *Amissio* ('Time' and 'Loss') have been announced as explicit themes from an early stage in the *Hypnerotomachia* (F.C. b5ᵛ).[135] But the 'Rape of Proserpina' episode gives us a vivid (indeed, visceral) sense of the two timescales operating in the work, the historical and the human. *Antiquitas* may endow the remains of the past with their beauty and their value, but it (or she) is also a destructive force.[136] And for human lives and human loves, Time is ultimately the agent of Loss.

CYTHEREA

The arrival of Cupid (in the context of an impending marriage celebration) in the following scene adds a further Apuleian dimension to Poliphilo's fears of a devouring snake-monster. It allows us to see the abandoned Polia—'watching for the arrival of our Lord' (G 242)—as a reprise of Psyche on the rock, waiting for the *saeuum atque ferum uipereumque malum* to come and claim her as his bride (*AA* 4. 33).[137] Indeed, Poliphilo articulates this anxiety about

[134] Poliphilo is *trepidante* ('trembling') when he reaches Polia (F.C. r5ʳ; G 273). Ovid uses the metaphor of 'boxwood pallor' (*buxoque simillimus . . . pallor*) in the tale of Ceyx and Alcyone (*Met.* 11. 416–17).

[135] Dronke, *Francesco Colonna*, 31. R.D.'s marginal gloss reduces these themes to issues of practical morality: 'Gift vainly bestowed, in time wantonlie spent, is a great losse, & breedeth repentance' (sig. E1ʳ; Gent, 33).

[136] Note Poliphilo's account of a mosaic that he encountered earlier: 'All the rest had been destroyed by insatiable and greedy time, by antiquity' (*Tuto il residuo, fue dalinsaturato, & uorace tempo absumpto, & dalla antiquitate . . .*, G 256; F.C. q4ᵛ).

[137] The description of Polia 'on the fresh and flowering grasses' (*sopra le fresche e florigere herbule*, G 239; F.C. p4ʳ) vaguely recalls the image of Psyche after Zephyrus has taken her off the mountain (*AA* 4. 35–5. 1).

the true nature of Love when Cupid appears in a boat and addresses Polia and Poliphilo as they kneel before him: 'It seemed likely, I thought, that he was comparing her in his mind with his beautiful Psyche, and, not without concupiscence, was finding her more lovely…' (F.C. r5ᵛ; G 275).

Apuleius' Psyche had been persuaded by her jealous sisters to cut off the head of the 'poisonous serpent' (*noxii serpentis, AA* 5. 20) that shared her bed and planned to eat her up (*AA* 5. 18). Colonna, in contrast, shows the God of Love in his fully revealed glory, borrowing Cupid's plumage (*plumule tenelle & delicatule… tremule… resultante,* G 278; F.C. r8ʳ) from Psyche's lamplit vision of her unknown husband (*plumulae tenellae ac delicatae tremule resultantes, AA* 5. 22). Colonna's account of the voyage to Cytherea also appropriates details from Apuleius' description of Venus' journey, transferring the 'sea-green beard' of 'Shaggy Portunus' (*Portunus caerulis barbis hispidus, AA* 4. 31) to Neptune (*cum la cerulea barba hispido,* F.C. r8ᵛ; G 279).[138]

Poliphilo addresses Polia's eyes in terms which make clear his identification not just with Lucius but with Psyche too:

O dulcissimi carnifici… Niento dimeno sempre mai piu gratiosi ui opto, & caldamente desidero, molto piu & sencia comparatione, che non desideraua in tante noxie erumne, & supreme, & mortale fatiche lo auriculato Lutiole uermiglie rose, & piu grati & opportuni che alla infoelice Psyche il socorso dilla granigera formicha, & il monito arundineo, & lo adiuuamento aquilare, & il punctulo innoxio dilla sagitta di Cupidine. (F.C. s1ᵛ)

(O charming and sweet executioners… Yet never have I found you more gracious and desirable, never wished for you with more ardour, incomparably more than long-eared Lucius, in his noxious pains and deadly fatigues, when he sought out the vermilion roses. You are more welcome and opportune to me than the grain-bearing ant which aided unhappy Psyche; than the swallow's warning, the eagle's help, or the painless prick of Cupid's arrow.) (G 282)

Poliphilo implores Cupid to 'Temper your burning torch a little' (*tempera alquanto le tue adurente facole*), appealing to him as a fellow-sufferer:

Tu alcuna fiata, signore mio, dilla bellissima Psyches te medesmo & cum le proprie crudele sagette uulnerasti, fina alla nouissima linea di ardore. quale gli mortali, essa extremamente amando, & ti piaque lei sopra tute puelle amare. Et assai te dolse il doloso consiglio dille inuide & fallace sorore, & sopra il nubilo cupresso contra essa cum diutino plangore cruciata, iracondo lamentabile querimonie, increpantila facesti. Vsa & exercita per tanto uerso me pietate, & considera experto la fragile qualitate degli cupidi amanti… (F.C. s4ᵛ)

(O my master, you once wounded yourself with your own arrows, and attained the utmost limits of ardour for beautiful Psyche. You loved her extremely, as mortals do,

---

[138] Pozzi (*Commento,* 193) notes a cluster of Apuleian borrowings in this section. One might add that Cupid's invocation of Zephyrus to propel the boat (Headnote, G 241; G 278) recalls the wind's role in transporting Psyche and her sisters to the Palace of Love (*AA* 4. 35).

and it pleased you to love her above all other girls. You were much hurt by the deceitful advice of the envious and lying sisters; in your pain you wept daily beneath the shady cypress-tree, and in your anger you rebuked her with lamentable complaints. Therefore use and exercise grace towards me, and consider, as one who has known it, the tender quality of lovers.) (G 288)

Book 1 reaches its climax on the island of Cytherea itself, interfusing a symbolic defloration—based on the piercing of the veil at the end of the *Roman de la Rose* (21,591 ff.)—with a vision of the 'holy Mother, Venus Erycine' (G 289) inspired by the Isiac theophany in Apuleius (*AA* 11). We are introduced to Cupid's 'divine wife Psyche' (G 331) who 'received her dear husband with kindly respect, in an unaffected and friendly manner, and with great reverence placed on his head a crown such as Hieron never consecrated' (G 338). And we are given an extended description of the Fotis-like hair of her companions (G 332–3) who almost immediately imperil Poliphilo's newly confirmed loyalty towards Polia.[139]

We should note that Colonna shares Beroaldo's positive attitude towards Apuleius' Isiac conclusion, as he continues his project of appropriation well into Book 11 of *The Golden Ass*. It is also clear that Colonna is concerned with depicting the full spectrum of desire.[140] Psyche's nymphs include Aschemosyne ('immodesty') who seems to be a grossly debased version of Fotis:

Et cum la dextera blandamente il longo capillamento apprenso extendersi supra le polpose & crissante nate, non consentiua, cum in uereconda petulantia, Quale petulca questulatrice, ma indicando Tribaba obscænissima insolentia cum extollentia di gliochii inconstanti & cesii . . . cum troppo lasciuientia infabre gestiente . . . (F.C. x6ʳ)

(. . . and with her right [hand] she seductively prevented her long hair from covering her plump and wriggling buttocks. She was in a truly wanton condition, making obscene tribadic motions and rolling her eyes . . . crudely gesturing with excessive lust . . .) (G 339)[141]

Polia and Poliphilo have their hands tied 'with ropes and garlands' by Plexaura ('binder') and Ganoma ('pleasure') while 'Inquisitive Psyche' follows immediately behind them, her cloak held together by a brooch with an intaglio engraved upon it 'representing Cupid cruelly wounding himself and Psyche rashly handling the arrow with its lethal prick' (G 341).[142] Venus and

---

[139] '. . . it was so pleasurable to my amorous eyes that I desired nothing else than to be able to gaze perpetually at these splendid nymphs . . . With such enticement, a man could give himself up willingly to cruel death' (G 336; cf. 337).

[140] Note the detail of the nymphs in the centre of the throng going naked (F.C. y6ᵛ; G 356).

[141] Cf. *AA* 2. 7: *lumbis sensim vibrantibus*; 2. 10: *morsicantibus oculis*.

[142] The 'proud vehicle of Amor's triumph' (G 342; F.C. x7ᵛ) is drawn by two oversized 'scaly skinks' with 'scaly tongues that flickered and flamed' (*vibramini*) in imitation of the serpents that guard the waterfall from which Psyche is required to fill a flask for Venus (*AA* 6. 15).

Cupid take the place of Isis and Osiris in Colonna's pantheon (G 361).[143] Inside the amphitheatre, 'Psyche reverently did honour to her beloved husband, returning his golden arrow with a smile', and presents Polia and Poliphilo 'before the sacrosanct Cytherian fount' (G 357). Psyche's companion, Synesia ('union'), has an obvious function in effecting the 'union' of the two lovers, but the marriage between Poliphilo and Polia might be read, at another level, as a union between ancient and contemporary, Classical and Christian, profane and sacred, carnal and spiritual.

Poliphilo takes the arrow from Synesia and pierces the velvet veil—embroidered with the letters *YMHN* ('Hymen', 'Marriage')—that hangs between two columns to reveal 'the divine form of her venerable majesty as she issued from the springing fountain, the delicious source of every beauty' (G 361). Far from being offended at the intrusion, the goddess welcomes Poliphilo:

... *dille plebee et uulgarie sorde quiui remundato, & da omni spurco impiamento, si forsa casitato fusse, dil mio rore perfuso expiato se purifichi* (F.C. z3^r)

(After being cleansed of every plebeian and vulgar stain, and from all unclean impiety into which he may have fallen, he shall be suffused with my [365] dew and purified) (G 364–5)

All of this suggests a fully integrated response to *The Golden Ass* on Colonna's part. Colonna appears to have recognized Lucius' asinification as a parody of the fate of Actaeon, resulting as it does from watching the naked Pamphile anoint herself (*AA* 3. 21).[144] Venus now plays the part of Diana in reverse, sprinkling Poliphilo with salt water from the shell in her hand:

Ne piu præsto benignamente facto hebbe et io di rore marino asperso & delibuto, che in me immediate excitati gli clarificati spiriti furono piu intelligibili. Et sencia praestolatione se conuertirono nel pristino stato li adusti & concremata membri & me senza fallire di digne qualitate ricentarme sentendo. . . . Et a me affectuosamente le plebarie toge dalle assignate nymphe exute, di candida & lautiuscula ueste di nouo me officiosamente uestirono. Et facti tranquillamente del nostro amoroso et corroborato stato securi et iucundissimamente rifocillati, consolabondi et di gaudio subitario et laetitia commoti et delibuti, repente ne feceron cum mustei osculamenti et cum linguario uibramine suauemente basiare et strictamente amplexare. Et cum simile modo luno & laltro le iucunde & festose Nymphe, nel suo sacro collegio nouo tirocinio et officio dilla foecunda natura receuendo, nui tutte dulcicule lepidamente ne basiorono.

Dique la Dea genitrice . . . cum diuino flato spirante geniale Balsamo dispensando cose illicite di propalatione & agli uulgari homini, non di relato effabile (z4^r)

---

[143] 'The Egyptians [338] showed no greater reverence to the images of Osiris, Isis, or Serapis . . . than the delicious and divine nymphs showed at the coming of their lord' (G 337–8).
[144] Cf. Petrarch, *Rime sparse* 23. 147–60.

(No sooner had she thus given her blessing by sprinkling and anointing me with sea-dew than I immediately found my mind clarified and my intelligence returning. My singed and cremated members found themselves unexpectedly restored to their pristine state[145] and I felt myself endowed, if I am not mistaken, with superior qualities .... Then the dutiful nymphs gently removed my plebeian rags and clothed me afresh in clean white garments. And now, being calm and secure in our mutually amorous state and consoled by our happy recovery, we were moved by a sudden influx of joy and gladness, so that we kissed, with kisses sweet as wine and with trembling tongues, and tightly hugged each other. Likewise the happy and festive nymphs, receiving us into their sacred college as novices and servants of abundant Nature, all gave us gracious little kisses.

Next the Mother goddess spoke ... exhaling her natural balsam with her divine breath, and told us things that it is unlawful to divulge to common people, which cannot be spoken here.)[146] (G 367)

The echoes of Lucius' retransformation and initiations are obvious, the *sacrosanctum collegium* of Isiac *pastophori* into which Lucius is admitted (*AA* 11. 17) having been replaced by a *sacro collegio* of Nymphs attendant upon *foecunda natura*. Yet this is less a travesty of the Isiac ending than an amplification of the erotic elements that suffuse Apuleius' narrative even in Book 11. Rather than rejecting Fotine pleasures out of hand, Colonna accommodates them within the full spectrum of desire that he presents in the *Hypnerotomachia*. But while the reclothing of Poliphilo thematically parallels the piece of linen-cloth (*linteam ... laciniam*) which Mithras orders to be given to the newly naked Lucius (*AA* 11. 14), the wording (*lautiuscula ueste*) actually echoes the 'rather elegant garment' (*uestem ... lautiusculam*) which the bandits bring to Tlepolemus when they elect him (in his guise as 'Haemus the Thief') to the generalship (*AA* 7. 9). Lexical traces such as these help us to reconstruct Colonna's configurative or typological reading of *The Golden Ass*. We realize (as Colonna seems to have done) that Tlepolemus' admission (on payment of 2,000 gold pieces) into the guild (*collegium*) of bandits is a foreshadowing (a proleptic parody, one might say) of Lucius' initiation into the *collegium* of *pastophori* (*AA* 11. 30).[147]

One can see (especially from a Winklerian perspective) how such parallels (between the *pastophori* and the bandits and the devotees of the Syrian goddess)

---

[145] This notion of a figurative death has a parallel in Lucius' account of 'treading the threshold of Proserpina' (*calcato Proserpinae limine*, *AA* 11. 23).

[146] Cf. *AA* 11. 23: *Ergo quod solum potest sine piaculo ad profanorum intelligentias enuntiari referam* ('I shall therefore relate only what may be disclosed without guilt to the minds of the uninitiated').

[147] Note that Lucius describes Tlepolemus' reclothing as a transformation (*Sic reformatus*, *AA* 7. 9), thus anticipating Lucius' return to human form through the intervention of the goddess (*hunc ... deae numen ... reformauit ad homines*, *AA* 11. 16).

can problematize orthodox readings of Book 11. The double Apuleian echo may equally encourage a suspicion that the resolution or synthesis achieved at this point in the *Hypnerotomachia* is illusory, or (at best) provisional. We should also bear in mind the possibility that Colonna is here articulating anxieties about fundamental aspects of the humanist enterprise. Poliphilo's notion of 'singed and cremated members' being 'restored to their pristine state' has an obvious parallel in the ideal of Renaissance philologists (one thinks of such works as Marcantonio Sabellico's dialogue *De latinae linguae reparatione*, 1493);[148] but, as we shall see in our next chapter, Colonna's account of Poliphilo's initiation may also have reminded contemporaries of the humanists' practice of initiating *fratres* into literary sodalities and academies such as those established by Leto, Aldus, and Conrad Celtis.[149]

BOOK 2

Book 2 of the *Hypnerotomachia* has a very different narrative structure, using analepsis and complex nesting techniques to recreate the inner experiences of the two main characters which have led to the dramatic climax that closed Book 1. It allows us, in particular, to hear Polia's side of the story as she relates her family's origins, her first sight of Poliphilo, her decision to dedicate herself to the cult of Diana after recovering from plague, and her struggle against the forces of Amor which have led her, from stony indifference towards Poliphilo, to her present state of union with him.

Apuleian input continues, however, to be high.[150] Poliphili experiences a symbolic death and rebirth and Polia herself undergoes a transformation of a kind. Polia's affinities with Psyche are stressed early on as she narrates the sufferings of her ancestors, the Lelli family of Treviso, who compared themselves to 'our lady Mother Cypria' and were punished by metamorphoses.[151]

---

[148] Mentioned by Lowry, *World of Aldus*, 29. R. Chavasse dates the work to 1491. See 'The *studia humanitatis* and the Making of a Humanist Career: Marcantonio Sabellico's Exploitation of Humanist Literary Genres', *RS* 17 (2003), 27–38, at 30.

[149] The graffiti in the catacombs refer to Pomponio Leto as *Pontifex Maximus* and to Pantagathus (identified by Palermino, 141, as Giovanni Domenico Capranica) as *Sacerdos Achademiae Romanae*. Antonio Parthenio, dedicating a 1486 edn. of a commentary on Catullus to Pomponio, refers to the 'followers of your Academy' (*Academiae tuae sectatores*) and to Pomponio himself as *Pontifex Maximus*. See Palermino, 141.

[150] This continuity might be used to refute the proposition that the two books are the work of different authors. Alternatively, it could suggest that the producer(s) of the 1499 *Hypnerotomachia* (Grassi or members of his circle) recognized the programme of Apuleian allusion in the 1467 draft (Book 2) and took pains to extend it through Book 1.

[151] The Lelli reference is particularly interesting as Teodoro Lelli was one of Paul II's chief advisers (*principali homini*) and was appointed bishop of Treviso in 1466 shortly before his

One such forebear was Murgania whom the people worshipped as though she were Venus (F.C. A2^{r-v}; G 383–4; cf. *AA* 4. 28–30). Polia is also linked, however, with one of Apuleius' earthier heroines when she recalls how Poliphilo first saw her as she stood on her balcony:

Dique io ardisco di dire, che cusi belli a Perseo non a parueron quegli di Andromeda. Ne quegli di Fotide a Lucio. Cusi ello cum intenti & mordaci risguardi accortose, sencia mensuratione & cum incremento damore repente se accense. (F.C. A3^v)

(I dare say that Andromeda's hair looked no more beautiful to Perseus, nor that of Fotis to Lucius, for he stared with intent and piercing gaze, suddenly taking fire with immeasurable and increasing love.) (G 386; cf. *AA* 2. 8–9)

As in Book 1, Colonna draws on moments of intense drama or emotion in *The Golden Ass* to furnish the diction for critical points in the development of the relationship between the two lovers. Reflecting on Polia's unkindness towards him the day before, Poliphilo conjures up an Ovidian episode (*Met.* 3. 138–252) as he imagines himself between the 'gnashing and foaming teeth of the Calydonian Boar' (*cum attrito di denti sonace & spumea del Apro Calidonio,* G 394; F.C. A7^v), but the language recycles Apuleius' description (*aper... dentibus attritu sonaci spumeus*) of the boar which (through the treachery of Thrasyllus) kills Charite's husband, Tlepolemus (*AA* 8. 4).

Addressing a desperate plea to the unrelenting Polia, Poliphilo raises his voice 'with his tears gushing forth' (*cum le promicante lachryme*) and falls to the ground as though dead (G 396; F.C. A8^v). His anguish draws on the tears of fear and humiliation that Lucius sheds at the end of the Festival of Laughter (*me renitentem lacrimisque rursum promicantibus*)—an experience which also leaves him feeling that he has died (*Nec... ab inferis emersi...* 'Nor did I emerge from the realms of the Dead...', *AA* 3. 10).

The most impressive feature of Book 2, however, is the presentation of Polia which Dronke has justly called 'one of the psychological heights in the genre of romance'.[152] Colonna's achievement is to represent the moral and emotional dynamics of Polia's conversion from Diana to Venus, not through the externalizing rhetorical structures of the Ovidian or Senecan *suasoria*, but as

---

death. Pastor (*History of the Popes,* iv. 112) notes that 'the Pope's relations with Lelli were of a very intimate character' and 'No letter, or decree of importance was issued until it had been examined by this excellent man.' Platina tells us ('Life of Paul II' (1888), 278), that after his first arrest (for threatening to call a council after Paul's dismissal of the abbreviators in 1464), the Pope sent 'Theodore, Bishop of Treviso' to examine him. The Bishop 'soon concluded me guilty for dispersing libels against Paul and mentioning a council'. See M. Billanovich, 'Francesco Colonna, il *Polifilo* e la famiglia Lelli', *IMU* 19 (1976), 419–28.

[152] *Francesco Colonna,* 11. Pozzi is very wide of the mark when he declares (Casella and Pozzi, *Colonna,* ii. 124) that 'di Polia il Colonna scopre il corpo soltanto'. Lefaivre, equally, fails to see the literary innovations of the *Hypnerotomachia* in blending very different traditions, when she says that the work is 'an anachronism' which 'adds nothing new to the amorous imaginary' (8).

inner experience. And in the three episodes which prove to be crucial to that conversion, Apuleius features prominently. After her display of 'more than bestial barbarism' (*immanitate piu che ferina*, F.C. B1ʳ) in dragging the senseless Poliphilo into a corner of Diana's temple, Polia escapes to her home. During her flight, however, she is whisked up by a whirlwind and deposited in a wild wood where she witnesses the hideous sight of two naked maidens (*fanciulle*) drawing a fiery chariot while being tormented by 'a winged youngster' (Cupid). The description of their 'tender, white, downy flesh' (*tenere & bianchissime & plumee carnee*) being burned by 'glowing chains' (*cathene candente*, F.C. B2ᵛ) while they are whipped incessantly seems to owe something to the episode following the *Risus* Festival where Lucius rejects the leather strap which the penitent Fotis offers him, deprecating the notion that it should even touch her 'downy and milk-white skin' (*plumeam lacteamque cutem*, AA 3. 14). However, the 'bristling-haired hunting dogs' (*uenatici cani horricomi*) which feed on the scattered remnants of the maidens once the 'boy' has stabbed and hewn them with his iron sword, are borrowed from Apuleius' account of the final canine assault (*canes etiam venaticos... horricomes*) on Thrasyleon in his disguise as a bear (AA 4. 19).

After witnessing this scene of erotic butchery, Polia is transported home and falls asleep in her locked bedroom, having summoned her aged nurse to keep her company. Her rest, however, is soon disturbed:

Ecco cum grande & strepente impeto ad me parue... di essere dimoti gli pessuli, & rapiti gli obiici, & da perfossori fracte le fere, & uiolentemente patefacti gli occlusi hostioli, & obserati limini della camera mia (F.C. B5ʳ)

(I seemed to hear a great noise as though bolts were being shot, locks forced, and burglars breaking the iron bars and violently throwing open the doors on the threshold of my bedroom) (G 405)[153]

Colonna makes the Apuleian subtext (AA 1. 11) clear when he has Polia say: 'I was in a worse agony than Andromeda on the seashore; in worse fear than Aristomenes under the table [*sic*] seeing Panthia and Meroe (*Et cum magiore terriculamento di Aristomene uedendo Panthia & Meroe testudinato*)' (G 406; F.C. B6ʳ).

But while the executioners resemble Socrates' attackers in their mode of ingress and their punitive intentions, their physical characteristics are drawn

---

[153] Such an episode has already been anticipated in Book 1 when Poliphilo, witnessing the spectacle of Cupid and his six nautical nymphs, asks rhetorically, 'what imprisoned and extinguished desire... would not have had its strong locks and painful bars vigorously shattered here...?' (*Et quale incarcerata & extincta concupiscentia... que gli tenaci claustri, & mordenti laquei quiui uigorosamente non hauesse disfracto*, G 278; F.C. r7ᵛ). The episode is echoed in Cupid's statement to Poliphilo's soul that he wants to 'break every barrier that resists the penetration of my will' (*confringere tutti gli obici repugnanti al mio uolante ingresso*, G 458; F.C. E7ᵛ).

from other episodes in *The Golden Ass*. Their 'bulging and swollen cheeks' (*lenfiate & tumide bucce*), 'goat-like hair' (*capelli hircipili*), and goatskin clothing (*Vestiti di Cyniphia sopra il nudo*, F.C. B5ᵛ) link them with the inflated goatskins that Lucius mistakes for brigands attacking Milo's house (2. 32).[154] And the detail of 'lowering their eyelids above their turgid cheeks' (*gli supercilii subducti, cum volto turgido*, G 406; F.C. B5ᵛ) derives from the description of Barbarus' face as he walks towards the forum holding the adulterer's sandals which he found underneath his bed (*uultu turgido subductisque superciliis incedit iratus, AA* 9. 21).[155]

The executioners threaten her with dismemberment in revenge for opposing 'the rule of the immortals' (*lo imperio, degli immortali Dii*) and drag her by the hair, but she is woken from the nightmare by her nurse. Her state— 'prostrate, utterly weary, more dead than alive...like a paralytic' (*del tuto prosternati di grande lassitudine, piu morta che uiua et quasi Clinica*, F.C. B6ᵛ)—resembles Aristomenes' at the end of the attack (*nunc humi proiectus, inanimis, nudus et frigidus...quasi...semimortuus, AA* 1. 14), one difference being that the witches' urine with which Aristomenes finds himself smeared (*lotio perlitus*) has been refined by Colonna into the 'flooding tears' (*irrorante lachryme*) which have soaked Polia's 'white linens' (*gli candidi linteamini*), leaving her 'fine shift...adhering damply to [her] virginal belly' (*la sutilissima Camisia al uirgonculo aluulo adherendo uda*, G 407; F.C. B6ᵛ).

The 'sagacious and experienced Nurse' (G 409) tries to 'remove this hardened mass of ice which time and habit had caused to grow and congeal' in Polia by citing a list of figures who suffered for opposing the gods, concluding with 'beautiful Psyche' who, 'for her disobedience, found herself condemned to hard and intolerable labours' (*Et per in obedientia ancora la formosa Psyche intante erumne & in tolerande fatiche perniciosamente si ritrouoe*, G 410; F.C. B7ᵛ). Cupid's anger towards chaste maidens who flee him is great, the nurse tells her: 'And if he could not prevent himself from falling in love with the fair Psyche, how could he be harmless to others?' (*Et si ello di se medesimo, non perdonoe, anamorarse della bella Psyche, como adaltri innocuo sarae?* (G 411; F.C. B8ʳ).

---

[154] The description of the executioners' hands as *perlite* ('besmeared') may echo Lucius' feeling of being polluted by the gore of the triple slaughter of wineskins (*caedis cruore perlitum, AA* 3. 1).

[155] The 'goat-like hair' (*capelli hircipili*) of the executioners is *semicani sordenti* (F.C. B5ᵛ), a feature borrowed from the witch who kills the cuckolded baker (*comae semicanae sordentes, AA.* 9. 30).

Milesian Discourse

The third exemplary episode is the story told by the nurse of a beautiful
woman (endowed with all of Polia's qualities and breeding and coming from
the same town), who suffered terribly from her rejection of an eligible lover.
In its framework, this *anilis fabula* resembles the consolatory tale of Cupid
and Psyche told to Charite by the old woman (*AA* 4 and 6); as a warning to
Polia not to reject Poliphilo's love, it serves the same function as the monitory
tale of Anaxarete told by Vertumnus (a supposed 'old woman') to Pomona
(Ovid, *Met.* 14. 695–764).[156] Having rejected the persistent suits of an eligible
youth, the woman finds herself, at the age of 28, consumed by desire. Concerned at her decline, her family marry her off to a rich old man, the least
disgusting of whose attributes is a white beard as coarse as 'the hair of a long-
eared ass' (*gli pili di uno auriculoso asino*, G 414; F.C. E[*sc.* C]1ᵛ).[157] The
immediate inspiration for this *contre-blason* is Agapes' tale in Boccaccio's
Ameto (xxxii. 7–28),[158] which we have already discussed as an example of an
intercalated narrative featuring a Milesian theme and a direct Apuleian
allusion.[159] But Colonna far surpasses Boccaccio in his litany of unattractive-
ness, while introducing a novel twist in the young woman's response. For
despite the fact that her husband's lips are as slimy as a snail, his breath sewer-
like, his eyes rheumy, his nostrils gaping and snotty (*Il naso ... hiulco, &
muculento*),[160] and his clothes give out 'a stench of stale piss' (*uno putore di
urina fetenti*, G 414; F.C. E[*sc.* C]1ᵛ), she is bitterly disappointed on their
wedding night:

> ... *la lasciuissima donna, de le sue uoluptuose appetiscentie totalmente frustrata, unque
> non pote (tuti gli conamini scortali, & di illustre meretricio perfuncta (excitare gli
> prosternati membri della enorme & exuigorata senecta. Hora aduiene che per longo
> tempo essa dal maluasio & tedioso uechio ocioso, Inerte, desidioso & Ignauo, piu Zelotipo
> del barbaro decurione, non potendo altro riceuere ne consequire, si non battiture (con-
> uertito in infinito Zelo) & iurgio, & garulosi cridi & freda & languida pigritia, &
> fastidioso te*[C2ʳ]*dio, & decepta del suo effrenato desio.* (F.C. C1ᵛ–2ʳ)

(The lascivious woman, totally frustrated in her voluptuous desire, tried every means
of seduction and every whorish trick, but was unable to arouse the flabby members of
excessive and enfeebled age. Thus, as time passed, she came to receive and expect

[156] Polia expresses her fear that she 'might share the fate of Anaxarete' (G 419; F.C. C4ʳ).
Vertumnus and Pomona appear in one of the *trionfi* (G 190–1; F.C. m3ᵛ–4ʳ).

[157] Note the earlier description of Apuleius' hero as *lo auriculato Lutiole* (F.C. s1ᵛ; = G 282).

[158] Pozzi and Ciapponi, ii. 248; Lefaivre, 62 (citing Popelin).

[159] See Ch. 3, *supra.* Cf. the descriptions of repulsive husbands given by Psyche's sisters (*AA*
5. 9–10).

[160] Pozzi and Ciapponi (ii. 408) suggest a lexical link to the 'distended nostrils' (*nares ...
hiulci*) of the broken-down draught animals in the baker's mill (*AA* 9. 13).

nothing from this obnoxious and tedious old man, who was so idle, inert, slothful, and sluggish, yet had become more jealous than Barbarus the decurion—nothing but blows, quarrels, garrulous cries, and a cold and languid boredom, a loathsome tedium and the utter disappointment of her unleashed desires.) (G 414)

Instead, however, of imitating Barbarus' wife Arete (*AA* 9. 17–21), or any of Apuleius' other adulteresses, Colonna's *lasciuissima donna* plunges a knife deep into her own heart. This interpolated narrative is a notable departure from the usual discourse of the *Hypnerotomachia*; and the effect is all the more marked since we hear the story from Polia's own chaste lips as she relates the events that led up to her decision to reciprocate Poliphilo's love.

We are familiar, from our reading of Petronius, Apuleius, and the *Decameron*, of the ways in which Milesian discourse is able to explore the lower reaches of human experience. The change in register is obvious in this passage of the *Hypnerotomachia*—we have moved from minute anatomizations of dentils, astragals, and nymphal tresses, to the full gamut of bodily secretions, a wallowing in snot, spittle, and piss. But this stylistic shift is an integral part of a more fundamental development in prose fiction—what can crudely be called the progress from romance to novel. Colonna is concerned in Book 2 with interiority, with mental and emotional process. These three experiences—vision, nightmare, and story—cause Polia to reflect, repent, and act. She returns to the Temple of Diana, succours the inert Poliphilo with kisses (not unlike Cupid saving the forgiven Psyche, *AA* 6. 21), and bares her 'white and apple-shaped breasts' to him 'with a tender expression and seductive eyes' (G 421). The High Priestess and her assistants, finding them 'joined and wound...in amorous embraces', attack them with rods and oak branches, dishevelling Polia's hair, lashing her shoulders, and exiling them from Diana's sanctuary (F.C. C6^v; G 424). Polia thus finds herself in the same position as the runagate Psyche, with Diana taking the role of the vengeful Venus (*AA* 6. 9).

Polia at this point undergoes an emotional metamorphosis: 'I...transformed (*conuertito*) my frigid breast into a furnace of burning love. I reformed (*remutati*) my beastly and cruel habits into a compliant disposition .... I transmuted (*tramutata*) my bashfulness into reckless passion' (G 425; F.C. C7^r). The transformation is marked by signs of celestial favour: Polia sees the chariot of Diana ('the cold and listless goddess who was menacing me with her hatred', G 425) being pursued by a second chariot (containing Venus and Cupid) which melts the first with its heat. When she looks down, Polia finds her lap and the bedroom floor strewn with 'fragrant red roses and twigs of flowering green myrtle' (G 425; F.C. C7^v).

We saw, on the island of Cytherea, how Venus and Cupid took the place of Isis and Osiris in Colonna's pantheon. Indeed, these Roman deities pose the same potential problem of plurality of worship that we find in Book 11 of *The Golden Ass*. Polia offers herself 'as a true and undaunted devotee of the venerable lady Mother' (G 427) but she also tells the High Priestess: 'I am certain that the mighty Son of divine Venus wields absolute dominion over the hot and starry heavens' (G 433; F.C. D3ᵛ).

When Poliphilo is asked to give an account of his courtship, he reproduces three letters, in the first of which he addresses Polia in terms which echo Lucius' veneration of Isis.[161] The 'Hyperborean gryphons' (*grypes hyperborei*) embroidered on the 'Olympian stole' that Lucius wears as an initiate (*AA* 11. 24) reappear in the peroration to Poliphilo's second letter: Jupiter 'has not created you among the Hyperborean gryphons' (*griphi hyperborei*, G 448; F.C. E2ᵛ). But having failed to receive any fruitful response even to his third letter, Poliphilo finds Polia alone in her temple and accosts her. Apuleius provides the climax to a seemingly bizarre tricolon: 'You have been more injurious to me than the stones of Britain to the honey-bees, more hostile, contrary and opposed to my will than Thetis rejecting Vulcan; more burdensome than the waving tail was to Lucius' (. . . *Et piu molesta che la instabile cauda a Lutio*) (G 453; F.C. E5ʳ). Poliphilo is once again echoing Lucius' delight at the disappearance, during the retransformation, of his tail—the thing which 'previously had been crucifying me most of all (*quae me potissimum cruciebat ante, AA* 11. 13). Given the phallic connotations of *cauda* that we discussed in the context of the Temple of Physizoa, the allusion seems to suggest that Polia serves, at this stage, as the focus for his 'inconstant' (*instabile*) sexual appetite. At the end of the *Ameto*, Boccaccio's regenerated hero acknowledges that 'there is desire that moves man to salvation' (*quivi disio movente omo a saluto*, xlix. 70, p. 144). Poliphilo, however, has not yet achieved that cognitive maturity, and while Polia's beauty ought to be bringing him closer to the angels, the lust it incites confirms him instead in his bestial state.

Polia is unmoved by his 'ardent affection or . . . abundant tears. Bereaved Isis did not weep so anxiously for her beloved Osiris' (*ne cum il mio succenso amore, ne cum abondante lachryme, che tanto anxiosamente non pianse per il caro Osiri, la afflicta Iside*, G 453; F.C. E5ᵛ). It is further evidence of Colonna's unitarian reading of Apuleius that he chooses to see Poliphilo's pursuit of Polia as comparable not only to Psyche's search for Cupid, but also to Isis' search for Osiris.

Poliphilo relates the story of his death in the temple, and his soul's ascent 'into the divine presence, before the high throne of the divine Lady Mother' (G 455) where it lodges a complaint over the behaviour of her son (G 456),

---

[161] e.g. *O Polia diua luce, & mia ueneranda Dea* ('O Polia, divine light, my venerated Goddess', F.C. D8ᵛ; G 444); *a questo mysterio necessaria sospitatrice* (F.C. E1ʳ; G 444). Cf. *iam sospitatricis deae . . . pompa* (*AA* 11. 9).

234

The Hypnerotomachia Poliphili

and is shown by Cupid 'the true and divine effigy of Polia' (G 457). His soul
re-enacts part of Lucius' infernal and celestial journeys after his return to
human form (*AA* 11. 23): *miraua in propatulo et palesemente mysterii et arcane
visione, raro agli mortali et materiali sensi permesso cernere* ('I beheld the open
revelation of mysteries and arcane visions that mortal and material senses are
rarely permitted to see' (F.C. E8ʳ; G 459). Polia's tresses are described as

looking more desirable than the sacred gold to wicked Atalanta or to Myrmex the
slave... To my burning fever, she was as a timely, healing, efficacious and speedy
medicine, far more acceptable than the puddle of muddy water seemed to Lucius
when the bag stuffed with tow caught fire (G 459)

*Piu desiderabile offerentise che lo sacro oro alla iniqua Atalanta. Et piu che a Myrmice
seruo... quale opportuna saluberrima et efficacissima et praesentanea medella essa al
mio fornaceo feruore, molto piu per acceptissima che il conceptabulo della lutulenta aqua
a Lucio cum lo ignito tomento stupeo appareua* (F.C. E8ʳ)

The juxtaposition of Atalanta and Myrmex is characteristic of Colonna's
approach, coupling a famous story (readily available in Ovid and other
sources) with an allusion to a fictional (but non-mythological) source accessible only to Apuleian initiates. The point of the puddle allusion soon becomes
clear in Poliphilo's description of how 'the amorous ferment grew wonderfully
within us' (*cum miro & amoroso fomento creue*, G 461; F.C. F1ʳ)—an echo of
the account of the flame being nourished in the load of tow on Lucius' back
(*fomento tenui calescens*, *AA* 7. 19). Colonna is evidently reading 'that most
wicked boy' (*puer ille nequissimus*, *AA* 7. 19) who torments Lucius when an
ass, as a type of Cupid who tortures mortals with desire.

The climax of the work, however, rewrites the ending of *The Golden Ass* to
make the theophany endorse human love rather than merely transcending it.
Polia is a 'glorious compound of virtue and physical beauty' (G 457), but the
osculatory consummation of their love is redolent of Fotis: 'Then with her
two nectar-and cinnamon-scented lips she gave me a dove-like kiss' (*Et cum
gemini labri nectarei, & Cynnamei columbaceamente sauiantime*).[162]

Colonna's final Apuleian allusion appears on the last page of the narrative
proper in the context of an *aubade*—'Why was I not given the Stygian sleep
from inquisitive Psyche's casket?' (*Et perche alhora non mi fue arrogato il
Stygio somno della Pyxide della curiosa Psyches?*, G 465; F.C. F3ʳ)—but even in
the act of acknowledging that everything he has experienced has been 'sweet

---

[162] G 462; F.C. F1ᵛ. Cf. *AA* 2. 10 (on Fotis): *iam patentis oris inhalatu cinnameo et occursantis
linguae illisu nectareo prona cupidine allibescenti*... Nectar also features in the false promise of
the laurel-roses (*AA* 4. 2) and the wedding-banquet of Cupid and Psyche (*AA* 6. 24). Note, too,
the reference to the 'cinnamon scents' (*cinnameos odores*) of the restorative roses that Lucius
anticipates shortly before his vision of Isis (*AA* 10. 29).

and loquacious illusion' (*di dolce, & argutula fallacia*, G 465; F.C. F3ʳ), Poliphilo recalls Thelemia and Fotis, both of whom are described as *argutula* (F.C. h8ᵛ; *AA* 2. 6).[163]

What are we to make, however, of the fact that the same word (a *hapax legomenon*) is applied (approvingly) by Polia to her nurse (*la perita ueteratrice mia Alumna*, G 417; F.C. C3ʳ) as was used of the witch who murders the baker (*ueteratricem quandam feminam, AA* 9. 29)? At the close of the work, Poliphilo describes his soul as being 'bound and entangled by its love of you' (*lanimo mio connexo & connodulato*, G 463; F.C. F2ʳ)... 'For you are...a miraculous image sent by heaven for my contemplation, through which I am bound by profound love in eternal fetters' (*Dal coelo al mio obtuto deiecta miranda imagine, per laquale cum profundo amore alligato sum alle aeterne pedice*). Is it problematic that the amatory binding celebrated here precisely echoes Byrrhena's description of the erotic bondage that Pamphile inflicts upon her lovers (*amoris profundi pedicis aeternis alligat, AA* 2. 5)? Or that Thrasyleon's (dramatically ironic) boast to the widow (*vides hominem ferreum et insomnium, certe perspicaciorem ipso Lynceo vel Argo, AA* 2. 23) is appropriated for the description of Cupid (*piu perspicace dil lynceo & di argo oculeo*, F.C. z2ᵛ; G 364)?

It might be argued that the Apuleian allusions help to establish a critical distance between Poliphilo's unalloyed appreciation of the cornucopia of sensory delights presented to him and the (initiated) reader's perception of them. How much authority we should attach to such moralizing structures remains, of course, open to debate: as with *The Golden Ass* itself, we are presented with a work which defies reductive and unitarian interpretations.

Colonna's evocation of erotic evanescence looks back to medieval dream-visions and forward to such works as *The Faerie Queene*, where Spenser vividly recalls Arthur's dream of lying with the 'Queene of Faeries' (*FQ* I. ix. 13–15). As a purely literary artefact, the *Hypnerotomachia* is valuable because it speaks to anyone who knows what it is to love and to lose. But we can also see in it an expression of Renaissance humanists' aspirations, reservations, and concerns at the very end of the quattrocento.

[163] Dronke, *Francesco Colonna*, 37 n. 54.

6

The Academical Ass: Apuleius and the Northern Renaissance

APULEIUS AND THE SODALITIES

We saw, in the last chapter, how the religious elements in Book 11 of *The Golden Ass* are transposed into the account of the erotic initiations at the close of Book 1 of the *Hypnerotomachia Poliphili*; and we suggested that Colonna might also be casting a sideways glance at the practices of humanist sodalities.[1] Pierio Valeriano's first collection of poetry, *Praeludia* (1509), includes a poem entitled *In sodales* in which the young poet asks to be admitted as the ninth member of a sodality (based at Padua and comprising such figures as Andrea Marone, Andrea Navagero, Paolo da Canal, Trypho Dalmata, and Girolamo Borgia), thus equalling the number of the muses.[2] Andrea Marone of Brescia (Andreas Maro Brixianus, 1475–1528) contributed the final set of liminary verses to the *Hypnerotomachia* in the form of a dialogue between an unnamed interlocutor and one of the Muses:

> *Cuius opus dic Musa? Meum est, octoque sororum.*
> *Vestrum? Cur datus Poliphilo titulus?*
> *Plus etiam a nobis meruit communis alumnus.*

---

[1] Andreas Meinhard's *Dialogus illustrate ac Augustissime urbis Albiorenae vulgo Vittenberg dicte*...(Leipzig: Martin Landsberg, 1508) also employs the convention of the dream-vision while exploring the themes of educational initiation and the *translatio studii et imperii* (Wittenberg is seen as the 'new Rome'). See Grossmann, *Humanism in Wittenberg*, 58–9.

[2] (Venice: Io. Tacuinus, 1509), sig. D3ᵛ. The poem is discussed by M. J. C. Lowry, 'The "New Academy" of Aldus Manutius: A Renaissance Dream', *BJRL* 58 (1976), 378–420, at 392, and Gaisser (*Valeriano*, 6 n. 18), though neither makes any connection to the *Hypnerotomachia*. Gaisser notes (274) that in a later collection (*Hexametri, odae et epigrammata* (Venice: Gabriel Giolito di Ferrariis, 1550), fol. 126ᵛ), the poem is retitled *In Sodales Patavii philosophantes*. The sodality poem gives a fresh resonance to a passage in Valeriano's *Leucippus* (an epyllion—first printed in the *Praeludia* of 1509—which has many points of connection with the *Hypnerotomachia*) where the eponymous hero is invited to enjoy the 'fellowship' (*commercia nostra*) of Daphne and her nymphs. See R. H. F. Carver, 'A New Source for Sidney's *Arcadia*: Pierio Valeriano's *Leucippus* (Text, Translation, and Commentary)', *ELR* 28 (1998), 353–71, at 363.

(Say, Muse, whose work is this?—Mine, and my eight sisters'.
Yours? Then why was the name of Poliphilo given?
It deserves rather to be the nursling of us all)

(G 8)

Valeriano's poem hardly constitutes 'proof' of a Paduan authorship of the *Hypnerotomachia*, but it does facilitate a reading of Andrea Marone's liminary verses as a coded memorial to the anonymous contributors to the work. Taken together, the two documents support our argument that the 1499 version of the *Hypnerotomachia* was a collaborative venture, drawing on the financial, artistic, and technical resources of the great cities of the Veneto (Venice, Padua, and Verona), involving men hailing from the extreme north of Italy (towns such as Belluno, Bolzano, and Pordenone), but also exploiting memories of, and continuing links with, the Rome of Bessarion, Bussi, Pomponio Leto, and their successors.[3] And the possibilty of its association with the Paduan sodality of Andrea Marone fits neatly with the view that the 'linguistic roots' of the book are 'grounded in a form of literary Italian that had developed in the area around Padua in the *quattrocento*'.[4]

In 1499, Giambattista Scita had provided the opening set of liminary verses to the *Hypnerotomachia* (F.C. 2ʳ; G 3). He died at the end of the following year and his funeral oration was delivered in Venice on 28 November 1500 by Marino Becichemo.[5] Becichemo (1468?–1526) was Albanian by birth (from Scutari, also known as Shkodër), but acquired Venetian citizenship around 1500 and taught at Brescia, Padua, and Venice. Further evidence of the Paduan and Venetian humanists' interest in Apuleius at the turn of the century is to be found in a letter from Becichemo to the Venetian humanist and bookseller Antonio Moreto of Brescia:

Facis tu, Morete mi, quod neque Tryphon, neque quisquam alius bibliopola priscis faciebat temporibus, ut non modo incorrecta serves auctorum monumenta, sed et ab erroribus obscuris et a paucissimis animadversis vendicare labores. De Apuleiani Asini titulo scribam, quod sentio. Tu Sabellicum nostrum et alios eruditos viros, qui quotidie ad te divertunt, consules, quodque magis vero proximum videbitur, sequeris.[6]

---

[3] Marone is explicitly counted as one of the *Transpadani* ('those from the other side of the Po') in Valeriano's *DLI* 25.

[4] M. Mancini, 'Intorno alla lingua del *Polifilo*', *R.R.-Roma nel Rinascimento, Bibliografie e note* 6 (1989), 29–48. The summary comes from Brown, *Venice & Antiquity*, 290. Both scholars support the claims of Fra Francesco Colonna of Venice.

[5] *DBI* vii. 512.

[6] *Centuria epistolicarum quæstionum*, cap. 57. The Apuleius passage is quoted (*en passant*) by Monfasani, 'The First Call for Press Censorship: Niccolò Perotti, Giovanni Andrea Bussi, Antonio Moreto and the Editing of Pliny's *Natural History*', 19 n. 75. Monfasani dates the letter to '[a]bout 1500'. Tryphon was Martial's bookseller at Rome (*Epig.* 4. 72 and 13. 3).

(You achieve, my dear Moreto, what neither Tryphon nor any other bookseller in ancient times managed to do: not only do you preserve the uncorrected monuments of authors, but you also labour to free them not only from intricate errors but even from the scarcely noticeable faults. As to the title of the Apuleian *Ass*, I shall write to you what I think. You should consult our Sabellico and the other learned men who daily drop by to see you, and you should follow whatever seems closer to the truth.)

The letter to Moreto appears in a collection of Becichemo's works edited by Angelus Britannicus and published in Brescia in 1505. The Venice edition of 1506 also contains a series of Becichemo's *castigationes* of the text of *The Golden Ass*.[7]

Moreto (Antonius Moretus Brixianus) had identified himself as a member of Pomponio Leto's Academia Romana in his edition of Terence in 1475, and had gone on to produce the third edition of Perotti's *Cornu copiae* (Venice: Baptista de Tortis, 19 October 1490).[8] He is also named in 1512 as one of the executors to the will of his brother-in-law (*sororius*), Alessandro Benedetti, a professor of medicine at the University of Padua, an editor of Pliny, and an acquaintance of Francesco Grassi (brother of Leonardo, the financier of the *Hypnerotomachia*). One clause in Benedetti's will stipulates that 'masses of Our Blessed Virgin Mary should be celebrated by the reverend Lord Master Francesco Colonna, friar in SS. Giovanni e Paolo' (*Item volo quod misse beate nostre Virginis Marie celebrentur per reverendum dominum magistrum Franciscum Colona, fratrem in sancto Ioanne Paulo*).[9]

We are thus able to identify an Apuleian context for the appearance of the *Hypnerotomachia* in Venice in 1499: a network of immediate readers with regional loyalties, but also strong connections to Rome, who could be relied upon to appreciate the layers of Apuleian allusion in the work. Becichemo's letter suggests that *Sabellicus noster* was part of a group of Venetian humanists with an interest in Apuleius congregating around Moreto.[10]

We might also note Sabellico's connections with Beroaldo. During the early 1490s, his *Emendationes seu annotationes in Plinium* were published in the same folio volume as Beroaldo's *Annotationes centum* (Venice: Baptista de Tortis, c.1490–3). A slightly later edition of Suetonius' *Vitae XII Caesarum* (Venice: Simon Bevilaqua, 1496) contained contributions from Sabellico,

---

[7] *Panegyricus ... Centuria epistolicarum quæstionum ... in qua sunt capita plura ad artem oratoriam & ad artificium orationum Ciceronis spectantia. Item sunt castigationes multæ in asinum aureum & in multa alio[rum] aucto[rum] o[per]a, etc.* (Venice: Bernardinus Venetus de Vitalibus, 1506).

[8] Monfasani, 'First Call for Press Censorship', 17 and 15.

[9] M. Billanovich, 'Francesco Colonna, il *Polifilo* e la famiglia Lelli', 420.

[10] Sabellico addresses a letter to Moreto on the penultimate page of his *De latinae linguae reparatione*. See *Marci Antonii Sabellici de Venetæ urbis situ liber primus ... Dialogus qui et latinae linguae reparatio inscribitur* ([Venice: Damianus de Mediolano de Gorgonzola, c.1494]), sig. hviii[r].

Beroaldo, and Battista Pio. The title page of the Venetian edition of 1500 shows Suetonius flanked by Beroaldo and Sabellico on either side.[11] And, as we saw in our previous chapter, the two humanists were brought together again (posthumously) in a collection of *Annotationes veteres et recentes* in which Sabellico uses an Apuleian *hapax legomenon* (*rimabundus*).[12]

The precise nature of Sabellico's relations with Aldus Manutius is difficult to gauge, but their circles clearly overlapped. Valeriano, for instance, was working with Aldus during the late 1490s, but it was at Sabellico's behest that he adopted the humanist monicker 'Pierius' ('the Pierian one', or, perhaps, 'Man of the Muses').[13] Indeed, many of the Paduan *sodales* were closely associated with Aldus.[14] The absence of a colophon identifying Aldus Manutius as the printer of the *Hypnerotomachia* does not mean that it was some freak emanation from the Aldine press or a mere piece of commissioned work.

At the very time when he published the *Hypnerotomachia*, Aldus was making plans for the 'Neacademy' that he proposed to establish in Venice. According to Lowry, 'Both on a personal and an intellectual level, Aldus seems...to have neglected his Roman [51] background'.[15] It was as *Aldus Romanus*, however, that the Venetian printer chose to present himself to the world. Indeed, as Lowry himself points out, the 1502 edition of Sophocles carries the colophon *Venetiis in Aldi Romani Academia* ('At Venice in the Academy of Aldus the Roman').[16] Despite the fact that his birthplace (Bassiano) was 46 miles south-west of Rome, Aldus was keen to stress the Rome–Venice axis. More radically, this might be taken as an expression of the complex dynamics of the *translatio studii* and the *translatio imperii*: the desire of a latter-day Roman to found a new Athens in *Gallia Togata*, a part of the Italian peninsula that had been a foreign province until it was tucked within the fold of Roman citizenship.[17]

---

[11] *Suetonius Tranquillus cum Philippi Beroaldi et Marci Antonii Sabellici commentariis. Cum figuris nuper additis* (Venice: Bartholomeus de Zanis de Portesio, 1500). Reprod. by Chavasse, 'The *studia humanitatis*', 32.

[12] (Venice: Ioa[n]. Tacuinus de Tridino, 1508), sig. A2ᵛ. E. Raimondi remarks that Beroaldo honoured 'la probità' as Sabellico's essential quality. See *Codro e l'umanesimo a Bologna* (Bologna: Zuffi, 1950; repr. Bologna: Il Mulino, 1987), 90. In the *De latinae linguae reparatione*, Sabellico acknowledges that he has heard favourable opinions of Beroaldo's commentary on Propertius (1486), but declines to speak of what he has not yet seen (*sed de his quæ non dum uidimus. quid dicam nihil habeo*, sig. hiiᵛ).

[13] See Gaisser, *Valeriano*, 282.

[14] Lowry, *World of Aldus*, 197, 213 n. 80; Gaisser, *Valeriano*, 6 n. 18.

[15] *World of Aldus*, 50–1. Lowry continues: 'A sincerely pious Christian, he may have been disturbed by the more bizarre antique posturings of Pomponio Leto and his circle, and by the suspicions of paganism or conspiracy which had fastened on them by 1468.'

[16] Lowry, *World of Aldus*, 196.

[17] Vincent Lang uses this very expression (*Petivimus tandem per togatam Galliam Bononiam*) when describing the journey from the Veneto to Bologna, where he hears Beroaldo whom he

CONRAD CELTIS

Aldus' vision of a Greek academy was not confined, however, to Venice, nor indeed to Italy. The 1490s had seen the Americas opened up to Europe; but this was also a time in which the Old World was being reconfigured, when the pre-eminence of Italy in respect of the *studia humanitatis* was being challenged. At the turn of the century, Aldus was corresponding with the German humanist Conrad Celtis (1459–1508), whose life and works provide one template for reading the *Hypnerotomachia*. The *Hypnerotomachia* and Beroaldo's *Commentary* both need to be seen in the context of the Great Jubilee of 1500, a year which also produced Albrecht Dürer's most famous self-portrait, Celtis' *Carmen saeculare* (a poem celebrating Germany's 'coming of age'), and the first German translation of *The Golden Ass*.

After crossing the Alps in the summer of 1487, Celtis had studied at Venice with Marcantonio Sabellico (who would become Leto's first biographer), at Padua with Marcus Musurus (a future member of Aldus' 'Neacademy'), and at Bologna with Beroaldo.[18] He had also made the acquaintance of Marsilio Ficino at Florence and Pomponio Leto at Rome (where he may have left his mark alongside those of the Pomponians in the catacombs), and he had gone on to found sodalities across Central Europe in conscious imitation of the Academia Romana.[19] In 1491 he wrote a short letter (from Ingoldstadt) to the jurist Sixtus Tucher, enclosing a copy of his *Epitoma in utramque Ciceronis Rhetoricam* and asking that Tucher, in turn, should send him copies of the *Noctes Atticae* and *The Golden Ass* (*Tu invicem, oro, aliquos libellos ad me*

---

describes as *in philosophia [morali], in oratoria et poetica interpretem fidelissimum et lectorem eloquentissimum, qui et soluta oratione et carmine scripsit complurima*. See *Der Briefwechsel des Konrad Celtis*, ed. H. Rupprich (Munich: Beck, 1934), nr. 256, p. 438.

[18] See *The Catholic Encyclopedia*, vol. iii (1908), s.v. 'Conrad Celtes'; L. W. Spitz, *Conrad Celtis: The German Arch-Humanist* (Cambridge, Mass.: HUP, 1957), 12, 61, 128. On Celtis and Musurus, see R. Pfeiffer, *History of Classical Scholarship, From 1300 to 1850* (Oxford: Clarendon, 1976), 63.

[19] Palermino (123) offers Celtis as a possible identity of *HERCIN* ('The man from Hercynia' in central Germany). Celtis co-founded the first of his sodalities, the *Sodalitas litteraria Vistulana*, in Cracow with Filippo Buonaccorsi (Callimachus Experiens), the member of the *Academia Romana* blamed by (the imprisoned) Pomponio Leto and Platina for sparking Paul II's fear of a conspiracy against him in 1468 (Palermino, 126). The interests and activities of Celtis' sodalities reveal many points of contact with the world of the *Hypnerotomachia*. There is, for example, a shared concern with trinitarian matters: 'Fascinated by numerical symmetries, the [Rhenish] sodality placed great emphasis upon the importance of the threefold name, the three sacred languages, and the threefold philosophy.' Celtis himself was known as the *triformis philosophiae doctor*. He was also the author of an ode (3. 9) 'dedicated to the German inventor of printing'. See Spitz, *Conrad Celtis*, 49, 51, 52.

mittas. Cupio autem ex te Aulum Gellium et Lucii Apulei fabulam). He also declared his desire to 'impel and arouse' his fellow countrymen to surpass his own achievements, so that 'the Italians may be forced to admit that not only the Roman Empire and military might, but also the splendour of literature, have migrated to the Germans' (*fateri cogerentur non solum Rhomanum imperium et arma sed et litterarum splendorem ad Germanos commigrasse*).[20]

After being invited to Vienna by the emperor in 1497, he gave lectures on Apuleius and published an edition of the *De mundo*.[21] Dedicating the work (on 1 November 1497) to the two leading figures in the Danubian sodality, Celtis adverts to his desire to increase 'the erudition of German youth' (*pro incremento . . . eruditione iuventutis Germanicae*) and describes his edition as 'a little morsel such as the merchants offer prospective customers so that they might be drawn as by an appetizing drink to the mysteries which are handled in philosophy and the divine poetry'.[22] Celtis is also highly conscious, however, of the congruence between political and discursive space. It is no accident that it is in Vienna, 'the residence and fatherland of Maximilian Caesar, Roman emperor and lord of all the world' (*Rhomani principis et domini orbis terrarum Maximiliani Caesaris domicilium et patria*), that he has chosen to present 'the *World* of Lucius Apuleius, who collected and compacted the entire fabric of the universe and its individual parts and workings so skilfully and extremely learnedly in the manner of an epitome'.[23]

Celtis' peroration contains a vague echo of the prologue to *The Golden Ass* (*aures . . . tuas benivolas . . . permulceam*, AA 1. 1) as he declines to go on, fearing lest he might 'appear to tickle your ears rather than soothing them' (*titillare . . . magis aures vestras quam mulcere videar*). And he ends with the promise that, if his present labour is welcomed 'with a cheerful countenance' (*hilari fronte*), his audience will be able to read 'the remaining books of Apuleius on Platonic majesty and sublimity' (*reliquos Apuleii libros de Platonica maiestate et sublimitate*), that is to say, the *De dogmate Platonis* and *De deo Socratis*.

---

[20] *Briefwechsel*, nr. 15, p. 29. It is interesting that he describes his *Epitome* as a *libellum nugas et ineptias meas continentem* which he 'blathered out' (*blatteravi*) during his peregrination among the Slavs. The echoes of Catullus 1 (*libellum . . . nugas*) are obvious, but *blatero* (a non-Ciceronian word) is used several times by Apuleius (e.g. of the old woman at AA 4. 24 and of the debauched devotees of the Syrian goddess at AA 8. 26). Letter to Tucher: partial translation by Spitz, *Conrad Celtis*, 95.

[21] *Lucij Apulei Platonici et Aristotelici philosophi Epitoma diuinum de mundo seu Cosmographia ductu Conradi Celtis impressum Uienne* (Vienna: J. Winterburger, 1497). See Spitz, *Conrad Celtis*, 128 n. 2. (For the lecture on Apuleius: see his *Ep*. 4. 44, 50). For a lucid introduction to the *De mundo* (and compelling arguments in favour of the attribution to Apuleius), see Harrison, *Latin Sophist*, 174–95.

[22] Spitz, *Conrad Celtis*, 66.

[23] *Delegi mihi narrandum Lucii Apulei mundum, qui totam illam universi orbis fabricam et eius singulas partes et operationes ita scite et admodum docte instar epitomatis collegit et contraxit.*

Celtis' activities in Vienna evidently caused something of a stir. Christopher Kuppner ('Pontanus'—another graduate in law from Bologna, 1490–2) reported back to him from Rostock on 1 January 1500 that he stood 'in the greatest peril of losing [his] good name' for having published (*sparsisse*) 'a certain book' (presumably the *De mundo*) in which he allegedly 'worshipped, venerated and adored Phoebus, Mercury, and Apollo as if [he] despised our saints and God like a gentile'. But while these accusations have been 'preached publicly by certain religious men in the University of Vienna', Celtis' teaching has won everybody over to his cause.[24]

In 1502, when Celtis (writing from Nuremberg) comes to dedicate his four books of *Amores* to Maximilian, he praises the emperor as 'a second Caesar Augustus who is restoring to us the former arts of Roman and Greek letters along with the Roman Empire' (*qui nobis cum Rhomano imperio ut alter Caesar Augustus priscas artes, Rhomanas et Graecas litteras . . . restituis!*). He discusses the respectable and the bestial forms of love: 'But concerning the power and impotence of each kind of love, I find nothing written by the poets more illuminating than that brilliant fable of Apuleius and those fifteen books of transformations that we have read of Ovid's' (*Quocirca de utriusque amoris vi et impotentia nihil unquam inlustrius scriptum a poetis invenio quam illam Lucii Apuleii speciosam fabulam et eos, quos de transformationis quindecim Ovidii libros legimus . . .*).[25]

EXOTICI AC FORENSIS SERMONIS RVDIS LOCVTOR:
TRANSFORMING THE BARBARIAN

What was it that attracted Germans like Conrad Celtis and Christoph Scheurl to Apuleius? The influence of Beroaldo in Bologna—the major training-ground for German jurists—was obviously enormous.[26] Johann Sieder

---

[24] Spitz, *Conrad Celtis*, 65. *Briefwechsel*, nr. 230, p. 384.

[25] *Briefwechsel*, nr. 275, pp. 498–9. The *Amores* contain woodcuts from the workshop of Albrecht Dürer and 'The architectonic arrangement . . . reveals again the author's fascination with Pythagorean numerology' (Spitz, *Conrad Celtis*, 86, 88).

[26] The introd. to Johann von Kitzscher's *Dialogus de sacri Romani imperii rebus* (wr. Bologna, 1498; pub. Wittenberg: Hermann Trebelius, 1504) consists of an imaginary letter to Beroaldo and a dream-vision in which Kitzscher is guided by Pico. See Grossmann, 51. Beroaldo's *Declamatio ebriosi, scortatoris, et aleatoris* ('Declamation of a Drunkard, a Whoremonger, and a Gambler') was translated twice into German, by Jakob Wimpheling (1513) and by Sebastian Brant (1539). See J. M. Weiss, '*Kennst Du das Land wo die Humanisten blühen?*: References to Italy in the Biographies of German Humanists', in *Germania latina/Latinitas teutonica: Politik, Wissenschaft, humanistische Kultur vom späten Mittelalter bis in unsere Zeit*, ed. E. Kessler and H. C. Kuhn (Munich: Fink, 2003), 439–55, at 444 n.26.

translated *The Golden Ass* into German within months of the publication of Beroaldo's commentary (1500), though a printed version did not appear until 1538.[27] Celtis' decision to produce an edition of the *De mundo* and the (unfulfilled) desire of Conrad Peutinger (a former student of Pomponio Leto at Rome and of Beroaldo at Bologna) to edit the *De herbarum medicaminibus* ascribed to Apuleius might be viewed as part of a concerted effort by German humanists to complement Beroaldo's work by editing the (pseudo-) Apuleian *residua*.[28]

But Apuleius also held out particular possibilities of self-transformation and cultural conquest. Notions of national and cultural identity are extremely fluid (indeed metamorphic) in his works. In the *Apologia* (24), Apuleius can describe himself as 'half-Numidian' (*seminumida*) and 'half-Gaetulian' (*semigaetulus*). In *The Golden Ass*, Lucius may be transformed into a donkey, but his author seems to be simultaneously Greek (*AA* 1. 1–2), Roman (*AA* 3. 29 and 4. 32), and African (*Madaurensis...pauper, AA* 11. 27). In Apuleius' prologue, the acquisition of Greek is depicted as a military campaign (*linguam Attidem primis pueritiae stipendiis merui*), while proficiency in Latin is achieved by dint of 'wretched toil' (*aerumnabile labore*). Non-Romans (and Germans, in particular) are likely to have noted the interplay of *aduena* ('newcomer', 'stranger', 'foreigner') and *indigena* ('native', 'indigenous'), the radical attractions of the author's claim of autodidacticism (*nullo magistro praeeunte*—a boast that Luther would echo), and the combination of aggression and cultivation in the phrase *aggressus excolui*.[29] The whole of the work thus becomes a vivid exemplification of what the 'rude speaker' (*rudis locutor*) could achieve.

Pomponio Leto's predecessor in the Studium at Rome, Lorenzo Valla (1407–57), had already established *Roma* as a linguistic construct, a culturally negotiable political space, when he wrote: *Ibi namque romanum imperium est ubique lingua dominatur* ('The Roman Empire exists wherever the Roman

[27] See R. Häfner, 'Ein schoenes Confitemini. Johann Sieders Übersetzung von Apuleius' *Goldenem Esel*: Die Berliner Handschrift Germ. Fol. 1239 aus dem Jahr 1500 und der erste Druck von 1538', *Beiträge zur Geschichte der deutschen Sprache und Literatur* 125/1 (2003), 94–136. Häfner tabulates some of the many differences between the manuscript and the printed version. I have not seen B. Plank's *Johann Sieders Übersetzung des 'Goldenen Esels' und die frühe deutschsprachige 'Metamorphosen'-Rezeption: ein Beitrag zur Wirkungsgeschichte von Apuleius' Roman* (Tübingen: Niemeyer, 2004).

[28] On Peutinger's *Annotationes* to the pseudo-Apuleian *De herbis* (1513), see M. Grünberg-Dröge, 'Peutinger, Konrad', *Biographisch-Bibliographischen Kirchenlexikons*, vol. vii (1994), 392–7. On Peutinger's association with Leto, see Palermino, 122. It may not be coincidental that Leonhard Pachel—who reprinted Bussi's edition of Apuleius' *Opera* (Milan, 1497)—was a native of Ingolstadt (where Celtis delivered his famous oration). See Cosenza, *BBDIP*, 453.

[29] *aggredior* can mean 'to approach' or 'to 'attack', while *excolo* can convey not only the growing of crops, but also the refining or polishing of speech as well as of marble.

language holds sway').[30] Glossing Apuleius' *in urbe Latia* (*AA* 1. 1), Beroaldo writes: *Romam significat. non solum latii sed & cunctarum terrarum caput: quæ communis patria authore Seneca dici potest* ('He signifies Rome, the capital not only of Latium but of all lands, which, on the authority of Seneca, may be called the homeland of all').[31] In response to the speaker's prefatory apology (*en ecce praefamur veniam, si quid exotici ac forensis sermonis rudis locutor offendero*, *AA* 1. 1), Beroaldo comments:

Exoticum sermonem appellat romanam linguam ueluti alienigenam ac insitiam sibique merito peregrinam cum ipse natione affer atticissare didicisset: & in patria stridulam barbariam puerilibus labris degustasset | exoticus enim significat peregrinum & externum: uocabulo quidem græco sed apud latinos usitatissimo.[32]

(He calls the Roman language an 'exotic discourse', as it were, alien and unfamiliar, and deservedly foreign to him, since he himself, an African by birth, had learned to atticize, and in his own homeland had tasted hissing barbarousness with his childish lips. For 'exotic' signifies 'foreign' and 'belonging to another country', by means of a Greek term indeed, but one most acclimatized among the Latins.)

It might seem natural for an Italian humanist to gloss this part of the prologue as an apology for 'speaking Latin like a foreigner', but Beroaldo is intent, instead, on legitimating subjectivity, validating other geographical 'centres of self', while recognizing that the very word by which Romans defined the 'foreign' (*exoticus*) was itself a borrowing, an artefact of Rome's long engagement with Greece in the *translatio studii et imperii*.

Beroaldo's Bologna was a place in which Germans (and other non-Italians) could be accepted as humanists without abandoning their sense of national identity. Scheurl 'was proud that he had been educated in Italy, and even that he pronounced Latin in the Italian way', but he was also a patriot.[33] In 1505, he delivered an oration at Bologna in which he refers to Beroaldo's laudatory poem on the Germans and to Beroaldo's 'opinion that the knowledge of the German language is indispensable, since it is next to Latin the most important language'.[34]

Colonna may have had Apuleius' prologue (*siquid exotici ac forensis sermonis rudis locutor offendero*, *AA* 1.1) at the back of his mind when he described Poliphilo's diffident response to the nymph whom he takes to be Polia:

[30] *Prosatori latini del Quattrocento*, ed. E. Garin (Milan: Ricciardi, [1952]), 596. Quoted by D'Amico, 'Progress', 353.

[31] *Commentarii … in Asinum aureum*, fol. 4ʳ.

[32] Ibid., fol. 4ʳ.

[33] Grossmann, *Humanism in Wittenberg*, 61.

[34] Ibid. 62. The oration, marking the appointment of a Saxon scholar, Dr Ketwig, as rector of the University of Bologna, was expanded for publication as the *Libellus de laudibus Germanie et ducum Saxoniae* (Bologna, 1506; Leipzig, 1508).

Et dubitando meritamente (chel non si conuerebbe unqua̲ntulo el mio rude & inculto parlare) di offenderla impudente, gia la calda uoce molte fiate essendo agli reticenti labri peruenuta, per tale ragione quella reprimeua (F.C. m1ʳ)

(I feared that my rude and uncultured manner of speech would offend her, and for that reason I repressed my ardent voice many times when it rose to my reticent lips) (G 185)[35]

Poliphilo longs, nonetheless, 'to be accepted here as a perpetual citizen' (*Quiui uolentieri essere io uorei connumerato municipe perpetuo*, F.C. m1ʳ; G 185).

The episode serves to articulate some of the fundamental anxieties pervading the whole humanist enterprise. At a time when reputation (not to mention employment prospects) depended upon the ability to reproduce, in speech as well as in writing, the language used fifteen centuries earlier, one can appreciate individuals' anxieties about their qualification for membership of the *respublica litterarum* or particular academies or sodalities.[36]

The nymphs find it 'extraordinary and unprecedented that a strange and foreign man should have chanced to arrive in this famous land' (*insolente gli apparue & inusitato. In quella celebre patria homo alieno & extrario cusi a caso essere peruenuto*, G 76; F.C. e2ᵛ). They welcome Poliphilo, but they also tease, humiliate, and frustrate him in the *Geloiastos* episode. The reception of foreigners in Italy could be equally complex. Looking back over the period 1450–1530, Valeriano affirms the humanist ideal of Rome as the 'common fatherland of the whole world' (*communem orbis totius patriam*) which is 'so fertile and abundant in its wealth of men of letters' (*ita litteratorum copia fertilem*) and which 'glories in the foreigners it has taken into its bosom and nurtured and fostered amongst its own' (*peregrinos gremio susceptos aluisse et inter suos fovisse gloriaretur*).[37] In a letter written in 1479 or 1480 during his trip to Germany, Pomponio Leto writes to Platina commending his host at Nuremberg (a certain Gottifredi) as someone worthy of 'enrolment' in *nostram Academiam*.[38] As Julia Gaisser has pointed out, however, 'The

---

[35] We might contrast the involuntary suppression of language that Lucius experiences when he tries to voice an explicitly Roman sense of moral outrage (*porro Quirites*) at the behaviour of the devotees of the Syrian goddess (*AA* 8. 29) and his earlier attempt to denounce the bandits to the civic authorities: 'Amongst these little crowds of Greeks, I tried to invoke the august name of Caesar in my native tongue' (*Inter ipsas turbelas Graecorum genuino sermone nomen augustum Caesaris invocare temptaui*). Lucius is able to produce 'an eloquent and powerful "O"' (*Et 'O' quidem tantum disertum ac ualidum clamitaui*), but is 'unable to pronounce the rest of Caesar's name' (*reliquum autem Caesaris nomen enuntiare non potui*, *AA* 3. 29). According to Sabellico (*Vita*, sig. n[vii]ʳ), Pomponio Leto 'declaimed in a voice that was melodious and pleasing, but not rapid, on account of a stammer' (*pronu̲nciabat canora voce & iucunda: minimeque concitata: ob linguæ titubantiam*).

[36] The charter for Aldus' New Academy stipulated fines for the mispronunciation of Greek (the money raised being used to fund *convivia*). See Lowry, 'New Academy', 380.

[37] *DLI*, Book 1, ch. 5.   [38] Palermino, 123.

world of Roman humanists, with its festivities and celebrations' could also be 'parochial and xenophobic'.[39]

Germans were particularly vulnerable to the charge of barbarism. As late as 1545, Martin Luther would recall the (alleged) behaviour of Giannantonio Campano (Pius II's court poet, a member of Leto's Roman Academy, and the apparent author of verses that came to be inscribed on a fountain modelled on the picture of the sleeping nymph in the *Hypnerotomachia*).[40] On reaching the Italian frontier after his stay at the Diet of Regensburg in 1471, Campano is reported to have 'turned his back on Germany, squatted, bared his behind, and said, *Aspice nudatas, Barbara terra, nates* ('Look, barbarous land, at my naked buttocks')'.[41]

Celtis objected to the tendency of modern historians like Marcantonio Sabellico to speak (in his *Decads*) of the most famous German leaders merely as 'barbarians' (*barbaros*), and he saw his race as 'the inheritors of the Roman Empire' (*Germanos, Romani reliquias imperii*).[42] He wanted, however, to transform both Germans themselves and also the way that they were perceived, especially in Italy. Hieronymus von Croaria writes to him from Ingolstadt on 19 April 1500: 'not only have you driven the barbaric language from our lands and introduced Latin, but by your works and writings, you have also laboured to atone for Germans' barbaric behaviour amongst other nations'.[43]

The metaphors that we usually associate with the Italian Renaissance—not merely 'rebirth' but 'renewal' (*renovatio*) or *instauratio* ('restoration')—were less obviously applicable to 'barbarians' such as the Germans who had chosen

[39] Gaisser, *Valeriano*, 30. The impeccable Ciceronian credentials of the Belgian humanist Christopher Longolius (Christophe de Longeuil) were not enough to save him from the wrath of the humanists who scuppered his election to Roman citizenship in 1519 by accusing him of treason (*Romanitas laesa*). See Rowland, *Culture*, 250–3; Gaisser, *Valeriano*, 302. According to Erasmus (*Ciceronianus* (1528)), Longolius' election was opposed because he was considered to be 'a barbarian and of undistinguished parentage' (*homo barbarus et obscurae familiae*). See K. Gouwens, 'Ciceronianism and Collective Identity: Defining the Boundaries of the Roman Academy, 1525', *JMRS* 23 (1993), 173–95, at 187. Cf. Erasmus, *Opera omnia* i–2 (Amsterdam: North-Holland, 1971) 695.

[40] Campano inscribed his name (*CAMPANVS ANTISTES PRECVTINVS*) alongside those of *Pomponius* and *Platina* in the catacomb of SS. Marcellino and Pietro. While imprisoned in the Castel Sant'Angelo, Pomponio Leto stated in his *Responsio* (Cod. Vat. Lat. 2934, fol. 307ʳ) that 'Bishop [Giannantonio] Campano can testify to his estimation of Callimachus as a man of bad character and of an insane state of mind.' See Palermino, 144 and 147, and 126–7 n. 36. On Campano's authorship of the verses, see Rowland, *Culture*, 183.

[41] *Against the Roman Papacy: An Institution of the Devil* (1545), trans. E. W. Gritsch, in *Luther's Works*, xli (1970), 257–322. I. D. Rowland, 'Revenge of the Regensburg Humanists, 1493', *SCJ* 25 (1994), 307–22, at 318 n. 25.

[42] *Oratio* 37 and 48; Spitz, *Conrad Celtis*, 27; *Selections from Conrad Celtis, 1459–1508*, ed. L. Forster (Cambridge: CUP, 1948), 46–77.

[43] *Briefwechsel*, nr. 237, p. 396.

in ancient times to reject the benefits of Roman civilization. For nations such as these, the notion of metamorphosis (both individual and collective) was particularly appropriate.

We have already discussed Beroaldo's identification of *inscitia* ('ignorance', 'inexperience') as one of the drugs inducing bestiality, and of *scientia* as the 'roses' which restore one from asinine to human form. Beroaldo's gloss certainly seems to have rubbed off on some of his German students at Bologna who became closely associated with Aldus' projects.[44] In a playful allusion to the activities of his own circle of humanists at Erfurt (the *Mutianus ordo* or *Mutianiscker Bund*), Konrad Muth (Conradus Mutianus Rufus, 1471–1526) explicitly identifies the 'humanization' of German men of letters (who discarded their baptismal names for Latin identities) as an Apuleian transformation:

Postquam vero renatus es et pro Iheger Crotus, pro Dornheim Rubianus salutatus, ceciderunt et aures prelonge et cauda pensilis et pilus impexus, quod sibi accidisse dicit Apuleius, cum adhuc asinus esset . . . restitueretur sibi, hoc est humanitati.

(But after you were reborn and greeted as *Crotus* instead of 'Jaeger', *Rubianus* instead of 'Dornheim', your enormously long ears fell off along with your drooping tail and uncombed hide, which is what Apuleius said happened to him when, having hitherto been an ass, . . . he was restored to his real self, that is, to humanity.)

Mutianus adds, 'You easily recognize the wretchedness of those who have not yet shed their barbarousness' (*facile cogniscis, quam miseri sint, qui nondum barbariam exuerunt*).[45]

Crotus Rubianus is best known as the co-author (with Ulrich von Hutten) of the satirical *Epistolae obscurorum virorum*, composed in 1515–17 in defence of one of Pomponio Leto's former pupils, Johann Reuchlin (1455–1522), the German Hebraist whose opposition to proposals by the Dominicans at

---

[44] Mutianus was in Italy from 1495 to 1502, taking his doctorate in canon law at Bologna. In a letter to Urbanus in Feb. 1506, Aldus writes: 'I most highly esteem S. Mutianus Rufus because of his learning and humanity and confess myself to be very much in his debt, on the one hand because he constantly speaks well of me, and on the other because he kindly procured for me the friendship of a man [Spalatin] decked out with learning and holy ways like you.' See *Der Briefwechsel des Conradus Mutianus*, ed. K. Gillert (Halle: O. Hendel, 1890), 37. Quoted by Webster Tarpley, 'The Role of the Venetian Oligarchy in the Reformation, Counter-Reformation, Enlightenment and the Thirty Years' War. Part II', *American Almanac* (5 Apr. 1993), reprod. on WWW (5. 1. Mutianus Rufus and Spalatin).

[45] *Der Briefwechsel des Conradus Mutianus*, nr. 260, p. 344. In a letter from 1506, Mutianus also echoes Apuleius (*AA* 10. 33) in his reference to 'vultures in togas': *blaterandi finem . . . togati vulturii . . . barbara pro Latinis habent*. See *Der Briefwechsel*, nr. 47, p. 61. Quoted by R. P. Becker, *A War of Fools: The Letters of Obscure Men: A Study of the Satire and the Satirized* (Bern: Lang, 1981), 66. Spitz (*Conrad Celtis*, 4) describes Mutianus as Celtis' 'most important pupil' at Erfurt, where Celtis taught for a period beginning in the winter of 1485/86.

Cologne to burn all Jewish literature apart from the Talmud made him the rallying point in the battle between humanists and scholastics.[46] Over the course of 119 fictitious letters, Reuchlin's opponents are made to expose their moral, intellectual, and linguistic deficiencies. In many respects, the work is a reverse image of the *Hypnerotomachia*. As Ulrich von Hutten puts it, *Barbare ridentur barbari* ('The barbarians are ridiculed in a barbaric language').[47] Ass insults and allusions occur frequently in the *Epistolae*.[48] None of these references is explicitly Apuleian—hardly surprising given the lament of 'Konrad Unckebunk' at the introduction into the University curriculum of 'Virgil and Pliny and the rest of the new-fangled authors' (*Virgilium et Plinium et alios noves autores*)—but they do manifest the ways in which the late medieval traditions of the ass (as a vehicle both for anticlerical satire and scholastic logic) could be yoked with the *Eselmensch* traditions of pseudo-Lucian and Apuleius.[49] 'Doctor Barthel Gowk', for example, boasts of how he used (defective) syllogism against a Reuchlinist (Martin Gröning) to prove that he (Gowk) was not an ass.[50]

In a supposed letter to Ortwin Gratius (Reuchlin's chief antagonist), 'Irus Perlirus' reports the threat made by one of his disgruntled students:

I shall go to *Italy*, where teachers do not cheat their pupils, and have no such mummery when they make their bachelors. If a man is learned the honour is conferred on him—if unlearned, he is treated like any other ass (*quando autem est indoctus, habetur sicut alius asinus*) . . . a friend told me that when he was resident at *Bologna* he observed that all the Masters of Arts from *Germany* were inducted like freshmen (*omnes magistri artium ex Almania deponebatur tanquam beani*); not so the mere students. For in *Italy* it is deemed a disgrace to hold the degree of Bachelor or Magister of a German University. (2. 58: pp. 255 and 51)

In the final letter of the collection, the ironical mask is allowed to slip, and the anti-Reuchlinists are openly attacked as 'double-headed asses and natural philosophers' (*bicipites asini et naturales Philosophi*). The letter is addressed to 'Mag. Ortwin Gratius, Champion of Barbarism and Mouthpiece of Cologne, who brayeth after the manner of a jackass against Poets and Scholars, and Greeks whose tongue he knows not' (*Qui clamat more asinino | Contra poetes et latinatos, Nec non Graecos peregrinos, Omnium Barbarorum defensori, Et Coleniensium praeconi famosiori . . .*).[51]

---

[46] On Reuchlin as a pupil of Leto's, see Cosenza, *BBDIH*, v. 375, and Palermino, 122.

[47] *Ulrichi Hutteni . . . opera*, ed. E. Böcking, 5 vols. (Leipzig: Teubner, 1856–61), i. 124. Quoted by E. Bernstein, 'Group Identity Formation in the German Renaissance Humanists: The Function of Latin', in *Germania latina / Latinitas teutonica* (WWW).

[48] i. 4, 24, 25, 28, and 35; ii. 10, 35, 58, 63, 66, 68, 69, and 70.

[49] *Epistola* 2. 46, pp. 229 and 485. When the schoolmen wish to show off their Classical learning, the limit of their repertoire is Ovid (e.g. *Epist. obs. vir.*, Book 2, pp. 216, 473).

[50] Ibid. 2. 10, pp. 154 and 418.   [51] Ibid. 2. 70, pp. 284 and 537.

The collection also includes an hilarious account of imperfect metamor-phosis.[52] A German schoolman ('Johann Arnoldi') has gone to Rome 'by ambulatory journeying' (*viatica ambulatione*), 'in contemplation of remu-nerative emolument flowing from the acquisition of a trifling foolish benefice' (*causa lucruli ad consarcinandum unum beneficiolum*). Exposed to humanist influences, he has been studying 'to acquire incomparable virtuosity in the Poetic Art' and so his 'diction differeth from its complexion of yore' (*Etiam sciveritis qualiter studuero hic per totum in poeseos artificiolo, et ergo fuerim aliter stilatus quam prius*), but he is no more successful in his linguistic efforts than Rabelais's Limousin scholar (*Pantagruel*, ch. VI), or Shakespeare's fop-pish courtier Osric (*Hamlet* II. ii)—they have all acquired a taste, but not the capacity, for big words.[53]

We see once more how notions of *transformatio*, *eruditio*, and *expolitio* create a matrix within the works of Colonna, Beroaldo, Celtis, and their associates. Beroaldo presents his commentary on Apuleius as 'a new image of my mind, thoroughly polished with versatile sculpting and careful elegance' (*Hoc vero novicium animi nostri simulacrum vario effigiatu cultuque laborioso perpolitum...*').[54] On the death of Beroaldo in 1505, Mutianus wrote: *Philippum sopor occupat. | Doctis flebilior quis potuit mori? | Non fame nocuit sopor, | Que splendet Pario marmore tersius* ('Sleep takes hold of Philip. Whose death could inspire more tears in learned men? Sleep has not harmed his reputation which shines with a higher polish than Parian marble').[55] In the *Oratio*—his inaugural lecture at Ingoldstadt (1492)—Celtis talked of the 'beauty and polish of words' (*verborum pulchritudo et expolitio*) as an essential requirement for the transformation of German youth.[56] On 27 May 1500, while Beroaldo's *Commentary* was going through the press, Joannes Rhagius Aesticampianus (Johann Rack of Somerfeld, 1460–1520) writes from Bologna, testifying to Celtis' success: 'I and many others... have been

---

[52] Ibid. 2. 36, pp. 210–11 and 467–8.

[53] We might compare the earlier example of Johannes Tinctoris of Braine-l'Alleud who registered himself on 1 Apr. 1463 as 'proctor of the German nation (i.e. Imperial subjects) at the University of Orléans'. What L. Holford-Strevens calls the 'peacock Latinity' of his entry in the register attracted marginalia: *Appuleio magis affectatus et stultior* ('More affected and foolish than Apuleius'); *Apulei asinus sivit docuit rudere* ('Apuleius' ass has dried up; he has taught [Tinctoris] to bray'); *rudit cum Apuleii asino: ride sesquipedalia verba buttubatte* [*sc. butubatta*] *stultiloqui. Parturiunt* [*sc. parturient*] *montes nascetur ridiculus mus* ('He brays with Apuleius' ass: Laugh at the sesquipedalian words, the trifles of this babbler. The mountains [will be] in labour: a ridiculous mouse will be born' (my translations; cf. Horace, *Ad Pisones*, 139)). See 'Humanism and the Language of Music Treatises', *RS* 15 (2001), 415–49, at 425. Holford-Strevens cites *Premier Livre des procurateurs de la Nation germanique de l'ancienne université d'Orléans 1444–1546*, ed. C. M. Ridderikhoff with H. De Ridder-Symoens (Leiden: Brill, 1971), 29–30.

[54] Beroaldo, fol. a2ʳ. Quoted by Gaisser, 'Teaching Classics in the Renaissance', 12.

[55] *Der Briefwechsel des Conradus Mutianus*, S. 319. Quoted by Krautter, 9.

[56] Forster, 64; Spitz, *Conrad Celtis*, 30.

polished in your workshop' (*ego et multi alii... in officina tua expoliti sunt*).⁵⁷
Celtis is vying with both the living (Beroaldo) and the dead (Leto): 'I see and
hear no-one here', Somerfeld tells him, 'to whom you yield in any mode of
discourse' (*cui hic in aliquo dicendi genere cedas, video et audio neminem*). In
Rome, meanwhile, 'the whole throng of learned men sacrifice religiously to
that Pomponio Leto whose tomb I saw recently when I was in the City.... And
so why, since glory comes too late to ashes, do we not erect altars to you while
you are still alive and believe you also to be a deity sent down from heaven in
order to expel ignorance, illuminate Germany and fill almost the whole world
with its name and most radiant writings?'⁵⁸ Celtis' role is presented here as
being very similar to that of Polia at the end of the *Hypnerotomachia*.⁵⁹

ACADEMIC DREAMS: ALDUS' NEW ACADEMY

Celtis' correspondence with Aldus Manutius shows him planning visits to
Venice in 1497, 1498, and 1501.⁶⁰ But the cultural traffic between Germany
and Italy was not one-way. On 23 April 1499 (just eight months before the
appearance of the *Hypnerotomachia*), Johann Reuchlin wrote to Aldus from
Heidelberg, referring elliptically to the failure of German humanists to secure
imperial patronage for a Greek academy in Germany: 'We are not worthy of
you.'⁶¹ By December 1505, however, John Cuno reports to Willibald Pirckhei-
mer that Aldus is 'preparing to move to Germany, to found a New Academy
under the protection of the King of the Romans'.⁶² Here we see, once again,
the instability of any fixed polarities between 'Roman' and 'barbarian', 'citizen'

⁵⁷ *Briefwechsel*, nr. 241, p. 403. On his 'occasional references' in 1508 to Apuleius, see C. E.
Lutz, 'Aesticampianus' Commentary on the *De Grammatica* of Martianus Capella', *RQ* 26/2
(1973), 157–66, at 163. Aesticampianus will be named as one of the prominent 'Reuchlinists' in
the *Epistolae obscurorum virorum*: 1. 7; 2. 9. *Epistola* 1. 17 depicts him lecturing on 'Pliny and the
other poets' (*Et ipse legit Plinium, et alios poetas*).
⁵⁸ *Briefwechsel*, nr. 241, p. 403.
⁵⁹ Cf. the concluding couplet of Johannes Camers' elegy on Celtis which appears above the
colophon of Celtis' *Libri odarum quatuor, cum Epodo, & saeculari Carmine* (Strasbourg: Schurer,
1513): *At pia turba poli letatur (credite) quare?* | *Quod retinent superi quem voluere virum* ('But
the pious throng of heaven (believe it!) rejoices. Why? | Because the gods above have hold of the
man they wanted.' Camers (aka Giovanni Ricuzzi Vellini) spent 39 years in Vienna and was a
friend of Marcus Musurus. See Cosenza, *BBDIH* v. 241.
⁶⁰ Spitz, *Conrad Celtis*, 61. On 13 Oct. 1497, Aldus sent Celtis a copy of the recently published
Greek grammar by Valeriano's uncle, Fra Urbano Bolzanio. See *Briefwechsel*, nr. 175, p. 288;
Lowry, *World of Aldus*, 265.
⁶¹ Lowry, 'New Academy', 404.
⁶² Dec. 1505: *Parat enim se idem Aldus migrare in Germaniam, sub titulo Regis Romanorum
neacademicam... instituere*. Trans. from Lowry, 'New Academy', 406.

and 'foreigner', 'republican' and 'imperial'. When Vincent Lang (writing from Rome in November or December 1500), refers to Aldus as *Graecanicae antiquitatis restaurator* ('the restorer of Greekish antiquity'), he uses an adjective which adroitly conveys the mediated nature of the ancient ideal being sought.[63] Earlier that year, Beroaldo had glossed Apuleius' *fabulam Graecanicam incipimus* (*AA* 1. 1) by observing (fol. 4ᵛ): *Differt autem græcanicus a græco: nam ut docet M. Varro libro sexto de Analogia græcanica aduenticia sunt de græcis ueluti notha … & ita hæc fabula ex græco Luciano deducta deriuataque est* ('But *Graecanicus* is different from *Graecus*; for, as Marcus Varro informs us in Book 6, 'On Analogy', *Graecanica* are things present by coming from abroad, as things known from the Greeks, and so this tale has been drawn and derived from the Greek Lucian.')[64]

A statute for Aldus' Greek Academy at Venice (datable to around 1502) proclaims the intentions of 'men who are already dreaming [ὀνειροπολεῖν] of a New Academy and have almost founded it in Plato's fashion'.[65] In fact, little came of Aldus' Venetian academy, and nothing of the imperial.[66] The ambiguous ending of the *Hypnerotomachia* (Polia—the dream-embodiment of *antiquitas*—dissolving in the very moment of Polifilo's embrace) seems prophetic of Aldus' own academic experience. It can certainly be seen as an allegory of antiquarianism, articulating anxieties about the limits of humanism, in general, and the feasibility (indeed, the value) of the sodality enterprise, in particular.

APULEIUS IN ITALY, 1501–1527

When the Roman Academy had re-formed in 1478, it had done so as a religious sodality, dedicated to Saints Victor, Fortunato, and Genesio, and placed 'under the protection of Cardinal Domenico della Rovere, one of Sixtus's nephews'.[67] It thus managed to operate within the (generously defined) parameters of the

---

[63] *Briefwechsel*, nr. 256, p. 436. Lang also refers to himself on occasion as 'Caius Plinius Secundus' (e.g. *Briefwechsel*, nr. 258, p. 445).
[64] Cf. Harrison and Winterbottom's observation that *Graecanicus* is a technical term used by Varro (*De lingua latina* 10. 70) for words which are 'Greek in origin but adapted for Latin use'. See 'Text, Translation, and Commentary', in *Companion to the Prologue*, ed. Kahane and Laird, 15.
[65] Lowry, 'New Academy', 382.
[66] Lowry (ibid. 415) observes: 'By the time of Erasmus' visit in 1508 the very [202] word "academy" had become a household joke: Aldus would utter it in a squeaky, broken voice, hinting that he would be senile if he ever lived to see such an institution.' See *Opus epistolarum Des. Erasmi Roterodami*, ed. P. S. Allen, 12 vols. (Oxford: Clarendon, 1906–58), iii. 404, no. 868.
[67] D'Amico, *Renaissance Humanism*, 96.

pagan/Christian synthesis that enforms the High Renaissance in Italy. This culture of accommodation was briefly threatened by the election, in January 1522, of a northern 'barbarian' (as the Romans styled him), the Dutchman Adrian Florensz Dedal. As Pope Hadrian VI, he planned 'to burn all the antique statues for lime' and he harboured a particular dislike of the Laocöon (unearthed in 1506).[68] Fortunately for the humanists, he only lasted a year.

Even within humanist circles, however, concerns were voiced about the limits of this pagan/Christian synthesis. In his *De Venere et Cupidine expellendis carmen* (1513), Pico's nephew, Giovanni Francesco Pico della Mirandola (a follower of Savonarola), presents the proliferation of pagan statuary in the Belvedere Garden (in particular, the group of Venus and Cupid recently acquired by Pope Julius II) as a physical manifestation of the intellectual and spiritual corruption of the Rome of the day. Like Beroaldo, he sees the *Esel-Mensch* of pseudo-Lucian and Apuleius as demonstrating Pythagorean notions of metempsychosis, though in this case, it is Christian Rome as a whole that has transformed itself:

> *Hinc syrii in brutum facies mutata sophistæ:*
> *In quod mox sese deceptus pyxide uertit*
> *Lucius / antiquæ renouans figmenta crotonis.*

> (Hence the form of the Syrian sophist was changed into a brute:
> misled by the box, Lucius soon turned himself into the same,
> reviving the fictions of ancient Croton.)[69]

In the accompanying letter to Lilio Gregorio Giraldi (Gyraldus), Pico explains that he does not envisage physically removing the pagan deities from the Belvedere Garden (*extra lucum*), but he does hope to drive them 'out of the minds of beasts. For—if any credence is to be given to Pythagorean fables— beasts were said to have once been men of that kind, and could be restored to their former selves by choosing Lucius' rose' (*ab animis ferarum. Nam si Pythagoreis non abroganda fides esset, dicerentur fuisse aliquando homines eiusmodi belluæ, inque illos ipsos selecta Lucii rosa posse restitui*).[70]

[68] Gaisser, *Valeriano*, 31, 33.

[69] (Rome: Jacobus Mazochius, 1513), sig. Aiv[v]; Gombrich, *Symbolic Images*, 105–7. Croton, in southern Italy, was the adoptive home of Pythagoras and hence associated with the theory of transmigration of souls. Jacopo Mazzocchi (or Mazzochio) collaborated with Mario Maffei in the production of the *Epigrammata antiquae urbis* (1520). See D'Amico, *Renaissance Humanism*, 86. Mazzocchi was one of the 'booksellers to the Roman Academy' (*bibliopolae Academiae Romanae*), and was involved with Angelo Colocci in Pope Leo's attempts to set up a Greek Academy in Rome. See Rowland, *Culture*, 217, 220.

[70] Sig. [Biv][v]. The Strasbourg edition is accompanied by a letter from Pico the Younger to Konrad Peutinger. See Gombrich, *Symbolic Images*, 223 n. 33. Rowland (*Culture*, 246) calls Pico the Younger 'a chronically disgruntled soul'. In the same year (or 1512), Pico was engaged in a public exchange of letters with Cardinal Pietro Bembo.

Pico's plea had little immediate effect. Raphael (Raffaello Sanzio, 1483–1520) had been born and spent his boyhood at Urbino during the dukeship of Guidobaldo da Montefeltro (dedicatee of the *Hypnerotomachia*). But, in around 1517, Raphael and his pupils (including Giulio Romano) were in Rome, decorating Agostino Chigi's villa (now the Villa Farnesina) in Trastevere with frescoes of Cupid and Psyche (the Loggia di Psiche).[71] In the Gonzagas' Palazzo Te in Mantua, Giulio Romano decorated the Sala di Psiche (completed 1528–9), drawing not only on Apuleius, but also, it would appear, on the *Hypnerotomachia*.[72] He seems, moreover, to have been influenced by Mario Equicola, who includes a discussion of 'Cupid and Psyche' in his *Libro di natura d'amore*.[73] Equicola had been a disciple of Pomponio Leto's in Rome, probably during the period 1482–92 (or 1484–94), and was connected with many of the figures we have been discussing: Angelo Colocci, Marino Becichemo, the Colonna family, and Battista Pio (who had preceded Equicola in Mantua as tutor to Francesco Gonzago's wife, Isabella d'Este, and may have already helped to sparked an interest in matters Apuleian).[74] Indeed, Equicola's and Pio's names are linked by an anonymous satire which parodies their (allegedly) Apuleian language, the *Dialogus in lingua mariopioneasive piomariana carmentali pulcherrimus* (1513).[75] Gonzaga's court at Mantua also appears to have enjoyed the performance, in November 1503, of 'what is possibly Italy's earliest five-act vernacular comedy', Publio Philippo Mantovano's *Formicone*, a dramatization of Apuleius' tale of adultery and a pair of slippers (*AA* 9. 17–21).[76]

Perhaps the most remarkable pictorial representations of all are to be found in the Rossi fortress (Rocca dei Rossi) at San Secondo, situated between Milan and Parma on the Via Francigena, the ancient pilgrim route which links those

[71] Rowland, *Culture*, 244. See K. Oberhuber, 'Raphael's Drawings for the Loggia of Psyche in the Farnesina', in *Raffaello a Roma*, ed. C. L. Frommel and M. Winner (Rome: Elefante, 1986), 189–208.

[72] Gombrich, *Symbolic Images*, 108; Acocella, *L'Asino d'oro nel Rinascimento*, 125–36. See, more generally, E. Verheyen, *The Palazzo del Te in Mantua: Images of Love and Politics* (Baltimore: Johns Hopkins UP, 1977).

[73] (Vinegia: Gabriel Giolito de Ferrari et fratelli, 1554). According to S. Kolsky, 'the first draft of the *Libro de natura de amore*' was 'begun in about 1495'. See *Mario Equicola: The Real Courtier* (Geneva: Droz, 1991), 42.

[74] For the (approximate) dates, see Kolsky, *Equicola*, 29. On Equicola's extensive network, see Kolsky's index. In his *De mulieribus* (written in Ferrara), Equicola addresses Leto as *Pythagoras meus* and claims that *divus ille Pomponius Laetus* 'was responsible for directing him towards the study of Plato' (Kolsky, 40).

[75] D'Amico, 'Progress', 377. Kolsky, *Equicola*, 59 and 104.

[76] Scobie, 'Influence', 213. Apuleius' characters—the jealous husband (Barbarus), the suborned slave (Myrmex, 'the ant'), and the young lover (Philesitherus, 'fond of chasing women')— are Italianized as Barbaro, Formicone, and Filetero. See *Formicone*, ed. L. Stefani (Ferrara: Bovolenta, 1980).

cities with Bologna (about 60 miles to the south-east), Florence, and Rome. The painter seems to be connected with the Raphael-Giulio Romano school, but the ceiling of the Sala dell'Asino d'Oro (*c.*1530) is unique in depicting scenes, not from 'Cupid and Psyche', but from the adventures of Lucius himself. The sixteen rectangular panels (with sixteen corner triangles) are set around a square centrepiece, and show the hero at various critical moments in the narrative: watching his hostess anoint herself; immediately after his own transformation, with his distraught lover standing with palms outstretched and one breast bared; having the load of sticks on his back set on fire by the malicious boy; fleeing with the abducted bride; carrying the statue of the goddess on his back; being spied upon by his new owners as he devours human food; having his head caressed by the naked *matrona* in front of a four-poster bed; and so on. The climax presented in the centrepiece, however, is drawn not from Apuleius but from the pseudo-Lucianic tradition, as mediated by Boiardo. There is no sign of Isis or Mithras: the ass kneels on the steps of a dais, surrounded by the trappings of civic and military authority, waiting to receive the transforming rose from the hand of the governor.[77]

In Rome, meanwhile, Angelo Colocci had lent Pomponio Leto's old garden on the Quirinal to the new Greek gymnasium and 'helped to set up a Greek press on the premises'. He acted as 'an archaeological consultant to Raphael' (Rowland, 221), and had installed a fountain modelled on the sleeping nymph in the *Hypnerotomachia* in his new gardens (the Horti Colotiani), an event celebrated by Girolamo Borgia (whom we mentioned earlier as a member of the Patavian sodality to which Valeriano sought entry).[78] During the reign of Leo X (1513–21), another erstwhile Patavian *sodalis*, Andreas Maro Brixianus (Andrea Marone of Brescia, 1475–1528), was a member of the sodality established at Rome by Coricius (Johann Goritz, *c.*1455–1527), a group memorialized by a collection of verses, the *Coryciana*, published in 1524.[79]

It was against this backdrop in Rome that Agnolo Firenzuola produced (during the period 1523–5) at least the first part of his *L'asino d'oro* (finally published in Venice in 1550, seven years after his death).[80] At the level of

[77] Cf. Acocella, 140–52.

[78] Rowland (*Culture*, 184) does not make the link with Padua. The inscription at the base of the fountain 'seems to have been written by the humanist Giannantonio Campano sometime before 1470' (ibid. 183). Campano, as we saw earlier, was a member of Leto's original Roman Academy and filled the post of *corrector* at Ulrich Hahn's press in Rome (Pastor, *History of the Popes*, iv. 71). See O. Kurz, '*Huius nympha loci*: A Pseudo-Classical Inscription and a Drawing by Dürer', *JWCI* 16 (1953), 171–7; P. P. Bober, 'The *Coryciana* and the Nymph Corycia', *JWCI* 40 (1977), 223–39; J. IJsewijn, 'De *huius nympha loci* (*CIL* VI/5, 3+ e) eiusque fortuna poetica syntagmation', *Arctos*, suppl. II (1985), 61–7.

[79] There is a modern edn., ed. J. IJsewijn (Rome: Herder, 1997).

[80] G. Fatini, introd., *Opere scelte di Agnolo Firenzuola*, 2nd edn. (Turin: Unione tipografico-editrice torinese, 1966), 10. Subsequent references are to this edn. According to D. Romei, the

individual words and phrases, it is, for large stretches, a relatively faithful translation; but in its overall conception, it is an extreme manifestation of those imaginative and appropriative tendencies that we saw within Pomponio Leto's circle and in Beroaldo's commentaries.[81] The autobiography and curriculum vitae given by Apuleius' narrator (*AA* 1. 1) are replaced by Firenzuola's own.[82] The *fabula Graecanica* (*AA* 1. 1) becomes *una tosca favola* ('a Tuscan tale') and the hero/narrator (Angelo), arriving in Book 1 with letters from Florence, no longer enjoys the miserly hospitality of Milo at Hypata, but of 'Petronio' at Bologna (236 ff.). The choice of towns can hardly have been accidental: Firenzuola's decision to name the slavegirl 'Lucia' (238) suggests that he may have consulted Beroaldo's gloss on *AA* 1. 23 (*Commentarii*, fol. 27^v) describing Fotis as a *lucida puella* (from φῶς, 'light'); and the narrator's description (241; = *AA* 2. 1) of Bologna as a city in which *tutto fusse per incanto trasmutata in quella forma* reads like a double-edged acknowledgement of the metamorphic effects of Beroaldo's commentaries.

The updating programme was not implemented uniformly. The story of Cupid and Psyche was preserved as a *favola* set *al tempo degli Iddii* ('in the time of the Gods', 305). The Isiac and Osirian ending of the original could not, however, be assimilated.[83] The contents of Book 11 of the *De asino aureo* are reduced to a mere three pages or so and are absorbed into Firenzuola's tenth (and final) book. The Egyptian gods are jettisoned: at the vision of the moon *nella sua maggiore grandezza* (463), Angelo is moved to consider his own sins (*la conscienza dalli miei grandi e moltiplici errori*, 464) and suddenly remembers that his ancestors had always sworn by one particular intercessor (*avocato*), 'that bearded old man' (*quel barbato vecchione*, that is to say, Saint Jerome) who had translated 'the mysteries of the ancient Hebrews' (*mistieri degli antichi ebrei*, 464). Angelo's prayer is answered by the voice of *un venerando vecchione* who says: *Vivi lieto, il mio Angelo, vivi lieto; penetrate sono le preci tue nel conspetto del primo Motore* ('Live happily, my Angelo; your prayers have penetrated the presence of the Prime Mover', 464). Firenzuola is careful, however, to recreate at least some of the feminine presence that is so

translation was completed in two phases, Books I–VII during Firenzuola's first period at Rome (1519–27, with a gap in 1522), and Books VIII–X in his final Roman sojourn (1532–4). See 'L'alfabeto segreto di Agnolo Firenzuola', http://www.nuovorinascimento.org/n-rinasc/saggi/html/romei/firenz93.htm. On Firenzuola's use of Beroaldo, see S. Maniscalco, 'Criteri e sensibilità di Agnolo Firenzuola, traduttore di Apuleio', *La rassegna della letteratura italiana* 82 (1978), 88–109.

[81] Firenzuola resists Pietro Bembo's call to take Boccaccio as the model for Italian prose, choosing instead to employ contemporary Tuscan speech.

[82] Carver, '*Quis ille?*', 174.

[83] Such reticence about pagan matters would fit Romei's theory that Book X was translated in the early 1530s, relatively shortly after the catastrophic Sack of Rome (1527).

marked in Apuleius' conclusion. The old man's voice tells Angelo to head for the city where the first lady he meets will be *una bellissima giovane, ma con aspetto infiammante i cuori degli uomini alle virtuti ed alle cose del cielo* ('a most beautiful young woman, but with a countenance that inflames the hearts of men to virtue and heavenly matters', 464). Angelo's *bellissima giovane* joins a long line (running from Dante's Beatrice to Colonna's Polia) of beautiful women who serve as celestial guides and salvific agents. Angelo has to be transformed spiritually before he is physically restored to his old shape. His *bellissima guida* takes him to a priest (*un sacerdote*) who removes each of his 'stains' (*ogni macchia*, 465), 'not by water, or lye, or any liquid, but by divine words' (465). The woman (identified as *la mercé d'Amore*, 465) leads Angelo to her house where she gives him *una ghirlonda di odorifere rose* and he returns to human form (465–6). In the final paragraph of his version, however, Firenzuola names 'Costanza' as the 'mistress of [his] soul' (*signora dell'anima*) and defines his metamorphosis not in religious terms, but in relation to the humanists' programme: *Questa fu quella che, trattomi dello asinino studio delle leggi civili, anzi incivili, mi fece applicare alle umane lettere* ('This was she who, when I was engaged in the asinine study of civil—nay, uncivil—laws, made me devote myself to literature'). Even after her death, it is Costanza (or the memory of Costanza) who has 'not allowed me to turn back into an ass' (*non mi ha mai lasciato all'asino ritornare*, 466).[84]

An even more metamorphic approach to the original is taken by the Ferrarese poet Curio Lancillotto Pasio in his *Bucolicorum Mimisis* (1506).[85] Pasio transforms Vergilian pastoral by introducing Milesian elements derived from Apuleius, but (partly, one suspects, for metrical purposes) he merges names and identities in a bravura performance. In Eclogue 9, a shepherd named Magirus complains to his friend, Caldius, about the baleful influence of a witch named 'Fotis'. The opening is markedly bucolic: 'I was singing happily, I remember, when a country-wench, Fotis, saw me—she who now bewitches me and my soft lambs' (*Cantabam, memini, laetus: me rustica vidit | Fotis, me et teneros ea nunc quae fascinat agnos*, vv. 5–6).[86] He proceeds, however, to relate the story of 'Telephron' and 'Byrrhenus' (i.e. Aristomenes and Socrates) and their nocturnal encounter with two witches at a tavern (cf. *AA* 1. 11–19). After recounting the death of 'Telephron', Magirus continues

---

[84] 'Costanza Amaretta' was the pseudonym given by Firenzuola to the (already married) object of his affections, a Roman gentlewoman who died, suddenly, early in 1525. See Fatini, *Opere scelte*, 10–12, 466.

[85] Pasio's eclogues survive only in manuscript (Bibl. Apost. Vat. Lat. 2866). I rely here on the extracts and summaries given by G. Pinotti, 'Curio Lancillotto Pasio e la *Bucolicorum Mimisis* dedicata a Niccolò da Correggio', *HL* 32 (1983), 165–96.

[86] Pinotti (194) identifies a collage of Vergilian phrases in this section of the poem.

his litany of Fotis' malevolent powers, before deciding to proceed to the city and denounce her 'to those who are charged, according to Holy Orders, with the task of burning ferocious witches in the dark flames' (*quis cura ex ordine sancto | est lamias atris saevas exurere flammis*, vv. 76–7).

In the tenth (and final) eclogue, Lucius tells the story of his own metamorphosis as a consolatory (and monitory) tale for his love-tormented friend Simulus. Having touched Meroe's ointment, Lucius has been transformed into an ass. He heads for the woods, unable to face his beloved Glaucia (a blending of Apuleian characters—Fotis and the libidinous *matrona*—with pastoral-mythological figures such as Daphne). Glaucia comes in search of Lucius who reveals his identity by writing in the sand. He invites her to dwell with him in a sheepfold (*abde in ovili*, v. 59), citing the example of Pasiphae who burned with desire for a young bull and managed 'to extinguish the sweet flames in its embrace' (*dulces complexa extinguere flammas*, v. 61; cf. *AA* 10. 19–22). Glaucia is moved to comply and they couple happily (vv. 62–9), but as soon as he returns to human form, she flees from him (*Induo cum faciem solitam, me Glaucia viso | aufugit*, vv. 75–6). This pastoral modulation of the comic ending to the pseudo-Lucianic *Onos* (ch. 56) converts Apuleius' narrative of (albeit problematic) redemption into a satire on female fickleness and appetite. The nymph Arethusa explains to the stricken Lucius the way of the world:

> *Nullus amor durat, gemitum nisi foemina sensit*
> *fructum nique atrox quasset te fronte superba.*

(vv. 87–8)[87]

(No love endures, unless the woman experiences the groan [of ecstasy], and unless, from a position of dominance, she shakes the forbidding fruit while you lie before her.)

Pasio dedicated his *Bucolicorum Mimisis* to Niccolò da Correggio, whose *Fabula Psiches et Cupidinis* was printed the following year (1507)—an early example of the huge vogue for poetic versions of 'Cupid and Psyche'.[88] In Florence, in about 1517, Niccolò Machiavelli was writing *L'asino d'oro*, a poem in *terza rime* which draws, like the *Hypnerotomachia*, on both Dante and Apuleius, but uses them to satirical effect, portraying a range of political

---

[87] Cf. the account of Fotis on top: *pendulae Veneris fructu me satiauit* (*AA* 2. 17).

[88] *Fabula Psiches et Cupidinis* (Venice: Manfrino Bono de Monteferrato, 1507). For a modern edn., see Niccolò da Correggio, *Opere: Cefalo, Psiche, Silva, Rime*, ed. A. Tissoni Benvenuti (Bari: Laterza, 1969), 49–96. On Correggio's treatment of Apuleius, see Acocella, 113–16. Galeotto dal Carretto's *Noze de Psyche & Cupidine* (Milan: A. de Vicomercato, 1520) provided a dramatization of the tale (Haight, *Apuleius*, 121). For a modern edn., see *Teatro del Quattrocento: Le corti padane*, ed. A. Tissoni Benvenuti and M. P. Mussini Sacchi (Turin: UTET, 1983), 611–725. Fumagalli (*Boiardo*, 145–50) discusses the verbal correspondences between Boiardo's translation and the adaptations of 'Cupid and Psyche' by Correggio and Carretto.

figures, transformed into beasts.[89] And the year 1520 saw the publication
in Naples of Girolamo Morlini's *Novellae*, a collection of Milesian tales
'remarkable for their Apuleian latinity and their emphatic focus on sex'.[90]

REVERTING TO TYPE: LUTHER AND THE SACK OF ROME

In Germany, however, the sodalities (inspired by Pomponio Leto, established by
Conrad Celtis, and cross-fertilized by Beroaldo) were assuming a rather different
shape. After completing his doctorate in jurisprudence at Bologna (where he had
purchased his copy of Beroaldo's Apuleius), Christoph Scheurl had returned to
Germany. As professor of law at Wittenberg (1507 to 1512), he instigated 'a
fundamental change' in the university, reshaping its curriculum along humanist
lines.[91] He then moved to Nuremberg where the *sodalitas Celtica* had become
known as the *Staupitziana* in honour of Johann von Staupitz, Vicar-General
of the German Congregation of Augustinians, and Martin Luther's spiritual
adviser.[92] In January 1517, Scheurl wrote to Luther asking him to join the
sodality.[93] For a brief period (from November 1517 until 1519), Luther began
styling himself in the humanist fashion as *Eleutherius* (variously translatable
as 'freeman', 'free-spirited', or—originally an epithet of Zeus—'Deliverer').[94]
In 1518, the Nuremberg *sodales* changed their name again to the *Martiniana*,
in honour of the reformer who had posted his Ninety-Five Theses at Wittenberg
the previous October.[95] Scheurl played an important part in the propagation
of Luther's challenges to papal authority, sending copies of the theses to prominent humanists and churchmen, including Johann Eck and Conrad Peutinger
(annotator of the *De herbarum medicaminibus* ascribed to Apuleius).[96]

Luther and the German humanists had certain interests in common: both
desired to loosen the grip of scholasticism while engaging with ancient texts in

[89] For a convenient summary, see S. Ruffo-Fiore, *Niccolò Machiavelli* (Boston: Twayne, 1982), 125–6.

[90] Scobie, 'Influence', 214. *Novellae, fabulae, comoedia* (Naples: Joan. Pasquet de Sallo, 1520).
For a modern edn., see Girolamo Morlini, *Novelle e favole*, ed. G. Villani (Rome: Salerno, 1983).

[91] Grossmann, 49.

[92] Bebb, 55.

[93] Bebb (59) cites *Willibald Pirckheimers Briefwechsel*, ed. E. Reicke (Munich: Beck, 1940),
vol. ii, ep. 310, p. 400.

[94] Spitz, 'Luther and Humanism', in *Luther and Learning*, ed. M. J. Harran (Selinsgrove:
Susquehanna UP; London: Associated University Presses, 1985), 69–94, at 71–2. Cf. Ulrich von
Hutten's use of the pseudonym 'Eleutherius Byzenus' for his *Triumphus Capnionis* (κάπνιος =
Reuchlin), a poem written in celebration of Reuchlin in 1514 (published in 1518). See *Ulrichi
Hutteni ... opera*, iii. 413–47. Queen Eleuterylida ('Free Will') provides a rather different 'take'
on freedom in the *Hypnerotomachia*.

[95] Bebb, 59.

[96] Bebb, 60. On Peutinger's *Annotationes* to pseudo-Apuleius (1513), see *supra*, p. 243.

their original languages (Latin, Greek, and Hebrew); theological and political opposition to papal supremacy overlapped with a more general inferiority/superiority complex with respect to Italian culture. As Luther made his semi-triumphal progress to the Imperial Diet of Worms (April 1521), he was met at the gates of Erfurt by Crotus Rubeanus who hailed him as 'a judge of evil, to see whose features is like a divine appearance'.[97] But Luther was not to retain this theophanous aspect for long—at least amongst humanists. We have seen Crotus being singled out by Mutianus as an example of the transformation of German asininity by the *studia humanitatis*—a shedding of 'barbarousness'. Luther's response to the problem of being German was in direct contrast to this: eschewing the humanists' concern with *expolitio*, he embraced his own 'roughness' as a *rusticus* and 'barbarous' Latinist, priding himself on his ability to pursue 'truth' without resorting to the Roman affectations of eloquence.[98]

As the full consequences of Luther's rebellion became apparent, many of his initial humanist supporters (Scheurl and Peutinger among them) turned back and reconciled themselves with the Catholic Church. Luther's diatribes became more extreme as he got older, but while he seldom refers directly to Apuleius, he makes copious use of ass-insults. In a late work like *Against the Roman Papacy: An Institution of the Devil* (1545), he hurls the charge of asininity back at Germany's usual attackers. A few selections will suffice:

Gently, dear Pauli [*sc.* Pope Paul III], dear donkey, don't dance around . . . [281] . . .

Why do you let yourselves imagine that you are better than crass, crude, ignorant asses and fools, who neither know nor wish to know what councils, bishops, churches, emperors—indeed, what God and his word—are? You are a crude ass, you ass-pope, and an ass you will remain!

I wanted to cover three things . . . third, whether it is true that he [290] has transferred the Roman Empire from the Greeks to us Germans, about which he boasts immeasurably and beats his breast. Should I then have some strength left, I shall again take up his bulls and briefs and try to see if I can comb out the crass, crude donkey's long unkempt ears for him!

He cannot consider me an ass, for he knows that I, by God's special grace, am more learned in the Scriptures than he and all his asses are . . .

. . . a donkey knows it is a donkey and not a cow. . . . But the mad [361] papal asses in Rome do not know they are asses . . .

---

[97] Spitz, 'Luther and Humanism', 69.
[98] *De servo arbitrio*, 101–2: 'I am an uncultivated fellow who has always moved in uncultivated circles'. See Spitz, 'Luther and Humanism', 76 and 91 n. 12.

Here now, papal ass, with your long donkey ears and accursed liar's mouth! The Germans have the Roman Empire not by your grace, but from Charles the Great and from the emperors in Constantinople...[99]

These passages bring together the issues of *inscitia, expolitio,* and *translatio imperii* that pervade the works of Colonna and Beroaldo, but in ways diametrically opposed to those of the humanists.

Indeed, it is one of the bitter ironies of history that, by propagating the words of Luther and his fellow 'reformers', the 'sacred art' (*sancta ars*) of printing (which Cusanus had wanted to bring from Germany) actually brought the barbarians back to Rome. The brief but brilliant world of Roman humanism was ruptured in May 1527 when Rome was sacked by German and Spanish troops of the emperor, Charles V. Palaces were ransacked, libraries destroyed, nuns raped, and a mob, baying beneath the walls of the Castel Sant'Angelo where Clement VII lay confined, swore their fidelity to 'Caesar' and cried *Vivat Lutherus pontifex!* ('Long live Pope Luther!').[100] Thousands died, humanists and ecclesiastics alike, including a priest murdered by Lutheran soldiers for refusing 'to administer Holy Communion to an ass'.[101]

Two prominent *sodales,* Johann Goritz (Coricius) and Andrea Marone (author of the commendatory verses to the *Hypnerotomachia*), died in the aftermath of the Sack. 'When the City was captured by the barbarians,' Valeriano tells us, '[Goritz] too was made captive by his fellow Germans' (*Capta a barbaris urbe, ipse quoque a Germanis suis captivus factus*).[102] Before the Sack, Marone was able to extemporize, by the thousand, 'erudite verses' (*carmina erudita*) which contained nothing 'muddy or unpolished' (*nil... lutulentum, inexpolitum*); but his death reads like a parodic apotheosis of the Poliphilian humanist: he remained in the city, 'held back by longing for his books and especially for his poems' (*librorum atque adeo poematum suorum desiderio detentus*). Jaundice left him looking 'paler than a gilded statue' (*inaurata pallidior statua videbatur*),[103] and he died, 'broken by such great

---

[99] *Luther's Works,* 55 vols. (St Louis: Concordia; Philadelphia: Fortress, 1958–86), xli. 263–376, at 280–1, 289–90, 344, 360–1, and 376. The translator, E. W. Gritsch, observes (261) that 'Luther's treatise was translated into Latin by Justus Jonas in Nov. 1545. Luther meant to edit the translation and send it to Trent, but was prevented from doing so by his illness; he died on February 18, 1546.'

[100] A. Chastel, *The Sack of Rome, 1527,* trans. B. Archer (Princeton: PUP, 1983), 106–7.

[101] C. Hibbert, *Rome: The Biography of a City* (Harmondsworth: Viking, 1985), 159. Chastel (*Sack of Rome,* 108) refers to the 'Feast of the Ass', citing a manuscript (now in the Biblioteca Angelica in Rome) mentioned by H. Schulz, *Der Sacco di Roma: Karls V. Truppen in Rom, 1527–1528* (Halle: Niemeyer, 1894), 71.

[102] This stands in ironic relation to Horace's encapsulation of the *translatio imperii et studii* in *Epistles* 2. 156–7: *Graecia capta ferum victorem cepit et artes intulit agresti Latio.*

[103] Cf. Poliphilo, G 77: 'with my voice and mind both paralysed, I remained half-dead, like a statue'.

evils' (*tantis malis fractus*), in 'a cheap little tavern' (*diobolari in tabernula*)—
the ultimate indignity for a hieratically minded humanist.[104]

Even among Luther's 'barbarian' followers, however, there was at least one
who was willing to engage with Apuleius, though the contrast with humanist
poets such as Curio Lancillotto Pasio could not be more marked. Close on the
heels of the first printing of a German translation of *The Golden Ass* (1538),
Hans Sachs (the cobbler-cum-*Meistersinger* of Nuremberg immortalized by
Richard Wagner) reduced the work to a simple 'parable' of sixty lines.[105]

> *Apuleius ein fabel*
> *schreipt zv einer parable,*
> *spricht: Als er in das lande*
> *thessalia genande*
> *kam in sein jungen jaren,*
> *zauberey zu erfaren,*
> *vnd thet in lieb hoffiren*
> *votis, einer haustiren,*
> *die in ains nachts lies schauen*
> *verwandlung irer frauen*
> *in ain grose nachtewlen,*
> *wie sie ausflueg mit hewlen.*

(Apuleius writes a story as a parable, saying: During his youth, he came into the
country of Thessaly to gain experience of magic. He wooed Fotis, a housemaid, who
one night allowed him to witness the transformation of her mistress into a large night-
owl which then flew out, screeching.)[106]

Sachs describes Fotis' unwitting confusion of ointments and Lucius' transformation, his sufferings at the hands of cruel fortune (*Ein jar durch ungluecks
gwalte | phielt er sein eselsgstalte*, 30–1), and his eventual restoration to human
form, not by divine intervention but by the eating of red roses. In the final
section (41–60), he draws the moral from the story:

---

[104] *DLI* 25; Gaisser, *Valeriano*, 186–7.

[105] Sachs (1494/7–1576) had celebrated Luther in his poem 'The Wittenberg Nightingale'
(1523). See *The Social History of the Reformation*, ed. L. P. Buck and J. W. Zophy (Columbus:
Ohio State UP, 1972), 23. Wagner's *Die Meistersinger* (1867) was used to open the Nazi Party
rallies at Nuremberg. See M. H. Kater, *The Twisted Muse: Musicians and their Music in the Third
Reich* (New York: OUP, 1997), 65.

[106] Meisterlied, *Der gulden esel* (8. 12. 1538), reprod. from Sächs. Landesbibl. Dresden, M 12,
56ᵛ–57ᵛ by Niklas Holzberg. I had the pleasure of hearing Prof. Holzberg perform Sachs's song
in Groningen at ICAN 2000. See his 'Staging the Fringe before Shakespeare: Hans Sachs and the
Ancient Novel', in *The Ancient Novel and Beyond*, ed. S. Panayotakis, M. Zimmerman, and
W. Keulen (Leiden: Brill, 2003), 393–400. Sachs produced many versions of classical subjects.
I am grateful to Dr Donata Kick for providing a working English translation of Sachs's song and
to Dr Barbara Ravelhofer for additional comments.

Der esel ist zv gleichen
den armen vnd den reichen,
die ir puelerey treiben
mit maiden vnd eweiben,
sint mutig, gail vnd gögel,
duncken sich frey nachtfögel
Wen sie sich recht thund schawen,
sint sie durch ir falsch frawen
paide an haut vnd hare
an sin vnd witzen gare
zv lauter esel worden
im puelerischen orden.
Da tragens haimlich leiden,
eyffern, senen vnd meiden,
menschlicher zucht vergessen,
pis das sie rosen essen
getrewer straff vnd lere.
Wer sich daran nicht kere,
der pleib mit andern pueben
ein esel pis int grueben.

(Such asses resemble the rich and the poor who commit indecency with virgins and wives and are lascivious, gay, and merry, thinking themselves free as the birds of the night. All of a sudden, they find that, by the fault of their false women, and by themselves lacking sense and wit, they all become asses, both skin and hair, in the vast crowd of adulterers. They bear secret passions, jealousies, desires, and secrecies, forgetting human moral behaviour until they eat roses, according to true punishment and teachings. Whoever doesn't pay attention to this, remains, along with other scoundrels, an ass until the grave.)

THE WARS OF IMITATION: CICERONIANISM, ECLECTICISM, AND APULEIANISM

Humanism in Rome was never quite the same again after the Sack of 1527. But the repercussions of the so-called 'Reformation' were felt throughout Italy. The pagan/Christian synthesis becomes less elastic as the movements later identified as the 'Counter-Reformation' gather force. Attitudes towards Apuleius and his *Ass* certainly become more polarized as humanism at Rome is increasingly identified with Ciceronianism.[107]

---

[107] See generally Gouwens, 'Ciceronianism and Collective Identity'; Rowland, 'Revenge', 308.

Lorenzo Valla (1407–57) had courted controversy early in his career through his advocacy of Quintilian.[108] Nevertheless, his *Elegantiae linguae Latinae* became a standard handbook of Latin style for over a century.[109] Antonio da Rho had dared to criticize the *Elegantiae*, and in his response (*In errores Antonii Raudensis adnotationes*), Valla made a passing reference to Apuleius which seems almost prophetic.[110] He derided da Rho for relying on Aulus Gellius, 'a man who spoke too elaborately and superstitiously' (*hominem curiose nimis, ac superstitiose loquentem*); but he then asked: 'what shall I say about Apuleius, especially in the work entitled *The Golden Ass*? If anyone were to imitate his style, he would seem not so much to be speaking goldenly as actually braying' (*quid dicam de Apuleio in eo præsertim opere, cuius nomen est de Asino aureo? cuius sermonem, si quis imitetur, non tam aureæ loqui, quam nonnihil rudere uideatur*).[111]

From Bussi to Beroaldo, Italian humanists seemed willing to 'bray', indeed, to 'bray goldenly'. In the cinquecento, however, Apuleius is cast as the *bête noire* of Latin purists: before the emergence of the Senecan and Tacitean stylistic schools at the end of the century, Apuleianism constituted the main rival of Ciceronianism. The paradox which twists the parameters of the whole debate is that while Tacitus' style, with its pointedness and asymmetry, is a conscious reaction *against* the balanced Ciceronian period, the florid extravagances of Apuleius can be seen as an extreme manifestation of the Asiatic rhetoric of which Cicero (in his 'copious' mode) was also a practitioner. The distinction between *copia* and *redundantia* will often be a subjective one.[112]

In a seminal essay, 'The Progress of Renaissance Latin Prose Style: The Case of Apuleianism', John F. D'Amico has described 'the creation of three distinct schools of imitation at the end of the Quattrocento and the beginning of the Cinquecento': eclecticism (or 'Quintilianism', which favoured 'Golden Age' Latin as the standard, but permitted non-Ciceronian words and neologisms where changing circumstances demanded them); Ciceronianism (the strictest form of imitation); and Apuleianism (the archaizing school).[113] These are

[108] Prete, 'La questione della lingua latina', 125–6.

[109] Erasmus wrote a précis of it in about 1488: *Paraphrasis seu potius epitome in elegantiarum libros Laurentii Vallae*. See P. G. Bietenholz, *Contemporaries of Erasmus*, 3 vols. (Toronto: U of Toronto P, 1985–7), iii. 372.

[110] On the dispute, see M. Regoliosi, 'Umanesimo lombardo: La polemica tra Lorenzo Valla e Antonio da Rho', in *Studi di lingua e letteratura lombarda offerti a Maurizio Vitale*, 2 vols. (Pisa: Giardini, 1983), i. 170–9.

[111] *Laurentii Vallæ elegantiarum libri sex. Item Adnotationes in Antonium Raudensem* (Strasbourg: Hulderichus Morhadus, 1521), fol. cxlvi[r].

[112] Gabriel Harvey draws just such a distinction in his comparison between Osirius and Cicero. See J. W. Binns, *Intellectual Culture in Elizabethan and Jacobean England: The Latin Writings of the Age* (Leeds: Francis Cairns, 1990), 275.

[113] *RQ* 37 (1984), 351–92, at 354.

certainly useful working categories, but the reality was more fluid and the debate cannot be reduced to a simple polarity between radical Apuleians and reactionary Ciceronians, with the advocates of eclecticism seated uncomfortably in the middle. Some of the most dismissive comments about Apuleius, Beroaldo, and the archaizers are made by the eclectics, who are themselves subjected to the vituperations of the Ciceronians. Moreover, individuals were capable of changing sides or holding seemingly contradictory positions. This was an age of lexical hypersensitivity in which Ciceronianism and Apuleianism can be seen as opposite sides of the same coin: each 'school' demands a detailed knowledge of the full range of Latin lexis. Ciceronians need to know which verbal 'rocks' (*scopuli*) to avoid if they are not to suffer shipwreck on the dangerous seas of language.[114] And to be a good Apuleian, one really needs to have mastered the arts of Cicero first. Paolo Cortesi (1465–1510) was such a linguistic purist that he translated a scholastic 'classic', the *Sentences* of Peter Lombard, into Ciceronian Latin.[115] By the time of his death, however, his tastes had broadened significantly. In a dedicatory epistle to the posthumously published *De cardinalatu* (Castrum Cortesium: Symeon Nardi, 1510), one of the editors, Raffaele Maffei of Volterra, describes him as 'eager to fish out new and almost Apuleian words' (*verba... nova ac fere Apuleiana expiscari curiosus*).[116] For D'Amico, Cortesi's renunciation of strict Ciceronianism and his embrace of Apuleian diction constitute not so much an act of tergiversation as an organic progression. But, in an earlier letter from Maffei (to Cortesi himself), we see even more clearly what was at stake for humanists. Maffei distinguishes between three classes of vocabulary in the *De cardinalatu:* familiar words (*satis trita*); 'somewhat obscure words which are nonetheless easily understood through dictionaries, which are in plentiful supply' (*recondita magis, attamen in lexicis, quorum magna est copia cognitu facilia*); and a 'third kind' which is 'entirely Apuleian and your own' and requires a mighty 'interpreter, without whom all the oracles and soothsayers celebrated by the ancients... could not have penetrated' the meaning (*Tertium genus Apuleianum totum ac tuum est, quod tantum interpretem requirebat, quo sine nec oracula cuncta aut mantea veteribus celebrata... penetrassent*).[117]

---

[114] See Schott's claim (*infra*) that Beroaldo, having produced good work on Cicero's *Tusculan Disputations*, then 'wrecked his ship' on 'the rock of Apuleius'. Cf. Accursio's subtitle to *Osci et Volsci*, describing archaic Latin words as needing 'to be avoided like rocks' (*tanquam scopulos esse fugienda*), and Erasmus' letter, attributing the rock simile to Octavian.

[115] Rowland, *Culture*, 201. In 'A Hitherto Unknown Portrait of a Well-Known Renaissance Humanist', *RQ* 43 (1990), 146–54, S. Poeschel has identified Cortesi as the young man who has usurped Cicero's position as the representative of Rhetoric in Pinturicchio's Sala delle Arti Liberali (Borgia Apartment, Vatican Palace, 1492–4).

[116] Latin text quoted by D'Amico, 'Progress', 374 n. 82.

[117] Ibid.

In some cases, one suspects that the humanists of the cinquecento are rewriting their own history. In the closing speech of Pierio Valeriano's *Dialogo della volgar lingua* (wr. 1516 or 1524; pr. 1620), 'Trissino' gives a heroicized account of the recent struggles over linguistic models:

> ... *alcuni si pensarono che 'l suo più bel fiore fosse lo stil Apuleiano, forse perch'era manco intelligibile, e così n'empirono tanti scartafacci, finché 'l Pontano, il Sabellico, il Bembo, il Sadoleto et alquanti altri galantomini comparsero, e con politissimo stil Romano cacciati d'Italia questi mostri, rimessero la lingua nella sua natural bellezza e purità.*[118]

(... some men reckoned that the Apuleian style was the more beautiful flower for them, perhaps because it was less intelligible, and so they filled up so much waste paper until Pontano, Sabellico, Bembo, Sadoleto and some other men of honour appeared, and, with the most polished Roman style, drove these monsters out of Italy, returning the language to its natural beauty and purity.)

Notions of *copia* in a negative sense (reams of waste paper) converge with those of metamorphosis ('monsters') and an ultimate return to the original state.

Valeriano makes many references to *The Golden Ass* in his *Hieroglyphica*, and he knew Sabellico well enough to change his own name at the latter's behest,[119] but the final speaker in his dialogue is unaware of (or has chosen to forget) Sabellico's interest in Apuleius, or the fact that even Pietro Bembo— the Arch-Ciceronian—had composed a collation of Apuleius in his youth.[120] Pietro's father, Bernardo Bembo ('Patrician of Venice'), owned a manuscript (E) of the *Metamorphoses* and the *Florida*, written in Italy in the fifteenth century.[121] According to M. R. James, the 'interest of this book consists in a number of pen and ink drawings by an Italian artist ... of very high artistic value'. These drawings, forty-nine in number, include illustrations of Fotis and Lucius kissing, Fotis bedecking Lucius with roses as he lies in bed, and

---

[118] *Dialogo della volgar lingua ... Non prima uscito in luce* (Venice: Battista Ciotti, 1620), 51–2. Quoted by P. Floriani, 'La "Questione della Lingua" e il "Dialogo" di P. Valeriano', *GSLI* 155 (1978), 321–45, at 343. For a modern edn., see *Discussioni linguistiche del Cinquecento*, ed. M. Pozzi (Turin: Unione tipografico-editrice torinese, 1988), 39–93, at 93.

[119] Gaisser, *Valeriano*, 281.

[120] C. Vecce, 'Bembo e gli antichi: Dalla filologia ai classici moderni', in *'Prose della volgar lingua' di Pietro Bembo: Gargnano del Garda (4–7 ottobre 2000)*, ed. S. Morgana, M. Piotti, and M. Prada (Milan: Cisalpino: Istituto editoriale universitario, 2000), 9–22, at 15.

[121] Eton College 147. Bernardo's inscription appears at fol. 122ᵛ: *Codex Bernardi Bembi patricii Veneti*. M. R. James notes that 'The MS was no doubt given to the College by Sir Henry Wotton.' Wotton had been the Ambassador at Venice and the bequest that he made to Eton (where he was Provost) in 1639 appears largely to have comprised items obtained from the collection of Bernardo the Younger, the son of Pietro Bembo. See *A Descriptive Catalogue of the Manuscripts in the Library of Eton College* (Cambridge: CUP, 1895), 76. Bernardo Bembo (b. 1433) was educated at the University of Padua, was in Rome in 1455, and returned to Venice in July 1499. He was the father (and teacher) of Pietro Bembo (1470–1547)—the correspondent of Marsilio Ficino. See *DBI* viii (1966), 103–11 and 133–50.

Fotis and Lucius lying in bed together.[122] Pietro was evidently well enough disposed towards his father's manuscript of Apuleius to hand it on to his own son, Bernardo Bembo the Younger.

In reality (at least in the quattrocento), the demarcations between different 'schools' of imitation were never so clearly drawn. Valeriano was associated with Beroaldo's nephew, Filippo Beroaldo the Younger, who, around 1503, had moved from Bologna to Rome where he served as secretary to Adriano Castellesi (1461?–1521?).[123] Yet, despite enjoying warm relations with his uncle and former teacher, the younger Beroaldo established his reputation as an eminent Ciceronian. In 1515, Castellesi's treatise *De sermone Latino* was published at Rome.[124] Castellesi begins by setting the context for his work—a discussion at Bologna where he discovers that the leading intellectuals of that university have been infected with the disease of Apuleianism:

Cum Bononiæ Viri me aliquot eruditi | officii causa conuenisset | commentaremurque inter nos (ut fit inter literarum studiosos) de Latini [II^v] sermonis elegantia | audiremque eorum plerosque Apuleii | Sidonii | Capellæ | Fulgentii | non tam uerbis | quam fœtoribus scaturire | uerbaque de industria promere aliorum etiam Autorum | quæ aut obsoleta nimis | aut noua | & omnino barbara uiderentur | multaque ego libere (ut soleo) contra eorum sermonis insolentiam (non sine stomacho) protulissem:[125]

(When I was at Bologna, several learned men gathered around me to pay their respects and we began to deliberate amongst ourselves—as happens with enthusiasts for literature—about the elegance of the Latin language. And I heard a great many of them gushing forth not so much with the words, as with the foul stenches, of Apuleius, Sidonius Apollinaris, Martianus Capella, and Fulgentius, and bringing to light, with great pains, words of other authors as well, which seemed either too worn out or too new, and altogether barbarous. And I—not without distaste—proffered, with my customary frankness, a good many words against the affectedness of their speech.)

In our last chapter, we noted Bussi's vision of printed texts 'stream[ing] forth and spread[ing] through the world in an abundant flood' (*scaturire et per omnem orbem uberrimo fonte diffluere*). Castellesi is here using *scaturire* (a word with sound Apuleian credentials) to describe an altogether fouler flood,

---

[122] Bernardo himself preferred to conduct a platonic affair with Ginevra de'Benci, and his departure from Venice has been thought, by some, to have caused the wanness of Ginevra's smile in Leonardo da Vinci's earliest surviving portrait, *c.*1474 (National Gallery of Art in Washington, DC). See M. D. Garrard, 'Leonardo da Vinci: Female Portraits, Female Nature', in *The Expanding Discourse: Feminism and Art History*, ed. N. Broude and M. D. Garrard (New York: IconEditions, 1992), 58–86.

[123] Gaisser, *Valeriano*, 267.

[124] *De sermone Latino, et modis Latine loquendi* (Rome: Marcellus Silber, 1515).

[125] fol. II^{r-v}. *Insolentia* can convey the senses both of 'unusualness' and of 'arrogance'—another example of the semantic multivalence which characterizes the diction of debates on Latin prose-style.

the 'stenches' and 'dregs' of a decayed Latinity.[126] And, for purposes of attack, he chooses to read only the surface of Apuleius' multi-layered prologue:

+ *Apuleius autem quem nostri temporis magis curiosi* | *quam eruditi sequi* | *& æmulari student* | *in principio operis sui* | *Latinas literas ignorare fatetur: In Vrbe inquit Latia aduena studiorum Quiritum indigenam sermonem erumnali labore nullo Magistro præeunte aggressus excolui* + *En ecce præfamur ueniam* | *si quid exotici* | *ac forensis sermonis rudis locutor offendero* | *iam hæc quidem ipsa uocis immutatio desultoriæ scientiæ stilo quem accesimus respondet* + *Quis rogo te ferat non tam Apuleium* | *qui vt mali ædificii dominus se Architectum non adhibuisse* | *ita literas sine Præceptore coluisse gloriatur* | *quam aliquos esse* | *qui malint fœtores* | *& quisquilias eius colligere* | *quam uerborum floribus perfectissimæ ætatis* | *quam signauimus* | *inhærere? Sed quod alii Apuleio similes insequentium ætatum Autores de seipsis* | *& tporum suorum inscitia balbutiant uideamus.*[127]

(But Apuleius, whom the elaborate rather than the erudite of our time are keen to follow and emulate, admits, at the beginning of his work, to being ignorant of Latin: 'In Rome,' he says, 'as a stranger to the learning of the Romans, I cultivated the native language, applying myself to it with wretched toil without any teacher leading the way. Lo and behold, we ask for pardon if I, the rude speaker of this foreign and marketplace language, should happen to give any offence. Now indeed, this change of tone which we have undertaken corresponds in style to the skill of the circus-vaulter.'[128] Who, I ask you, would not hold both Apuleius (who thus boasts—as the master of a badly-built house might boast of not having employed an architect—of tending to his letters without a guide) and some others to be those who, rather than sticking to the verbal bouquets of that most perfect age which we have described, prefer to collect its stenches and dregs? But let us see what other authors, similar to Apuleius, in subsequent ages, stammer about themselves and the ignorance of their times.)

Erasmus and the Ciceronians

Castellesi had been appointed papal nuncio to Henry VII of England in 1490. He was, in Cosenza's phrase, 'a great favourite' of the king, becoming bishop of Hereford and (from 1504 to 1518) bishop of Bath and Wells.[129] Another

---

[126] Matteo Maria Bandello appears to be referring to this passage in his dedicatory letter to Marco Antonio Sabino. See *Matthaei Bandelli Opera latina inedita vel rara*, ed. C. Godi (Padua: Antenore, 1983), 63. Quoted by Fumagalli, *Boiardo*, 98.

[127] *De sermone Latino*, fol. V[r]. Cf. the third fragment in the so-called 'False Preface' to the *De deo Socratis* (s. 108), where Apuleius compares his extempore speechifying to the haphazard building of a rough stone wall.

[128] *OLD*, s.v. *desultor*: 'A rider in the circus who jumped from one horse to another.' We might note that Pio described his exposition (written for Isabella d'Este) of the *Tabula Cebetis* as an *interpretatio desultoria*—perhaps in homage to Apuleius' approach: *Cebetis Tabulae interpretatio desultoria Pii.* See D'Amico, 'Progress', 362 n. 36.

[129] For most, if not all, of this time, however, Castellesi (Hadrianus Castellensis or Cornetanus) held his bishoprics *in absentia*. See Cosenza, *BBDIH* v. 890; *DBI* xxi. 665–71. He first visited

humanist who enjoyed warm relations with the Tudor court was Desiderius Erasmus, but his attitude towards Apuleius was rather more ambivalent. The first authorized edition of the *De copia* appeared in Paris in 1512. Dedicated to John Colet and his new school, St Paul's, it became one of the most famous and popular educational treatises of the sixteenth century. At the beginning of the *De copia* (1. 9), Erasmus holds up Apuleius as a model of the rich style, to be observed and emulated:

Praecipuam autem vtilitatem adferet, si bonos auctores nocturna diurnaque manu versabimus, potissimum hos, qui copia dicendi praecelluerunt: cuiusmodi sunt Cicero, A. Gellius, Apuleius, atque in his vigilantibus oculis figuras omneis obseruemus, obseruatas memoria recondamus, reconditas imitemur, crebraque vsurpatione consuescamus habere in promptu. (Erasmus, *Opera omnia*, I–6, p. 34)

(But it will be of especial advantage if, night and day, we turn over in our hand the good authors, most of all, those who excel in the copiousness of their speech—of such a kind are Cicero, Aulus Gellius, and Apuleius. And with ever-wakeful eyes, we should observe all their figures of speech; having observed them we should store them in the memory; having stored them, we should imitate them; and, by frequent employment, we should become accustomed to having them at the ready.)

The injunction to thumb Cicero, Aulus Gellius, and Apuleius 'night and day' is nicely edged—Erasmus is himself imitating a passage in the *Ars poetica* (268–9) where Horace criticizes the unmusical verses of Ennius and enjoins his readers to 'turn over the Greek models in your hand by night, turn them over by day' (*vos exemplaria Graeca | nocturna versate manu, versate diurna*). It is a neat irony that the Horatian formula should be employed in endorsing two such un-Horatian writers as Gellius and Apuleius, Gellius (an affecter of archaism) being an avowed admirer of Ennius. The coupling of the 'Father of Eloquence' with the exemplars of 'degenerate Latinity' is nevertheless remarkable, especially in a textbook composed for the use of impressionable pupils in a model school designed by a high-minded educationalist like Dean Colet.

In Book 2 of the *De copia*, Erasmus twice praises Apuleius' description of Hippias in the *Florida* and cites, as an imitative model in his chapter on place-description (*Loci descriptio*), the palace in Book 5 of *The Golden Ass* (*Regia Psyches apud Apuleium*).[130] Erasmus' comments in other and later works,

England in 1488 and was employed by Henry VII as his agent in Rome. While in England in 1490, he was appointed collector of the papal tribute called 'Peter pence'. On 10 May 1492, Henry VII 'granted him the prebend of Ealdland in St Paul's Cathedral and a week later Cardinal Morton presented him to St Dunstan-in-the-East'. He returned to Rome in 1492 as Henry VII's ambassador, and in 1504, he was enthroned by proxy in the bishopric of Bath and Wells, his proxy being his kinsman Polydore Vergil. See T. F. Mayer, 'Castellesi, Adriano (*c.*1461–1521)', *ODNB*. Vergil had come to England (probably at Castellesi's instigation) in 1501 or 1502 and was naturalized in 1510.

[130] *Opera omnia*, i. 6, 198, 208 (Hippias), 214 (Psyche's Palace).

however, appear to support D'Amico's claim that he 'developed a critical attitude toward both Apuleius and Aulus Gellius as stylists and in this he seems to have been influenced by his reading of Lorenzo Valla'.[131] Yet such an analysis is oversimplistic. Erasmus made many changes to the *De copia* over the years, but the final authorized edition (that of Froben published at Basel in 1534, two years before the author's death) contains the same praise of Apuleius as the first, the same exhortations to read and imitate him. His response to Cicero and Apuleius is almost as ambivalent as his reaction to the early upheavals of the Reformation. The evidence suggests that Erasmus' quarrel was not with Apuleius himself, but with those who slavishly imitated him by darkening their Latin prose-style with affected archaism and deliberate obscurantism. Writing to Guillaume Budé in 1517, he expresses his disdain for the two extremes of imitation—slavish Ciceronianism and affected Apuleianism:

Inter tot scriptorum species nullos minus fero [471] *quam istos quosdam Ciceronis simios, a quo genere non ita multum mihi videtur Pontanus; nam Apuleianos* τερατολόγους *et pueri rident.*[132]

(Amongst so many sorts of writers, I tolerate none less than those apes of Cicero, from which category Pontano does not seem to me to be far removed; for even children laugh at those Apuleian marvel-mongers.)

In 1521, Budé's disciple Nicolas Bérault of Orléans (*c.*1470–*c.*1545) attacked the archaizing school in his preface to Valla's *Elegantiae*:

Porro cum idem moneat, optimum ac candissimum quenque & statim & semper esse legendum, mirum cur nonnulli, ex eijs etiam qui uulgo docti ac eloquentes, sibi doctissimi eloquentissimique uidentur, Apuleium, Apollinarem, Sidonium, Gellium, aliosque innumeros, Ciceroni, Sallustio, Liuio, Columellæ, Fabio, tot iam annos ita proposuerint, ut hos nunquam attingunt, illos semper habeant in manibus, euoluant, mirentur, ediscant. Ex eis cum quidam mihi familiariter amicus, sed præposteris literis imbutus, ad me consilij gratia uenisset, rogassetque, ecquem potissimum sibi putarem legendum, qui ad latini sermonis splendorem, & copiam non parum conduceret, egoque Ciceronem unum id optime præstare dixissem, Cicero, inquit ille, [A2ᵛ] *mihi frigere uidetur præ Apuleio, ac Gellio. Nam quæ apud Ciceronem leguntur omnia, inquit, peruulgata sunt ac quotidiana. Gellius uero, reconditis uulgoque ignotis uocibus ludit, arridet, titillat, Cicero eadem toties repetens ac inculcans, ut citharædus chorda, qui semper oberrat eadem, non sine molestia legitur.*[133]

[131] D'Amico, 'Progress', 379 n. 99. D'Amico quotes J. Chomarat, 'Erasme lecteur des *Elegantiae* de Valla', in *Acta Conventus Neo-Latini Amstelodamensis*, ed. P. Tuynman et al. (Munich: Fink, 1979), 206–43, at 241–2 n. 107.

[132] *Opus epistolarum*, ed. P. S. Allen, ii, Letter 531, pp. 470–1.

[133] *Elegantiarum libri sex*, sig. A2ʳ⁻ᵛ.

(Moreover, when the same man advises that each [writer] should be read immediately and for evermore as the best and most dazzling, is it a wonder that several of those who seem learned and eloquent to the masses—and most learned and most eloquent to themselves—should for so many years now have preferred Apuleius, Sidonius Apollinaris, Gellius, and countless others to Cicero, Sallust, Livy, Columella, Fabius? As a result, they never touch the latter, but always have the former in their hands: they turn them over; they admire them; they learn them by heart. When one of these—an intimate friend of mine but infected with this perverted literature—came to me for advice and asked me whom, above all, I most thought he should read as contributing in no small way to the splendour and copiousness of one's Latin speech, and I said that Cicero, alone, provided that best, he said: 'To me, Cicero seems frigid compared with Apuleius and Aulus Gellius. For all the words that are read in Cicero', he said, 'are overcommon and everyday. But Gellius—he sports, he amuses, he titillates with words that are obscure and concealed from the masses. Cicero, returning to the same words so many times and stuffing them in, like a lute-player who always blunders on the same string, is not read without disgust.')[134]

This sardonic account seems to have met with Erasmus' approval, for in the following year he dedicated to Bérault his *De conscribendis epistolis*, quoting a tag on the importance of avoiding the 'unusual word' (*verbum insolens*) in one's speech and endorsing the deriding of 'certain Apuleians' of his own age, and those who affect an obsolete archaic style (*Et merito ridentur hoc nostro seculo quiddam Apulejani, & obsoletæ antiquitatis affectatores*).[135]

In his *Dialogus de pronunciatione* (1528), Erasmus alludes, in the voices of the Lion and the Bear, to the proclivities of the archaizers:

LE. . . . *Sunt & qui suum quoddam scripturae affectant, ita scri*[926]*bentes Latina, ut parum exercitato Graeca videri possint.*
UR. *Ridendos mihi narras, non imitandos, nisi forte placent Apuleji & Isidonii* [sic], *aut, ut recentiores attingam, Baptistae Pii; qui quum suppetant probata, splendida, accommodaque vocabula, tamen confictis impudenter novis malunt suo more loqui, perinde quasi nihil possit esse praeclarum quod sit usitatum.*[136]

(LION: And there are those who affect an individual script, writing Latin in such a way that they can seem, to the untrained eye, to be writing in Greek.

---

[134] For the reference to the lyre-player clanging on the same string, see Horace, *Ars poetica* 355–6.

[135] *De conscribendis epistolis, cap. IV: De perspicuitate epistolæ*, in *Opera omnia*, i. 347. For the dedication (to Nicolaus Beraldus Aurelius), see Bietenholz, i. 126; *CWE* ix, Ep. 1284. Erasmus, once again, is cautious about committing himself too strongly to any particular position: *Mihi* [348] *non displicet illud Octavii Cæsaris, non aliter in sermone fugiendum verbum insolens quam in cursu scopulum* ('I am not dissatisfied with that saying of Octavius Caesar's, that the unusual word is to be avoided in speech, as a rock is in a voyage').

[136] *Opera omnia*, i. 925–6.

BEAR: You are telling me of men who should be laughed at, not imitated, unless, perhaps, one likes those Apuleiuses and Sidoniuses or, to mention more recent ones, the Battista Pios who, when well-tried, noble, and appropriate words are available, nevertheless prefer to speak in their own way, shamefully coining new words, as though nothing could be splendid which was familiar.)

The most famous and controversial work to emerge from the debate over style is Erasmus' *Ciceronianus*, a dialogue between Nosoponus and Bulephorus published in 1528. In Nosoponus, Erasmus was seen to be caricaturing, in general, the extreme Ciceronians (who were mainly Italian) and, in particular, Christopher Longolius (Longueil)—the brilliant young Belgian scholar who had died in Reginald Pole's arms, exhausted by his pursuit of Ciceronian purity. In the course of the dialogue, Bulephorus (a vehicle, apparently, for some of Erasmus' own views) succeeds (with the help of a friend) in liberating Nosoponus from his harsh Ciceronian fetters. Here, however, they consider the merits of Apuleius' works in relation to Cicero's:

B. *Sed heus,* Apuleius *nobis præteritus est.* N. *Hunc Ciceroni conferam, quum libebit, graculum comparare luscinie.* B. *Sit sane, in* Asino *& Floridis, at in Apologiis accedit.* N. *Minus quidem abest,* [106] *sed immenso sequitur intervallo. Cæterum &* Martianum Capellam *oblitus, si tales libet proferre.*[137]

(BULEPHORUS: But look—we've left out Apuleius.

NOSOPONUS: I shall compare him with Cicero, when I'm willing to compare a jackdaw with a nightingale.

BULEPHORUS: That may well be the case in *The Golden Ass* and the *Florida,* but in the *Apology* he comes close.

NOSOPONUS: Certainly, he is less far away, but he's separated by an immense distance. But you've forgotten Martianus Capella, if you're going to produce such writers.)

The impact of Erasmus' *Ciceronianus* (the same name is used by several polemicists in the sixteenth century for their own treatises on the subject) was immense and lasting, and the reaction to it, often virulent.[138] In 1534, Bérault was provoked to shed his Ciceronian toga and assume the more variegated mantle of an Erasmian eclectic with a dialogue (which owes much to Erasmus' *Ciceronianus*) caricaturing the slavish imitation demanded by Ciceronianism.[139] But Étienne Dolet (Stephanus Doletus) responded to the original

---

[137] Erasmus, *Dialogus, cui titulus Ciceronianus: siue de optimo genere dicendi* (Neustadt an der Haardt: Henricus Starckius, 1617), 105–6.

[138] See G. W. Pigman III, 'Imitation and the Renaissance Sense of the Past': The Reception of Erasmus' *Ciceronianus*', *JMRS* 92 (1979), 155–77.

[139] See *Nicolai Beraldi Aurelii dialogus: quo rationes quædam explicantur, quibus dicendi ex tempore facultas parari potest: deque ipsa dicendi ex tempore facultate: ad reuerendiss<imum>. Cardinalem Oddonem Castelioensem, tituli diuorum Sergij, Bacchi, Apuleij uirum utriusque linguæ peritissimum* (Lyons: Seb. Gryphius, 1534); and Pigman, 'Imitation', 162.

attack on Longolius with his *Dialogus de imitatione Ciceroniana aduersus Desiderium Erasmum Roterodamum, pro Christopher Longolio* (1535). One of the interlocutors, Villanovus, describes Erasmus as being Apuleian in style and Lucianic in content. 'What sort of mask', he asks, 'has Erasmus adopted in his writings?' He answers his own question:

Duplici ea quidem, & utraque deformi atque horrida, neque inter doctos satis tolerabili, verborum personam (da nos ita loqui posse, licet asperè & nouè) Horatij Hemistichijs Apulei impuris uocibus, Beroaldi adagijs sibi ipse confecit, tandem post inanes labores in eum modum stilo inquinatus, quo leprosi facies, maculis tum marcentibus, tum pallentibus & sanie immundas plenis, turpiter misereqúe fœdata. sentientiarum Laruam (hic etiam uerbi ueniam à te peto) unde nisi à Luciano assumspit, autore omnium ma-
[90]*ximè dicaci & conuitioso, religionis experti, dei ignaro, & ad omnia tum sacra, tum profana ridenda proiecto . . .*[140]

(A double one, indeed, and doubly misshapen and ugly, not to be tolerated among learned men. He has forged for himself a verbal persona—if this expression is permissible, although novel and inelegant—out of Horatian rags, filthy language from Apuleius, and the adages of Beroaldus; and after long and worthless labours his style has become impure like the face of a leper, repulsive and wretchedly disfigured with pallid, rotten sores full of foul matter. And where has he got his *sententia*-mask from—here again I beg you to excuse the expression [sc. *sententiarum Larvam*]—if not from Lucian, that most scurrilous and immoral of all authors, an expert on religion but ignorant of God and inclined to laugh at all things, both sacred and divine)[141]

Having lambasted Erasmus and More, Dolet turned his attentions in 1540 to Francesco Florido (1511–47) who underlines the fact that an Erasmian-style eclectic could still be an avowed anti-Apuleian.[142] As late as 1539, Florido was lamenting the legacy of Beroaldo, who 'was held in great esteem when he was alive, not only by the Italians, but also by foreign nations, and was preferred, by the general consensus of the ignorant masses, not only to mediocre men of letters, but to those most excellent heroes, Angelo Poliziano, Giovanni Pico, Ermolao Barbaro, and Rudolf Agricola'. So pervasive and pernicious was his influence (his readers were 'emptied of any desire' to read other authors' writings) that

he seemed to have wanted not to cultivate the Latin language, but either to extinguish or destroy it completely. Since he was indeed the first, in his own times, to stimulate

---

[140] Latin text from *L'Erasmianus siue Ciceronianus d'Étienne Dolet (1535)*, facs. edn., ed. E. V. Telle (Geneva: Droz, 1974), 89–90.

[141] English trans. (slightly adapted) from T. Cave, *The Cornucopian Text* (Oxford: Clarendon, 1979), 49–50.

[142] *Stephani Doleti Galli Aurelii liber de imitatione Ciceroniana aduersus Floridum Sabinum* (Leiden: Étienne Dolet, 1540).

that utterly corrupt form of writing from Apuleius, Martianus Capella, and Sidonius Apollinaris and those who are rather uncultivated and so spread it into many parts of Europe—from which listeners flocked around him on all sides—that many vestiges survive even now and could not be completely effaced unless either all those whom he taught were to leave the land of the living, or, by Senatorial edict, a ban were to be placed on selling his works in public.[143]

Beroaldo's archaizing influence was most visible in his 'disciple' Giovanni Battista Pio. The account given by Paolo Giovio (1483–1552) acknowledeges Pio's talents while lamenting their misuse:

Non erit vllo seculo, agrestibus præsertim grammaticis in gratum Pij nomen, vrbanis autem & elegantibus viris nunquam iniucundum. robusto enim ingenio, tenacique memoria præualidus, doctissimi famam meruit, quum obscuros authores interpretandos suscepisset, inepta quidem Beroaldi præceptoris æmulatione, cuius in Asinum Apuleij commentationes exierant. in ijs fuêre Fulgentius, Sidonius, & e poetis Plautus, Lucretius, & Valerius Flaccus. Exoleta [188] *enim rancidæ vetustatis vocabula delectu insano sectabatur, admirante quidem discipulorum inscia turba, quum planè à non insulsissimis rideretur.*[144]

(In no age will the name of Pio be disagreeable, especially to boorish grammarians, but to cultured and refined men, it will never be unpleasant. Powerful in his strength of intellect and retentive memory, he earned his reputation of being deeply learned, when he undertook—in foolish emulation, admittedly, of his teacher, Beroaldo, whose commentaries on the *Ass* of Apuleius had come out—the explication of obscure authors. Amongst these were Fulgentius, Sidonius, and the poets, Plautus, Lucretius, and Valerius Flaccus. Indeed, with an insane delight, he used to hunt out the obsolete words of rank antiquity, to the admiration of an ignorant crowd of disciples, when he was simply laughed at by all but the most foolish.)

---

[143] *Philippus Beroaldus . . . in magno dum viueret honore, non ab Italis modo, verum ab exteris quoque nationibus habitus, neque mediocribus solum literatis, sed excellentissimis illis heroibus Angelo Politiano, Ioanni Pico, Hermolao Barbaro, Rodulphoque Agricolæ, communi imperitæ multitudinis consensu prælatus . . . Quæ enim ab ipso auctore ad fastidium vsque vbique commendata, non pauci admirabantur, ea tam sinistre ab iis, qui omni affectu vacui aliorum scripta & legere, & diligenter excurere solent, accepta fuerunt, vt Latinam linguam non excolere, sed vel exstinguere, vel prorsus labefactare voluisse videatur. Siquidem vitiosissimum scribendi genus ex Apuleio, Martiano, Sidonio, & iis qui sunt duriores, primus suis temporibus excitauit & in multas Europæ partes, a quibus vndique ad eum confluebant auditores, ita diffudit, vt plurima adhuc super sint eius vestigia, neque penitus deleri possint, nisi aut quotquot ille instituit, inter vivos esse desinant, aut principium edicto, ne qua illius opera publice væneant caueatur.* See *Francisci Floridi succesiuarum lectionum libri III* (Basel, 1539). Quotation here is taken from Jan Gruter's *Lampas, siue fax artium liberalium, hoc est thesaurus criticus, etc.*, vol. i (Frankfurt: Jonas Rhodius, 1602), containing *Francisci Floridi Sabini lectionum subcisiuarum*, 2. 9 (*De Philippi Beroaldi in Seruium annotationibus*), 1121.

[144] *Elogia virorum literis illustrium* (Basle: Peter Perna, 1577), 187–8. The phrasing is slightly different in the Basle edn. of 1527: *Quaesebat rancidae vetustatis vocabula iam plane repudiata a sanis scriptoribus* (102). See R. Sabbadini, *Storia del Ciceronianismo e di altre questioni letterarie nell'età della rinascenza* (Turin: Loescher, 1886), 43.

Giovio echoes Castellesi with his notion of 'rank antiquity'. *Rancidus* suggests not merely moral corruption but corporeal decomposition, and it provides an implicit criticism of the archaeological humanism which was so prevalent in Leto's circle and so manifest in the *Hypnerotomachia*. We see here the conflicting views as to which words should form part of a living (but, necessarily, resurrected) Latin language. The discovery, in April 1485, of the body of a girl—perfectly preserved in 'a coating of aromatic paste' in a tomb on the Via Appia—has been hailed by historians such as Burckhardt as one of the defining moments in the Renaissance.[145] Thousands flocked to see the prodigy, not least because, as Daniele da San Sebastiano reported, the removal of myrrh and balm revealed a face 'so lovely, so pleasing, so attractive, that, although the girl had certainly been dead fifteen hundred years, she appeared to have been laid to rest that very day'.[146] Hartmann Schedel (who had earlier recorded the price of the *editio princeps* of Apuleius' *Opera* as 'three papal ducats') satisfies his correspondent's 'eagerness for novelties' with a slightly ironic account of the affair: 'One would think there is some great indulgence and remission of sins to be gained by climbing that hill, so great is the crowd, especially of women, attracted by the sight.'[147] Apuleian initiates might read the scene as an inverted image of Psyche, thronged by admirers, but soon to be laid out as a bride-corpse on a mountain-top (*AA* 4. 28–35).

More generally, 'By seeing a great antique beauty as deathless, Renaissance viewers are realizing the culture's erotic dreams in their most absolute classical and humanistic form.'[148] One might well apply this observation to the *Hypnerotomachia*: the Roman Girl's beauty had been embalmed for her Renaissance admirers by techniques derived from the Egyptian god Anubis. Polia has been preserved as the embodiment of antiquity by a superior process: the wonders of print technology combine with Apuleian language as a kind of embalming ointment to create what the epitaph calls a *myropolium* ('perfumery').[149] Alexander ab Alexandro's account of the Roman Girl describes 'the ointment which filled the bottom of the coffin as having

[145] *The Civilization of the Renaissance in Italy*, 183–4 ('Part 3: The Revival of Antiquity: The Ruins of Rome'); R. Lanciani, *Pagan and Christian Rome* (London: Macmillan, 1892), 294–301; Barkan, *Unearthing the Past*, 57–63. Conrad Celtis devotes an epigram (*De puella Romae reperta*) to the discovery. See *Selections from Conrad Celtis*, ed. Forster, 34.

[146] Letter to Giacomo Maffei (like Grassi, a citizen of Verona). See Lanciani, 296; Barkan, *Unearthing the Past*, 57. Barkan observes (58) that 'much of the paper trail surrounding the event is composed by individuals in the avant garde of classical and antiquarian enthusiasm (often in the circle of Pomponio Leto)'.

[147] Munich Cod. 716. Quoted by Lanciani, 298.

[148] Barkan, *Unearthing the Past*, 62.

[149] G 466; F.C. F3ᵛ. Note Andreas Maro's paradoxical apostrophe to Polia: 'O how happy you are, unique among all mortals, | Polia, who lives even better in death' (G 8).

the appearance and scent of a fresh perfume', but other documents reveal that the girl's skin quickly began to blacken upon exposure to the air, and the putrefying body was either reinterred at the base of the city walls or thrown into the Tiber.[150] The end of the *Hypnerotomachia* also acknowledges the impossibility of maintaining a grip on the vision of Polia, but ambivalence pervades the whole work: triumphalist humanism is always on the cusp (at least) of ridiculousness. Giovio's claim that Pio was 'laughed at by all but the most foolish' recalls the criticisms of Erasmus detailed above (*rident*; *ridentur*; *Ridendos mihi narras, non imitandos*), but it would also appear that the archaizers could laugh at themselves.

Andreas Schott

The most comprehensive attack upon Apuleianism comes not from the sixteenth but from the seventeenth century, in a treatise by the Jesuit Andreas Schott (1552–1629) which provides a retrospective on the whole debate.[151] Addressing the 'Consuls and Senators' of Antwerp, Schott adduces Cicero as both 'the most eloquent of all Romans—whoever were, are or will be in any time' and also as the saviour of his country (from the conspiracy of Catiline), thus reaffirming the link commonly made between eloquence, moral integrity, statesmanship, social harmony, and civilization.[152] Schott mentions other authors who offend against his sense of classical decorum, but it is clear that he sees the primary divide as being between Ciceronianism and Apuleianism:

At qui æuo nostro non defuere, qui, quantum in Apuleio operæ posuerunt, tantum CICERONI dedissent, horas sibi posterisqúe meliùs collocassent. (p. 61)

(But in our own age, there was no lack of people who, had they given as much attention to Cicero as they put into Apuleius, would have invested their hours far better for their descendants.)

In praising Cicero, he adapts the same Varronian figure that Beroaldo had used more than a century earlier to extol Apuleius:

---

[150] Lanciani, 299 and 301.

[151] *Tullianorum quæstionum de instauranda Ciceronis imitatione libri III* (Antwerp: Jan Moretus, 1610). Schott was the author of another treatise, *Cicero a calumniis vindicatus* (Antwerp, 1613), mentioned by J. E. Sandys, *History of Classical Scholarship*, 3 vols. (Cambridge: CUP, 1908–21), ii. 305. By translating the *Bibliotheca* into Latin, he also made available Photius' synopses of lost ancient fiction such as Antonius Diogenes' *Wonders beyond Thule*. See *Le incredibili avventure al di là di Tule*, ed. M. Fusillo (Palermo: Sellerio, 1990).

[152] Schott, sig. *2ʳ.

*Equidem Musas, si Latinè loqui vellent (quod de Accio Plauto M.Varro iudicauit)
CICERONIS potiùs ore locuturas existem.* (p. 9)

(Indeed, if the Muses wanted to speak in Latin—the judgement Marcus Varro made of
Accius Plautus—I should think they would rather speak with the mouth of Cicero.)[153]

And he repeats Castellesi's charge that Apuleius is condemned by his own
prologue:

Appuleius in Asino *(cum quo rudere hoc sæculo plerique, quàm cum* CICERONE *loqui
malunt) operis initio Latinæ sese linguæ rudem atque imperitum* fatetur, *aduenamque
studiorum Quiritium, vt Afrum* αὐτοδίδακτον, *nullo magistro præeunte Latinè didicisse*
ærumnabili [45] *(vt ipsius verbis vtar) labore.* (pp. 44–5)

(In the *Ass,* Apuleius—a great many in this age prefer to bray with him than to speak
with Cicero—admits, at the beginning of the work, that he is 'unskilled and inexperi-
enced' in the Latin language and that, as a stranger to the Romans' studies, as a self-
taught African, with no teacher leading the way, he learned Latin with—to use his own
words—'wretched toil'.)

One of the Apuleian 'brayers' that Schott had in mind may have been his
old friend from Louvain, the great Flemish scholar (and founding father of
neo-Stoicism) Justus Lipsius (Joost or Josse Lips, 1547–1606).[154] In *De Lipsii
latinitate (vt ipsimet antiquarii Lipsii stylum indigitant) Palaestra I* (Frankfurt:
[Stephanus], 1595), Henri Estienne attacked Lipsius for 'abandoning
the moderate Ciceronianism of his earlier Letters and his *Variae lectiones*
for a new style founded on Tacitus and Seneca, and even on Gellius and
Apuleius'.[155]

Schott employs two strategies to find Apuleius guilty by association: one
geographical, the other chronological. First, he firmly places Apuleius in the
(now generally discredited) category of 'African Latin':

*In gentibus eadem dicendi scribendíque varietas obseruata. Afri, vt ingenio moribusqúe
vafri sunt, callidi, versipilles; sic & in dicendo acuti, breues nimis, atque hinc adeò
obscuri, vt Milesiarum scriptor de asino Appuleius Madaurensis, & Martianus Cappella
in Philologiæ nuptiis. Docti sunt, at obscuri, Tertullianus atque Arnobius.* (p. 16)

---

[153] Varro's judgement is quoted by Quintilian: *Licet Varro Musas, Aeli Stilonis sententia,
Plautino dicat sermone locuturas fuisse, si Latine vellent.* See *Quintiliani institutionis oratoriae
liber X,* ed. W. Peterson, 2nd edn. (London, 1903; repr. Chicago: Bolchazy-Carducci, 1981), 19.

[154] Lipsius' literary executor was Jan Wower (editor of Apuleius) who appears with Lipsius in
Rubens' painting, 'The Four Philosophers'. See, generally, L. Deitz, 'Ioannes Wower of Hamburg, Philologist and Polymath. A Preliminary Sketch of his Life and Works', *JWCI* 58 (1995),
132–51.

[155] Sandys, *History of Classical Scholarship,* ii. 304. Lipsius' *Opera omnia quæ ad criticam
proprie spectant* (Antwerp: Christophe Plantin, 1585) include five books of *Antiquarum lectionum* (devoted principally to Plautus) and a *Satyra Menippæa* entitled *Somnium,* directed against
the critics of his age (*lusus in nostri æui criticos*). Cf. D. C. Allen, 'On Spenser's *Muiopotmos', SP*
53 (1956), 141–58, at 147–8 n. 3.

(The same diversity of writing and speaking is observed amongst races. Just as the Africans are artful, cunning, and crafty in their character and morals, so too in their speech, they are too concise and hence so obscure, as is Apuleius of Madaura, the author of Milesian tales concerning the ass, and Martianus Capella in the *Marriage of Philologia*. Learned, but obscure, are Tertullian and Arnobius.)[156]

Qui aridi sunt ac ieiuni, Appuleium, Symmachum, Sidonium, & Afros sic laudant, vt ceteris præferant. (p. 17)

(Those who are parched and barren praise Apuleius, Symmachus, Sidonius, and the Africans to such an extent that they prefer them to the rest.)

Secondly, he links the decline in Latin style with the decline of civilization itself. Having discussed Quintilian, Valerius Maximus, the two Plinies, Suetonius, and Tacitus, Schott turns, in chapter 16, to 'The Death of Latinity' (*De Latinitatis interitu*):

Secutum hinc corruptum vitiosumqúe tempus, quo non solùm deteriora studia redderentur, sed & degenerarent penitus, & omnino perirent. Nam in Italicum sermonem mutatus Latinus est, & Atticus Græcorum in vulgarem, vt nominant, barbararum gentium irruptionibus; ibi Gotthorum colluuie, hîc Turcarum tyrannide, qua litteræ omnino in Græcia exstinctæ ac sepultæ, heu, iacent. (p. 43)

(There followed on this, a corrupt and depraved time in which not only were studies rendered poorer, but they degenerated utterly and began to perish completely. For the Latin language was adulterated into the Italian, and the Attic of the Greeks into the demotic—as they call it—by the invasions of barbarian races: in the former case, by the conflux of Goths, in the latter by the tyranny of the Turks, whereby all literature in Greece, alas, lies dead and buried.)

By a convenient ignorance of (or indifference to) the true chronology, Apuleius (who was born about 123 and flourished under the celebratedly pacific Antonines) is made a contemporary of writers from the barbarian-infested fifth and sixth centuries:

Vixerunt autem in hac temporum infelicitate balbi potiùs quam diserti scriptores, Symmachus, Appuleius, Cassiodorus, Sidonius Apollinaris, Fulgentius Planciades, Martianus Capella, & Boëthius. *In quibus illustrandis hac tempestate recentiores tantum operæ ac diligentiæ posuisse vehementer equidem miror; neglectis interim melioris notæ auctoribus, vt CICERONE ac Philosophorum schola vniuersa.* (p. 44)

(There lived, in these unfortunate times, writers who were rather stammerers than fluent: Symmachus, Apuleius, Cassiodorus, Sidonius Apollinaris, Fulgentius Planciades, Martianus Capella, and Boëthius. I do indeed marvel greatly that in this period more recent writers have put so much effort and care into elucidating them, while,

---

[156] As J. G. F. Powell points out, the 'concept of "African Latin"... is not prima facie ridiculous, and should not be treated as such, but one must be careful.' See 'Some Linguistic Points in the Prologue', in *Companion to the Prologue*, ed. Kahane and Laird, 27–36, at 27.

Apuleius and the Northern Renaissance

meantime, authors of greater note like Cicero and the whole school of Philosophers are neglected.)

But the climax of Schott's attack is his reproduction of an excerpt from an earlier parody of Apuleian style by Mariangelo Accursio of l'Aquila (1489–1546):

De Appuleio verò Metamorphoseos ex Lucio Patrensi, seu Luciano scriptore, audi, amabò, quæ in Dialogo olim ante hosipsos octoginta annos à Mariangelo Accursio (homine, vt illis temporibus, pererudito, quíque Nasonem, Ausonium, ac Solinum Diatribâ illustrarit) Oscè ac Volscè conscripto, vt sæculi degenerantis nimiùm à prisca Eloquentia insaniam veluti aceto aspersa Satyra perstringeret: audi, inquam, & risum contine, si potes: Ego pol, id spontaliter, cupienterqúe, præclariter factitarem, si L. Appuleij multiloquentiæ lineamentationem leuigatiusqúe veriuerbium saturantiùs ac non nepa lyra concallerem. Illam, inquam, suauiloquentiam facundiosam; & Oratorum melos quo ipsum Asinum, cognomento Aureum, auratiorem auro fastigauit. Est quippen tanta eius altiloquentia, vt præ huius no<u>mine</u> non vatracen Arpinatem polylogum, blacteratorem, lingulacam, immoderatam suam eloquentiam pro rostris dixe credam *En grande sophos, en os ferreum, vel nulla potiùs frons huius Antiquarij, qui CICERONI Arpinati Apuleij Asinum præferre non dubitet: fremant licet qui in alia omnia discesserunt: dicam quod sentio: miseret me sanè illorum,* [60] *& helleborum Anticyris propinari exoptem, qui has delitias non modò occæcati priuatim amplectuntur, sed & publicè prædicant, glorioséque iactant Abderitanis non absimiles, qui cùm Democritum sæculi sui vitia ridentem in stultis numerarent, accito etiam publicè Hippocrate, qui insaniæ morbum depellerat, se insanos esse, præposteriqúe iudicij vitio laborare minimè animaduerterent. Doleo sanè* Phil. Beroaldum, *maiorum memoria, multæ quidem lectionis virum potiùs, quàm iudicij, quíque CICERONIS Tusculanas Lutetiæ publicè explanasset, atque adeo commentando illustrasset; mutata mox velificatione in hunc veluti Apuleij scopulum naue fracta impegisse, & omnem dicendi formam peruertisse potiùs, quàm vertisse. Hoc amplius, vastos ac laboriosos in Asinum Commentarios reliquisse: nimirum vt flores inde legeret Budæus, quibus Iuris Pandectas illustraret. Eius Bononiæ auditor, Eloquentiæ & ipse doctor* Baptista Pius, *Deus bone, quàm ridiculus, dum Fulgentij Plauti, ac Sidonij Apollinaris, quàm CICERONI similior esse & haberi vult.* (pp. 59–60)

(But as for Apuleius, who wrote the *Metamorphoses* on the model of Lucius of Patrae or Lucian, listen, please, to what was once [written] eighty years ago in *Oscus and Volscus* by Mariangelo Accursio—in those times a man of great erudition who elucidated Ovid, Ausonius, and Solinus in learned discussion—in order to censure, in a satire sprinkled, as it were, with vinegar-wit, the madness of an age which had degenerated too much from its former eloquence. Listen, I say, and contain your laughter if you can:

'By Pollux! I would practise it voluntarily and eagerly and excellently, if I could be skilled more smoothly in the lineamentation of Lucius Apuleius' multiloquence and more abundantly in his veracity and not with a Scorpion for a Lyre. That fluent suaviloquence, I say, and the song of Orators with which he exalted the very Ass, surnamed Golden, to be more golden than gold. So great indeed is his high-flown eloquence that compared with this man's name, I should not believe that club-footed, wordy, [Cicero] of Arpino, the bleater, the chatterbox, declared his immeasurable eloquence on the Rostra.'[157]

Behold the mighty sophist, behold the iron mouth or rather the complete lack of shame [*nulla frons*] of this Antiquarian, who does not hesitate to prefer the Ass of Apuleius to Cicero of Arpino. Those who have taken complete leave of their senses may snarl if they like; I shall say what I think. I should very much like the hellebore of the [three] Anticyras to be furnished to those blinded men who not only embrace these delights in private but vaunt them in public and flourish them boastingly, not unlike those fools of Abdera who, when they numbered among the stupid, Democritus (who was laughing at the vices of his age) even after summoning Hippocrates to drive away the disease of madness, did not notice that they themselves were mad and suffering from the defect of perverted judgement.[158] I do indeed grieve that, in our ancestors' memory, Filippo Beroaldo (a man rather of great reading, than of good judgement) who had publicly expounded Cicero's *Tusculan Disputations* at Paris and illuminated them by his commentary, in a quick change of tack, struck, as it were, against this rock of Apuleius, wrecking his ship, and perverted rather than transformed the whole model of speaking. He left, in abundance, his vast and laborious commentaries on the *Ass,* doubtless so that Budé could choose from them the flowers with which to elucidate [Justinian's] *Encyclopædia of Law.* His pupil at Bologna (and himself a Doctor of Eloquence), Battista Pio, wants (Good God, how ridiculous!) to be (and be held to be!) more like Fulgentius, Plautus, and Sidonius Apollinaris than Cicero.)

In Book 2, Schott provides 'The Judgements of the Ancients and More Recent Writers as to the Best Method of Imitation'. Amongst these, he adduces the testimony of Marc-Antoine de Muret (1526–85) who depicted an age of errant Apuleians and archaizers, drawn back in the wisdom of maturity, to the Ciceronian flock:

M. Ant. Muretus. Orat. XII.

Olim plerisque sæpiùs in manibus erat Appuleius, aut Sidonius Apollinaris, quàm CICERO: Persium quàm Horatium, Lucanum aut Claudianum [184] *quàm* Virgilium *libentius, & maiore cum studio peruolutabant. Animaduertit hunc errorem aetas, &* Bembi, Sadoleti *ac similium & exemplo & auctoritate commota, ad vetustiorum lectionem imitationemque*

---

[157] See *Osco, Volsco, Romanaq., eloquentia interlocutoribus, dialogus, ludis Romanis actus: In quo ostenditur, verbis publica moneta signatis utendum esse, prisca vero nimis, et exoleta, tanquam scopulos esse fugienda* ([Rome?: s.n.], 1531). D'Amico ('Progress', 377) dates the work to 1513.

[158] Antiquity boasts three places called Anticyra—frequently confounded (and usually associated) with the production of hellebore, a plant used by the ancients for the treatment of mental disorders. Cf. Horace, *Ars poetica,* 300. Abdera is the name of a town in Thrace (birthplace of the philosophers Protagoras, Democritus, and Anarchus) noted for the stupidity of its inhabitants.

reuocata est. Hi præter CICERONEM, Cæsarem, Sallustium, & si fortè aliquot alios eidem ætati suppares tum ex Poëtis præter Catullum, Lucretium, Virgilium, tres aut quatuor alios damnare cœperunt.[159]

(There was a time when Apuleius (or Sidonius Apollinaris) was in most hands more often than Cicero: they used to read Persius more willingly than Horace; Lucan or Claudian with greater zeal than Vergil. The following age realized this error and, moved by the example and authority of Bembo, Sadoleto, and similar men, was recalled to the reading and imitation of the ancients. These men began to condemn writers other than Cicero, Caesar, and Sallust—though you might perhaps throw in a few others of the same period, and then, of the poets, three or four besides Catullus, Lucretius, and Vergil.)

Yet once again, Schott is telling only part of the story. He knew Muret well enough to write his *Vita*, but in this discussion he overlooks the fact that in other works Muret championed Tertullian, Cassiodorus, and Apuleius.[160]

The controversy over the correct models and modes of imitation in Latin prose composition was evidently neither a short-lived nor a clear-cut phenomenon. The pervasiveness of Apuleian diction in the *Hypnerotomachia*, for example, does not necessarily mean that its author(s) sanctioned its use in daily affairs. The *Hypnerotomachia* is, first and foremost, a lexical, literary, architectural, pictorial, and typographical performance. It is fundamentally dialogic. But we should not neglect the epideictic aspect even in avowedly anti-Apuleian works. When Mariangelo Accursio composes *Oscus et Volscus*, he is not merely exposing the archaizers (above all, Battista Pio) to ridicule; he is also demonstrating his rhetorical (and lexical) virtuosity. Schott uses *Antiquarius* as a derogatory term when he discusses the target of Accursio's satire; but Accursio was in a position to parody the style of the Renaissance Apuleians in part because he shared some of their archaeological interests, producing a ground-breaking edition of an extravagant Late-antique stylist (Ammianus Marcellinus), and being a student of classical inscriptions.[161]

---

[159] *De optimâ Imitandi ratione veterum recentiumqúe Iudicia* (Schott, 183–4). See *M. Antonii Mureti, presbyteri, J. C. et civis Rom. Orationum volumina duo* (Cologne: Antonius Hierat, 1614).

[160] Cf. M. W. Croll, 'Muret and the History of "Attic Prose"', in his *'Attic' and Baroque Prose Style: The Anti-Ciceronian Movement*, ed. J. Max Patrick et al. (Princeton: PUP, 1966, repr. 1969), 107–62, at 161: 'Challenged to defend his championship of later Latin authors, [Muret] encouraged his pupils to study Tertullian, Apuleius, and Cassiodorus.'

[161] *Ammianus Marcellinus a Mariangelo Accursio...purgatus* (Augsburg: Silvan Otmar, 1533). On Accursio's interest in classical inscriptions from Augsburg and Regensburg, see M. Ott, *Die Entdeckung des Altertums: Der Umgang mit der römischen Vergangenheit Süddeutschlands im 16. Jahrhundert* (Kallmünz: Lassleben, 2002), 184–92. P. S. Allen notes (*Opus epistolarum Des. Erasmi Roterodami*, i. 185), that a copy (Schlettstadt, Cat. Rhen. 197) of *Osci et Volsci Dialogus* was 'sent to Beatus Rhenanus from Rome by Michael Hummelberg on 18 Aug. 1514'.

The Stylistic Debate in England

In England, the debate never reached the levels of vitriol achieved on the Continent and J. W. Binns is, broadly speaking, correct when he characterizes the English school as one of 'moderate Ciceronianism'.[162] Nevertheless, Philip Sidney, writing on 18 October 1580 to his brother Robert, was impelled to say:

So you can speake and write Latine not barbarously I never require great study in Ciceronianisme the chiefe abuse of Oxford, Qui dum verba sectantur, res negligunt. My toyfull booke I will send with Gods helpe by February, at which time you shall have your mony.[163]

Sidney recalls, through inversion, the injunction attributed to Cato the Censor (*rem tene, verba sequentur*), condemning what he sees amongst Ciceronians as the vice of concentrating on style at the expense of content.[164] In the *Apologie for Poetrie* (wr. pre-1586, pr. 1595), Sidney refers, somewhat disdainfully, to 'Nizolian Paper-bookes of figures and phrases'—the *Thesaurus Ciceronianus* compiled by Mario Nizzoli (1498–1576), which allowed servile imitators to assemble a 'pure' Latin style, using nothing but authenticated Ciceronian constructions.[165] And it is hardly surprising, given the close connection with England of several of the principal combatants (More, Erasmus, Castellesi, and Lipsius) that the controversy figured large in English intellectual life and that Apuleius (*pace* Binns) was an integral part of it.[166]

England's interest in Apuleius had clearly survived the departure of Erasmus and the execution of More. Roger Ascham, tutor to the Princess Elizabeth and author of an educational treatise (*The Scholemaster*) and a book on archery (*Toxophilus*) began his correspondence with Johann Sturm (humanist, Ciceronian, and rector of the gymnasium at Strasburg) on 4 April 1550.[167] Writing from St John's College, Cambridge, Ascham refers to the fine achievements of

---

[162] Binns, *Intellectual Culture*, 289.

[163] *The Complete Works of Sir Philip Sidney*, ed. A. Feuillerat, 4 vols. (Cambridge: CUP, 1912–26), iii. 132.

[164] For the attribution to Cato, see Julius Victor, *Ars rhetorica*.

[165] *Nizolius sive Thesaurus Ciceronianus*, ed. Marcello Squarcialupo of Piombino (Basle: Eusebius Episcopius, 1576).

[166] On 17 Mar. 1586, Justus Lipsius dedicated to Sidney his *De recta pronunciatione Latinae linguae dialogus* (Leiden: F. Raphelengius, 1586). See J. A. van Dorsten, *Poets, Patrons, and Professors: Sir Philip Sidney, Daniel Rogers, and the Leiden Humanists* (Leiden: Sir Thomas Browne Institute, 1962), 119 and 215–16. The Anglo-Dutch circle patronized by Leicester and Sidney in Leiden at this time also included Petrus Colvius who would publish his edn. of Apuleius' *Opera omnia* in 1588 (van Dorsten, 131–2).

[167] Ascham named his second son 'Sturm' in honour of his friend. See R. O'Day, 'Ascham, Roger (1514/15–1568)', *ODNB*; and, generally, L. W. Spitz and B. Sher Tinsley, *Johann Sturm on Education: The Reformation and Humanist Learning* (St Louis, Mo.: Concordia, 1995).

classical scholars at his own university, and then turns his attention to the rival school of learning:

Quid omnes Oxonienses sequuntur, plane nescio, sed ante aliquot menses, in Aula incidi in quendam illius Academiæ, qui nimium præferendo LUCIANUM, PLUTARCHUM et HERODIANUM, SENECAM, AULUM GELLIUM, et APULEIUM, utramque linguam in nimis senescentem et effœtam ætatem compingere mihi videbatur.[168]

(Clearly, I do not know what all the Oxonians are engaged upon, but a few months ago at Court, I chanced upon a certain man from that university who, by an excessive preference for Lucian, Plutarch, Herodian, Seneca, Aulus Gellius, and Apuleius, seemed to me to confine each language to an excessively decaying and worn-out age.)

Lawrence Ryan comments on this passage that Ascham's conversation at Court

shocked his own more orthodox humanism and made him suspect that Oxonians were on the verge of decadence. They were, if one might credit what this person had told him, interested mainly in authors of the declining periods of Greek and Roman eloquence...To Ascham such 'corrupted' taste was a sure forewarning of the demise of true learning at the sister university.[169]

From the passage itself, there is no way of telling, for certain, whether this purported zeal for Apuleius related to his philosophical, rhetorical, or imaginative works; yet the fact that the 'decadent', extravagantly Asiatic, rhetoric for which Apuleius is usually criticized is confined almost exclusively to the *Metamorphoses* and the *Florida,* suggests that at least one of these works was being read (perhaps even taught) at Oxford.[170]

In the third book of *The Arte of Rhetorique* (1553), Thomas Wilson includes Apuleius in his discussion of two 'kyndes of Exornacion': 'Lyke endyng' (*Similiter desinens,* e.g. 'wickedly'/'naughtely') and 'Lyke falling' (*similiter cadens,* e.g. 'trauaile'/'auaile'). 'Diuerse in this our tyme', Wilson declares, 'delite muche in this kynd of writyng, whiche beeyng measurably vsed, deliteth muche the hearers, otherwyse it offendeth, and werieth mens ears'. This tendency to overuse the devices was apparent even in the time of Tacitus but had become rampant by the age of Augustine:

---

[168] Ascham, Letter XCIX, To Sturm (i. 2), in *The Whole Works of Roger Ascham,* ed. J. A. Giles (London: John Russell Smith, 1865), i, pt. 1, p. 190. Cf. A. Feuillerat, *John Lyly: Contribution à l'histoire de la renaissance en Angleterre* (Cambridge: CUP, 1910), 461. Ascham's Latin letters were first published in 1576 by Edward Grant.

[169] L. V. Ryan, *Roger Ascham* (London: OUP, 1963), 117.

[170] His philosophical works, besides being written in a relatively straightforward style, were also unoriginal. With the humanistic revival in interest in the original Greek texts of Plato, the attraction of Apuleius' popularizations must have severely diminished.

the people were suche wher he liued, that they toke muche delite in rimed sentences, & in Orations made ballade wise. Yea thei were so nyce & so waiwarde to please, that excepte the Preacher from tyme to tyme coulde ryme out his Sermon, they woulde not long abide the hearyng.... So that for the flowyng stile, & ful sentence, crept in mynstrelles elocution, talkyng matters altogether in rime, & for weightinesse & grauitie of wordes, succeded nothyng els but wantonnesse of inuencion. Tullie was forsaken, with Liuie, Cesar, & other: And Apuleius, Ausonius, with such mynstrell makers were altogether folowed.[171]

Apuleius also features in Richard Sherry's *A Treatise of the Figures of Grammer and Rhetorike* (1555). Discourse is 'ungarnished' 'when eyther there lacketh order, or beautifying in the wordes'. One 'fault' is 'Aschematon, when in the oration there is no varietie, nor pleasauntnes, but it is all alike, and by no varietie taketh away tediousnes'. But the 'contrary' fault is 'Ποικιλογιά When in the oration ther is nothing rightly and properly spoken, but all is to muche befigured and begayed. Such is the writing of Apuleius.'[172]

A generation later, another Cambridge scholar, Gabriel Harvey, provides, in his *Rhetor* (1577), an indictment of Apuleianism which culminates in the cry: μεταμόρφωσιν exspecto; non illam quidem ex asinis in homines, sed ex Apuleijs in Ciceronis ('I await a metamorphosis—not, indeed, from asses into men, but from Apuleiuses into Ciceros').[173]

Apuleianism enjoyed an extraordinary longevity. In a provincial school play, *Apollo Shroving* (1627), William Hawkins shows Gingle being overawed by the ink-horn terms of Captain Complement, a professed 'teacher of gestures and fashions' who descends from the same tradition as Rabelais's Limousin scholar (*Gargantua and Pantagruel*, II. vi), Sidney's Rhombus (*The Lady of May*), and Shakespeare's Holofernes (*Love's Labour's Lost*):

Ging. What starre is that, &c O excellent! All the world could neuer haue furnisht me with such a Tutor.
Comp. Say rather all the habitable circumference of this muddy massy earthy globe could not haue affoorded and suppeditated vnto me so mellifluous an Indoctrinator, as is the curious Captaine *Complement.*
Ging. O that I could by Metamorphasis be transformed into this eloquent man.

---

[171] ([London]: Richard Grafton, 1553), fol. 108[r—v].

[172] (London: Richard Tottel, 1555), sig. Bii[v]. The noun presumably derives from ῥοικός 'crooked' or from ῥοϊκός, 'flowing, fluid, *hence* weak, failing ... suffering from a flux; diarrhoea, or the like' (L&S).

[173] *Gabrielis Harueii rhetor, vel duorum dierum oratio, de natura, arte, & exercitatione rhetorica: ad suos auditores* (London: Henry Binneman, 1577), sig. D.ij[r]. The *Rhetor* appeared in the same year as the *Ciceronianus* in which Harvey mocked the slavish Ciceronianism of his own youth. See *Gabriel Harvey's 'Ciceronianus'*, ed. H. S. Wilson, trans. C. A. Forbes (Lincoln, Nebr.: U of Nebraska, 1945).

Complement's page, Jacke Implement (a *servus callidus* played by the 11-year-old Joseph Beaumont), immediately quips:

Imp. Thou hadst better bee transformed with *Apuleius* into a golden Asse.[174]

As late as 1642, Milton could use Apuleius as ammunition in his anti-prelatical tract *An Apology for Smectymnuus*, when he attacks the 'Clerks' of the University:

How few among them that know to write, or speak in a pure stile... declaming in rugged and miscellaneous geare blown together by the foure winds, and in their choice preferring the gay ranknesse of *Apuleius, Arnobius,* or any moderne fustianist, before the native *Latinisms* of *Cicero*.[175]

OTHER EDITIONS

Yet however well or badly Apuleius fared in such controversies, demand for his works continued unabated. Continental editions of Apuleius were clearly available in England in the early part of the sixteenth century. The Probate Inventories from Cambridge alone record four individuals possessing Latin texts (and one a French translation) in the period 1537 to 1558.[176] We should not assume, however, that all of the Latin editions in English hands were by Beroaldo. Three editions of the collected works appeared early in the century: one in 1512, by a Florentine priest, Marianus Tuccius (who saw his task as restoring to its pristine form a text mutilated by the vicissitudes of chance and the bonfires of barbarians);[177] another by Aldus' brother-in-law Gian Francesco Torresani (Franciscus Asulanus) in Venice in 1521 (the Aldine);[178] and a

---

[174] *Apollo Shrouing, Composed for the Schollars of the Free-schoole of Hadleigh in Suffolke. And acted by them on Shroue-tuesday, being the sixt of February, 1626* (London: Robert Mylbourne, [1627]), Act IV, sc. i, p. 61. Hawkins had been a sizar at Christ's College, Cambridge (BA, 1623; MA, 1626). See R. Cummings, 'Hawkins, William (*d.* 1637)', *ODNB*. Beaumont (identified in the list of players on p. 2 of *Apollo Shrouing*) would go on to compose *Psyche, or, Love's Mystery* (1648), a religious epic in 30,000 verses.

[175] *Complete Prose Works of John Milton,* gen. ed. D. M. Wolfe, 10 vols. (New Haven: YUP, 1953–82), i. 934.

[176] E. S. Leedham-Green, *Books in Cambridge Inventories: Book-Lists from Vice-Chancellor's Court Probate Inventories in the Tudor and Stuart Periods,* 2 vols. (Cambridge: CUP, 1986), ii. 32. Three of the four Latin works are described as *apuleius de asino aureo* (in one case the words *per beraldum* [*sic*] make the editorship explicit) but the description *apuleius* in one instance suggests a copy of the *Opera omnia*.

[177] *De asino aureo libelli xi, etc.* (Florence: Philippus de Giunta, 1512).

[178] *L. Apuleii Metamorphoseos, siue lusus asini libri XI. etc.* (Venice: In ædibus Aldi & Andreæ soceri, 1521).

third, in Florence in 1522, by Bernardus Philomathes.[179] None of these three editions supplied commentaries, but they had the advantage over Beroaldo of providing the whole works of Apuleius in a more readable (because less contracted), less bulky, and less expensive octavo format. Asulanus appears to have entertained no high opinion of his author. Dedicating his edition to the French king's ambassador in Venice, he begins by citing Cicero's judgement that the 'perfect orator and the supreme master of eloquence is the man who can say small things softly, middling things with moderation, and great things seriously'.[180] He goes on to chart the decline in the purity of the Latin language, and having considered (amongst others) Seneca and Pliny, continues:

Horum autem ætati successerunt nonnulli, qui corruptum quoddam latinitatis genus inuexerunt, [Aii^v] *cuius author, & princeps Apuleius fuit Madauræ ortus, uir excellenti ingenio, et potius ad multa uersanda, quàm ad percipienda aptus. nam Platonicæ philosophiæ discreta perplexe tradidit. id quod colligere possumus ex multis eius libris. & quæ ex Aristotele literis prodidit, non usquequaque Peripateticam disciplinam sapiunt.*

(But after their age there followed several who introduced a certain corrupted sort of Latinity, the originator and leader of which was Apuleius—born at Madaura, a man of exceptional talent, better suited to trying his hand at many things than at understanding them. For he handed down the principles of Platonic philosophy confusedly. What we can assemble from his many books and what he produced from Aristotle's writings do not always have the flavour of Peripatetic teaching.)

Asulanus' blunt appraisal of Apuleius' capacities as a philosopher is in line with the modern-day consensus and contradicts the tradition of editors who (into the sixteenth century, and beyond) continued to give a high place to the thought of the man whom posterity had lauded with the epithet *philosophus Platonicus*.[181] There is no suggestion, in Asulanus' preface, of the *Metamorphoses* having any moral or allegorical significance. Asulanus even changes the alternative title of the work from *De asino aureo* to *Lusus asini* ('The Jest of the Ass'), a hermeneutic shift which removes the novel from the realms of Platonic myth and brings it closer to the Cynical world of Lucianic satire.

---

[179] *L. Apuleij Madaurensis, Metamorphoseon siue de asino aureo. Libri XI, etc.* (Florence: Per hæredes Philippi Iuntæ, 1522). See Bibliography for full list of contents.

[180] *PERFECTVM Oratorem, summumq́ue eloquentiæ magistrum iudicauit M.Tullius eum esse, qui eleganter posset parua summisse, modica temperate, magna grauiter dicere* (sig. Aii^r).

[181] The epithet appears as early as Sallustius' *subscriptio* to the *De magia*.

APULEIUS IN RENAISSANCE DICTIONARIES
AND THE CATHOLIC *INDEX*

The passionate debates over Apuleius' (de)merits as a stylist may account for the curious anomalies that we find in Renaissance dictionaries, which serve both as mythological source-books and also as establishers of classical norms.[182] Robert Estienne's *Dictionarium proprium nominum* (1512) has entries for such writers as Vergil and Lucan, but makes no mention of Apuleius or Psyche.[183] At the other end of the century, Natale Conti (Natalis Comes) presents ten books of *Explicationes fabularum* which again make no reference to Apuleius or Psyche, even though nearly twelve pages (drawn from a host of ancient authors) are devoted to an investigation of Cupid's nature and genealogy, divinity, or humanity.[184] Thomas Elyot's *Dictionary* (1538) was 'the first Latin-English dictionary to be based on Renaissance humanist ideals of classical learning'.[185] Elyot made no attempt, in his first lexicographical foray, to include an expansive list of proper nouns, so that there is no account of individual authors; but the margins of the first edition are peppered with references to the provenance of particular words. Seven such words or phrases are attributed to 'Apuleius', though no indication of the precise location is given: *Altrinsecus, Circumsecus, Macilentus, Multicolorus, Reducere, Reijcio,* and *Auribus prouehi.* For some of these, clearly, he was indebted to the lexicographer Calepinus, but his explanation of the Latin phrase indicates a close familiarity with the text itself:

Auribus prouehi, to be carried by the eares, it is proprely vsed, where we wyl declare, that being in iourney with one, we delyte so moch in his communication, that we fele no labour or payne by going or riding. So may we say, *auribus prouehimur,* in hering of hym our paynes are relieued, or in heryng him talke, our iorney semeth shorte, or is abbreuiate.

Elyot takes his phrase from the beginning of Book 1 of *The Golden Ass* where the grim tale of Aristomenes and Socrates elicits Lucius' appreciation of the way in which the hearing of a *lepida fabula* can alleviate the tedium of a long journey:

---

[182] See generally D. T. Starnes and E. W. Talbert, *Classical Myth and Legend in Renaissance Dictionaries* (Chapel Hill: U of North Carolina P, 1955).

[183] (Paris: Robertus Stephanus, 1512).

[184] *Natalis Comitis mythologiae, siue explicationum fabularum, libri decem: in quibus omnia prope naturalis & moralis philosophia dogmata continentur* (Paris: Arnoldus Sittart, 1583), lib. IV, cap. xiv.

[185] R. C. Alston, ed., *Thomas Elyot: Dictionary 1538* (Menston: Scolar P, 1970).

Quod beneficium etiam illum vectorem credo laetari: sine fatigatione sui me usque ad istum civitatis portam non dorso illius sed meis auribus prouecto. (A.A 1. 20)

(I believe even my horse rejoiced in this support for I was carried as far as that city-gate (with no weariness on his part) not on his back but on my ears.)

Henry VIII had himself intervened in the printing of the *Dictionary*, encouraging Elyot in his endeavours and making his own library available for the further revision of the work.[186] Elyot's 'correction and amplifycation' of the *Dictionary* of 1538 resulted in the *Bibliotheca Eliotæ*, first published in 1542. His proclaimed brief is moral as well as encyclopaedic: he desires to make 'a general collection by the order of letters' of things topographical, zoological, botanical, geological, and medicinal, providing

Fynally the names of moste notable personages, who from the fyrst Adam vntyll thre hundred yeres after the incarnation of CHRISTE, dyd any thynge worthy a speciall remembrance, expedient and necessary to the moderation of our actes and proce-dynges, with the hystoryes or lyues of the sayd persones compendyousely gathered. I haue not omytted fables and inuentions of paynymes, for the more easy vnderstand-ing of poetes. I also thought it necessary to enterlace the detestable heretykes ... to the intente that those heresyes beinge in this wyse diuulgate, may be the sooner espyed and abhorred in suche bokes, where they be craftily interlaced with holsome doctrine.

The work is thus seen to act as a reinforcer of moral orthodoxy, and the entry for 'Cicero' is accordingly eulogistic: he is not only the greatest orator of all, but also the greatest statesman. Apuleius elicits a rather different response:

Apuleius, a phylosopher borne in Aphrica, not withstanding he florished in Athenes, & after wrate in latin diuers stiles, as De uita & moribus Platonis, & de Deo Socratis, in a ryght eloquent and temperate style. In his bokes callyd Floridorum & De asino aureo, he wrate so affectately and flouryshingly, that he is therfore more to be mocked than praysed. He made also a ryght commendable boke of the names and vertues of herbes, he was about the yere of our lorde. 300.

No mention is made of the *Apologia*, Elyot, instead, praising the pseudo-Apuleian *Herbarius*; and the *floruit* given (AD 300) is about a century and a half later than that assigned by modern scholars. What is most interesting is the contrast between the disdain Elyot expresses for *The Golden Ass* in the second edition, and his readiness to quote from it in the first.[187] The 1542 entry for Apuleius reappears, almost unchanged, in the revised editions of the *Bibliotheca Eliotæ* produced by Thomas Cooper in 1548 and 1552, and is

---

[186] Elyot, 'The Preface' to *The Dictionary* (1538), sigs. Aii^v–iii^r.

[187] Elyot's dismissal of *The Golden Ass* is also interesting in the light of the fact that he translated a dialogue of Lucian's in about 1535.

incorporated into the most influential Latin-English dictionary of all—Cooper's own *Thesaurus linguæ Romanæ & Britannicæ*.[188]

This ambivalence towards Apuleius—an interest in him coupled with a reluctance to be *seen* to be enjoying him—is representative: Apuleius has always inhabited the borderlands of respectability. Robert Graves makes the bald statement that 'The Inquisition was very hot against the book and succeeded in mutilating all the editions except the Editio Princeps Andrew, Bishop of Aleria published in 1469.'[189] In fact, the position is more complicated: Apuleius escaped the censure of the *Index* published in 1558 and the revised *Index* of 1627.[190] He did, however, fall foul of the *Spanish* Inquisition, appearing in the *Nouissimus librorum prohibitorum et expurgandorum index* published in 1640; though this proscribes only translations into vernacular languages (*APVLEYO. Su Libro intitulado, Asno de oro, en Romance, ò en qualquier lengua vulgar*) together with the critical work of certain (heterodox) Apuleian scholars: the Dedication and Preface of Marcus Hopperus Basiliensis to his new edition of Apuleius' *Opera* (1614), Isaac Casaubon's edition of Apuleius' *Apologia* (1594), and Scipio Gentilis' commentary on that work.[191] The Latin text itself escapes unscathed.

APULEIUS AND HUMANIST ATTITUDES TOWARDS FICTION

Apuleius also features prominently in Renaissance debates over the value and function of fictions. In Book II of *De copia*, both Lucian and Apuleius furnish examples to illustrate Erasmus' account of 'Fictional Narratives' (*De fictis narrationibus*):

Porro, quae risus causa finguntur, quo longius absunt a vero, hoc magis demulcent animos, modo ne sint anicularum similia deliramentis, et eruditis allusionibus doctas

---

[188] *Thesaurus linguæ Romanæ & Britannicæ* (London: Henry Wykes, 1565), sig. C1ʳ and (London: Henry Bynneman, 1584), sig. Bbbbbbb.3ᵛ. In the *Thesaurus*, Cooper removes the proper names to a supplementary *Dictionarium Historicum & Poeticum* wherein Apuleius appears in an entry virtually identical to Elyot's except in orthography and the use of the phrase 'diuers woorkes' instead of 'dyuers styles'.

[189] Introd. to trans., *The Transformations of Lucius* (Harmondsworth: Penguin, 1950), 20.

[190] *Index auctorum et librorum qui ab officio sanctae Rom. uniuersalis inquisitionis caueri ab omnibus et singulis in uniuersa Christiana republica mandantur* (Rome: Pope Paul IV, 1558); *Nouus index librorum prohibitorum* (Cologne: Ex commissione S. R. E. Inquis., 1627).

[191] (Madrid: Supreme Senate of the Inquisition, 1640), 68. Marcus Hopperus, 766; Casaubon, 675; Scipio Gentilis, 84. According to Scobie ('Influence', 219), Cortegana's Spanish trans. was placed on the *Index expurgandorum* published at Seville in 1559.

etiam aures capere possint. Quo de genere sunt Luciani Verae narrationes, et ad huius exemplum effictus Asinus Apulei; praeterea Icaromenippus, et reliqua Luciani pleraque (Erasmus, *Opera omnia*, i–6, p. 257)

(But those works which are devised for the sake of amusement allure minds the more, the further they are from the truth, provided that they do not resemble the absurdities of little old women, and that they are also able to capture learned ears with their erudite allusions. Of this type are the *True History* of Lucian and the *Ass* of Apuleius (fashioned on Lucian's model) as well as the *Icaromenippus* and a great many of the other works of Lucian.)

Erasmus appears to be undercutting his own distinction when he separates Apuleius from the *anicularum deliramenta*, given the fact that the narratrix of 'Cupid and Psyche' is described as a *delira... anicula* ('a silly little old woman', *AA* 6. 25). Yet comparison with a passage from the *Institutio principis christiani* would suggest that the *deliramenta* he envisages here are the 'unlearned' chivalric romances.[192] Erasmus shows no inclination to read allegorical significance into *The Golden Ass*, or derive from it moral or spiritual edification: the fictions are there to amuse (*risus causa*), the intellectual component being the interplay between the ingenious author who garlands his narrative fancies with 'erudite allusions' and the educated readers who delight in their ability to recognize and appreciate those allusions.

This is a critically significant view of reading—it is not merely a passive matter of receiving instruction or edification (*utile*) through the pleasant and palatable medium (*dulce*) of the text, or of being mentally refreshed by works which allow a return to weightier matters (as in the Horatian and Lucretian models); it is an act of participation. The medieval perspective of a hierarchical transmission of knowledge from venerated *auctor* to receptive *lector* gives way to a reader-based view: Erasmian *aures* are already *doctae* before they encounter the reading in which they delight.[193]

---

[192] Carver, ' "True Histories" ', 334–5. In his *Institutio principis christiani* ('The Education of a Christian Prince', 1516), Erasmus condemns the continuing vogue (*permultos videmus... delectari*) for 'stories of Arthur, Lancelot, and the rest' which are 'not only abounding in tyranny, but also utterly unlearned, foolish, and old-womanish' (*non solum tyrannicis, verum etiam prorsus ineruditis, stultis & anilibus*). Erasmus, however, adds a significant coda: 'It would be more profitable [for the young prince] to invest [his] hours in comedies or the fables of the poets than in absurdities of this kind' (*consultius sit in comoediis aut poetarum fabulis horas collocare, quam in eiusmodi deliramentis*). See Erasmus, *Opera omnia*, iv-1, pp. 179–80; C. S. Lewis, *English Literature in the Sixteenth Century, Excluding Drama* (Oxford: Clarendon, 1954), 28; Adams, 'Bold Bawdry', 41.

[193] Erasmus' view of reading is not, of course, an innovation, merely the reassertion of literary values that dominated the Roman literary world until the beginning of the Middle Ages. It would be unwise, however, to generalize too much from this passage. Erasmus, in other works, was capable of endorsing extremely orthodox theories about the function of reading. What is significant is the attitude he expresses, here, towards the particular class of writings comprised by Apuleius and Menippean satire.

One hesitates to attribute any notion of a 'coherent evolution' to so protean a mind as Erasmus', given his ability to express what to our ears seem 'modern' sentiments even as he affirms the most medieval pieties. Yet there is surely a contradiction between the high moral claims that he makes for Lucian in the preface to the *Luciani somnium siue gallus* and the acknowledgement, here, of the primacy of the function of erudite entertainment. It may well be that his representation of Lucian in the preface was not entirely ingenuous to begin with—that his initial delight in the scoffing brilliance of the Syrian led to the attempt to accommodate Lucian to the prevailing theoretical model of his day, the Horatian *utile/dulce* formula. But it is also possible that Erasmus' perception of the relative functions of instruction and entertainment had actually altered, and that this change was prompted by (or at least resulted in) a new appreciation of such narratives as *The Golden Ass*.

Yet the humanist response to Apuleius remains profoundly ambivalent. Luther and the elder Scaliger might attack Erasmus for his Lucianism, but humanists of the Erasmian camp were more willing to express their admiration for the Syrian than for the Madauran.[194] Writing from Louvain in 1516, Adriaan Cornelissen van Baerland gives his brother Cornelis a catalogue of Erasmus' writings in which he praises the latter's Latin translation of Lucian's dialogues and commends them to be learned by heart.[195] He then refers to Erasmus' *Concio de puero Iesu* and remarks:

hanc orationem non dubito quin aliquando legeris; fuisti enim à primis annis earum rerum studiosior, quæ ad mores animi tui componendos attinerent: lascivas vero poetarum fabulas & pestilentissimas Apulei facetias, recte semper contemsisti: nam quid, per Deum immortalem, poetæ talibus nugis docent, nisi peccare, nisi à virtutum castris ad vitia transfugere, atque desciscere?

(I have no doubt that you have read this speech at some time; for you were always, from your earliest years, fond of those things which concerned the formation of your mental character. But you have always rightly spurned the lascivious fables of poets and those most pestilent jests of Apuleius. For what, by immortal God, do poets teach by this nonsense, except how to sin, except how to desert the camps of Virtues and go over to Vices?)

A letter from the same period to Erasmus demonstrates even more graphically the critical position of *The Golden Ass* in the interaction of medieval and Renaissance thought. In Maarten van Dorp (1485–1525) we see a man stretched by the opposing vectors of scholasticism and humanism. At the

---

[194] See C. R. Thompson, *The Translations of Lucian by Erasmus and St. Thomas More* (Ithaca, NY: n.pub., 1940), 45, for Luther and the elder Scaliger's attack on the 'Lucianic' Erasmus.
[195] Latin text from *Opera omnia*, vol. iiib, *Epistola* XCVIII, p. 1583.

University of Louvain, he taught in both the faculties of arts and theology. In 1508 and 1509, he staged two of Plautus' plays; in 1510, he delivered a public *Oratio in laudem Aristotelis.*[196] Dorp (who was also a friend of van Baerland) had advised Erasmus against publishing his edition of the Greek New Testament and, in the course of his letter, he attacks the paganism and stylistic fetishism of those humanists who disdain the reading of patristic authors because their prose-style falls short of their own exacting standards. With fine irony, he concedes the need of theologians to submit to the manifest superiorities of the New Learning:

Et praestiterit forte ex mediis Turcis accersere viros eloquentes bonis literis absolute eruditos, qui Dei ecclesiam illustrent, hoc est fabulas Ouidii, Apulei Asinum, Lutiani somnia publice doceant . . .[197]

(And perhaps it would be better to summon, from the midst of the Turks, eloquent men, thoroughly versed in belles-lettres, who could enlighten the Church of God, by publicly teaching the fables of Ovid, the *Ass* of Apuleius, the dreams of Lucian.)

Erasmus suppressed his own reply to the letter but Thomas More also responded on Erasmus' behalf and More's letter (though likewise suppressed by its author) survives. More does not mention Apuleius in his response; but *The Golden Ass* was clearly a work that More knew well, for his Latin poems published in 1518 contain one epigram which has been overlooked by students of Apuleius' *Nachleben*:

> *IN CHELONVM*
> Cur adeo inuisum est pigri tibi nomen aselli?
>   Olim erat hoc magnus, Chelone, philosophus.
> Ne tamen ipse nihil differre puteris ab illo
>   Aureus ille fuit, plumbeus ipse magis.
> Illi mens hominis asinino in corpore mansit
>   At tibi in humano est corpore mens asini.[198]

(Why is the name of the sluggish ass so hateful to you?
Once, Chelonus, there was a philosopher who was great in this;
Lest you should be thought, however, to differ in no way from him,

---

[196] Bietenholz, *Contemporaries of Erasmus*, i. 398–404.
[197] *Opus epistolarum Des. Erasmi*, ii. 128.
[198] My trans. Latin text from *The Complete Works of St. Thomas More*, ed. R. S. Sylvester et al., vol. iii, pt. 2 (New Haven: YUP, 1984), 272–4. The 1518 and 1520 edns. have the title, *IN CELONIVM*, but the Yale editor follows the 1563 emendation to *IN CHELONVM*, observing (at 412) the derivation of the name from the words χηλή ('hoof') and ὄνος ('ass'). The editor notes that 'The philosopher (in a loose sense) who was great because of an ass is probably Apuleius, author of *The Golden Ass*. In *Lucius or the Ass* Lucian told the same story of a lively young man changed into an ass.' The use of *aureus* in line 4 of the poem, however, makes the reference to Apuleius unambiguous.

He was golden, you are more leaden.
He retained the mind of a man in an ass's body;
    But you have the mind of an ass in a man's body.)

An English version appeared in 1577 in *Flowers of epigrammes* by Timothy Kendall ('late of the Vniuersitie of Oxford: now student of Staple Inne in London'):

> *Against Chelonus.*
>
> WHy dost thou loth *Chelonus* so,
>   the name of lumpish asse?
> The learned *Lucius Appuley,*
>   an asse he sometyme was.
> But thou dost differ muche from hym,
>   (he had a learned head)
> He was a golden asse perdy,
>   thou art an asse of Lead.
> A manly mynd, and body of
>   an asse he had, we finde:
> But thou a manlike body hast:
>   a doltishe asselike minde.[199]

It is often said that, in his later years, More repented of his youthful literary diversions and sought a more sober course. Yet Apuleian diction is found not only in *Utopia* (1516) but even in his *De tristitia Christi*, a work composed in the Tower in 1534/5 as he awaited execution.[200] This is not to say that More was consciously alluding to *The Golden Ass* in either of these works, but it does suggest that he was not only intimate with the novel, but also willing to allow its influence to be shown in his own prose-style.

We should note, too, that when Erasmus comments on *The Golden Ass* in his chapter *De fictis narrationibus* (*De copia*), he has no expectation of verisimilitude—narratives which blur the boundary between Truth and Fiction might offend his Platonist instincts. The work for which he is most famous today— *The Praise of Folly* (*Moriae Encomium*), first published in 1511—acknowledges (in the preface) both Lucian's and Apuleius' *Ass* as satirical precedents; but while Erasmus manages to elaborate such rhetorical tropes as prosopopoeia far beyond the usual confines of pseudo-doxology (so that Folly threatens to

---

[199] (London: [By John Kingston], by Ihon Shepperd, 1577), sig. L1^{r-v}.

[200] In the *Utopia*, he uses *dissitus* (52/11, 144/24) and *nugamentum* (154/15). See *The Complete Works of St. Thomas More*, vol. iv, ed. E. Surtz (New Haven: YUP, 1965), 580. In the *De tristitia Christi*, More uses *curiosulus*, a diminutive known in Latin only from *AA* 10. 31 (where it describes the wind uncovering 'Venus' in the pantomime). See *The Complete Works*, xiv/2, 1019.

become not merely a didactic tool but an autonomous 'character'), there is very little about the work that could be called 'novelistic'. The closest he comes to such a use of fiction is perhaps in 'The Shipwreck' (*Naufragium*), one of the best known of Erasmus' *Colloquia* (1518), those delightfully dramatized dialogues whose influence can still be seen in Cervantes' *Novelas ejemplares* (1613). Both More and Erasmus are typical of northern humanists in their subordination of fiction to didactic (or merely epideictic) ends. If humanists have a preferred mode of fiction, it takes the form of satire (whether called Varronian, Menippean, Lucianic, or Erasmian).

Juan Luis Vives

The range of such works is enormous, even extending to satirical fictions about Fiction itself. One of the most entertaining of these is a dialogue entitled *Veritas fucata, sive de licentia poetica, quantum Poetis liceat a Veritate abscedere* ('Truth Falsified, or Concerning Poetic Licence: To what Extent Poets are Permitted to Depart from the Truth'), composed by Vives in 1522 or 1523. The opposing kingdoms of Truth and Falsity have called a truce and Falsity sends a delegation to persuade Truth to submit to them, since she cannot survive unsupported by fiction. The delegation is led by Homer and Hesiod, with Apuleius and Lucian as the two footsoldiers (*ille* [sc. *Homerus*] *quidem Hesiodo comitatus & duobus a pedibus Luciano atque Appuleio iter ingressus est*).[201] Apuleius is delighted to hear Lucian remark that he was once turned into an ass, since he himself has been 'changed into an ass by a great many people, above all by Martianus Capella, Sulpicius Apollinaris, Battista Pio, and Filippo Beroaldo'. While they await Truth's answer, Plato and Homer swap insults and Varro and Ausonius become argumentative. In order to jolly the party along (*Ad exhilarandum conuiuium*, sig. Cii^r), Apuleius 'said something about his Ass' while 'Lucian expounded his *True (Hi)stories* which neither he nor anyone else either saw or heard or will believe' (*Lucianus suas veras narrationes exposuit. quas nec ipse, nec alius, quisquis vel vidit vel audiuit, vel credet*, sig. Cii^r). Truth, meanwhile, stays up all night, turning these matters over in her mind. She shudders at the thought of being dressed up in counterfeit colours (*fucata*), but acknowledges that she will have to

---

[201] (Louvain: Theodornecus Martinus Alostensis, 1523), sig. Biv^r. Lucian and Apuleius also feature in two Menippean satires by Nicolas Rigault, *Asinus sive de Scaturigine Onocrenes* (1596) and *Funus parasiticum* (1599). See I. De Smet, *Menippean Satire and the Republic of Letters, 1581–1655* (Geneva: Droz, 1996), 118–23. Another Menippean satire, *Amator ineptus* (probably printed by Jean Maire in Leiden in 1633) makes frequent use of Apuleian language. For example, 'Psyche' (one of the objects of the Clumsy Lover's attentions) is described in the same terms as Fotis (8. 8: *moribus ludicra prorsusque argutula*; cf. *AA* 2. 6). See I. De Smet, 'Amatus Fornacius, *Amator Ineptus* (Palladii, 1633): A Seventeenth-Century Satire', *HL* 38 (1989): 238–306, at 260 *et passim*.

make some concessions if she is to have any impact on the obstinate minds of men. Accordingly, she decides that the orders of Falsity should be accepted, but with certain conditions: Fiction is neither to be accepted nor rejected completely (*fucum in totum nec admitti nec reiici*). Homer is ordered to take back to the kingdom of Falsity ten conditions, the ninth of which provides a carefully delimited place for Milesian Tales: anyone who freely chooses to be a devotee (*assectari*) of Falsity and turns his back on morality and utility (*nec ad mores aut vitae vsum deflexerit*, sig. C[iii]ᵛ), may be given Milesian Citizenship and go and live in voluptuousness with Apuleius, Lucian, and Clodius Albinus.[202]

The whole of Vives's dialogue, of course, is so highly ironic that one cannot put too much store by these concessions and it is perhaps significant that the *Veritas fucata* (1522/3) was generally not included in the major editions of Vives's works—he may have felt (with the benefit of hindsight) that he had already compromised himself enough.

The general tenor of his comments is hostile. In 1529, Vives condemns, as being designed merely to 'stimulate pleasures', the works of certain poets, as well as

the fables of Milesius, as that of the Golden Ass, and in a manner all Lucian's works, and many others which are written in the vulgar tongue as of Tristan, Launcelot, Ogier, Amadís, and of Arthur the which were written and made by such as were idle and knew nothing. The books do hurt both man and woman, for they make them wily and crafty, they kindle and stir up covetousness, inflame anger and all beastly and filthy desire.[203]

voluptates titillant pleraque Poetarum opera, et Milesiae fabulae, ut Asinus Apuleji, et fere Luciani omnia, quales crebrae sunt in linguis vernaculis scriptae Tristani, Lanciloti, Ogerii, Amadisii, Arturi, et his similes; qui libri omnes ab otiosis hominibus, et chartarum abundantibus, per ignorantiam meliorum sunt conscripti: hi non feminis modo, verumetiam viris officiunt, quemadmodum ea omnia, quibus nutus iste noster ad pejora detruditur, ut quibus armatur astutia, accenditur habendi sitis, inflammatur ira, aut cujuscunque rei turpis atque illicita cupiditas.[204]

For Vives, these sorts of fictions pollute both home and state.

Apuleius, however, was clearly an author whom Vives knew intimately. In his commentary on Augustine's *City of God* (composed at the prompting of Erasmus, and dedicated to King Henry VIII), Vives refers to *The Golden Ass*, *Apologia*, and *Florida* repeatedly, and his criticism is tempered by obvious affection:

---

[202] The conditions are usefully summarized by W. Nelson, *Fact or Fiction: The Dilemma of the Renaissance Storyteller* (Cambridge, Mass.: HUP, 1973), 46–7.

[203] Vives, *The Office and Duetie of an Husband*, trans. Thomas Paynell (London: John Cawood, c.1558), sig. O7ʳ⁻ᵛ; W. B. Ife, *Reading and Fiction in Golden Age Spain: A Platonic Critique and Some Humanist Replies* (Cambridge: CUP, 1985), 14.

[204] Vives, *De officio mariti* (Bruges: [De Molendino?], 1529); Ife, *Reading and Fiction*, 177.

Hee was of *Madaura*, a *Platonist*, a great louer and follower of antiquitie, both in learning and language. His *Asse* hee had from *Lucian*, but added much to the translation.[205]

Of the wickednesse of arte Magicke, depending on these wicked Spirits ministery. CHAP. 19.

Now extant] His two Apologies concerning Magicke: wherein hee leaueth all his luxurious phrase, and his fustian tearmes, and goeth to it like a plaine lawyer: yet not so well but he flies out here and there and must bee *Apuleius* still. (8. 19, p. 326)

Of the deuills power in transforming mans shape: what a Christian may beleeue herein. CHAP. 18.

...Apuleius] Hee was a magitian, doubtlesse: but neuer turned into an asse. *Augustine* saw how incredible that was, but <hauing> not red many Greekes, he could not know whence he had his plot of the *golden asse:* for <he> names none that he followes, as hee doth in his cosmography. But *Lucian* before him <wrote> how hee beeing in Thessaly to learne some magike was turned into an asse in stead of a <?bird, not> that this was true: but that *Lucian* delighted neither in truths, nor truths likelihoods. <This work>e did *Apuleius* make whole in latine, adding diuers things to garnish it with more delight to such as loue Melesian tales, and heere and there sprinckling it with his antiquaries <phrases>, and his new compositions, with great liberty, yet some-what suppressing the absurdity <of the the>ame. But wee loue now to read him because hee hath said some things there in that <?new> dexterity, which others seeking to imitate, haue committed grosse errors: for I thinke <that> grace of his in that worke, is inimitable. But *Apuleius* was no asse, only he delights mens <eares wi>th such a story, as mans affection is wholy transported with a strange story. (18. 18, p. 695)

In chapter 5 (*De historia*) of his *Declamatio de incertitudine et vanitate scientiarum atque artium* (1530), Heinrich Cornelius Agrippa von Nettesheim (1486–1535) lumps together (as *fabulosae historiae*) Lucian, Apuleius, and the Arthurian romances, condemning them as *fabulosa ac simul inerudita deliramenta poetarum, comoediis ac fabulis fabulosiora* ('fabulous and, at the same time unlearned absurdities of the poets, more fabulous than comedies and fables').[206] In the *De occulta philosophia*, however, Agrippa draws extensively on *The Golden Ass*. In his dedicatory epistle to Johannes Trithemius

---

[205] *St. Augustine, Of the citie of God vvith the learned comments of Io. Lod. Viues. Englished by I.H.* (London: George Eld, 1610), 2. 2, p. 157. (*EEBO* images based on poor microfilm).

[206] (Antwerp: Johannes Graphaeus, 1530), fol. E. 4ᵛ. Of course, nothing in the *Declamatio* should be taken at face value. See, generally, E. Korkowski, 'Agrippa as Ironist', *Neophilologus* 60 (1976), 594–607; and M. H. Keefer, 'Agrippa's Dilemma: Hermetic Rebirth and the Ambivalences of *De Vanitate* and *De Occulta Philosophia*', *RQ* 41 (1988), 614–53.

(1462–1516), he quotes Socrates' account of Meroe's powers (*AA* 1. 8: *et divini potens... Tartarum ipsum illuminare*).[207] Within the body of the work, we find the following references (by no means an exhaustive list):

Bk 1, ch. 50: the incestuous stepmother's entreaty to her stepson (*AA* 10. 3)

Bk 1, ch. 58: Zatchlas causing the dead man to speak (*AA* 2. 28–9)

Bk 1, ch. 71: Psyche's prayer to Ceres (*AA* 6. 2)

Bk 1, ch. 72 : the alleged power of magic (*AA* 1. 3: *Magico susurramine... noctem teneri*)

Bk 2, ch. 10: Lucius dipping his head in the water seven times (*AA* 11. 1)

Bk 3, ch. 2 : Mithras taking hieroglyphic texts from the sanctuary (*AA* 11. 22: *peracto... munita*)

Bk 3, ch. 32: the old man's entreaty to Zatchlas before he reanimates the dead nephew's corpse (*AA* 2. 28: *per coelestia sydera... et sistra phariaca*)

CONCLUSIONS

The common denominator of Apuleian influences in the Renaissance is controversy. Platonists use him in their struggle with the Aristotelians; he becomes a focal point in the bitter debates over Latin prose-style; and he features prominently in discussions of the function and value of fiction. The debate over imitative models was no frigid academic exercise—it was a battle to establish the very fabric of intellectual discourse, spoken as well as written. Language is fundamental to thought; style is inextricably linked with character; and Apuleianism was regarded as much as a moral and political threat as an aesthetic one. Cicero was not only the most eloquent of the Romans; he was also the most virtuous—his statesmanship and his balanced periods are reflections of each other—and though denied the benefit of Revelation, he came closer in his philosophy to the teachings of Christ than any of his countrymen. The decline in Latinity that produced Apuleius is linked by the polemicists with the decay of classical civilization itself; and the contemporary threat to Ciceronian orthodoxy posed by the resurgence of Apuleianism is made analogous.

Of the ancients who resurfaced in the Renaissance, Lucian is perhaps the most prominent, and it is no coincidence that two of the greatest literary

---

[207] Agrippa had sent Trithemius a draft of the work in 1510, but it was not until 1533 that the (much revised and expanded) work was printed. See *De occulta philosophia libri tres*, ed. V. Perrone Compagni (Leiden: Brill, 1992), 31. Agrippa also quotes from the *Apologia*, the *De deo Socratis*, the *De mundo*, and the pseudo-Apuleian *Herbarius*.

works produced by sixteenth-century humanists—*Utopia* and the *Praise of Folly*—are essentially Lucianic. Lucian's blasphemous irreverence placed him beyond the pale for the likes of Luther and the more conservative humanists, but the purity of his Attic made him pedagogically attractive (Erasmus learned most of his Greek by translating Lucian, and educationalists wrote him into their curricula) and though his use of *joco-serium* violated the prevailing Aristotelian and Horatian precepts of generic uniformity, the Erasmians were able to accommodate him by stressing his 'delightful teaching'. Yet the fascination that Apuleius held for the Renaissance is evident at every stage. Here was another joco-serious author (Erasmus once called him 'a philosopher but without a trace of a frown'[208]), as eloquent and amusing as Lucian, and equally controversial. But humanism had not yet developed the theoretical apparatus necessary to assimilate Apuleius completely. Lucianic fictions could be defended because they were satirically pointed. In contrast, the ostensible *telos* of *The Golden Ass*—Isiac initiation—was obviously unacceptable, and the Beroaldian exegesis of the work as a warning against voluptuary indulgence must have seemed as artistically unattractive as it was intellectually unconvincing. The real imaginative appeal of Apuleius' novel lay in its presentation of non-teleological, 'autonomous' fictions and in the dialectic established between the 'credible narrations' contained within the work and its fantastical superstructure. Erasmus made frequent use of fictive devices in his writings, but even if the 'fictional overlay' became, on occasions, 'distracting' (as in the *Shipwreck*), he retained what Douglas Duncan calls a 'basic mistrust of fictions *per se*'.[209] This tension is evident even in the work of Rabelais's who famously claimed Erasmus as both father and mother to his work. Apuleius figures in the Land of Satin in the posthumously-published and possibly spurious *Cinquiesme Livre*: 'J'y vy la peau de l'asne d'or d'Apulée' ('I saw the Skin of Apuleius's golden Ass', ch. 30, 974), but Rabelais's obvious master in the exposition of the ludicrous and the fantastic is Lucian; if one wished to add an 'Ancient Novelist' as a significant influence, it would have to be Petronius (minus his *Cena*). For while Rabelais, by extending the limits of Menippean satire, opens up new possibilities for the literary artist wanting to explore 'the human condition' in all its aspects, he provides none of the narrative structure that will be necessary for the emergence of a recognizable novel. The triumph of the autonomous fiction was still to come.

---

[208] *philosophum quidem illum sed fronte ne utiquam tetrica.* See *Opus epistolarum Des. Erasmi,* i. 185.

[209] *Ben Jonson and the Lucianic Tradition* (Cambridge: CUP, 1979), 47, 50.

7

The Golden Asse of William Adlington (1566)

By 1566, Apuleius had already played a pivotal role in Italian humanism and had long been prominent in the controversies of the Northern Renaissance; but it was the publication of William Adlington's translation that unlocked, for a much larger audience of English readers, the heavy casket of Apuleius' Latin and allowed the succeeding generations to plunder the riches within. The years of 1565 to 1567 witnessed the publication of four of the most influential works of the English Renaissance, Adlington's translation appearing in the same year as William Painter's *The Palace of Pleasure*, sandwiched between the first instalment of Golding's Ovid (1565) and Thomas Drant's rendering of Horace's *Ars poetica* (1567).[1] The Register of the Company of Stationers records during the period 22 July 1565 to 22 July 1566:

Wekes. Recevyd of henry Wekes for his lycense for pryntinge of a boke intituled *the hole boke of* LUCIOUS APELIOUS of ye golden asse . . . . viijd.[2]

Henry Wykes had been an apprentice of Thomas Berthelet (d. 1555) and had continued to print in the Fleet Street shop after the death of Berthelet's nephew, Thomas Powell (1564).[3] Adlington himself has proved to be an elusive figure. Although he signs his dedicatory epistle 'From Vniversity Colledge in Oxenford, the xviij. of September, 1566', he has left no trace in the university or college archives.[4] Charles Whibley suggested that he may

---

[1] Apuleius appears in *The Palace of Pleasure*, ed. J. Jacobs, 3 vols. (London: David Nutt, 1890), i. 9, as the penultimate entry in the first of Painter's two lists of 'Authours out of whom these Nouelles be selected, or which be remembred in diuers places in the same': 'Titus Liuius. Herodotus. Aelianus. Xenophon. Quintus Curtius. Aulus Gellius. S. Hierome. Cicero. Polidorus Virgilius. Aeneas Syluius. Paludanus. Apuleius. L. Cælius Rhodoginus.' The remaining books of Golding's *Metamorphoses* were published in 1567.

[2] *A Transcript of the Registers of the Company of Stationers of London, 1554–1640 A.D.*, ed. E. Arber, 5 vols. (London: priv. printed, 1875–94), i, fol. 138ᵛ.

[3] On Wykes's career, see R. B. McKerrow, gen. ed., *A Dictionary of Printers and Booksellers in England, Scotland and Ireland, and of Foreign Printers of English Books 1557–1640* (London: Bibliographical Soc., 1910), 304, and *STC* iii. 192.

[4] The subscription is printed in the BL's copies of the 1566, 1571, and 1582 edns. but has been added by hand to the Bodleian copy of the 1596 edn. A county-by-county survey of the

have been the 'W.A.' responsible for the publication in 1579 of a pious work entitled *A Speciall Remedie against the furious force of lawlesse Love*, but William Averell is another candidate.[5] To this meagre stock, we can now add two possible clues. The Records of the Prerogative Court of Canterbury contain the will of William Adlington or Adlyngton, Gentleman of London, made on 14 April 1571, and proved on 12 May 1571.[6] The will makes no mention of books or literary activity, and there is nothing to tie the testator to the translator beyond the fact that the death date would explain our Adlington's disappearance from the literary scene. It may also be worth noting that the will of Philip Henslowe (*c.*1555–1616) specifies an annuity of £30 to his sister, 'Mary Walter, *alias* Adlington'.[7]

Some background information can also be gleaned from Adlington's dedication of the work to Thomas Radcliffe, third Earl of Sussex (1526?–83).[8] Sussex had been one of the canopy-bearers at the funeral of Henry VIII (1547) and in 1556, Queen Mary sent him, accompanied by Sir Henry Sidney (his new brother-in-law), as lord deputy of Ireland. On news of Mary's death in 1558, he handed Ireland over to Sidney and returned to England, but in the following year he was appointed lieutenant-general by Elizabeth and governed Ireland (incurring much criticism) until 1564.[9] He enjoyed strained relations with Robert Dudley, Earl of Leicester, and opposed the notion of the latter's match with Elizabeth, favouring instead, the Austrian Archduke Charles:

In summer 1565 and again a year later there were open confrontations between the earls.... A public reconciliation enforced by the queen papered over the quarrel, but

incidence of the name in the International Genealogical Index suggests that Adlingtons, in the 15th cent., were concentrated in two large groupings, in Lancashire and in London. The abstracts of charters relating to the Adlingtons at Adlington Manor in Chester contained in BL Add. Mss. 6032. ff. 27, 28 are restricted to the 14th cent. and consequently yield no useful information about the translator's origins. I am grateful to the Fellow Archivist at University College, Oxford, for checking the college archives. The 'Buttery Books' are missing for this period and Adlington's name does not appear elsewhere.

[5] *The Golden Ass of Apuleius: Translated out of the Latin by William Adlington*, ed. W. E. Henley, introd. C. Whibley (London: David Nutt, 1893), p. xxviii. On the *Remedie* (reprinted by the Roxburghe Society in 1844), *STC* (item 982) says, 'possibly not by Averell'. W. E. Burns (*ODNB*, s.v. 'Averell, William') makes no attempt to claim the *Remedie* for Averell.

[6] Catalogue ref. PROB 11/53; image ref. 242/196. Downloaded from PRO's Documents Online (6 May 2005). Adlington's bequest of six pounds 'to each of my Mrs children Margyt Marke Steven and Will̲i̲a̲m' seems to suggest that he had married a widow with children from her former marriage.

[7] Mentioned, *en passant*, by C. Sisson, 'Henslowe's Will again', *RES* 5 (1929), 308–11, at 310. On Henslowe's involvement in a production of Dekker's *Cupid and Psyche*, see Ch. 8, *infra*.

[8] On Sussex, see W. T. MacCaffrey, 'Radcliffe, Thomas, third earl of Sussex (1526/7–1583)', *ODNB*.

[9] Sussex had married Frances, daughter of Sir William Sidney (and aunt of the infant Philip Sidney) in 1555.

in the winter of 1565–6 adherents of the two rivals sported coloured badges, purple for the Norfolk and Sussex followers, yellow for Leicester's; and the courtiers went about armed. The continued pressure on the queen to marry, focused in the 1566 parliament, pushed her to act and in November of that year she appointed Sussex to a mission to Vienna to discuss marriage. Royal vacillation delayed his departure to June 1567.[10]

But besides being a 'perfect courtier and diplomat', Sussex was also, it has been said, 'a scholar saturated in the new learning, a patron of the drama in its infancy, and of rising literary genius'.[11] 'Genius' is a strong word to apply to a literary circle that probably reckoned Anthony Munday its brightest luminary, but Adlington may have offered Sussex something to appeal to diplomat as well as *littérateur*.[12] Golding, in 1565, had dedicated his (Ovidian) *Metamorphosis* to 'Robert, Erle of Leycester',[13] and there is surely an irony (if not a covert political reference) in Adlington's dedication (to a nobleman negotiating a royal match with Leicester's rival) of a work which advertises, on its title-page, 'an excellent Narration of the Mariage of Cupide and Psiches'.

THE TRANSLATION

Sources

The Golden Ass acquired an English complexion relatively late: by 1566 there were already two translations in Italian, three in French, one in German, and one in Spanish. The versions of Boiardo (1518) and Firenzuola (1550) are so distant—in word and spirit—from the original, that they can be dismissed as potential sources; and the improbability of Adlington's knowing German would seem to rule out Sieder's translation (1538). But Adlington gives a clue to the underpinnings of his own translation when he justifies his not having 'so exactly passed through the Authot [*sic*], as to point euerie sentence according as it is in Latine, or so absolutely translated euerie word, as it lieth in the prose', by the practice of his Continental predecessors: '(for so the

---

[10] Sussex had married Frances, daughter of Sir William Sidney (and aunt of the infant Philip Sidney) in 1555.

[11] R. Dunlop, 'Radcliffe, Thomas', *DNB* xlvii (1896), 136–44, at 143.

[12] F. B. Williams, Jr., *Index of Dedications and Commendatory Verses in English Books before 1641* (London: Bibliographical Soc., 1962), 153. I am grateful to Dr L. G. Black for referring me to this work.

[13] *The Fyrst Fower Bookes of ... Metamorphosis* (London: William Seres, 1565), sig. [*j]ᵛ. The dedication is dated 23 Dec. 1564.

French and *Spanish* translatours haue not done)'.[14] The only Spanish version
available to him was that of Diego López de Cortegana (*c.*1513) but '[c]areful
examination fails to bring out any connection between the two'.[15] As to the
French influence, Charles Whibley's analysis has gone virtually unchallenged
since the appearance of his much-praised introduction to the reprint of
1893.[16] Whibley refers to the translations by Guillaume Michel (1522) and
Georges de la Bouthière (1553),[17] but decides that la Bouthière was not used
by Adlington, Michel instead being the 'guide, and too often a blind guide,
unto Adlington's footsteps':

> A comparison of the two versions sets the matter beyond uncertainty. If again and
> again the same inaccuracy glares in English and French, it is obvious that the one was
> borrowed from the other.[18]

One voice alone seems to have questioned Whibley's pronouncements. In
1908, Adolf Hoffmann contended that Adlington also made use of la
Bouthière, citing, in support of his claim, Adlington's translation of Venus'
sarcastic welcome to Psyche (*Tandem inquit dignata es socrum tuam salutare?*)

---

[14] Adlington, sig. A3[r]. Except as otherwise indicated, all quotations are taken from the
Bodleian's copy of *The eleuen Bookes of the Golden Asse* (London: Valentine Symmes, 1596).
According to MacCaffrey (*ODNB* entry), Sussex (Adlington's patron) was 'at home in Latin' and
had 'essayed to learn Spanish' during the reign of Queen Mary (1553–8) when he was appointed
'gentleman of the privy chamber' to Mary's husband, King Philip II of Spain.

[15] H. B. Lathrop, *Translations from the Classics into English from Caxton to Chapman,
1477–1620* (Madison: U of Wisconsin, 1933; New York: Octagon, 1967), 160. Lathrop's work
is riddled with errors: e.g. 'Lopez de Castegone', 'Thomas Adlington' (in the text), and 'John
Adlington' (in the Index). Walsh's reference (*Roman Novel*, 233) to Spanish versions by 'Medina
del Campo' (1543) and 'Amberes' (1551), results from mistaking the place of publication for the
name of the translator. My own (rather cursory) inspection of the Spanish text failed to unearth
any compelling evidence of dependency, but Adlington's prefatory matter may owe something
to Cortegana's. See, generally, C. G. Gual, 'Sobre la version espanola de *El asno de oro* por
Diego López de Cortegana', in *Homenaje al profesor Antonio Vilanova*, ed. A. Sotelo Vázquez and
M. C. Carbonell, 2 vols. (Barcelona: Dept. de Filol. Espanola, U of Barcelona, 1989), i. 297–307;
J. Gil, 'Apuleyo en la Sevilla renacentista', *Habis* 23 (1992), 297–306; F. P. Rubio, 'La traducción
española del *Asínus Aureus* de Apuleyo de Diego López de Cortegana', *Livius* 4 (1993), 157–68.

[16] It is called a 'magnificent introduction' in the anonymous foreword to the Abbey Classics
reprint of the 1639 edn.: *The Golden Asse of Lucius Apuleius* (London: Simpkin Marshall, n.d.),
p. xii. The editor of the original Loeb edn., S. Gaselee (1915), calls it (at p. viii) 'an elaborate and
clear-sighted criticism of the merits and failures of Adlington's translation' and (at p. ix) praises
Whibley for his 'great ingenuity' in having 'tracked down the particular [French] rendering
he employed'.

[17] Guillaume Michel, trans., *Lucius Apuleius de Lasne dore* (Paris: Philippe le Noir, 1522);
George de la Bouthière, trans., *Métamorphose* (Lyons: Jean de Tournes & Guillaume Gazeau,
1553). The colophon to the 1522 edn. of Michel states that the translation was made in 1517,
and H. Le Maitre, *Essai sur le mythe de Psyché dans la littérature française des origines à 1890*
(Paris: Boivin, n.d.), 361, cites actual edns. for 1517 and 1518, though he puts the view that these
might be but one edn.

[18] Whibley, p. xxvi.

as 'O goddesse, goddesse, you are now come at length to visit your husband'.[19] Hoffmann quotes la Bouthière's translation, *Dea, dea, dit elle, tu as daigné à la parfin venir saluer ta belle mere,* and concludes:

Verzeihlicherweise hat der Engländer die Interjektion 'dea' (afr. dea, dia) mit der Bedeutung 'wahrhaftig!', 'wirklich!', 'traun!' missverständlich mit dem lat. Vocativ 'dea', 'Göttin' verwechselt und mit 'goddess' übersetzt.

Im Übrigen besteht kein Zusammenhang zwischen Bouthieres und Adlingtons Version unseres Märchens. Der Engländer hat im löblichen Gegensatz zu der Mehrzahl seiner Kollegen dem knappen Text des Originals den Vorzug gegeben vor der an tausend Stellen abweichenden, in die Breite fliessenden, französischen Übersetzung.[20]

(The Englishman, with excusable misunderstanding, has confused the [French] interjection *dea*, meaning 'really!', 'truly!', 'indeed!', with the Latin vocative *dea*, and translated it as 'goddess'. As for the rest, there exists no [other] connection between la Bouthière and Adlington's version of our tale. The Englishman has, in commendable contrast to the majority of his colleagues, given preference to the concise text of the original, rejecting the flowing breadth of the French translation which departs [from the original] in a thousand places.)

Neither Whibley nor Hoffmann, however, seems to be aware of the existence of a third French translation, made in 1553 by Jean Louveau.[21] Francis Douce, who bequeathed to the Bodleian Library copies of Michel, la Bouthière, and Louveau, noted in the front of his own copy of the 1596 edition of *The Golden Asse*: 'I suspect that Adlington has rather translated from the French of Louveau than the Latin of Apuleius.'[22] Douce died in 1834 and no one, until now, appears to have repeated his observation.[23] In the passage quoted by Hoffmann, Louveau is even closer than la Bouthière to Adlington:

Dea, dea, tu es venuë finalement saluer ta belle mere, ou tu es venuë visiter ton mary qui est en danger de sa vie pour la playe que tu lui as faicte? (Louveau, p. 190)

---

[19] A. Hoffmann, *Das Psyche-Märchen des Apuleius in der englischen Literatur* (Strasbourg: Huber, 1908), 8–9; Beroaldo (*Commentarii*, 1500), fol. 122ᵛ [= *AA* 6. 9]; Adlington, ch. 22, p. 95.

[20] Hoffmann, 9; la Bouthière, 303.

[21] *Luc. Apulée de lasne doré: contenant onze livres* (Lyons: Jean Temporal, 1553). Le Maitre (*Essai*, 48) records six 16th-cent. edns. of Louveau, to which list one might add a seventh (Lyons: N. Perrineau for I. Temporal, 1558). All quotations in this chapter are taken from the Bodleian's copy, *Luc. Apulee de l'ane dore, xi liuures* (Paris: Claude Micard, 1584). Walsh's statement (*Roman Novel*, 233) that 'There were two French versions in the sixteenth century, that of Temporal and that of Louveau d'Orleans' confuses the publisher of the 1558 edn. ('I. Temporal') with the translator ('I. Louueau').

[22] Bodleian, Douce A. 252.

[23] For an account of this discerning and engaging collector, see S. G. Gillam et al., *The Douce Legacy* (Oxford: Bodleian Library, 1984).

Such instances could be repeated ad infinitum, but one might single out the concluding sentence of the novel:

Rursus denique quam raro [sic] *capillo collegii uetustissimi: & sub illis Syllæ temporibus conditi munia* [280ᵛ] *non obumbrato: uel obtecto caluicio: sed quoquouersus obuio: gaudens obibam.* (Beroaldo, fol. 280ʳ⁻ᵛ [= AA 11. 30])

Michel's version bears only the vaguest relation to the Latin:

Je feiz tout ce que le dieu me commanda. Je alloye nue teste pour monstrer lhumilite | & lobseruation de la loy si que ie donnasse bon exemple. Je viuoye chastement | subuenoye au poure peuple | porioye bonne doctrine | sou-[clxviᵛ]*tenoie les pupilles et poures | et me resiouyssoie en la vie contemplatiue dedans la saincte cite de Romme.* (Michel, fol. clxviʳ⁻ᵛ)

Louveau is far more literal, and is followed, almost word for word, by Adlington:

Et depuis me feit auoir place, & office dedans l'ancien palais, qui fut erigé au temps de Sylla, ou ie faisois mon office en grande resiouissance, ayant la teste rasee. (Louveau, p. 409)

and after he appointed me a place within the ancient pallace, which was erected in the time of *Silla*, where I executed my office in gret ioy with a shauen crowne. (Adlington, ch. 48, p. 208)

Even at the level of structural organization, Adlington follows Louveau almost exactly, occasionally compressing two of the Frenchman's chapters into one, or dividing a longer one into two.²⁴ Our Louveau-thesis still needs to be tested, however, against the evidence for Michel provided by Whibley, the strongest of which is the occurrence (with no authority, we are told, in the Latin) of the name *Britunis* in Adlington and *Brulinus* in Michel:²⁵

After that we had passed many smal villages, we fortuned to come to one *Britunis* house, whereat our first entrie they began to hurle themselues hether and thether, as though they were mad. (Adlington, ch. 36, p. 140 [= AA 8. 27])

Et apres quilz eurent en aulcunes maisons erre vindrent en aucun villaige chiez vng riche laboureur nomme Brulinus: qui possedoit ledit villaige / cest assauoir quelque bel heritaige Quant ilz furent la chascun commenca a vller et crier heultement (Michel, fol. 109ʳ)

---

²⁴ There are no chapters in the early printed edns. of Apuleius. The text flows, thick and stolid, through the casing of Beroaldo's commentary, broken only by the ends and beginnings of its eleven books. La Bouthière continues the practice. The French edns. of Michel and Louveau, however, are clearly divided, a summary of the contents of each chapter appearing in the chapter heading.

²⁵ Whibley, p. xxvii.

One might want to make the preliminary objection that the degree of similarity between 'Britunis' and 'Brulinus' is hardly sufficient to constitute evidence of dependence; but where could Michel and Adlington have found such names, given that the Latin text, as we know it today, says nothing of either character?:

Nec paucis pererratis casulis ad quandam uillam possessoris beati perueniunt et ab ingressu primo statim absonis ululatibus constrepentes fanatice prouolant (Budé edn., AA 8. 27)

The simple answer is provided by Beroaldo, the ultimate source of the anomaly:

nec paucis pererratis casulis: ad quandam uillam possessoris britini perueniunt. (Beroaldo, fol. 186ᵛ)²⁶

But it is in Louveau that we find Adlington's immediate source:

Apres qu'ils eurent esté par quelques maisons, nous arriuasmes à la maison d'vn nommé Britinus, ou de premiere entree ils commencerent à vrler, & faire vn grand bruit, comme hors du sens. (Louveau, p. 273)

Whibley observes that 'This strange correspondence in error might be enforced by countless examples.'²⁷ In fact, in all but one of the examples cited by Whibley, Adlington is actually closer to Louveau than to Michel. Of the three Frenchmen, la Bouthière was the best equipped, linguistically, to penetrate the lush jungle of Apuleius' Latin, but where Apuleius is copious, la Bouthière is merely verbose. Worse still (at least, from a twenty-first-century perspective) is his willingness to excise or adapt portions of the text where the subject matter is not to his liking—most obviously (as we shall see below) in the replacement of Book 11 with an adaptation of the pseudo-Lucianic *Onos*.²⁸ Louveau's, on balance, is the best of the three versions, but it is certainly not perfect, often (despite its protestation of independence) being merely a revision of Michel's, and frequently reproducing the latter's mistakes or interpolations. Apuleius' introduction to the encounter between Aristomenes and Meroë is translated correctly (if prolixly) by la Bouthière:

Hæc adhuc me suadente: insolita uinolentia: ac diuturna fatigatione pertentatus bonus Socrates iam sopitus stertebat altius. (Beroaldo, fol. 16ᵛ [= AA 1. 11])

Ie nauois encores du tout paracheué mon dire que le bon Socrates (pour le bon vin quil auoit beu ce soir, par plusieurs iours à lui desia desaccoutumé, ou bien pource quil estoit

---

²⁶ Marianus Tuccius and Franciscus Asulanus both give the same reading, *Britini*. La Bouthière (468) merely speaks of *la maison du Seigneur dudit lieu*.

²⁷ Whibley, p. xxvii.

²⁸ Cf. the practice of Firenzuola described in Ch. 6, *supra*.

grandement las & abatu des tra[34]*uaux sus mentionnez) subitement fut endormi.* (la Bouthière, p. 33)

Adlington and Michel, however, both include explanatory material bridging chapters—whence Whibley (p. xxvi) deduces an interdependence:

En luy disant ces parolles et ladmonnestant nous departir du logis pour paour que meroe la magicienne ne nous enchantast comme elle auoit fait aultres plusieurs | ia se ndormoit Socrates car il estoit fort trauaille. Pareillement auoit il beu plus quil nauoit de coustume ... (Michel, fol. vii^r)

In speaking these words, and deuising with my selfe of our departing the next morrow, lest Meroe the Witch should play by vs, as she had done by diuers other persons: it fortuned that Socrates did fal asleepe, and slept very soundly, by reason of his trauel and plentie of meate and wine, where withall he filled himselfe. (Adlington, ch. 5, p. 9)

Adlington, however, is merely following Louveau who has himself followed Michel:

En luy disant ces paroles, & l'admonestant nous de partir du logis, de peur que Meroë la magicienne ne nous enchantast, & feist comme elle auoit fait à plusieurs autres, ia s'endormoit le bon Socrates, & ronfloit bien fort, à cause du trauail qu'il auoit prins, & aussi d'autant qu'il auoit beu plus que de coustume ... (Louveau, p. 17)

The same can be said of the passage from the beginning of Book 4 quoted by Whibley (at p. xxxvii):

nec me cum asino uel equo meo compascuus cœtus attinere potuit: adhuc insolitum alioquin prandere fœnum. Sed plane pone stabulum prospectum hortulum: iam fame perditus. fidenter inuado. & quamvis [75^r] *crudis oleribus: affatim tamen uentrem sagino* ... (Beroaldo, fols. 74^v−75^r [= *AA* 4. 1])

(The idea of forming a dining society with an ass and my own horse didn't exactly grab me since I was not yet used to lunching on hay. But behind the stable I could see, in full view, a little garden. Being now perished with hunger, I burst boldly in; and although the vegetables were unripe, I nonetheless crammed my belly till I was full.)

Adlington and Michel both interpret Lucius' removal to the garden as a result of social exclusion rather than an exercise of gastronomic discrimination:

touteffoys mon cheual et lautre beste lasne de [xxxix^r] *milo ne me voulurent souffrir auec eulx paistre: car point ne me congnoissoyent encore | parquoy ie men entray en vng beau iardin qui pres de la estoit comme tout pery de fain | ie trouuay la assez a menger* (Michel, fols. xxxviii^v−xxxix^r)

but mine owne horse and Miloes asse, woulde not suffer me to feede there with them, but I must seeke my dinner in some other place. Wherefore I leaped into a garden behinde the stable, and being welnigh perished with hunger, though I could find nothing there, but raw and greene sallets, yet I filled my hungrie guts therwithall abundantly... (Adlington, ch. 18, p. 56)

But here, once again, the apparent correspondence between Michel and Adlington is due to Louveau's own dependence upon Michel:

toutefois mon cheual & l'asne de Milo, ne me voulurent onques souffrir paistre auecques eux pour la premiere fois: parquoi i'entrai dedans vn iardin que i'auois veu derriere l'estable, & pour la grand faim que i'auois, ie m'empli le ventre de herbes qui estoient dedans... (Louveau, p. 107)

Adlington was evidently following the Latin as well, since he gives to *fame perditus, crudis holeribus,* and *affatim* a literal force not found in either French version.

The only remaining pillar of Whibley's Michel-thesis is the correspondence between Adlington's 'a certaine cobler' and Michel's *quelque sauatier* in Milo's tale of the myopic seer Diophanes:

Nam die quadam: cum frequentis populi circulo septus coronæ circunstantium fata donaret. Cerdo quidam nomine negociator: accesit: eum diem commodum peregrinationi cupiens: (Beroaldo, fol. 43[r] [= *AA* 2. 13])

(For one day when, surrounded by a circle of thronging people, he was doling out fortunes to the ring of bystanders, a certain trader, Cerdo by name, approached, wanting to know what day would be suitable for making a journey.)

La Bouthière and Louveau give *Cerdo quidam nomine negociator* its obvious meaning:

de cas fortuit vn marchand nommé Cerde lui vint demander vn iour prospere & destiné à faire vn voyage... (la Bouthière, p. 76)

vn certain facteur appellé Credo, s'aprocha de luy, desirant sçauoir le temps commode à son voyage, auquel il promit de la faire... (Louveau, p. 53)

Both Michel and Adlington, however, by mistaking the proper noun for a common noun, turn the trader into a cobbler:

car vng iour comme il bateloit & predisoit les fortunes des gens tout enuironne de moult de peuple | vint a luy quelque sauatier bonnegociateur linterrogant de sa fortune pource quil vouloit faire quelque voyage (Michel, fol. xix[r])

For being on a day amongst a great assembly of people, to tel the simpl [*sic*] sort their fortune a certaine cobler came vnto him and desired him to tell when it should be best for him to take his viage, the which he promised to do... (Adlington, ch. 10, p. 28)

The pun in Apuleius depends upon the relationship between the business-man's name and the Greek word for profit (κέρδος) and Beroaldo supplies this etymology; but he goes on (in contrast to la Bouthière, Louveau, and modern translators) to link *nomine* not with *Cerdo* but with *negociator*, so that the sense becomes 'a profiteer named Trader' rather than the more obvious 'a trader named Profit'. Michel's and Adlington's mistake (*pace* Whibley, p. xxvii) is quite understandable. Adlington had only to open a copy of Thomas Cooper's dictionary to see the following entry:

cerdo, onis, m.g. a cobblar, sometyme generally all that vse any vile handy craft to geat moneie by, are called *cerdones*, for *cerdos*, in Greke, is *lucrum*, gaine.[29]

And either translator could have seized upon the additional (and, in this context, irrelevant) note provided by Beroaldo's commentary: *uulgo cerdonem uocitant sutorem ueterum calceorum* ('people commonly use the name *cerdo* for a mender of old shoes').

Yet having laid the Michel-thesis firmly to rest, we are forced, Zatchlas-like, to resurrect it for a moment in response to data quite independent of Whibley.[30] Adlington's use of Louveau is evident from the outset:

Qui est celuy? Entens vn peu, & tu congnoistras qui c'est: qui t'escrit: Hymette, Atticque, Istme, Ephire, & Tenare Spartiaque, terres fertiles & abondantes en blez, sont (croyez tousiours aux bons liures) mon antique race: là (di-ie) estant, i'ay eu ma premiere ieunesse estudié, puis apres, commes estrange & nouueau venu i'arriuay à Rome, auquel lieu i'apprins la langue Latine auec grande peine & sans maistre, ie vous prie donc me vouloir pardonner, si ie blesse voz douces oreilles par rude & rustic langage: Et certes desia le changement de voix respond au stille de la science legere: & inconstante que i'ay aprise: ie commence donc à te raconter vne fable Grecque, de laquelle preste moy l'oreille, Lecteur, & tu y prendras plaisir. (Louveau, sig. [Aviij]^v [= AA I. 1])

WHAT and who he was attend a while, and you shall vnderstand that it was euen I, the writer of mine owne Metamorphosie, and strange alteration of figure, *Hymettus, Athens, Isthmia, Ephire, Tenaros*, and *Sparta*, beeing fat and fertill soiles (as I pray you giue credit to the bookes of more euerlasting fame) be places where mine ancient progenie and linage did somtime flourish: there I say, in *Athens* when I was yong, I went first to schoole. Soone after (as a stranger) I arriued at *Rome*, whereas by great industrie and without instruction of any schoolemaster I achieued to the ful perfection of the Latin tongue: behold, I first craue and beg your pardon, lest I should happen to displease or offend anie of you by the rude and rustike vtterance of this strange and forin language. And verily this new alteration of speech doth correspond to the enterprised matter, whereof I purpose to entreate, I will set foorth vnto you a pleasant Grecian iest. Whereunto gentle reader, if thou wilt give attendant eare, I wil minister vnto thee such delectable matter as thou shalt be contented withall. (Adlington, sig. [A4]^v)

---

[29] *Bibliothecæ Eliotæ*, ed. Thomas Cooper (London: Thomas Berthelet, 1552), sig. Oij^r.

[30] Zatchlas, in *AA* 2. 28, persuades the spirit of the young man murdered by his wife to speak.

Much of the phrasing and syntax is very close: Louveau's *rude & rustic* (the original reads *exotici ac forensis*), Adlington does not need to change at all (though he produces a doublet—'strange and forin'—by attempting to accommodate the Latin).[31] Yet one might easily think that Adlington had Michel's version to hand; for while Louveau merely terms the passage a *Proème*, Adlington calls it 'The Preface of the Author to his sonne, Faustinus And unto the Readers of this Book', which closely resembles Michel's title: *Prologue de Lacteur ¶ La proposition de lacteur a son filz Faustinus & auy lecteurs de ce present liure.*[32] Michel's Prologue, however, deviates wildly from the original and exerted no discernible influence upon Adlington. Two possibilities therefore present themselves. The first is that Adlington set about translating Apuleius with only Michel as his guide, but chancing, almost before he had begun, upon the infinitely more legible and manifestly more accurate Louveau, retained from the earlier French version nothing more than the title to the preface. The second possibility is that Adlington had no knowledge of Michel at all but relied (as Michel had no doubt done) upon Beroaldo's note on the opening words, *at ego sermone*:

Lusurus Asinum aureum exorditur ab epigrammate iambico bimembri quo faustinum filium siue lectorem alloquens instar poetarum summatim proponit quid fit toto in opere edisertaturus.[33]

(Being on the point of performing *The Golden Ass*, he begins with an epigram in double iambics in which, addressing his son Faustinus or the reader, he sets out briefly, in the manner of the poets, what he is going to relate in the work as a whole.)

One other set of contrary data remains to be considered. Adlington's translation of the novel owes nothing, we have argued, to la Bouthière. Yet there are marked similarities between their prefatory discussions of method:

En quelle entreprinse ne me suis voulu assuiettir de le rendre mot à mot, ni clause à clause, comme font daucuns, defraudans en ce, nostre riche langue de sa naïue grace, celebre copiosité, & douce mignardise: ains selon lexigence de la matiere, & que le lieu le requeroit, m'accommodant aux affections, iay vsé de Phrases & circonlocutions qui m'ont

---

[31] Adlington's 'the writer of mine owne Metamorphosie and strange alteration of figure' finds authority, however, neither in Apuleius nor Louveau, but it may derive from Beroaldo's gloss (fol. [3]ᵛ) on *Quis ille* ('Who is this?', *AA* 1. 1): *extrinsecus subintelligendum sit. qui in alias imagines conuersus & in se rursum refectus fuerit: significatur autem ipsemet Apuleius* ('This might be understood superficially as the man who has been changed into different appearances and restored again to his old shape; but Apuleius himself is being intimated').

[32] Michel, fol. iiᵛ. La Bouthière uses the phrase PROLOGVE DE LAVTEVR.

[33] Beroaldo, fol. 3ʳ. One might add a third possibilty that Adlington and Michel had independent access to some other (Latin or vernacular) version (presently unknown to us) which supplied both of them with the reference to Faustinus. The name 'Faustinus' forms no part of the text of Apuleius' *Metamorphoses*. Beroaldo would have derived it from the opening of Book 2 of the *De dogmate Platonis* or from the *De mundo*.

semblé plus propres & conuenables: sans interrompre toutefois & discontinuer lordre & vray fil du suiet: ni en rien l'imminuer & changer, fors en ce qui sest trouué totalement indigne & aborrent de toute lecture. (la Bouthière, p. 12)

Howbeit I haue not so exactly passed through the Authot [*sic*], as to point euerie sentence according as it is in Latine, or so absolutely translated euerie word, as it lieth in the prose, (for so the *French* and *Spanish* translatours haue not done) considering the same in our vulgar tongue would haue appeared verie obscure and darke, and thereby consequently, loathsome to the Reader, but nothing erring (as I trust) from the giuen and natural meaning of the Author, haue vsed more common and familiar words (yet not so much as I might do) for the plainer setting forth of the same. (Adlington, sig. A3^r)

To such correspondences in sense and (superficial) similarities in diction (e.g. *aborrant de toute lecture* and 'loathsome to the reader'), we might add parallel phrases like 'vulgar tongue'/*vulgaire François* and 'now a daies'/*pour le iourdhui*:

iay bien voulu prendre ceste honneste hardiesse, de traduire cest ancien auteur Latin en nostre [7] *vulgaire François. Que si nest à tous permis & concedé d'approcher de la douce phrase & heureux langage de plusieurs doctes & eloquents traducteurs, qui pour le iourdhui fleurissent en nostre France:* (la Bouthière, pp. 6–7)

I purposed according to my slender knowledge (though it were rudely and farre diagreeing from the fine and excellent doings now a daies, to translate the same into our vulgar tongue, to the end, that amongst so many sage and serious workes) (as euerie man welnigh endeauors daily to encrease) there might be some fresh and pleasant matter, to recreate the minds of the readers withal: (Adlington, sig. [A2]^v)

Both translators express reservations about the suitability of their offering:

De quelle ferme confidence muni & poulsé, ie me suis ingeré mettre en lumiere ceste mienne traduction, qui vous est auec moymesmes dediee: encores que le subiet me semblast aucunement indigne de vos doctes & chastes oreilles, volontiers tousiours occupees à ouir choses graues & serieuses. Toutefois persuadé que vostre seigneurie, à son acoutumee louable, prendra le tout en bonne part: s'arrestant plustot au bon zele & affectionné vouloir de son humble seruiteur, qui ne tend que à la faire rire, que à la matiere, en son endroit parauenture impertinente: ie nay point trop ceremonieusement craint de vser de ce moyen pour m'insinuer de plus en plus en vostre bonne grace. (la Bouthière, p. 8)

And after long deliberation had, your honourable Lordship came to my remembrance, a man much more worthy than vnto whome so homely and rude a translation should be presented. But when I againe remembred the iesting and sportfull matter of the booke vnfit to be offered to euery man of grauitie and wisedome, I was wholly determined to make no Epistle Dedicatorie at all: til as now of late, perswaded thereuuto [*sic*] by my friends, I haue boldely enterprised to offer the same vnto your Lordship, who (as I trust) wil with no lesse good will accept the same, then if it did intreate of some serious and loftie matter, considering that although the matter therein seeme very light and mery, yet the effect thereof tendeth to a good & vertuous moral.... (Adlington, sig. [A1]ᵛ)

And each ends with a commitment to some worthier project in the future:

Parquoy soyez asseuree que si ie congnois ceste mienne diligence, conceüe dune enuie de vous plaire, estre de vous, tant soit peu, fauorisee, ie me tiendray trop plus qu'assez satisfait: & me induirez à mieux continuer, voire de me attaquer par ci apres à matieres plus hautes & plus graues, selon quil plaira au souuerain Createur men donner la grace. (la Bouthière, p. 9)

The which if your honorable Lordship shal accept and take in good part, I shal not onely thinke my small trauel and labour well employed but also receiue a further comfort to attempt some more serious matter, which may be more acceptable to your Lordship: desiring the same to excuse my rash and bold enterprise at this time, as I nothing doubt in your Lordships goodnes. (Adlington, sig. [A2]ʳ)

The correspondences seem close: the plea for patronal indulgence (*vostre seigneurie... prendra le tout en bonne part* / 'if your honorable Lordship shal accept and take in good part') coupled with the promise to undertake 'some more serious matter' (*matieres plus hauts & plus graues*). But both of these are dedicatory commonplaces. Louveau, moreover, also asks his dedicatee to excuse *la hardiesse que maintenant ay prinse enuers vous. En ce faissant me donnerez courage d'entreprendre petit à petit plus hautes matieres*, a passage which resembles not only the undertaking to 'attempt some more serious matter' but also Adlington's request 'to excuse my rash and bold enterprise'.[34] The resemblances between Adlington and la Bouthière are likely, therefore, to be merely coincidental, and Louveau remains the only proven source.

Yet while Adlington's dependence on the French was heavy, it was not exclusive. He depreciates, as we saw, his own 'slender knowledge', but he makes a real (if not fully sustained) attempt to grapple directly with the Latin. 'One advantage at least', Whibley tells us, 'was enjoyed by Adlington':

He studied Apuleius in the native Latin, using, we may believe, the famous folio of 1500 (*cum Beroaldi commentariis*), prefaced by that *Vita Lucii Apuleii summatim relata*, which he paraphrased in English with his accustomed inaccuracy.[35]

Critics tend to speak as though the 1500 folio of Beroaldo were the only Latin edition of Apuleius available to the Renaissance. This original edition is certainly a beautifully produced book, but the ratio of commentary to text, the use of the colon as the principal unit of punctuation and of small letters

[34] Louveau, sig. Aiiʳ.   [35] Whibley, p. xxv.

for proper nouns, together with the plethora of contractions can seem
intimidating, especially to the modern reader unfamiliar with the typographical conventions of *incunabula*. Adlington might well have used one of the
later editions of Beroaldo (which are punctuated more according to modern
style) or even chosen from the range of editions by Marianus Tuccius,
Franciscus Asulanus, and Bernardus Philomathes. For the *Vita*, after all,
Adlington was not so much paraphrasing Beroaldo as translating Louveau.[36]
But only Beroaldo provided a commentary, a means of penetrating Apuleius'
'darke and high' style, his 'strange and absurd words', and his 'new inuented
phrases', and Adlington clearly took advantage of this.[37]

We have to picture Adlington, then, with the French and the Latin text
open on the desk before him, favouring one above the other as his interest
inclined him or his linguistic abilities constrained him. Louveau, it is true,
sometimes led him astray when he should have kept a more vigilant eye on the
Latin, but there are, equally, cases where Adlington follows the Latin more
faithfully than his predecessors. In Book 9, for example, as the Gardener is
returning with Lucius from a bloody banquet, he is confronted by a bullying
soldier who demands to know *quorsum uacuum duceret asinum* ('whither he
was leading a burdenless ass').[38] The Latinless gardener, not understanding
the question, makes no reply, and is rewarded with a beating. Louveau is
content with the vernacular (*demanda... ou il menoit ainsi son asne à
vuide*), but Adlington converts Apuleius' indirect question into a direct one:
Quorsum vacuum ducis Asinum?[39]

In Book 11, he transliterates the (corrupt) Greek passage in Beroaldo (*Laois
Aphesus* for τὰ πλοιαφέσια, 'the start of the navigation season', *AA* 11. 17) and
combines it with the gloss that Louveau had himself taken from Beroaldo
('which signified the end of their diuine seruice, and that it was lawful for
euery man to depart').[40] When a *pastophor* appears to Lucius in a dream,

---

[36] Whibley assumes that Adlington's 'Life of Lucius Apuleius Briefely Described' has been
lifted—without acknowledgement—from Beroaldo's *Vita Lucii Apuleii Summatim Relata* but
here—as so often—Adlington is actually following (almost *verbatim*) Louveau who says merely,
La Vie de LApuleius sommairement escrite. The only apparent difference between Adlington's and
Louveau's version is the colour attributed to Apuleius' eyes. Louveau talks of *les yeux verds ou
bleuz*, but Adlington's 'gray eied' (sig. A3^v) is an exact translation of Apuleius' *oculis cesiis*
(Beroaldo, fol. 2^r), indicating Adlington's readiness to follow the original when his linguistic
competence enabled him. And where Louveau refers to Apuleius' *quatre liures des Florides*,
Adlington repeats Beroaldo's genitive plural with 'the foure books named *Floridorum*' (sig.
[A4]^r).
[37] 1636 edn. The 1596 edn. (sig. [A2]^v) does not include the adjectives 'darke' or 'absurd'.
[38] Beroaldo, fol. 217^v (= *AA* 9. 39).
[39] Louveau, 322; Adlington, ch. 43, p. 164.
[40] Adlington, ch. 47, p. 199; Beroaldo, fol. 270^r; Michel, fol. 105^v; Louveau, 392. The other
Latin edns. use the same Greek words.

thyrsos & hederas...gerens (11. 27), Adlington, presented with Louveau's *tenant en ses mains des fueilles de lierre, & de vigne,* chooses to say 'holding in his hands speares wrapped in Iuie'—an abberation, we might think, until we see Thomas Cooper's gloss on *Thyrsus*: 'some take it for a speare with a sharpe head, which had boowes and leaues of iuie wrapped about it.'[41]

The story of the Boy and the Bear (which may have attracted Shakespeare when he devised the death of Antigonus in *The Winter's Tale,* III. i) is another such example:

Dumque in ista necis meæ decontor electione: matutino me rursum puer ille peremptor meus circa montis suetum ducit uestigium. Iamque me de cuiusdam uastissimæ ilicis ramo pendulo destinato: paululum uiam supergressus: ipse securi lignum: quod deue- heret: recidebat. & ecce de proximo specu uastum attolens caput funesta proserpit ursa: quam simul conspexi: pauidus & repentina facie conterritus: totum corporis pondus in postremos poplites recello. arduaque ceruice sublimiter eleuata: lorum quo tenebar rumpo (Beroaldo, fol. 161ᵛ [= AA 7. 24])

Cependant qu'on estoit en telle deliberation de ma mort, ce faux garson me mena le lendemain bien matin à la montaigne, pour querir du bois, ou il me lia à la branche d'vn arbre: & cependant que i'estoit lié, il couppoit du bois pour me charger: Lors voicy arriuer vne merueilleuse, & terrible Ourse qui sailloit d'vne cauerne, & si tost que ie l'euz veüe, elle me feit si grand peur que ie me laissay tomber sur les genoux en rompant mon licol: (Louveau, p. 240)

While I deuised with my selfe in what manner I might end my life, the roperipe boy on the next morrow lead me to the same hil againe, and tied me to a bow of a greate Oke, and in the meane season he tooke his hatchet and cut wood to load me withal, but behold there crept out of a caue by, a maruailous great Beare, holding out his mightie head, whom when I saw, I was sodeinly strocken in feare, and (throwing all the strength of my body into my hinder heeles) lifted vp my strained head & brake the halter, wherwith I was tied (Adlington, ch. 30, p. 122)

Adlington's 'roperipe boy' excited Whibley's admiration (p. xix), but the word (meaning 'Ripe for the gallows; fit for being hanged') is not, for the Tudors, exceptionally uncommon and conveys precisely the opposite mean-ing to the Latin's *puer ille peremptor meus* ('that boy, my destroyer').[42] Adlington's attempt is superior, however, to Louveau's ineffectual epithet *ce faux garson*. His 'marueilous great beare' suggests that he was still looking at Louveau (*vne merveileuse, & terrible Ourse*), but, faithful to the Latin, he restores Lucius to his suicidal deliberations (Louveau's ass was merely the object of the robbers' murderous intentions). Adlington is more specific than Louveau, correctly rendering *ilex* as an 'Oke' (Louveau simply calls it *vn*

---

[41] Louveau, 405; Adlington, ch. 48, p. 206; *Bibliotheca Eliotæ*, sig. AAaaiijᵛ.
[42] *OED*, s.v. 'rope-ripe'.

arbre), conveying the detail of *uastum attolens caput* ('holding out his mightie head') and *arduaque ceruice sublimiter eleuata* ('lifted vp my strained head'), and mastering the complex construction *totum corporis pondus in postremos poplites recello* ('throwing all the strength of my body into my hinder heels') which Louveau mangled (*ie me le laissay tomber sur les genoux*).

Yet Adlington can also be a botcher. He seems to have grown more careless as he neared the end of his labour, for he follows Louveau into error by calling the town of Cenchreae (*oppidum . . . nobilissimæ coloniæ corinthiensium*) 'the most famous Towne of all the *Carthaginians*' (*la plus noble ville des Carthaginiens*);[43] and his response, in Book 11, to the return of Lucius' horse shows him as insensible to the straightforward French as to the Latin:

Et ecce superueniunt de patria quos ibi reliqueram famuli. cum me fotis malis [271ᵛ] *incapistrasset erroribus: cognitis. scilicet famulis meis: necnon & equum quoque illum meum reducentibus: quem diuerse distractum: notæ dorsualis cognitione recuperauerunt.* (Beroaldo, fol. 271ʳ⁻ᵛ [= AA 11. 20])

Et tout soudain voicy arriuer des seruiteurs que i'auois laissez au païs, lors que Fotis [395] *m'accoustra si bien, & amenerent mon cheual qui auoit esté recouuré par aucuns signes qu'il auoit sur le dos.* (Louveau, pp. 394–5)

By and by beholde arriued my seruaunt which I had left in the countrey, when *Fotis* by errour made me an Asse, bringing with him my horse, recouered by her through certaine signes and tokens which I had vpon my backe. (Adlington, ch. 48, p. 201)

Whibley singles out for special mention Adlington's response to Fotis' grisly description of Pamphile's love-potion, the ingredients of which include 'detached skulls torn from the teeth of wild animals' (*extorta dentibus ferarum trunca caluaria*)—a phrase rendered (unaccountably in Whibley's view) as 'the iaw bones and teeth of wild beasts'.[44] The Latin is not easy to begin with, and Adlington was led astray by Louveau's *les mantibules des bestes,* but he still kept at least one eye on the original, for while Louveau translates the previous phrase (*trucidatorum seruatus cruor*) as *le sang de ceux qui auoient esté tuez,* Adlington restores (where he could equally well have left out, since the term is redundant) the sense of *seruatus*: 'the bloud which she had reserued of such as were slaine'.

No such excuse is available, however, for his treatment of the unwelcome rewards given to Lucius after Charite's deliverance from the bandits' cave:

præsepium meum ordeo passim repleri iubet. fœnumque camelo bactrinæ sufficiens apponi. (Beroaldo, fol. 153ᵛ [= AA 7. 14])

---

[43] Beroaldo, fol. 251ʳ (= AA 10. 35); Adlington, ch. 46, p. 189; Louveau, 370.

[44] Beroaldo, fol. 67ᵛ (= AA 3. 17); Whibley, p. xxii; Adlington, ch. 15, p. 49; Louveau, 93.

(She gives orders for my stall to be filled with barley, and enough hay provided to satisfy a Bactrian camel.)

La Bouthière manages the essential phrase (*qu'il eust basté a suffi à vn chameau*) and Michel and Louveau deal with the problem of the dromedary simply by ignoring it;[45] but Adlington attempts, heroically, to engage with the Latin—with risible results:

Then my good mistris...commaunded...that my maunger should be filled with barley, and that I should haue hay and oats aboundantly, and she woulde call me her little Camell. (Adlington, ch. 27, p. 116)

Critics however, have been more than willing to forgive such deficiencies in scholarship. Adlington may refer to his 'homely and rude' translation, 'barbarously and simply framed in our English tongue',[46] but the lucidity and economy of his version have been highly praised:

...his translation is often better literature than the work of Apuleius, seeing that it is always fresh, direct, and simple.[47]

Adlington, a sober man, had moreover little relish for the profuse verbiage of his subject.[48]

...for my part I think the translation better than the original, for I am unable to read Apuleius without having my attention drawn so constantly [160] away to the oddity and difficulty of the language that I lose the thrill of the situation, and thus the language comes into conflict with the substance.[49]

'Sober' Adlington may have been, but when he appears to be making a conscious stylistic decision in telescoping an elaborate description of the arrival of night or dawn into a single phrase, he is really only following Louveau.[50] And Lathrop's comment that Adlington 'substitutes for the abrupt and chiming rhythm of Apuleius an ample and flowing manner, using connectives and filling up omissions, and balancing large groups unostentatiously but harmoniously' needs to be tempered by the revelation that his

---

[45] La Bouthière, 387; Michel, fol. 91^v; Louveau, 232.

[46] Adlington, sig. [A1]^v.

[47] E. B. Osborn, introd., *The Golden Asse of Lucius Apuleius*, repr. of 1639 edn. (London: Abbey Library, Murrays Book Sales, n.d.), p. xvi.

[48] Anon., *The Golden Asse of Lucius Apuleius* (London: Abbey Classics, Simpkin Marshall, n.d.), p. xii.

[49] Lathrop, *Translations*, 159–60.

[50] Whibley, p. xx. Thelyphron's *cum ecce crepusculum...et iam nox tempesta* (*AA* 2. 25) is laconically rendered by Adlington as 'til it was midnight' (ch. 11, sig. F2^r) in response to Louveau (66).

syntactical structure, the word-order, his 'ample and flowing manner', are almost entirely dictated by Louveau.[51]

ADLINGTON THE MORALIST

Propter honestatem

Similar considerations of source may also affect our perception of the moral orientation of the translation. Adlington, we are told, 'was something of a prig in morals, as his Preface, Dedication and the occasional notes on the events of the story show'.[52] Some support for this view is given by the marginal note to be found, in the first edition, at the end of his account of Lucius' congress with the onophilic *matrona* (*AA* 10. 22): *Here I haue left out certain lines propter honestatem.*[53] Critics have seen such considerations of propriety operating throughout the translation. Hoffmann, for example, cites, as an instance of Adlington's 'Neigung, schlüpfrige Wendungen des Originals zu vermeiden' ('his tendency to avoid the obscene turnings of the original'), his rendering of Venus' promised reward to the finder of Psyche.[54] The Latin is enticingly erotic, Michel suggestive, Adlington austere:

accepturus indicii nomine: ab ipsa Venere. vii. sauia suauia. & unum blandientis adpulsum linguæ longe mellitum. (Beroaldo, fol. 122[r] [= *AA* 6. 8])

et la auroit pour son loyer ce quil demanderoit | et dauantaige sept gracieux baisiers de la propre bouche de celle Venus: et le huytiesme doulx et poignant entre les aultres | (Michel, fol. lxxv[v])

and for reward of his paines, he should receiue seauen sweet cosses of *Venus* (Adlington, ch. 22, p. 94)

Such austerity, however, is proof less of moral restraint than of indebtedness to Louveau:

& pour le salaire de sa peine, il baisera sept fois la deesse Venus. (Louveau, p. 189)[55]

Adlington's version of the *matrona* scene, on the other hand, is certainly more chaste than Beroaldo's, Apuleius' detailed description of the consummation

[51] Lathrop, *Translations*, 161.

[52] F. J. Harvey Darton, ed. and introd., *The Golden Ass of Lucius Apuleius in the Translation by William Adlington* (London: Navarre Soc., 1924), 35–7.

[53] The note appears adjacent to the lines, 'When night was passed, with muche ioye and small sleape . . .' in the 1566 edn. (ch. 46, fol. 110[r]), but it is not in the 1596 edn.

[54] Hoffmann, 6.

[55] Adlington must have been looking at Beroaldo to get 'sweet' from *suauia,* but he was probably deflected from the rest of the Latin not so much by its explicitness as by its difficulty.

being reduced to a 'therwithall she eeftsoones embraced my bodie round about, & had her pleasure with me'.[56] But in all this, he is simply following the French example. There is only one point where he can be said to be imposing independent censorship: Louveau's Lucius is *en grande peine, considerant comment... elle qui estoit encores si ieune, & tendre, pourroit endurer vn si grand & deshonneste membre*, while Adlington's ass merely wonders 'how she, who was yong and tender, could be able to receiue me'.[57] Louveau, in fact, is easily the most explicit of the French translators and Adlington, his follower, seems liberal by comparison with Michel and la Bouthière. Michel's *noble matrosne* is infatuated by the sight of the asinine Lucius but is unable, given the natural order of things, to satisfy her desire; while la Bouthière introduces, in place of the libidinous noblewoman, *vne femme qui fort ressembloit à la gentle Fotis* upon whom the ass makes amorous (and successfully resisted) advances.[58]

In the first love-scene between Lucius and Fotis, la Bouthière is evasive while Michel is positively coy: *En disant ces ioyeuses parolles nature nous admonnete* [xxᵛ] *et enseigna ce que nous debuions faire.*[59] Louveau, in contrast, gives a fairly faithful rendering of the Latin:

Hæc simul dicens: inscenso: grabattulo super me sessim residens: ac crebra subsiliens lubricisque gestibus mobilem spinam quatiens: pendule ueneris fructu me satiauit, usque dum lassis animis: & marcidis artubus defatigati: simul ambo corruimus: inter mutuos amplexus animas anhelantes. (Beroaldo, fol. 46ʳ [= AA 2. 17])

(At the same time that she said these words, she climbed onto the little couch and, sinking down on me and springing up repeatedly, shaking her mobile backbone with slippery motions, she sated me with the fruit of pendular Venus until, exhausted, with our spirits tired and our limbs enervated, we both sank at the same time amongst our mutual embraces, breathing out our souls.)

En disant ces paroles là, elle monta sur le lict, & se ietta sur moy tout doucement, souuentefois sautant sur moy, & me faisant iouir du doux fruict de Venus, iusques à ce que noz esprits & noz corps demourerent tous las, & demo-[58]*rasmes tous deux embrassez auec la grosse alaine.* (Louveau, 57–8)

Adlington's reduction of the scene to a bare 'In saying these words she came to me to bed, and embraced me sweetely' is a clear example of independent censorship, but the phenomenon is a comparatively rare one.[60]

---

[56] Adlington, ch. 46, p. 181.   [57] Louveau, 354; Adlington, ch. 46, p. 180.

[58] Michel, fol. cxlᵛ; la Bouthière, 606.   [59] La Bouthière, 80–1; Michel, fol. xxʳ⁻ᵛ.

[60] Adlington, ch. 10, p. 30. Cf. Firenzuola's heavily abbreviated account of Agnolo's love-making with Lucia: *entrati nel letto, cogliemmo gli ultimi frutti d'amore* (252). Firenzuola also omits the whole account of their first embrace and kiss, from *Et cum dicto artius eam complexus* down to *ex animo proeliabor* (= AA 2. 10). Lucia merely promises to visit Agnolo at night (248).

In Book 7, Lucius is 'accused of Lecherie by the boie' who claims that, while carrying wood in the mountains, he will attack women and men and assault them:

humi prostratis illis inhians illicitas atque incognitas temptat libidines & ferinas uoluptates auersam uenerem [sc. *auersa uenere*]: *inuitat ad nuptias* (Beroaldo, fol. 159ᵛ [= *AA* 7. 21])

Louveau compresses Apuleius' description of the unnatural assault into a single word, *efforcer*:

il court apres, & les iette par terre en les voulant efforcer: dauantage en les voulant baiser il les mord par la bouche: (Louveau, 238)

But Adlington (doubtless influenced by Beroaldo's gloss, *Auersa uenere. concubitum puerilem*) captures, almost exactly, the sense of *ferinas uoluptates auersa uenere inuitat ad nuptias*:[61]

he wil stride ouer them to commit his buggerie and beastly pleasure, moreouer he wil faine as though he would kisse them, but he will bite their faces cruelly... (Adlington, ch. 29, p. 120)

Adlington, in sum, is more prepared than Louveau to dilute the strength of the original but (unlike the other Frenchmen) he does not go out of his way to censor Apuleius.

'[I]n this feined iest': Adlington the Exegete

...Adlington was of [xxv] those who would allegorize both mythology and romance...And, as if to excuse the translation of a 'meere jeast and fable,' he addresses to the reader a most solemn homily, setting forth the example of Nebuchadnezzar and upholding the efficacy of prayer.[62]

The relationship between Book 11 and the rest of the novel is, we have argued, the central interpretative problem posed by *The Golden Ass*. To la Bouthière (and the Italian translators before him), the Isiac ending was simply repellent:

i'y trouuay si peu de gout & de grace, que à peine péuz ie prendre patience de le prelire. Icelui ne traitant que daucuns ceremonies, pompes, processions, & sacrifices des prestres de la Deesse Isis. Le tout tant prolixe et ennuieux, que ie fuz grandement desgouté le mettre au rang des autres. (la Bouthière, p. 13)

---

[61] The lemma in the subscribed commentary indicates that the intended reading in the text was *auersa uenere*.
[62] Whibley, pp. xxix–xxx.

And since la Bouthière, as a translator, *ne tend que à la faire rire*, nothing was to be lost in replacing the whole of the final book with a seven-and-a-half-page adaptation from what (perpetuating the common error of the Renaissance) he terms the *premier original Grec de Lucian, dont le tout auoit esté premierement tiré.*[63]

Michel's approach could hardly be more different. Book 11 is retained but the name 'Isis' is replaced, throughout, by that of 'Ceres' who, by a curious act of thematic reorientation, provides the subtitle to the translation: *de la couronne Ceres.* The *Sens nouuel sur les liures de Lucius Apuleius de Lasne dore* appended to Michel's translation interprets Lucius' journey to witch-ridden Thessalia as the passage of *lhomme viateur* from the land of earthly will to *lestat de la spiritualite*, his desire to be metamorphosed into a bird representing the individual's attempt to fly, by means of good works, to the celestial state—an attempt frustrated, in Lucius' case, by his surrender to *lamour de la chambriere Fotis*, who symbolizes *la temptation du dyable.*[64] This analysis is followed (somewhat contradictorily) by a sort of 'Sermon against Flying' (berating the hubris of the over-curious human intellect), and the work closes with an identification of Ceres (who incorporates, amongst other entities, the moon, Juno, and Diana) with *la glorieuse vierge Marie.*

Adlington, in contrast, follows the example of Louveau who preserves Apuleius' ending (as an intrinsic and essential part of the novel) in its pristine form:

parce qu'en iceluy onziesme est contenu le but où semble que nostre Auteur Apulee ayt voulu tirer, pour y traiter le recouurement de sa premiere forme: ioint qu'il est plein de belles antiquitez & plaisantes fables pour cause des cerimonie & superstition des anciens Payens, desquelles Lucien n'a fait aucune mention: ainsi i'espere que ne trouuerez moins beau l'onziesme liure que les autres precedens. (Louveau, sig. Aiiij^r)

Louveau steers between the frenetically exegetical Michel and la Bouthière (who considers the novel to have no metaphorical or metaphysical significance). He omits Beroaldo's *Scriptoris intentio atque consilium*, providing instead a *Sonnet du traducteur, comprenant la principale intention de l'Auteur en sa Philosophie.*[65] In his prefatory *Epistre*, however, he includes some exegetical material which makes the conventional attribution of Lucius' asinine fate to his bodily and intellectual indulgences:

---

[63] La Bouthière was following the example of Boiardo whom he calls (at 13) *un autre doctissime traducteur Tuscan.* Firenzuola also rewrote the ending of Apuleius' novel but, instead of turning to ps.-Lucian, he converted Mithras, the priest of Isis, into a Catholic priest. See Scobie, 'Influence', 215–17; and Ch. 6, *supra.*

[64] Michel, sigs. oo ii^v–oo iii^r.

[65] Louveau, sig. [Avii]^v.

Toutefois si nous voulons esleuer noz esprits vn peu [a iii^r] *plus hault, & entre les espines cueillir la rose, nous trouuerons que non sans cause l'Autheur (qui estoit grand Philosophe) a prins vn tel suiect: demonstrant que par nos appetits desordonnez, vie lubrique & charnelle, sommes faits semblables aux bestes brutes & specialement à l'Asne, qui est le plus lourd & ignorant entre tous les animaux, & le plus souuent tombons en maintes seruitudes & miseres, comme lui aduint par sa luxure & trop grande curiosité. Tant y a que son intention & vrai but semble tirer à nostre doctrine & reformation de vie:* (Louveau, sigs. [Aii]^v–[Aiii]^r)

Louveau's is a suggestive, rather than a prescriptive, explication: *neantmois,* he concludes, *ie remets le tout à vostre iugemen, & de tousbons esprits.*

Adlington, in his address 'To the Reader', plays the part of the exegetical convert surprised by meaning. Initially, he resembles la Bouthière, attracted by the 'exceeding plentie of mirth' of Apuleius' 'pleasant and delectable ieasts' and deciding to translate them so that 'there might bee some fresh and pleasant matter to recreate the mindes of the Readers withall.'[66] He is 'driven from my purpose', however, first by the difficulty of the Latin, and secondly by the apparently 'frivolous and trifling' nature of Apuleius' book '(which seems a meere ieast and fable, and a worke to be laughed at . . .)'.[67] Once, however, he has 'thoroughly learned the intent of the Author, and the purpose why hee invented so sportfull a iest', he decides to attempt

(God willing) as nigh as I can, to vtter and open the meaning thereof, to the simple and ignorant, whereby they may not take the same, as a thing onely to iest and laugh at (for the fables of *Æsope,* and the faining of Poets were neuer written for that purpose) but by the pleasantnesse thereof, be rather induced to the knowledge of their present estate, and thereby transforme themselues into the right and perfect shape of men. (Adlington, sig. [A2]^v)

The exegesis that follows owes much to Beroaldo's *Scriptoris intentio atque consilium*:[68]

. . . *Verum sub hoc transmutationis inuolucro* | *naturam mortalium & mores humanos quasi transeunter designare uoluisse. ut admoneremur ex hominibus Asinos fieri: quando uoluptatibus belluinis immersi Asinali stoliditate brutescimus* | *nec ulla rationis uirtutisque scintilla in nobis elucescit:* . . . *Rursus ex Asino in hominem reformatio significat calcatis uoluptatibus exutisque corporalibus deliciis rationem resipiscere: & hominem interiorem* | *qui uerus est homo ex ergastulo illo cenoso* | *ad lucidum habitaculum* |

---

[66] In this he resembles the Latin preface to de Cortegana's Spanish version: *gratia laxandi animam.* See *Lucio Apuleyo del asno de oro, Corregido y anadido* (Medina d'l campo: P. de Castro, 1543), sig. ai^v.

[67] sig. [A2]^v.

[68] Michel also includes (at sig. Ai^v) *Lintencion de lacteur de ce present liure. Par Berould introduict,* but there is nothing in the phrasing to suggest an influence upon Adlington's exegesis.

Virtute & religione ducibus remigrasse: Ita ut dicere possimus iuuenes illicio uoluptatum possessos | in Asinos transmutari | mox senescentes | oculo mentis uigente | maturescentibusque uirtutibus exuta bruti effigie humanam resumere | Scribit enim Plato in symposio quod tunc mentis oculus acute incipit cernere cum primum corporis oculus deflorescit . . . Quibus anima consopita brutescit. donec gustatis rosis hoc est scientia | quæ mentis illustratio est | cuiusque odor suauissimus | auide hausta in humanam formam hoc est rationalem intelligentiam reuertatur exuto asinali corio | idest deposito inscitiæ & rerum terrenarum crassiore uelamento. (Beroaldo, fol. 2ᵛ)

(. . . Truly, under the wrapper of this transformation he wanted (as it were, in passing) to represent the nature of mortal men and human customs, so that we might be warned against changing from men into asses; when, having been sunk in beastly pleasures, we become brutish with the stupidity of an ass and no spark of reason and virtue shows itself in us . . . The restitution from ass back into man signifies the recovery of reason when pleasures are trampled underfoot and corporeal delights cast off and the return of the inner man (who is indeed a man in that foul penitentiary), with virtue and religion as his guides, to the dwelling-place full of light. Thus we can say that young men, possessed by the allurement of pleasures, are transformed into asses. Soon, growing old, as the eye of the mind flourishes and their virtues mature, they shed their brutish form and resume their human <form>. For Plato writes in *The Symposium*: 'The eye of the mind begins to discern clearly as soon as the eye of the body withers.' . . . The soul, stupefied by [Forgetfulness, Error, Ignorance], becomes brutish until, with the tasting of the roses, that is, with knowledge (which is the illumination of the mind and whose smell is most sweet) having been avidly devoured, he returns to human form (that is the rational intelligence) having shed his asinine hide, that is, having laid aside the heavier covering of ignorance and earthly things.)

Verely vnder the wrap of this transformation, is taxed the life of mortal men, whenas we suffer our mindes so to be drowned in the sensual lusts of the flesh, and beastlie pleasure thereof: (which aptly may be called, the violent confection of Witches) that wee leese wholly the vse of reason and vertue (which properly should be in man) and plaie the parts of brute and sauage beasts . . . [A3ʳ] . . . But as *Lucius Apuleius* was changed into his humane shape by a Rose, . . . so can we neuer be restored to the right figure of our selues, except we taste and eat the sweet Rose of reason and vertue, which the rather by meditation of praier we may assuredly attaine.

    Againe, may not the meaning of this worke be altered and turned in this sort: A man desirous to apply his mind to some excellent art, or giuen to the studie of any of the sciences, at the first appeareth to himself an Asse without wit, without knowledge, and not much vnlike a brute beast, till such time as by much paine and trauell he hath atchiued to the perfectnes of the same, and tasting the sweet floure and fruit of his studie, doth thinke himselfe well brought to the right and verie shape of a man. Finally, the Metamorphosie of *Lucius Apuleius,* may be resembled to youth without discretion, and his reduction to age, possessed with wisedome and vertue. (Adlington, sigs. [A2]ᵛ–A3ʳ)

G. N. Sandy calls Adlington's preface 'a paraphrase' of Beroaldo, but the description is inaccurate.[69] The opening words of each version are, it is true, very close (metaphrase, in fact, rather than paraphrase) but Adlington transposes and reduplicates. For Beroaldo, it is the roses of 'knowledge' (*scientia*)—the 'illumination of the mind'—which restore the bestialized intelligence to human form. Adlington, in contrast, identifies 'the sweet Rose' (to be gained by 'meditation of praier') with the 'reason and vertue' which figured in Beroaldo's account of the *effects* of succumbing to 'beastly pleasures'. Beroaldo's spiritual sense of *scientia* is then transposed down an octave to supply the second (far more mundane) interpretation of the work: as an allegory of a man 'giuen to the studie of any of the sciences'. And Adlington's sturdy, Anglo-Saxon empiricism leads him to ignore Beroaldo's allusion to the Platonic 'eye of the mind' when he interprets the story, finally, in terms of the 'reduction to age' of 'youth without discretion'.[70] Beroaldo, as we argued in Chapter 4, was actually far more interested in the necromantic and linguistic content of the novel than in any spiritual edification it might afford, but he does at least allude to the Pythagorean and Platonic notions of metempsychosis. Adlington is resistant to all such metaphysical tendencies, eschewing mention even of the word 'soul' and concentrating, in its stead, on the need to 'regenerate' the 'mind'.[71] Beroaldo's abstract, philosophical interpretations are converted into quotidian prescriptions:

Now since this booke of *Lucius* is a figure of mans life, and toucheth the nature and manners of mortal men, egging them forwarde from their Asinal forme to their humane and perfect shape, beside the pleasant and delectable iests therein contained, I trust if my simple translation be nothing accounted, yet the matter it selfe shall be esteemed by such, as not onely delight to please their fancie in reading the same, but also take a patterne thereby, to regenerate their minds, from brutish and beastly custome. (Adlington, sig. A3ʳ)

The problem of reconciling the 'iesting and sportfull matter of the booke' with the 'good & vertuous moral' to which it 'tendeth' is addressed in conventional Lucretian terms:

although the matter therein seeme very light and mery, yet the effect thereof tendeth to a good & vertuous moral... For so haue al Writers in times past imploied their labors, that posteritie might receiue some fruitfull profit by the same. And therefore the Poets fained not their Fables in vaine, considering that children in time of their first studies, are much allured thereby to proceede to more graue and deepe disciplines,

---

[69] 'Book 11: Ballast or Anchor?', in *Aspects*, ed. Hijmans and van der Paardt, 138.

[70] De Cortegana (sig. a iᵛ) prescribes the roses 'of discretion and reason' (*prudencie ac rationis*).

[71] Taking *anima* (as the ancients themselves were inclined to do) as the equivalent of *animus*.

whereas otherwise their mindes would quickely loathe the [A2]ʳ wise works of learned men, wherein in such vnripe yeers they take no sparke of delectation at al. And not only that profit ariseth to children by such fained Fables, but also the vertues of men are couertly therby commended, and their vices discommended and abhorred. (Adlington, sigs. [A1]ᵛ–[A2]ʳ)

> sed vel uti pueris absinthia taetra medentes
> cum dare conantur, prius oras pocula circum
> contingunt mellis dulci flavoque liquore,
> ut puerorum aetas inprovida ludificetur
> labrorum tenus, interea perpotet amarum
> absinthi laticem deceptaque non capiatur,
> sed potius tali facto recreata valescat [72]

(in the same way that doctors, when they are trying to give foul wormwood to children, first smear the rims of the cups with honey—sweet, golden and runny—so that unsuspecting childhood may be deluded as far as the lips, swallowing, in the process, the bitter fluid of wormwood and, though deceived, being unharmed, but instead restored by this means, growing stronger)

In both cases, the alluring medium (Horace's *dulce*) entices the reader to an understanding of the message (the *utile*) which he would otherwise find unpalatable. Such a theory has obvious attractions: one can enjoy the wit and titillation of the *inuolucrum* ('wrapper'), safe in the knowledge that one is receiving moral edification from what it conceals. But the approach ignores the danger that the trappings or medium might actually contradict or subvert the tenor of the perceived 'message'.

The problem is highlighted by the marginal *sententiae* which have especially exposed Adlington to the charge of priggishness.[73] At times, however, the moralizing is so effusive that a discrepancy appears between the rectitude of the moral pronouncement and the attention given to the turpitude which prompted it. In Book 9, a baker returns from a dinner where his friend, a fuller, has discovered his wife hiding an adulterer. The baker recounts the story to his own wife, only to find that he has just been cuckolded in exactly the same way. He appears to behave very kindly to his wife's young lover, reassuring him that he means him no harm:

---

[72] *T. Lucreti Cari de rerum natura libri sex*, ed. J. Martin (Leipzig: Teubner, 1969), i. 936–42.

[73] Some of the marginal notes are simply clarificatory, explaining classical allusions ('Cerberus is the dog of hel fained by poets to stand at Plutoes gate', 12), adding topographical detail (Thessaly is 'A countrey where are many inchantresses & witches', sig. B1ʳ), or helping the reader to understand the flow of Apuleius' narrative by indicating changes in narrative point of view ('He speaketh to Apuleius', 15). We should not necessarily assume, however, that the marginal notes came from Adlington's hand. They may have originated with Henry Wykes (the printer of the first edn.) and then been incorporated into subsequent edns.

ac ne iuris quidem seueritate: lege de adulteriis ad discrimen uocabo capitis: tam uenustum atque pulchellum puellum.... Talis sermonis blandicie cauillatum deducebat ad torum nolentem puerum: sequentem tamen: & pudicissima illa uxore alterorsus disclusa: solus ipse cum puero cubans: gratissima corruptarum nuptiarum uindicta perfruebatur. sed cum primum rota solis lucida diem peperit: uocatis duobus e familia ualidissimis: quam altissime sublato puero: [209ᵛ] *ferula nates eius obuerberans.* (Beroaldo fols. 208ᵛ–209ᵛ [= AA 9.27–8])*

nor wil I not punishe thee according to the rigour of the lawe of Iulia, which commaundeth that adulterers should be put to death: No, no, I will not execute my crueltie against so faire & [158] comely a young man as you be,... with these and like wordes hee lead the young man to his chamber, whereby hee might reuenge his enemie at his pleasure. On the next morrowe, hee called two of the most sturdiest seruants of his house, who helde vp the young man, while he scourged his buttockes welfauoredly with roddes like a childe. (Adlington, ch. 41, pp. 157–8)

The Latin's comedy of gender (*pulchellus puellus*) and the ironic epithet applied to the wife (*pudicissima uxor*) are lost in the translation, and Apuleius' description of the baker's retribution ('Lying alone with the boy, he enjoyed a delightful revenge for his marred marriage') is certainly toned down in Adlington's 'reuenge his enemie at his pleasure'.[74] But the comic reversal of sexual fortunes is retained, and the collocation of 'chamber' and 'pleasure' leaves us in no doubt as to what form the baker's revenge took. Indeed, it is significant that the very words, 'whereby hee might reuenge his enemie at his pleasure' are omitted in the 1639 edition, published (we must assume) long after Adlington's death. And when Adlington comments in the margin, 'Such young men are worthie<r> to be beaten with rods then to lye with women', the piety of the statement enhances the already rich blend of righteous punishment and sexual opportunism.[75] In the same way, Louveau's bland chapter heading describing the suicide of a woman *à cause que son mary ioussoit d'autre que d'elle* becomes relishingly aspirated in Adlington's phrase 'because her husband haunted harlots'.[76] How far Adlington himself was aware of these tensions and discrepancies is uncertain: it is very difficult at this distance to recover the true register of his comments. But it is certainly true that the moralizing notes hang particularly loosely on the body of the work.

[74] Depending on whether one takes *nuptiarum corruptarum* as an objective or subjective genitive, one can also translate the phrase as 'enjoyed the vengeance of corrupt intercourse' (*nuptiae* can also mean 'intercourse'). Adlington here merely follows Louveau's *se vengea à son aise de son ennemy* in the same way that 'the rigour of the lawe of Iulia' is imported from Louveau's *La loy rigoureuse Iulia* (Louveau, 308).

[75] Adlington, ch. 41, p. 158.

[76] Louveau, 283; Adlington, ch. 35, p. 137; AA 8. 22.

Arthur Golding had already addressed similar problems a year before Adlington in his introduction to *The Fyrst Fower Bookes of P. Ouidius Nasos worke, intitled Metamorphosis*. In his dedication, he asks forgiveness for 'my maymed and vnperfect translation' and talks of

the nomber of excellent deuises and fyne inuentions contriued in the same, purporting outwardly moste pleasant tales & delectable histories, and fraughted inwardlye with moste pithie instructions and wholsome examples, and conteynyng bothe wayes moste exquisite connynge and deepe knowledge. (Golding, sig. [*j]ᵛ)

The tradition of *Ouidius moralizatus* is, of course, a long and elaborate one. The greater bulk of *The Golden Ass*, on the other hand, is peculiarly resistant to allegorical exegesis. Something obviously could be made of the central motif of the man transformed through venery and curiosity, but the 'pleasant tales' which constitute most of the novel contain neither 'pithie instructions' nor 'wholsome examples'.[77] The virtuous suffer and the evil go unpunished in a world controlled by Tyche ('Chance').[78]

In his verse preface 'To the Reader', Golding again anticipates Adlington:

> But if wee suffer fleshly lustes as lawlesse lordes too reigne,
> Than are wee beastes, wee are no men, wee haue our name in vaine.
> And if wee be so drownd in vice that feeling ones bee gone,
> Then may it well of vs be sayd, wee are a blocke or stone.
> This surely did the Poets meane when in such sundry wise
> the [*sic*] pleasant tales of turned shapes they studied too deuise.
> Their purpose was too profit men, and also too delight.
>
> (Golding, sig. *iiiʳ)

The Lucretian influence appears once more in the claim that poets needed to adorn the 'playne and naked tale' with 'pleasant terms and art' if the reader were 'to print it in his hart'; but Golding guards himself against the charge of collusion in immorality by characterizing two kinds of wrong reader: first, the 'naughtie persone' who 'seing vice shewd lyuely in his hew, | Dooth take occasion by and by like vices too ensew'; secondly, the extremist who,

> ...beyng more seuere than wisdome dooth requyre,
> Beeholding Vice (too outward shewe) exalted in desyre,
> Condemneth by and by the booke and him that did it make,
> and willes it too bee burnd with fyre for leud examples sake.
> Theis persons ouershote themselues, and other folkes deceiue:
> Not able of the Authors mynd the meanyng too conceyue.

---

[77] The Psyche myth, of course, is a case apart.

[78] The baker, for example, having exacted his revenge upon the adulterer, is murdered by his wife (*AA* 9. 30).

The Authors purpose is too paint and set before our eyes
The lyuely Image of the thoughts that in our stomackes ryse.
Eche vice and vertue seemes too speake and argue too our face,
With such perswasions as they haue their dooinges too embrace.
And if a wicked persone seeme, his vices too exalt,
Esteeme not him that wrate the woorke in such defaultes too halt.
But rather with an vpright eye consyder well thy thought:
See if corrupted nature haue the lyke within thee wrought.

(Golding, sig. *iii^v)

Golding then tries a new (and somewhat contradictory) tack, akin to the tricksters' ruse in the story of 'The Emperor's New Clothes'. The response to an ambiguous work of art becomes a test of the reader's purity:

Then take theis woorkes as flagrant flowers most full of pleasaunt iuce.
The whiche the Bee conueyng home may put too wholsome vse:
And which the spyder sucking on too poyson may conuert,
Through venym spred in all her lymbes and natiue in her hart.
For to the pure and godly mynde, are all thynges pure and cleene,
And vntoo such as are corrupt the best corrupted beene:

(Golding, sig. [*iv]^r)

The rules of intellectual property are not amenable to time-travel. If Adlington seems, to modern sensibilities, a plagiarist, he probably did not seem so to his contemporaries, for his reference to 'the *French* and *Spanish* translatours' suggests little attempt to conceal his borrowings. Yet while it would be anachronistic to condemn Adlington for his appropriations, our appraisal of his own moral, spiritual, and intellectual commitment to the exegetical position he adopts is surely qualified by the fact that almost the whole of his expository work is patched together from other sources. Golding may be building on theoretical sand, but he has at least constructed some sort of coherent moral framework for his translation. Adlington, by comparison, is only a half-hearted moralist—and the most nominal of allegorists. Golding and Sandys (and the gamut of medieval and Renaissance commentators before and after them) seem to have believed sincerely in allegory; Adlington's dedicatory explications of Ovidian myths are mere commonplaces: 'The fall of *Icarus*, is an example to prowde and arrogant persons that weeneth to clime vp to the heauens. By *Midas*... is carped the foule sin of auarice.'[79] Yet these very exegetical deficiences are, in a way, part of the translation's strength. The 'excellent narration of the marriage of *Cupid* and *Psyches*' is boldly advertised on the title page and is accorded (in a departure from the practice of the Latin

---

[79] Adlington, sig. [A2]^r.

and French sources) a separate chapter; but there is not a single exegetical reference to the myth in the whole apparatus of the translation. Psyche has been both boon and bane to *The Golden Ass*: the jewel in the dung that ensured the novel's survival from antiquity; but also the neck about which was hung an allegorical yoke that all but strangled the beast as a creative entity.

Textual critics will usually prefer the lazy or ignorant medieval scribe, who faithfully reproduces an unintelligible passage, to the cleverer *emendator* who, by introducing his own conjectures, takes us further away from the original. Adlington's case is analogous: erratic his translation may be, but the numerous errors are mere blemishes compared with the disfigurements inflicted upon Apuleius' text by a much better scholar like la Bouthière. In a few places, it is true, Adlington chose to censor Louveau, but he emerges, in comparison with both proven and potential sources, as far more liberal a translator than his critics have allowed. What he gave to English readers was considerable: a reasonably complete, adequately accurate, and eminently readable *Ass*, unburdened by the weight of Beroaldo's commentary or the exegetical yoke of Fulgentius, Boccaccio, and Michel, but spared the emasculating knife wielded by Boiardo, Firenzuola, and la Bouthière. English literature has much to thank him for.

8

After Adlington: Apuleius in England
(1566–1660)

THE ELIZABETHAN *ASS*

One of the earliest and most interesting responses to Apuleius in English is provided by George Gascoigne (1534/5–77). Gascoigne's *A Hundreth Sundrie Flowres* (the 'richest collection of early Elizabethan poetry') was printed in or around April 1573 and contains a triplet of sonnets on the theme of Lucius' affair with Fotis.[1] Upon his return from 'service with the vertuous Prince of Orenge' in Holland, Gascoigne found that the poems had 'bene offensive for sundrie wanton speeches and lascivious phrases' and had been 'doubtfully construed'.[2] He then published the work in a revised form, 'gelded from all filthie phrases ... and beautified with additions of many moral examples'.[3] *Posies* ('Corrected, perfected, and augmented by the Authour') appeared in 1575, two years before his death. The 'deformed youth' had become 'a reformed man' and, in an attempt to give a moral complexion to the work, Gascoigne redistributed his poems into three horticultural categories: 'Floures' ('beeing more pleasant than profitable'), 'Hearbes' ('more profitable than pleasant'), and 'Weedes' which

> might seeme to some judgements, neither pleasant nor yet profitable.... But as many weedes are right and medicinable, so may you find in this none so vile or stinking, but it hath in it some vertue if it be rightly handled.[4]

The depiction of vice, we are told, can have the salutary effect of indicating what is to be avoided. Gascoigne ends his address 'To the Readers' with a request:

---

[1] The accolade is Tucker Brooke's, in *A Literary History of Britain*, ed. A. C. Baugh, 2nd edn. (London: RKP, 1967; repr. 1976), 394.

[2] *George Gascoigne: The Posies*, ed. J. W. Cunliffe (Cambridge: CUP, 1907), 3.

[3] Ibid. 6. The preamble was addressed to the 'reverende Divines', identified as 'the Queen's Majesty's Commissioners' by C. T. Prouty, *George Gascoigne: Elizabethan Courtier, Soldier, and Poet* (New York: Columbia UP, 1942), 79.

[4] *The Posies*, 13.

...I pray thee to smell unto these posies, as *Floures to comfort, Herbes to cure,* and *Weedes to be avoyded.* So have I ment them, and so I beseech thee Reader to accept them. Farewell.[5]

Gascoigne's Apuleian sonnets appear in both collections—somewhere towards the middle of *A Hundreth Sundrie Flowres,* and, in *Posies,* as the penultimate entry in 'Weedes':

Three Sonets in sequence, written uppon this occation. The devizer hereof amongst other friends had named a gentlewoman his Berzabe, and she was content to call him hir David. The man presented his Lady with a Booke of the Golden Asse, written by Lucius Apuleius, and in the beginning of the [138] Booke wrote this sequence. You must conferre it with the Historie of Apuleius, for els it will have small grace.[6]

> THIS *Apuleius* was in Affricke borne,
>   And tooke delight to travayle *Thessaly,*
> As one that held his native soyle in skorne,
> In foraine coastes to feede his fantasie.
> And such a gaine as wandring wits find out,   5
> This yonker[7] woon by will and weary toyle,
> A youth mispent, a doting age in doubt,
> A body brusd with many a beastly broyle,[8]
> A present pleasure passing on a pace,
> And paynting playne a path of penitence,   10
> A frollicke favour foyled with foule disgrace,[9]
> When hoarie heares should clayme their reverence.
> Such is the fruite that growes on gadding[10] trees,
> Such kynd of mell most moveth busie Bees.
>   *For Lucius he,*   15
> Esteeming more one ounce of present sporte,
> Than elders do a pound of perfect witte:
> Fyrst to the bowre of Beautie doth resort,

---

[5] *The Posies,* 17.

[6] Text (but not notes) from *George Gascoigne's 'A Hundreth Sundrie Flowres',* ed. C. T. Prouty (Columbia: U of Missouri, 1942), 137–9. The latest edn. is by G. W. Pigman (Oxford: Clarendon, 2000), 256–7 and 622–4. The version in *Poesies* (ed. Cunliffe, 463–4) is identical except for minor points of orthography and the preliminary note which begins: '¶ *Davids salutacions to Berzaba wherein are three son*ets' etc. Gascoigne's Apuleian sonnets are cited and discussed by Tobin, *SFN,* 31–2.

[7] *Yonker:* 1) A youth of high rank; 2) 'a fashionable young man'. The glosses are all based on the 2nd edn. of the *OED.*

[8] *Broyle* ('broil'): 'tumult' or 'turmoil', with perhaps a nuance (from the verb) of something mixed confusedly.

[9] 'A mirthful countenance defiled with foul disgrace.'

[10] *Gadding:* 'spreading hither and thither', 'straggling in growth'; with perhaps a moral reflection on Lucius' behaviour given by the figurative meaning of 'gad': 'to go wandering, in desire or thought; to leave the true path'. Cf. 'gadding gyrles' in line 38.

And there in pleasure passed many a fitte,[11]
His worthy race he (recklesse) doth forget, 20
With small regard in great affayres he reeles,
No counsell grave nor good advice can set,
His braynes in brake that whirled still on wheeles.
For if *Birhena* could have held him backe,
From *Venus* Court where he nowe nousled was, 25
His lustie limbes had never found the lacke
Of manly shape: the figure of an Asse,
Had not bene blazed on his bloud and bones,
To wound his will with torments all attonces.
                                    But Fotys she, 30
Who sawe this Lording whitled[12] with the cuppe,
Of vaine delight wherof he gan to tast:
Pourde out apace, and filde the Mazor[13] up,
With dronken dole,[14] yea after that in hast.
She greasd[15] this gest with sauce of Sorcery, 35
And fed his mind with knacks[16] both queynt and strange:
Lo here the treason and the trechery,
Of gadding gyrles, when they delight to raunge.[17]
For *Lucius* thinking to become a foule,
Became a foole, yea more than that, an Asse, 40
A bobbing blocke, a beating stocke, an owle,[18]
Well wondred at in place where he did passe:
And spent his time, his travayle and his cost,
To purchase paine and all his labour lost.
                                    Yet I pore I, 45

[11] *Fitte* ('fit'): Obsolete sense of 'a position of intense excitement', perhaps with a further notion of the 'paroxysm' associated with love-making.

[12] *Whitled* ('whittled'): 'excited by drink, intoxicated'.

[13] *Mazor* ('mazer'): 'hardwood drinking-bowl, usu. silver-mounted'; cf. *FQ* II. xii. 49. 3.

[14] *Dole*: perhaps playing on three senses of the word: (1) 'something distributed or doled out'; (2) 'grief, sorrow, mental distress'; (3) 'guile, deceit, fraud'.

[15] *Greasd*: the main sense of 'grease' here is 'to gull, cheat'; but it may also suggest erotic lubrication (cf. the *matrona* in *AA* 10. 21 anointing herself and Lucius with oil of balsam before their congress) while anticipating the smearing of the body with ointment prior to transformation (*AA* 3. 21 and 25).

[16] *Knacks*: 'tricks, artifices, devices'; but also, in the gastronomic context, 'a choice dish, a delicacy, a dainty'.

[17] *Raunge* ('range'): 'to rove, roam, wander about'; 'to change from one attachment to another, to be inconstant'.

[18] *Bobbing block* ('bobbing' = 'beating, striking') appears to mean the same thing as *Beating stock*: 'A jocular title given to one who is subjected to beating.' *Owl* may seem to be an infelicitous term given that Lucius was trying to be turned into an owl (bird of Athena, wisdom) when he was changed into an ass. But 'Owl' could be used in the 16th cent. 'in allusion to an appearance of gravity and wisdom (often with implication of underlying stupidity)'. Lucius, who thought himself wise, was shown to be asininely stupid.

Who make of thee my *Fotys* and my freende,
In like delights my youthfull yeares to spend:
Do hope thou wilt from such sower sauce defend,
                    David thy King.

                Meritum petere grave.

This is an odd poem in many respects. Plato would have used it to good effect in his attack on poetry in the *Republic*, since it exhibits mimesis at so many removes from reality. The poet (Gascoigne) creates two (unnamed) lovers who assume the roles of David and Bathsheba. 'David' then takes the part of Poet, composing a sonnet-sequence on the inside cover of a copy of (what appears to be Adlington's translation of) *The Golden Asse* which he presents to 'Berzabe'. The whole poem is thus veiled in several layers of irony—a case of fictitious lovers trying to exchange their feigned biblical identities for fictional identities drawn from a pagan author, Apuleius.[19]

The tale of David and Bathsheba (Gascoigne seems to have confused her name with Beersheba, the place of Abraham's sojourn in the land of Canaan) is well known.[20] The king, smitten by the sight of Bathsheba bathing, summons and impregnates her, then disposes of her husband, Uriah, by sending him into the forefront of the battle and ordering his comrades to retire. Subsequently, he takes Bathsheba to wife but is divinely punished by the death of the son she bears him. The key elements in the biblical tale—adultery, murder, and divine retribution—are matched by the fornication, necromancy, and poetic justice in Apuleius. Gascoigne's poem is typical of the Renaissance attitude towards Fotis evident in the works of Beroaldo, Guillaume Michel, and Adlington: they are happy to enjoy her charms even as they condemn her.[21] Gascoigne makes the causality explicit: it is the amorous entanglement from which Byrrhena failed to save Lucius that leads to his destruction.[22] As Pigman points out, Gascoine omits any reference to Lucius' ultimate redemption.[23]

---

[19] Gascoigne had already exploited the technique of linking three sonnets (*Terza sequenza*) in the opening section of *The Adventures of Master F.J.*, a proto-novel composed of poems connected by prose which appears at the beginning of *A Hundreth Sundrie Floures*. A further link is F.J.'s poem about 'Fayre Bersabe the bright' and 'King David'. See Pigman's edn., 146 and 562.

[20] 2 Samuel 11–12.

[21] It may be worth observing that the poet's father, Sir John Gascoigne, was charged before Cardinal Pole with having committed adultery with his servant-girl, Anne Dowry. See Prouty, *George Gascoigne*, 11.

[22] The account of Lucius' affair given by Prouty (*A Hundreth Sundrie Flowres*, 269) seriously distorts Fotis' role in the metamorphosis. Lucius, we are told, was unwilling to follow Birhena's exhortation to leave Pamphile's house because 'he had fallen in love with Milo's servant girl, Fotis'. He desired to be transformed into an owl, but, 'by a trick of Fotis' he became, instead, an ass'.

[23] *A Hundreth Sundrie Flowres* (2000), 622.

Gascoigne supplies one of Renaissance England's few direct allusions to Fotis. Thomas Watson's allusion to Psyche in Sonnet LXXVI of *The Heka-tompathia* (1582) is far more representative:

In this Sonnet the Author being, as it were, in halfe a madding moode, falleth at variance with *Loue* himselfe, & blasphemeth his godheade, as one that can make a greater wounde, then afterwardes he him selfe can recure. And the chiefe cause that he setteth downe, why he is no longer to hope for helpe at *Loues* hande, is this, because he him selfe could not remedie the hurt which he susteyned by the loue of faire *Psyches*.

> Thou foolish God the Author of my griefe,
> If *Psyches* beames could set thy heart on fire,
> How can I hope, of thee to haue reliefe,
> Whose minde with mine doth suffer like desire?
> Henceforth my heart shall sacrifice elswhere
> To such a *Sainte* as higher porte doth beare... [24]

In this same year, the acidulous Stephen Gosson was including 'the *Golden Asse*' and 'the *Æthiopian historie*' among those works which 'haue beene throughly ransackt to furnishe the Playe houses in London'. Gosson names one such play when he attacks drama in Platonic terms for its distortion of reality: 'The perfectest Image is that, which maketh the thing to seeme neither greater nor lesse, then in deede it is. But in Playes, either those thinges are fained, that neuer were, as *Cupid* and *Psyche* plaid at *Paules*...'.[25]

None of these plays has survived, but John Lyly's *Sapho and Phao* (1584) is an almost contemporary example of a drama with Apuleian content being performed for the Queen by the boys of St Paul's, London. Venus, besotted with Phao, tells her son: 'O Cupid, thy flames with *Psyches* were but sparks, and my desires with *Adonis* but dreames, in respecte of these vnacquainted tormentes'.[26] In Lyly's *Mydas* (perf. 1589; pr. 1592), we find—in addition to the inevitable play on asinine ears—a chiastic allusion to *The Golden Ass*:

Myd. Ah *Mydas*, why was not thy whole body metamorphosed.... Vnfortunate in thy wish, vnwise in thy iudgement; first a golden foole, now a leaden asse.[27]

[24] *The hekatompathia or Passionate centurie of loue* (London: John Wolfe for Gabriell Cawood, 1582), sig. K2^r. A marginal note adjacent to the first mention of 'Psyches' reads 'Vide Apul.' Cf. *The Complete Works of Thomas Watson (1556–1592)*, ed. D. F. Sutton, 2 vols. (Lewiston, NY; Lampeter: Edwin Mellen P, 1996), i. 214.

[25] *Playes Confuted in Fiue Actions* (London: Thos. Gosson, 1582), sigs. D5^v and D4^v; repr. in *The English Drama and Stage under the Tudor and Stuart Princes, 1543–1664*, ed. W. C. Hazlitt (London: Roxburghe Library, 1869), 188.

[26] (London: Thomas Cadman, 1584), IV. ii, sig. E3^v. The subtitle reads: *Played beefore the Queenes Maiestie on Shrouetewsday, by her Maiesties Children, and the Boyes of Paules*.

[27] John Lilly, *Six Court Comedies* (London: Edward Blount, 1632), sig. X8^r. For the dating of *Mydas*, see G. K. Hunter, 'Lyly, John', *ODNB*.

In Lyly's *Gallathea* (III. iv), Telusa says: 'We have brought the disguised nymph, and have found on his shoulder Psyche's burn, and he confesseth himself to be Cupid.' Diana declares: 'Thine own arrow shall be shot into thine own bosom, and thou shalt be enamored not on Psyches but on Circes.' Diana proceeds (like Venus in *AA* 6. 10–21) to set a series of impossible tasks.[28]

The Apuleian and the Heliodorean intersect briefly in *The Historie of Forbonius and Prisceria* (1584) which Thomas Lodge dedicated to Sir Philip Sidney. Prisceria is the granddaughter of '*Theagines* of *Greece,* the copartener of sorrowe with *Caricleala,* the straunge borne childe of the *Aegyptian* king'. In the final poem of the romance, Apuleius' Zephyrus is invoked:

> Her cherie lips doth daunt the morning hiew,
> From whence a breath so pleasant did insew,
> As that which laide faire *Psiches* in the vayle,
> Whome *Cupide* woode and woed to his auayle.[29]

In Robert Greene's *Menaphon* (1589)—generally considered his best romance—Melicertus and Democles compete in bucolic encomia. Amongst the 'rare conceipts' of Melicertus' *blason* of his beloved's charms is the image of Cupid and Psyche sporting in Sephestia's dimple:

> Whilome, while *Venus* sonne did seeke a bowre,
> To sport with *Psiches* his desired deare,
> He chose her chinne; and from that happy stowre
> He neuer stints in glorie to appeare.[30]

And in one of the most important of the Elizabethan anthologies, *The Phoenix Nest* (1593), 'T. W. Gent.' (possibly Thomas Watson again) eulogizes the 'dainty paradise' of Sibilla's breasts as being

> As white as snowe, as smooth as Iuorie,
> As faire, as Psyches bosome, in that howre,
> When she disclosde the boxe of Beauties Queene,[31]

John Donne uses the same image in one of his *Elegies*, 'The Comparison', which, according to the general critical consensus, 'ingeniously blends . . . the

---

[28] '*Gallathea*' and '*Midas*', ed. A. Begor Lancashire ([London]: Arnold, 1970), 47, 48, and 52.

[29] *An alarum against vsurers . . . Heereunto are annexed the delectable historie of Forbonius and Prisceria* (London: T. Este, for Sampson Clarke), fols. 21ᵛ and 30ᵛ. Cf. *The Complete Works of Thomas Lodge*, 4 vols. ([Glasgow]: Hunterian Club, 1883), i. 53–84, at 72.

[30] *The Life and Complete Works of Robert Greene, M.A.*, ed. A. B. Grosart, 10 vols. (London: Huth Library, 1881–6), vi. 127 and 128.

[31] *The Phoenix Nest 1593*, ed. H. R. Rollins (Cambridge, Mass.: HUP, 1931), 106–7. On the identification with Watson, see Rollins, p. xix.

Petrarchan and anti-Petrarchan tradition in Italian poetry'[32] as the poet contrasts 'his own woman's perfections' with 'the filthy deformities of another's'.[33] The anti-Petrarchan tradition can be seen in the 'skumme' and 'Chaos', the 'worme eaten trunkes' and 'ragged carrets', which compose the portrait of the addressee's consort; but it is more difficult to identify the genuinely Petrarchan component in the presentation of the poet's own mistress. In the course of the poem, the beloved's head is compared with the apples which precipitated the Sack of Troy (line 16) and the Fall of Man (line 18); her 'best lov'd part' is equated with an alchemist's alembic (lines 36–8); and their love-making is likened to the 'reverent sacrifice' of priests and to a surgeon 'searching wounds' (lines 49–52). Apuleius, however, provides the clinching evidence in the middle of the poem, where the poet praises the beloved in the following terms:

> Like Proserpines white beauty-keeping chest,
> Or Joves best fortunes urne, is her faire brest.

(lines 23–4)[34]

Critics duly note the allusion in the first line to Book 6 of *The Golden Ass* where Psyche is required 'to take down to Hell a box (*pyxis*) and beg from Proserpina a little beauty for Venus'.[35] They overlook, however, the revealed reality of the goddess's chest:

When *Psyches* was returned from hel, to the light of the world, she was rauished with great desire, saying: Am not I a foole, that knowing that I carrie here the diuine beutie, wil not take a little thereof to garnish my face, to please my loue withal? And by and by she opened the box [101] where she could perceiue no beutie nor any thing else, saue onely an infernall and deadly sleepe, which immediately inuaded all her members as soone as the boxe was vncouered, in such sort that she fel downe vpon the ground, and lay there as a sleeping corps.[36]

The contents of 'Proserpines white beauty-keeping chest' are not only illusory but deadly. The more one reads the poem, the narrower becomes the distance between the two female objects. Far, in fact, from presenting to view a pair of diametrical opposites, the poem enacts the argument of the final line: 'comparisons are odious'. The difference between 'sweat drops' and 'Ranke sweaty froth', between a 'fired gunne' and a 'Lymbecks warme wombe', is, one

[32] H. Gardner, ed., *John Donne: 'The Elegies' and 'The Songs and Sonnets'* (Oxford: Clarendon, 1965, repr. 1978), 119.
[33] J. Carey, *John Donne: Life, Mind and Art*, 2nd edn. (London: Faber, 1990), 16. Cf. R. Donald, 'Another Source for Three of John Donne's *Elegies*', *ELN* 14 (1977), 264–8, at 267: 'In contrast to this anathema is Donne's mistress, whose virtues are balanced against the other's vices.'
[34] *The Elegies and The Songs and Sonnets*, ed. Gardner, 5.
[35] Gardner, 121.   [36] Trans. Adlington (1596 edn.), 100–1 (= *AA* 6. 20–1).

begins to feel, almost arbitrary—a function merely of the poet's argumentative shaping of language. John Carey cites the poem as an example of one side
of Donne's personality, 'the desire for a single, all-encompassing viewpoint';[37]
but it surely serves, conversely, to illustrate the other aspect of Donne which
Carey has elucidated so well: his frequent refusal, perhaps even his inability, to
commit himself unequivocally to any one position.

Early evidence of Apuleius' reception in Scotland is provided by Alexander
Montgomerie (d. 1598), 'master poet' to James VI and crypto-Catholic.[38] In
'Lyk as Aglauros, curious to knau…', Montgomerie's (male) speaker likens
his predicament as a lover ('wondring on a deitie divyne—| The Idee of
perfectione in this eird', vv. 16–17) to the consequences for Psyche of glimps-
ing Cupid, though (perhaps influenced by *Partonopeu de Blois*) he blames
Psyche's mother (rather than her sisters) for persuading her to violate her
husband's injunction:

> Or as Psyches (by her Mother mov'd
> Hir sleeping Cupid secreitly to sie)
> Resav'd the lamp to look him vhom sho lov'd
> Quhais hevenly beutie blind't hir amorous ee
> That sho forȝet to close the Lamp till he
> In wrath auok and fleu sho wist not vhair
> And left his deing Lover in dispair,
> Euen so am I.[39]

In Sonnet XXVI of *Parthenophil and Parthenophe* (1593), Barnabe Barnes
(1571–1609) writes:

> When louely wrath my mistresse hart assaileth,
> Loues golden dartes take ame from her bright eyes:
> And Psiche Venus rosie couche empayleth
> Plac'd in her cheekes, with lillyes where she lyes…[40]

---

[37] Carey, *Life, Mind and Art*, 16.

[38] See, generally, R. D. S. Jack, 'Montgomerie, Alexander (early 1550s–1598)', *ODNB*.

[39] vv. 8–15. In *The Poems of Alexander Montgomerie*, ed. D. J. Parkinson, 2 vols. (Edinburgh:
Scottish Text Soc., 2000), i. 50.

[40] (London: J. Wolfe, 1593), sig. Ciijʳ (xxvi. 1–4). In the preceding sonnet, Barnes may be
drawing (even if at one or more removes) on the story of Meroe and Socrates (*AA* 1. 12–19) as
Parthenophil describes how Parthenophe 'did deadly wound me | And with her bewties balme
tho dead keepes liuely | My liuelesse body, and by charmes hath bound me | For thankelesse
meede to serue her' (xxv. 9–12). In the final poem (Sestine 5) of the sequence, Barnes traduces
the Petrarchan tradition by having Parthenophil invoke Hecate and the 'auenge-full furies' to
bring Parthenope to him upon the back of a goat, 'naked and bare', so that they can 'conioyne
this heauenly night' (p. 145). According to J. D. Cox ('Barnes, Barnabe', *ODNB*), Elizabeth (the
Virgin Queen) is imaged in Parthenophe, while Parthenophil's 'stance of frustrated expectation,
occasioned by an unyielding and unapproachable female, seems appropriate to one of Essex's
party in the early 1590s'.

In John Dickenson's Arcadian romance *Arisbas, Euphues amidst his Slumbers: or Cupids iourney to hell* (1594), Arisbas' wanderings echo those of Psyche:

Ungentle *Cupid*, hast thou deeming my *Timoclea* fairer then thy *Psyche*, renewed thy doting humor? if so, then wert thou cruell in thy change, but more in thy choise, enforcing mee to loue whome thy selfe didst like. I haue wandered through the earth, augmenting the springs with streames of my teares, filling the woods with rebounding Ecchoes of my woes, tracing the plaines with restlesse steps, yet haue I mist *Timoclea*, and not finding her, haue lost my selfe.[41]

An even more daring inversion of gender occurs in the 'vnexpected discourse' about the youth Hyalus given by the shepherd Damon to comfort Prince Arisbas. Hyalus' beauty is such that 'Shepherds doted on him, Lasses droupt on him', 'Pan sighed to see him, remembring by him his Syrinx, though of an other sexe', and 'Hamadryades flocked to view him, wishing him one of their troupe' (E3[r–v]). Snatched from Arcadia by the amorous Zephyrus and conveyed to 'the fortunate Islands', he is laid down 'in a medowe on a bed of floures' and then taken to the god's palace, 'a most pleasant coole edifice', where he is

serued by vnseene attendants that waited with diligence on their Lords dearling. Varietie of daintiest fare, choise of wines, change of meates, store of delicates, were plenti [E4[v]] fully brought or rather blowne in at appointed houres, tables couered, all things furnished with more then princely magnificence, yet no servitour appearing, diuine melodie on windie instruments fild his eares with continuall charmes of harmonious sounds. Oft he walked abroade to viewe the perfections planted in that soyle, and being weary or wanton, roade backe in an ayrie Chariot. But all this could not content him, who wanting his wonted companions, seemed to leade a life voyde of comfort.[42]

Zephyrus, being 'vnable to deny him anything', agrees to return Hyalus to Arcadia ('Truce was taken, and the composition sealed with many kisses'), on condition that he 'shunne the sight of *Pomona*' and avoid all other lovers (E4[v]). Pomona, however, imprisons Hyalus, and is only persuaded to release him by the intervention of Boreas who blasts Arcadia with icy winds. Having finally been set free, Hyalus falls asleep 'neere a pleasant Spring':

In this sleepe, strange sleepe, the late sexe was chaunged, and of a faire boy a fairer maide fashioned. Awaking and musing much at this metamorphosis, she was in the midst of her dumps raisde with a strong gale, & carried to a place neere the streights of

[41] (London: Thos. Creede for Thos. Woodcocke, 1594), sig. B2[r]; repr. in *Prose and Verse by John Dickenson*, ed. A. B. Grosart ([Blackburn]: priv. printed, 1878), 35.
[42] sig. E4[r–v] (= *Prose and Verse*, 62). There is a detailed description of 'CVPIDS PALACE' at 71.

Thermopyles, where was a Temple dedicated to Æolus, wherein the lovely maide was consecrated a Priest to that God, and continued there the whole tearme of her life a spotlesse virgin. (sig. F2ʳ)

In its homoerotic dimensions, the story of Hyalus shows strong affinities with Sidney's *Arcadia*, Marlowe's *Hero and Leander*, and Shakespeare's Sonnet 20; but Dickenson (conscious, perhaps, of the precedent set by *Partenopeu de Blois*) makes specific use of 'Cupid and Psyche' to play boldly (and ironically) with gender, bringing to the surface some of the latent ambiguities about sexual identity that are such a feature of early modern romance. Moreover, the conclusion of the tale (unusually) blends 'Cupid and Psyche' with its outer frame, playing on corporeal metamorphosis (ass to man / boy to girl) and spiritual transformation (abstemious *pastophor*/virgin priest[ess]).

The tale of Hyalus is immediately followed by one of Arisbas' own poems, 'The strife of Loue and Beautie', in which the story of 'Cupid and Psyche' is deployed by each of the disputants:

> He said beautie nere preuailed,
> But where Loue the heart assailed.
> Beautie for it selfe admired,
> His shafts causde to be desired.
> For where Loue bred no remorse,
> There had beautie litle force.
> Psyche was more faire then any:
> Loude of few, though likde of many.
> Yet so likde that not affected:
> Sisters sped, but she reiected.
> Yet, quoth Beautie Psyche gainde
> Cupids heart to her enchainde.
> Where was then his wonted might?
> Vanquishde by a womans sight?[43]

Sonnet V of *Diella* (1596) by 'R. L.' (Richard Linche?) repeats Dickenson's conceit (sig. B2ʳ) of Psyche being displaced in Cupid's affections by the poet's own love:

> THE little Archer, viewing well my loue,
>   stone-still amaz'd, admired such a sight,
> And swore he knew none such to dwell aboue,

---

[43] sig. F3ʳ (= *Prose and Verse*, 69). The passage is incorporated by John Hind into his *Eliosto Libidinoso* (London: Valentine Simmes, 1606), Book I, 44–5. Earlier in the romance, Amasias (lovestruck by Florinda) asks himself: 'Can Beautie (fond foole) be resisted, which makes the gods to bow? Love himselfe yeelded to the feature of *Psyche*, and thinkest thou thy fancie to be of greater force?' (8).

> though many faire, none so conspicuous bright:
> With that inrag'd, (flamigerous as he is)
> 　he now gan loathe his *Psiches* louely face,
> And swore great othes to rob me of my blisse,
> 　saying that earth for her was too too base;
> But *Cytherea* checkt her lordly sonne,
> 　commaunding him to bring no giglet thether,
> Fearing indeed, her amorous sports were done
> 　with hote-spur *Mars*, if hee should once but see her.
> If then her beauty moue the Gods aboue,
> Let all men iudge if I haue cause to loue.[44]

In *Alba* (1598) by Robert Tofte (1561–1620), the beloved's hand is said to be 'no hand, it is the daintie Glove, | Which *Psyches* ware, when she was wed to LOVE'.[45] Psyche is also alluded to in *A Herrings Tayle* (1598), a mock epic of 1026 alexandrines on the theme of a snail's contention with a weathercock, by the Cornish antiquary Richard Carew (1555–1620). Æolus manages to steal one of the peacocks that draw Juno's chariot:

> Now fortune (Louers friend) so guided *Æolus*,
> That one of those he got, and gaue to *Zephirus*
> Sweet breathed *Zephirus*, who (*Psyche* like) away
> With bloomie gale him bare, and in sure guard did lay... [46]

In his risible continuation of Marlowe's *Hero and Leander* (1598), Henry Petowe writes:

> This *Psiches* had no Cupid, love was bannisht,
> And love from love exild, love needs must famish.[47]

On or around the first of May 1600, the manager of the Rose and Fortune theatres, Philip Henslowe (d. 1616), recorded a payment of 30 shillings to Thomas Dekker and John Day, 'in earnest of a booke Called The golden Ass & Cupid & Psiches'. It would appear that Henry Chettle 'was called in on the collaboration', for he shares with Dekker and Day in a further payment of £3

---

[44] *Diella, Certaine Sonnets, adioyned to the amorous Poeme of Dom Diego and Gineura* (London: H. Olyney, 1596), sig. B3ʳ. On the identity of 'R. L.', see S. Massai, 'Linche, Richard (*fl.* 1596–1601)', *ODNB*.

[45] 'The First Part of the Months Minde of A Melancholy Lover', Stanza [XIV] (= vv. 323–4), repr. in *The Poetry of Robert Tofte, 1597–1620*, ed. J. N. Nelson (New York: Garland, 1994), 101 (= sig. [B8ʳ] of original edn.). Concerning the influence on Tofte of Thomas Watson's *Hekatompathia*, see Nelson's introd., pp. xxi–xxiii.

[46] *A Herrings Tayle: Contayning a Poeticall Fiction of Divers Matters Worthie the Reading* (London: Matthew Lownes, 1598), vv. 346–9.

[47] *The Second Part of Hero and Leander* (1598), vv. 327–8. In *Elizabethan Narrative Verse*, ed. N. Alexander (London: Arnold, 1967), 128.

(10 May) and a final payment (14 May) of 30 shillings (for 'the gowlden asse
cuped & siches'). Henslowe also notes that he 'Lent vnto Thomas dowton [*sc.*
Downton] the 5 of June 1[59]600 to bye a sewt for his boye in the playe of
cvped & siches the some of xxxxs'.[48]

The play itself is lost, but at least two portions of it seem to have been
preserved in *Englands Parnassus: or The choysest Flowers of our Moderne Poets,
with their Poeticall comparisons*, compiled by Robert Allott and published in
1600.[49] In the section devoted to descriptions of 'Groaues', we find a fragment
of the scene in which Psyche's sisters relate how they were brought down to
see her:

> —When many a weary step
> Had brought vs to the top of yonder mount,
> Milde *Zephirus* embrac'd vs in his armes,
> Cast vs into the lap of that greene meade,
> Whose bosome stucke with purple Violets,
> Halfe budded Lillies, and yoong Musk-rose trees,
> About whose waste the amorous woodbine twines,
> Whilst they seeme maidens in a louers armes,
> There on the curled forehead of a banke,
> That sweld with camomill, ouer whose bewtie
> A wanton Hyacinth held downe his head,
> And by the winds helpe oft stole man a kisse[.][50]
> He sate vs downe, and thus we did ariue.
>
> *Th. Dekkar.*

Dekker seems to have been influenced by the long description of the 'lowly
vale, *Tempe* yclipt' in which Carew's Zephirus had placed the peacock two
years earlier:

> All in a vesture of greene grasse apparelled,
> With guard of roses and sweet flowers embrodered,
> And entersowed trees (like ouches) yeeld a grace,
> Whose waste the climing Iuie and woodbine embrace:

---

[48] *Henslowe's Diary*, ed. R. A. Foakes, 2nd edn. (Cambridge: CUP, 2002), 133–5; W. L.
Halstead, 'Dekker's *Cupid and Psyche* and Thomas Heywood', *ELH* 11/3 (Sept. 1944), 182–91,
at 182.

[49] (London: For N. L[ing,] C. B[urby] and T. H[ayes], 1600), 372–3 and 478. The anthology
also includes (under the heading, 'Pleasure', 229) three lines ('*Physche* in stedfast loue...')
adapted from Spenser's *FQ* III. vi. 50. 6–8. For a modern edn., see *Englands Parnassus Compiled
by Robert Allott, 1600*, ed. C. Crawford (Oxford: Clarendon, 1913), sections 1988, 2052, 2232.

[50] This variant reading (found, e.g., in the Harvard UL copy) is an (imperfect) correction to
the 'And by the winds helpe oft stole may abide' given in (e.g.) the Huntington and Folger copies
(478). For 'man a kisse', we should read 'many a kisse'. See Halstead, 'Dekker's *Cupid and Psyche*',
186 n. 13.

> But they scorne proffred loue, and without spreaded armes
> Protect the nursling herbes from *Phoebus* firie harmes . . . [51]

And parts of at least two passages from Dekker's play (those reproduced in *Englands Parnassus*) will find their way into Thomas Heywood's *Loves Maistresse, or, The Queens Masque* (1636).[52] There is also an obscure allusion to Apuleius in Dekker's play *A Knight's Conjuring* (1607):

Who breedes this disease, in our bones? Whores? No, alack let's doe them right, t'is not their fault but our mothers, our cockering mothers, who for their labour make us to be call'd Cockneys, or to hit it home indeed, those golden asses our fathers.[53]

Apuleius lends something to the physiognomy of the river deity, Isis, in Book I of Edward Wilkinson's *Thameseidos* (1600):

> Her Eye-lids blacke, of Heben arches made,
> VVere like the bow that *Psiches* husband had;
> In which so liberall was Nature to her,
> That euery one suspected (that did view her)
> She onely 'made faire *Isis* to deceaue them:
> And both of sight and iudgement to bereaue them.

In Book II, Cupid perceives that Neptune has been 'enchaunted by [Isis'] beautie' and

>   being very glad,
> That then the long desired meane he had
> T'auenge him for the enuious tale he tolde,
> Vnto his mother then, when faine he would
> Haue maried *Psiches*: straight he to the hart
> Strake *ISIS* with a leaden headed dart:
> Then with an other all of burnisht gold,
> He warmd his hart, that had long time been cold;
> And made him supplyant, craue remedie
> For those hot flames that in his brest gan frie . . . [54]

In *Tom Tel-Troths Message and his pens complaint* (1600), John Lane (*fl.* 1600–30) turns his satirical gaze on the followers of Pride and her 'handmaides . . . Fancie and Vanitie':

---

[51] *A Herrings Tayle*, vv. 354–9.
[52] Halstead, 183–7.
[53] ed. E. F. Rimbault, in *Early English Poetry, Ballads, and Popular Literature of the Middle Ages*, vol. v (London: Percy Soc., 1842), 29. The margin contains a sententia: 'wise mothers make foolish children'.
[54] (London: W. W[hite] for Simon Waterson, 1600), sigs. B1ʳ (i. 215–20) and C1ʳ (ii. 47–56).

Bedawbd with gold like *Apuleius* Asse
Some princk and pranck it: others more precise,
Full trick and trim tir'd in the looking-glasse,
With strange apparell doe themselues disguise.
  But could they see what others in them see,
  Follie might flie, and they might wiser bee.

(lines 253–8)[55]

THE STUART *ASS* (1603–1660)

Ben Jonson (1572–1637) owned at least one copy of Apuleius' *Opera*, and his own works contain several Apuleian allusions.[56] At the beginning of *The Haddington Masque* (perf. 1608; pr. 1616), Venus descends to earth in search of Cupid who has run away. She fears that 'he hath surpris'd | A second PSYCHE, and liues here disguis'd', and she offers a 'kisse' as a reward for finding him.[57] Poem XXXIII of *The Underwood* ('An Epigram to the Councellour that pleaded and carried the Cause') makes use of Lucius' condemnation of lawyers as *togati vulturii* (*AA* 10. 33):

But when I read or heare the names so rife
Or hirelings, wranglers, stitchers-to of strife,
Hook-handed Harpies, gowned Vultures, put
Upon the reverend Pleaders…

(lines, 7–10)[58]

Jonson makes far more explicit allusion to *The Golden Ass* than Shakespeare ever did; but the differences in their approach to Apuleius are telling. In the scholarly apparatus to the royal presentation copy of *The Masque of Queenes* (performed 2 February 1609), Jonson refers to Apuleius as one of his 'authorities' (alongside Bodin and the *Malleus maleficarum*):

These powers of troubling *Nature* are, frequently, ascrib'd to Witches, and challeng'd by them-selues; where euer they are induc'd by *Homer, Ouid, Tibullus, Pet. Arbiter,*

---

[55] (London: R. Howell, 1600), 21.

[56] Jonson's copy of Petrus Colvius' edn. of the *Opera omnia* (Leiden: Ex Officina Plantiniana apud Franciscum Raphelengium, 1588) is in the Bodleian Library (8 A. 15 Art. Seld.). It includes extensive underlining and marginal marking (in pencil) to the *Florida* and *Apologia*, and to Book 1 of the *Metamorphoses*. See R. C. Evans, *Habits of Mind: Evidence and Effects of Ben Jonson's Reading* (Lewisburg: Bucknell UP; London: Associated University Presses, *c.*1995), 89–133 ('Jonson's Apuleius: The *Apologia* and *Florida*'). I am grateful to Dr Mark Bland for bringing Jonson's copy to my attention.

[57] *Ben Jonson*, ed. C. H. Herford and P. Simpson, 11 vols. (Oxford: Clarendon, 1925–52), vii. 251–2.

[58] Ibid. viii. 18. *The Underwood* was posthumously published in 1640.

Seneca, Lucan, Claudian, to whose authorities I shall refer more, anone. For the present, heare *Socrat. in Apul. de Asin. aureo. lib. j.* describing *Meroë* the witch: *Saga, & diuinipotens . . . Tartari ipsum illuminare.*[59]

I haue touchd at this before (in my note, vpon the first) of the vse of gathering flesh, bones & sculls: to which I now bring that peice of *Apuleius, lib. iij de Asino aureo* of Pamphile: *Priusque apparatu solito instruxit . . . trunca caluaria.* And, lib. Ij. Byrrhena to Lucius of Pamphile, *Maga primi nominis . . . & id Chaös mergit.*[60]

Jonson quotes Henry Cornelius Agrippa (*De occulta philosophia* 4) and observes:

which doctrine he had from *Apuleius,* without all doubt, or question. Who in *lib. iij. de* [297] *Asin. aur.* publisheth the same: *Tunc decantatis spirantibus . . . ducebat exuuiarum veniunt.* All wch are mere arts of Sathan, when eyther himselfe will delude them wth a fallse forme, or, troubling a dead body, make them imagine these vanities the meanes . . . [61]

In *Timber, or Discoveries,* Jonson makes a marginal note, *Vide Apuleium,* and the editors of the Oxford edition refer us to *AA* 1. 8: *At ille digitum a pollice proximum ori suo admovens in stuporem attonitus 'Tace, tace', inquit.*[62] Elsewhere in *Discoveries,* he adapts the terms of Apuleius' *Apologia* to his own defence.[63] Jonson uses Apuleius in the manner of a scholar, to flesh out footnotes, in contrast to Shakespeare who assimilates Apuleian material into the fabric of his drama so thoroughly that the original lineaments are all but defaced.

In Nathan Field, John Fletcher, and Philip Massinger's *The Honest Man's Fortune* (perf. 1613; pr. 1647), the asinine transformation is used as a positive reinforcement of social hierarchies. Veramour is reunited with his old master, Montaigne (now fallen into distress), and invites him to 'leane on my shoulder', declaring:

> I would be changd
> Like *Apuleius,* weare his Asses eares,
> Provided I might still this burthen beare.[64]

---

[59] Ibid. vii. 289. Cf. *AA* 7. 8.   [60] Ibid. 291. Cf. *AA* 3. 17 and 2. 5.

[61] Ibid. 296–7.   [62] Ibid. viii. 575 and xi. 225.

[63] Ibid. viii. 604–5; xi. 253: *Quippe insimulari quivis innocens potest: revinci . . .* Cf. *Apologia* 1. 5; and Mason, *Humanism and Poetry,* 269.

[64] *The Dramatic Works in the Beaumont and Fletcher Canon,* gen. ed. F. Bowers, 10 vols. (Cambridge: CUP, 1966–96), x. 62 (= Act III, sc. i, 203–5). The editor, Cyrus Hoy (x. 4), ascribes this section of the play to Field. The exchange may relate to an emblem from the early 1580s showing a servant with an ass's head. See, generally, M. T. Burnett, 'The "Trusty Servant": A Sixteenth-Century English Emblem', *Emblematica* 6/2 (1992), 1–17; and M. DiGangi, 'Asses and Wits: The Homoerotics of Mastery in Satiric Comedy', *ELR* 25 (1995), 179–208, at 181 n. 7.

Contrariwise, in Thomas Tomkis's *Albumazar* (performed before James I on 9 March 1614/15 at Trinity College, Cambridge), Apuleius is invoked in the satirical context of a social transformation from yeoman ('Trincalo') to gentleman ('Antonio') engineered by the play's eponymous 'astrologer':

> *Albumazar.* Stand forth transform'd *Antonio* fully mued
> From browne soare feathers of dull yeomanry
> To th'glorious bloome of gentry, prune your selfe slick,
> Sweare boldly y'are the man you represent
> To all that dare deny't.

Initially, Trincalo is sceptical:

> TRI.   Give me a looking-glasse
> To read your skill in these new Lineaments.
> ALB. I'de rather giue you poyson: for a glasse
> By secret power of crosse reflections,
> And opticke vertue, spoiles the wondrous worke
> Of transformation, and in a moment turnes you [F3ᵛ]
> Spight of my skill, to *Trincalo* as before.
> We read that *Apuleius* by a rose
> Chang'd from an Asse to Man: so by a mirrour,
> You'l loose this noble lustre, and turne Asse.⁶⁵

Trincalo's delusion of having been transformed continues, however, for most of the play. Despite his proclamation, 'I feele my vnderstanding is enlarg'd | With the rare knowledge of this latter age' (III. v, sig. F4ʳ), he is repeatedly characterized in asinine terms. In a scene which plays both on the story of the Corinthian *matrona* (*AA* 10. 19–22) and the reception of Bottom by Titania (*A Midsummer Night's Dream*, III. i and IV. i), Trincalo is entertained by Bevilona, a 'curtezan' posing as the real Antonio's mistress:

> TRI. Sweete Lady pardon mee, I'le follow you.
> Happy *Antonio* in so rare a Mistresse!
> But happier I, that in his place enioye her:
> I say still, there's no pleasure like Transforming.⁶⁶

⁶⁵ (London: Nicholas Okes for Walter Burre, 1615), Act III, sc. iv, sig. F3ʳ⁻ᵛ. The Apuleian allusions remain in Okes's 1634 edn. ('*Newly revised and corrected by speciall Hand*'). While on the subject of mirrors, we might note the existence of a curious poem by Richard James in 92 heroic couplets based on the *Apologia* (13–16) and entitled, 'An Apologie for a Looking Glasse by Apuleius against one Æmilian' (*c.*1620–38). See Bodleian Lib., Oxford, MS James 35; printed in *Poems of Richard James*, ed. A. B. Grosart (priv. pr., 1880), 203–7. On the popularity of *Albumazar* (itself an adaptation of Giambattista della Porta's *L'astrologo* [pr. Venice, 1606]), see S. P. Cerasano, 'Tomkis, Thomas (*b. c.*1580, *d.* in or after 1615)', *ODNB*.

⁶⁶ III. viii, sig. G3ʳ.

When Bevilona's 'husband' Ronca returns home 'unexpectedly', however, the model changes to Apuleius' tale of the fuller's wife (*AA* 9. 24–5). Trincalo is forced to hide in a beer barrel, while Bevilona and Ronca collude to maximize his discomfiture:

> *TRI.* Pox of all Transmutation, I am smother'd.
> Lady, as you loue mee, giue the Hogshead vent.
> The beere that's in't will worke and breake the vessell.
> *BEV.* Signior *Antonio*, as you loue your life
> Lie still and close, for if you stirre you die.
> *RON.* So, so, now shake it, so, so.
> *TR.* Oh I am drown'd, I drowne!
> *RON.* Whence come's this hollow sound?
> *TR.* I drowne, I smother!
> *RON.* My life 'tis *Trincalo*, For I haue heard that Coxcombe,
> That Asse, that Clowne, seekes to corrupt my wife,
> Sending his fruite and dainties from the Country.
> O that 'twere he. How would I vse the villaine!
> First crop his eares, then slit his nose, and gueld him,
> And with a red hot Iron seare his raw wounds;
> Then barrell him againe, and send the Eunuch
> To the great Turk to keep his Concubines.
> Tick, tock, who's within heere?[67]

Towards the end of the play, Trincalo meets Cricca, servant of his landlord Pandolfo:

> *CR.* No, feare it not: 'tis plaine: *Albumazar*
> Hath cheated my old master of his plate.
> For here's the Farmer, as like himselfe as euer;
> Onely his cloathes excepted. *Trincalo*!
> *TRI. Cricca*, where's *Trincalo*? Do'st see him here?
> *CR.* Yes, and as ranke an Asse as e're he was.
> *TRI.* Thou'rt much deceiu'd, thou neither see'st nor know'st me.
> I am transform'd, transform'd.
> *CR.*   Th'art still thy selfe.[68]

Despite its academical provenance, Tomkis's play has much in common with Jacobean City Comedy in its concern with satirizing social ambition. The presence, however, of James I (who, in 1611, had incurred obloquy by instituting the practice of selling baronetcies as a source of revenue) must have added a certain piquancy to Tomkis' depiction of an aspirant ass.

---

[67] III. ix, sig. G3^v.   [68] IV. viii, sig. I1^r.

On 13 February 1617, Christ Church College in Oxford hosted a performance of *Technogamia, or The Marriages of the Arts*, an academical comedy by Barten Holyday (1593–1661). Holyday was praelector in rhetoric and philosophy (1617–21) and had translated Persius' *Satires* (1616).[69] In *Technogamia*, he plays within the venerable tradition of the Seven Liberal Arts as he depicts Geometres' misguided attempts to win the love of Astronomia by means of Magus' magic:

> *Geom.* . . . ah, were it the will of the gods, I had but halfe of this skill, I'de giue all that I haue, and get more as I could; but can you doe all these Wonders?
> *Magus.* Farre stranger, farre stranger; most amazing transformations; why, there was *Apuleius* so skilfull in this Arte, that he turn'd himselfe into an Asse, and *Lucian* was turn'd into an Asse, before he studi'd it.

Geometres fails to see the irony of Magus' boast, but pedagogical orthodoxy is reinforced at the end of the play when Magus is banished (along with Astrologia) from the 'Common-wealth' of learning. Holyday uses the earlier scene to take a gentle swipe at the *magia*-minded humanists:

> *Geom.* O strange! but can a Spirit giue Learning?
> *Magus.* Oh, there was *Hermolaus Barbarus*, when he studied Philosophie, and lesse vnderstood any place, hee would call vp a Spirit to instruct him; so the famous *Cardans* father carryed one alwaies in a Ring on his finger; and *Agrippa* had his Dogge with a Characteriz'd Collar.[70]

Technogamia was performed again on 26 August 1621 before James I at Woodstock in Oxfordshire, but the king was not impressed. It is possible, however, that Holyday's time at Oxford bore Apuleian fruit in John Price (1602?–76) who went up to Christ Church in 1617. Price (Pricaeus) would go on to edit Apuleius' *Apologia* (Paris: Simon Fevrier, 1635) and *Metamorphoses* (Gouda: Willem van der Hoeve, 1650).[71]

The 'famous *Cardan*' mentioned by Holyday was Girolamo Cardano (1500/1–76), mathematician, physician, and astrologer—a man notorious for his supposed 'atheism'. Cardano had visited Scotland and England in 1552, staying in London with John Cheke.[72] In his autobiography, *De vita propria liber* (1575), Cardano devotes a chapter to 'Utterly Supernatural Things' (*Res prorsus supra naturam*), amongst which he includes the tale of how he came to

[69] F. D. A. Burns, 'Holyday, Barten (1593–1661)', *ODNB*.
[70] *ΤΕΞΝΟΓΑΜΙΑ* (London: William Stansby for John Parker, 1618), III. iii, sig. G2ʳ. The play was reprinted in his lifetime (London: J. Haviland for R. Meighen, 1630). There is a critical edn. by Sister M. Jean Carmel Cavanaugh (Washington, DC: Catholic U of America P, 1942).
[71] See, generally, M. H. Crawford, 'John Price', *ODNB*.
[72] J. Stoner, introd., *The Book of My Life (De Vita Propria Liber)* (London: Dent, 1931), p. xii.

learn Latin instantly and, as it were, by magic, upon purchasing a gilded copy of Apuleius:

Quis fuit ille qui mihi vendidit Apuleium iam agenti annum ni fallor xx. Latinum, &
statim discessit, ego verò qui eovsque neque fueram in ludo literario nisi semel, qui
nullam haberem Latinæ linguæ cognitionem, cùm imprudens emissem quod esset aur-
atus, postridie euasi qualis nunc sum in lingua Latina, nec non & Græcam quasi simul,
& Hispanicam, & Gallicam accepi, sed dumtaxat vt libros intelligam: ignarus sermonis,
& narrationum, & regularum Grammaticæ prorsus?[73]

(Who was that man who sold me an Apuleius in Latin when I was—if I'm not mistaken—in my twentieth year and immediately vanished? I had, in fact, until that time been in elementary school only once, and had no knowledge of the Latin tongue. Having rashly bought the book because it was gilded, I emerged, the following day, as proficient in the Latin language as I am now, and also acquired Greek, almost at the same time, and Spanish and French, though only to the extent that I can understand books, being utterly ignorant of how to speak or write them, or of the rules of grammar.)

It is hard to tell, as a modern audience, how we should read something so patently ridiculous, though the fact that the binding is said to be gilded (*auratus*) while the contents, we know, are golden (*De asino aureo*) suggests that Cardano's stretching of credibility is, at least, knowingly playful. More-over, the claim of instantaneous proficiency in Latin stands in ironic contrast to Apuleius' prologue in which the narrator talks of acquiring Latin *aerumn-abili labore* ('by great industrie', as Adlington puts it).[74]

   Robert Burton (1577–1640) makes frequent reference to *The Golden Ass*, the *Florida*, and the *De deo Socratis* in the *Anatomy of Melancholy*, proclaiming in the 'Satyricall Preface': 'We are apish in it [*sc.* the world], *asini bipedes*, and every place is full *inversorum Apuleiorum*, of the metamorphised and two-legged Asses'.[75] In his 'Digression of the Misery of Schollers', he ingeniously distorts the real reason for Psyche's spinsterhood (her beauty is such that she is admired as a perfectly polished statue, *AA* 4. 32) by observing that 'none would marry her, *quòd indotata*, faire Psyche had no money'.[76] But another passage

---

[73] Ch. 43, *Res prorsus supra naturam*, in *Hieronymi Cardani…opera omnia*, ed. Charles Spon, 10 vols. (Lyons: Jean-Antoine Huguetan and Marc-Antoine Rauaud, 1663), i. 38. Cf. D. C. Allen, 'Three Italian Atheists: Pomponazzi, Cardano, Vanini', in his *Doubt's Boundless Sea: Skepticism and Faith in the Renaissance* (Baltimore: Johns Hopkins P, 1964), 49. See, generally, A. Grafton, *Cardano's Cosmos: The Worlds and Works of a Renaissance Astrologer* (Cambridge, Mass.: HUP, 1999).

[74] Cardano's *Quis fuit ille* also plays on Apuleius' *Quis ille?* (*AA* 1. 1). In ch. 27, Cardano shows his stylistic orthodoxy by referring to Cicero as the 'Father of Eloquence'.

[75] 'Democritus to the Reader', in *The Anatomy of Melancholy*, ed. T. C. Faulkner et al., 6 vols. (Oxford: Clarendon, 1989–2000), i. 30.

[76] Ibid. i. 322 (Part. 1. sec. 2. Memb. 3. subs. 15).

in 'Democritus to the Reader' gives a more accurate sense of the work's genealogy: 'I did sometime laugh and scoffe with *Lucian,* and satyrically taxe with *Menippus*'.[77] And the motto, *Omne tulit punctum qui miscuit vtile dulci,* which adorns the title page of the fourth edition (1632) confirms our suspicions that the *spoudogeloion* ('jocoseriousness') that informs the *Anatomy* is akin to Jonson's: of the Lucianic kind, but brought under the sway of Horace.

In the *Pseudodoxia Epidemica* (1646–72)—a work which owes much to the *Anatomy*—Sir Thomas Browne refers to 'those famous Bookes, Entituled Lucius by the one, and Aureus Asinus by the other'; he cites 'the fable of the Fullers wife' (*AA* 9. 25) in his chapter 'Concerning Sternutation, or Sneezing, and the custome of saluting or blessing upon that motion'; and he quotes Lucius' oath to Fotis, *Adjuro per dulcem capilli tui nodulum* (*AA* 3. 23).[78]

In *Histriomastix* (1633), the Puritan pamphleteer William Prynne (1600–69) quotes from the *praeludia* to the festival of Isis (*AA* 11. 8) in order to demonstrate

one particular abuse, of mens acting female parts in womens apparell and haire in Enterludes; *Vbi alius soccis obauratis, indutus serica veste, mundoque pretioso, & adtextis capite crinibus, incessu perfluo fœminam mentitur,* as Apuleius expresseth it. Which practise is diametrally contrary to *Deut.* 22. 5. *The woman shall not weare that which pertaineth to a man, neither shall a man put on a womans garment; for all that doe so, are an abomination to the Lord thy God.*[79]

The work cost him part of his ears (as well as a fine of £5,000) because of its supposedly 'seditious' slight to Queen Henrietta Maria who participated in court masques in that same year. By a nice irony, William Laud—the Archbishop of Canterbury who was responsible for the shearing of Prynne's ears (cropped in 1633 and removed completely in 1637) and who faced Prynne, in turn, at his own trial for treason (1644)—owned a manuscript entitled *Lucij Apuleij madaurensis metamorphoseon,* which he donated to the Bodleian Library (MS Laud Lat. 55).[80] H. O. Coxe ascribed it, in his original Quarto Catalogue of the Laudian Manuscripts, to the fourteenth century, as did D. S. Robertson, but R. W. Hunt, the corrector of the 1973 reprint of Coxe's

[77] Anatomy of Melancholy, i. 5.

[78] ed. R. Robbins, 2 vols. (Oxford: Clarendon, 1981), i. 34 (Bk I, ch. 6); i. 320 (Bk IV, ch. 9); i. 427 (Bk V, ch. 22).

[79] *Histrio-Mastix. The Players Scovrge, or Actors Tragœdie, Divided into Two Parts. Wherein it is largely evidenced, by divers Arguments . . . That popular Stage-playes (the very Pompes of the Divell which we renounce in Baptisme, if we beleeve the Fathers) are sinfull, heathenish, lewde, ungodly Spectacles, and most pernicious Corruptions* (London: for Michael Sparke, 1633), Part II, Act II, sc. ii, p. 879.

[80] Laud's inscription appears at the bottom of fol. 57r: '*Liber Guil: Laud Archie~pi Cant. & Cancellar: Vniuersit: Oxōn: 1637.*'

Catalogue, reascribes it to the fifteenth century.[81] At fol. V[v] appears the inscription *Jo. Priceus Anglo-Britannicus emi Venetiis 1629* ('I, John Price, an Anglo-Briton, bought this in Venice, 1629'). Hunt notes:

In the preface to his edition of the *Metamorphoses* of Apuleius (Gouda, 1650) Price says that he had given the manuscript to Laud: '*Sequentes libros contulimus cum uno tantum MS. Codice, quem a nobis acceptum Gulielmus nuperus Cantuariae Archiepiscopus (Vir literis ornandis attentissimus) donavit Oxoniensi Bibliothecae*.'[82]

William Browne, Thomas Heywood, and Shakerley Marmion

Britannia's Pastorals established William Browne of Tavistock (1590/1–1645?) as one of the seventeenth century's most prominent Spenserian poets.[83] The first two books appeared in 1613 and 1616, with commendatory verses by the likes of Michael Drayton, John Selden, and Ben Jonson, and have been admired (and imitated) by poets as eminent as Milton, Coleridge, and Keats. The fragmentary third book has come down to us in a single manuscript copy preserved in the library of Salisbury Cathedral.[84] The second song of this third book may be the earliest surviving attempt in English literature at an extended treatment of the Cupid and Psyche myth.[85]

Browne introduces the story as a 'faieryes song', sung by an 'elfe' to 'all yee merry westerne swaynes,[86] | And ev'ry gentle shepherdesse that deignes | A kinde attentive eare to what I sing'. The opening is very close to the original:

[81] See H. O. Coxe, *Bodleian Library Quarto Catalogue, II: Laudian Manuscripts* (1858–85), corr. edn., introd. R. W. Hunt (Oxford: Bodleian Library, 1973), 27.

[82] 'I have compared the following books with only one manuscript book—the one which William, the late Archbishop of Canterbury (a man most attentive to the ornamenting of literature), once received from us and donated to the Library of Oxford.' See Hunt's Coxe, p. xxvii; *Metamorphoseos libri XI* (Gouda: Gulielmus vander Hoever, 1650); L. C. Purser, 'Laud's Manuscript of Apuleius', *Hermathena* 35 (1909), 425–37; Fumagalli, *Boiardo*, 69 n. 30.

[83] See M. O'Callaghan, 'Browne, William (1590/91–1645?)', *ODNB*.

[84] The MS. was edited by T. Crofton Croker for the Percy Society in 1852. Cf. *The Poems of William Browne of Tavistock*, ed. G. Goodwin, 2 vols. (London: Routledge, 1894), ii. 1–75.

[85] F. Moorman dates the Third Book 'between 1624 and 1628', though (relying on perhaps questionable 'internal evidence') he concludes that 'the whole of the Second Song...was probably composed at an earlier period. The last Stanza addressed to Caelia places it somewhere within the years 1617–24, in which we find him wooing this lady. The subject-matter, the verse, in which stanzas replace the heroic Couplets of all the other songs, and the lightness of tone point to the fact that it was composed as an independent poem, and afterwards added to the story of the Pastorals.' See *William Browne: His 'Britannia's Pastorals' and the Pastoral Poetry of the Elizabethan Age* (Strasbourg: Trübner, 1897), 15–16. J. Holmer suggests a date of 1624–5 for the composition of the first and second songs. See 'Internal Evidence for Dating William Browne's *Britannia's Pastorals*, Book III', *PBSA* 70 (1976), 347–64, at 362–4.

[86] Browne's 'swaynes' may owe their 'westerne' orientation to Adlington's opening, 'There was sometimes, a certaine Kinge, inhabityng in the Weast partes...' Apuleius is non-directional (*Erant in quadam ciuitate, AA* 4. 28).

> Of royall parents in a country rich
>> Were borne three daughters, with all beautyes crownde
> That coulde the eyes of men or gods bewitch,
>> Or poets sacred verse did ever sounde;
> But Natures favour flewe a higher pitch,
>> When with the youngest she enrich'd this round,
> Thoughe her first worke for prayse much right might holde,
> Her last outwent yt, and she broke the molde.[87]

(lines 1–8)

Browne was obviously following the Latin (*Sic effata et osculis hiantibus filium diu ac pressule saviata*, AA 4. 31) rather than Adlington ('When she had spoken these woordes, she embrased and kissed her sonne') in his description of Venus' farewell to Cupid:

> Thus spoke she, and a winning kisse she gave,
>> A long one with a free and yeelding lipp,
> Unto the God;

(lines 193–5)

The poem contains much, however, of Browne's own embroidery. The offended Venus seeks her son 'among th' Elizian groves', but finds him instead 'with a shepheard . . . on the playnes', whom he loved 'for his verse, | Thoughe lowe and tuned to an oaten reed'. Venus commands Cupid to

> make that glorious mayde
> Slave in affection to a wretch as rude
> As ever yet deformitie araydc
> Or all the vices of the multitude.
> Lett him love money! and a friend betrayde
>> Proclayme with how much witt he is indude;
> Lett not sweet sleepe but sicknes make his bedd!
> And to the grave bring home her maidenhead.

(lines 177–84)

Browne develops Apuleius' suggestion of ill health (*incolumitas*, AA 4. 31), but he transforms social and economic deficiencies (lack of rank and money) into moral failings (avarice and treachery). Venus' departure marks the end of the Apuleian material in the poem. Browne then devotes twelve stanzas to Cupid's first sight of Psyche, including a *blason* of her cheeks, lips, voice, smile, hair, fingers, palms, wrists, arms, and (finally) breasts:

---

[87] Ed. T. Crofton Croker.

Nature, when she made woemens brests, was then
    In doubt of what to make them, or how stayned;
If that she made them softe, she knewe that men
    Woulde seeke for rest there, where none coulde be gayned:
If that she made them snow-like, they agen
    Woulde seeke for colde where loves hote flamings reigned;
She made them both, and men deceaved soe,
Finde wakefullnes in downe, and fyre in snowe.

Such were faire Psyches lillyed bedds of love,
    Or rather two new worlds where men would faine
Discover wonders by her starres above,
    If any guide coulde bring them back againe.
But who shall on those azure riveretts move,
    Is lost, and wanders in an endles mayne;
Soe many graces, pleasures, there apply them,
That man should need the worlds age to descry them.

(lines 257–72)

The poem concludes abruptly, however, after only three hundred lines. There is a half-hearted attempt at disguising the narrative truncation in the final stanza: Psyche's charms are transferred (none too successfully) to the beloved Coelia, the poet flattering her with the claim that her 'blest endowments are my verses mothers'. But Browne evidently lacked the energy or the inclination to sustain his grand scheme, and was perhaps daunted by the challenge of marrying the mythological and pastoral elements in the poem.

The Caroline period can, however, boast two large-scale versions of 'Cupid and Psyche', one dramatic, the other narrative. Thomas Heywood's *Loves Maistresse, or, The Queens Masque* (pr. 1636) brings together many of the themes explored so far in this chapter: the linking of Apuleius' transformation with that of Midas (cf. Lyly); the blending of 'Cupid and Psyche' with pastoral (Psyche's father Admetus is variously described as King of Thessaly and King of Arcadia). It appears to incorporate passages (and, doubtless, themes) from Dekker, Chettle, and Day's lost play 'The golden Ass & Cupid & Psiches' (1600).[88] But, in its revamped form, it enjoyed two royal performances, the second of them occurring (at Henrietta Maria's invitation), on 19 November 1634, in honour of the king's birthday.[89] In the prologue added for the occasion, Heywood compliments the queen by adapting the conceit of Psyche being displaced in her husband's affections: Cupid declares that he recognizes his surroundings

[88] Halstead ('Dekker's *Cupid and Psyche*', 184) notes that there is no evidence that Heywood collaborated on this play, but he may have been an actor in it.

[89] F. S. Boas, *Thomas Heywood* (London: Williams & Norden, 1950), 150.

by one face,
To which my Mistris Psiche must give place.
A presence; that from Venus takes all power,
And makes each place she comes in, Cupids bower.[90]

Heywood acknowledges the contribution to the masque's success of 'the rare decorements which new apparell'd it' supplied by 'that admirable Artist, Mr. Inego Jones, Master surveyor of the Kings worke'. But he also makes high claims for the moral and intellectual content of his piece:

The Argument is taken from *Apuleius*, an excellent Morrall, if truely understood, and may be called a golden Truth, conteined in a leaden fable, which though it bee not altogether conspicuous to the vulgar, yet to those of Learning and judgement, no lesse apprehended in the Paraphrase, then approved in the Originall: of which, if the perusers hereof were all *Apuleians*, and never a *Midas* amongst them, I should make no question.[91]

At the opening of the masque, Apuleius appears in person, carrying 'a pair of Asses eares in his hand', the significance of which he explains in his soliloquy:

How art thou Apuleius retransform'd?
Or else how cam'st thou metamorphis'd first
Into an Asse? Why to so dull a beast,
Of slow, and so obtuse a memory?
I had a braine aym'd at inscrutable things,
Beyond the Moon; what was sublunary,
Me thought was for my study all too meane;
Therefore, I therefore was I thus transhap'd:
That knowing man who keeps not in his bounds,
But pryes into heavens hidden Mysteries
Further than leave, his dulnesse is increast,
Ceaseth to be a man, and so turnes beast:
And thus I fell, yet by the selfe same power,
That calls all humane wisedome foolishnesse,
Am once more to my pristine shape restor'd;
Only to show how vaine my ambitions were,
This follies crest I still about me beare:

The contrast with George Gascoigne is marked. There is no mention of Lucius' erotic entanglements with Fotis: Apuleius is cast in Icarian, Adamic, and Faustian terms as the proto-humanist who misapplied his intellect and 'fell'.

---

[90] Cf. the address to Cupid in Robert Baron's 'Upon a Black Patch on Eliza's Breast Cut in the Form of a Dart': 'You gaz'd so long her eyes upon | Far brighter than thy Psyche's own . . . | Alas! you lost your levell'd aime' (vv. 13–17). See the *Eliza* section of his *Pocula Castalia* (London: W. H. for Thomas Dring, 1650), 97.

[91] *Dramatic Works of Thomas Heywood*, 6 vols. (London: Pearson, 1874), v. 85.

The reformed Apuleius is shocked by the boorishness of Midas whom he encounters in his search for 'the *Muses* Temple':

> *Ap.* If men be growne thus savage; oh you powers,
> Remetamorphise mee into an asse;
> 'Tis lesse inglorious, and lesse griefe to live
> A beast amongst wilde beasts, then to see man
> Bruite-like to blemish his creation.

Apuleius resolves to show Midas

> a story of mine owne,
> Of *Cupids* love to *Psiche*, sit and see't;
> I'll make thee then ingeniously confesse
> Thy treason 'gainst the Muses Majesty;
> Withall, not only whatsoever's mine,
> But all true Poets raptures are divine.

At the end of each act, Apuleius provides the dull-witted, ass-eared Midas, with a commentary on the action:

> *Mi.* And for thy Scene; thou brings't heere on the stage
> A young green-sicknesse baggage to run after
> A little ape-fac'd boy thou term'st a god;
> Is not this most absurd?

> *Ap.* Mis-understanding foole, thus much conceive,
> *Psiche* is *Anima, Psiche* is the Soule.
> The Soule a Virgin, longs to be a bride,
> The soule's Immortall, whom then can shee wooe
> But Heaven? whom wed, but Immortality:

> *   *   *

> By *Venus* heere, is meant intemperate lust:
> Lust woes her son *Desire,* to inflame the soule
> With some base groome, that's to some ugly sinne.
> *Desire* is good and ill; the evill sweares
> To *obay* his mother *Venus,* and vexe *Psiche*:
> But *Cupid* representing true desire,
> Doates on the Soules sweete beauty, sends his seruant
> *Zephirus;* In whom, Celestiall pleasur's meant,
> To entice his love, the Soule, to his chast bed,
> Giving her heaven for her lost maiden-head.[92]

---

[92] Ibid. 106–7.

Psyche's decision to climb the 'rock' by herself (Heywood's innovation)

> ... shewes how many strong adversities,
> Crosses, pricks, thornes, and stings of conscience,
> Would throw the ambitious soule affecting heaven,
> Into despaire and fainting diffidence,
> Which Psiche must passe through; the soule must fly
> Through thousand letts, to seek eternity.

And Psyche's sisters are

> The restlesse sins that travell night and day,
> Envying her blisse, the sweet soule to betray.
>
> (Act II)

At the dramatic level, Heywood also seems to have sensed the affinity between Psyche's sisters and Shakespeare's Goneril and Regan. Admetus' renunciation of Psyche after her banishment by Cupid recalls *King Lear*:

> I have three daughters; thou of all the rest,
> Hads't in my true conceptions greatest share,
> For which, I call'd thee Psyche, that's the soul,
> For as my soul I lov'd thee; now I abjure
> All interest in thy birth; hence from my court!
> My hand shall ne'er lay blessing on thy head.
> Nor my tongue grace thee with a daughter's name;
> Thou art not mine, but the base birth of shame.
>
> (iii. ii. p. 46)[93]

Heywood makes three important changes to his source: he destroys the 'blessed bower' after Psyche's trangression;[94] he makes her ugly; and he exiles her:

> *Boreas,* I charge thee by *Orithias* love,
> Lay waste and barren this faire flowrie grove,
> And make this Paradise a den of snakes;
> For I will have it uglier than hell,
> And none but ghastly scrietch-owles heere shall dwell;
> Breath winters stormes upon the blushing cheekes
> Of beautious *Psiche;* with thy boystrous breath,
> Rend off her silkes, and cloathe her in torne raggs;
> Hang on her loath's locks base deformity,

---

[93] Cf. *King Lear*, i. i. 112–15: 'Here I disclaim all my paternal care, | Propinquity and property of blood, | And as a stranger to my heart and me | Hold thee from this for ever.'

[94] The same thing happens in what is perhaps the best adaptation of 'Cupid and Psyche' in modern times—C. S. Lewis's *Till We Have Faces: A Myth Retold* (London: Bles, 1956), ch. 15.

> And beare her to her father, leave her there,
> Barren of comfort, great with child of feare;

(III, p. 123)

This is the most forceful and intense part of the masque. The intonation is biblical when Cupid asks Psyche, 'How durst thou violate my dread command?'[95] Psyche's sin, like Adam and Eve's, has universal consequences:

> Bid famine ride upon his frozen wings,
> Till they be blasted with his poysonous breath;
> Musick, be turn'd to sorrow, smiles to teares,
> Pleasures to shreiks, felicitie to feares.

(II, p. 122)

Cupid's 'plague' upon women recalls God's punishment of Adam and Eve in Genesis (3: 16–19: 'in sorrow thou shalt bring forth children' and 'In the sweat of thy brow thou shalt eat bread'):

> No, for thy sake, this plague pursue thy sex;
> You shall have appetites, and hot desires,
> Which though supplied, shall nere be satisfied;
> You shall be still rebellious, like the Sea,
> And like the Windes inconstant; things forbid
> You most shall covet, loath what you should like;
> You shall be wise in wishes but enjoying
> Shall venture heavens losse for a little toying.

(II, p. 122)

> *Mi.* But why did *Cupid* hide himself from *Psiche?*
> *Ap.* Oh who dares prie into those misteries,
> That heaven would have conceal'd; for this shee's charged
> Not to see *Cupid's* face, to shun her sisters.

(II, p. 120)

At the end of the third act, 'Apuleius' explains Psyche's fate:

> ... but because poore soule,
> She aym'd to search forbidden mysteries,
> Her eyes are blasted, *Cupid* loathes her sight,
> Hee leaves her ugly, and his blessed bower
> Is rent in pieces; for heaven seemes to fall
> When our poore soules turn diabollicall.

(III, p. 134)

---

[95] Fulgentius had drawn a parallel between Cupid's injunction against sight and Adam's failure to 'see that he is naked'. See Ch. 1, *supra*.

> *Mi.* . . . Why left he *Psiche* when she lost his love,
> Yet mourn'd when shee was left of all her friends.
> *Ap.* All bid the wretched soule run to despaire,
> When leprous sin deformes her, but even then,
> When the gods hate her? When shee's scorn'd of men?
> *Cupid* hangs in the ayre; his divine eyes
> Shed teares for her, comforts her miseries.
> *Mi.* Yet hee forsooke her too.
> *Ap.* Till Psiche bee made faire and angel-white,
> Shee's not to stand in Cupid's glorious sight.

(iii, p. 134)

Heywood is at pains to tighten the narrative logic of his source, filling in the causal gaps which make a reading of Apuleius so curious and tantalizing. Psyche is given a practical reason for opening the box of Proserpina's beauty: she is not merely insatiably curious; she wants to redress the leprous ugliness of her face:

> It's beauty Psyche, and celestial,
> And thou art ugly;

(p. 172)

The ending is even more harmonious than Apuleius': Psyche's sisters are forgiven. And in the closing lines of *Love's Mistress,* Cupid arbitrates between Midas and Apuleius with the words, 'Keep thou the Asses eares, the Lawrell thou': 'Ignorance' (Midas) has been overcome by 'Art' (Apuleius).

Heywood's practice of alternating action with exegesis runs the risk of creating an absolute dichotomy between the *dulce* and the *utile* of the Horatian formula.[96] But the running altercation between Apuleius and Midas also has a meta-dramatic function: it invites us to reflect on the purpose(s) of masques, on the relationship between text, spectacle, meaning, and morality. And, of course, court masques are, of their nature, ineluctably political phenomena. We have raised doubts, elsewhere in this book, about the stability of Apuleius' resolutions. Knowing what the following decade will bring the Stuarts, we can hardly avoid infusing the close of Cupid's prologue with a sense of historical irony:

> Long as the spheares continue, may you Raigne
> In Majesty, in power, in issue blest,
> Be all these with your fortunate yeeres Increast;
> Till Cupid (ever yong) with Time grow old . . .

---

[96] The Horatian tag, *Aut prodesse solent aut delectare,* appears (as it does in many of Heywood's works) on the title page of the 1640 edition of *Loves Maistresse.*

Shakerley Marmion's *Cupid and Psiche, or an Epick Poem of Cupid, and his Mistress*, emerges from the same cultural milieu as *Love's Mistress*, and the dedication ('To the High and Mighty, Charles Lodovick, Prince Elector') shows that Marmion (1603–39) shares Heywood's belief in the edifying content of the story:

And, however in the outward bark and title thereof, it appear painted with vanity, yet is that but as a light garment to cover more deep and weighty mysteries.[97]

Heywood reiterates the sentiments in the commendatory poem which he addresses to Marmion:

> The Argument is high, and not within
> Their shallow reach to catch, who hold no sin
> To tax what they conceive not; the best minds
> Judge trees by fruit, not by their leaves and rinds.
> And such can find (full knowledge having gain'd)
> In leaden fables, golden truths contain'd.[98]

The metaphors being used are precisely those employed by Stefano Colonna, almost three hundred years before, to justify his reading of *The Golden Ass*.[99] Yet while Heywood uses the figure of 'Apuleius' to incorporate details from Fulgentius' exegesis into the text itself, Marmion simply prefaces his work with a 'Mythology: or, Explanation of the Argument' (drawn almost verbatim—and without acknowledgement—from Fulgentius' *Mitologiae*) before embarking upon a pretty poem which immediately forgets any pretension to profundity.[100]

Other Treatments

Whatever the merits and demerits of their versions, Heywood and Marmion certainly manifest (and perhaps helped to create) a vogue for Apuleius during the Caroline period, for in 1639 (after a gap of forty-three years) there appeared a new edition of Adlington's translation.

 In *Love's Riddle. A Pastorall Comædie, written, at the time of his being Kings scholler in Westminster Schoole* (1638), Abraham Cowley (1618–67) uses an Apuleian allusion to underscore the social divide between wooer and wooed, when Florellus (a gentleman) invokes Cupid:

---

[97] *Minor Poets of the Caroline Period*, ed. G. Saintsbury, 3 vols. (Oxford: Clarendon, 1906), ii. 6.
[98] Ibid. 8.
[99] See Ch. 3, *supra*.
[100] *Minor Poets*, 9.

> Direct me now good love, and teach my tongue
> Th'inchantments that thou woo'dst thy *Psyche* with.

Bellula (a shepherdess) rejects him ('Fortune and nature have forbidden it, |
When they made me a rude and homely wench') and Florellus resolves to
transform his appearance and 'wooe her | In Sylvan habit'.[101]

Milton may have attacked the 'Clerks' of the University for 'preferring the
gay ranknesse of *Apuleius* ... before the native *Latinisms* of *Cicero*', but he was
ready to use the novel when it suited him.[102] In *Areopagitica* (1644), he writes:

> Good and evill we know in the field of this World grow up together almost insepar-
> ably; and the knowledge of good is so involv'd and interwoven with the knowledge of
> evill, and in so many cunning resemblances hardly to be dicern'd, that those confusd
> seeds which were impos'd on Psyche as an incessant labour to cull out, and sort
> asunder, were not more intermixt.[103]

In *Colasterion* (1645), he says: 'I may chance not fail to endorse him on the
backside of posterity, not a *golden*, but a leaden Asse.'[104] And in *Comus* (more
correctly, *A Maske Presented at Ludlow Castle, 1634*), he incorporates Apuleian myth (with Miltonic variations) into the warp of his poetry:

> But far above in spangled sheen
> Celestial Cupid her famed son advanced.
> Holds his dear Psyche sweet entranced
> After her wandering labours long,
> Till free consent the gods among
> Make her his eternal bride,
> And from her fair unspotted side
> Two blissful twins are to be born,
> Youth and Joy, so Jove hath sworn.[105]

J. J. M. Tobin, however, has also made extensive claims for Apuleian
presence in Milton's greatest poetry, citing numerous correspondences (in
theme as well as diction) between *The Golden Ass* and *Paradise Lost* (particularly in Books IV and IX of that poem).[106] None of the alleged parallels is
convincing on its own (many, indeed, seem far-fetched) but the evidence he

---

[101] (London: John Dawson, for Henry Seile, 1638), III. i. See *The English Writings of Abraham
Cowley: Essays, Plays and Sundry Verses*, ed. A. R. Waller (Cambridge: CUP, 1906), 67–148, at 99,
101, and 102.

[102] *An Apology for Smectymnuus* (1642), in *Complete Prose Works*, i. 934. See Ch. 6, *supra*.

[103] *Complete Prose Works*, ii. 514.

[104] Ibid. 757.

[105] *Comus*, 1002–10, in *The Poems of John Milton*, ed. J. Carey and A. Fowler (London:
Longman, 1968, repr. 1972), 227–8.

[106] 'Apuleius and Milton', *RPL* 7 (1984), 181–91.

amasses has a certain cumulative weight. He finds a congruence between the poem and the novel (and 'Cupid and Psyche' which enacts, in miniature, the plot of the whole) in the themes of 'curiosity' and 'sin, suffering, and redemption'.[107] In reaction to this, one might, of course, object that these thematic correspondences could merely be the result of the structural affinities between 'Cupid and Psyche' and Milton's own source, Genesis (the disobedience-and-punishment motif being common to both). But if we allow Tobin's claims for verbal parallels, then we can say, equally well, that Milton's use of Apuleius follows the pattern that we discerned in Sidney and Spenser: the Apuleian elements emblematize the unresolved dialectic between medium (*dulce*) and message (*utile*). Readers have generally found Comus a more engaging figure than the virtuous lady he fails to seduce, and the 'Satanic' interpretations of *Paradise Lost* made by Dryden, Blake, and Shelley are well known. Comus' 'stately palace, set out with all manner of deliciousness: soft music, tables spread with all dainties' recalls the 'royal meats and deintie dishes' accompanied by an invisible 'harmonie of the instruments' which greet Psyche upon her arrival at Cupid's 'Princely edifice'.[108] But the Spirit's 'epiloguizing' of 'Celestial Cupid' and Psyche's 'fair unspotted side' seems incongruous in a masque whose ostensible theme is Chastity.[109] Cupid, after all, has merely succeeded (where Comus fails) in using supernatural powers to gain the object of his desire (and Comus has at least tried persuasion before applying other means). And while Psyche may believe in the validity of the nuptials, Venus is unpersuaded, referring derisively to 'her great belly which she hath gotten by playing the whore'.[110] It is only the heavenly wedding that legitimates Cupid's union with Psyche.[111] In *Comus* and *Paradise Lost*, as in *The Faerie Queene*, an awareness of Apuleian sources (or even mere analogues) highlights the thematic and artistic stresses with which each work is fraught.

In Book VI of *Parthenissa, a Romance* (1655), Roger Boyle, the first Earl of Orrery (1621–79), shows the two heroes, Artabbane and Artavasde, inspecting the 'adornings' (p. 538) in the 'Temple of the Goddesse of Love' (which owes much of its embellishments, directly or indirectly, I suspect, to the *Hypnerotomachia Poliphili*). We are treated to a long series of mythological

---

[107] Ibid. 190.

[108] *The Poems of John Milton*, 209; Adlington, ch. 22, p. 75; *AA* 4. 3.

[109] On the controversy regarding the theme of Chastity, see Carey and Fowler, *The Poems of John Milton*, 172.

[110] Adlington, ch. 22, p. 95; *AA* 6. 9.

[111] Venus observes that the earthly marriage was invalid because 'made betweene vnequal persons, in the field without witnesses, and not by the consent of their parents' (Adlington, ch. 22, p. 95; *AA* 6. 9).

ecphrases, climaxing in the two 'Tables' depicting Psyche and Leucothoe who serve as representatives of the heroes' own loves:

And though all those Tables were so admirably represented, that to know the Story, [545] you needed but to see the Pictures, yet there were two others which so intirely tooke up our Hero's [*sic*] contemplation, that after the sight of them, they esteem'd none of the remaining ones worthy of theirs; The first was of a Beautie which could not but be excelent, since in Artabbanes's owne opinion, she resembl'd the faire Parthenissa. 'Twas that of the lovely Psiche, she that captivated the God of Love himselfe, & was so long taken for Venus, that had she bin immortall, she had eternally (as she did for a time) rob hir of hir votaries & Altars; The Artist had so well represented this Nymph, that it Authoriz'd Venus's Enuy and Mens mistake. There was in this representation, how the King of Milesia hir Father,[112] by the command of an Oracle, abandon'd hir to the Gods upon a Mountaine, how the Zephirs carry'd hir on their wings, into the fortunate Island to the Palace of Love, which 'till then, nor ever since, could boast of so admirable an Adornment; how the fair Psiche's two Sisters, at hir request were brought thither by the Zephirs, who envying their Sisters felicity, perswaded hir 'twas not a God, but a Serpent [546] she blest with hir embraces; how the credulous Nymph contrary to hir engagement, conceal'd a Lampe by hir Bedds side, with which when the little God had stupify'd his Sences by too-much satisfying them, she resolv'd hir doubts, but by so unfortunate a way that a drop of Oyle fell upon Cupid, who immediatly wak'd & flew away: There were further represented the tragick Death of the fair Psiche's Sisters; The Miseries which after that fatall Night befell hir; hir descent into Hell, & at length hir ascent into Heaven, to marry hir God, who now had pardon'd hir Cryme, & thereby deriv'd a more sublime satisfaction from his mercy, than he could have had in his Revenge.[113]

THE GREENE–HARVEY–NASHE CONTROVERSY

Apuleius also features prominently in the so-called Greene–Nashe–Harvey controversy.[114] In Robert Greene's *A Qvip for an Vpstart Courtier* (1592), *The Golden Asse* serves as an inverted image of social transformation. Frequent

[112] As Stephen Harrison points out to me, Boyle's 'King of Milesia' seems to be a mistranslation of *Milesiae conditor* (*AA* 4. 32).

[113] *Parthenissa, a Romance* (London: Henry Herringman, 1655), 544–6. On the date, see C. W. Miller, 'A Bibliographical Study of *Parthenissa* by Roger Boyle, Earl of Orrery', *SB* 2 (1949), 115–37. On *Parthenissa*, see P. Salzman, *English Prose Fiction, 1558–1700: A Critical History* (Oxford: Clarendon, 1985), 190–200.

[114] Although the dispute seems to have had its origins in John Lyly's response to Gabriel Harvey's supposed slight on Lyly's patron, the earl of Oxford, it soon became inextricably intertwined with another famous controversy, that of the Martin Marprelate tracts. See *The Works of Thomas Nashe*, ed. R. B. McKerrow, 5 vols. (London: A. H. Bullen/Sidgwick & Jackson, 1904–10), v. 65–110. All quotations are taken from this edn.

reference is made, throughout the controversy, to the Harvey brothers' humble origins as the sons of a 'rope-maker' from Saffron Walden. Greene's narrator ('Cloth breeches') claims to be writing on behalf of 'auntient Gentility and yeomanrie' against the 'vpstart Courtier' ('Veluet breeches') who, 'sprang of a Peasant will vse any sinister meanes to clime to preferment, being then so proude as the foppe forgets like the Asse that a mule was his father'.[115] The debate is presented as a dream vision in which Cloth breeches, wandering in 'a vale tapestried with sweet and choice flowers', sees one particular herb, 'the Courtiers comfort, Time':

I might perceiue certaine clownes in clowted shoone gather it, & ease of it with gréedinesse: which no sooner was sunke into their mawes, but they were metamorphosed, and lookt as proudly, though pesants, as if they had beene borne to be princes companions. (sig. A3ʳ)

Cloth breeches addresses Veluet breeches directly:

I will not denie, but there be as fantasticall fooles as your selfe, that perhaps are puft vp with such presuming thoughts, and ambitiously aime to trick themselues in your worships masking sutes, but while such climbe for great honours, they often fall to great shames. It may be therevpon you bring in *Honos alit Artes*, but I gesse your mastership neuer tried what true honour meant, that truss it vpe within the compasse of a paire of veluet-breeches, and place it in the arrogancy of the hart; no, no: say honor is idolatry, for they make fooles of themselues, and idols of their carcases: but he that valueth honour so, shall reade a lecture out of *Apuleius* golden asse, to learne him more wit. (sig. B4ʳ)

Greene's confrère Thomas Nashe declares in *Pierce Pennilesse* (1592):

We want an *Aretine* here among vs, that might strip these golden asses out of their gaie trappings, and after he hath ridden them to death with railing, leaue them on the dunghill for carion. (*Pierce Pennilesse* (1592), *Works*, i. 242)

   In *Pierces Supererogation, or A New Praise of the Old Ass* (1593), Harvey tries to neutralize the asinine insults by invoking the pseudo-doxological tradition of the ass:

Balaams Asse was wise, that would not run vpon the Angels sword: *Æsops Asse* no foole, that was gladd to fawne vpon his master, like a Dogge: *Lucians Asse*, albeit he could not fly, like the witch his hostisse, (whose miracles he thought to imitate, had not her gentle maide coosened him with a wrong boxe) yet could he Politiquely saue himselfe, please or ease his masters, delight his mistrisses, shew many artificiall feates, amaze the beholders, drinke the purest wine in Thessalonica, and finally eate roses, aswell as thistles: *Apulius* [*sic*] *Asse* was a pregnant Lucianist, a cunning Ape, a loouing worme, and (what [248] worthyer prayse?) A golden Asse: *Machieuels Asse* of the same

---

[115] (London: John Wolfe, 1592), sig. A2ᵛ.

mettal, and a deepe Politician like his founder, could prouide for One, better then the Sparrow, or the Lilly: *Agrippas Asse,* a woonderfull compound, and (may I say?) a diuine beast, knew all things, like Saloman, and bore all burdens like Atlas. (*Pierces Supererogation,* Grosart, ii. 247–8.)[116]

We note the priority accorded the (pseudo-)Lucianic *Onos* and the characterization of Apuleius as a 'pregnant Lucianist'. Machiavelli's *L'asino d'oro* had been published in London in 1588 by John Wolfe,[117] while Agrippa's *De incertitudine & vanitate scientiarum, & artium* (e.g. Paris, 1531) had appeared in English in 1569, with 'A Digression in praise of the Asse' in chapter 102:

and it is read that *Abraham* father of the elect, rode onely vpon Asses, so that this old Prouerbe among the people is not spoken in vaine, which saithe: that the Asse carieth mysteries, wherefore I wil now aduertise you famous professours of sciences, naye rather *Cumane* Asses, that if the vnprofitable burdens of humane knowledges be not set aparte, and that Lyons borrowed skinne put of, (not of that Lyon of the Tribe of *Iuda,* but of him whiche goeth about howlinge, and seekinge whome he may deuoure) yée be not tourned againe into bare and mere Asses, that yée be vtterly and altogether vnprofitable to carrie the mysteries of diuine wisdome: neither had that *Apuleius* of *Megara* euer bene admitted to the holy mysteries of Isis, if first he had not of a Philosopher ben tourned into an Asse.[118]

Harvey names Apuleius sixteen times in *Pierces Supererogation,* identifying him explicitly with Nashe:

Let his owne mouth / be his pasport, or his owne penne his warrant: & who so honest, as his deerest frend, villany: or so learned, as his learnedest counsell, vanity: or so wise, as his profoundest Autor, young Apuleius. What familiar spirite of the Ayre, or fire, like the glibb, & nimble witt of young Apuleius? or where is the Eloquence that should describe the particular perfections of young Apuleius? Prudence, may borrow, with discretion: Logique, arguments; Rhetorique, coulours; Phantasy, conceites; Steele, an edge; and Gold, a luster, of young Apuleius. O the rare, and queint Inuention. ô the gallant, and gorgeous Elocution: ô the braue, and admirable amplifications: ô the artificiall, and fine extenuations: ô the liuely pourtraitures of egregious prayses, and disprayses: ô the cunning, and straunge mingle-mangles: ô the pithy iestes, and maruelous girdes of yong Apuleius: the very prodigality of Art, and Nature. What greater [40] impossibility, then to decipher the high and mighty stile of young Apuleius, without a liberall portion of the same eleuate Spirite? Happy the father, that begat, and thrise happy the sweete Muses, that suckled, and fostered young Apuleius. (*Pierces Supererogation,* Grosart, ii. 39–40)

---

[116] Unless otherwise indicated, all quotations are from *The Works of Gabriel Harvey, D.C.L.,* ed. A. B. Grosart, 3 vols. (London: Huth Library, 1884).

[117] F. Raab, *The English Face of Machiavelli* (London: RKP, 1964), 52.

[118] *Of the Vanitie and Uncertaintie of Artes and Sciences, Englished by Ja[mes]. San[ford]. Gent.* (London: Henry Wykes, 1569), fol. 184ᵛ.

This is as much a critique of Apuleius' style as of Nashe's, the most important element for our purposes being the 'straunge mingle-mangles'—the mixed-modes which (in different ways) put Nashe and Apuleius beyond the bounds of Horatian decorum. The identification between Nashe and Apuleius is repeated throughout the work:

I come not yet to the Praise of the olde Asse: it is young Apuleius, that feedeth vpon this glory. (*Pierces Supererogation*, Grosart, ii. 52)

and finally discouer young Apuleius in his ramping roabe; (ibid. 119)

Sweet Apuleius, when thou hast wiped thy mouth with thine owne Asse-dung; and thine owne Tounge hath sayd vnto thy Pen, Pen thou art an Asse...But Asses carry mysteries: and what a riddle is this? that the true man should be the counterfait; and the false fellow the true Asse. (ibid. 250)

I were best to end, before I beginne; and to leaue the Autor of Asses, where I found the Asse of Autors. When I am better furnished with competent prouision, (what prouision sufficient for so mighty a Prouince?) I may haply assay to fulfill the Prouerbe, by washing the Asses headd, and setting the crowne of highest praise vpon the crowne of young Apuleius, the heire apparant of the old Asse, the most glorious Olde Asse.

I haue written in all sortes of humours priuatly I am perswaded, more then any young man of my age in England. They be the wordes of his owne honorable mouth: and the golden Asse, in the superabundance of his rich humours, promiseth [266] many other golden mountaines; but hath neuer a scrat of siluer. (ibid. 265–6)

Accounts of the controversy tend to depict Harvey as the lumbering pedant, consistently outscored in the fencing ring by the more nimble-footed Nashe. This is overly simplistic: Harvey is willing to deploy the same rhetorical weapons as Nashe, and he often gives as good as he gets; but he also expresses at times a very different view of the proper ends of discourse:

I deeme him wise that maketh choice of the best, auoideth the worst, reapeth fruite by both, despiseth nothing that is not to be abhorred, accepteth of any thing that may be tollerated, intertaineth euery thing with commendation, fauour, contentment, or amendment. Lucians asse, Apuleius asse, Agrippas asse, Macchiauels asse, miself since I was dubbed an asse by the only Monarch of asses, haue found sauory herbes amongst nettles, roses amongst prickles, berryes amongst bushes, marrow amongst bones, graine amongst stubble, a little corne amongst a great deal of chaff. (*Pierces Supererogation*, Grosart, ii. 292)

If he *is* an ass, Harvey suggests, he is, at least, capable of finding the 'roses' that will ensure his transformation, unlike Nashe, who, for all his 'pithy iestes, and maruelous girdes', remains the 'Monarch of asses'.

The most notable use of Apuleius, however, is to be found in Harvey's *The Trimming of Thomas Nashe Gentleman* (1597). Nashe, at this time, was incarcerated in the Fleet Prison for his part in the satirical comedy, *The Isle of Dogs*. Harvey uses his antagonist's discomfiture to blend the familiar (Platonic) notion of the body as the gaol-house of the Soul, with an evocation of the punishment threatened to Charite (*AA* 6. 31–2) after her attempted escape from the cave where she had just been told the story of 'Cupid and Psyche':

O double vnhappie soule of thine, that liues so doubly imprisoned, first in thy bodie, which is a more stinking prison than this where thou art; then, that it accompanieth thy bodie in this prison. Were it not sufficient that one prison should tortor thy soule enough? No, first because thy soule hath too deepe a hand in all thy knaueries, tis so imprisoned and fettered to thy bodie, that it cannot go without it Poore Soule more miserable than the kings daughter captiuated & long time kept imprisoned in the Theeues houses, at last offering [E4ᵛ] to breake away, was condemned to be sewed into the asses bodie & there to dye; for the asses bodie was dead, and nothing aliue in the asse (the prison) to trouble the Maid the prisoner. But thy prison is aliue, and all the affections in thy bodie are as stinking vermine & wormes in it, that crawle about thee, gnawing thee, and putting thee to miserie. She in short time was sure to die, and so to be free againe; thou art still in dying, and hoping for freedome, but still liuest, and this augments thy calamitie: she should haue had her head left out to breathe into the aire, but thou breathest into thy prison thy bodie, that corrupts within thee, and so retournes to bee thyne owne poyson. Thus much miserie (poore soule) thine owne bodie affoords thee, and by being with thy bodie in the second prison, all this is doubled. Now if thou wouldest bee free from thy prisons, make a hoale in thy first prison, breake out there, and so thou escapest both, thou neuer canst be caught again: and by this thou shalt crie quittance with thy bodie, that thus hath tormented thee, and shalt leaue him buried in a perpetual dungeon. (sig. E4ʳ⁻ᵛ)

How much significance should we attach to Harvey's labelling of Nashe as 'little Apuleius'? The invective of the dispute is often indiscriminate; the adversaries have a habit of appropriating each other's ammunition; and there is, in all of it, a degree of disingenuousness. Harvey's marginalia and Letter Book reveal the high (if uneasy) regard with which he privately viewed Lucian, Rabelais, and Aretino and, for all his Ciceronian protestations, he attempts to fight Nashe using Lucianical weapons.[119] Harvey, moreover, was doubtless attracted by the concinnity of the 'Nashe'/'ass' coupling, and the term 'Apuleius' allowed him to suggest asininity without directly charging hebetude (given Nashe's obvious cleverness, a foolish accusation to make).

Nashe himself, alas, is little help. He had already made an Apuleian allusion in his first major work, *The Anatomie of Absurditie* (1589):

---

[119] e.g. *Letter-Book of Gabriel Harvey, A.D. 1573–1580*, ed. E. J. L. Scott (London: Camden Soc., 1884), 134, 143; Duncan, *Ben Jonson and the Lucianic Tradition*, 84.

Were it that the infamie of their ignoraunce did redound onelie vppon themselues, I could be content to apply my speech otherwise, then to their *Apuleyan* eares; but sith they obtaine the name of our English Poets, and thereby make men thinke more baselie of the wittes of our Countrey, I cannot but turne them out of their counterfet liuerie, and brand them in the foreheade, that all men may know their falshood. (*Works*, i. 24)

In *Pierce Pennilesse* (1592), he alludes to the daemonological content of the *De deo Socratis*.[120] He appears, however, to make only one direct response to the 'little Apuleius' sally:

Sa ho: hath *Apuleius* euer an Atturney here? One *Apuleius* (by the name of *Apuleius*) he endites to be an engrosser of arts and inuentions, putting downe *Plato, Hippocrates, Aristotle,* and the *Paragraphs* of *Iustinian. Non est inuentus:* there's no such man to be found; let them that haue the Commision for Concealments looke after it, or the Man in the Moone put for it. (*Haue with you to Saffron-walden* (1596), *Works*, iii. 118)

Yet the invective does show that Harvey saw in Nashe a fusion not only of grotesque Rabelais, scoffing Lucian, and railing Aretino, but also of Apuleius with his 'gorgeous Elocution', 'straunge mingle-mangles', and 'high and mighty stile'. So it is that Harvey, talking of Nashe in *A New Letter*, can say 'the sweet Youth haunted *Aretine*, and *Rabelays*, the two monstrous wittes of their [273] languages' and then, a page or so later, revert to Apuleian nomenclature: 'But, I thanke God, I have some-thing else to dispute: and if young Apuleius be not still the sonne of old Apuleius'.[121]

The Greene–Harvey–Nashe quarrel cannot really be said to be *about* any one thing in particular, but occasional intrusions of literary theory reveal, behind the invective, fundamental questions as to the nature of discourse and the function of fiction, and remind us that Apuleius had been (since Late Antiquity) very much a part of this debate. In the third of his *Foure Letters* (1592), Harvey writes:

Euen Lucians true tales are spiced with conceite: and neither his, nor Apuleius' Asse, is altogether an Asse. It is a piece of cunning in the most fabulous Legends, to interlace some credible narrations, & verie probable occurrences, to countenance and authorize the excessive licentiousnesse of the rest. Vnreasonable fictions palpably bewray their odious grossnesse: (*Foure Letters*, Grosart, i. 200)

This could well serve as a critique of Nashe's own literary achievement—the very qualities of wit and invention that attract us to his works are also those that define its limitations. The consequence of his 'Lucianical' (the 'diabolical' extreme of 'Lucianic') temperament—his unfettered proteanism, the 'excessive

---

[120] *Works*, i. 227, 235.   [121] ed. Grosart, i. 272–4.

licentiousnesse' of his imagination—is an inability (or, at least, a refusal) to sustain 'credible narrations'. In *The Unfortunate Traveller* (1594), of course, Nashe wrote, as he puts it, in 'a cleane different vaine from other my former courses of writing' and he came closest to creating what we would today term a 'novel'.[122] He begins in the familiar mode of the pamphleteer, with a series of 'jests' to illustrate his youthful 'knavery',[123] interlaced with satirical jabs and glib one-liners, and displays, in his anachronistic mingling of historical figures and events, the artistic license that characterizes Lucian's *True Histories*.[124] But in the latter part of the work he presents extended narratives of a different kind—the story, say, of Heraclide's ravishment and suicide, or the death (through confusion of poisons) of Iuliana—which reproduce the typical configurations of an Apuleian tale;[125] and Jack Wilton is shown to have several features in common with Lucius: the youthful good looks which attract the attention of women; a quality of passivity which exposes both heroes to capital charges for crimes they did not commit; and a shared resolve to reform at the end of their adventures. It may be no more than coincidence that during this period Shakespeare and Nashe shared a dedicatee in the Earl of Southampton; but it is certainly true that as Nashe became less Lucianical, less labile, in *The Unfortunate Traveller*—more willing to allow sustained and 'credible narrations'—he moved closer towards the kind of controlled proteanism that informs much of Shakespeare's greatest achievement.[126]

[122] *The Unfortunate Traveller* (1594), *Works*, ii. 201.

[123] Ibid. 262.

[124] Ibid. 227: 'I must not place a volume in the precincts of a pamphlet'; ibid. 246: the satirical attack on Ciceronianism; ibid. 213: 'beeing by nature inclined to *Mercie* (for in deede I knewe two or three good wenches of that name)'. On *The Unfortunate Traveller* and 'the Lucianic or menippean tradition', see L. Hutson, *Thomas Nashe in Context* (Oxford: Clarendon, 1989), 141 ff.

[125] *Works*, ii. 292–5, 319.

[126] Extensive claims have been made for the presence of allusions to the Greene–Harvey–Nashe quarrel in *Love's Labour's Lost*. See the New Arden edn. by R. W. David, 5th edn. (London: Methuen, 1956; repr. 1983), pp. xxxiv ff.

9

The Arcadian Ass: Sir Philip Sidney and Apuleius

At his death in 1586, Sidney left behind two versions of *Arcadia*: the so-called *Old Arcadia*, a pastoral tragicomedy 'in five books or acts' completed in about 1581 (which circulated in manuscript and then disappeared from view for several centuries, only appearing in print in 1926);[1] and what we term, for convenience, the *New Arcadia*, a much revised and expanded version in two and a half books which was abandoned in 1584—two years before the skirmish at Zutphen that cost him his life. This incomplete version was published in 1590, breaking off mid-sentence at a critical point in the action.[2] In an attempt to 'repair' this 'disfigured face', Sidney's literary executors presented 'the conclusion, not the perfection of *Arcadia*' in the 1593 edition, 'supplying the defectes' to the *New Arcadia* by tacking on the last two books of the *Old*.[3] Subsequent editions carried a supplement, bridging the gap between the two versions.

Even in this grotesquely hybrid form, the *Arcadia* was a huge success. The seventeenth and early eighteenth centuries saw no fewer than fifteen English editions of the work and it was translated into French (1624–5), German (1629), and Dutch (1639).[4] Sidney's influence on later literature was enormous. John Barclay's *Argenis* (1621)—neo-Latin best-seller and one of Europe's first *romans à clef*—shows clear traces of the *Arcadia*. Indeed, a significant proportion of seventeenth- and eighteenth-century fiction was written in imitation of, or reaction against, the Sidneian tradition of prose romance.[5]

---

[1] *The Countess of Pembroke's Arcadia (The Old Arcadia)*, ed. J. Robertson (Oxford: Clarendon, 1973) (= *OA*).

[2] *The Countesse of Pembrokes Arcadia* (London: John Windet for William Ponsonbie, 1590); *The Countess of Pembroke's Arcadia (The New Arcadia)*, ed. V. Skretkowicz (Oxford: Clarendon, 1987) (= *NA*).

[3] Hugh Sanford's prefatory remarks to *The Countesse of Pembrokes Arcadia. . . . Now since the first edition augmented and ended* (London: William Ponsonbie, 1593), sig. ¶4^r.

[4] Skretkowicz, *NA*, p. xliv.

[5] See, generally, Salzman, *English Prose Fiction, 1558–1700*.

Given such a pedigree, it is no mere postmodernist affectation to talk about the 'influence of Sidney' on the ancient novels. Our interest in ancient fiction—indeed, our very capacity to conceptualize it—is determined, at least in part, by the modern novel's status as the dominant literary mode. But that pre-eminence was by no means inevitable. Since the *Arcadia* serves as one of the principal mediators between the two forms, Sidney's decisions assume a special significance. He was, after all, 'the first modern European to compose a full-scale novel in the ancient pattern'.[6]

THE *OLD ARCADIA* AND ITS SOURCES

The contributions of Jacopo Sannazaro's *Arcadia*, Jorge de Montemayor's *Diana*, Heliodorus' *Aethiopica*, Achilles Tatius' *Leucippe and Clitophon*, and the *Amadis de Gaule* to Sidney's work have long been recognized, but the role of Apuleius has been underestimated.[7] William Ringler, in 1962, noted 'the possible derivation of the trial scene and denouement of the *Old Arcadia* from Book X of Apuleius'.[8] Jean Robertson elaborated on the point, offering a précis of Apuleius' story of the Phaedra-like stepmother whose amorous advances towards her stepson are rebuffed:

the frustrated stepmother turns against him, and prepares poison; her own son drinks it and dies. She complains to her husband that the stepson had tried to seduce her, and that when he failed, he poisoned her own son. The father begs the justices to condemn his son to be stoned to death; but the truth emerges at the trial, where the poison turns out to have been a sleeping potion, much as the effect of Gynecia's potion wears off, and Basilius is restored to life after sentence of death has been passed on Gynecia and the princes.[9]

Sidney had already reworked the Phaedra-Hippolytus myth in the Second Eclogues, though his immediate model for Amasis and his stepmother was

[6] V. Skretkowicz, 'Sidney's Tragic *Arcadia* and the Ancient Novel', ICAN 2 paper, abstracted in *The Ancient Novel*, ed. Tatum and Vernazza, 52. Jacopo Sannazaro's *Arcadia* (1504) consists merely of twelve verse eclogues interposed with twelve short prose descriptions. *Diana*, the Spanish prose romance by Jorge de Montemayor (continued by Gil Polo), and the multi-authored *Amadis de Gaule*, are both indebted to Heliodorus, but the one is too static, the other too hydra-headed, to qualify as a novel.

[7] A. C. Hamilton asserts that the Latin novel 'may be ignored: while it provided Sidney with some matter... it did not serve him as an "imitative pattern"'. See *Sir Philip Sidney: A Study of his Life and Work* (Cambridge: CUP, 1977), 189 n. 1. According to Robertson (*OA*, p. xxiv), Longus' *Daphnis and Chloe* 'had no detectable influence on the *Old Arcadia*'.

[8] W. A. Ringler, ed., *The Poems of Sir Philip Sidney* (Oxford: Clarendon, 1962), p. xxiv.

[9] *OA*, p. xxiii; cf. Tobin, *SFN*, p. xiii.

Heliodorus' story of Cnemon and Demaenete (itself a Euripidean derivative) in the *Aethiopica* (1. 9–17, *CAGN*, 359–68). On second reading, however, we can see Amasis' tale as a kind of liminary admonition, for the Second Eclogues lead into the cave-scene of 'The Third Book or Act' where Gynecia uncovers her passion to Pyrocles. Gynecia, as mother to his beloved Philoclea, stands in much the same relation to Pyrocles as a stepmother, and the violence of her passion turns her, for moments at least, into a monster worthy of Seneca or Euripides, eager to commit 'a notable example of revenge' upon her own daughter: 'that accursed cradle of mine shall feel the smart of my wound' (*OA*, 184). A combination of details suggests, however, that the operative model for the story of Gynecia (easily the most richly delineated of the characters in the *Old Arcadia*) was found in *The Golden Ass*.

Apuleius begins his story in Book 10 with a warning: 'Gentle reader, thou shalt not reade of a fable, but rather a tragedie'.[10] Gynecia, at her first repulse, proclaims 'I will not be the only actor of this tragedy!' (*OA*, 184). In the Euripidean, Senecan, and Heliodorean stories, the stepsons all reject their stepmothers out of hand. In Apuleius, in contrast, the young man 'although he abhorred to commit so great a crime, yet hee would not cast her off with a present deniall, but warilie pacified her mind with delaie of promise'.[11] Pyrocles, doubly beset, decides that 'there was no way but to yield to the violence of [the Duke and Duchess'] desires, since striving did the more chafe them' (*OA*, 184). *The Golden Ass* was not the only potential source of the poison that turns out to be a sleeping-potion—Sidney could have found such a device in any version of the story that Shakespeare was to adapt in *Romeo and Juliet*[12]—but Gynecia's 'bottle of gold' (*OA*, 224) has a peculiarly Apuleian provenance. In each case, the potion is unwittingly intercepted by a thirsty innocent (the woman's young son and the duchess' husband, respectively) whose apparent death leads to a trial on capital charges. Tragedy, however, is miraculously transformed into comedy by the sudden restoration to life of the 'murdered' victim when the effect of the potion wears off (*OA*, 415). Apuleius can thus be seen to be supplying important narrative material for the conclusion of the novel.

No one, however, has commented on the Apuleian elements in the beginning of the *Old Arcadia* which opens, like 'Cupid and Psyche', with an oracle. Oracles, of course, are common enough in literature, but Sidney's is far closer to Apuleius' than to those found, say, in the *Amadis* (Book VIII),

---

[10] Adlington, ch. 44, p. 168 [= *AA* 10. 2].

[11] Ibid. p. 169 [= *AA* 10. 4].

[12] See *Brooke's 'Romeus and Juliet'*, ed. J. J. Munro (London: Chatto & Windus, 1908), pp. ix–lx. The original version, *Giulietta e Romeo* by Matteo Bandello (1485–1561), may itself be indebted to Apuleius.

Leucippe and Clitophon (2. 14), or the *Aethiopica* (2. 26, 36).[13] Apuleius' king is concerned to find a husband for his neglected daughter. Sidney's Basilius has less good cause:

not so much stirred with the care for his country and children as with the vanity which possesseth many who, making a perpetual mansion of this poor baiting place of man's life, are desirous to know the certainty of things to come, wherein there is nothing so certain as our continual uncertainty . . . (*OA*, 5)

The effect on both rulers, however, is the same:

The king, sometimes happie when he heard the prophesie of *Apollo,* returned home sad and sorrowful . . . (Adlington, ch. 22, p. 73 [= *AA* 4. 33])

. . . his amazement was greater than his fore curiosity—both passions proceeding out of one weakness: in vain to desire to know that of which in vain thou shalt be sorry after thou hast known it. But thus the duke answered though not satisfied, he returned into his country with a countenance well witnessing the dismayedness of his heart; (*OA*, 5)

Already we can see that Sidney shares Apuleius' interest in *curiositas*—one of the controlling factors of *The Golden Ass.*[14]

Psyche's father is told:

> Her husband is no wight of humane seede,
> But Serpent dire and fearce as may be thought.
> Who flies with winges aboue in starrie skies,
> And doth subdue ech thing with fierie flight.
> The gods themselues, and powers that seem so wise,
> With mightie Ioue be subiect to his might,
> The riuers blacke and deadly flouds of paine,
> And darknes eake, as thral to him remaine.

> (Adlington, ch. 22, p. 73 [= *AA* 4. 33])

The oracle appears at once both to fulfil and contradict Venus' curse upon Psyche that she might 'fal in loue with the most miserablest creature liuing, the most poore, the most crooked, and the most vile, that there may be none found in al the world of like wretchednes'; and Sidney seems to have had both curse and oracle in mind when he inspired 'the woman appointed to that impiety' to declare Philoclea's fate: 'Thy younger shall with nature's bliss

---

[13] J. J. O'Connor links Sidney's oracle to Book VIII of the *Amadis*, where the princess Niquée is sequestered by her father after an astrologer divines 'that any man who sees her will either go mad for love or die within a brief time'. See *Amadis de Gaule and its Influence on Elizabethan Literature* (New Brunswick, NJ: Rutgers UP, 1970), 187.

[14] The oracle is essential to the development of the narrative in each case, the difference being that Psyche's father is not criticized for consulting it.

embrace | An uncouth love, which nature hateth most' (*OA*, 5).[15] In both instances, of course, the husband proves to be a paragon of beauty; but the terms of the oracles are not entirely violated: Cupid may be 'the most meeke and sweetest beast of al beasts', but he is described, nevertheless, as a 'beast' (satisfying at least part of the prediction, *sæuum atque ferum uipereumque malum*), as well as being a powerful primal force, with sway, as in the oracle, over gods and nature.[16] Pyrocles, likewise, though a comely 'Cleophila', is an 'uncouth love' by virtue of his unnatural disguise.

Apuleius has also been credited as the possible source of two of Sidney's names.[17] When Musidorus ('Dorus') tricks his obstructive host into taking a horse to dig for hidden treasure beneath an oak, 'Dametas wished himself the back of an ass to help to carry away the new-sought riches—an unfortunate wisher, for if he had as well wished the head, it had been granted him' (*OA*, 188). The ass-reference may help to signpost the Apuleian humour buried in the 'box of cypress with the name of the valiant Aristomenes graven upon it' which Dametas comes across in the course of his digging (*OA*, 187). The 'valiant' Aristomenes of the *Old Arcadia* is ultimately indebted to Pausanias,[18] but Sidney may also have had in mind the Apuleian namesake—the all-too-unheroic narrator of the first tale, who watches, from his hiding-place under the bed, the evisceration of his friend, Socrates, before being discovered, in turn, by the witches who 'clapped their buttockes vpon my face, and all be pissed me til I was wringing wet'.[19]

Musidorus disposes of his host's wife, Miso, by fabricating a tryst between Dametas and a certain 'Charita' (*OA*, 168), comic effect perhaps being heightened here by giving a fictitious rustic adulteress the name of the nobly born romantic heroine ('Charite' in Apuleius, 'Charites' in Adlington's version) who is abducted on her wedding day and told the consolatory tale of 'Cupid and Psyche' in the robbers' cave. If the passage works, then it does so by playing upon the discrepancy between the rustic and the sophisticated response to the same clues. While Miso flies out of the house to catch Dametas and 'Charita' in Oudemian ('No one') Street, only to find that no such place exists, the literate reader smiles at the Homeric deceit.[20]

It is hard, however, to know how far one should follow the lines of Apuleian allusion in these two scenes. Nowhere is Apuleius' predilection for narrative

[15] Adlington, ch. 22, p. 72 [= *AA* 4. 32].

[16] Ibid., p. 85 [= *AA* 5. 22]; Beroaldo, fol. 98ᵛ [= *AA* 4. 33].

[17] e.g. *OA*, p. xxiii; Tobin, *SFN*, p. xiii.

[18] R. H. F. Carver, ' "Valiant Aristomenes": A Messenian Hero in Sidney's *Old Arcadia*', *N&Q* 239 (1994), 26–8.

[19] Adlington, ch. 5, p. 11 [= *AA* 1. 13].

[20] Cf. Odysseus (*Od.* 9. 366) giving his name as 'Nobody' to the Cyclops: Οὖτις ἐμοί γ᾽ ὄνομα.

nesting so evident as in the Chinese-boxes arrangement of 'Cupid and Psyche', where he plays at alternating fictions and realities within the total fictional framework. Something similar is happening with Sidney: Musidorus entraps Dametas' family by using a fictitious Charita (in Apuleius, the 'real' hearer of a fictitious story) as the bait. Yet Dametas, attempting, in 'real life', to forestall Pamela and Musidorus, catches Pyrocles and Philoclea in bed together by acting out the part of Psyche—the heroine of the story told to Charite. Every door in the house has been locked by Pyrocles, but Dametas enters through a trapdoor and comes

to the bedside of these unfortunate lovers, who at that time, being not much before the break of day—whether it were they were so divinely surprised to bring their fault to open punishment; or that the too high degree of their joys had overthrown the wakeful use of their senses; or that their souls, lifted up with extremity of love after mutual satisfaction, had left their bodies dearly joined to unite themselves together so much more freely as they were freer of that earthly prison; or whatsoever other cause may be imagined of it—but so it was that they were as then possessed with a mutual sleep, yet not forgetting with viny embracements to give any eye a perfect model of affection. But Dametas, looking with the lamp in his hand, but neither with such a face nor mind, upon these excellent creatures, as Psyche did upon her unknown lover, and giving every way freedom to his fearful eyes, did not only perceive it was Cleophila (and therefore much different from the lady he sought), but that this same Cleophila did more differ from the Cleophila he and others had ever taken her for. (*OA*, 273)

Sidney's parenthetical qualification ('but neither with such a face nor mind') suggests the primary intention of the Apuleian allusion: to highlight the comic incongruity of a rustic boor being likened to the wife of the god. But both scenes share the shock of a central discovery—the anagnorisis for their respective tales: Psyche's 'unknown lover' is suddenly revealed as the God of Love; the alluring Amazon is finally uncovered as a male. There is also a comparable convergence of malice and wonder. Psyche, persuaded by her wicked sisters that her husband is a serpent intent on eating her, comes to the bedside armed with a lamp and a razor to cut off his head. The lamp is an ambiguous figure, manifesting Psyche's irreligious *curiositas*—the violation of her uxorial oath—while retaining the more obvious connotations of revelation. It is the sight of Cupid that saves the god's head, though it is the same 'rash & bold lampe' that burns him and causes him to fly away and desert Psyche.[21] Dametas' purpose is also malicious, but the malice is directed at another target altogether—Pamela and Musidorus—the epiphany afforded by Pyrocles and Philoclea being purely serendipitous. And while both scenes privilege the observers (and us, their audiences) with a forbidden view, the

[21] Adlington, ch. 22, p. 86 [= *AA* 5. 23].

play of perspectives is quite different. Psyche moves from the role of love-making with her husband, to armed aggressor, to amorous onlooker and penitent caresser, to oil-spiller and deserted transgressor; the actor is converted into an observer but, by disturbing the observed, is drawn into the action in an unforeseen way. Sidney, in contrast, presents us with a topologist's paradox: the lovers' private world of abandoned conscience and lost consciousness is deftly invaginated—not only made public, but rendered into a self-conscious artefact ('not forgetting with viny embracements to give any eye a perfect model of affection'). The observer, Dametas—quite unequal, imaginatively and aesthetically, to what he sees, but the 'instrument', nonetheless, employed by 'the everlasting justice' (*OA*, 265) to enforce the objective moral code which the lovers have violated—retreats from the scene, leaving the observed (for the time being, at least) intact. Our response in each case is ambivalent: our sense of the wrongness of the protagonists' actions (the disobedience of Psyche, the fornication of Pyrocles and Philoclea) is mitigated, in Psyche's case, by compassion at the harshness of her punishment and, in the case of Pyrocles and Philoclea, by appreciation of the counter-system of aesthetic and moral values established in their embrace.

Yet the allusion to Psyche is also appropriate in the context of Sidney's expatiations upon the lovers' souls.[22] Beroaldo had employed the Platonic commonplace of the body being the prison of the soul in his commentary on *The Golden Ass*:

Rursus ex Asino in hominem reformatio significat calcatis uoluptatibus exutisque corporalibus deliciis rationem resipiscere: & hominem interiorem | qui uerus est homo ex ergastulo illo cenoso | ad lucidum habitaculum | Virtute & religione ducibus remigrasse: (Beroaldo, fol. 2ᵛ)

(The restitution of ass back into man signifies the recovery of reason, when pleasures are trampled underfoot and corporeal delights cast off, and—under the guidance of Virtue and Religion—the return of the inner man (who is the true man) from that foul penitentiary to the dwelling-place full of light)

Sidney, in contrast, presents his lovers in the throes of Platonic ecstasy, the intensity of their love-making having released their souls from their 'earthly prison'.[23] But any self-respecting Renaissance Platonist would recognize this as a distortion of the tradition of amatory *ekstasis*.[24]

---

[22] Sidney may be playing on the butterfly/soul meanings of ψυχή when he describes Pyrocles as being 'as close as a butterfly with the lady Philoclea' (*OA*, 274).

[23] On the Renaissance tradition of Platonic ecstasy (especially in the work of Leone Ebreo), see app. D of *John Donne: The 'Elegies' and 'The Songs and Sonnets'*, ed. Gardner, 259–65.

[24] Contrast Donne's 'The Ecstasy' or the near-fatal (but non-genital) embrace of Theagenes and Chariclea after their reunion in *Aethiopica* 2. 6 (*CAGN*, 382). Cf. *An Æthiopian Historie*, trans. Thomas Underdowne (London: Frauncis Coldocke, 1577), sig. [E.viii]ᵛ.

The union of souls ought to be a precondition of physical union rather than a consequence of it. In the context of Arcadia, spiritual union requires the approval of religion and state: without such sanction, the congress of Pyrocles and the princess, however attractively presented, is not only fornication, but treason. Readers with an Apuleian cast of mind may well recall the first bed-scene involving Lucius and Fotis: *simul ambo corruimus: inter mutuos amplexus animas anhelantes* ('we both collapsed at the same time amongst our mutual embraces, breathing out our souls').[25] In both cases, sexual fulfilment is followed by catastrophe. Pyrocles is arrested on capital charges; Lucius stands trial as part of the *Risus* Festival and is subsequently transformed into an ass, a calamity which Mithras (and the majority of critics) attribute to his 'having descended into slavish pleasures' (*ad seruiles delapsus uoluptates, AA* 11. 15).[26]

The Golden Ass can thus be seen to be supplying Sidney with the narrative devices needed to initiate (oracle) and conclude (sleeping-potion) the *Old Arcadia*, as well as featuring in its erotic climax. Dorothy Connell flirts with the idea of Apuleian influence when she says that Sidney's 'theme of love's transforming power...has roots in the *Metamorphoses* of Ovid, as well as in the *Golden Ass* of Apuleius (where the theme has both comic and mystical overtones)'.[27] And Jean Robertson (*OA*, p. xxiv) suggests that

The Golden Ass may also have been Sidney's model for the way in which he switches from the serious troubles of his main personages to the farce of the deceptions practised by Musidorus on Dametas, Miso, and Mopsa, so that he can elope with Pamela. After his complaints in the *Defence of Poesy* against the lack of decorum in tragicomedies, Sidney goes out of his way to justify Apuleius's practice...

---

[25] Beroaldo, fol. 46^r (= *AA* 2. 17). It might seem rash to argue for a direct allusion to the Fotis-scene here, given that, in Adlington's version, the Platonic ecstasy is ignored completely (Bk II, ch. 10, p. 30). Amongst the 'Poems Attributed to Sir Philip Sidney', however, Ringler (*Poems*, 340) prints one entitled 'Wooing-Stuff' which begins, 'Faint Amorist: what, do'st thou think | To tast Loves Honey, and not drink | One dram of Gall? or to devour | A world of sweet, and tast no sour?' This is reminiscent of Fotis' response to Lucius' first kisses: *Heus tu Scholastice ait: dulce & amarum gustulum carpis. Cave ne nimia mellis dulcedine diutinam bilis amaritudinem trahas* ('Hey there, Scholar,' she said, 'You snatch a little foretaste, sweet and bitter. Watch out that you don't contract, with too much sweetness of honey, the lasting bitterness of bile', Beroaldo, fol. 40^v; = *AA* 2. 10). Of course, the tradition of Love as bitter-sweet is a very long one, but Sidney's poem is closer in phrasing to the Latin than to Adlington ('O scholler, thou hast tasted nowe both honnie and gall, take heede that thy pleasure doe not turne into repentance', Bk II, ch. 9, p. 26) suggesting that Sidney read the (pseudo-)ecstatic love-scene in the original.

[26] But see R. H. F. Carver, '*Serviles Voluptates* and *The Golden Ass* of Apuleius: A Defence of Fotis', abstracted in *The Ancient Novel*, ed. Tatum and Vernazza, 55–6.

[27] *Sir Philip Sidney: The Maker's Mind* (Oxford: Clarendon, 1977), 25.

THE DEFENCE OF POESY

Sidney's remarks on *The Golden Ass* occur in his analysis of tragedy. Having criticized modern dramatists who defy the unities of place and time, he considers the unity of action, attacking contemporary English plays for being

neither right tragedies, nor right comedies, mingling kings and clowns, not because the matter so carrieth it, but thrust in the clown by head and shoulders to play a part in majestical matters with neither decency nor discretion, so as neither the admiration and commiseration, nor the right sportfulness, is by their mongrel tragi-comedy obtained. I know Apuleius did somewhat so, but that is a thing recounted with space of time, [115] not represented in one moment; and I know the ancients have one or two examples of tragi-comedies, as Plautus hath *Amphitryo;* but, if we mark them well, we shall find that they never, or very daintily, match hornpipes and funerals.[28]

J. J. M. Tobin talks of Sidney's 'appropriate neo-classical discrimination between what is legitimate in pure tragic drama, as opposed to what is proper for fictional narrative'.[29] But Sidney's qualifications ('because the matter so carrieth it', 'I know Apuleius did somewhat so', and 'never, or very daintily') amount to taxonomic fudgings. Apuleius, in fact, so mingles his elements that the pure tragic response is seldom permitted to occupy the mind for an adequate period before being displaced by a comic or bathetic effect.

Sidney's remarks actually reveal a fundamental ambivalence towards mixed modes in general and *The Golden Ass* in particular.[30] Sidney refuses to condemn Apuleius, apparently feeling an aesthetic attraction to Apuleius' complex shifts of register, but the discipline of crystallizing his views of literature in the *Defence* seems to have forced him to consider more critically the very inconsistencies which make the *Old Arcadia* so interesting.[31]

---

[28] *A Defence of Poetry*, in *Miscellaneous Prose of Sir Philip Sidney*, ed. K. Duncan-Jones and J. van Dorsten (Oxford: Clarendon, 1973), 114–15.

[29] *SFN*, p. xiii.

[30] At *Defence*, 94, Sidney defends mixed modes like tragicomedy and heroical-pastoral by observing that 'if severed they be good, the conjunction cannot be hurtful'. But his remarks on 'mongrel tragi-comedy' reveal the prejudices he shares with Horace: *denique sit quod uis, simplex dumtaxat et unum* ('whatever kind of work it is, let it at least be unmixed and uniform', *Ars poetica*, 23).

[31] For a fuller discussion, see R. H. F. Carver, '"Sugared Invention" or "Mongrel Tragi-Comedy": Sir Philip Sidney and the Ancient Novel', *GCN* 8 (1997), 197–226.

'SUGARED INVENTION': THE HELIODOREAN MODEL

The major thrust of the *Defence of Poesy* is its attempt to legitimate 'feigning'. For Sidney, the essence of *poesy* is 'making': ποιεῖν. Indeed, 'it is not rhyming and versifying' but 'that feigning notable images of virtues, vices, or what else, with that delightful teaching which must be the right describing note to know a poet by'. Poets, he tells us,

> do merely make to imitate, and imitate both to delight and teach; and delight, to move men to take that goodness in hand, which without delight they would fly as from a stranger; and teach, to make them know that goodness whereunto they are moved...[32]

Sidney's paradigm for this notion is a work of idealized history, the *Cyropaedia* of Xenophon, which has been called 'the first extant novel'.[33] For Sidney, the value of the work is its ability 'to bestow a Cyrus upon the world to make many Cyruses'.[34] But Xenophon, whatever his appeal as an educator, could not satisfy Sidney's needs as a narrative artist. These had to be met by the 'zodiac of his own wit' and by the available resources of fiction, chief among them the *Aethiopica* of Heliodorus.[35]

The Renaissance reception of the *Aethiopica* may seem a striking instance of the misguided application of Aristotelian literary principles, but it had important implications for the development of the European novel: here was a work of prose fiction of which even Humanists could approve.[36] Heliodorus was not only popular with the general readership; he received the highest accolades from influential literary theorists.[37] Julius Caesar Scaliger advises the aspiring epic poet to read the *Aethiopica* 'with the utmost care' (*accuratissimè*) and 'set it before his eyes as his best model' (*pro optimo exemplari*

---

[32] *Defence*, 81.

[33] P. Stadter, 'Fictional Narrative in the *Cyropaideia*', *AJP* 112 (1991), 461–91, at 461. Cf. J. Tatum, *Xenophon's Imperial Fiction: On the Education of Cyrus* (Princeton: PUP, 1989).

[34] *Defence*, 79.

[35] Ibid. 78.

[36] As G. N. Sandy observes, da Pazzi's Latin translation of the *Poetics* appeared in 1536, just two years after the publication (at Basel) of the *ed. princ.* of Heliodorus. See 'Classical Forerunners of the Theory and Practice of Prose Romance in France: Studies in the Narrative Form of Minor French Romances of the Sixteenth and Seventeenth Centuries', *Antike und Abendland* 28 (1982), 169–91, at 169.

[37] Joseph Hall (author, *inter alia*, of a Theophrastan work, *Characters of Virtues and Vices*, 1608) observes (in 1620), 'What Schole-boy, what apprentice knows not Heliodorus?' Quoted by D. Bush, *English Literature in the Earlier Seventeenth Century, 1600–1660*, 2nd edn. (Oxford: Clarendon, 1962), 53. Cf. G. N. Sandy, 'Ancient Prose Fiction and Minor Early English Novels', *Antike und Abendland* 25 (1979), 41–55, at 41.

sibi proponendum).[38] This may seem strange counsel indeed; for while the *Aethiopica* shows some structural affinities with epic (the *in medias res* beginning is the most obvious), the experience of reading it is quite un-Homeric.[39] Yet Tasso, for one, endorsed Scaliger's views. In his early critical work *Del poema eroica*, Tasso approved Macrobius' distinction between edifying fictions and those (like Apuleius') where 'the poet wishes only to please the ears and make, as it were, a profession of falsehood and of lying' (*il poeta vuol solo piacere a gli orecchii e fa quasi professione di falsità e di bugia*);[40] and in the *Gerusalemme liberata* he partly modelled the character of Clorinda upon Chariclea.[41] Later critics, such as Alonso López Pinciano, went so far as to equate Heliodorus with Vergil and Homer.[42]

The conflict between Apuleian and Heliodorean impulses can also be seen in the work of Miguel de Cervantes. Apuleian influence has long been recognized in *Don Quixote* (1605) where Cervantes set out to destroy the influence of the chivalric romances (*libros del caballerías*).[43] The most obviously Apuleian moment is the episode in Part I (chapter 35) where Don Quixote wakes in the innkeeper's loft (which he takes to be part of a castle) and slaughters the wineskins which have been placed near his bed.[44] The episode interrupts the conclusion of the interpolated 'Tale of the Foolishly Inquisitive Man' (*La nouela del Curioso impertinente*, chs. 32–5) and the complex is indicative of the transformation that Cervantes' discursive method

---

[38] *Poetices libri septem* (Lyons: Antonius Vincentius, 1561), 144.

[39] e.g. the Homeric tags (*Iliad*. 4. 51; 8. 65) in a battle-scene (*Aethiopica* 1. 30) which turns out to be a squabble between rival gangs of bandits motivated not by heroic valour but by financial greed.

[40] Quoted in A. K. Forcione, *Cervantes, Aristotle, and the 'Persiles'* (Princeton: PUP, 1970), 181. See *Tasso: Discourses on the Heroic Poem*, trans. M. Cavalchini and I. Samuel (Oxford: Clarendon, 1973), 26.

[41] e.g. *G.L.* xii. 21 ff. See W. Stephens, 'Tasso's Heliodorus and the World of Romance', in *Search for the Ancient Novel*, ed. Tatum, 67–87.

[42] *Philosophia antigua poetica* (Madrid: Thomas Iunti, 1596), 262. For Scaliger and Pinciano, see T. Hägg, *The Novel in Antiquity* (Oxford: Blackwell, 1983), 1, 200.

[43] In the celebrated discussion of Don Quixote's 'books of chivalry', the canon declares: 'in my opinion, this sort of composition falls under the heading of Milesian Fables, which are extravagant tales, whose purpose is to amaze and not to instruct; quite the opposite of Moral Fables, which delight and instruct at the same time' (*Y, según a mí me parece, este género de escritura y composición cae debajo de aquel de las fábulas que llaman milesias, que son cuentos disparatados, que atienden solamente a deleitar, y no a enseñar; al contrario de lo que hacen las fábulas apólogas, que deleitan y enseñan juntamente* (Cervantes, Part i, ch. 47). See *The Adventures of Don Quixote*, trans. J. M. Cohen (Harmondsworth: Penguin, 1950), 424–5; *Don Quijote de la Mancha I*, ed. J. B. Avalle-Arce (Madrid: Alhambra, 1979), 566. For a fuller analysis, see R. H. F. Carver, ' "True Histories" and "Old Wives' Tales": Renaissance Humanism and the "Rise of the Novel" ', *Ancient Narrative* 1 (2000–1), 322–49.

[44] Cf. Lucius' encounter with the inflated wineskins at *AA* 2. 32.

has undergone—a change from (parodic) romance to something approaching *sermo Milesius*.[45]

In another episode (Part 1, chapter 43), the Knight has his hand fixed by the innkeeper's daughter and Maritornes—like the bandit chief (named Lamachus in a parodic reference to the famous Athenian general) whose hand is nailed to the inside of the door by the owner of the house he and his band are trying to rob (*AA* 4. 10). But there are many more pervasive levels of Apuleian influence. Don Quixote shares with Lucius a tendency to credulity and an eagerness for novelty. Like Lucius, he is a well-born and perniciously curious man who has been metamorphosed, not by magic, but by the wicked influence of fictions.[46] There is a great deal of self-conscious play with notions of wise donkeys (who understand human speech and emotions) and asininely foolish humans. Cervantes goes to extraordinary lengths to emphasize the 'friendship and loyalty' between Sancho and his ass, Dapple. Characters like the Canon express amazement that Don Quixote (despite his transformation) displays such good sense, such powers of reasoning and discourse on every subject other than chivalry (e.g. Part I, chapter 49, p. 435).

Don Quixote comes back from his first adventure, battered and mounted on his neighbour's ass (Part I, chapter 5). Just as Lucius escapes his captors by spraying them with liquid dung (*AA* 4. 3), so Don Quixote secures his release from the cage by threatening the priest and canon with offensive smells if he is not allowed to relieve himself in the fields (Part I, chapter 49, p. 435). Indeed, Sancho uses the urge to excrete as a kind of reality test (Part I, chapter 48, p. 433).

But mastery of comic or realist fiction was evidently not enough, for in *Los Trabajos de Persiles y Sigismunda* (1617), Cervantes strove to 'competir con Heliodoro' by constructing romance on an epic scale.[47] *Persiles* was an initial

---

[45] *La nouela del Curioso impertinente* belongs to a narrative tradition that leads back, through the *novelle* of Boccaccio's *Decameron*, to the adultery stories of *The Golden Ass*. It is, essentially, a Milesian tale.

[46] At the heart of *Don Quixote* is the notion of metamorphosis, of the fluidity of identity, of the shifting borders that separate appearance and reality. Cognates of 'transformation' (e.g. *transformaciones*, Part I, chs. 37, 44) and 'metamorphosis' (e.g. *metamorfoseos*, Part I, ch. 37) recur. Don Quixote begins with self-conscious transformations, metamorphosing himself (Part I, ch. 5, p. 53: 'he lost his senses and changed himself from a quiet gentleman into a knight errant'), his horse, and the farm girl Aldonza Lorenzo.

[47] Prologue to the *Novelas Ejemplares* (1613). Cf. C. Gesner, *Shakespeare and the Greek Romance: A Study of Origins* (Lexington: UP of Kentucky, 1970), 45. Cervantes could not, however, banish *The Golden Ass* completely. In *Cervantes's Theory of the Novel* (Oxford: Clarendon, 1962), 207, E. C. Riley cites Apuleius as a background presence for a passage in the *Persiles* where Cervantes 'allows an unsuitable comic irony to break in'. And a 'dialectical imitation' of Cupid and Psyche has been identified in Cervantes' tale of the avenging Scottish countess (*Persiles*, iii. 16–17). See D. de Armas Wilson, 'Homage to Apuleius: Cervantes' Avenging Psyche', in *Search for the Ancient Novel*, ed. Tatum, 88–100.

success but its relative obscurity today may tell us something about the narrative possibilities afforded by these two models for prose fiction, the *Aethiopica* and *The Golden Ass*.

In the *Defence*, Sidney describes the *Aethiopica* (along with the *Cyropaedia*) as 'an absolute heroical poem', singling out for special praise Heliodorus' 'sugared invention of that picture of love in Theagenes and Chariclea'.[48] His revision of the *Arcadia* seems to be an attempt to refashion the work along Heliodorean lines.[49] In formal terms, Sidney wanted to move towards the grander design, and the example of the *Aethiopica* allowed him to satisfy the desire for narrative multiplicity—the sense of fictive fecundity—which romance offered, while working within the structure of epic. Hence the *in medias res* beginning of the *New Arcadia*, the more convoluted plotting, the introduction of siege and battle scenes, and so on.

The *Aethiopica* could also more easily be promoted as an edifying work than *The Golden Ass*—suffused with erotic suggestion but untouched by the explicit carnality that so marks the Roman novel.[50] And while Adlington (or his first printer) felt obliged to impose his own marginal moralizations upon a generally recalcitrant text, Thomas Underdowne needed only to add quotation marks to highlight the *sententiae* already included by Heliodorus.[51] Most importantly of all, while *The Golden Ass* is devoid of exemplary characters, the *Aethiopica* swarms with them.[52] As Underdowne points out in his preface to his translation:

This booke punisheth the faultes of euill doers, and rewardeth the well liuers. What a king is *Hidaspes*? What a patterne of a good [¶iii^v] prince? What a lewde woman was *Arsace*? What an euill end had shee? Thus might I say of many other.[53]

Such a reading, of course, will seem crude and simplistic to an audience of modern scholars familiar with the subtleties of Heliodorus' narrative.[54] But

[48] *Defence*, 81.

[49] See V. Skretkowicz, 'Sidney and Amyot: Heliodorus in the Structure and Ethos of the *New Arcadia*', *RES* 27 (1976), 170–4.

[50] e.g. the description of the gold snakes in Chariclea's bosom (3. 4; Underdowne, sig. C.vi^r, *CAGN*, 412). Even Underdowne entertained some doubts as to the edifying nature of the work, ending his preface with the imprecation, 'God graunt that my labour be profitable to all, (for I feare not, but that it wilbe pleasaunt to many) and that none thereby take occasion of offence or dooinge amisse' (sig. ¶ iii^r).

[51] e.g. 'Suche is the nature of theeues, they esteeme more money then their owne liues' (Underdowne, sig. C. iii^r).

[52] The tragic fate of Charite and Tlepolemus makes them a parody of the exemplary lovers of the Greek romances from which they are drawn.

[53] 'To the gentle reader', sig. iii^r–^v.

[54] Even Heliodorus has a share of morally ambiguous figures: e.g. Knemon, the nobly born Athenian and tragic victim, torn between altruism and self-interest; or Thyamis, the virtuous man who turns bandit after being cheated of his priesthood, falls in love with Chariclea, tries to

Underdowne's appraisal fits the critical needs of the day, confirming Sidney's assertion of the quality 'particular to Poetry' that 'therein a man should see virtue exalted and vice punished'.[55]

The problem with Sidney's notion of 'the speaking picture of poesy' is that it furnishes a static model for the relationship between aesthetics and morality in fiction. Sidney's theory allowed for negative ideal figures, but it did not permit the mixing of virtues and vices in the one character. That would vitiate the integrity of the Platonic Idea or the Aristotelian universal:

> If the poet do his part aright, he will show you in Tantalus, Atreus, and such like, nothing that is not to be shunned; in Cyrus, Aeneas, Ulysses, each thing to be followed; where the historian, bound to tell things as things were, cannot be liberal (without he will be poetical) of a perfect pattern, but, as in Alexander or Scipio himself, show doings, some to be liked, some to be misliked.[56]

Sidney, however, has been rather selective in his illustrations. The theory may work with the *Cyropaedia* which offers, in place of characterization, a sustained exercise in *effictio* (the representation of the exemplary leader's virtues)—but it cannot account for the complex achievements of what would more usually be considered 'heroical' poems.[57] How, for instance, do we fit an Agamemnon or an Achilles, a Dido or a Turnus into this rigid framework? Sidney made earlier mention of Achilles as 'a perfect pattern' of 'valour',[58] but (as Horace observes, *Epistles* 1. 2. 14) his intemperate wrath costs his comrades dear, and his petulance leads Dryden (a century after Sidney) to liken him to 'a Booby... complaining to his Mother'.[59] Heliodorus, indeed, makes the problem explicit when he says that Theagenes exhibits all the virtues of Achilles 'Sauing that he is not so arrogant and proude'.[60]

---

murder her when faced with her loss (killing Thisbe instead, 1. 30), and is finally restored to his priesthood—but they are only minor characters and all (with the exception of the satrap, Oroondates) are cleared out of the way well before the dénouement. On related problems, see J. J. Winkler, 'The Mendacity of Kalasiris and the Narrative Strategy of Heliodoros' *Aithiopika*', *YCS* 27 (1982), 93–158.

[55] *Defence*, 90.

[56] Ibid. 88. By the end of the 17th cent., critical theory had accommodated the notion of mixed character. Dryden, for example, tells us (*Works*, v. 271): 'The Courage of *Achilles* is propos'd to imitation, not his Pride and Disobedience to his General, nor his brutal Cruelty to his dead Enemy, nor the selling his Body to his Father. We abhor these Actions while we read them, and what we abhor we never imitate: The Poet only shews them like Rocks or Quicksands, to be shunn'd.'

[57] Cicero describes the *Cyropaedia*—in a letter to Quintus quoted by Sidney (*Defence*, 81)— as an *effigiem iusti imperii* ('the portraiture of a just empire') rather than an attempt at historical verisimilitude.

[58] *Defence*, 86.

[59] *Dedication of the Æneas*, in *The Works of John Dryden*, 20 vols. (Berkeley: U of California P, 1956–2000), v. 291.

[60] Underdowne (sig. Gii^v), recalling Diomedes' description of Achilles (*Iliad* 9. 699). Cf. *CAGN*, 428 (4. 5).

And this, it appears, is precisely what endeared him to the neo-Aristotelian literary theorists of the Renaissance: in respect of characterization, at least, Heliodorus could actually surpass his epic masters.

Yet the writing of the *Defence* must have made Sidney aware of the contradiction between his theory of exemplary characterization and his own practice in the *Old Arcadia*. As Katherine Duncan-Jones observes:

Sidney's complex presentation of the two princes, in which he plots the ever-widening discrepancy between their idealized pretensions and their actual self-interest, yet keeps them always the heroes, is one of the special strengths of the 'old' version. The more dignified and idealized treatment of them in the revised version is one of the changes that made the story uncompletable on the old lines.[61]

The princes' lapses are well known: abandoned to the cause of love, they exchange manly armour for rustic weeds and womanish disguise, neglecting the pressing business of rescuing Erona, abusing the trust of their hosts, and causing consternation on all sides—especially to the all-but-ruined duchess. And while Musidorus almost rapes Pamela, Pyrocles succeeds in seducing Philoclea.[62]

If such elements make the ending of the *Old Arcadia* problematic for modern readers, we ought to remember that problems of closure seem to have weighed less heavily on our forebears. Achilles Tatius, who gave Sidney the names of Clitophon, Clinias, and Leucippe for the *New Arcadia*, also provided, in Melite's generous but adulterous passion for Clitophon, a model for Gynecia's fixation with Pyrocles in the *Old*.[63] In both cases the hero dissembles, promising a consummation which he means to withhold—although Clitophon ultimately succumbs while Pyrocles (albeit sorely tempted) resists the corporeal riches uncovered by Gynecia and contrives a stratagem whereby the duchess does commit adultery—but with her own husband. Yet both women are ultimately hailed as paragons of wifely virtue, Melite because she can truthfully swear that she remained faithful for the whole of her husband's absence (she seduces Clitophon on the night of Thersandros' return), Gynecia because of Basilius' obliviousness and the silence of Pyrocles and Philoclea.[64]

---

[61] K. Duncan-Jones, ed., *Sir Philip Sidney: The Countess of Pembroke's Arcadia (The Old Arcadia)* (Oxford: OUP, 1985), p. xvi.

[62] *OA*, 177, 211.

[63] S. L. Wolff, *The Greek Romances in Elizabethan Prose Fiction* (New York: Columbia UP, 1912), 314.

[64] *OA*, 360. Leucippe, similarly, is celebrated for preserving her virginity throughout her torments and captivities, but is only prevented, at the beginning of the work, from surrendering her maidenhead to Clitophon by the eruption of her dream-ignited mother into her bedroom. And Clitophon, of course, while enjoying Leucippe's appreciation of his supposed fidelity, conceals the fact of his congress with Melite.

The Gynecia-Melite parallel introduces a nice irony—a touch of realism—to the *Old Arcadia*, but it augments rather than undermines the element of seriousness which permeates the last third of the work. Chivalric romance is remarkably liberal in its moral dispensations: the premarital consummation of Pyrocles' love for Philoclea is quite in keeping with the spirit of the *Amadis*. But the *Old Arcadia* interrogates the conventions of romance even as it exploits them. The youth, beauty, and noble birth of the two princes, their martial prowess and comradely devotion, initially endear them to their audience, ensuring that excesses are indulged in them that would not be tolerated in others. But this immunity from quotidian moral responsibilities is neither absolute nor permanent. Sidney brings the romance tradition into collision with Protestant principles of individual accountability—with powerful results.

During the trial, the princes are forced to acknowledge the full consequences of their actions. But the harsh sentence, the miraculous reprieve occasioned by the wearing-off of the love-potion (itself an Apuleian device), and the matrimonial reparations that follow, make amends (more or less) for their youthful transgressions.[65] And Gynecia is able 'in the remnant of her life' to 'purchase' 'with observing all duty and faith' that 'most honourable fame' which her adulterous conduct had before unfairly earned (*OA*, 416). The characterization, in other words, is (in contrast to that in Heliodorus) not only dynamic (liable to change) but also organic (able to develop). Sidney has achieved a more subtle kind of *paideia*—one in which the central characters are schooled, through error, in the virtues which they are meant to embody.[66]

Yet Sidney was obviously dissatisfied with the finished product. The urge to Heliodoreanize is evident in the *New Arcadia*'s attempt to rewrite Pyrocles and Musidorus as 'absolute heroical' figures. The near-rape of Pamela and the premarital consummation-scene between Pyrocles and Philoclea could find no place in the revision.[67] As a general rule, the good are made better, the baser sort degraded even further (Dametas' faults, for instance, are so darkened that buffoonery is transformed into vice) and the postlapsarian 'infected will' that caused the princes in the *Old Arcadia* to fall short of their ideal gives ground, in the *New*, to a notion of externalized evil, embodied in Cecropia.[68] Conversely, the criticism of Basilius (who appears as something

---

[65] As Pyrocles says (*OA*, 394–5), 'the salve of her honour... [395]... must be my marriage and not my death, since the one stops all mouths, the other becomes a doubtful fable'.

[66] Compare Spenser's method in *The Faerie Queene* (the instruction in virtue of a character like the Redcrosse Knight in Bk. 1).

[67] *NA*, 429. In the hybrid edn. of 1593, Pyrocles goes to Philoclea to persuade her to elope, rather than to seduce her, and the 'too high degree of their joys' that renders them unconscious on the bed at *OA*, 236 becomes, in *Sir Philip Sidney: The Last Part of the Countesse of Pembrokes Arcadia*, ed. A. Feuillerat (Cambridge: CUP, 1912), 90, 'the unresistable force of their sorrowes'.

[68] On the conflict between fallen Man's 'erected wit' (lifted up to its divine source) and his 'infected will', see *Defence*, 79.

of a doting fool in the *Old Arcadia*) is tempered by praise in the *New*, and his behaviour in the face of the siege is made to show that, whatever his private susceptibilities, his kingly qualities can assert themselves when the commonweal is imperilled.[69]

Ancient romances like those of Achilles Tatius and Apuleius establish a dynamic between randomness and determinism: the characters are constantly berating what they see to be a blind and malevolent fortune, but their opinions are reversed by the affirmation of Divine Providence in the conclusion. The *Old Arcadia*, accordingly, is full of attacks upon 'filthy fortune'; but all is redeemed (in rhetorical terms, at least) by Basilius' observation that everything has worked out in terms of the oracle.[70] When it came to the revision, Sidney seems to have been unhappy with the facility of this resolution and, striving to surpass Heliodorus (who gives his main characters a far firmer sense of their assured destiny than the other novelists),[71] he put in Pamela's mouth an apology for Divine Providence reputedly sufficient to move Charles the First to adopt her prayer as his own on the eve of his execution.[72]

All in all, the revision is given a firmer moral structure. Sidney's revised plan would (if followed through) have necessitated the rejection of the proteanism that accounts for much of the interest of the old version. The transformation, however, was never completed. For a start, there is enough unassimilated erotic material in the *New Arcadia* to show how difficult Sidney found his self-appointed task.[73]

'MONGREL TRAGI-COMEDY'?

Strains in the new design are evident even in the first two books—especially in the Arcadian revolt. The attempt at laconic humour in the description of the princes dispatching the rustics and mechanicals is, of course, repugnant to modern taste but, more importantly from the point of view of Sidney's poetic,

---

[69] Criticism of Basilius tempered by praise, *NA*, 16.

[70] Basilius (*OA*, 416) considers that 'all had fallen out by the highest providence'. On Fortune, see e.g. *OA*, 285.

[71] The Heliodorean sense of resolved contraries is made explicit in the last book where the populace perceives the working of Divine Providence: 'Surely, they [the Gods] made very contrarye thinges agree, and ioyned sorrow and mirth, teares and laughter together, and turned fearefull, and terrible [T.v^v] thinges into a ioyfull banquette in the ende ...' (Underdowne, sig. T.v^{r-v}; = 10. 38). Cf. J. R. Morgan's translation: 'the same divine force that had staged this whole drama and that now produced a perfect harmony of diametric opposites' (*CAGN*, 586).

[72] Skretkowicz (*NA*, p. li) cites Gauden's *Eikon Basilike* (1649). The king's use of the prayer may well be apocryphal.

[73] e.g. the bathing-scene (*NA*, 189–95).

the tone of epic burlesque jars violently with the new work's apparent commitment to realizing an 'absolute heroical poem'.[74]

For Amphialus, at least, the intervention of Helen, Queen of Corinth, holds out some prospect of redemption;[75] but no such consolation is available in the case of Argalus and Parthenia. Their joyful reunion after long trials (*NA*, 45) is the due reward for their constancy; and by replacing 'sugared invention' with moral delight, Sidney has actually surpassed Heliodorus' 'picture of love in Theagenes and Chariclea'.[76] But the narrative is sheared by an Apuleian transformation. For just as Charite and Tlepolemus (whose separation, travails, and ultimate marriage in *The Golden Ass* could be taken straight from the idealized Greek romances) suffer a tragic sequel to the romantic comedy of their reunion, so too, the happy ending of Argalus and Parthenia is trumped by a turn of Fortune which claims both their lives (*NA*, 378, 397). Yet this Apuleian reversal comes shortly after Pamela's celebrated affirmation of Divine Providence (*NA*, 359 ff) and it directly contradicts Sidney's theory of poetic justice.[77] There is an irrevocability about these deaths of the good and the beautiful that no narrative trick can undo.

But worse is to follow. The tragic tale of Argalus' death is followed immediately by what Wolff calls the 'comic relief' of Dametas' challenge to Clinias.[78] Hamilton tells us that Sidney's

skill is so assured that he can balance such pathos with a superbly comic account of the 'combat of cowards', Dametas and Clinias, 'mingling kings and clowns' with 'decency' and 'discretion' because 'the matter so carrieth it'.[79]

The terms Hamilton quotes remind us that Sidney is attempting here to produce tragicomedy along the permitted Apuleian lines, in contrast to the 'mongrel tragi-comedy' which he explicitly proscribes in the theatre.[80] Yet the result reads strangely—more narrative jerk than dramatic balance; and it

---

[74] 'Zelmane striking the farmer to the heart with her sword as before she had done with her eyes' (*NA*, 290); the cobbler's attempt to mend his damaged face: 'but as his hand was on the ground to bring his nose to his head, Zelmane with a blow sent his head to his nose' (*NA*, 281); the miller offering Dorus 'two milch-kine and four fat hogs for his life' only to have a sword thrust 'quite through from one ear to the other (*NA*, 282).

[75] In Gervase Markham's *The English Arcadia, Alluding his Beginning from Sir Philip Sydnes Ending* (London: Edward Allde for Henrie Rocket, 1607), Helen succeeds in curing Amphialus and marries him.

[76] The story of Argalus and Parthenia was enormously popular: Francis Quarles's reworking of it (1629) went through many editions.

[77] *Defence*, 90 (discussed above).

[78] Wolff, *Greek Romances*, 331; *NA*, 379–86.

[79] Hamilton, *Sir Philip Sidney*, 162.

[80] O'Connor (*Amadis de Gaule*, 191) links the 'combat of cowards' to the contest between Darinel and Mardoquée in *Amadis* ix. xxxiv.

affords us perplexity rather than any 'relief'—perplexity of a kind familiar to us from our reading of Apuleius.

Some trace of the Apuleian vapours which permeate the *New Arcadia* may be evident in the preface to the hybrid edition of 1593, produced at the instigation of Sidney's sister Mary, the Countess of Pembroke.[81] In the address 'To the Reader', 'H.S.' (Hugh Sanford) attacks those readers who had criticized the presentation of 'the conclusion, not the perfection of *Arcadia*':

Neuer was *Arcadia* free from the comber of such *Cattell*. To vs, say they, the pastures are not pleasaunt: and as for the flowers, such as we light on we take no delight in, but the greater part growe not within our reach. Poore soules! what talke they of flowers? They are Roses, not flowers, must doe them good, which if they finde not here, they shall doe well to go feed elswhere: Any place will better like them: For without *Arcadia* nothing growes in more plenty, then *Lettuce* sutable to their *Lippes*...[82]

The allusion is, as A. C. Hamilton has observed, to the plight of Apuleius' protagonist: only the eating of roses can restore him to human form.[83] Sanford is trying to distance himself from the asininely ignorant readers who are unable to reach up to eat the moral and artistic flowers of Sidney's work that might redeem them from their bestial state.

CONCLUSIONS

The *Arcadia* is a Janus-figure, looking backwards as well as forwards. The revision manifests contradictory impulses—an attempt to Heliodoreanize the work, to render it more serious, edifying, and stable, coupled with a centrifugal tendency to explore more dynamic possibilities of narrative and characterization (including those provided by *The Golden Ass*). The paradox is that the very qualities—the moral and imaginative dynamics—which invest the *New Arcadia* with such interest, also account for its formal failure. But that failure was as productive as it was inevitable. The *Arcadia* is one of the earliest examples of comparative criticism of the ancient novels and it serves as a case study of the sorts of tensions and possibilities facing early-modern writers of fiction.

[81] One might also note (with Skretkowicz, 'Sidney's Tragic *Arcadia*') the correspondence between Pyrocles' inability to interpret the monitory images in Kalander's house (the first being of 'Diana, when Actaeon saw her bathing', *NA*, 15) and Lucius' failure to read the warning against *curiositas* contained in the sculpture of Actaeon and Diana in Byrrhena's house (*AA* 2. 4).

[82] H[ugh]. S[anford]., ed., *The Countesse of Pembrokes Arcadia* (London: William Ponsonbie, 1593), sig. ¶ 4ᵛ.

[83] Hamilton, *Sir Philip Sidney*, 171, 208.

10

Psyche's Daughter: Pleasure and *The Faerie Queene*

To perceive a tension in *The Faerie Queene* between the high-mindedness of its declared aims and the sensual exuberance of its execution has become a commonplace of Spenserian criticism.[1] C. S. Lewis gave the problem its most famous formulation in *The Allegory of Love* where he tackled the question of 'actual sensuality and theoretical austerity'.[2] But for all its elegance, Lewis's solution has never seemed wholly convincing. Whatever metaphor we use to describe *The Faerie Queene*—tapestry or mosaic, palimpsest or labyrinth— the difficulty is the same: the manifold sources from which Spenser has drawn his threads or *tesserae*; the layers of classical, medieval, Italian, and Celtic writing that underlie his text; and the maze of narratives and meanings which he has fashioned and generated within it, all ensure that the poem resists easy summation. Yet, if we had to reduce *The Faerie Queene* to a single concern, we might well choose Pleasure. The problem of pleasure pervades the whole of Spenser's epic.[3] For the individuals within the poem, the problem concerns the proper function of sensual, aesthetic, philosophical, and spiritual pleasure in the context of the virtuous life. For the poet and the reader, it also involves a consideration of the relationship between textual pleasure and moral purpose, between delectation (*dulce*) and edification (*utile*).

It is thus significant that Pleasure should appear in person in what is generally regarded as one of the finest and most important sections of the poem: the description of the Garden of Adonis (*FQ* III. vi). Spenser's use there of 'Cupid and Psyche' is well known.[4] The naughty Cupid has run away and

---

[1] A. C. Hamilton cites Legous and Sir Herbert Grierson as early promulgators of this view. See *Structure of Allegory in 'The Faerie Queene'*, 6.

[2] (Oxford: Clarendon, 1936), 322, 324.

[3] 'Pleasure' in its singular, plural, and possessive forms appears 142 times in Spenser's poems (78 of them in *FQ* alone). See C. G. Osgood, *A Concordance to the Poems of Edmund Spenser* (Washington: Carnegie Institute, 1915), 654.

[4] In *Classical Mythology in the Poetry of Edmund Spenser* (Princeton: PUP, 1932), 104, H. G. Lotspeich observes that 'From his very brief treatment, it is impossible to decide whether [Spenser] knew Apuleius, *Metamorphoses* 5, 6, at first hand, or uses Boccaccio's rather full paraphrase of it (5. 22).' The *Genealogia* was apparently well known to Spenser but, in the Renaissance as a whole, it is Fulgentius rather than Boccaccio whose interpretation is consistently quoted.

Venus engages the assistance of Diana's nymphs as she searches for her son.[5] In the course of their quest, they chance upon the lately conceived and newly born babies of the sleeping Chrysogone (III. vi. 26). Diana takes one 'To be vpbrought in perfect Maydenhed' and calls her '*Belphoebe*'.[6] The other is taken by Venus, 'To be vpbrought in goodly womenhed.' She calls the infant '*Amoretta*,' 'to comfort her' for the loss of Cupid. There follows a long description of the '*Gardin of Adonis*' (III. vi. 39) where, miraculously, Adonis 'liues in euerlasting ioy' (III. vi. 49), keeping company with such gods as Cupid

> Who when he hath with spoiles and cruelty
> Ransackt the world, and in the wofull harts
> Of many wretches set his triumphs hye,
> Thither resorts, and laying his sad darts
> Aside, with faire *Adonis* playes his wanton parts.

> And his true loue faire *Psyche* with him playes,
> Faire *Psyche* to him lately reconcyled,
> After long troubles and vnmeet vpbrayes,
> With which his mother *Venus* her reuyled,
> And eke himselfe her cruelly exyled:
> But now in steadfast loue and happy state
> She with him liues, and hath him borne a chyld,
> *Pleasure*, that doth both gods and men aggrate,
> *Pleasure* the daughter of *Cupid* and *Psyche* late.

> Hither great *Venus* brought this infant faire,
> The younger daughter of *Chrysogonee*,
> And vnto *Psyche* with great trust and care
> Committed her yfostered to bee,
> And trained vp in true feminitee:
> Who no lesse carefully her tendered,
> Then her owne daughter *Pleasure*, to whom shee
> Made her companion, and her lessoned
> In all the lore of loue, and goodly womanhead.

> In which when she to perfect ripeness grew,
> Of grace and beautie noble Paragone,
> She brought her forth into the worldes vew,
> To be th'ensample of true loue alone,

---

[5] Spenser draws here (*FQ* III. vi. 11–26) upon two traditions: the 'Hue and Cry after Cupid', familiar from the *First Idyll* of Moschus, and the Ovidian myth of Diana and Actaeon (*Met.* 3. 155 ff.). A translation of Moschus' 'Idyllion of Wandring Loue' (possibly mediated via Politian's Latin version) appears in E. K.'s list of Spenser's 'lost' works in the *Shepheardes Calender*.

[6] All references are to *The Faerie Queene*, ed. T. P. Roche, Jr. (Harmondsworth: Penguin, 1978; repr. 1984).

> And lodestarre of all chaste affectione,
> To all faire Ladies, that doe liue on ground.
> To Faery court she came, where many one
> Admyred her goodly haueour, and found
> His feeble hart wide launched with loues cruell wound.

(FQ III. vi. 50–2)

Spenser had already placed Cupid's daughter in a similar *locus amoenus* in 'An Hymne in Honour of Love', composed, according to the dedication of 1596, 'in the greener times of my youth':

> So thou thy folke, through paines of Purgatorie,
> Dost beare unto thy blisse, and heavens glorie.

[41]

> There thou them placest in a Paradize
> Of all delight, and joyous happie rest,
> Where they doe feede on Nectar heavenly wize,
> With *Hercules* and *Hebe*, and the rest
> Of *Venus* dearlings, through her bountie blest,
> And lie like Gods in yvorie beds arayd,
> With rose and lillies over them displayd.

[42]

> There with thy daughter *Pleasure* they do play
> Their hurtlesse sports, without rebuke or blame,
> And in her snowy bosome boldly lay
> Their quiet heads, devoyd of guilty shame,
> After full joyance of their gentle game,
> Then her they crowne their Goddesse and their Queene,
> And decke with floures thy altars well beseene.[7]

A. C. Hamilton argues that in Books III and IV of *The Faerie Queene*, Spenser was able to 'reduce the nightmare world of romance to the ordered dream of faery land by treating thematically two classical myths, Venus and Adonis, and Cupid and Psyche'. These two myths are 'definitively rendered in the Garden of Adonis' where

the 'efficacie of nature' (to use Sidney's term)[8] is expressed through the love between Venus and Adonis...[139]...What the [Venus and Adonis] myth expresses upon the cosmic level, [the Cupid and Psyche myth] expresses upon the human or psychological:

---

[7] *The Yale Edition of the Shorter Poems of Edmund Spenser*, ed. W. A. Oram et al. (New Haven: YUP, 1989), 704–5.

[8] [Hamilton's note:] *Apol.*, p. 9.

Psyche is herself the pattern of 'true feminitie' who may teach Amoret 'all the lore of loue, and goodly womanhead'. (III. vi. 51)[9]

Spenser had thrown the bait to the Neoplatonizers by calling Adonis the 'Father of all formes' (III. vi. 47. 8), and Roche, extrapolating, identifies Venus with 'matter'.[10] But a closer reading of the two texts may lead us to check some of our allegorizing impulses. The grace of the description of the Garden of Adonis should not blind us to its strangeness. The Garden is not merely a source of generation but a locus of resolution and renewal: Adonis is restored to Venus; Psyche is 'reconcyled' to Cupid. Most remarkable of all, however, is the degree of rapprochement established between Venus and Psyche. For most of Apuleius' narrative, Venus plays two roles: the first, that of the offended deity, jealous of the due reverence that Psyche's beauty has alienated from her; the second, that of the wicked witch, devising all manner of cruel and unnatural trials to punish her de facto daughter-in-law. It is only at the end of the story, at the marriage-feast which has conferred immortality upon Psyche, that Venus enters into the harmony of the resolution; and she does so through the impersonal agency of dance (*AA* 6. 24). Spenser's Venus, on the other hand, has put the 'long troubles and vnmeet vpbrayes' with which she had 'reuyled' Psyche (*FQ* III. vi. 51) sufficiently far behind her to feel sanguine about committing Amoret to Psyche's care.

Such a volte-face may make us suspicious about the facility of the resolutions in the Garden as a whole; and closer examination confirms that we are right to be so. Half of the mythic content of the Garden is distanced from the narrator at the outset by the qualification in the line, 'There yet, some say, in secret he doth ly' (III. vi. 46. 4).[11] There is also a problem with temporal sequence. Adonis is himself a paradox—'subiect to mortalitie' yet 'eterne in mutabilitie'—but (if we can believe what 'some say') he is at least firmly entrenched in his Garden. Psyche too, to judge from stanzas 50–2, is a permanent resident. Cupid, on the other hand, seems to be one of Adonis' occasional visitors, 'resorting' thither whenever 'he hath with spoiles and cruelty | Ransackt the world' and feels like 'laying his sad darts | Aside' for a while. This continued existence as 'winged boy' (wreaking his wonted havoc) and gay bachelor ('with faire Adonis playes his wanton parts') sits uncomfortably with the description of his new domestic arrangements: 'But now in stedfast loue and happy state | She with him liues and hath him borne a chyld'.

These fudgings are perhaps a necessary response to the contradictions inherent in the source material. In Apuleius' text, Jove makes explicit his

[9] Hamilton, *Structure of Allegory*, 138–9. This book incorporates the argument of 'Spenser's Treatment of Myth', *ELH* 26 (1959), 335–54.

[10] Roche, Penguin edn., 1153, and *The Kindly Flame* (Princeton: PUP, 1964), 123.

[11] Spenser's 'some say' is equivalent to the *ferunt* or *fertur* beloved of classical poets.

reasons for consenting to the union: the constraints of marriage will put an end to Cupid's libertine ways.[12] For Renaissance writers, this presents a problem. Apuleius had provided them with an attractive tale, but the binding of Cupid to Psyche robs love-elegy, mythological narrative, and comedy of one of their principal agents: the 'winged boy' whose 'sad darts' set so many plots and poems in motion. It may be for this reason that Psyche's appearances in Renaissance English verse seem infrequent relative to the influence of *The Golden Ass* during the period. Throughout the sonnet sequences of Spenser, Sidney, Daniel, Shakespeare, and Drayton, the name Psyche occurs only once—when Drayton 'conjures' Cupid 'By thine owne loved PSYCHES' to 'wound her Heart, whose Eyes have wounded me'.[13]

An anonymous poem in *A Poetical Rhapsody* (1602) expresses the problem perfectly:

> *Cupids Mariage with Dissimulation.*
>
> A New-found match is made of late,
>   Blinde *Cupid* needs will change his wife;
> New-fangled Loue doth *Psyche* hate,
> With whom so long he led his life.
>   Dessembling, shee
>   The Bride must bee,
>   To please his wanton eye.
>   *Psyche* laments
>   That Loue repents,
>   His choyce without cause why.[14]

The union of Cupid and Psyche represents a dramatic and narrative stasis; it translates well into the visual and plastic arts, but to fulfil the dynamic needs of literature, the bond needs to be broken. In chapter 8 (*supra*), we saw John Dickenson (*Arisbas*), R.L. (*Diella* V), and Ben Jonson (*The Haddington Masque*), toying with the same conceit of Cupid being tempted to break his faith with Psyche.

Spenser's response to these iconographical problems is to depict Cupid as simultaneously wanton imp and faithful husband. In this he is merely

---

[12] *tollenda est omnis occasio et luxuria puerilis nuptialibus pedicis alliganda* ('Every opportunity must be removed and his boyish wantonness must be bound in the fetters of marriage', *AA* 6. 23).

[13] Sonnet 36 of *Idea* (1619), in *The Works of Michael Drayton*, ed. J. W. Hebel et al., 5 vols. (Oxford: Shakespeare Head P, 1931–41; repr. 1961), ii. 328.

[14] *A Poetical Rhapsody 1602–1621*, ed. H. R. Rollins, 2 vols. (Cambridge, Mass.: HUP, 1931), i. 164. Rollins refers to a handwritten list which includes this poem as one of the compositions of 'A.W.' and (at ii. 53–71) reluctantly endorses the view that these initials refer to 'Anonymous Writers'. To my knowledge, neither this poem nor that contained in *The Phoenix Nest* has been noted by commentators on Apuleius' *Nachleben*. The poem reappears in Samuel Pick's *Festum Uoluptatis* (1639).

exploiting (as Apuleius had done) a long-standing ambiguity.[15] The representation of Love oscillates between the Hesiodic-Parmenidean-Platonic Eros (as depicted, say, in Plato's *Symposium* and *Phaedrus*) and the more familiar Cupid of love elegy. Eros is the primal deity, begetter of the world, 'Victor of gods, subduer of mankynde' ('Hymne in Honour of Love', lines 75, 45). Cupid is the wayward boy: mischievous and capriciously tyrannical, yet indispensible.

Olympian burlesque is at least as old as Homer; but in the case of 'Cupid and Psyche', Apuleius comes close to subverting cosmic in favour of merely comic resolution: the gods face fines for non-attendance; Jupiter chastises Cupid for causing him to transgress the Julian statute against adultery (*AA* 6. 22–3), and reassures Venus that he will make the marriage legitimate and in accordance with civil law (*AA* 6. 23). Yet Venus dances her all-resolving dance and the union brings forth its strange fruit, Voluptas. Critics often fail to observe, however, that the 'happily ever-after' ending of 'Cupid and Psyche' is placed in perspective by the tragic frame-tale of Charite and Tlepolemus. The resolution in the Garden of Adonis is similarly fraught. It may be no more than coincidence that the deaths of both Adonis and Tlepolemus are occasioned by wild boars (Spenser, after all, is constrained by his Ovidian source, *Met.* 10. 710 ff.); but it is significant that the heroines of both frame-tales meet similar fates. Charite, having been delivered from the robbers' cave where Psyche's tale was told, falls victim to the murderous lust of Thrasyllus. Amoret is handed over to Psyche to be 'trained vp in true feminitee', but Psyche's careful nurture and Pleasure's sisterly companionship are not enough to protect her from the vile clutches of Busirane.[16]

Indeed, it could be argued that Apuleius creates, in 'Cupid and Psyche', a deceptive centrepiece, an apparent resolution which, while pointing the way towards some final (and, in turn, ambiguous) resolution, is itself illusory. Spenser, I suggest, produces something similar in the Garden of Adonis. The context of the Garden is as important as its content. Book III opens with 'the captiu'd *Acrasia*' (III. i. 2. 1) being sent under guard to 'Faerie court'. The 'pleasures vaine' of Phædria's island (II. vi) and the necromantic pleasures of the Bower of Bliss (II. xii) apparently give way to the birth of '*Pleasure,* the daughter of *Cupid* and *Psyche* late' (III. vi. 50. 9). But even if we accept that we are dealing with distinct *kinds* of sensual experience, we may still find it incongruous that Spenser, who appends so many opprobrious

---

[15] Apuleius' Cupid appears both as boyish mischief-maker and authoritative husband.

[16] *FQ* III. xi–xii. Tobin (*SFN*, p. xvii) links the cardial wounding of Amoret (*FQ* III. xii. 20–1) with Meroë's removal of Socrates' heart. The wounding is immediately followed in the Masque of Cupid by the appearance of 'the winged God himselfe' who 'much reioyced in his cruell mind' at the sight of the 'dolorous | Faire Dame' (*FQ* III. xii. 22. 7–9)—a silent commentary (if such were needed) on the resolution in the Garden of Adonis (Cupid, we should remember, is foster-father to Amoret). Scudamour is shown at II. xi. 7 in armour decorated with images of Cupid.

epithets to images of pleasure, should give Pleasure so central a place in
perhaps the most important canto in the poem.[17] The birth of Voluptas at
the end of 'Cupid and Psyche' may seem similarly incongruous when one
considers the Isiac Priest's condemnation of *seruiles uoluptates* (*AA* 11. 15).
There is, in fact, in the works of both Apuleius and Spenser, a fundamental
ambivalence towards 'pleasure'.

Such ambivalence has, of course, linguistic as well as philosophical precedent. Cicero gives a concise distinction between the physical and spiritual
aspects of *voluptas:*

*Huic verbo omnes qui Latine sciunt duas res subicient, laetitiam in animo, commotionem
suavem iucunditatis in corpore.*[18]

(Everyone who knows Latin understands by this term two things: happiness in mind,
the sweet agitation of delight in body.)

The first meaning links *voluptas* with the Platonic notion of *eudaimonia*; the
second with sensual delights. Spenser, one might argue, makes a subdivision
between lawful and illicit sensual pleasures (though the distinction is not
always clear), but he also invokes the Lucretian notion of pleasure as an all-
encompassing generative power. In the opening of the *De rerum natura* (1. 1–2),
Lucretius addresses 'Nurturing Venus, mother of the stock of Aeneas, delight of
men and gods' (*Aeneadum genetrix, hominum divomque voluptas,* | *alma Venus*).
Her significance is tripartite: ancestor (through Aeneas) of the Roman people in
general and of Caesar in particular; embodiment and provider of divine, as well
as mortal, pleasure; and cosmic, life-giving force. Spenser imitates this passage in
Book IV (x. 44–7) when he addresses 'Great Venus, Queene of beautie and of
grace, | The ioy of Gods and men':

> So all the world by thee at first was made,
>   And dayly yet thou doest the same repayre:
>   Ne ought on earth that merry is and glad
>   Ne ought on earth that louely is and fayre,
>   But thou the same for pleasure didst prepayre.
>   Thou art the root of all that ioyous is,
>   Great God of men and women, queene of th'ayre,
>   Mother of laughter, and welspring of blisse,

(*FQ* IV. x. 47. 1–7)

At some stage in antiquity, the abstraction, *voluptas,* became personified
into a goddess and given the alternative name of Volupia. The classical
provenance of this deity is rather obscure. As early as the beginning of the

---

[17] e.g. 'Pleasure's poisoned bait', etc.   [18] Cicero, *De finibus* 2. 4. 13.

second century BC, Plautus was ridiculing the deification of such abstractions as *voluptas*; a practice which also caused Cicero to scoff.[19] But a passage in the *De lingua latina,* where Varro mentions the *Volupiae sacellum* ('Chapel of Volupia') to pinpoint the location of the *porta Romanula,* indicates that Rome actually had a temple to the goddess.[20] St Augustine delights in appropriating such material to his attack on pagan polytheism in the *De ciuitate dei.* Drawing on Varro's lost *Antiquities,* he names Volupia amongst the plethora of risible gods:

Neque enim in hoc tam praeclaro opere et tantae plenissimo dignitatis audent aliquas partes deae Cluacinae tribuere aut Volupiae, quae a voluptate appellata est, aut Lubentinae, cui nomen est a libidino, aut Vaticano, qui infantum vagitibus praesidet aut Cuninae, quae cunas eorum administrat . . .[21]

(For in such a distinguished work and one so full of dignity, they do not dare to bestow any parts to Cluacina [Goddess of Sewers] or to Volupia, who is named after Pleasure, or Lubentina, whose name comes from Desire, or Vaticanus, who watches over the wailings of infants, or Cunina, who takes charge of their cradles.)

As a goddess, it seems, Voluptas (or Volupia) was not regarded terribly seriously, even amongst classical pagans. To the Renaissance, however, she was a source of some fascination. Voluptas insinuated herself into the trinity of the Graces, appearing in such paintings as Botticelli's *Primavera* (to the left of Castitas and Pulchritudo) and Raphael's *The Three Graces* (on the right).[22] And she (or, at least, the concept she embodied) gave her name to one of the earliest works of the Neoplatonist Marsilio Ficino whose influence upon Spenser is well attested.[23]

What are we to make, then, of Spenser's introduction of Cupid and Psyche's daughter into the Garden of Adonis? She is clearly no mere mythological ornament. The Platonic associations of the Apuleian tale demand, at the very least, consideration within the philosophical context of the *The Faerie Queene*; and by making Pleasure the foster-sister of Amoret (who engages our sympathies as much as any character in the poem), Spenser draws her into the human web of the work. But the Apuleian vignette also gives formal expression to the tensions in the poem as a whole: Pleasure is not only a personified

---

[19] Plautus, *Bacchides* 115; Cicero, *De natura deorum* 2. 23; Macrobius, *Saturnalia* 1. 10.

[20] Varro, *De lingua latina* 5. 34. 164.

[21] Augustine, *De ciuitate dei* 4. 8.

[22] See E. Wind, *Pagan Mysteries in the Renaissance* (rev. edn., Oxford: Clarendon, 1980), 61.

[23] Ficino, *De voluptate.* Book 10 of his *Epistolae* includes two *Apologi de uoluptate* ('Fables of Pleasure'). See *Opera . . . omnia* (Basle: Heinrich Petri, 1576), i. 921–4. For Ficino's reference (*Commentary on Plato's Symposium,* vii. 4) to 'that . . . of which the Platonist Apuleius complains' (*AA* 10. 3), see Ch. 5, p. 212 n. 110, *supra.*

abstraction, introduced into the text at a particular point (iii. vi. 49); it is also an inseparable part of the text itself.

Herein lies Spenser's problem. The Letter to Raleigh encapsulates the 'generall end' of *The Faerie Queene* as being 'to fashion a gentleman or noble person in vertuous and noble discipline'; and supporting authorizing structures are provided in the poem itself by the quatrains at the head of cantos, the allegorical machinery appropriated from the medieval tradition, and the narrator's own intrusions and asides. A text can be concerned with Virtue; it can contain poetic patterns which may guide the reader towards the Virtuous Life; but it cannot, in itself, be virtuous. Pleasure, on the other hand, is the very stuff of poetry. Poets realized early on that unpackaged Virtue was not a particularly saleable commodity; and the formulations of both Lucretius (honey and wormwood) and Horace (*omne tulit punctum qui miscuit utile dulci*) express, in their own (albeit oversimplistic) ways, a sense of the necessary relation between edification and delectation. Spenser may have succeeded (where Milton, arguably, was to fail) in 'convincing us of the loveliness of virtue',[24] but we shall see that his decision to emblematize Pleasure threatens to fracture the already fragile crucible in which the reactive elements of the poem are held.

THE CAVE OF MAMMON

Apuleian influence has also been discerned in two other 'crucial scenes' in *The Faerie Queene*: the Cave of Mammon (ii. vii), and '*Isis* Church' (v. vii).[25] A. C. Hamilton was the first to link Guyon's sojourn in the garden of Proserpina with Psyche's subterranean adventure:

When Guyon, like Psyche, descends to the garden of Proserpina he is tempted to eat and rest, and upon leaving falls asleep. Psyche is rescued by Cupid who relents her punishment through love, while Guyon is rescued by the Angel. But such an angel, Spenser tells us in rapturous terms unique in Book II 'of wondrous beautie, and of freshest yeares,' whose face 'diuinely shone,' and whose wings were 'decked with diuerse plumes, like painted Iayes': 'like as *Cupido* on *Idæan* hill, / When hauing laid his cruell bow away, / And mortal arrowes...' (ii. viii. 5, 6)[26]

The first thing to note, of course, is that both Apuleius and Spenser are playing upon a long tradition of catabasis: the descriptions of descents into

[24] P. C. Bayley, ed., *Faerie Queene Book I* (Oxford: OUP, 1966), 10.

[25] Tobin (*SFN*, p. xiv) calls the Cave, the Church, and the Garden of Adonis (*FQ* iii. vi) 'three of the most crucial scenes in the poem'.

[26] *Structure of Allegory*, 148.

the Underworld found in the *Odyssey* (11. 568–635), the *Georgics* (4. 467–84), the *Metamorphoses* (4. 432–80), and (above all) the *Aeneid* (6. 268–899) are all, directly or indirectly, exerting their pressure on the two passages. Yet while Spenser's angel may have borrowed some feathers from the wings of Tasso's Gabriel, there is nothing in the classical or Italian models to compete with Apuleius as the source of salvific intervention at the point of re-entry into the upper world.[27] Spenser seems to have been, as Tobin puts it, 'at some pains not to conceal his source', since he chooses to paint his angel so emphatically in the colours of Cupid; and Tobin uses this as his base for linking the themes of avarice and, more profoundly, curiosity in the two texts.[28] But besides falling into the trap that frequently awaits the over-exuberant source-hunter, Tobin misses (as Hamilton had done) the most important relation between the two passages. Psyche, faced with her final trial, is neither wiser nor more resolute than she was when confronted by the first. She is fortified against the suicidal despair to which she is all too prone by the advice of the tower, and resists all the temptations in the Underworld itself, but in the course of her anabasis she succumbs to vanity as well as curiosity when she opens the box of Proserpina's beauty only to be overcome by infernal sleep. Cupid, at this point, suddenly appears and wipes the sleep from her eyes to restore her to life—*a deus ex machina* who functions (according to one's viewpoint) either as a symbol of the dependence of divine intervention (as with Lucius and Isis) on the needs, rather than deserts, of the recipient; or as yet another expression of the narrative's subordination to the arbitrary whims of its author. Guyon, in contrast, survives the temptations of the Underworld for three days; it is only when he emerges, victorious but exhausted, and falls into a sleep that is Psyche-like in depth though not in origin, that the angel comes to his assistance. Both Psyche and Guyon depend for salvation on some form of divine intervention, but the deserts of the recipients are very different.

'*ISIS* CHURCH'

In Book V, canto vii, Britomart, on her way to release Artegall from the clutches of Radigund, enters the temple of Isis, where she receives a strange vision which, we are told, 'did close implie | The course of all her fortune and

---

[27] Torquato Tasso, *Gerusalemme liberata*, introd. G. Petrocchi (Basiano: Bietti, 1968), I. 13, 14. See *The Works of Edmund Spenser: Variorum Edition*, ed. E. Greenlaw, C. G. Osgood, and F. M. Padelford, 11 vols. (Baltimore: Johns Hopkins P, 1932–57), *ad loc.*

[28] An extreme instance of Tobin's ingenuity is his attempt (*SFN*, pp. xv–xvi) to derive Spenser's linking of Pilate and Tantalus from Psyche's words, '*Ecce ... tantillum*'.

prosperitie' (v. vii. 12. 8–9). The main sources for this scene are traditionally held to be Plutarch's *De Iside et Osiride* and Diodorus Siculus' *Bibliotheca* (1. 11 ff.), with Natalis Comes (*Myth.* 5. 13) perhaps supplying 'some additional suggestions'.[29] The Variorum editor, however, provides a further perspective:

> Strangely enough every commentator has overlooked the obvious traces in this passage of Spenser's reading in the *Metamorphoses* of Apuleius. The experience of Britomart in 'Isis Church'—the vigil, the dream, the investure for the sacrifice, the encounter with the high priest at dawn—is all clearly based upon that of Lucius the Ass in *Metamorphoses* 11. 4–8, where Isis restores him to human form and he becomes a priest of Isis and then of Osiris.[30]

When Apuleius' narrator claims descent from Plutarch at the beginning of *The Golden Ass* (1. 2), he is also sketching a literary genealogy for the work. Apparent links between Book 11 of the novel and Book V of *The Faerie Queene* need, therefore, to be referred to the earlier Greek treatise which served as a common source for Spenser and Apuleius. Adlington describes how Lucius went to worship Isis in Rome where he was 'a stranger to her Church' (ch. 48, p. 206; *AA* 11. 26), but apart from this correspondence in nomenclature, there is little, if anything, in '*Isis* Church' that could not be accounted for in terms of the *De Iside* or the *Bibliotheca*. Britomart's visit to the temple involves a formal incubation—the sleeping in hallowed precincts for the express purpose of receiving a vision—whereas Lucius merely falls asleep by the side of the water and is woken by a vision of the moon that comes unbidden. And while Isis tells Lucius exactly what to do, the vision she sends to Britomart is as impenetrable as it is disturbing, and requires the assistance of the priest to release its meaning. The recipients' reactions are also profoundly different: Lucius is so moved by the experience that he delivers himself up, body, purse, and soul, to the devotion of the goddess; Britomart, in contrast, distributes her largesse and goes upon her way, fortified in spirit by the expectation of reunion, but without having undergone any change to her essence.

Tobin, however, while making no reference to Osgood, takes the Apuleian connection one stage further by asserting that Spenser

> based the dream of Britomart and the impregnating serpent (amphibian) lover upon the experience of Psyche whose initially invisible husband she thought to be a monstrous serpent. That the crocodile in Britomart's dream should represent her true love even as Osiris is the true love of Isis is in keeping with the ultimately

---

[29] Lotspeich, *Classical Mythology*, 73 (cited in Variorum edn., v. 215). Spenser may have read Plutarch in a Latin translation or the French version by Amyot (*Moralia*, 1572).

[30] C. G. Osgood, Variorum edn., v. 216; cf. H. Maclean, ed., *Edmund Spenser's Poetry* (London: Norton, 1982), 371 n. 2.

sacramentalized marriage of Cupid [xv] and Psyche, a Grecian pair of immortal lovers who are an elegantly refracted image of Osiris and Isis.[31]

These claims need to be qualified, once again, by an awareness of Plutarch—in this case, his 'Life of Alexander' wherein the great king's conception is anticipated in the fiery dream visited upon his mother, Olympias, in whose bed a serpent was reputed to have been found.[32] But Tobin's comments upon the appropriateness of the Osiris/crocodile identification should remind us that in a work so manifestly concerned with interpretation—with the act of reading as a learning experience—we ought, as readers 'well auis'd', to be prepared for the possibility of misinterpretation.[33] There is, in fact, a similar degree of rightness and wrongness about the interpretations offered by the two priests. Both seem to have access to information about the protagonists' fortunes and lineage that could only be derived from a supernatural source, but each interpretation is attended by misrepresentation or simple error.[34] One 'palpable gross' instance of this is the Priest's account of Britomart's dream:

> For that same Crocodile doth represent
> The righteous Knight, that is thy faithfull louer,
> Like to *Osyris* in all iust endeuer.
> For that same Crocodile *Osyris* is,
> That vnder *Isis* feete doth sleepe for euer:
>   To shew that clemence oft in things amis,
> Restraines those sterne behests, and cruell doomes of his.
>
> (*FQ* v. vii. 22. 3–9)

Edwin Greenlaw has pointed out some of the difficulties in Spenser's iconography:

Spenser's representation of Isis with one foot on the crocodile is not a happy one if, as he says, the crocodile is her lover Osiris; that is, it is not a happy one for the lover, or for romantic views of the marital relation. Plutarch is more satisfying. To him Typhon, the crocodile, is the passionate, irrational and brutal part of the soul. Isis therefore represents the reason subduing this irrational principle. This symbolism would fit Spenser's treatment of the legend of Guyon.[35]

---

[31] Tobin, *SFN*, p. xiv.

[32] Thus Maclean, *Edmund Spenser's Poetry*, 374 n. 4.

[33] The Bower contains ivy made of gold, 'so colored | That wight, who did not well auis'd it view, | Would surely deeme it to be yvie trew' (*FQ* ii. xii. 61). Cf. Apuleius' address to the *lector scrupulosus* (*AA* 9. 30).

[34] On lineage, see *FQ* v. vii. 21; *AA* 11. 15. On Mithras' 'misinterpretation', see Winkler, *Auctor & Actor*, 209–15.

[35] 'Some Old Religious Cults in Spenser', *SP* 20 (1923), 216–43, at 239, quoted in Variorum edn., 215.

Spenser's identification of Osiris with the crocodile is not only 'unhappy'; it is jarringly incongruous since the two animals most famously identified with Typhon—the murderer of Osiris and the arch-enemy of Isis—are the crocodile and the ass.

Plutarch is also explicit on the subject of the Isiac tonsure, and *The Golden Ass* leaves us with our gaze firmly fixed on the bald dome of Lucius' head; but Spenser stresses—not once, but twice—the 'long locks' of the priests of Isis.[36] Greenlaw opines that 'Spenser has transferred, consciously or unconsciously, to the priests of Isis some of the characteristics of the galli' (the priests of the Phrygian goddess Cybele) but offers no suggestion as to the hermeneutic implications of this transference; while others have attempted to explain it in syncretistic terms.[37] Syncretism has a place, of course, in *The Golden Ass,* and Isis identifies the Phrygian *deum mater* as one of the alternative forms in which she is worshipped (*AA* 11. 5). But while Apuleius' *galli* are presented as catamitic charlatans, the *pastophores* of Isis are depicted as sincere practitioners of their beliefs. Yet, as Winkler suggests, the distinction is not quite so clear as it might at first appear. Lucius is disgusted by the extortionate tricks of Philebus and his band in Books 8 and 9, but a good deal of Book 11 is devoted to the practicalities of financing his initiation into the Isiac and Osiric mysteries—outlays which at one stage reduce him to selling the robe off his back (*AA* 11. 27). For the most part, he is only too keen to oblige, but the steady toll of new initiations leads even Lucius to suspect that 'the former priests had giuen me ill counsell'.[38]

There is, similarly, something vaguely unsettling about Britomart's munificent response to the priest's prophetic exegesis:

> And on those priests bestowed rich reward:
> And royall gifts of gold and siluer wrought,
> She for a present to their Goddesse brought.

> (*FQ* v. vii. 24. 3–5)

It is all suspiciously reminiscent of the priests of Apuleius' Syrian Goddess (*AA* 8. 25) who go from town to town, extracting money by 'diuination, and porgnostication [*sic*] of things to come'.[39] And Adlington's marginal note on

[36] *De Iside et Osiride*, 4; *FQ* v. vii. 4. 5; v. vii. 20. 7.

[37] Greenlaw, 'Old Religious Cults', 239. One might note that the mitres which feature in Spenser (and Plutarch) appear, in Apuleius, in the description of the priests not of Isis but of the Phrygian goddess. The debauched priest Philebus is described as having long hair around a bald dome (*AA* 8. 24).

[38] Adlington, ch. 48, p. 207 (= *AA* 11. 29). Cf Winkler, *Auctor & Actor*, 215–23.

[39] Ibid., ch. 39, p. 146 (= *AA* 9. 8). Philebus and his motley crew are subsequently arrested for the theft of a gold cup taken from the temple of the Mother of the Gods (= *AA* 9. 9).

the *galli,* 'So used faigned Egyptians of late years in England', suggests the resonance of chicanery that the term 'Egyptian' might have carried for an Elizabethan audience.

Other critics have taken pains to purge such terms as 'morrow Mas' (*FQ* v. vii. 17. 8) of any papistical taint. But the obvious suggestion of Catholic targets in terms like 'Idoll' (v. vii. 8. 1) and 'robe of scarlet red', and the correspondence (noted as early as Saint Isidore) between the cults of Isis and the Blessed Virgin Mary, should nurture our suspicions that a profound vein of irony runs through the whole episode.[40]

Such suspicions may be confirmed by our reading of the sequel to the temple visit. All in all, the canto is profoundly puzzling. Britomart, in the figure of Isis trampling upon the crocodile, is meant (on the priest's reckoning) to embody that 'clemence' which 'oft in things amis, | Restraines those sterne behests, and cruell domes of his'; but Talus (whose chief function seems to be the doing of Artegall's dirty work) is only constrained, late in the day, from leaving 'not one aliue' in Amazonia by the 'very ruth' of Britomart—a momentary impulse (inspired by the sight of 'heapes' of 'slaughtered carkasses') to temper her 'reuengefull vow'.[41]

Then there is the paradox that it is during her reign 'as Princes' (v. vii. 42. 3) in the land of the Amazons that Britomart 'The liberty of women did repeale' (v. vii. 42. 5)—a paradox which reflects the fundamentally ambivalent view of the proper relations between the sexes expressed in the priest's identification of the idol and the crocodile with Isis and her lover Osiris.[42] Thirdly, the prophecy proves to be, if not illusory, then certainly premature. Britomart had been much 'eased in her troublous thought' (v. vii. 24. 2) by the priest's promise of a fruitful (re-)union with her beloved, but the restoration of Artegall does not produce the expected result. She defeats Radigund (at no small cost to herself), releases her beloved from the 'Yron prison' where he lies 'disguiz'd in womanish attire' (v. vii. 37. 2, 7), and makes the other captive knights his liegemen, only to be rewarded by the sight of Artegall, 'now well recur'd' (v. vii. 43. 7), departing—without so much as a word of thanks—to continue 'Vppon his first aduenture' (v. vii. 43. 9) in the service of another woman.

[40] Isidore, *Ep.* 4. 31. 28. Cited by Greenlaw, 'Old Religious Cults', 233. Cf. the representation (still standard in statues in Roman Catholic churches) of Our Lady trampling the serpent underfoot.

[41] v. vii. 22. 8–9; v. vii. 36. 'Clemence' was conspicuously absent in her decapitation of the prostrate Radigund (v. vii. 34).

[42] In his discussion of the aetiology of the Isiac and Osiric cults, Diodorus Siculus remarks: 'It is for these reasons, in fact, that it was ordained that the queen should have greater [87] power and honour than the king, and that among private persons, the wife should enjoy authority over her husband'. See *Diodorus of Sicily: The Library of History,* trans. C. H. Oldfather, 10 vols., Loeb Library (London: Heinemann, 1933), vol. i, bk i, ch. 27, pp. 86–7.

Hough says of 'Britomart's sojourn in Isis's Church' that it 'looks as though it were meant to come to something but it hardly does so'.[43] From the point of view of static, authorizing structures, this is certainly true, but as a catalyst for the dynamic exposition of themes, the scene is richly effective, even if the ensuing dialectic issues in no resolution.

THE PSYCHE MOTIF

The further we stray from the indisputably Apuleian content of the Garden of Adonis, the more speculative our claims for Apuleian presence must be. Romantic epic is a fraught genre to begin with: classical and medieval, pagan and Christian elements are drawn into a dense but uneasy skein. A single stanza of *The Faerie Queene* may generate pages of passages for comparison in the Variorum edition, but the quest for a hermeneutic resolution of these putative ingredients is altogether more elusive. Everything, it seems, influences everything else. Thus frustrated, one may well find comfort in Barthes's strictures on the 'myth of filiation' and, making a virtue of failure, surrender oneself to the ineluctable tug of the intertext. Much of *The Golden Ass* is a dense web drawn from earlier classical literature (in particular from Vergil and Ovid) so that apparent similarities between passages in Spenser and Apuleius may indicate, not a filial, but a collateral, relationship due to descent from a common source. To complicate matters further, Spenser's most important predecessors were themselves indebted to Apuleius. In the *Orlando furioso*, Ludovico Ariosto (1474–1533) intended to perfect what Matteo Maria Boiardo (d. 1494) had begun in his *Orlando innamorato*. Boiardo is credited with producing the first translation of *The Golden Ass*, the *Apulegio volgare*, composed, according to some scholars, between 1478 and 1479,[44] and Apuleian material is present in at least two scenes in the *Orlando furioso*: Canto XII, 86 ff. and Canto XXI.[45]

---

[43] G. Hough, *A Preface to 'The Faerie Queene'* (London: Duckworth, 1962; repr. 1982), 200.

[44] The oldest verifiable edn. seems to be one from 1518. On the role possibly played by Boiardo's grandfather, Feltrino Boiardo (d. 1456), see Ch. 6, *supra*. The work must have circulated in manuscript for at least a decade or two before the appearance of the first edn. See Scobie, 'Influence', 214–15. Some of the elements of Psyche's razor-wielding visit to Cupid (*AA* 5. 21–3) are redeployed by Boiardo when Malagise (a Christianized magus) is overcome by the sleeping Angelica's beauty as he is about to slit her throat (*OI* i. i. 45). Cf. Cavallo, *Boiardo's 'Orlando innamorato'*, 34.

[45] Isabella, trapped in the brigands' cave and rescued by Orlando (Canto XII), resembles Charite. According to Moreschini ('Sulla fama di Apuleio nel medioevo e nel rinascimento', 475), the story of the adulterous murderess, Gabrina (Canto XXI), 'è probabilmente un' imitazione di una delle novelle tragiche di Apuleio (x. 23–8)'. See *Orlando furioso*, ed. M. Turchi and E. Sanguineti (Milan: Garzanti, 1974; repr. 1985).

What appears to be an Apuleian echo in Spenser may well turn out to be merely an echo of an echo.

The same caveat extends to the deeper structures in the poem. A. C. Hamilton sees an Apuleian archetype operating throughout *The Faerie Queene*:

> What appeals most strongly to Spenser's imagination is the quest of the beautiful and virtuous woman for her lover…
>
> Psyche, rather than Venus, is his pattern for woman.[46]

Hamilton finds Psyche-elements in the depiction of Una, Britomart, Belphoebe, and Amoret.[47] Even Arthur resembles Psyche in his enjoyment of 'that brief vision of his love which leads him to wander throughout the world'. But the 'chief Psyche figure', Hamilton tells us, 'is Florimel'.[48]

Psyche and the heroines of *The Faerie Queene* certainly draw upon a common archetype—the woman separated from the object of her love—but it is less clear that Apuleius is the direct or only source for these characterizations. Bradamante's quest for Ruggiero in the *Orlando furioso* furnishes the most immediate model, and an ultimate source is suggested either by Isis' search for the *disiecta membra* of Osiris, or by Ceres' quest for her beloved daughter Proserpina.[49]

Nonetheless, the special, almost emblematic, positioning of the Apuleian vignette in the Garden of Adonis gives it a privileged status in the text and may even authorize us to accord priority to *The Golden Ass* over competing possible sources in the elucidation of particular passages in the poem. By calling attention, in this specific instance, to its own relation to the novel, the poem can be said to be inviting a closer and more general inter-reading of the two texts. The legitimacy of such an intertextual methodology remains controversial, but clad, proleptically, in the Apuleian arms of Book 3, we can approach the opening of the poem and see what develops.

Beneath the surface of the accounts of Psyche's exposure on the 'rock of yonder hill aloft' and her proposed marriage to 'no wight of human seed' (*AA* 4. 33) lie the ancient myths describing the virtuous maiden who is sacrificed to the beast to save her city, and the unseen husband who is actually a serpent.[50] A partial adumbration of this first buried myth is present in the

---

[46] *Structure of Allegory*, 140, 143.

[47] Ibid. 140, 143, 145.

[48] Ibid. 140, 147.

[49] Plutarch, *De Iside et Osiride*; Ovid, *Met.* 5. 538 ff. The quest for Proserpina is one of the bases for Apuleius' own account of Psyche's search for Cupid—as Heywood realized when he combined the two stories in *Loves Maistresse*.

[50] e.g. Andromeda and Perseus. See Scobie, *Apuleius and Folklore*. It is interesting that C. S. Lewis (who made no use of Apuleius in his analysis of Spenser) should have responded to the

poem in the figure of the 'huge dragon' which has kept Una's regal parents
shut up for many years in a 'brasen castle', having 'with foule vprore |
Forwasted all their land, and them expeld'.[51] Such similarities in deep mythic
structures are complemented by closer parallels between the novel and poem.

When Una and Redcrosse appear at the beginning of *The Faerie Queene*,
their relationship seems to be purely that of a knight in the service of a lady
beset by adversity.[52] Their interactions are formal ('Ah Ladie', 'Sir knight') and
any potential sexual energies are sublimated into desire for chivalrous action
(as in the battle with the beast, Error, where Redcrosse is described as being
'full of fire and greedy hardiment', I. i. 14. 1). There is no indication of
anything more personal. When, at the end of the first canto, Redcrosse lies
awake after seeing the counterfeit Una at his bedside, his concern is not for an
emotional breach, but for a violation of the chivalric code. He is 'Much
grieued to thinke that gentle Dame so light, | For whose defence he was to
shed his blood' (*FQ* I. i. 55. 2–3). By the time of his flight at the beginning of
the second canto, however, the situation has changed significantly. Rising in
the morning, Una

> Lookt for her knight, who far away was fled,
> And for her Dwarfe, that wont to wait each houre;
> Then gan she waile and weepe, to see that woefull stowre
>
> (*FQ* I. ii. 7. 7–9)

Una has been transformed from the noble Lady, intent on delivering her
homeland from the ravening beast, to the deserted lover, searching 'every hill
and dale, each wood and plaine'

> . . . sore grieued in her gentle brest,
> He so vngently left her, whom she louest best.
>
> (*FQ* I. ii. 8. 8–9)

The pivot on which the characterization turns is Spenser's appropriation of
the discovery-scene in Apuleius. Psyche, lamp and blade in hand, comes to the
bed of the husband she believes to be a serpent, intending to cut off his head.
Uncovering the lamp, however, she sees Cupid for the first time and, amazed

---

underlying mythic structures when he transformed Apuleius' story in *Till We Have Faces: A
Myth Retold* (1956; repr. London: Collins, 1979). Lewis' Psyche becomes the 'Great offering' to
'the Brute' (56).

[51] Letter to Raleigh and I. i. 5. 7–8. Spenser's description of Una in the Letter as 'a faire Ladye
in mourning weedes, riding on a white Asse' may contain a trace of the Apuleian oracle
commanding that Psyche be exposed to the 'serpent dire': 'Let Psyches corps be clad in
mourning weede' (Adlington, ch. 22, p. 73; *AA* 4. 33).

[52] 'Whom to auenge, she had this Knight from far compeld' (I. i. 5. 9).

by his beauty, 'thought to hide the razor, yea verily in her own heart'.[53] It is in
this mingled state of contrition and desire, heaping eager kisses upon her still-
sleeping husband, that she accidentally scorches him with the lamp and causes
him to wake. Redcrosse, 'Bathed in wanton blis and wicked ioy', dreams that

> his Lady by him lay,
> And to him playnd, how that false winged boy,
> Her chast hart had subdewed, to learn Dame pleasures toy.

> (*FQ* i. i. 47. 6–9)

When he wakes, 'as seeming to mistrust, | Some secret ill, or hidden foe of his',
he sees 'Una' beside him:

> Lo there before his face his Lady is,
> Vnder blake stole hyding her bayted hooke,
> And as halfe blushing offred him to kis,
> With gentle blandishment and louely looke,
> Most like that virgin true, which for her knight him took.

> (*FQ* i. i. 49. 5–9)

In each case there is a threat (or, in Redcrosse's case, the perceived threat) of
physical violence ('Some secret ill, or hidden foe of his') which is subsequently
sublimated into something amorous but no less menacing. The two agents are
similarly contrite. Psyche wants to kill herself with the razor; 'Una' expresses
her subordination to the commands of 'the blind God': 'Yet thus perforce he
bids me do, or die. | Die is my dew: yet rew my wretched state' (i. i. 51. 6–7).
The murderous razor has been transformed into the 'bayted hooke', but the
ultimate effect is the same. Cupid and Redcrosse, outraged by a perceived
betrayal of faith, both 'fly' from wife and lady.[54]

Spenser uses the Dream-Counterfeit sequence to create psychological
depth by proxy—a sort of vicarious characterization which allows him to
maintain allegorical integrity while introducing human colour. Redcrosse's
dream of 'loues and lustfull play' (i. i. 4. 4) is sent by Archimago, so that,
officially, the knight's psyche is unimpeached. Yet the fact remains that he has
dreamt (all too humanly) of lying with Una, and is uncertain of his ability to
control his desires: 'wonted feare of doing ought amis' (i. i. 49. 2). Una, too, is
officially innocent, but reacts as though partially guilty. Rather than feeling
righteous indignation that her knight has deserted their noble quest (and, in
so doing, sullied her own honour), Una behaves as a forsaken lover, like
Psyche, at once both wrong and wronged. The fudging in narrative causality

---

[53] Adlington, ch. 22, p. 85; *AA* 5. 22: *et ferrum quaerit abscondere, sed in suo pectore.*
[54] *tacitus auolauit*, 5. 23; *FQ* i. ii. 6. 9.

resembles the complex textual logic operating in *The Golden Ass.* The difference is that Una, unlike Psyche, is completely innocent at all times: she sleeps,
chaste and unwitting, while Redcrosse (the victim of Archimago's fabricated
dream) is tormented by 'this great passion of vnwonted lust' (I. i. 49. 1)
and deceived by the sight of the 'false couple' in their 'lewd embracement'
(I. ii. 5. 4–5).

When we return to read the account of the counterfeit Una, we can detect
the (typically Spenserian) signposts indicating the divide between attractive
appearance and sinister reality:

> ... *as* halfe blushing ...
> Most *like* that virgin true ...
>
> *seemd* to bereave
> (*FQ* I. i. 49. 7–9; I. i. 52. 3)[55]

Yet if we read the speech of the *counterfeit* as though it were spoken by the *real*
Una, it has a curiously human quality:

> Your owne deare sake forst me at first to leaue
> My Fathers kingdome ...
>
> ... My weaker yeares
> Captiu'd to fortune and frayle worldly feares,
> Fly to your faith for succour and sure ayde
>
> (*FQ* I. i. 52. 1–6)

Psyche has been snatched from her father's kingdom by Cupid's desire and,
when the God flies from her, she catches hold of him and is carried into the air
until weariness constrains her to let go (*AA* 5. 24). 'Una', in a moment of
(understandable and attractive) weakness, seeks comfort from the Knight, her
defender. Her 'halfe blushing' offer 'him to kis' (I. i. 49. 7) is made sinister
only by Redcrosse's interpretation of it. It is the coincidence of her appearing
in fulfilment of his dream, rather than any 'holiness of affections', that
engenders the 'hasty heat'[56] of his instinctive response:

> All cleane dismayed to see so vncouth sight,
> And halfe enraged at her shamelesse guise,
> He thought haue slaine her in his fierce despight:
>
> (*FQ* I. i. 50. 1–3)

The subsequent wanderings of Una who 'In wildernesse and wastefull
deserts strayd | To seeke her knight' (I. iii. 3. 4–5), recall how '*Psyches* hurled
her selfe hither and thither, to seeke her husband' (Adlington, ch. 22, p. 91;

[55] Emphasis added.   [56] Hamilton, *Structure of Allegory*, 143.

AA 6. 1). Meeting a lion who takes 'pittie' on her 'sad estate' (i. iii. 7. 5)—
reminiscent of the animals who take 'pittie' on Psyche in her 'great difficultie
and labour'[57]—Una bewails her fate and speaks of Redcrosse in a manner far
more suited to the God of Love than to an ordinary knight:

> How does he find in cruell hart to hate
> Her that him lou'd, and euer most adord.
> As the God of my life? Why hath he me abhord?
>
> (*FQ* i. iii. 7. 7–9)

Two other scenes reinforce Una's relation to Psyche. In Canto vi, the
'Faunes and Satyres' (i. vi. 7. 7), having rescued Una from Sansloy's attempted
rape, 'Do worship her, as Queene, with oliue girlond cround' (i. vi. 13. 9),
according her the same reverence paid to Psyche:

For why euery person honoured and worshipped this maide insteed of Venus. And in
the morning at her first comming abroad, offered vnto her oblations, prouided
bankets, called hir by the name of *Venus* that was not *Venus* indeed, and in her
honour presented floures and garlands in most [72] reuerent fashion. (Adlington,
ch. 22, pp. 71–2; *AA* 4. 29)

> And old *Syluanus* selfe bethinkes not, what
> To thinke of wight so faire, but gazing stood,
> In doubt to deeme her borne of earthly brood;
> Sometimes Dame *Venus* selfe he seemes to see,
> But *Venus* neuer had so sober mood;
>
> (*FQ* i. vi. 16. 3–7)[58]

Spenser's 'light-foot Naiades' respond in the manner of Apuleius' Venus and
'enuie her in their malitious mind' (i. vi. 18. 6), while the Satyrs' reaction is to
'scorne their woody kind' (i. vi. 18. 8) in the same way that the worshippers of
Psyche show 'such a contempt...towards the goddesse *Venus*'.[59] The crucial
difference is that while Psyche allows the worship to continue and thus incurs

---

[57] Adlington, ch. 22, p. 96; *AA* 6. 10.

[58] The paragonic beauty of the heroine (and/or hero) is a topos of the Greek novel (e.g.
Longus, *Daphnis and Chloe*, 4. 33. 3–4, Heliodorus, *Aethiopica* 2. 33. 3) but it is only in *Chæreas
and Callirhoe* that the heroine is identified explicitly with Aphrodite (1. 1. 2)—and Chariton is
not an author whom Spenser could have known since the *ed. princ.* of his romance did not
appear until 1750. In Musaeus' *Hero and Leander* (available to the Elizabethans in Latin and
French translations), Hero is called a 'new Cypris' (l. 68), but her admirers' response is not to
worship her but to try to take her to bed. See Kenney, ed., *Cupid and Psyche*, 116; and L. C.
Martin's incautious attribution of Marlowe's lines to Apuleius in *Marlowe's Poems* (London:
Methuen, 1931), 34–5. Cf. Tobin, *SFN*, p. xvii.

[59] Adlington, ch. 22, p. 71; *AA* 4. 29.

the wrath of Venus, Una reaffirms the true, orthodox, divine order and tries to wean the 'saluage nation' (I. vi. 11. 3) away from idolatry:

> During which time her gentle wit she plyes,
> To teach them truth, which worshipt her in vaine,
> And made her th'Image of Idolatres;
> But when their bootlesse zeale she did restraine
> From her own worship, they her Asse would worship fayn.[60]
>
>   (*FQ* I. vi. 19. 5–9)

After Psyche's desertion by the oil-scorched Cupid, she surprises us by her ruthless disposal of the sisters she had loved. Both are led 'by the stratagem of their sister'[61] to hurl themselves from the cliff in the belief that Zephyrus will carry them down to their prospective husband Cupid. The punishment may be appropriate to their crimes, but Psyche's assumption of the role of executioner catches us unawares. This is yet one more manifestation of the kind of incongruities that we come to expect (and, in a disturbed kind of way, even relish) in the novel. When Arthur kills Orgoglio, Una says of Duessa,

> Ne let that wicked woman scape away;
> For she it is that did my Lord bethrall,
> My dearest Lord, and deepe in dongeon lay,
> Where he his better dayes hath wasted all.
>
>   (*FQ* I. viii. 28. 5–8)

There is more than a hint here of vindictive jealousy. Una's links with the protagonists of the ancient novels are underscored by her exclamation, 'And fie on Fortune mine auowed foe' (I. viii. 43. 3), and Arthur offers her a chance to re-enact the retribution exacted by Psyche:

> And loe that wicked woman in your sight,
> The roote of all your care, and wretched plight,
> Now in your powre, to let her liue, or dye
>
>   (*FQ* I. viii. 45. 4–6)[62]

---

[60] In the figure of Una's ass, Spenser unites the Psyche story with the Aesopic tradition of the over-weening, idol-bearing ass—a tradition which had been contaminated as early as the emblematist Alciati by contact with the Apuleian story of the ass reformed in the procession of Isis. See, e.g., J. M. Steadman, 'Una and the Clergy: The Ass Symbol in *The Faerie Queene*', *JWCI* 21 (1958), 134–7.

[61] *fallacie germanitatis* (5. 27). Adlington omits these lines.

[62] Note how Duessa is made the sole 'roote' of Una's 'care' and 'plight'—a description more accurately applicable to Archimago and one which absolves Redcrosse from all responsibility.

Una, magnanimous where Psyche was unrelenting, replies:

> To do her dye (quoth Vna) were despight,
> And shame t'auenge so weake an enimy;
> But spoile her of her scarlot robe, and let her fly.
>
> (*FQ* I. viii. 45. 7–9)

Yet even as we affirm the moral superiority that Spenser establishes for Una over Psyche, we should be conscious of the tonal and ethical complexities of the scene. Una's intercession demonstrates her clemency, but it also allows a previously jilted lover to humiliate her rival, sexually, by having her stripped before the eyes of her knight and her deliverer.

A 'VIOLENT CONFECTION OF WITCHES'

While Una wanders, Psyche-like, 'from one to other *Ynd*' (I. vi. 2. 7), Redcrosse acquires a 'new Lady' (I. ii. 29. 7), 'Fidessa', whose 'forged beauty' (I. ii. 36. 1) conceals the inner vileness of Duessa. In search of shade, they encounter Fradubio and Frælissa who have been transformed by Duessa into 'two goodly trees' (I. ii. 28. 3).[63] Fradubio relates how he staged a beauty contest between the two ladies: 'A Rosy girlond was the Victors meede' (I. ii. 37. 5). Duessa won the contest 'by her hellish science' (I. ii. 38. 5) and Fradubio took her as his 'Dame' until one day

> I chaunst to see her in her proper hew,
> Bathing her selfe in origane and thyme:
> A filthy foule old woman I did vew,
>
> (*FQ* I. ii. 40. 6–8)

Behind Spenser's Duessa and Acrasia lie Ariosto's Alcina and Tasso's Armida; behind all of them, the Homeric archetype Circe. The primary source for the revelation-scene is doubtless the moment in the *Orlando furioso* where Ruggiero, disenchanted by the Ring of Reason (*l'annello . . . de la ragion*, viii. 2), sees Alcina not as a vision of peerless beauty but as an ancient crone, wrinkled and hollow-cheeked (*crespo e macilente*, vii. 73).[64] Poetry has an inherent propensity for voyeurism, especially when it involves the kind of

---

[63] The figure of the man turned into a tree or plant, most famously presented in Vergil's Polidorus, has a long and rich history: e.g. *Aen.* 3. 27–42; Ariosto, *OF* vi. 26–53; Tasso, *GL* xiii. 41–2.

[64] Cf. *Sir John Harington's Translation of 'Orlando furioso'* (1591), ed. G. Hough (London: Centaur, 1962), vii. 62. 'Her neather partes misshapen, monstrous' (*FQ* I. ii. 41. 1) may derive, ultimately, from Dante's picture of Fraud swimming in the Styx. See Variorum edn., i. 205.

literary iconography in which Spenser delights; and (male) poets, of course, have long colluded with their (male) audiences in catching women in the act of bathing. The vision of Duessa is the grotesque counterpoint of the two Spenserian appropriations of the Ovidian myh of Diana and Actaeon.[65] The power of Thessalian witches was familiar to the Renaissance from a variety of sources, Lucan supplying an epic description of their horrors in his account of Erictho, while the elegiac poets forged the link between magic and the darker sides of love.[66] But the Apuleian witches (like Tasso's, Thessalian) furnish a useful parallel. When Lucius watches Pamphile strip and besmear herself with 'ointment' and change herself into an 'Owle', he 'seemed not to haue the likenesse of Lucius, for so I was banished from my sences' (Adlington, ch. 16, p. 51; *AA* 3. 21–2).

Duessa, too, has been transformed in Fradubio's mind, and he resolves to 'refrain' 'from her most *beastly* companie' (*FQ* i. ii. 41. 5–6—emphasis added). She, however,

> Perceiu'd my thought, and drownd in sleepie night,
> With wicked herbes and ointments did besmeare
> My bodie all, through charmes and magicke might,
> That all my senses were bereaued quight.

> (*FQ* i. ii. 42. 2–5)

The passage combines the two parts of the Lucius/Pamphile episode: the effect upon Fradubio's 'senses' and his actual metamorphosis:

And then I put off all my garments and greedely thrust my hand into the boxe, and tooke out a good deale of ointment and rubbed my selfe withal. (Adlington, ch. 16, p. 52; *AA* 3. 24)

In both the Spenser and the Apuleius, the calamitous transformation can be (and has been) read as the direct result of the surrender of the well-meaning but weak-willed man to the blended vices of witchcraft and sensuality.

Redcrosse and Duessa are parted in Canto v when the witch descends into hell to revive Sans-foy, and the knight escapes from the House of Pride after discovering the secrets of its dungeons.[67] But in Canto vii, Duessa comes

---

[65] Venus surprising Diana in iii. vii. 17–19; and Faunus spying upon her in *Mutabilitie*, vi. 42–7.

[66] Lucan, *De bello ciuili* 6. 438 ff. Ovid (*Amores* 3. 7. 27) asks, rhetorically, if his impotence is the result of Thessalian drugs or witches' charms and curses. Cf. Tibullus, 2. 4. 56 and Propertius, 1. 5. 6.

[67] The 'sinfull house of Pride' shares some features with the house of Cupid ('The house of mightie Prince it seemd to bee', *FQ* i. iv. 2. 7; 'princely Edifice', Adlington, ch. 22, p. 98; *domus regia*, *AA* 5. 1) but not enough to make a conclusive Apuleian identification. In the parade of sins, *Idlenesse* 'chose to ryde' 'vpon a slouthfull Asse', but it does not seem to be a particularly Apuleian ass.

upon Redcrosse resting from the 'boyling heat' in 'a gloomy glade, | About the fountains like a girlond made'.[68] Duessa is merely called 'The Witch' (*FQ* I. vii. 3. 6), a name which darkens the sensuousness of the reconciliation scene:

> Vnkindnesse past, they gan of solace treat,
> And bathe in pleasaunce of the ioyous shade,
>
> (*FQ* I. vii. 4. 2–3)

The stream has been cursed by Diana (goddess of Chastity) because of the lethargy of one of her nymphs, and when Redcrosse

> ... lying downe vpon the sandie graile,
> Drunke of the streame, as cleare as cristall glas,
> Eftsoones his manly forces gan to faile,
> And mightie strong was turnd to feeble fraile.
>
> (*FQ* I. vii. 6. 2–5)

Witchcraft, sensual indulgence, and chastity combine in the one passage. The first interpolated tale in *The Golden Ass* is that told by Aristomenes. His friend, Socrates, has been ensnared by the 'carnell desire' of Meroë—a witch who shares Duessa's Circean penchant for metamorphosing ex-lovers—and when he escapes, she gives pursuit. Catching him at night, she

thrust her sword vp to the hilts into the left part of his necke, and receiued the bloud that gushed out ... and ... thrust her hand downe into the [11] entrailes of his body, and searching about, at length brought forth the heart of my miserable companion Socrates, who (having his throat cut in this sort) yeelded out a doleful crie, and gaue up the Ghost. (Adlington, ch. 5, pp. 10–11; *AA* 1. 13)

In the morning, however, Socrates appears to be alive and perfectly well. He and Aristomenes resume their journey and everything seems to be normal until they begin to recount the horrors of the night and Socrates says:

the remembrance thereof makes me now to feare for my knees do tremble[69] that I can vneth go anie further ... (Adlington, ch. 5, p. 14; *AA* 1. 18)

Aristomenes relates how he

gaue him bread and cheese, and we sate downe under a great plaine tree and I eate part with him, and while I beheld him eating greedely, I perceiued that he waxed meigre and pale, and that his liuely colour faded away ... but when that Socrates had eaten snfficiently [*sic*], he waxed very thirstie ... and behold euill fortune, there was behind the plaine tree a pleasant running water as cleere as Christal, and he rose and came to

---

⁶⁸ *FQ* I. vii. 4. 5. We have already noted the dangerous associations of 'girlonds'.
⁶⁹ Cf. 'trees did tremble' (*FQ* I. vii. 7. 7).

the Riuer, and kneeled downe vpon the side of the banke to drinke, but he had scant touched the water with his lips, whenas behold the wound of his throate opened wide, and the Sponge sodainely fell into the water, and after issued out a little remnant of bloud, and his body (being then without life) had fallen into the riuer, had I not caught him by the leg, and so pulled him up.[70] (Adlington, ch. 5, p. 14; *AA* 1. 19)

At the beginning of the second book, Guyon 'Findes Mordant and Amauia slaine | With pleasure poisoned baytes.' Amavia (not dead, in fact, but dying) recounts how her Lord, Mordant, was 'beguiled' by '*Acrasia* a false enchaunteresse' (*FQ* ii. i. 51. 3) in the Bower of Bliss:

> Him so I sought, and so at last I found,
>> Where him that witch had thralled to her will,
>> In chaines of lust and lewd desires ybound,
>> And so transformed from his former skill,
>> That me he knew not, neither his owne ill;
>> Till through wise handling and faire gouernance,
>> I him recured to a better will,
>> Purged from drugs of foule intemperance;
> Then meanes I gan deuise for his deliuerance.
>
> Which when the vile Enchaunteresse perceiu'd,
>> How that my Lord from her I would repriue,
>> With cup thus charmd, him parting she deceiu'd;
>> Sad verse, giue death to him that death does giue,
>> And losse of loue, to her that loues to liue,
>> So soone as *Bacchus* with the Nymph does lincke,
>> So parted we and on our iourney driue,
>> Till coming to this well, he stoupt to drincke:
> The charme fulfil'd, dead suddenly downe did sincke.
>
> (*FQ* ii. i. 54–5)

In terms of Apuleian drama, this is the full performance for which the well-scene with Duessa and Redcrosse was the dress rehearsal. All the Apuleian elements are now present: witch and sexual indulgence, water and death.[71]

---

[70] The Latin actually reads: *argento uel uitro aemulus in colorem* ('rivalling silver or glass in colour', 1. 19). It might be tempting to see, in the similarity of such phrasing as 'the stream, as cleare as cristall glas' and 'a pleasant running water as cleere as christal', evidence of Spenser's familiarity with Adlington's translation; but the crystallinity of water is manifest not only in classical literature (e.g. Horace, *Odes* 3. 13. 1: *o fons Bandusiae splendidior vitro*) but also in the Italian of Ariosto (*un rivo che pare a cristallo*, *OF* xxiii. 100).

[71] The sense-bereaving effects shared by Lucius and Mordant are here transferred to Guyon: 'And his fresh bloud did frieze with fearfull cold, | That all his senses seemd bereft attone' (ii. i. 42. 3–4). Amavia's role as loyal lady resembles Aristomenes' role as loyal friend, her attempt by 'wise handling and faire gouernance' to redeem Mordant counterpointing Aristomenes' clothing, bathing, feeding, and counselling of Socrates (*AA* 1. 7). After the death of Socrates, Aristomenes deserts his wife and children to go into exile; Amavia, with Mordant slain,

Mordant is described as being 'transformed from his former skill' (II. i. 54. 4)—a metaphorical transformation which prefigures the physical transformations occasioned by Acrasia and reflects a recurrent concern of *The Faerie Queene*: the metamorphic power of mental states and bodily indulgences.[72]

In the last stanza of Book II, Guyon says:

> See the mind of beastly man,
> That hath so soone forgot the excellence
> Of his creation, when he life began,
> That now he chooseth, with vile difference,
> To be a beast, and lacke intelligence.
>
> (*FQ* II. xii. 87. 1–5)

Sir John Harington, in 1591, offers a similar gloss to the metamorphosis of Astolfo (*Orlando furioso* vi); but Guyon's speech is closer to Adlington (and Beroaldo) than to Ariosto:

Verely vnder the wrap of this transformation, is taxed the life of mortal men, whenas we suffer our mindes so to be drowned in the sensual lusts of the flesh, and beastlie pleasure thereof: (which aptly may be called, the violent confection of Witches) that wee leese wholly the vse of reason and vertue (which properly should be in man) and plaie the parts of brute and sauage beasts: By like occasion we reade, how diuers of the companions of *Vlysses*, were turned by the maruellous power [A3ʳ] of Circe into swine. (Adlington, 'To the Reader', sigs. [A2]ᵛ–A3ʳ)

The same theme is present in each passage: the intelligent mind's indulgence in beastly pleasures transforms the possessor in the manner of a 'violent Confection of Witches'.

We need to have the deaths of Mordant and Amavia in mind when we meet Acrasia in Book II, Canto xii. Guyon's destruction of the Bower of Bliss has drunk rivers of critical ink. The lushness of Spenser's description, the allure of the Bower's manifold delights, and the violence of Guyon's response to it have prompted the charge that Spenser, at heart, was of Acrasia's party. The complaint is a familiar one—Milton, we all know, gave the devil the best tunes. In Blake's words:

---

abandons her 'bloodie babe'. Before the throat-slitting episode, Socrates pinpoints the original cause of his misfortune as being his 'desire to see a game of triall of weapons' (*uoluptas gladiatorii spectaculi*, *AA* 1. 7; Adlington, ch. 3, p. 3). Mordant desires 'to seeke aduentures wilde' (II. i. 50. 6) in the martial manner befitting a knight.

[72] e.g. the drunken, Gluttony, 'In shape and life more like a monster, then a man' (I. iv. 22. 9); or 'that great proud king of *Babylon*' 'Into an Oxe he was transform'd of yore' (I. v. 47. 1, 5); or Malbecco.

The reason Milton wrote in fetters when he wrote of Angels & God, and at liberty when of Devils & Hell, is because he was a true Poet and of the Devils party without knowing it.[73]

The question in *The Faerie Queene* is whether the distinction between low and high pleasures can survive the transfer from philosophical treatise to poetic text. In order to represent higher Pleasure, the poet has chosen to employ the images of sensual pleasures; and what differentiates the Garden of Adonis from the 'false delights' of Phædria's island, or the prurient sterility of Acrasia's Bower, is uninhibited and fruitful sexual gratification:

> Franckly each paramour his leman knowes
> Each bird his mate, ne any does enuie
> Their goodly meriment and gay felicitie.
>
> (*FQ* III. vi. 41. 7–9)

C. S. Lewis' defence of Spenser's moral and artistic technique in the Bower of Bliss falters, however, at two points. Is it really appropriate, we must first ask, to base the condemnation of the Bower as much upon its 'artifice' as its supposed 'sterility' when artifice is the excellent quality which informs the work as a whole? Secondly, are the pleasures in the Garden of Adonis really so very different from those in the Bower of Bliss? Lewis argues that while the Bower may seem attractive on cursory inspection, it does, in fact, contain nothing but 'male prurience and female provocation.'[74] Yet the argument that the sexuality of the Bower is merely voyeuristic overlooks (as Hough wittily points out) the pearly drops obtained on Acrasia's brow 'Through languor of her late sweet toil'.[75] And who is doing the looking anyway? To whom do the 'hungrie eies' belong, if not to Guyon and the Palmer, as well as to the narrator, poet, and reader? Part of Spenser's problem here is a function of the inherent limitations of poetry (or, more fundamentally, language) as a mimetic medium. Music can probably create the most convincing simulacrum of purity; and it is certainly possible, through painting or sculpture, to represent without prurience the beauty of the naked human form. But when it comes to matters sexual, poetry does seem instinctively disposed towards the devil's party—the lord of carnal or sensual desires—and, by an ironic twist, poetry is actually more prone to scopophilia than the pictorial arts. Moreover, when one reads the description of Venus' love-making with Adonis, it is hard (*pace* Lewis) to see these pleasures as being any less predatory than those of the Bower of Bliss:

---

[73] *The Marriage of Heaven and Hell*, in *William Blake: The Complete Poems*, ed. A. Ostriker (Harmondsworth: Penguin, 1977), 182.
[74] *The Allegory of Love*, 332.   [75] *FQ* II. xii. 78. Hough, 164.

... reape sweet pleasure of the wanton boy;

... when euer that she will,
Possesseth him, and of his sweetnesse takes her fill.

(*FQ* III. vi. 46. 3, 8–9)

As to the actual destruction, whatever moral endorsements we may make cannot wholly displace our aesthetic response. Spenser himself does little to check such lectorial tendencies since even the adjectives refuse to cooperate in the presumed moral judgement: 'But all those pleasant bowres and Pallace braue | Guyon broke downe' (II. xii. 83. 1–2). It is a victory without triumph, a curtain-fall that elicits no applause.

Yet the effect is surely calculated. To create an engaging and convincing poem, temptations obviously must *tempt*. The 'false delights' and 'pleasures vaine' must outwardly appear sufficiently attractive to demonstrate how easy it is, even for the virtuous like Guyon, to be tempted by them. Spenser has chosen, in fact, to suppress the most important justification for Guyon's destruction of the Bower: Acrasia is a murderess, and the Bower, as the means whereby she seduces her victims, is a candidate ripe for demolition. Guyon's violence, on this reading, is merely the fulfilment of the solemn oath made at the end of Canto i to exact 'dew vengeance' for the deaths of Amavia and Mordant (II. i. 61. 7). Yet for most of Book II (and certainly in the Bower itself) we are allowed to forget these deaths.[76] The destruction is *meant* to come as a shock to us, meant to appear as Guyon's repressive response to the cupidinous feelings engendered in his own breast by the sight of the 'lilly paps' of the 'naked Damzelles' (II. xii. 63–8).

Mordant's stream is obviously closer to Socrates' deadly waters than is Redcrosse's, but it would be rash to call either an explicit allusion to Apuleius. These passages (unlike the 'Cupid and Psyche' vignette at III. vi) are perfectly explicable without reference to Apuleius—it is easy to see, independently of *The Golden Ass,* that the enervation of Redcrosse and the death of Mordant after drinking from the streams are merely the physical manifestations of the spiritual enervation that results from their dalliance with the sexually bewitching enemies of Truth and Virtue. The Apuleian parallels, however, augment the Circean and, by giving a more sinister colouring to the consequences of sensual indulgence, help to justify Guyon's actions.

---

[76] The vigilant reader is, however, given clues. The mythological scenes adorning Armida's palace (*GL* xvi. 1–7) depict men (Hercules and Antony) degraded by their passion for women (Iole and Cleopatra); Acrasia's Bower, in contrast, shows us the atrocity-engendering love of Jason and Medea (*FQ* II. xii. 44).

PHÆDRIA

If the importation of Apuleian material into the necromantic episodes actually serves to bolster the endorsed meanings of the poem, the character of Phædria, whom we meet six cantos before we enter Acrasia's Bower, is altogether more problematic. Her luscious island in the middle of the '*Idle lake*' seems to prefigure the Bower of Bliss; but Spenser is no mere recycler of imagery: Phædria's island is distinguished from Acrasia's Bower of Bliss, as the Bower is from the Garden of Adonis.

A source for Phædria has long been claimed in Tasso's *fatal donzella* whose gondola carries Carlo and Ubaldo towards Armida's palace where Rinaldo lies enthralled.[77] As Harold Blanchard points out, however, Tasso's *donzella* is as virtuous as she is fair, bringing her passengers swiftly and faithfully to their desired destination. Phædria, in contrast, 'misleads' Sir Guyon and instead of taking him to the other side of the water attempts to beguile him on her island with the same charms that have enchanted Cymochles. Blanchard derives Phædria, not from Tasso, but from a passage in Boiardo where the 'damsel is described *con faccia ridente*, suggesting at once the seductive mirth of [838] Phædria':

> A l'altra ripa stava una donzella
> Vestita a bianco, e con faccia ridente,
> Sopra a la poppa d'una navicella.
> Diceva: O cavalieri, o belle gente,
> Se vi piace passare, entrate in barca,
> Però che altrove il fiume non si varca.[78]

C. W. Lemmi, on the other hand, contends that Trissino's *L'Italia liberata* was Spenser's source for the outline and some of the detail in Book II—a view given qualified support by Graham Hough who finds a counterpart for Phædria in Trissino's 'minor enchantress called Ligridonia'.[79] The influence on Spenser of the lesser-known romantic epics remains controversial, and had the claims for Boiardo and Trissino not been made, it would still be possible to account for the structure and characterization of Book II of *The Faerie*

[77] *GL* xv. 3 ff.

[78] Boiardo, *OI* ii. ix. 49–53; H. H. Blanchard, 'Spenser and Boiardo', *PMLA* 40 (1925), 828–51, at 837–8. Cited in Variorum edn., ii. 241.

[79] C. W. Lemmi, 'The Influence of Trissino on the *Faerie Queene*', *PQ* 7 (1928), 220–3; Hough, 161. The congruence between the names of the enchantresses in Trissino and Spenser (Acratia and Acrasia) sounds persuasive, but one would be more readily convinced if Lemmi had given some account of the availability of *L'Italia liberata* in England or shown some contemporary reference to it.

Queene largely in terms of the transposition of materials found in Tasso and Ariosto. The Bower owes much of its detail to Tasso's garden, but its occupant, Acrasia, is indebted less to the Dido-like Armida than to Ariosto's altogether more sinister enchantress, Alcina.[80] And the idea for Phædria's 'immodest Merth' may have flowed from the *fonte del riso,* the deadly fountain of laughter found on the plain outside Armida's palace (*GL* xiv. 74).

Nothing, however, in the Italian predecessors supplies a clue to Phædria's name. The only other Phædrias known are male—young reprobates in Terence's *Phormio* and *Eunuchus*—but the name may also carry resonances of its more famous cognates. One thinks of Phaedra, whose 'outrageous loues' for her stepson Hippolytus are described by Spenser twice in the same poem—the poet (perhaps significantly) declining in both instances to speak of the 'wanton stepdame' by name.[81] Plato's *Phaedrus* may also come to mind; while a more recondite reference from Diogenes Laertius is provided in the *Thesaurus* of Henri Estienne (*Thesaurus Stephani*). Phaedrion, we are told, was the slave-girl of Epicurus—famed exponent of a pleasure-goaled philosophy.[82] According to J. W. Draper:

Phædria, described as 'Immodest Mirth' (I,vi arg.) owes something to the adjective φαιδρόν, gay. The word often had a bad connotation in Greek as it had in Spenser, and was used on the comic stage for a young man sowing his wild oats (e.g. Terence, *Phormio*). Apparently this is the particular sort of temptation Guyon is allegorically experiencing in Canto vi.[83]

A. C. Hamilton's gloss on 'Phædria' as 'glittering, cheerful (φαιδρός) referring to her superficial pleasure and superfluous frivolity' is fuller than Draper's, but Roche's 'the shining one' is the most literal of the three. Φαιδρός, the adjective formed from φαιδρόομαι ('beam with joy'), derives, ultimately, from τό φάος which carries both the literal sense of light and the metaphorical sense of 'illumination of the mind'. As a name for the personification or embodiment of 'immodest Merth', therefore, 'Phædria' is both descriptively accurate ('fresh and faire', I. vi. 3. 1, and joyous) and metaphorically ironic (the light she shines is a false one).

The extent of Spenser's knowledge of Greek is a matter of some dispute, but Draper cites the use of abstruse etymologies in the devising of names as evidence that Spenser 'apparently addressed the *Faerie Queene,* from first to

---

[80] In 'The Bower of Bliss and Armida's Palace', *CL* 6 (1954), 335–47, R. M. Durling tends, however, to overemphasize the differences between the two: 'Acrasia and Alcina are true Circes, while Armida remains virtuous until she falls in love with Rinaldo.' But see *GL* xiv. 50 for her Circean tendencies: 'turn'd them first to monsters vile'.

[81] *FQ* I. v. 37–9; v. viii. 43.

[82] Diogenes Laertius, 10. 21; Stephanus, *Thesaurus,* 1865.

[83] J. W. Draper, 'Classical Coinage in the *Faerie Queene*', *PMLA* 47 (1932), 97–108.

last, to the aristocracy; for he gave certain parts of the poem an esoteric sense that only they could understand'.[84] Draper's conclusions may be questionable (Spenser seems to have been addressing several sorts of readers, and Elizabeth's proficiency in Greek should not be taken as being representative of the Court as a whole), but the presence of significant names in the poem is incontrovertible, and if Spenser's own Greek was unequal to the challenge of the subtle etymologies pressed upon him by modern critics, there was always 'Hobbinol' to help him out. Gabriel Harvey, for all the obloquy heaped upon him by Nashe, was one of the most learned men in England, and as one-time lecturer in Greek at Pembroke Hall, Cambridge, he would have been in a perfect position to advise his friend on the finer points of etymology.

The etymological significance of Fotis' name has been discussed elsewhere. Beroaldo, as early as 1500, identified Fotis with τό φῶς, the Greek word for light. This is the contracted form of τό φάος (the root of Phædria's name) and the stem of the verb φωτίζω ('to shine, give light, teach, illuminate with spiritual light'). Spenser was certainly familiar with the uncontracted root of Fotis' name (τό φάος) since he called two of his other characters in the *Faerie Queene*, Phao.[85] Is it overly ingenious to suggest that Spenser was aware of the etymological affinities of the names Fotis and Phædria?

The visual detail for the Phædria scene derives from a variety of sources—Italian romantic epic, as well, perhaps, as Celtic folklore—while the moralizing input in the first stanza comes from Aristotle's *Ethics* (2. 3). But the dramatic and thematic functions of Phædria bear a striking resemblance to those of Fotis in *The Golden Ass*. Both Phædria and Fotis serve lustful witches, and both have been held to be shiners of false light. The Fotis scenes have always been among the most popular in the novel, and it is possible that Spenser, in giving an Apuleian gilding to the Italian boat-girl, was responding not only to *The Golden Ass* itself but to an intermediate source, George Gascoigne's triplet of sonnets on Lucius' affair with Fotis which we encountered in Chapter 8.[86]

There are external, as well as internal, reasons for linking Gascoigne with Spenser. In his notes to 'November' in *The Shepheardes Calender* (1579), 'E.K.' (possibly Edward Kirke, but more probably a literary veil for Spenser and Harvey) refers to Gascoigne (d. 1577) as 'a wittie gentleman, and the very chefe of our late rymers'.[87] Gascoigne's literary patron was Arthur Grey,

[84] J. W. Draper, 107. On Spenser's knowledge of Greek, see A. C. Judson, *The Life of Edmund Spenser* (Baltimore: Johns Hopkins P, 1945; repr. 1947), 14.

[85] A Nereid, '*Phao* lilly white' (IV. xi. 49. 5) and 'th' Ægyptian *Phæo*' (III. ii. 20. 3).

[86] There may be a link between Spenser's 'Bowre of Blisse' (*FQ* II. xii) and Gascoigne's account of how Lucius 'Fyrst to the bowre of Beautie doth resort, | And there in pleasure passed many a fitte'.

[87] On 'E. K.', see A. Hadfield, 'Kirke, Edward (1553–1613)', *ODNB*.

fourteenth Baron Grey of Wilton (1536–93), who subsequently enjoyed the
secretarial services of Spenser during his governorship of Ireland and provided the model for Arthegal in Book V of *The Faerie Queene*.[88] A composite
edition, *The Pleasauntest Workes of George Gascoigne Esquyre: Newlye compyled into one volume*, appeared in 1587,[89] and Spenser may have been
alluding to the 'Weedes' section of this in the Proem to Book IV of *The Faerie
Queene* where he spoke of the 'rugged forhead' (traditionally identified as
William Cecil, Lord Burleigh) who had disapproved of his 'looser rimes':[90]

> For praising loue, as I haue done of late,
> And magnifying louers deare debate;
> By which fraile youth is oft to follie led,
> Through false allurement of that pleasing baite,
> That better were in vertues discipled,
> Then with vaine poemes weeds to haue their fancies fed.

> (*FQ* IV, Proem, i. 4–9)

Spenser was obviously sensitive to such criticism; and he had cause to be. The
ambiguities (moral and aesthetic) of the Garden of Adonis and the Bower of
Bliss are characteristic of the *The Faerie Queene* as a whole. Knights and Ladies
wander, unchaperoned, through the tapestried plains and forests of the poem,
espousing the codes of chivalry and chastity, but their actual practice of those
codes is often ambiguous.[91]

Apuleius was only one of many sources used by Spenser in constructing *The
Faerie Queene* and it would be rash, given the prior claims of Circe and her
Italian daughters, to advance Meroë or Pamphile as sole models for Duessa or
Acrasia. But there is a structural as well as a hermeneutic symmetry in the
roles of Phædria and Fotis which is critically illuminating, even if we are only
prepared to accept one as the analogue to the other. Moreover, the cumulative
evidence makes it worth at least staking the claim that Fotis contributes
directly to the character and thematic function of Phædria.

The Spenserian potential of what Gascoigne terms Fotis' 'bowre of Beautie'
needs no elucidation; the 'loud lay' with which Phædria charms Cymochles
ends with the injunction, 'Refuse such fruitlesse toile, and present pleasures
chuse', recalling Gascoigne's description of 'presaunt pleasure' and 'one ounce
of present sport.'[92] Other similarities establish, if not filiation, then at least
significant parallelism:

[88] A. C. Baugh, ed., *A Literary History of Britain*, 395, 485. G. W. Pigman III, 'Gascoigne, George (1534/5?–1577)', *ODNB*.
[89] (London: Abell Iesses, 1587), 294–6.
[90] Thus Collier (1862), Variorum edn., iv. 164.
[91] e.g. VI. ii. 16; VI. iii. 20; and Calidore and Pastorella in VI. xi. 38.
[92] *FQ* II. vi. 14. 8; II. vi. 17. 8.

> And all the way, the wanton Damzell found
> New merth, her passenger to entertain:
> For she in pleasant purpose did abound,
> And greatly ioyed merry tales to faine,
> Of which a store-house did with her remaine,
>
> (*FQ* ii. vi. 6. 1–5)

Fotis is similarly described as being 'beautifull, wanton, and pleasant in talke' while Phædria's effect upon Cymochles parallels Lucius' response to Fotis 'mincing of meat and making pottage' in the kitchen:

> Her light behauiour, and loose dalliaunce
> Gaue wondrous great contentment to the knight,
>
> (*FQ* ii. vi. 8. 1–2)

her loines and hips did likewise moue and shake, which was in my mind a comely sight to see. (Adlington, ch. 9, p. 24; *AA* 2. 7)[93]

Fotis, we should recall, is neither sinister nor evil (her affection for Lucius is sincere and her confusion of the ointments which leads to his transformation is a genuine mistake) but, from the moral viewpoint of the priest of Isis in Book 11, she appears not only as the embodiment of the *seruiles uoluptates* that led to Lucius' beastly transformation but also as 'une lumière de l'erreur, qui luit pour ceux dont l'âme n'a pas été préparée à discerner la vérité'.[94]

Yet Book 11 cannot exercise complete control over our reading (or, rather, re-reading) of the first ten books, and while, from our Isiac perspective, we may acknowledge the ramifications of Lucius' dalliance with a slave-girl, the Fotis episode continues to impress itself upon us as a beautiful and sensual experience. We enjoy being seduced by Fotis again and again, even when we are fully aware of the consequences.

Phædria, similarly, is not, in herself, malicious or evil. Her Fotis-like fondness for 'gaudie girlonds' (ii. vi. 7. 4) and 'sensuall delight' (ii. vi. 8. 7) is actually rather engaging. Cymochles is utterly entranced:

> Thus when she had his eyes and senses fed
> With false delights, and fild with pleasures vaine,
> Into a shadie dale she soft him led,
> And laid him downe vpon a grassie plaine;
> And her sweet selfe without dread, or disdaine,
> She set beside, laying his head disarm'd
> In her loose lap, it softly to sustaine,

---

[93] Adlington, ch. 8, p. 42; *Nam et forma scitula et moribus ludicra et prorsus argutula est* ('For she is pretty in appearance, sportive in behaviour, and truly loquacious', *AA* 2. 6).

[94] P. Grimal, 'A la recherche d'Apulée', *REL* 47 (1969), 94–9, at 98.

Where soone he slumbred, fearing not be harm'd,
The whiles with a loud lay she thus him sweetly charm'd.

$$(FQ\ \text{ii. vi. } 14)$$

Spenser calls them 'false delights' and 'pleasures vaine' but once again his negative adjectives do not entirely cancel the positive force of the nouns. Phædria, in Graham Hough's view, is 'a flittertigibbet, but no worse; and it is hard to resist the feeling that Spenser treats her with a good deal of indulgence.'[95]

In the introduction to Book I of *The Faerie Queene*, P. C. Bayley writes:

His great achievement . . . is his success in convincing us of the loveliness of virtue. It is this which makes *The Faerie Queene* the greatest of all English imaginative works of high seriousness and moral purpose. We all know the complaint that Milton's Comus is more beguiling and attractive than the Lady, God and Christ pale and cold beside the human warmth of Satan, however fallen. Milton wrote of 'virtue in her shape how lovely' but was unable to convince us of the loveliness of virtue. Spenser leaves us in no doubt, and, as far as any work of literature can influence a man's [11] life, he makes us love virtue and want to be virtuous.[96]

There is a good deal of truth in this appraisal—even modern readers will testify that the experience of reading the poem can be, if not morally uplifting, then at least morally sobering—but in itself it is too simplistic. We have argued that the proper uses of pleasure (and the corresponding abuses) form the fundamental concern of *The Faerie Queene*. Spenser succeeds in showing us the duplicity of Duessa and (ultimately, at least) the viciousness of Acrasia, just as he had shown us the goodness and beauty of Una. But the island of Phædria is not a place of 'vicious pleasure' as Acrasia's Bower is.[97] Certainly, it contradicts the martial ethos espoused by the knights in the poem, playing upon the ancient theme (most famously represented in Odysseus' dallyings with Calypso and Aeneas' sojourn with Dido) of the warrior-voyager being detained from his heroic purpose by sensual or emotional indulgence. It is generally said that Phædria's song (*FQ* ii. vi. 15–17) derives from the passage in Tasso where Armida's nymph sings to Rinaldo (*GL* xiv. 62–4); but her theme there is merely *carpe diem* (*Folli, perché gettate il caro dono, | che breve è sì, di vostra età novella?*, xiv. 63. 1–2) and we have to wait for the 'naked wantons' of Book XV before we hear, in the song sung to Carlo and Ubaldo, any of the *militia amoris* elements found in Phædria's 'loud lay'.[98]

Phædria parts the embattelled Guyon and Cymochles with the words:

[95] Hough, 159.   [96] Bayley, ed., *Faerie Queene Book I*, 10–11.
[97] Lewis, *Allegory of Love*, 333.
[98] Hough, 159. The *locus classicus* for the identification of love with warfare is Ovid's *Amores* 1. 9 (*Militat omnis amans*, 'Every lover is a soldier').

> But if for me ye fight, or me will serue,
>> Not this rude kind of battell, nor these armes
> Are meet, the which doe men in bale to sterue,
> And dolefull sorrow heape with deadly harmes:
> Such cruell game my scarmoges disarmes:
> Another warre, and other weapons I
>> Doe loue, where loue does giue his sweet alarmes,
> Without bloudshed, and where the enemy
> Does yeeld vnto his foe a pleasant victory.

> (*FQ* II. vi. 34)

Tasso's nymph invites the knights to

> Put off those arms, and fear not Mars his rage,
>> Your sword, your shield, your helmet needless is;
> Then consecrate them here to endless rest,
> You shall love's champions be and soldiers blest.
>
> The fields for combat here are beds of down,
>> Of heaped lilies under shady brakes:

> (*GL* xv. 63. 5–8; 64. 1–2)[99]

But Fotis' parting injunction to Lucius before the night of their first love-making is much closer to Spenser than is Tasso:

go and prepare your selfe, for I intend valiantly & coragiously to encounter with you this night. (Adlington, ch. 9, p. 26; *AA* 2. 10)

Once they are alone, Lucius shows to Fotis his 'great impatience' and says: 'as you see I am now prepared vnto the battell, which you your selfe did appoint'.[100] Fotis replies:

Now (quoth shee) is come the houre of justing, now is come the time of warre, wherefore shew thy selfe like unto a man, for I will not retyre, I will not fly the field, see then thou bee valiant, see thou be couragious, since there is no time appointed when our skirmish shall cease. In saying these words she came to me to bed, and embraced me sweetly, and so wee passed all the night in pastime and pleasure, and never slept until it was day...

Cymochles is so delighted by Phædria,

> That of his way he had no souenance,
> Nor care of vow'd reuenge, and cruell fight,
> But to weake wench did yeeld his martiall might.

---

[99] Torquato Tasso, *Jerusalem Delivered*, trans. Edward Fairfax (1600), ed. and introd. R. Weiss (London: Centaur, 1962).

[100] Adlington, ch. 10, p. 30; *AA* 2. 16.

So easie was to quench his flamed mind
With one sweet drop of sensuall delight,
So easie is, t'appease the stormie wind
Of malice in the calme of pleasant womankind.

(*FQ* II. vi. 8. 3–9)

Cymochles' counterpart, Lucius, is similarly affected and declares:

I am so striken and subdued, with thy shining eyes, ruddy cheekes, glittring haire, sweete cosses, and lilly white paps, that I neither haue minde to go home, nor to depart hence, but esteeme the pleasure which I shal haue with thee this night, aboue al the ioyes of the world. (Adlington, ch. 15, p. 50; *AA* 3. 19)

The irony in the Apuleian case is that Lucius, unlike his epic counterparts, has no compelling heroic quest from which he is being detained. The traditional opposition between the *militia amoris* and the true vocation of the martial man is recalled when Ubaldo comes upon Rinaldo, steeped in sloth and wantonness, in the garden of Armida.[101] Ubaldo is able to rouse him to conscience with a rebuke that carries real force:

Va l'Asia tutta e va l'Europa in guerra:
chiunque e pregio brama e Cristo adora
travaglia in arme or ne la siria terra.
Te solo, o figlio di Bertoldo, fuora
del mondo, in ozio, un breve angola serra;
te sol de l'universo il moto nulla
move, egregio campion d'una fanciulla.

(*GL* xvi. 32)

(Ubaldo took the time, and thus begun,
'All Europe now and Asia be in war,
And all that Christ adore and fame have won,
In battle strong, in Syria fighting are;
But thee alone, Bertoldo's noble son,
This little corner keeps, exiled far
From all the world, buried in sloth and shame,
A carpet champion for a wanton dame.')[102]

The external world has compelling demands to make upon the individual. But Spenser's problem is that there is, as Lewis puts it, 'no *situation* in *The Faerie*

[101] Cf. Hector's rebuke when he finds Paris dallying in Helen's boudoir (*Iliad* 6. 325 ff.).
[102] *Godfrey of Bulloigne, or The Recoverie of Ierusalem*, trans. Edward Fairfax (London: A. Hatfield for J. Jaggard, 1600), repr. in *Jerusalem Delivered: A Poem by Torquato Tasso*, ed. H. Morley (London: Routledge, 1890), 327.

Queene, no when nor where', no 'core of momentous historical truth'.[103]
The *raison d'être* of Spenser's knights is merely the 'pursuit of praise and
fame' (ii. i. 23. 2) and their behaviour, it must be said, often resembles that of
bellicose schoolboys. Set against this, the image of the warrior, Cymochles,
lying 'Disarm'd' in Phædria's 'loose lap' (ii. vi. 14. 6–7) is actually rather
appealing.

We should bear in mind, however, Phædria's relation to Acrasia and Fotis'
to Pamphile. Phædria's ambiguous role is expressed in her conversation with
Cymochles:

> Vaine man (said she) that wouldst be reckoned
> A stranger in thy house, and ignorant
> Of *Phædria* (for so my name is red)
> Of *Phædria*, thine owne fellow seruant;
> For thou to serve Acrasia thy selfe doest vaunt.[104]

(*FQ* ii. vi. 9. 5–9)

Phædria (like Fotis) is a mediatrix. Cymochles is detained when he goes *away*
from the Bower of Bliss ('thy house') to enact the violent purposes of Atin
against the virtuous person of Guyon; Guyon is diverted as he journeys
towards it to wreak just vengeance upon the murderous Acrasia. Both Phædria
and Fotis maintain a considerable degree of autonomy on island and in
bedroom; there is nothing sinister *per se* in their dallyings with Cymochles
and Lucius.[105] But one is the servant, the other a slave, to evil witches, and
both characters are susceptible to moralizing readings which link their amorous activities with the pernicious propensities of their mistresses.[106] Guyon
and Cymochles are both placed in the same position as Lucius; Guyon alone
resists the temptation.

[103] *Allegory of Love*, 310, 309. Merlin speaks of Artegall being brought back 'to withstand |
The powre of forrein Paynims, which inuade thy land' (*FQ* iii. iii. 27. 8–9), but such a
circumstance is never developed to provide a 'situation'.

[104] In his edn. of the *FQ* (London: Longman, 1977), *ad loc.*, Hamilton gives the gloss ' "since
you serve Acrasia, I serve you". Preferable to the weaker, "I am a servant of Acrasia even as you
are." ' The latter may be dramatically the weaker, but, thematically, it is very important. Phædria
is actually the servant of Acrasia.

[105] Tasso's nymph, in contrast, is employed to beguile Rinaldo into sleep so that Armida can
wreak her vengeance upon him (*GL* xiv. 65).

[106] We can also make a link between Phædria—described as 'immodest Merth' (Argument to
FQ ii. vi)—and her mistress through etymology, ἀκρασία meaning 'incontinence', 'licentiousness', 'immoderate character'.

MUIOPOTMOS OR THE FATE OF THE BUTTERFLIE

Something should be said at this point about another of Spenser's works in which Apuleian elements feature prominently. Only a year separates the publication of *Muiopotmos* from the first appearance of *The Faerie Queene* and the two poems share much in the way of theme and imagery. The Bower of Bliss is partially restored in Clarion's 'gay gardins' where 'Arte with [Nature] contending, doth aspire | T'excell the naturall, with made delights'; the lush pleasures of each provoking in us a similarly ambiguous response.[107] And not content with using 'Cupid and Psyche' as a narrative centrepiece for *The Faerie Queene*, Spenser makes explicit use of the story in the first of his two aetiological narratives—the transformation into a butterfly of Venus' flower-gathering nymph Astery,

> Who being nimbler joynted than the rest,
> And more industrious, gathered more store
> Of all the fields honour, than the others best;
> Which they in secret harts envying sore,
> Tolde *Venus*, when her as the worthiest
> She praisd', that *Cupide* (as they heard before)
> Did lend her secret aide, in gathering
> Into her lap the children of the spring.
>
> Whereof the Goddesse gathering jealous feare,
> Not yet unmindfull, how not long agoe
> Her sonne to *Psyche* secrete love did beare,
> And long it close conceal'd, till mickle woe
> Thereof arose, and manie a rufull teare;
> Reason with sudden rage did overgoe,
> And giving hastie credit to th'accuser,
> Was led away of them that did abuse her.
>
> Eftsoones that Damzel by her heavenly might,
> She turn'd into a winged Butterflie,
> In the wide aire to make her wandring flight;
>
> (*Muiopotmos*, 121–39)

---

[107] *Muiopotmos*, 165–6. All quotations are taken from *The Shorter Poems of Edmund Spenser*, ed. Oram et al. Books I–III of *The Faerie Queene* were published in 1590. The volume of *Complaints* in which *Muiopotmos* appeared in 1591 contains much early work but, as Oram points out (218), *Muiopotmos*' 'very sophistication implies maturity'. According to Maclean (*Edmund Spenser's Poetry*, 484), the poem was probably written in 1590.

Venus' injunction to her Nymphs 'To gather flowres her forhead to array' (line 117) is doubtless based on Ovid's description (*Met.* 5. 391–4) of Proserpina and her flower-laden companions just before her rape; but the gathering is an analogue to the cruel task which Apuleius' Venus sets Psyche of separating the mixed heaps of grain. Astery's success arouses the jealousy of her fellow nymphs in the same way that Psyche's wealth and happiness enrage her sisters; and the nymphs charge that Cupid 'Did lend her secret aide', just as Venus protests to Psyche that 'This is not the labour of thy hands, but rather of his that is amorous of thee'.[108] Venus' response in *Muiopotmos* is swift and drastic, but in seeking to avoid a repetition of the Psyche affair, she actually turns Astery into another sort of ψυχή— the butterfly that commonly appears in ancient art as a symbol of the winged soul.[109]

So far, so good. But to move from the poem to the criticism is to begin to suspect that the coruscating surface of *Muiopotmos* conceals a fundamental opacity.[110] To see it (as many critics have done) merely as a *jeu d'esprit* is to ignore the lapsarian resonance in the description of Clarion's death: 'For loe, the drerie stownd is now arrived, | That of all happines hath us deprived' (414–15).[111] But the allegorizing approach of D. C. Allen, first used in an article in 1956 and then, four years later, in *Image and Meaning*, is also problematic.[112] Allen speaks, in the article, of 'a higher seriousness' in *Muiopotmos* and says of the (notorious) opening lines, 'I am inclined to believe this stanza solemnly intended.'[113] In the revised version, he discusses the

[108] Adlington, ch. 22, p. 96; *AA* 6. 11.

[109] We find (almost contemporaneous) evidence for the play between the spiritual and the entomological significances of Psyche's name in *The Silkwormes and their Flies* (London: V[alentine] S[immes] for Nicholas Ling, 1599), where Thomas Moffet addresses the silkworms' flies with the words, 'Go worthy soules (so witty *Greeks* you name)', explaining the pun in a marginal note at the end of Book 1: 'Ψύχή [*sic*] is all one name in Greeke for a soule and a butterflie' (40). See the facsimile edn. with commentary by V. H. Houliston (Binghamton, NY: MRTS, 1989). D. C. Allen ('On Spenser's *Muiopotmos*', 150) refers us to Scapula's Greek dictionary of 1587.

[110] Recent studies include: R. A. Brinkley, 'Spenser's *Muiopotmos* and the Politics of Metamorphosis', *ELH* 48 (1981), 668–72; A. D. Weiner, 'Spenser's *Muiopotmos* and the Fates of Butterflies and Men', *JEGP* 84 (1985), 203–20; J. H. Morey, 'Spenser's Mythic Adaptations in *Muiopotmos*', *Spenser Studies* 9 (1988): 49–59; J. Dundas, '*Complaints: Muiopotmos, or The Fate of the Butterflie*', in *The Spenser Encyclopedia*, ed. A. C. Hamilton (Toronto: U of Toronto P, 1990), 186–7; E. Mazzola, 'Spenser, Sidney, and Second Thoughts: Mythology and Misgiving in *Muiopotmos*', *Sidney Journal* 18/1 (2000), 57–81; E. C. Brown, 'The Allegory of Small Things: Insect Eschatology in Spenser's *Muiopotmos*', *SP* 99 (2002), 247–67.

[111] Hallet Smith calls the poem 'a light, delicate, *jeu d'esprit*' in 'The Use of Conventions in Spenser's Minor Poems', in *Form and Convention in the Poetry of Edmund Spenser*, ed. W. Nelson (New York, 1961), 122–45, extracted in *Edmund Spenser's Poetry*, ed. Maclean, 714.

[112] *Image and Meaning: Metaphoric Traditions in Renaissance Poetry* (Baltimore: Johns Hopkins P, 1960; rev. 1968).

[113] 'On Spenser's *Muiopotmos*', *SP* 53 (1956), 141–58, at 146, 143.

interpretations of 'Cupid and Psyche' given by Martianus, Fulgentius, and Boccaccio, and continues:

The legend of Cupid and Psyche, hallowed by the Platonic associations of its author, was read as an allegory of the rational soul bound in marriage to Divine Love but disturbed in its marital duties by the lower levels of the mind... [30]... If Spenser had read Apuleius in an original text, he would have learned from the margins what it meant in a spiritual sense. It is not impossible, therefore, that this myth is the key to a possible allegory hidden beneath the literal text of the 'Muiopotmos'... [31]... the *Muiopotmos* could be an allegory of the wandering of the rational soul into error. The title then is not so ironic as it seems, for πότμος as Spenser surely knew, was reserved by the Greeks for the destiny of great heroes: πότμον ἐπισπεῖν, as Homer is accustomed to say. On the literal level there is irony, but it washes away as the allegory unfolds. The clear soul, faultless and sinless, sponsored by piety and wisdom (Minerva) yet ballasted in part by the senses (Venus), can come through heedlessness into the web of evil. For this tragedy, πότμος is an exact term, and Melpomene the proper muse.[114]

F. E. Court rejects, or at least qualifies, Allen's Apuleian exegesis:

... for Allen's interpretation to be completely satisfactory, the Christian Cupid should symbolize the body that seeks and finally unites happily with Psyche, the soul. Allen's analysis seems to me to presuppose a happy ending. But *Muiopotmos* ends tragically with the brutal death of Clarion, and there is not even a suggestion in the final stanzas that Clarion will enjoy an afterlife... I believe... that the reason Spenser did not explicitly use the Cupid-Psyche myth, even if he might have [10] had it in mind, is precisely because it does end happily. He therefore invented the Astery story to reveal the usual fate of mortals who dare for any reason to arouse the anger of the gods. In Spenser's invention Venus reacts in a fashion more traditional with her nature than one would infer from the outcome of the Cupid-Psyche story.[115]

There are, however, more fundamental objections to Allen's approach. Allen assumes that the mythology associated with Psyche is a stable, uniform entity and that we can treat the versions and interpretations of Apuleius, Martianus Capella, Fulgentius, and Boccaccio as though they were interchangeable. 'The Psyche legend... was one of the few pagan myths accepted by early Christians', he tells us, apparently unaware that the Christian use of the butterfly/soul motif on funerary monuments owes nothing to Apuleius.[116] He assumes, moreover, that Renaissance readers were bound

---

[114] *Image and Meaning*, 29–31.

[115] 'The Theme and Structure of Spenser's *Muiopotmos*', *SEL* 10 (1970), 1–15, at 9.

[116] *Image and Meaning*, 30. Allen (30) attributes to Beroaldo in 1500 (rather than Johannes Andreas of Buxis in 1469) the *ed. princ.* of *The Golden Ass* and he perpetuates a common error in making the allegorization of Ovid the work of Thomas Wallensis rather than Petrus Bechorius (39).

to interpret Apuleius' story strictly in terms of the older (often incompatible) exegeses.

In the earlier paper, Allen dismisses the historical allegorizations of the poem with the flourishing observation that 'the art of the poet and that of the historian have almost nothing in common. They cannot wear each others' masks and to suggest that they can is an unhappy error in critical strategy'.[117] Allen fails, however, to perceive that the work of the philosopher and the art of the poet are also fundamentally different. A poet may be inspired by philosophical ideas to write a poem, but the process of poetic composition subjects those ideas to transmutational forces which are beyond the control of the philosopher (and often, indeed, of the poet himself). Once poetry goes beyond explicit didacticism (as found, say, in Lucretius), it ceases to be an unadulterating vessel for ideas.[118] Allen's analysis sounds plausible, cogent even, when separated from the text, but as soon as we put the ideas back into the poem, they cease to be discrete. Allen's pietistic exegesis misrepresents not only the tone, but also the meaning, of the works both of Apuleius and Spenser. The poem takes much of its formal structure from the conventions of mock-epic and pseudo-doxology (the praising of trivial things) and it is impossible, on any reasonable, sensitive reading, to ignore the inflated, mock-heroic, elements: the overstated alliteration of the opening ('I sing of deadly dolorous debate'); the tautologies and pleonasmus of such lines as 'two mightie ones of great estate' (line 3), 'Drawne into armes, and proofe of mortall fight' (line 4), 'sdeignfull scorne' (line 7), 'Full of brave courage and bold hardyhed' (line 27); the comic, legalistic, anthropomorphism of the description of Clarion as 'the eldest sonne and haire' (line 22); the (slightly camp) distorted proportions in the comparison of the 'hairie hide of some wilde beast' which Clarion wears 'about his shoulders broad' (lines 65–6) with the lion's skin worn by Hercules (line 71). The opening stanza may be serio-comic—it may have serious implications—but it is certainly not 'solemnly intended'.

Allen's error, then, is his attempt to articulate the poem too strictly in terms of the medieval interpretations foisted upon the story. We need to distinguish here between what might be called *teleological* and *epideictic* allegory—the one aimed at drawing the reader, through the veil of poetry or fiction, to an understanding of something he otherwise would not know or fully fathom; the other designed

---

[117] 'On Spenser's *Muiopotmos*', 142. My own reading does not preclude the possibility of historical allusion, but since Apuleius' story has no light to shed on the matter, I have hazarded no guesses.

[118] It might be argued that even the *De rerum natura* sets up a dynamic between form and content—it seems strange, after all, to begin a poem extolling Man's freedom from the supernatural with an invocation to the goddess Venus.

to display the artist's skill in weaving, into the weft of his work, philosophical, religious, historical, or political material that will tease and delight the reader in the enactment of discovery and recognition of things already fathomed or familiar. In practice, of course, these categories are not discrete—committed allegory would be crude and doomed if not relieved by some unalloyed display, and performance allegory usually subsumes into itself something of its ostensibly underlying subject-matter—but, broadly speaking, we can say that while *The Pilgrim's Progress* (or even *Animal Farm*) belongs to the category of teleological or committed allegory, both Apuleius' 'Cupid and Psyche' and Spenser's *Muiopotmos* are products of the epideictic school.[119]

Weaving is the obvious metaphor to invoke in describing Spenser's mythographical technique, the embroidered motif of the butterfly being used to connect three separate myths: those of Psyche, Astery, and Arachne. Spenser's treatment of the contest between Arachne and Minerva involves a kind of reactionary subversion—the turning of a received (but in itself subversive) myth into one which reaffirms traditional hierarchies. In Ovid, it is true, Arachne is punished for her hubristic challenge to the goddess and so could appear, to mediaeval and Renaissance exegetes, as an *exemplum* of overweening pride.[120] But the sympathy of the poet(ry) and the audience is clearly on the side of the girl.[121] She not only challenges, she actually defeats, Minerva who rends the victorious tapestry in indignant rage, then drives the girl to suicide by beating her with the shuttle (6. 130–3). Arachne's success can be related to her use of energy, her ability to encapsulate, in living form, what Marlowe was to call the 'headdie ryots, incest, rapes' of the Olympian deities, in contrast to the reasserted divine order, the achieved stasis, of Minerva's picture.[122] There can hardly fail, therefore, to be some irony, some level of self-consciousness or empathetic identificaton, in an artist's depiction of Arachne. Yet Spenser transforms Ovid's account. Not only is his Minerva the true victor of the contest, Arachne's metamorphosis is self-initiated, the spontaneous manifestation of her 'poysonous rancor' (line 344) and envious 'dryrihed' (line 347). Some vestige, some ghost presence, of Ovid's Arachne remains, nevertheless, to haunt *Muiopotmos,* calling attention to the contradictions inherent in the attempt of a poetic artist to condemn the mythological exemplar of the artist's craft. William Nelson's view of *Muiopotmos* as 'a

---

[119] The categories are most obviously mixed in a genre like political satire, particularly in the splenetic form displayed by Swift in *Gulliver's Travels.* (According to these criteria, *Animal Farm* is a political fable rather than a political satire—it lacks the requisite spleen.)

[120] *ut tamen exemplis intelligat aemula laudis,* | *quod pretium speret pro tam furialibus ausis... Met.* 6. 83–4. Thus, e.g., Golding.

[121] Ovid's phrase *caelestia crimina* (*Met.* 6. 131) captures this ambivalence splendidly.

[122] *Hero and Leander,* 144.

delightful teaching of the heavenly lesson that on earth happiness is its own destruction, that only in heaven or by heavenly intervention is the fruitful olive victorious over chaos and death' ignores the Ovidian subtext to Minerva's victory and overlooks the fact that Venus' 'heavenly intervention' is anything but salutary.[123]

Tensions such as these transect the poem as a whole. Apart from the coincidence of names (Ovid's Arachne depicts Asterie in the eagle's grip though Spenser's Astery owes nothing to this particular mythological victim), there is no natural or necessary connection between Spenser's two *aetia*. The linkage between them is (as we often find to our delight in Ovid) quite arbitrary, dependent only upon the token presence in each of a butterfly. And the Astery story merely reinforces the doubts we expressed in our discussion of the Apuleian material in the Garden of Adonis. In *Muiopotmos*, Cupid (at least in his mother's eyes) and Venus herself have both reverted to type—the incorrigible philanderer and the jealous (or over-protective) mother-in-law. The resolution of 'Cupid and Psyche' (already fragile in Apuleius and fractured in *The Faerie Queene*) here disintegrates completely.

Yet this instability in the Apuleian story does not preclude the presence of allegorical elements in the poem. The butterfly's pride-induced destruction is linked implicitly with the Adamic Fall (line 416) and is associated, via etymology and explicit mythological allusion, with the fate of the Soul. At issue is not the presence or absence of such allegorical elements, but the way in which they relate to the poem as an entity. The allegory is not static but dynamic, dialectical. *Muiopotmos*, we have argued, is an epideictic allegory, concerned, first and foremost, with revealing the poet's skill. It invites the reader to discover deeper significances below its glittering surface, even as it destroys the possibility of facile exegetical resolutions. The poetic structure, then, is crystalline; the hermeneutic content, fluid. *Muiopotmos* is both an affirmation and a denial of the primacy of the artistic act, and whether we see it ultimately as exquisite embroidery or ravelled skein, the poem stands as an ironic tribute to Arachne's craft.

CONCLUSIONS

We have seen that Spenser used different parts of *The Golden Ass* in various ways and with varying degrees of success. Meroë and Pamphile contributed to the pool of attributes from which Duessa and Acrasia emerged, and the

---

[123] W. Nelson, *The Poetry of Edmund Spenser: A Study* (New York: Columbia UP, 1963), 74. Quoted by Maclean, ed., *Edmund Spenser's Poetry*, 485.

combination of Homeric, Italian, and Apuleian elements was, by and large, an effective one. The account of Psyche's fall supplied a screen behind which Una could be clothed in the human colours that strict allegory would deny her, while Apuleius' description of her exile and her responses to trials and adversity provided a backdrop against which the virtues both of Una and Guyon could be measured. But it is when Spenser—in *Muiopotmos* as well as in *The Faerie Queene*—makes explicit reference to 'Cupid and Psyche' that the difficulties really begin. The problem with Hamilton, Roche, and Allen is not that they incorporate the philosophical or religious content of 'Cupid and Psyche' into Spenser's narratives, but that they do so statically, rather than dynamically or dialectically. Whether Spenser was attempting Neoplatonic allegory or not in his uses of 'Cupid and Psyche', he cannot have been unaware of the wider, non-allegorical, significance of the novel from which that story derived. The myth enabled Spenser to give a semblance of iconographic resolution to some of the moral and aesthetic tensions within *The Faerie Queene,* yet the resolution proves to be illusory. If we see this failure of resolution as the unforeseen (and/or inevitable) consequence of an Elizabethan's attempt at static allegory, we are likely to belong to one of two classes of readers: those who regard the poem from the point of view of literary history as a kind of cultural dinosaur, impressive in itself and important in its influence on the greater works that succeeded it, but ultimately small-brained and doomed to extinction; or those (the 'perverse school') who detect, behind the Protestant mask of 'our sage and serious Spenser', a poetic Acrasian, unable to restrain himself from undermining the proclaimed 'generall end' of the poem.

It would be difficult (even were access possible) to love the mind of a man who had written *A General View of Ireland*, let alone the man himself who had put such ideas into practice; and what we know of Spenser suggests that we should perhaps join the first class of readers and take (and damn) him at his own word. Modern critical fashion (as promoted by Stanley Fish) would incline us to the second class, seeing the text as, inevitably, 'a self-consuming artifact' and the unfinished condition of the poem would support such a view.[124] But whether we think in terms of authorial intention or of the repeated, renewing constituting, through reading, of a text composed in an alien age, a third option is available: to see the whole of *The Faerie Queene* in those dramatic, dynamic, dialectical terms of which we have spoken. Large parts of the poem are, of course, read in such a way by the vast majority of critics. Everyone agrees that characters like Redcrosse and Guyon, though

---

[124] See, generally, *Self-Consuming Artifacts: The Experience of Seventeenth-Century Literature* (Berkeley and Los Angeles: U of California P, 1972).

allegorical, are not infallible: they are tempted, they are ignorant, they are led into error and then led back (together, it is hoped, with the reader) to the ways of understanding. And in the allegorical depictions, say, of the destructive force of the Reformation or the execution of Mary, Queen of Scots, we are meant to feel the aesthetic and human costs of what are presented as morally necessary events. But the Apuleian exegesis provided here suggests that the dialectic is far more profound and pervasive than is generally credited, drawing into itself the Apuleian figure of Pleasure (unstably emblematized in the Garden of Adonis) and the Fotis-like Phædria who mediates deliciously between the often unattractive (and morally uncompelling) world of Spenser's knights and the superficially appealing (but ultimately sinister) Bower of Bliss. Yet this is dialectic without resolution: the thesis (Virtue) and antithesis (Pleasure) do not produce a stable synthesis. Apuleius fabricated such a resolution of opposing modes in the eleventh book of *The Golden Ass*, but he appears (to Winklerians, at least) to have taken pains to make that resolution as problematic as possible. Spenser, faced with an increasingly violent dialectic that no rhetorical sleight of hand could resolve, chose a different course. Not only does he destroy (in a brilliant feat of imaginative transposition) the iconographic foundation of the poem by elevating his own love (instead of Queen Elizabeth) to be a fourth Grace (*FQ* vi. x. 27), he signals the approaching close of the work by making his alter ego, Colin Clout, break his bagpipe (vi. x. 18. 5).[125]

[125] Cf. *Shepheardes Calender*, 'April', lines 113–16, and 'January', line 72.

11

Shakespeare's Bottom and Apuleius' *Ass*

Shakespearian criticism has been slow to embrace *The Golden Ass* as a significant source. As long ago as 1807, Francis Douce discerned a relationship between the witches in *Macbeth* ('grease that's sweaten | From the murderer's gibbet', IV. i. 65–6) and Pamphile's tendency to cut 'the lumps of flesh from such as were hanged' (*AA* 3. 17). Douce noted that Adlington's translation was 'a book certainly used by Shakespeare on other occasions'; but it was not until the 1940s that interest was renewed.[1] In a ground-breaking study, D. T. Starnes detected Apuleian influence in one of Shakespeare's poems (*Venus and Adonis*) and eight of his plays, concluding that 'Shakespeare seems to have read *The Golden Ass* shortly before the beginning of his dramatic career' and then reread it 'after a period of almost ten years'.[2]

Starnes's main findings can be summarized as follows:

The Comedy of Errors: Antipholus of Syracuse's impressions of Ephesus ('Dark-working sorcerers that change the mind, | Soul-killing witches that deform the body', I. ii. 99–100) echo Lucius' response to Hypata (*AA* 2. 1) and the powers of Thessalian witches (as ascribed to Meroe and Pamphile, and described by the mutilated Thelyphron). The 'recurrent statements of Dromio that he is transformed into an ass and does the service of that beast' (1022) reflect the experience of Lucius.

The Two Gentlemen of Verona: Valentine's rescue of Silvia (IV. i and V. iii–iv) mimics Tlepolemus' deliverance of Charite (*AA* 7. 5–13).

A Midsummer Night's Dream: Bottom's affair with Titania (III. i; IV. i) reflects Lucius' encounter with the Corinthian *matrona* (*AA* 10. 19–22).

Macbeth: The witches' incantation (IV. i) adopts 'the basic pattern' (1036) from Fotis' description of Pamphile (*AA* 3. 17–18).

Antony and Cleopatra: The Queen's abuse of the messenger (II. v. 24 ff.) recalls Venus' treatment of Psyche (*AA* 6. 9). The description of Venus in the

---

[1] *Illustrations of Shakspeare and of Ancient Manners*, 2 vols. (London: Longman, Hurst, Rees, & Orme, 1807), i. 398.

[2] 'Shakespeare and Apuleius', *PMLA* 60 (1945), 1021–50, at 1050.

pantomime at Corinth lends details to Enobarbus' portrait of Cleopatra in her barge (II. ii. 202–18).

Cymbeline: Cornelius fills the role of Apuleius' 'sage and ancient Physitian' in the story of the wicked stepmother (*AA* 10. 2–12), averting the Queen's murderous design by supplying a sleeping-potion in place of poison. Cymbeline's exclamation at the restoration of Imogen and his lost sons ('O, what am I? | A mother to the birth of three?', v. v. 368–9) derives from the conclusion of the same tale: 'Behold how the fortune of the old man was changed, who thinking to be deprived of all his race and posterity, was in one moment made the father of two Children' (Adlington, ch. 44; = *AA* 10. 12).

The Winter's Tale: The devouring of Antigonus by a bear (III. iii) resembles the fate of the boy who tormented Lucius (*AA* 7. 24–6). The punishments which Autolycus imagines for the shepherd and his son (IV. iv. 798 ff.) derive from the tortures proposed for Charite (*AA* 6. 31–2) and those actually inflicted upon the adulterous servant (*AA* 8. 22).

The Tempest: Ariel and the invisible spirits owe something to Zephyrus and to Psyche's experience in the palace of Cupid. The masque of Iris, Ceres, and Juno celebrating the betrothal of Miranda and Ferdinand (IV. i) draws on Psyche's encounter with Ceres and Juno (*AA* 6. 2–4) and the wedding entertainments (*AA* 6. 23–4).

Venus and Adonis: The descriptions of the boar and the death of Adonis absorb details from the hunting scene involving Tlepolemus and Thrasyllus (*AA* 8. 4–6).

The last sixty years have seen a trickle of articles (mainly directed towards elucidating Apuleian presence in *A Midsummer Night's Dream*) and a monograph.[3] In *Shakespeare's Favorite Novel: A Study of 'The Golden Asse' as Prime Source*, J. J. M. Tobin confirms and extends Starnes' discoveries, concluding that Shakespeare relied on Apuleius throughout his career, and made 'use of *The Golden Asse* in more than thirty of his works'.[4] Indeed, the importance to Shakespeare of Apuleius was 'scarcely surpassed by Holinshed, Ovid, and Plutarch'.[5]

Tobin has exposed many important congruences between Apuleius' narrative and Shakespearian drama, but his analysis is often marred by a reluctance

---

[3] Studies by Sister M. Generosa, J. Dover Wilson, F. Kermode, J. A. McPeek, and A.-P. de Prinsac are discussed *infra*.

[4] (Lanham, Md: UP of America, 1984), 161. The only plays or poems in which Tobin (*SFN*, 165) does not discern Apuleian influence are *1* and *3 Henry VI*, *The Taming of the Shrew*, *The Rape of Lucrece*, *King John*, *Richard II*, *The Merchant of Venice*, *As You Like It*, *Twelfth Night*, *Henry VIII*, and *The Two Noble Kinsmen*.

[5] Tobin, *SFN*, p. xi.

to admit that other influences might account for an alleged Apuleian presence in any one passage.[6] Tobin wishes to take us 'as close as we can get' to 'the heart of Shakespeare's creative imagination' (1), and much of his argument depends on minute verbal correspondences which would only be apparent to someone making a close comparison of the three texts (Apuleius, Adlington, and Shakespeare). In many instances, one can only say that one is unconvinced by the supposed parallels, and uncertain what their hermeneutic significance would be, were the case for them made out. It is difficult, for example, to be persuaded by Tobin's identification of Polonius with Apuleius' fishmonger (*AA* 1. 24–5), or by his attempt to link Ophelia's 'They say the owl was a baker's daughter' (IV. v) with Pamphile's avine metamorphosis and with the baker's daughter who learns of her father's murder in a dream (*AA* 9. 31).[7]

Tobin does, however, identify several examples of Apuleian influence which deserve to be better known. In the *Merry Wives of Windsor* he reveals (60–2) an Apuleian dimension to the themes of transformation, and connects Falstaff's ''Tis time I were choked with a piece of toasted cheese' (v. v. 138–9) to Lucius' account (*AA* 1. 4) of eating meat 'fried with the flower of cheese and barly' which sticks in his throat so that 'I was well nigh choked' (Adlington, ch. 2). Tobin indicates (62–7) how the asininity of Dogberry in *Much Ado about Nothing* derives not only from Apuleius directly but also from intermediate sources such as Harvey's *Pierce's Supererogation* which includes the *apologia* of asses that we encountered in Chapter 8 (*supra*).

It is among the tragedies, however, that Tobin locates the most persuasive and enriching parallels. He demonstrates the many uses to which Shakespeare put the mandragora motif from *AA* 10. 2–12, most obviously in *Romeo and Juliet* and *Cymbeline*, but also in *Hamlet*.[8] The Gertrude-Claudius-Hamlet nexus involves what he calls 'the diffraction' of the narrative of the wicked stepmother (*AA* 10. 2–12) 'into the elements of the sexual tension between a son and a mother (one married to the son's step-father), a bedchamber interview, and the subsequent drinking of poisoned wine by an unintended victim'. Tobin sees Ophelia as a passive Psyche figure, deriving hints for her suicide from Psyche's determination to drown herself after Cupid's desertion (*AA* 5. 25); and he suggests that Shakespeare 'modelled the watery descent of Ophelia upon the airy flight of Psyche' who was

caried from the hill with a meek winde, which retained her garmentes up, and by little and litle brought her downe into a deepe valley, where she was laide in a bedde of most sweete and fragrant flowers'.[9]

---

[6] The review by R. F. Hardin, *RPL* 8 (1985), 297–9, tempers damning criticism with limited praise.

[7] Tobin, *SFN*, 74–5 and 76–8.

[8] Ibid. 41–2.   [9] Adlington, ch. 22; *AA* 4. 35; Tobin, *SFN*, 84.

Ophelia falls from the boughs of a willow overhanging

> the weeping brook. Her clothes spread wide
> And, mermaid-like, awhile they bore her up

(IV. vii. 176–7)

Hamlet is usually dated to 1600, and we can buttress Tobin's claim by glancing across to an exactly contemporary passage influenced by Apuleius, the account (preserved in Allott's *Englands Parnassus*, 1600) of Psyche's sisters' Zephyr-assisted descent which (as we saw in Chapter 8) probably derives from the play ('a booke Called The golden Ass & Cupid & Psiches') produced by Dekker, Chettle, and Day in the same year. Dekker's 'purple Violets' may have influenced the 'long purples' in the 'coronet weeds' that Ophelia tries to hang on the 'pendant boughs' (IV. vii. 70–3); and the description of 'the curled forehead of a banke, | That sweld with camomill, ouer whose bewtie | A wanton Hyacinth held downe his head' may have provided an imaginative bridge between Psyche's descent and the riparian aspects of Ophelia's death.[10] We might also observe (as another addendum to Tobin's account) the similarity between Ophelia's funeral cortège (the King and Queen coming after the coffin) and the procession of mourners accompanying Psyche (daughter of a king and queen) to the rock: 'they went to bringe this sorrowfull spouse, not to her marriage, but to her final ende and buriall' (Adlington, ch. 22; *AA* 4. 34). Queen Gertrude laments for the daughter-in-law that should have been:

> I hop'd thou shouds't have been my Hamlet's wife;
> I thought thy bride-bed to have deck'd, sweet maid,
> And not have strew'd thy grave

(V. i. 267–9)

Psyche's wedding to a 'high-born husband' (*generosum . . . maritum, AA* 4. 34) led to marital desertion and the contemplation of suicide by drowning and by leaping from a height—but the eventual outcome was happy. An awareness of the comedic configurations of this underlying myth enhances the poignancy of Ophelia's tragedy.

In *King Lear*, Shakespeare seems to have recognized an affinity between Goneril and Regan, the jealous sisters of Psyche, and the wicked sisters of the Cinderella fairy-tale tradition. Tobin also traces the influence of 'Cupid and Psyche' in *Othello*, finding a close correspondence between the murder scene (V. ii: '*Desdemona in her bed. Enter Othello with a light*') and Psyche's approach—razor in hand—to the sleeping Cupid (*AA* 5. 22–3). Othello's

---

[10] Similarly, in Adlington's translation (ch. 22), the *fontem vitreo latice perlucidum* which she sees (*AA* 5. 1) is 'a runninge river as cleere as Cristall'.

address to his light ('thou flaming minister') echoes Apuleius' apostrophe ('O rashe and bolde lampe the vile ministery of love', Adlington, ch. 22). The 'rasor turned his edge' at the sight of Cupid, while Othello, having kissed Desdemona, declares: 'O balmy breath, that dost almost persuade | Justice to break her sword!' (v. ii. 16–17). Othello's tears wake his intended victim just as the oil from Psyche's lamp wakes Cupid.

While the play hinges on the transformation engendered in Othello by Iago who revels in the thought of being rewarded 'for making him egregiously an ass' (ii. i. 317–18), Shakespeare uses Apuleius' *Apologia* in constructing Othello's defence of himself (i. iii) 'against the charge that he had gained the love of his wife by the use of charms, drugs, and magic'.[11] Tobin illuminates at least one aspect of what Coleridge called Iago's 'motiveless malignity' by showing that 'Iago's Spartan taciturnity in the face of torture at the end of the play derive[s] from the behavior of the guilty servant exposed by the ancient physician': 'neither the feare of the wheele or any other torment according to the use of the Grecians, which were ready prepared, no, nor yet the fire could enforce him to confesse the matter, so obstinate and grounded was he in his mischievous mind'.[12]

The remarkable climax of *The Winter's Tale* is an obvious reworking of the Pygmalion myth as the 'statue' of Hermione appears to come to life (v. iii), but it has an Apuleian inflection. The Third Gentleman describes the statue as 'a piece... newly perform'd by that rare Italian master, Julio Romano, who, had he himself eternity and could put breath into his work, would beguile nature of her custom, so perfectly is he her ape' (v. ii. 104–8). Explicit references to artists are rare in Shakespeare, and Tobin usefully draws our attention to Giulio Romano's Sala di Psiche in the Palazzo Te in Mantua and to the eye-deceiving realism of the statuary in Byrrhena's house.[13]

A MIDSUMMER NIGHT'S DREAM

Of all Shakespeare's works, the play in which a man is given an ass's head would seem to offer the greatest potential as a locus of Apuleian influence. Francis Douce identified the 'receipt for making a man resemble an ass' given in Scot's *The Discoverie of Witchcraft* (1584) as the immediate source of Bottom's transformation.[14] Other critics have seen, as a more important

---

[11] Tobin, *SFN*, 87.   [12] Ibid. 90; Adlington, ch. 44; = *AA* 10. 10.

[13] Tobin, *SFN*, 152–3; *AA* 2. 4–5.

[14] *Illustrations of Shakspeare*, i. 193. The passage occurs in Bk xiii, ch. 19 of Reginald Scot, *The Discoverie of Witchcraft*, ed. B. Nicholson (London: Elliot Stock, 1886), 258.

influence, the quip made about '*Bodins* asseheaded man' during the discussion of asinine transformations in Book V (where Scot twice mentions Apuleius).[15] Scot's task is to expose ('discover') the illusory nature of necromancy and, in so doing, protect English women from the hysterical attacks on alleged witches being made on the Continent.

The Renaissance treatises on witchcraft address issues which are fundamental to all verbal art: the relationship between reality and illusion, essence and appearance, reason and imagination. In depicting Bottom's asinine 'translation' on stage, Shakespeare is giving dramatic form to a debate that has profound philosophical, theological, and social implications for both the Middle Ages and the Renaissance. The issue is this: can the Devil or his agents (witches and demons) transform men into beasts? The metamorphosis of Lucius is intimately involved in this debate.[16]

The specific details of Bottom's 'translation' may owe more to the tradition of assification preserved by Augustine, William of Malmesbury, Jean Bodin, and Reginald Scot, than to Apuleius, but other instances put it beyond question that Shakespeare was drawing widely and deeply on *The Golden Ass* in constructing the play. Puck's knavish tricks recall those of the naughty Cupid; Oberon inflicts upon Titania ('Wake when some vile thing is near', II. ii. 33) the same punishment unsuccessfully prescribed by Venus for Psyche; and the assified Lucius enjoys the love of a noblewoman, rich and beautiful, while Bottom enchants, at first sight, 'a spirit of no common rate' (III. i. 147).[17]

Annie-Paule de Prinsac also draws a comparison between Bottom's 'désir profond de multiplicité' (his wish to play all parts: tyrant, Thisbe, lion, 'sucking dove', and nightingale) and Lucius' desire to indulge his curiosity by becoming an owl.[18] Both are rewarded for their metamorphic aspirations by being transformed into the antitheses of what they desired. The differences, however, are significant. Lucius is the handsome young nobleman, credulous, curious, prone to flights of airy fancy. Bottom is the 'shallowest thick-skin' of the 'rude mechanicals', indomitable in his literal-mindedness.[19] Lucius is desperate to escape his asinine form, acutely conscious of the contrast between his bestial appearance and the human intelligence (and appetite) it

---

[15] '*Bodins* asseheaded man must either eat haie or nothing', Scot, Bk. v, ch. 5, p. 79. For Apuleius, see Bk. v, ch. 1, pp. 72–3, and Bk. v, ch. 4, p. 78.

[16] See, e.g., *Ioannis VVieri de praestigiis daemonum, & incantationibus ac ueneficiis libri sex*, 5th edn. (Basil: Ex officina Oporiniana, 1577), col. 268. For a much more detailed discussion, see R. H. F. Carver, 'The Protean Ass' (University of Oxford D.Phil Thesis, 1991), 279–87.

[17] For a broader summary, see Tobin, *SFN*, 32–40.

[18] 'La Métamorphose de Bottom et *L'Âne d'or*', *Études anglaises* 34 (1981), 61–71, at 63.

[19] III. ii. 13 and 9.

conceals. Bottom (whose asininity is merely cephalic) is unaware of his own translation (his retort to Snout, 'You see an ass-head of your own, do you?', is dramatically ironic).[20] Bottom is loquacious where Lucius is dumb. Lucius, repelled by the hay provided, longs for human food, while seeking the roses that will restore him to his original form. Bottom, in contrast, nurtures a bestial appetite in a still-human belly ('good hay, sweet hay, hath no fellow', IV. i. 33), while enjoying the attentions of Titania, whose promise to 'stick musk-roses in thy sleek smooth head' (IV. i. 3) gains added irony from its Apuleian significations.[21]

It can, of course, be dangerous to cite differences between texts as evidence of filiation; but the Apuleian echoes are sufficiently loud to suggest that Shakespeare is consciously playing on the figure of Lucius, creating a rich resonance through disparity. Prinsac observes, 'Il semble même que Shakespeare soit complu à certains jeux de miroirs, ne nous donnant que des images inversées de l'original'.

Some critics go even further, making *The Golden Ass* a hermeneutic key to the play. James McPeek uses, as a metaphor for Shakespeare's reworking of 'Cupid and Psyche', the image of a mosaic, 'shattered into its original *tesserae*, which Shakespeare has picked up and rearranged to suit his own design'.[22] Yet he is also at pains to read the play in terms of the story:

In her final patient submission to Oberon's will (IV. i. 60–66), Titania becomes a Psyche, whose patient submission to the will of Venus attests her worthiness of Cupid's love.

Frank Kermode writes:

On this narrative of Apuleius, for the Renaissance half-hidden in the enveloping commentary of Beroaldus, great superstructures of platonic and Christian allegory had been raised; and there is every reason to suppose that these mysteries are part of the flesh and bone of *A Midsummer Night's Dream*.[23]

Tobin carries this even further:

One can argue that Cupid and Psyche, like Pyramus and Thisbe, had been allegorized as the soul's search for Christ and that the presence of both myths in the comedy, implicitly and explicitly, indicates that all this funny business about error, love and

---

[20] III. i. 110–11. Bottom's remark, 'I am such a tender ass, if my hair do but tickle me, I must scratch' (IV. 1. 25), is in a similarly ironic vein. It recalls Lucius' narrational asides, 'poor ass'.

[21] Roses, we remember, are the means whereby Lucius can be restored to his human form.

[22] 'The Psyche Myth and *A Midsummer Night's Dream*', *SQ* 23 (1972), 69–79, at 69. Cf. Tobin, *SFN*, 38.

[23] 'The Mature Comedies', in *Stratford-upon-Avon Studies 3: Early Shakespeare*, ed. J. R. Brown and B. Harris (London: Arnold, 1961), 211–27, at 218.

blindness, might be more serious than audiences in the theatre and study usually view it. But we correctly think of Shakespeare as being unlike his contemporaries in his avoidance of allegorized myth.[24] Nevertheless, *A Midsummer Night's Dream* is a special play and a specific asinine transformation is a most special occurrence on the stage. Accordingly, there have interpretations of the play which suggest that a philosophical meaning is clearly present in the comedy.[25]

Just how allegorical a reading one wishes to elicit from the play in light of the allegorical tradition of the tale and the ambivalent ass-motif as understood in the Renaissance will depend upon one's willingness to admit *A Midsummer Night's Dream* as a special case within a canon of non-allegorical plays. It is a special case and we should, like Lucius, be sufficiently curious to take a chance, for whatever the initial humiliating experience the ultimate reward is very great indeed.[26]

To Kermode and Tobin one might say several things: Beroaldo's is the most famous, but it is certainly not the only Latin edition of the Renaissance. The novel was available to sixteenth-century readers in editions without any 'enveloping commentary' and, more importantly, in the vernacular. Adling-ton's prefatory material makes no mention of 'Cupid and Psyche' (though the title page advertises 'an excellent Narration of the Mariage of Cupide and Psiches'—the emphasis being surely upon the narrative power of the tale rather than upon any allegorical attractions). There is, moreover, nothing explicitly Christian about Adlington's exegesis of the book as a whole (the closest he comes is his mention of the punitive transformation of 'Nabuchad-nezzar' and 'the sweet Rose of reason and vertue, which the rather by meditation of praier we may assuredly attaine'). Beroaldo (1500) and Bussi (1469) merely refer us to Fulgentius who identifies Psyche's royal father with God (the Queen being Matter) and Cupid with Desire ('which is attracted both to good and evil'). Boccaccio does indeed identify Cupid as 'honourable Love or God himself' (though—under the influence of Martianus Capella— he gives the same godly role to Psyche's father, Apollo), but he is careful to remain within the borders of Platonic and Aristotelian theology, and makes no attempt to interpret the myth in the light of Christian revelation. The first English work which allegorizes the tale as the 'soul's search for Christ' is Dr Joseph Beaumont's massive poem *Psyche, or Love's Mystery*, 'displaying the intercourse betwixt Christ and the soul', which did not appear until 1648.

All three critics rely on elastic and conflationary readings of the two texts. 'It is scarcely conceivable, though the point is disputed,' Kermode declares,

---

[24] [Tobin's note:] Douglas Bush, 'Classical Myth in Shakespeare's Plays', in *Elizabethan and Jacobean Studies Presented to F. P. Wilson*, ed. H. Davis and H. Gardner (Oxford: Clarendon, 1959), 71.

[25] Tobin, *SFN*, 38.   [26] Ibid. 40.

'that the love-affair between Titania and Bottom is not an allusion to *The Golden Ass*.'[27] Venus' attempt to make Psyche 'fall in love with the most miserablest creature living, the most poore, the most crooked, and the most vile' is echoed in Oberon's vindictive decree that Titania should 'Wake when some vile thing is near' and be immediately enamoured; while Bottom's 'most rare vision' recalls Lucius' Isiac epiphany at the beginning of Book 11:

What they [*sc.* Lucius and Bottom] have in common is transformation and an experience of divine love. Bottom has known the love of the triple goddess in a vision.

The only problem with Kermode's analysis is that, in conflating (as Shakespeare himself has done) the figures of Titania, Psyche, and Isis, he overlooks the most important parallel between the play and novel: the love of Titania for Bottom and of the Pasiphaë-like *matrona* for the asinine Lucius.[28] This association with bestiality should be sufficient, in itself, to scotch any attempt at a discrete identification of Titania with Isis (though it need not preclude an assimilation of Isis into the already complex hermeneutics of the Titania-Bottom interlude).

Titania and the Libidinous *Matrona*

Most critics today are willing to concede that the Titania–Bottom interlude owes at least something to Apuleius' account of the libidinous *matrona* in Book 10. Where they differ is in the degree of resonance they are prepared to allow between the two texts. C. and M. Martindale, while endorsing the recent critical emphasis on 'the erotic nature of the play', refer to those 'salacious' critics who 'speculate on whether Titania actually copulates with Bottom'.[29] Such speculation is not, however, merely prurient. One has only to turn to Leviticus to see the orthodox position on such congresses:

And if a woman come to anie beast, and lie therewith, then thou shalt kil the woman and the beast: they shal dye the death, their blood *shal be* vpon them.[30]

[27] 'The Mature Comedies', 218.

[28] Ovid, *Met.* 8. 131–7, relates how Pasiphaë, the wife of Minos, fell in love with a bull and bore a 'hybrid offspring' (*discordis...fetus*, 8. 133)—the Minotaur.

[29] *Shakespeare and the Uses of Antiquity*, 66. According to Brooks (Arden edn., p. cxv n. 1), 'even a controlled suggestion of carnal bestiality is surely impossible: jealous Oberon will not have cast his spell to cuckold himself. Her dotage is imaginative and emotional.'

[30] Lev. 20: 16. *The Geneva Bible: A Facsimile of the 1560 Edition*, introd. Lloyd E. Berry (Madison: U of Wisconsin, 1969), fol. 55ᵛ.

Bottom, it might be argued, is only a beast from the neck up, and references to bestiality are therefore unwarranted. But the use of partial attributes to suggest a whole is a well-established dramatic convention and Bottom's own bestial appetites ('good hay, sweet hay, hath no fellow', iv. i. 33) as well as Titania's perception of him ('Methought I was enamour'd of an an ass', iv. i. 76) establish him, at important moments in the text, as being fully asinine.[31] The ass, for the Renaissance, is a many-hided beast, but the attributes paramount here are those of foolishness (compare the ass's ears of Midas and those mentioned by Benvolio in *Doctor Faustus*, iv. v. 22, as well as Oberon's caustic 'Hateful fool', iv. i. 48) and of lasciviousness (the ass was credited with being, proportionally, the best endowed of all beasts). Certainly, Titania's language ('Lead him to my bower'; 'Lamenting some enforced chastity', iii. ii. 190, 194) and the timing of her exits and her entrances, imply that she has in mind something more than chaste caresses (Oberon's complex simile, 'Like tears, that did their own disgrace bewail', iv. i. 55, is surely suggestive). This leads to yet another joke within a joke. In pseudo-Lucian and Apuleius, it is the size of the hero's member, as much as his clever tricks, that attracts the attention of the young noblewoman.[32] Titania, condemned to a degrading passion for an ass, cannot even enjoy the compensation of an ass's generous endowment.

Shakespearian plays are generally reticent about their debts to earlier texts, but no one who has read Apuleius' account (and our research has shown that we can reasonably expect an educated Elizabethan to have been familiar with *The Golden Ass*, and a regular theatregoer to have come into contact with at least some of it) can fail to retain it as a ghost presence when confronted by the love-scenes between Titania and Bottom. Apuleius supplies the erotic details that Shakespeare, out of a sense of theatrical propriety or in the spirit of intertextual delight, chose to suppress.[33] McPeek observes:

The resemblances in manner are patent, the essential difference between the two episodes being that Shakespeare's delicate scene from its first staging up to recent times has apparently conveyed to its audience no hint of forbidden lust (Jan Kott's view presents a Shakespeare all too modern).[34]

[31] On the dramatic convention, see C. and M. Martindale, *Shakespeare and the Uses of Antiquity*, 65.
[32] In pseudo-Lucian's *Onos* (56), when the hero returns, in human form, to the woman he had pleasured as an ass, he is rudely ejected when she discovers that he has lost the only thing that had attracted her to him in the first place.
[33] Prinsac argues (70) that Shakespeare 'ait choisi d'effacer toute référence sexuelle' in the very place 'où il aurait pu être le plus grivois'. The description of the Bottom–Titania interlude may not be 'saucy', but it is certainly suggestive.
[34] 'The Psyche Myth', 77.

Harold F. Brooks follows Dover Wilson in seeing this delicacy as the result of a modulation of key:

a modulation of the coarse love made to the ass by a lascivious matron, into the key of the blandishments lavished upon him by a charming captive princess would yield something like Titania's courtship of Bottom.[35]

David Ormerod characterizes Apuleius' account as 'a graphic and debauched description of the depths of bestial love'; but this is misleading.[36] In fact, the tonal divergence between the two passages (at least in translation) is not particularly great. The love-scene deserves quoting in full:

There fortuned to be amongst the assembly, a noble and rich matron, that conceiued much delight to behold me, and could find no remedy to her passions and disordinate appetite, but continually desired to haue her pleasure with me, as *Pasiphae* had with a Bull. In the end she promised a great reward to my keeper for the custodie of me for one night . . . [180] there were foure Eunuchs that laie on a bed of down on the ground with boulsters accordingly for vs to lie on, the couerlet was of cloth of gold, and the pillowes soft and tender, whereon the delicate matron had accustomed to lay her head, then the Eunuches not minding to delay any longer the pleasure of their mistres, closed the doors of the chamber and departed away: within the chamber were lamps that gave a clear light al the place ouer: Then she put off all her garments to her naked skinne, and taking the lamp that stood next to her, began to annoint al her body with balme, and mine likewise, but especially my nose, which done she kissed me, not as they accustome to do at the stewes, or in brothell houses, or in the curtisant schooles for gaine of mony, but purely, sincerely, and with great affection, casting out these and like louing words: Thou art he whom I loue, thou art he whome I only desire, without thee I cannot liue, and other like preamble of talk, which women can vse well inough, whenas they minde to shew or declare their burning passions and great affection of loue: Then shee tooke me by the halter and caste me downe vpon the bed, which was nothing strange vnto me, considering that she was so beutifull a matron, and I so wel bolen out with wine, & perfumed with balme, whereby I was readily prepared for the purpose: But nothing greeued me so much as to thinke how I should with my huge and great legs imbrace so faire a matron, or how I should touch her fine, deintie, and silken skinne, with my hard hoofes, or howe it was possible to kisse her soft, pretie and ruddie lips, with my monstrous mouth and stonie teeth, or how she, who was yong and tender, could be able to receiue me.

And I verely thought, if I should hurte the woman by any kinde of meane, I should be throwne to the wild beastes: But in the meane season she kissed me, and

---

[35] Introd. to Arden edn. (London: Methuen, 1979), p. lix; cf. J. Dover Wilson, *Shakespeare's Happy Comedies* (London: Faber, 1962), 215–19. Titania's offer to send a 'venturous fairy' to 'fetch thee new nuts' (IV. i. 34–5) is held to be an echo of Charite's offer to the (asinine) Lucius as he carries her in flight from the robbers' cave (*AA* 6. 28).

[36] 'A *Midsummer Night's Dream*: The Monster in the Labyrinth', *Shakespeare Studies* 11 (1978), 39–52, at 45. Cf. Tobin, *SFN*, 39.

loo[181]ked in my mouth with burning eyes, saying: I hold thee my cunnie, I holde thee my nops, my sparrow, and therwithall she eftsoones imbraced my bodie round about, & had her pleasure with me, wherby I thought the mother of *Minotarus* did not causelesse quench her inordinate desire with a Bull. When night was passed, with much joy and smal sleepe. The Matrone went before day to my keeper, to bargaine with him another night ... [37]

Adlington's marginal comment, 'Here I have left out certain lines *propter honestatem*' serves the dual purpose of advertising the translator's modesty while inviting the curious reader to consult the (readily available) original:

Sed angebar planè, non exili metu reputans, quemadmodum ... quamquam ex vnguicu-lis perpruriscens, mulier tam vastum genitale susciperet. Heu me, qui dirupta nobili femina, bestiis obiectus, munus instructurus sim mei domini! ... vanas fuisse cogitationes meas, ineptumq́ue monstrat metum. artissimè namq́ue complexa, tum me prorsus, sed totum recipit. Illa verò, quotiens ei parcens nates recellebam; accedens totiens nisu rabido, & spinam prehendens meam, appliciore nexu inhærebat: vt hercules etiam deesse mihi aliquid, ad supplendam eius libidinem crederem: (ed. Colvius, 1588)

(Yet I was wracked by no small fear as I considered how ... the woman, although itching from the tips of her toes, could receive so vast a member. Woe unto me: were the noblewoman to be ruptured, I should be thrown to the beasts and provide my master with a public entertainment.... [S]he showed me that my thoughts were in vain and my fear unfounded. For, locking me tight in her embrace, she drew in absolutely all of me— yes, all of me. Indeed, as often as I shoved my buttocks back to spare her, she came onto me with a frenzied pressure and, gripping my spine, clung in a closer embrace, so that, by Hercules, I believed that even I did not have enough to satisfy her desire ...)

Tonally, this is a complex scene. We experience a kind of defamiliarization in reverse. Apuleius makes the unnatural appear surprisingly natural: *nil noui, nihilque difficile.*[38] Critics have noted the correspondence between the four eunuchs in the *matrona's* bedchamber and the four fairies who attend Bottom, and between the endearments of the *matrona* and those used by Titania. But there are also more subtle congruences. The comedy in the Bottom–Titania scene comes from the interplay between the panegyrical language of the enamoured Titania and the complacent opportunism of her asinine swain. In the Apuleian version, it depends upon the contrast between the delicacy of the *matrona's* endearments ('my nops, my sparrow') and her importunate receptivity to the ass's member.

[37] Adlington, ch. 46, pp. 179–81 (1596). I have only found the marginal note *propter honestatem* in the the 1566 edn.

[38] It is just possible that Bottom's indomitable complacency was suggested by this single line in Apuleius: 'which was nothing strange vnto me, considering that she was so beutifull a matron, and I so well bolen out with wine, & perfumed with balme' (*quippe cum nil noui nihilque difficile facturus mihi videre ...,* Adlington, ch. 46, p. 180; *AA* 10. 21).

Prinsac, commenting on the Titania–Bottom scene, speaks of a 'union qui, par une étrange alchimie, dépasse le burlesque'.[39] This, surely, is exactly right. The scene is not merely ridiculous. The normal aesthetic and moral parameters are displaced: Bottom actually becomes—at least for a few moments—beautiful. Where Prinsac stumbles is in her evaluation of the tonal complexity of Apuleius. She talks of a 'moralisme intransigeant, qui noircit Lucius afin de le mieux blanchir ensuite', contrasting the achievement of Shakespeare who, 'avec beaucoup plus de nuances, substitue un esthétisme qui rapelle d'avantage les *Métamorphoses* d'Ovide'.

There is no shortage of nuance in Apuleius—he is, after all, in many respects, a prose-Ovid. If the description of the *matrona*'s fragile innocence (ambrosial lips, milk-and-honey limbs) competes with the evidence of her carnal capacity, so too, the purity and sincerity of her kisses are undercut by the business-like efficiency of her love-making. The ablative absolute, *operosa et pervigili nocte transacta*, contains the modern sense of a transaction fulfilled, and the moral order invoked by her pre-dawn departure (*vitata lucis conscientia*) is promptly dispelled by her bargaining for another night's services.[40]

Shakespeare's love-scenes are similarly complex. Titania's famous speech, 'Sleep thou, and I will wind thee in my arms' (IV. i. 39 ff.) is as troubling as it is beautiful. Brooks concludes a long note on the woodbine/honeysuckle/ivy/ elm passage with the question: 'Does Shakespeare deliberately substitute the ivy for the vine because Titania's embrace, like that of the ivy in *Err.* (l. 178), is not marital?'[41] Brooks overlooks a fact well known to Shakespeare's contemporaries: that the 'female ivy' that 'Enrings' the elm eventually kills it.[42] Titania's injunctions, 'Out of this wood do not desire to go' and 'Tie up my lover's tongue; bring him silently', evoke a more sinister side of the relationship.[43] Much of the comic power of the scene comes from the sight

---

[39] Prinsac, 71.

[40] The primary meaning of *vitata lucis conscientia facessit mulier* is doubtless that she left before dawn to avoid making her shameful conduct public; but there may be an accessory sense of personal shame made manifest to the self by the incursion of light.

[41] Brooks, 89.

[42] In *A Display of Heraldrie* (London: William Hall for Raphe Mab, 1610), John Guillim describes 'the Iuie' as 'a *Type* of *Lust* rather than of *Loue*' in contrast to 'The *woodbine*' ('a louing and amarous plant, which embraceth al that it growes neere unto; but without hurting of that which it loueth'). See Sect. III, ch. 7, p. 107; and A. D. Nuttall, *The Stoic in Love: Selected Essays on Literature and Ideas* (London: Harvester Wheatsheaf, 1989), 91. Tamsin Simmill has kindly pointed out to me that in *Faunus and Melliflora* (1600), John Weever uses the ivy growing around the oak as a simile for the enervating effects of an amorous embrace. See the edn. by A. Davenport (London: UP of Liverpool, 1948), lines 821–4, p. 34. Ronsard provides even earlier examples.

[43] III. i. 145; III. ii. 194. Brooks adopts Pope's emendation, 'my love's tongue', *causa metrica*, but I have preserved the reading of F and Qq because of its greater explicitness.

of the proud Titania in thrall to a monstrous Bottom who is himself quite unfazed by the experience. Yet she is, paradoxically, also in command. In this respect, she resembles the witches mentioned by Augustine, William of Malmesbury, Bodin, and Scot who keep their men-turned-asses in a state of servitude for years. But while an awareness of the Apuleian episode adds to the erotic potential of Shakespeare's scene—a fact which could have been used by Jan Kott and Peter Brook to support their radical view of the play—it also heightens the comedy by emphasizing what is not happening in actuality. Bottom—metamorphosed into the bestial embodiment of sexual desire—is more concerned with getting a 'bottle of hay' to eat than with satisfying any other kind of appetite. If you take away his 'sleek smooth head' and 'fair large ears' and substitute an elongated phallus—as in Brook's RSC production (1970), itself influenced by Kott's *Shakespeare Our Contemporary* (1964)— you upset the delicate balance of the scene.

Where, then, does all this take us? For Prinsac, the absence of any 'mouvement inexorable' leading Bottom to Titania renders otiose the search for intellectually coherent meaning: 'Ceux qui cherchent une raison morale ou psychologique à tout cela s'égarent'.[44]

Hermeneutic Key

The problem with the approach of critics such as Kermode and Tobin is the positing of a separable 'philosophical meaning'. As we have seen, *The Golden Ass* is subject, from the fourteenth to the seventeenth century, to a form of double-reading. While enjoying its erotic and rhetorical content, readers were at pains to extract from it moral, philosophical, or spiritual meaning, partly, perhaps, to justify an otherwise illicit pursuit, but also from a genuine sense that *The Golden Ass,* for all its tricks and hermeneutic elusiveness, is involved, at some level, with profound issues: obvious ones such as sin, retribution, revelation, and salvation; and more complex ones, like reality and illusion.

Allegorical, philosophical, and perhaps even religious resonances may be generated by the mythological material that has been imported into the play, but such significations operate, by their nature, dynamically, flowing with, and cutting against, the thematic movements. The Apuleian material which is undoubtedly present in *A Midsummer Night's Dream* does not enable us to construct a hermeneutic key which will open to us the hidden meanings of the play. If we invoke all the Apuleian parallels, we are forced to identify Titania not only with Psyche, Charite, Venus, and Isis, but also with the libidinous

---

[44] Prinsac, 71.

matrona and the captivating witch.[45] The play, like the novel, resists mono-lithic interpretations: meaning is elusive, or else it emerges only from the interaction of opposites contained within the text. But an awareness of the Apuleian subtext can enrich our reading of the play; and it should also alert us to possible similarities in narrative/ dramatic technique.

Far more profound an influence than the Platonic ramifications of 'Cupid and Psyche' is Apuleius' tendency to subvert the facility of his own resolu-tions. Apuleius did this most obviously in his counterpointing of 'Cupid and Psyche' with the story of Charite and Tlepolemus, the fairy-tale resolution of the one being offset by the tragic resolution of the other.[46] Shakespeare, I suggest, does something similar in *A Midsummer Night's Dream*, providing an apparent harmonization of conflict through a triple wedding which cannot wholly obscure the mythological 'reality' that the ducal union is destined to lead to Hippolyta's death, Theseus' remarriage, and the loss of their son, Hippolytus, to the incestuous passion of the new wife, Phaedra.

CONCLUSIONS

Are we to conclude, then, that *A Midsummer Night's Dream* is not a comedy at all, but a crypto-tragedy? Clearly not. It would be quite wrong of the Jan Kott/ Peter Brook school to prescribe their dark reading of the play as the only legitimate one; their interpretation involves an extreme (perhaps, extremist) accentuation of the darker elements which are unquestionably present within a texture that is predominantly light. The play is sufficiently well constructed to bear the weight of very different interpretations: a Mendelssohnian lush-ness and a Brookian harshness. Here we see the difference between novel and play: both can be performed in the theatre of the mind where parallel interpretations can be staged simultaneously; the play proper can only be presented in one interpretation at a time.

A Midsummer Night's Dream is more self-referential than most of Shake-speare's plays: there is a good deal of talk about poetry, the relation of art and imagination to reality, and the function of the dramatist. Theseus uses fine poetry to denounce poets, one of whom has given him his 'local habitation'.[47] The ballad that Bottom proposes to sing is, in a sense, the play before us (or, at

[45] Oberon, similarly, must play Venus to Titania's Psyche (though he resembles Cupid in his final forgiving intervention) while Bottom takes the parts of Cupid (lover of Psyche/Titania) and Lucius (lover of *matrona*/Titania).

[46] Subversion operates more subtly (and even more controversially for modern critics) in the Isiac resolution to the novel as a whole. See Introduction, *supra*.

[47] As Brooks acknowledges, p. civ.

least, a good part of it), Peter Quince's relation to Shakespeare having something in common with that of Colin Clout to Spenser. And modern advocates of authorial death might make some capital out of Theseus' quip, 'if he that writ it had played Pyramus, and hanged himself in Thisbe's garter, it would have been a fine tragedy' (v. i. 343–6).

It is in an unexpected place, however, that we find the most important discussion. Theseus, faced with the prospect of 'tragical mirth' in the 'tedious brief scene of young Pyramus | And his love Thisbe', delights in Peter Quince's flights of oxymoron:

> Merry and tragical? Tedious and brief?
> That is hot ice, and wondrous strange snow!
> How shall we find the concord in this discord?
>
> (v. i. 58–60)

This could almost serve as Shakespeare's *Ars poetica*. The topos of *Impossibilia* is, of course, an old and familiar one; but, in the case of Shakespeare, this oxymoronic mode is frequently extended to become part of the thematic structure of the plays.[48] Brooks's note points us sensibly towards Sidney's discussion of 'mongrel tragi-comedy' in *An Apology for Poetry* and suggests that Shakespeare has managed to avoid the failing that Sidney condemns. Significant for our purposes is Sidney's special pleading for Apuleius: 'I know that Apuleius did somewhat so but that is a thing recounted with space of time, not represented in one moment.'[49] Much of Shakespeare's achievement lies in his ability to draw concord from discord (the characteristic *telos* of the comedies); but a good deal of the comic richness and complexity is actually generated by his ability to maintain discord within concord. It is in this shared talent for harmonious discordance that the genius of Apuleius and Shakespeare is often most manifest.

It may be merely that Shakespeare's natural genius made him a particularly acute reader of *The Golden Ass*. But the accumulated evidence of Apuleian presence in the Shakespearian corpus suggests that *The Golden Ass* exerted a profound influence, providing a rich resource of interactive elements which contributed to the proteanism of his own dramatic art.

Bottom's famous speech, 'Man is but an ass, if he go about to expound this dream' (iv. i. 205–6), could almost serve as a motto for Shakespeare's own aesthetic philosophy. Shakespeare's genius (and much of his enduring appeal) is, to an extent, a function of his escape from allegory, his rejection of the exegetical tradition that dominates the Middle Ages and pervades the

---

[48] On the topos, see A. D. Nuttall, 'Fishes in the Trees', in *The Stoic in Love*, 68–81.
[49] Shepherd, 135.

Renaissance. His contemporaries may equal or surpass him on one point or another, but no one matches Shakespeare's ability to invest characters with dramatic autonomy, with the capacity to exist outside of the text that incarnates them. Shakespeare is far more focused on the *cortex* than the *medulla* or *nucleus*, on the vehicle of the dramatic fiction than on the abstract meaning it might contain, on the *dulce* than on the *utile*. Bottom's joyful cry, 'It shall be called Bottom's Dream, because it hath no bottom', holds, in rich dialectic, two contrary senses: the dream lacks any 'fundamental character, essence, reality'—it has, ultimately, no meaning—but it is also 'unfathomable', having an 'inexhaustible' profundity.[50]

Even if we 'take a chance', as Tobin urges us, in adopting an allegorical approach, what is our reward? Apuleius supplies no keys to unlock the closed meanings of the play. A comparison between the two works can tell us much, however, about Shakespeare's technique of source-adaptation and the way he read Apuleius; and it can give us a means of mapping the hermeneutic complexities of both texts. The subversive reading of *The Golden Ass* is not an invention of post-structuralism. Shakespeare was undermining the monolithic interpretations four centuries before John J. Winkler.

[50] *OED*, s.v. 'bottom', 12 and 2b.

Epilogue

'And all your notes,' said Dorothea, whose heart had already burned
within her on this subject so that now she could not help speaking with
her tongue. 'All those rows of volumes—will you not now do what you
used to speak of?—will you not make up your mind what part of them
you will use, and begin to write the book which will make your vast
knowledge useful to the world?'

(George Eliot, *Middlemarch*)[1]

The ghost of Mr Casaubon is likely to haunt anyone who embarks upon a study
of the reception of a Classical text without imposing clear boundaries in space
and in time. Casaubon's ambition to produce the 'Key to All Mythologies' makes
him the collector of almost every fact and every opinion, but (as even Lucius
admits), to be *multiscius* is not necessarily to be *prudens* (*AA* 9. 13). Filippo
Beroaldo, taking a wife in late middle age, saw, in the fruit of Cupid and Psyche's
union, an augury for his own marriage.[2] The desiccated Mr Casaubon, honey-
mooning with his young bride in Rome, is quite incapable of such an act of
intellectual and emotional integration:

'Should you like to go to the Farnesina, Dorothea? It contains celebrated frescoes
designed or painted by Raphael, which most persons think it worth while to visit.'

'But do you care about them?' was always Dorothea's question.

'They are, I believe, highly esteemed. Some of them represent the fable of Cupid and
Psyche, which is probably the romantic invention of a literary period, and cannot,
I think, be reckoned as a genuine mythical product. But if you like these wall-paintings
we can easily drive thither; and you will then, I think, have seen the chief works of
Raphael, any of which it were a pity to omit in a visit to Rome. He is the painter who
has been held to combine the most complete grace of form with sublimity of
expression. Such at least I have gathered to be the opinion of cognoscenti.'

---

[1] *Middlemarch* (1871–2), ed. W. J. Harvey (Harmondsworth: Penguin, 1965), ch. 20, p. 232.
[2] See Ch. 4 (*supra*). Like Mr Casaubon, Beroaldo (1453–1505) died within a few years of his
marriage. On the Casaubon archetype, see A. D. Nuttall, *Dead from the Waist Down: Scholars
and Scholarship in Literature and the Popular Imagination* (New Haven: YUP, 2003) esp. 26–71.

As a result of such exchanges, Dorothea

was gradually ceasing to expect with her former delightful confidence that she should see any wide opening where she followed him. Poor Mr Casaubon himself was lost among small closets and winding stairs, and in an agitated dimness about the Cabeiri, or in an exposure of other mythologists' ill-considered parallels, easily lost sight of any purpose which had prompted him to these labours.[3]

I am conscious not merely of 'small closets and winding stairs', but of whole buried cities that I have left uncharted or unexplored in this study. We have touched, for instance, upon Raphael's paintings in the Villa Farnesina, but made no attempt at any systematic coverage of pictorial representations of 'Cupid and Psyche'. Little has been said (beyond Erasmus) about the Dutch reception of Apuleius, and nothing at all about the Portuguese.[4] And while the interplay of Apuleian and Heliodorean impulses in Cervantes has been adumbrated, scant attention has been paid to Hans Jakob Christoffel von Grimmelshausen's *Der abentheurliche Simplicissimus* (1669), or to the relationship between *The Golden Ass* and the development of the picaresque.[5]

In England, Apuleius continues to exert his influence well beyond Milton. The story of 'Cupid and Psyche' will feature repeatedly (if with little distinction) in seventeenth-century literature. One thinks of Thomas Shadwell's *Psyche. A Tragedy* (1675); Thomas Duffett's *Psyche Debauch'd. A Comedy* (1678); Aphra Behn's *Sir Patient Fancy: A Comedy* (1678) and *The Amours of Philander and Silvia* (1687); and Thomas D'Urfey's *A New Opera Call'd Cinthia and Endimion, or The Loves of the Deities* (1697). At the very end of the eighteenth century, Thomas Taylor the Platonist will produce the first instalment of his translation of Apuleius' collected works.[6] At the beginning of the nineteenth century, the story of 'Cupid and Psyche' will have a particular

[3] *Middlemarch*, ch. 20, p. 229.

[4] On Dutch receptions, see R. Th. van der Paardt, 'Three Dutch Asses', *GCN* 2 (1989), 133–44. For an example of the influence of 'Cupid and Psyche' in Portuguese, see T. F. Earle, *Theme and Image in the Poetry of Sá de Miranda* (Oxford: OUP, 1980), 12–19. Earle notes that Sá de Miranda (*c*.1481–*c*.1558) offers in his eclogue *Encantamento* 'only a truncated version' (15) of the story and may have made use of Fulgentius. Earle also points (16) to a *Psyche* in twelve books by the Spanish poet Juan de Mal Lara (1524?–71).

[5] Cf. W. Riggan, 'The Reformed Picaro and His Narrative: A Study of the Autobiographical Accounts of Lucius Apuleius, Simplicius Simplicissimus, Lazarillo de Tormes, Guzman de Alfarache, and Moll Flanders', *Orbis litterarum* 30 (1975), 165–86.

[6] *The Fable of Cupid and Psyche . . . to which are added, a poetical paraphrase on the speech of Diotima, in the Banquet of Plato; four hymns, &c.* (London: T. Taylor, 1795); *Apuleius' Golden Ass, or, The Metamorphosis: and other Philosophical Writings* (London: T. Rodd, 1822; repr. Frome: Prometheus Trust, 1999).

resonance for the Romantics.[7] The most famous expression of that interest is, of course, Keats's 'Ode to Psyche':

> O latest born and loveliest vision far
> Of all Olympus' faded hierarchy!
> Fairer than Phoebe's sapphire-region'd star,
> Or Vesper, amorous glow-worm of the sky;
> Fairer than these, though temple hast thou none...

Though Psyche was born 'too late for antique vows | Too, too late for the fond believing lyre', the poet promises to devote himself to her service:

> Yes, I will be thy priest, and build a fane
> In some untrodden region of my mind...

For Keats, the Psyche story was a highly creative influence. The 'Ode' seems to have unlocked a new poetic store, inaugurating the sequence of odes of 1819 in which he realized his greatness.

It has to be admitted, however, that many of the poetic and pictorial effusions inspired by 'Cupid and Psyche' have been bland, trite, or insipid.[8] Indeed (at the risk of simplifying crudely), we might say that the 'Victorian attitude' to Apuleius is encapsulated by John Evelyn Barlas in 'Cupid and Psyche' (1884):

> I found a fallen rose-bud
> Where the mire lay gross and crass,
> One sweet Milesian story
> In the filthy Golden Ass...[9]

Walter Pater's retelling of 'Cupid and Psyche' in *Marius the Epicurean* (1885) retains its power to charm, but there is little sense (in this or other versions from the period) of the creative possibilities of the 'gross and crass' 'mire' from which that 'fallen rose-bud' had been plucked, nothing to parallel Flaubert's delight in the mixing of 'urine' and 'incense' in the novel. We have to wait until the twentieth century to enjoy the kinds of integrated responses to *The Golden Ass* that we have seen (if only fitfully) during the Renaissance.

---

[7] See, generally, J. H. Hagstrum, 'Eros and Psyche: Some Versions of Romantic Love and Delicacy', *Critical Inquiry* 3 (1977), 521–42. A fragment survives in the Bodleian Library of Mary Shelley's translation of the tale. See *Mary Shelley's Literary Lives and Other Writings*, vol. iv, gen. ed. N. Crook (London: Pickering & Chatto, 2002). I am grateful to Prof. Pamela Clemit for bringing to my attention the appearance of this fragment in print and to Prof. Michael O'Neill for the Hagstrum reference.

[8] The versions by Mrs Tighe (*Psyche, or The Legend of Love*, 1805), William Morris (Part 3 of *The Earthly Paradise*, 1868), and Robert Bridges (*Eros and Psyche*, 1886) are among the best known. Cf. Haight, *Apuleius*, 149–59.

[9] Evelyn Douglas (pseud.), *Poems, Lyrical and Dramatic* (London: Trubner, 1884), 230.

APPENDIX

Putative Apuleius Glosses in the *Abolita* Glossary[1]

Apuleius, *AA*, Book 1

Mutuo : vicissim aut de accepto fenore dono (*MU* 9). Cf. *AA* 1. 1: *mutuo nexu.*

Praestinaturus : praemercaturus (*PR<A>E* 31). Cf. *AA* 1. 5 (Aristomenes, hastening to Hypata to purchase cheese at a good price): *festinus accucurri id omne praestinaturus.* Cf. *AA* 9. 8 (the all-purpose prophecies given by the priests of the Syrian goddess): *Si possessiones praestinaturus quaereret...*

Pube tenus : usque ad inguinem (*PU* 26). Cf. *AA* 1. 6 (Socrates baring his loins as he covers his face out of shame): *faciem suam... prae pudore obtexit ita ut ab umbilico pube tenus cetera corporis renudaret.* But cf. *Aen.* 3. 427 (the half-human Scylla): *virgo | pube tenus.*

Lubentia : libidinem (-do) vel voluptas. Cf. *AA* 1. 7 (an apparent improvement in Socrates' spirits under Aristomenes' ministrations): *Iam adlubentia proclivis est sermonis et ioci....*

Scitulum : cultulum (*SC* 18). Cf. *AA* 1. 7 (description of Meroe): *anum sed admodum scitulam.*

Marcidus : lassus, gravatus (*MA* 3). Cf. *AA* 1. 15 (Socrates, following the nocturnal visit of the eviscerating witches): *marcidus et semisopitus.*

Exanclasti : ex<h>austi (*EX* 53). Cf. *AA* 1. 16 (Aristomenes addresses the bed that has shared his troubles): *Iam, iam, grabatule... qui mecum tot aerumnas exanclasti.*

Mantica : bisaccia (*MA* 39). Cf. *AA* 1. 18 (Aristomenes taking the sack from his shoulder to hand Socrates some bread and cheese): *mantica<m> mea<m> umero exuo.* Cf. *Mantica : bargila* (*MA* 66) and Petronius, *Satyricon* 31, (the panniers on the little bronze donkey on Trimalchio's sideboard): *asellus erat Corinthius cum bisaccio positus....*

---

[1] The 'evidence' presented here is based mainly on the researches and conjectures of W. M. Lindsay. Additional candidates proposed by me are marked with an asterisk. In the *Praefatio* to his edn. of the *Abolita* glossary (*Goss. Lat.* iii. 95), Lindsay admits that he has 'sought in vain for such definite proof' of an Apuleian source as he has established for Festus, Terence, and Vergil (*Frustra tamen quaesivi tam certa indicia...*), and he leaves it to his reader to weigh the evidence and 'give judgement' (*perpende quanti valeant sigla huius fontis in meo libro posita, tum dato iudicium*). I offer this appendix in a similarly tentative spirit. In many instances, Lindsay's identification of an Apuleian context for a relatively common word depends upon the gloss's occurrence within a supposed Apuleian 'batch'. To appreciate Lindsay's rationale, one needs to read the glosses in the (semi-alphabetical) order given in the *Abolita* glossary itself. I have reordered the glosses here so as to indicate the attention that different portions of *The Golden Ass* may have received from 7th-cent. readers. I am grateful to Dr David Daintree, Rector of St John's College, University of Sydney, for reading a draft of this appendix.

Gurgu<s>tiolum : *angusta <h>abitatio et latens; tractum a gurgite* (*GU* 4). Cf. *AA*
1. 23 (Milo apologizing for the meanness of his house): *ergo gurgustioli nostri ne
spernas peto.* Cf. *AA* 4. 10 (Chryseros climbing onto the roof of his hut after nailing
Lamachus' hand to the door): *gurgustioli sui tectum ascendit.*

Commodum : *ipsum quod eodem tempore;* and *Continantur* : *congrediuntur* (*CO* 94 and
95). Cf. *AA* 1. 24 (Lucius being joined by Pythias just as he is leaving the market):
Inde me commodum egredientem continatur Pythias. Cf. *AA* 5. 8 and v. 31, *infra.*

Salebra : *via inaequalis* (*SA* 8). Cf. *AA* 1. 26 (Lucius slurring his words to Milo through
tiredness): *incerta verborum salebra balbuttire.*

Book 2

*Obgannire : *obcanere* (*OB* 29). Cf. *AA* 2. 2 (the old man muttering in Byrrhena's ear
on meeting Lucius): *incertum quidnam in aurem mulieris obganniit.* But Lindsay
(app. crit.) suggests Terence, *Phormio* 1030(?).

Oculi caesii : *gattinei* (*OC* 4). Cf. *AA* 2. 2 (Byrrhena remarking upon Lucius' eyes):
oculi caesii quidem, sed vigiles et in aspectu micantes.[2]

Gestiunt : *requirunt* (*GE* 10). Cf. *AA* 2. 8 (Lucius' contention that most women, when
they wish to prove their attractiveness, desire to show their beauty naked): *nudam
pulchritudinem suam praebere se gestiunt.*

Intuitus sum : *aspexi* (*IN* 19a). Cf. *AA* 2. 8 (Lucius' habit of staring at women's hair):
intueri.

Ciruleus (*caer-*): *viridis vel glaucus* (*CI* 10). Cf. *AA* 2. 9 (Fotis' hair): *nunc corvina
nigredine caerulus columbarum collis flosculos aemulatur.*

Congermanescere : *coniungi[er]* (*CO* 105). Cf. *AA* 2. 10 (Fotis and Lucius kissing):
Iamque aemula libidine in amoris parilitatem congermanescenti mecum; but cf.
Nonnius, p. 90, 16 sq.: *coalescere, coniungi vel consociari.*

*Petulans: inverecundus, inportunus.—ntia : *inportunitas.* Cf. *AA* 2. 16 (Lucius being
aroused by Fotis): *ad libidinem inquies et petulans.*

*Diribitores: divisores; et diribitores dicebantur qui suffragia populi divisa in loculos
tributim separabant* (*DI* 65). Cf. *AA* 2. 19 (brilliantly robed waiters at Byrrhena's
banquet): *Diribitores plusculi splendide amicti fercula copiosa scitule sumministrare.*

Obtutus : *aspectus* (*OB* 66); and *Secubat* : *sequestrate cubat* (*SE* 48). Cf. *AA* 2. 20
(Byrrhena's guests turn their attention to the reclusive Thelyphron): *omniumque
ora et optutus in unum quempiam angulo secubantem conferuntur.*

Book 3

Circumforaneus (*-eis*) : *cir<c>a fara* (*fo-*) *ductis* (*CI* 11). Cf. *AA* 3. 2 (Lucius being
paraded through the streets on the way to his 'trial'): *et in modum eorum quibus*

---

[2] The gloss *gattinei* (sc. *cattinei*, 'cat-like') may be derived from Aelius Donatus' gloss (*glaucis
oculis, quasi felis oculos habens et glaucos*) on Terence, *Hecyra* 3. 4. 26 [line 440 overall] (*caesius*).

lustralibus piamentis minas portentorum hostiis circumforaneis expiant circumductus angulatim, forum eiusque tribunal astituor.

Eiulantes : ululantes (EI 4). Cf. *AA* 3. 8 (women wailing over 'corpses' at *Risus* trial): *plangore sublato se lugubriter eiulantes.*

*Luctatur : pugnat (LU 18) and, *Instaurat : redintegrat (IN* 34). Cf. *AA* 3. 9 (Lucius' reluctance to 'refresh' his earlier crime by uncovering the 'corpses' at his trial during the Festival of Laughter): *Luctantem me ac diu renuentem praecedens facinus instaurare nova ostensione.*

Beaedi (Boeoti) : Thebani (BE 4). Cf. *AA* 3. 16 (Pamphile's love for a Boeotian youth): *adulescentum quendam Boeotium.* Cf. *Boeotio* at *AA* 3. 17 and 18.

Mancipatum (quasi municipatus) : honor civicus qui capitur ex loco (MA 25) and *Mancipatus : vinctus (MA* 38). Cf. *AA* 3. 19 (Lucius declaring his willing bondage to Fotis): *mancipatum teneas uolentem.*

Obsistit : resistit (OB 67). Cf. *AA* 3. 28 (the robbers occupying Milo's house repel a relief party): *auxiliis hinc inde convolantibus obsistit discursus hostilis.*

Obsepta : circumclausa (OB 68). Cf. *AA* 3. 28 (the robbers using axes on Milo's securely locked storeroom): *Tunc horreum quoddam satis validis claustris obsaeptum obsertumque . . . securibus validis aggressi diffindunt.*

Book 4

Frutectum : arborum contextus (FU [sic] 31). Cf. *AA* 4. 1 (Lucius looks for a means to eat roses without being seen): *si devius et protectus <emend. frutectis>.*[3]

Scaturribat : ebulliebat (SC 16). Cf. *AA* 4. 6 (torrent flowing down the robbers' mountain): *De summo vertice fons affluens bullis ingentibus scatturibat.*

Obtionem : electionem (OB 70). Cf. *AA* 4. 15 (robbers select Thrasyleon from those volunteering for the mission of impersonating a bear): *Quorum prae ceteris Thrasyleon factionis optione delectus.*

Lemores (-mur-) : daemones (LE 18). Cf. *AA* 4. 22 (robbers disguised as goblins): *in Lemures reformati.*

Tibia zigia (zy-) : a coniungendo dicta (TI 8); and **Modus Lydius : qualis in celebrando funere a Lydiis dictum (dicitur?) (MO* 50). Cf. *AA* 4. 33 (Psyche's funereal wedding procession to the rock): *sonus tibiae zygiae mutatur in querulum Ludii modum.*[4]

Book 5

Annuit : consentit (AN 10). Cf. *AA* 5. 5 (Psyche's assent to Cupid's demand that she ignore her sisters): *Annuit et ex arbitrio mariti se facturum spopondit.*

---

[3] MSS read *protectus*, but many editors adopt the Juntine edn.'s *frutectis.*

[4] F and φ read *gygiae* and *gigie*, respectively. Beroaldo restores *zygiae*. Note 'Zygia' as a name for Juno (*AA* 6. 4). Lindsay (*Gloss. Lat.* iii. 147) curiously ignores *AA* 4. 33, suggesting *Florida* 4 instead. Vat. 3321 reads *Modus liuius qualis in celebrandum funere a lydiis dictum.* MS Cassin. 439 provides the readings *Modus lidius* and *celebrando.*

Commodum : ipsum quod eodem tempore (*CO* 94). Cf. *AA* 5. 8 (Psyche's description of her husband as just beginning to show a downy beard on his cheeks): *commodum lanoso barbitio genas inumbrantem.* Cf. *AA* 5. 5 *supra.*

*Indulge : da operam, da veniam, praesta aut ignosce (*IN* 122). Cf. *AA* 5. 13 (Psyche requests from Cupid the boon of her sisters' embrace): *germani complexus indulge fructum.*

Ingluvies: gula vel guttur (*IN* 35). Cf. *AA* 5. 17 (the sisters' description of Psyche's husband as a monstrous snake): *veneno noxio colla sanguinantem hiantemque ingluvie profunda.*

Roborare : confortare.—atus : confortatus (*RO* 16). Cf. *AA* 5. 22 (Psyche, on the point of killing her husband): *fati tamen saevitiae sumministrante viribus roboratur.*

Titubare : claudicare [vel dubitare]—bans : nutans (*TI* 9–9a). Cf. *AA* 5. 25 (Pan's consolation of Psyche): *ab isto titubante et saepius vacillante vestigio.*

Confarreatis nuptiis : multis modis nuptiae fiunt etc. (*CO* 102). Cf. *AA* 5. 26 (Psyche exacting vengeance by telling her sister that Cupid wants to marry her): *Ego vero sororem tuam . . . iam mihi confarreatis nuptiis coniugabo.*[5]

Caeleps inves<tis> : innupta (-tus) (*CE* 51). Cf. *AA* 5. 28 (Venus' description of her son): *puerum ingenuum et investem.*

Investem : inberbem (*IN* 224). Cf. *AA* 5. 28 (Venus' description of her son): *puerum ingenuum et investem.* Cf. *Investis : sine barba* (*IN* 21).

Nugorem (-onem) : inutilem (*NU* 14). Cf. *AA* 5. 30 (Venus decides to employ Sobrietas to punish her good-for-nothing son): *quae castiget asperrime nugonem istum.*

Continantur : congrediuntur (*CO* 95). Cf. *AA* 5. 31 (Ceres and Juno joining the enraged Venus): *Sed eam protinus Ceres et Iuno continantur.*

Book 6

Sustulit : nutrivit (*SU* 74). Cf. *ΛΛ* 6. 8 (the effect on Psyche of Mercury's proclamation of Venus' reward of seven kisses): *Quae res nunc vel maxime sustulit Psyches omnem cunctationem.*

Delibare : deminuere (*DE* 20). Cf. *AA* 6. 20 (Psyche deciding to open the jar of Proserpina's beauty): *inepta ego . . . quae nec tantillum quidem indidem mihi delibo*).

Infamatum : infamem, turpem, abiectum (*IN* 109). Cf. *AA* 6. 23 (Jupiter on the need to bridle Cupid's excesses): *Sat est cotidianis eum fabulis ob adulteria cunctasque correptelas infamatum.*

---

[5] Lindsay (*Gloss. Lat.*, iii. 113, app. crit.) suggests that the long gloss on the different types of marriage given here (identical, except for a change in tense, to Servius Auctus' gloss on *Georgics* 1. 31) has driven out a shorter gloss on *AA* 10. 29 where Lucius anticipates being publicly mated with the condemned woman (*Talis mulieris publicitus matrimonium confarreaturus*). But the lemma is identical to the restored text of *AA* 5. 26 (F, by a dittography of *confestim* from the previous sentence, reads *confestim arreathis*). However, cf. *Gai Institutiones or Institutes of Roman Law by Gaius*, ed. and trans. E. Poste (4th edn.), revd. E. A. Whittuck, introd. A. H. J. Greenidge (Oxford: Clarendon, 1904), 1 § 136: *Praeterea mulieres quae in manum conveniunt, in patris potestate esse desinunt, sed in confarreatis nuptiis de flaminica Diali senatusconsulto ex relatione Maximi*, &c.

Tuburcinati : p[r]opinati (TU 18); and *Amfractibus : circumflexionibus (AM* 8). Cf. *AA* 6. 25 (after bolting down their dinner, the robbers take out Lucius and his horse, returning them later, laden with loot and exhausted by the hills and circuitous routes): *Prandioque raptim tuburcinato... multisque clivis et anfractibus fatigatos.* But cf. Nonnius, 179, 21.

Erciscendae : evocandae, [in] devidendae (div-) (ER 3). Cf. *AA* 6. 29 (Lucius and Charite 'arguing' over which direction to take after escaping from the robbers' cave): *Sic nos diversa tendentes et in causa finali de proprietate soli, immo viae herciscundae contendentes.*

Fartilem : plenum; unde fartores <qui aves saginant> (FA 35). Cf. *AA* 6. 31 (the robber's proposal to slit Lucius' throat, stuff his belly with the naked Charite, and expose them on a rock): *et fartilem asinum exponere.*

Book 7

Grassator : latro, depraedator (GR 7). Cf. *AA* 7. 7 (Tlepolemus, disguised as 'Haemus', refers to his band operating as thieves): *grassabamur.*

*Pulvinar: capitale (PU 17). Cf. *AA* 7. 9 ('Haemus' taking his place at the head of the robbers): *Sic reformatus, singulos exosculatus et in summo pulvinari locatus cena poculisque magnis inauguratur.*

Gregatim : globatim (GR 4). Cf. *AA* 7. 11 (robbers returning to camp with livestock): *gregatim pecua comminantes.*

Crapula : nausia vel comesatio (CA [*sic*] 49). Cf. *AA* 7. 12 (Tlepolemus forcing wine on the robbers): *sauciis illis et crapula vinolentiaque madidis ipse abstemius non cessat impingere.* Cf. *AA* 8. 13 But and also: 3. 18: *crapula madens.*

Saginatur : nutritur. –na : pinguedo (SA 22–22a). Cf. *AA* 7. 14 (proposal that Lucius be rewarded for saving Charite by being kept at home with nothing to do but eat): *Placuerat uni domi me conclusum et otiosum hordeo lecto fabaque et vicia saginari.*

Insaciabilis (-sat-) : qui saciari non potest (IN 215). Cf. *AA* 7. 17 (the insatiability of Fortune's cruelty to Lucius): *Verum Fortuna meis cruciatibus insatiabilis.*

Concipilabo : concidam minutatim (CO 100). Cf. *AA* 7. 18 (the cruel boy tormenting Lucius): *immo vero et ipsis auribus totum me complicabat [cidit] fusti grandissimo, donec fomenti vice ipsae me plagae suscitarent.* But cf. Plautus, *Truculentus* 621: *iam concipilabo.*

Iners : piger vel tardus. Cf. *AA* 7. 23 (a rustic recommends castration as a solution to the licentiousness of 'lazy asses'): *asinos inertes.*

Book 8

Infortunio : infelicitate (IN 110). Cf. *AA* 8. 1 (report of the death of Charite and 'the fall from fortune of her whole household'): *de eius exitio et domus totius infortunio.*

Infecta : non facta, vel tincta (IN 111). Cf. *AA* 8. 5 (Thrasyllus' bloodstained hands): *manus infectus humano cruore.*

Decipulum : deceptionem (*DE* 21). Cf. *AA* 8. 5 (Thrasyllus' ploy to kill Tlepolemus): *nactus fraudium opportunum decipulum.*

Interula : tunica interior (*IN* 201). Cf. *AA* 8. 9 (Charite tearing her nightgown after the appearance of Tlepolemus' ghost): *discissaque interula decora bracchia saevientibus palmulis converberat.*

Ultroneus : sponte volenti; and *Infesti : invidentes* (*UL* 1 and *IN* 112). Cf. *AA* 8. 14 (Thrasyllus' cry as he immures himself in the tomb of Tlepolemus and Charite): *Ultronea vobis, infesti manes, en adest victima.* But cf. *AA* 2. 30: *in exanimis umbrae modum ultroneus gradiens;* and 4. 7: *infesti.*

Inclamant : vocant (*IN* 78). Cf. *AA* 8. 21 (companions searching for young man eaten by giant snake): *illum iuvenem frequenter inclamant.*

Stipite : arbor<e> nudata foliis (*ST* 27). Cf. *AA* 8. 22 (the adulterous steward, smeared with honey and tied to a tree-trunk): *cuius in ipso carioso stipite inhabitantium formicarum nidificia bulliebant* [F = *borri<e>bant*]; But cf. *Aen.* 3. 43 etc.

Absonum : non simile sono (*AB* 36) *and Succedaneum : successor* (*SU* 62). Cf. *AA* 8. 26 (the catamites' cry of joy at the expectation of a new slave-boy quashed by the sight of the asinine Lucius): *effeminata voce clamores absonos intollunt... Sed postquam non cervam pro virgine, sed asinum pro homine succidaneum videre...*

Infet (-it): infatur, hoc est dicere incipit (*IN* 113); and *Dissignat: ordinat, distribuit* (*DI* 68). Cf. *AA* 8. 28 (a devotee of the Syrian goddess concocting a justification for his self-flagellation): *Infit vaticinatione clamosa conficto mendacio semet ipsum incessere atque criminari quasi contra fas sanctae religionis dissignasset aliquid.* But cf. *AA* 2. 19: *cum infit ad me Byrrhaena.*

Incutit : in[d]icit, ingerit (*IN* 80). Cf. *AA* 8. 28 (Lucius' alarm at the profusion of flagellants' blood): *Quae res incutiebat mihi non parvam sollicitudinem.*

Book 9

Concipilassent : minuatim concidissent (*CO* 96). Cf. *AA* 9. 2 (Lucius believes that he would have been hacked into pieces had he not escaped to a bedroom): *Nec dubio me lanceis illis vel venabulis, immo vero et bipennibus... membratim compilassent.*[6]

Famigerabilis : famae devulgatae (*FA* 36). Cf. *AA* 9. 5 (the adulterous wife in the Tale of the Tub): *postrema lascivia famigerabilis.*

Inprovisus : inspiratus (-sper-), inperitus (*IN* 173). Cf. *AA* 9. 5 (while the wife and her lover grapple, the unwitting husband returns home unexpectedly): *Ac dum Veneris colluctationibus securius operanter, maritus, ignarus rerum ac nihil etiam tum tale suspicans, inprovisus hospitium repetit.* NB The gloss appears to be responding to the context (*ignarus*) by suggesting that he is both 'unexpected' (*insperatus*) and 'unforeseeing' (because he is *inperitus*).

---

[6] J. van der Vliet, ed., *Metamorphoseon libri XI* (Leipzig: Teubner, 1897), emends the MSS' *compilassent* to *concipilassent.* See his '*Compilare—concipulare*', *Archiv für Lateinische Lexikographie und Grammatik* 9 (1896), 461. Note also *Abolita's Concipilabo : concidam minutatim* and *AA* 7. 18. Cf. Van der Vliet's note on *compilabat [cidit].* Hanson suggests that *cidit* came from a gloss (*concidit*).

Homuncio : non grandis formae homo (*HO* 1). Cf. *AA* 9. 7 (the lover dismissively addressing the husband): *Quin tu, quicumque es, homuncio.* But cf. Terence, *Eunuchus* 591.

Pusio : unde diminutive pusillus (*PU* 9). Cf. *AA* 9. 7 (the young lover having his way with the wife while her husband cleans out the storage jar beneath them): *At vero adulter, bellissimus ille pusio, inclinatam dolio pronam uxorem fabri superincurvatus secure dedolabat.*

Anstistites : principes. Cf. *AA* 9. 10 (the devotees of the Syrian goddess defending themselves as 'high priests of her cult'): *religionis antistites.*

Vibices : plagae in corpore sine sanguine[m] (*VI* 32). Cf. *AA* 9. 12 (the welts on the skin of the slaves in the mill): *vibicibus lividis totam cutem depicti.*

Virosa mulier : virorum appetans (*VI* 33); **Ebrius : ad tempus multum bibens.—iosus : semper multum bibens* (*EB, EC* 2–2a);[7] and *Pervicax: valde verbosus* (*PE* 64).[8] Cf. *AA* 9. 14 (the baker's wife): *saeva scaeva, virosa ebriosa, pervicax pertinax.*

Sequester : interpres (*SE* 50). Cf *AA* 9. 15 (the old woman acting as the baker's wife's go-between): *anus quaedam stuprorum sequestra et adulterorum internuntia.*

Caperratum supercilium : triste s<uperciliu m> (*CA* 50). Cf. *AA* 9. 16 (the young cuckolder shudders at the 'wrinkled eyebrow' of the baker): *Caperratum supercilium ignaviter perhorrescit.*

Saliares cenas : quae fiunt a Saliis (*SA* 16); and *Tuccetum : bubula apud Albinos (Alp-) condita* (*TU* 16). Cf. *AA* 9. 22 (the baker's wife prepares her lover a meal fit for a priest): *At pudica uxor statim cenas saliares comparat, vina pretiosa defaecat, pulmenta recentia tuccetis temperat.*

Naccam : fullonem (*NA* 16). Cf. *AA* 9. 22 (the baker, meanwhile, is dining with the fuller): *Nam et opportune maritus foris apud naccam proximum cenitabat.*[9]

Angiportus : aedium materia (mac-) [vel aediculae] (*AN* 12) and ***Angiportum : androna biforium, vel callem.* Cf. *AA* 9. 25 (the fuller drags his wife's lover—half-dead from the sulphur fumes—out into the nearest alley): *semivivum illum in proximum deportat angiportum.*

Intempestivum : intemperatum (*IN* 8). Cf. *AA* 9. 28 (the baker to the youthful cuckolder): *et intempestivum tibi nomen adulteri vindicas?*

Veteratricem : callidam in circumscribendo. Cf. *AA* 9. 29 (the baker's wife seeks out a witch): *magnaque cura requisitam veteratricem quandam feminam, quae devotionibus ac maleficiis quidvis efficere posse credebatur, multis exorat precibus multisque suffarcinat muneribus.*

Exoliscere : est in duritiam verti gratiamque aetatis amittere (*EX* 54). Cf. *AA* 9. 32 (Lucius and the gardener dining on over-ripened lettuce): *lactucae veteres et insuaves illae, quae seminis enormi senecta ad instar scoparum in amaram caenosi sucus cariem exolescunt.*

---

[7] Lindsay (*Gloss. Lat.* iii. 121, app. crit.) notes Isidore, *Diff.* 205 (*Ebrius ad tempus multum bibit. Ebriosus semper multum bibit*) with the query '*ex Festo?*'

[8] Cf. *PE* 5 (*Pervicax : constans, perseverans.* [Lindsay suggest 'Festus?']) and *PE* 25 (*Pervicax : intentione ductus [durus].* [Lindsay points us to Terence, *Hecyra*, 547]).

[9] The gloss is unattributed in *Gloss. Lat.* (iii. 149, *NA* 16), but elsewhere (*Ancient Lore*, 4) Lindsay supplies references both to Apuleius and to Festus (166: *Naccae appellantur vulgo fullones, ut ait Curiatius, quod nauci non sint*).

Instruit : componit vel docet (*IN* 23). Cf. *AA* 9. 37 (the young man 'arranges' himself as a 'hideous banquet' for the wealthy landowner's dogs): *saeuisque illis ac ferocissimis canibus instruit nefariam dapem.*

Cerebrum : narium altitudo (*CE* 52). Cf. *AA* 9. 40 (the gardener being beaten by the soldier): *Sed ubi ... advertit ... cerebrum suum diffindere.*

Book 10

Eculeum : genus poenae (*EB, EC* 4); and *Equuleus : genus tormenti* (*EQ* 1). Cf. *AA* 10. 10 (the slave facing torture on suspicion of poisoning): *Nec rota vel eculeus more Graecorum tormentis eius apparata iam deerant.*

Pulvillum (-us) : plumacium (*PU* 22). Cf. *AA* 10. 20 (eunuchs making a bed of pillows for Lucius and the onophilic matrona): *Quattuor eunuchi confestim pulvillis compluribus ventose tumentibus pluma delicata terrestrem nobis cubitum praestruunt...*

**T<a>enias : vittae sacerdotium; apud Praenestinos flagra* (*TE* 22)[10] and **Papillae : mamillae vel (mamillarum?) capita* (*PA* 14). Cf. *AA* 10. 21 (the Corinthian matrona undressing): *tunc ipsa cuncto prorsus spoliata tegmine, taenia quoque qua deuinxerat papillas.* But cf. *Aen.* 11. 803 etc.

**[Lupanaria : cellulae mereticum]* (*LU* 43).[11] Cf. *AA* 10. 21 (the Corinthian *matrona*'s un-whorish kisses): *non qualia in lupinari solent basiola iactari uel meretricum poscinummia uel aduentorum negantinummia...*

**Expiare : emundare* (*EX* 18) and ***Spurcitia : inmunditia* (*Abstrusa* glossary, *SP* 26). Cf. *spurcum additamentum: Chiae rosae lotionibus expiauit ac dein digitis hypato, lichano, meso, parameso et neto hastam inguinis mei spurcitia pluscule excorians emundauit.*

**Lustrum: quinquenni tempus aut lumen* (*LU* 6)[12] and **autumabam : aestimabam (exist-?)* (*AU* 23). Cf. *spurcum additamentum: modicum illud morulae qua lustrum sterni mandauerat anni sibi reuolutionem autumabat.*

Flagris : flagellis (*FL* 10). Cf. *AA* 10. 24 (Jealous wife strips and beats her husband's sister): *primum quidem nudam flagris ultime verberat.*

Nubilum : umbrosum (*NU* 12). Cf. *AA* 10. 28 (Doctor's wife collapses after denouncing her poisoner): *repente mentis nubilo turbine correpta.*

Solabar : dolores levabam (*SO* 24). Cf. *AA* 10. 29 (Lucius comforting himself with the expectation of Spring and roses): *Plane tenui specula solabar clades ultimas.*

Nundinat : mercatur (*NU* 13). Cf. *AA* 10. 33 (Lucius attacking lawyers as 'vultures in togas'): *Quid ergo miramini, ... togati vulturii, si toti nunc iudices sententias suas pretio nundinatur ... ?*

Gremio fovet : qui sinu[m] sustinet (*GR* 9). Cf. *AA* 10. 35 (Lucius lying down on the beach): *in quodam mollissimo harenae gremio lassum corpus porrectus refoueo.*

---

[10] Lindsay attributes this gloss to Festus.

[11] Lindsay brackets this as a gloss which has crept in from the *Abstrusa* glossary.

[12] Weak evidence, since the *lustrum* being glossed is merely a homonym of *lustrum* ('place of debauchery'), though Spurcus' *anni ... reuolutio* could have generated confusion.

Book 11

Byssum : sericum tortum (*BI* 2). Cf. *AA* 11. 3 (Isis' tunic): *Tunica multicolor, bysso tenui pertexta.* Cf. Martianus Capella, 2. 114.

Luna semestris : medii mensis (*LU* 28). Cf. *AA* 11. 4 (the image of the full moon on Isis' cloak): *semenstris luna flammeos spirabat ignes.*

Iniurius : iniquius, iniustus (*IN* 155). Cf. *AA* 11. 6 (Isis explaining to Lucius why he owes her all that remains of his life): *Nec iniurium, cuius beneficio redieris ad homines, ei totum debere quod vives.*

Materiam : occasionem (*MA* 46). Cf. *AA* 11. 15 (Mithras' dismissal of Blind Fortune): *Eat nunc et summo furore saeviat et crudelitati suae materiam quaereat aliam.*

Carc<h>es[s]ium est in summo malo na<vis> (*CA* 51). Cf. *AA* 11. 16 (ship dedicated to Isis): *Iam malus insurgit pinus rotunda, splendore sublimis, insigni[s] carchesio conspicua.*

Semota : obtecta vel sequestrata (*SE* 68). Cf. *AA* 11. 23 (the dismissal of the crowds prior to Lucius' initiation): *Tunc semotis procul profanis omnibus.*

Fovendis : amandis (*FO* 14). Cf. *AA* 11. 25 (Lucius' prayer to the statue of Isis): *semper fovendis mortalibus munifica.*

Beluae : bestiae marinae (-ris?) (*BE* 6). Cf. *AA* 11. 25 (Lucius' prayer to the statue of Isis): *Tuam maiestastem perhorrescunt... beluae ponto natantes.*

Inlustrat : illuminat, visitat, vel honore sublimat (*IN* 156). Cf. *AA* 11. 27 (Lucius discovers that he has not yet been enlighted by the mysteries of Osiris): *At magni dei deumque summi parentis, invicti Osiris, necdum sacris inlustratum).*

Bibliography

Primary Sources

Manuscripts

Eton College. MS 147.
London. British Library, MS Harley 4838.
Oxford. Bodleian Library, MS Laud. Lat. 55.
Vatican City. Biblioteca Apostolica Vaticana, MS Vat. Lat. 3384.

Editions of Apuleius

Bussi, Giovanni Andrea de (Johannes Andreas de Buxis), ed., *Lucii Apuleii platonici madaurensi philosophi metamorphoseos liber: ac nonnulla alia opuscula eiusdem: necnon epitoma Alcinoi in disciplinarum Platonis desinunt* (Rome: [C. Sweynheim & A. Pannartz], 28 Feb. 1469).

Celtis, Conrad, *Lucij Apulei Platonici et Aristotelici philosophi Epitoma diuinum de mundo seu Cosmographia ductu Conradi Celtis impressum Uienne* (Vienna: J. Winterburger, 1497).

Beroaldo, Filippo, ed., *Commentarii a Philippo Beroaldo conditi in asinum aureum Lucii Apulei* (Bologna: Benedictus Hectoris, 1 Aug. 1500).

Tuccus, Marianus, ed., *Quæ præsenti enchiridio continentur. De asino aureo libelli xi. Florida. De dogmate Platonis. De philosophia item liber unicus. Asclepius... item in calce L. Apuleii orationes duæ pro se ipso* (Florence: Philippus de Giunta, 1512) (First Juntine).

Asulanus, Franciscus, ed., *L. Apuleii Metamorphoseos, siue lusus asini libri XI. Floridorum IIII. De deo Socratis I. De philosophia I. Asclepius Trismegisti dialogus eodem Apuleio interprete. Eiusdem Apuleii liber de mundo... Apologiæ II. Isagogicus liber Platonicæ philosophiæ per Alcinoum philosophum græce impressus* (Venice: In ædibus Aldi & Andreæ soceri, 1521).

Bernardus Philomathes Pisanus, ed., *Quæ in toto opere continentur. L. Apuleij Madaurensis, Metamorphoseon siue de asino aureo. Libri XI. Floridorum. Libri IIII. De deo Socratis libellus. Apologiæ. Libri II. Trismegistus dialogus. De mundo siue de cosmographia liber I* (Florence: Per hæredes Philippi Iuntæ, 1522) (Second Juntine).

Colvius, Petrus, ed., *L. Apulei Madaurensis opera omnia quæ exstant, emendata & aucta: curâ Petri Colvi Brugensis: cum eiusdem ad omnia uberioribus notis* (Leiden: Ex Officina Plantiniana apud Franciscum Raphelengium, 1588).

Wower, Jan, ed., *L. Apuleii Madaurensis Platonici opera. Iohan. à Wouuer ad veterum librorum fidem recensuit, infinitis locis emendauit, nonnullis auxit* ([Basle:] Froben, 1606).

Price, John, ed., *L. Apulei Madaurensis, philosophi Platonici Apologia* (Paris: Simon Fevrier, 1635).

—— ed., *L. Apuleii Madaurensis Metamorphoseos libri XI, cum notis & amplissimo indice Ioannis Pricæi* (Gouda: Willem van der Hoeve, 1650).

Butler, H. E., and A. S. Owen, eds., *Apulei Apologia sive Pro se de Magia Liber* (Oxford: Clarendon, 1914).

Robertson, D. S., ed., *Apulée: Les Métamorphoses*, vol. i (Paris: Budé, 1940).

Vallette, Paul, ed. and trans., *Apulée: Apologie, Florides*, 2nd edn. (Paris: Budé, 1960).

Beaujeu, Jean, ed., *Apulée: Opuscules philosophiques* (Paris: Budé, 1973).

Translations from Apuleius (and Pseudo-Apuleius)

Renaissance Translations

Adlington, William, *The xi Bookes of the Golden Ass, Conteininge, the Metamorphosie of Lucius Apuleius, enterlaced with sondrie plesant and delectable Tales, with an excellent Narration of the Mariage of Cupide and Psiches, set out in the iiij v and vi Bookes. Translated out of Latine into Englishe by William Adlington* (London: Henry Wykes, 1566).

—— *The eleuen Bookes of the Golden Asse containing, the metamorphosie of Lucius Apuleius, enterlaced with sundry pleasant & delectable tales, with an excellent narration of the marriage of Cupid and Psyches, sette out in the fourth, the fifth, and the sixt Bookes. Translated out of Latin into English by William Adlington* (London: Valentine Symmes, 1596).

Boiardo, Matteo Maria, *Apulegio volgare, tradotto pe el conto Mattheo Maria Boiardo* (Venice: Nicolò d'Aristotele da Ferrara and Vincenzo de Polo da Venetia, 1518).

Bouthière, George de la, *Metamorphosie, autrement, l'asne d'or de L. Apulee de Madaure Philosophe Platonique | Traduite de Latin en nostre Vulgaire par George de la Bouthiere Autunois* (Lyons: Iean de Tournes & Guillaume Gazeau, 1553).

Cortegana, Diego Lopez de, *Lucio Apuleyo del asno de oro, Corregido y anadido* (Medina d'l campo: P. de Castro, 1543).

Firenzuola, Agnolo, *L'asino d'oro d'Apuleio* (1550?), in *Opere scelte di Agnolo Firenzuola*, ed. Giuseppe Fatini, 2nd edn. (Turin: Unione tipogafico-editrice torinese, 1966).

Louveau, Jean, *Luc. Apulée de lasne doré: contenant onze livres. Traduit en François par Iean Louueau* (Lyons: Jean Temporal, 1553).

—— *Luc. Apulee de l'ane dore, xi. liures. Traduit en François par. I. Louueau d'Orleans, & mis par Chapitres & Sommaires auec vne table en fin, plus y a sus les 4. 5. 6. liures traitons de l'amour de Cupido & de Psyches xxxii huictains mis en leur lieu, traduits sus d'autres qui ont esté trouuez taillez en cuiure en langue Italique* (Paris: Claude Micard, 1584).

Michel, Guillaume, *Lucius Apuleius de Lasne dore autrement dit de la couronne Cere* |
  *conte̲nant maintes belles hystoires delectantes fables et subtilles inue̲ntions de diuers
  propos Speciallement de philosophe e Tra̲nslate de Latin en langaige Francoys* (Paris:
  Philippe le Noir, 1522).

Modern Translations

Copenhaver, Brian P., trans., *Hermetica: The Greek 'Corpus Hermeticum' and the Latin
  'Asclepius' in a New English Translation* (Cambridge: CUP, 1992).
Gaselee, Stephen, trans., *The Golden Ass*, Loeb Library (London: Heinemann, 1915;
  repr. 1977).
Graves, Robert, trans., *The Transformations of Lucius* (Harmondsworth, Penguin,
  1950).
Hanson, J. A., trans., *Apuleius: Metamorphoses*, Loeb Library (London: Heinemann,
  1989).
Harrison, S. J., ed., *Apuleius: Rhetorical Works*, trans. Stephen Harrison, John Hilton,
  and Vincent Hunink (Oxford: OUP, 2001).
Kenney, E. J., trans., *Apuleius: The Golden Ass: or, Metamorphoses* (London: Penguin,
  1998.
Taylor, Thomas, trans., *The Fable of Cupid and Psyche ... to which are added, a poetical
  paraphrase on the speech of Diotima, in the Banquet of Plato; four hymns, & c.*
  (London: T. Taylor, 1795).
—— *Apuleius' Golden Ass, or, The Metamorphosis: and other Philosophical Writings*
  (London: T. Rodd, 1822; repr. Frome: Prometheus Trust, 1999).
Walsh, P. G., trans., *Apuleius: The Golden Ass* (Oxford: Clarendon, 1994).

Other Primary Sources

Accursio, Mariangelo, *Osco, Volsco, Romanaq. eloquentia interlocutoribus, Dialogus,
  ludis Romanis actus, in quo ostenditur, verbis publica moneta signatis utendum
  esse, prisca vero nimis et exoleta tanquam scopulos esse fugienda*, etc. ([Rome: n.
  p.], 1531).
—— *De antiquato et obsoleto sermone fugiendo, dialogi duo, etc. (Osci, et Volsci.-
  Lexiphanes. Simylus Sopolis)* [ed. L. Margonius] (Strasbourg: A. Bertramus, 1610).
—— ed. *Ammianus Marcellinus a Mariangelo Accursio mendis quinque millibus pur-
  gatus, & libris quinque auctus ultimis, nunc primum ab eodem inventis* (Augsburg:
  Silvan Otmar, 1533).
Agrippa, Henricus Cornelius, *Declamatio de incertitudine et vanitate scientiarum atque
  artium* (Antwerp: Johannes Graphaeus, 1530).
—— *Henrie Cornelius Agrippa. Of the Vanitie and Uncertaintie of Artes and Sciences,
  Englished by Ja[mes]. San[ford]. Gent* (London: Henry Wykes, 1569).
—— *De occulta philosophia libri tres*, ed. V. Perrone Compagni, Studies in the History
  of Christian Thought 48 (Leiden: Brill, 1992).
Alanus de Insulis, *De planctu Naturae*, ed. N. M. Häring, *Studi medievali*, 3rd ser. 19
  (1978), 797–879.

Alanus de Insulis, *Alan of Lille: The Plaint of Nature*, trans. J. J. Sheridan (Toronto: PIMS, 1980).

Alberti, Leon Battista, *On Painting and On Sculpture: The Latin Texts of 'De pictura' and 'De statua'*, ed. and trans. Cecil Grayson (London: Phaidon, 1972).

—— *Sur la cryptographie* [*De componendis cifris*], trans. Martine Furno, *De Petrarque à Descartes* 68 (1999), 705–28.

Allott, Robert, ed., *Englands Parnassus: or The choysest Flowers of our Moderne Poets, with their Poeticall comparisons* (London: For N. L[ing,] C. B[urby] and T. H[ayes], 1600).

—— *Englands Parnassus Compiled by Robert Allott, 1600*, ed. Charles Crawford (Oxford: Clarendon, 1913).

Amatus Fornacius (pseudonym), *Amator ineptus*, ed. Ingrid de Smet: 'Amatus Fornacius, *Amator Ineptus* (Palladii, 1633): A Seventeenth-Century Satire', *HL* 38 (1989), 238–306.

Anonymi contra philosophos, ed. Diethard Aschoff, CCSL 58A (Turnhout: Brepols, 1975).

Anthologia Latina, ed. F. Buecheler and A. Reise, 2 vols. (Leipzig: Teubner, 1894–1906).

Apianus, Petrus (Peter Bienewitz), ed., *Inscriptiones sacrosanctae vetustatis* (Ingolstadt: Petrus Apianus, 1534).

Arber, Edward, ed., *A Transcript of the Registers of the Company of Stationers of London, 1554–1640 A.D.*, 5 vols. (London: priv. printed, 1875–94).

Ariosto, Ludovico, *Orlando furioso*, ed. Marcello Turchi and Edoardo Sanguineti (Milan: Garzanti, 1974; repr. 1985).

—— *Sir John Harington's Translation of 'Orlando furioso'* (1591), ed. Graham Hough (London: Centaur, 1962).

Ascham, Roger, *The Whole Works of Roger Ascham*, ed. J. A. Giles, 3 vols. (London: John Russell Smith, 1864–5).

Ausonius, *Decimi Magni Ausonii Burdigalensis opuscula*, ed. Sextus Prete (Leipzig: Teubner, 1978).

—— *The Works of Ausonius*, ed. R. P. H. Green (Oxford: Clarendon, 1992).

Bandello, Matteo Maria, *Matthaei Bandelli Opera latina inedita vel rara*, ed. Carlo Godi, Medioevo e umanesimo 52 (Padua: Antenore, 1983).

Barlow, William (or Jerome), *Rede me and be nott wrothe* (Strasbourg: Johann Schott, 1528).

Barnes, Barnabe, *Parthenophil and Parthenophe* (London: J. Wolfe, 1593).

Baron, Robert, *Pocula Castalia: The authors motto. Fortunes tennis-ball. Eliza. Poems. Epigrams, & c.* (London: W. H. for Thomas Dring, 1650).

Becichemo, Marino, *Marinus Becichemus... salutem omnibus... Hoc libro continentur hæc opera Becichemi. Panegyricus... Principi Leonardo Lauretano et... Senatui Veneto dictus. Centuria epistolicarum quæstionum... in qua sunt capita plura ad artem oratoriam & ad artificium orationum Ciceronis spectantia. Item sunt castigationes multæ in asinum aureum & in multa alio[rum] aucto[rum] o[per]a, etc.* (Venice: Bernardinus Venetus de Vitalibus, 1506).

Benedict of Nursia, St., *Regula Benedicti*, ed. Rudolf Hanslik, 2nd edn., CSEL 75 (Vienna: Hoelder-Pichler-Tempsky, 1977).

Bérault, Nicholas, *Nicolai Beraldi Aurelii dialogus. Quo rationes quædam explicantur, quibus dicendi ex tempore facultas parari potest: deque ipsa dicendi ex tempore facultate: ad reuerendiss<imum>. Cardinalem Oddonem Castelionensem, tituli diuorum Sergij, Bacchi, Apuleij uirum utriusque linguæ peritissimum* (Lyons: Seb. Gryphius, 1534).

Bernardus Silvestris, *Cosmographia*, ed. Peter Dronke, Textus Minores 53 (Leiden: Brill, 1978).

—— *The 'Cosmographia' of Bernardus Silvestris*, trans. Winthrop Wetherbee (New York: Columbia UP, 1973).

—— *The Commentary on Martianus Capella's 'De nuptiis Philologiae et Mercurii' Attributed to Bernardus Silvestris*, ed. Haijo Jan Westra, Studies and Texts 80 (Toronto: PIMS, 1986).

—— *The Commentary on the First Six Books of the 'Aeneid' of Virgil Commonly Attributed to Bernardus Silvestris*, ed. J. W. Jones and E. F. Jones (Lincoln, Nebr.: U of Nebraska P, 1977).

Beroaldo, Filippo, *Orationes et poemata. Orationes Philippis Beroaldi uiri q[ui] clarissimi Bononiae litteras bonas docentis* ([[Lyons]: [Johannes Trechsel], [4 Sept. 1492]).

—— *Commentarii a Philippo Beroaldo conditi in asinum aureum Lucii Apulei* (Bologna: Benedictus Hectoris, 1 Aug. 1500).

—— *Varia Philippi Beroaldi opuscula* (Basle: J. Froben, 1513).

Bessarion, John, *Bessarionis cardinalis Sabini & Patriarche Constantinopolitani libri aduersus calumniatorem Platonis* (Rome: C. Sweynheym & A. Pannartz [before 28 Aug. 1469]).

Boccaccio, Giovanni, *Amorosa Visione: Bilingual Edition*, trans. Robert Hollander, Timothy Hampton, and Margherita Frankel, introd. Vittore Branca (Hanover, NH: UP of New England, 1986).

—— *Genealogiæ deorum gentilium* (Venice: Wendelm of Speier, 1472).

—— *Ioannis Bocatii peri genealogias deorum, libri quindecim, cum annotationibus Iacobi Micylli* (Basle: Io. Hervagius, 1532).

—— *Boccaccio-Funde: Stücke aus der bislang verschollenen Bibliothek des Dichters darunter von seiner Hand geschriebenes Fremdes und Eigenes*, ed. Oskar Hecker (Brunswick: Westermann, 1902).

—— *Boccaccio on Poetry: Being the Preface and the Fourteenth and Fifteenth Books of Boccaccio's 'Genealogia Deorum Gentilium' in an English Version with Introduction, Essay and Commentary*, trans. and introd. Charles G. Osgood (Princeton: PUP, 1930).

—— *Genealogie deorum gentilium libri*, ed. Vincenzo Romano (Bari: Laterza, 1951).

—— *Opere latine minori*, ed. Aldo F. Massèra, Scrittori d'Italia 111 (Bari: Laterza, 1928).

—— *Comedia delle ninfe fiorentine (Ameto)*, ed. A. E. Quaglio, in *Tutte le opere di Giovanni Boccaccio*, gen. ed. Vittore Branca (Verona: Mondadori, 1964), ii. 665–835.

Boccaccio, Giovanni, *L'Ameto*, trans. Judith Serafini-Sauli, Garland Library of Medieval Literature 33 (New York: Garland, 1985).

Boiardo, Matteo Maria, *Orlando innamorato*, ed. Giuseppe Anceschi, 2 vols. (Milan: Garzanti, 1978).

Botfield, Beriah, ed., *Prefaces to the First Editions of the Greek and Roman Classics and of the Sacred Scriptures* (London: Bohn, 1861).

Boyle, Roger, First Earl of Orrery, *Parthenissa, a Romance. In Four Parts. Dedicated to the Lady Northumberland, And the Lady Sunderland. The Fourth Part* (London: Henry Herringman, 1655).

Brooke, Arthur, *Brooke's 'Romeus and Juliet'*, ed. J. J. Munro (London: Chatto & Windus, 1908).

Browne, Thomas, *Sir Thomas Browne's Pseudodoxia Epidemica*, ed. Robin Robbins, 2 vols. (Oxford: Clarendon, 1981).

Browne, William, *The Poems of William Browne of Tavistock*, ed. Gordon Goodwin, introd. A. H. Bullen, 2 vols. (London: Routledge, 1894).

'Burley, Walter' (attrib.), *Liber de vita ac moribus philosophorum poetarumque veterum. Ex multis libris tractus necnon breuiter & compendiose per venerabilem virum magistrem Walterum Burley compilatus* [Cologne: U. Zell, after 1469].

—— *Gualteri Burlaei Liber de Vita et Moribus Philosophorum mit einer altspanischen Übersetzung der Eskurialbibliothek*, ed. Hermann Knust, Bibliothek des litterarischen Vereins in Stuttgart 177 (Tübingen: Litterarischer Verein in Stuttgart, 1886).

Burton, Robert, *The Anatomy of Melancholy*, ed. Thomas C. Faulkner et al., 6 vols. (Oxford: Clarendon, 1989–2000).

Bussi, Giovanni Andrea de (Johannes Andreas de Buxis), *Giovanni Andrea Bussi: Prefazioni alle edizioni di Sweynheym e Pannartz prototipografi Romani*, ed. Massimo Miglio (Milan: Edizioni il Polifilo, 1978).

Calcidius, *Platonis Timaeus interprete Chalcidio cum eiusdem commentario*, ed. Johann Wrobel (Leipzig: Teubner, 1876).

Calepino, Ambrogio, *Ambrosii Calepini Bergomatis ordinis Eremitarum obseruantium professoris deuotissimi vocabularius. Thesaurus copiosissimus* (Frascati: Alexander Paganinus, 1522).

Cardano, Girolamo, *Hieronymi Cardani Mediolanensis philosophi ac medici celeberrimi opera omnia*, 10 vols., ed. Charles Spon (Lyons: Jean-Antoine Huguetan and Marc-Antoine Rauaud, 1663).

—— *The Book of My Life (De Vita Propria Liber) by Jerome Cardan*, trans. Jean Stoner (London: Dent, 1931).

Carew, Richard, *A Herrings Tayle: Contayning a Poeticall Fiction of Divers Matters Worthie the Reading* (London: Matthew Lownes, 1598).

Carretto, Galeotto dal, *Noze de Psyche & Cupidine celebrate per lo magnifico Marchese Galeoto dal Carreto: poeta in lingua Tosca non uulgare* (Milan: A. de Vicomercato for I. I. & fratelli de Legnano, 1520).

—— *Noze de Psiche e Cupidine*, in *Teatro del Quattrocento: Le corti padane*, ed. Antonia Tissoni Benvenuti and Maria Pia Mussini Sacchi (Turin: UTET, 1983), 611–725.

Cartari, Vincenzo, *Imagini degli dei degli antichi* (Venice: Marcolini, 1556).

Casaubon, Isaac, *Isaaci Casuboni de satyrica Græcorum poesi, & Romanorum satira libri duo. In quibus etiam poetæ recensentur, qui in vtraque poesi floruerunt* (Paris: Ambrosius & Hieronymus Drouart, 1606).

Cassiodorus, *Cassiodori Senatoris institutiones*, ed. R. A. B. Mynors (Oxford: Clarendon, 1937; repr. 1963).

Castellesi, Adriano, *De sermone Latino, et modis Latine loquendi* (Rome: Marcellus Silber, 1515).

Castelvetro, Lodovico, *Castelvetro on the Art of Poetry: An Abridged Translation of Lodovico Castelvetro's 'Poetica d'Aristotele vulgarizzata et sposta'*, trans. Andrew Bongiorno, MRTS 29 (Binghamton: Medieval & Renaissance Texts & Studies, 1984).

Celtis, Conrad, *Libri odarum quatuor, cum Epodo, & saeculari Carmine* (Strasbourg: Schurer, 1513).

—— *Der Briefwechsel des Konrad Celtis*, ed. Hans Rupprich (Munich: Beck, 1934).

—— *Selections from Conrad Celtis, 1459–1508*, ed. Leonard Forster (Cambridge: CUP, 1948).

Cervantes Saavedra, Miguel de, *Don Quijote de la Mancha I*, ed. J. B. Avalle-Arce (Madrid: Alhambra, 1979).

Chaucer, Geoffrey, *The Riverside Chaucer*, gen. ed. Larry D. Benson (Boston: Houghton Mifflin, 1987).

Chrétien de Troyes, *Kristian von Troyes: Cligés*, ed. Wendelin Foerster (Halle: Niemeyer, 1921).

—— *Arthurian Romances*, trans. D. D. R. Owen (London: Dent, 1987).

Christodorus of Thebes, Ἔκφρασις, in *The Greek Anthology*, ed. and trans. W. R. Paton, 5 vols. (London: Heinemann, 1917–18), i. 58–91.

Chronicon Salernitanum: A Critical Edition with Studies on Literary and Historical Sources and on Language, ed. Ulla Westerbergh, Acta Universitatis Stockholmiensis, Studia Latina Stockholmiensia 3 (Stockholm: Almquist & Wiksell, 1956).

Claudianus Mamertus, *Claudiani Mamerti opera*, ed. August Engelbrecht, CSEL 11 (Vienna: Geroldi Fil., 1885).

Colonna, Francesco (attrib.), *Francesco Colonna: Hypnerotomachia Poliphili (Venetiis, Aldo Manuzio, 1499)*, facs. edn., introd. Peter Dronke (Saragossa: Ediciones de Pórtico, 1981).

—— *Francesco Colonna: Hypnerotomachia Poliphili. Edizione critica e commento*, ed. Giovanni Pozzi and Lucia A. Ciapponi, 2 vols., 2nd edn. (Padua: Antenore, 1980).

—— *Francesco Colonna: Hypnerotomachia Poliphili: The Strife of Love in a Dream*, trans. and introd. Joscelyn Godwin (London: Thames & Hudson, 1999).

Conquestio uxoris Cavichioli papiensis (aka *De Cavicholo*), in *Teatro goliardico dell' Umanesimo*, ed. Vito Pandolfi and Erminia Artese (Milan: Lerici, 1965), 31–45.

Conti, Natale, *Natalis Comitis mythologiae, sive explicationum fabularum, libri decem: in quibus omnia prope naturalis & moralis philosophia dogmata continentur* (Paris: Arnoldus Sittart, 1583).

Cooper, Thomas, *Thesaurus linguæ Romanæ & Britannicæ, tam accurate congestus, vt nihil penè in eo desyderari possit, quod vel Latinè complectatur amplissimus Stephani thesaurus, vel Anglicè, toties aucta Eliotæ bibliotheca: opera & industria Thomæ Cooperi Magdalensis* (London: Henry Wykes, 1565).

Correggio, Niccolò da, *Fabula Psiches et Cupidinis* (Venice: Manfrino Bono de Monteferrato, 1507).

—— *Opere: Cefalo, Psiche, Silva, Rime*, ed. Antonia Tissoni Benvenuti, Scrittori d'Italia 244 (Bari: Laterza, 1969).

Cortesi, Paolo, *De cardinalatu* (Castrum Cortesium: Symeon Nardi, 1510).

Coryciana, ed. Jozef IJsewijn, Varia (Academia Latinitati Fovendae) 7 (Rome: Herder, 1997).

Cowley, Abraham, *Love's Riddle. A Pastorall Comædie, written, at the time of his being Kings scholler in Westminster Schoole* (London: John Dawson, for Henry Seile, 1638).

—— *Essays, Plays and Sundry Verses*, ed. A. R. Waller (Cambridge: CUP, 1906).

D[allington], R[obert], trans., *Hypnerotomachia. The Strife of Loue in a Dreame* (London: Simon Waterstone, 1592), facs. edn., introd. Lucy Gent (Delmar, NY: Scholars' Facsimiles & Reprints, 1973).

Dante Alighieri, *The Divine Comedy*, trans. John D. Sinclair, 3 vols. (London: Bodley Head, 1939).

Decembrio, Angelo Camillo, *De politia litteraria*, ed. Norbert Witten, Beiträge zu Altertumskunde 169 (Munich: Saur, 2002).

Dekker, Thomas, *A Knight's Conjuring* (1607), ed. E. F. Rimbault, vol. v (London: Percy Soc., 1842).

Dickenson, John, *Arisbas, Euphues amidst his Slumbers: or Cupids iourney to hell* (London: Thos. Creede for Thos. Woodcocke, 1594).

—— *Prose and Verse by John Dickenson*, ed. Alexander B. Grosart ([Blackburn]: priv. printed, 1878).

Diodorus Siculus, *Diodorus of Sicily: The Library of History*, trans. C. H. Oldfather, 10 vols., Loeb Library (London: Heinemann, 1933).

Dolet, Étienne, *Stephani Doleti Dialogus de imitatione Ciceroniana aduersus Desiderium Erasmum Roterodamum, pro Christopher Longolio*, facs. edn., ed. E. V. Telle, in *L'Erasmianus siue Ciceronianus d'Étienne Dolet (1535)*, Travaux d'humanisme et renaissance 138 (Geneva: Droz, 1974).

—— *Stephani Doleti Galli Aurelii liber de imitatione Ciceroniana aduersus Floridum Sabinum* (Leiden: Étienne Dolet, 1540).

Donne, John, *The 'Elegies' and 'The Songs and Sonnets'*, ed. Helen Gardner (Oxford: Clarendon, 1965).

Drayton, Michael, *The Works of Michael Drayton*, ed. J. W. Hebel et al., 5 vols. (Oxford: Shakespeare Head P, 1931–41; repr. 1961).

DuVal, John, trans., and Raymond Eichmann, eds., *Cuckolds, Clerics, and Countrymen: Medieval French Fabliaux* (Fayetteville: U of Arkansas P, 1982).

Elyot, Sir Thomas, *Thomas Elyot: Dictionary 1538*, ed. R. C. Alston, English Linguistics 1500–1800: A Collection of Facsimile Reprints 221 (Menston: Scolar P, 1970).

—— *Bibliotheca Eliotæ. Eliotes Dictionarie the second tyme enriched, and more perfectly corrected, by Thomas Cooper, schole master of Maudlens in Oxforde* (London: Thomas Berthelet, 1552).

Epistolae Academicae Oxon. (Registrum F): A Collection of Letters and Other Miscellaneous Documents Illustrative of Academical Life and Studies at Oxford in the Fifteenth Century, ed. Henry Anstey, 2 vols. (Oxford: Oxford Historical Soc., 1898).

Equicola, Mario, *Libro di natura d'amore di Mario Equicola. Di nuouo con somma diligenza ristampato e corretto da M. Lodouico Dolce. Con nuoua tauola delle cose piu notabili, che nell'opera si contengono* (Venice: Gabriel Giolito de Ferrari et fratelli, 1554).

Erasmus, *Des. Erasmi Roterod. Dialogus, cui titulus Ciceronianus: siue de optimo genere dicendi* (Neustadt an der Haardt: Henricus Starckius, 1617).

—— *Desiderii Erasmi Roterodami, de duplici copia rerum ac verborum commentarij duo* (Strasbourg: Matthias Scheurer, 1513).

—— *Desiderii Erasmi Roterodami opera omnia* (Leiden: Peter Vander, 1703; Facs. London: Gregg P, 1962).

—— *Opus epistolarum Des. Erasmi Roterodami,* ed. P. S. Allen, 12 vols. (Oxford: Clarendon, 1906–58).

—— *That chyldren oughte to be taught and brought vp gently in vertue and learnynge, and that euen forth wyth from theyr natiuitie: A declamacion of a briefe theme, by Erasmus of Roterodame* (London: John Day [1551]).

—— *Opera omnia Desiderii Erasmi Roterodami* (Amsterdam: North-Holland, 1969–).

—— *Praise of Folly,* trans. Betty Radice, introd. A. H. T. Levi (London: Penguin, 1971).

Estienne, Henri, *De Lipsii latinitate (vt ipsimet antiquarii Lipsii stylum indigitant) Palaestra I, Henr. Stephani, Parisiensis: nec Lipsiomimi, nec Lipsiomomi, nec Lipsiocolacis: multoque minus Lipsiomastigis. Libertas volo sit Latinitati, sed licentia nolo detur illi. Hic multa non vulgaria vulgi literatorum linguis de Latinitate illa antiquaria tantumnon digladiantibus opponuntur. Molestia huius litis est sermonibus implicita multis, auferunt qui taedium, et liticulas tibi ad alias qui conferunt* (Frankfurt: [Stephanus], 1595).

Estienne, Robert, *Dictionarium propriorum nominum virorum, mulierum, populorum, idolorum, vrbium, fluuiorum, montium, cæterorúmque locorum quæ passim in libris prophanis leguntur* (Paris: Robertus Stephanus, 1512).

Fazio degli Uberti, *Il Dittamondo,* ed. Giuseppe Corsi (Bari: Laterza, 1952).

Ficino, Marsilo, *Commentary on Plato's Symposium on Love,* trans. Sears Jayne, 2nd edn. (Dallas: Spring Publications, 1985).

Field, Nathan, John Fletcher, and Philip Massinger, *The Honest Man's Fortune,* in *The Dramatic Works in the Beaumont and Fletcher Canon,* gen. ed. Fredson Bowers, 10 vols. (Cambridge: CUP, 1966–96), x. 1–144.

Firenzuola, Agnolo, *Opere scelte di Agnolo Firenzuola,* ed. G. Fatini, 2nd edn. (Turin: Unione tipogafico-editrice torinese, 1966).

Firenzuola, Agnolo, *On the Beauty of Women*, trans. and ed. Konrad Eisenbichler and Jacqueline Murray (Philadelphia: U of Pennsylvania P, 1992).

Floire et Blancheflor, ed. Margaret M. Pelan, 2nd edn. (Paris: Les Belles Lettres, 1956).

Florido, Francesco, *Francisci Floridi Sabini lectionum subcisiuarum*, in *Lampas, siue fax artium liberalium, hoc est thesaurus criticus*, ed. Jan Gruter, vol. i (Frankfurt: Jonas Rhodius, 1602).

Fournival, Richard de, *La Biblionomia de Richard de Fournival du Manuscrit 636 de la Bibliothèque de la Sorbonne: Texte en facsimilé avec la transcription de Léopold Delisle*, ed. H. J. Vleeschauwer, Mousaion 62 (Pretoria: n.pub., 1965).

Fulgentius, *Enarrationes allegoricæ fabularum* [ed. with comm. by Joannes Baptista Pius] (Milan: V. Scinzenzeler, 1498).

—— *Fabii Planciadis Fulgentii V. C. opera*, ed. Rudolph Helm (Leipzig: Teubner, 1898).

—— *Fulgentius the Mythographer*, trans. Leslie Whitbread ([Columbus]: Ohio State UP, 1971).

Garin, Eugenio, ed., *Prosatori latini del Quattrocento*, La letteratura italiana: storia e testi (Ricciardi) 13 (Milan: Ricciardi, [1952]).

Gascoigne, George, *The Pleasauntest Workes of George Gascoigne Esquyre: Newlye compyled into one volume* (London: Abell Iesses, 1587).

—— *George Gascoigne's 'A Hundreth Sundrie Flowres'*, ed. C. T. Prouty, U of Missouri Studies 17/2 (Columbia: U of Missouri, 1942).

—— *A Hundreth Sundrie Flowres*, ed. G. W. Pigman III (Oxford: Clarendon, 2000).

—— *The Posies*, ed. John W. Cunliffe (Cambridge: CUP, 1907).

Geoffrey of Monmouth, *Historia Regum Britanniae: A Variant Version Edited from the Manuscripts*, ed. Jacob Hammer, Mediaeval Academy of America Publication 57 (Cambridge, Mass.: Mediaeval Academy of America, 1951).

—— *The 'Historiae Regum Britanniae' of Geoffrey of Monmouth*, ed. Acton Griscom (London: Longmans, Green, & Co., 1929).

Gerald of Wales, *Giraldi Cambrensis opera*, Rerum britannicarum medii aevi scriptores 21, 8 vols. (London: Longmans, 1861–91), vol. v, ed. James F. Dimmock.

Giovio, Paolo, *Pauli Iouii Nouocomensis episcopi Nucerini elogia virorum literis illustrium, quotquot vel auorum memoria vixere* (Basle: Peter Perna, 1577).

Glossaria Latina iussu Academiae Britannicae edita, vol. iii. *(Abstrusa, Abolita)*, ed. W. M. Lindsay and H. J. Thomson (Paris: Société anonyme d'édition 'Les Belles lettres', 1926).

Golding, Arthur, trans., *The Fyrst Fower Bookes of Ouidius Nasos worke, intitled Metamorphosis* (London: William Seres, 1565).

Gosson, Stephen, *Playes Confuted in Five Actions* (London: Thos. Gosson, 1582); repr. in *The English Drama and Stage under the Tudor and Stuart Princes 1543–1664*, ed. William Carew Hazlitt (London: Roxburghe Library, 1869), 157–218.

Greene, Robert, *A quip for an vpstart courtier: or, A quaint dispute betvveen veluet breeches and cloth-breeches Wherein is plainely set downe the disorders in all estates and trades* (London: John Wolfe, 1592).

Greg, W. W., ed., *A Companion to Arber: Being a Calendar of Documents in Edward Arber's 'Transcript of the Registers of the Company of Stationers of London, 1554–1640': With Texts and Calendar of Supplementary Documents* (Oxford: Clarendon, 1967).

Guillaume de Lorris, and Jean de Meun, *Le Roman de la Rose*, ed. Félix Lecoy, 3 vols. (Paris: Librairie Honoré Champion, 1965–70; repr. 1973–85).

—— —— *The Romance of the Rose*, trans. Charles Dahlberg (Hanover, NH: UP of New England, 1983).

Harvey, Gabriel, *Gabrielis Harueii Rhetor, vel duorum dierum oratio. De natura, arte, & exercitatione rhetorica. Ad suos auditores* (London: Henry Binnemann, 1577).

—— *The trimming of Thomas Nashe Gentleman, by the high-tituled patron Don Richardo de Medico campo, barber chirurgion to Trinitie Colledge in Cambridge* [i.e. Richard Lichfield] (London: Printed [by E. Allde] for Philip Scarlet, 1597).

—— *Gabriel Harvey's 'Ciceronianus'*, ed. Harold S. Wilson, trans. Clarence A. Forbes (Lincoln, Nebr.: U of Nebraska, 1945).

—— *Letter-Book of Gabriel Harvey, A.D. 1573–1580*, ed. Edward John Long Scott (London: Camden Soc., 1884).

—— *The Works of Gabriel Harvey, D.C.L.*, ed. A. B. Grosart, 3 vols. (London: Huth Library, 1884).

Hawkins, William, *Apollo Shroving. Composed for the Schollars of the Free-schoole of Hadleigh in Suffolke. And acted by them on Shroue-tuesday, being the sixt of February, 1626* (London: Robert Mylbourne, [1627]).

Henslowe, Philip, *Henslowe's Diary*, ed. R. A. Foakes, 2nd edn. (Cambridge: CUP, 2002).

Heywood, Thomas, *Dramatic Works of Thomas Heywood*, 6 vols. (London: John Pearson, 1874).

Hind, John, *Eliosto Libidinoso* (London: Valentine Simmes, 1606).

Holyday, Barten, ΤΕΞΝΟΓΑΜΙΑ [*Technogamia*] *or The marriages of the arts: A comedie written by Barten Holyday, Master of Arts, and student of Christ-Church in Oxford, and acted by the students of the same house before the Vniuersitie, at Shroue-tide* (London: William Stansby for John Parker, 1618).

—— *Technogamia*, ed. Sister M. Jean Carmel Cavanaugh (Washington, DC: Catholic U of America P, 1942).

Hooper, John, *Early Writings of John Hooper, D.D. Lord Bishop of Gloucester and Worcester, Martyr, 1555*, ed. Samuel Carr (Cambridge: Parker Soc., 1843).

Hugh of Fleury [Hugo de Sancta Maria], *Hugonis Floriacensis monachi Benedictini Chronicon, quingentis ab hinc annis & quod excurrit, conscriptum*, ed. Bernhard Rottendorf (Monasterium Westphaliae: Bernard Raesfeld, 1638).

Hutten, Ulrich von, *Ulrichi Hutteni . . . opera*, ed. E. Böcking, 5 vols. (Leipzig: Teubner, 1856–61).

Index, *Index auctorum et librorum qui ab officio sanctae Rom. uniuersalis inquisitionis caueri ab omnibus et singulis in uniuersa Christiana republica mandantur* (Rome: Pope Paul IV, 1558).

Index, *Nouus index librorum prohibitorum* (Cologne: Ex commissione S.R.E. Inquis., 1627).

—— *Nouissimus librorum prohibitorum et expurgandorum index* (Madrid: Supreme Senate of the Inquisition, 1640).

Isidore of Seville, *Sancti Isidori Hispalensis episcopi, opera omnia quæ extant*, ed. Frater Iacobus du Breul (Paris: Michael Sonnius, 1601).

—— *The Etymologies of Isidore of Seville*, ed. and trans. Stephen A. Barney et al. (Cambridge: CUP, 2006).

James, Richard, *Poems of Richard James*, ed. A. B. Grosart (priv. pr., 1880).

Jewel, John, *The Works of John Jewel, Bishop of Salisbury. The Third Portion, Containing Apologia Ecclessiæ Anglicanæ. An Apology of the Church of England. The Defence of the Apology, Parts I–III*, ed. John Ayre (Cambridge: Parker Soc., 1848).

John of Salisbury, *Ioannis Sareberiensis Episcopi Carnotensis Policratici sive De Nugis Curialium et Vestigiis Philosophorum Libri VIII*, ed. Clemens Webb, 2 vols. (Oxford: Clarendon, 1909).

—— *Policraticus: Of the Frivolities of Courtiers and the Footprints of Philosophers*, ed. and trans. Cary J. Nederman, Cambridge Texts in the History of Political Thought (Cambridge: CUP, 1990).

—— *The Letters of John of Salisbury*, ed. W. J. Millor, H. E. Butler, and C. N. L. Brooke, rev. edn., 2 vols. (Oxford: Clarendon, 1979–86).

Jonson, Ben, *Ben Jonson*, ed. C. H. Herford and Percy Simpson, 11 vols. (Oxford: Clarendon, 1925–52).

Julianus the Theurgist, *The Chaldean Oracles: Text, Translation, and Commentary*, ed. Ruth Majercik (Leiden: Brill, 1989).

Keil, Heinrich, ed., *Grammatici Latini*, 7 vols. (Leipzig: Teubner, 1857–80).

Kendall, Timothy, *Flovvers of epigrammes, out of sundrie the moste singular authours selected, as well auncient as late writers. Pleasant and profitable to the expert readers of quicke capacitie: by Timothe Kendall, late of the Vniuersitie of Oxford: now student of Staple Inne in London* (London: [By John Kingston] by Ihon Shepperd, 1577).

King, John, *Lectures upon Ionas, Deliuered at Yorke in the Yeare of our Lord 1594. By John Kinge* (Oxford: Joseph Barnes, 1597).

—— *A sermon preached at White-Hall the 5. day of November. ann. 1608* (Oxford: Joseph Barnes, 1608).

Lactantius, *Lactance: Institutions Divines Livre V, Tome I*, ed. and trans. *Pierre Monat*, Sources Chrétiennes 264 (Paris: Éditions du Cerf, 1973).

Leigh, Edward, *A Treatise of Religion and Learning* (London: A[braham]. M[iller]. for Charles Adams, 1656).

Lewis, C. S., *Till We Have Faces: A Myth Retold* (1956; London: Collins, 1979).

L[inche], R[ichard], *Diella, Certaine Sonnets, adioyned to the amorous Poeme of Dom Diego and Gineura* (London: H. Olyney, 1596).

Lipsius, Justus, *Iusti Lipsi opera omnia quæ ad criticam proprie spectant* (Antwerp: Christophe Plantin, 1585).

Lodge, Thomas, *An alarum against vsurers . . . Heereunto are annexed the delectable historie of Forbonius and Prisceria* (London: T. Este for Sampson Clarke, 1584).

—— *The Complete Works of Thomas Lodge*, 4 vols. ([Glasgow]: Hunterian Club, 1883).

Lucian, *Luciani Samosatensis opera, quæ quidem extant, omnia, a græco sermone in Latinum conuersa, nunc postremùm multo diligentius & melius quàm antè, ad Græcum exemplar correcta & emendata* [ed. Jacob Moltzer] (Paris: Michael Vascosanus, 1546).

—— *Luciani viri quam disertissimi complura opuscula longe festiuissima ab Erasmo Roterodamo & Thoma moro interpretibus optimis in latinorum linguam traducta* ([Paris:] Ascensianus, 1506).

—— *Lucian*, trans. A. M. Harman, 8 vols., Loeb Library (London: Heinemann, 1921).

Luther, Martin, *Against the Roman Papacy: An Institution of the Devil* (1545), trans. Eric W. Gritsch, in *Luther's Works*, 55 vols. (St Louis: Concordia; Philadelphia: Fortress, 1958–86), xli. 263–376.

Lydus, Johannes Laurentianus, *Ioannis Lydi Liber de mensibus*, ed. Richard Wünsch (Stuttgart: Teubner, 1898; repr. 1967).

Lyly [Lilly], John, *Sapho and Phao. Played beefore the Queenes Maiestie on Shrouetewsday, by her Maiesties Children, and the Boyes of Paules* (London: Thomas Cadman, 1584).

—— *Sixe Court Comedies* (London: Edward Blount, 1632).

—— *'Gallathea' and 'Midas'*, ed. Anne Begor Lancashire, Regents Renaissance Drama ([London]: Arnold, 1970).

Macrobius, *Macrobii Aurelii Theodosii viri consularis et illustris in Somnium Scipionis expositionis quamelegantissimae libri. Macrobii . . . Saturnaliorum libri* (Venice: N. Jensen, 1472).

—— *Ambrosii Theodosii Macrobii commentarii in Somnium Scipionis*, ed. James Willis (Leipzig: Teubner, 1970).

—— *Macrobii Ambrosii Theodosii commentariorum in Somnium Scipionis libri duo: Introduzione, testo, traduzione e note*, ed. Luigi Scarpa (Padua: Liviana, 1981).

Maffei, Raffaele, *Commentariorum vrbanorum Raphaelis Volterrani octo et triginti libri* (Basle: Froben and Episcopius, 1559).

Mantovano, Publio Philippo, *Formicone*, ed. Luigina Stefani, I presupposti teatro 1 (Ferrara: Bovolenta, 1980).

Map, Walter, *De nugis curialium. Courtly Trifles*, ed. and trans. M. R. James, rev. C. N. L. Brooke and R. A. B. Mynors (Oxford: Clarendon, 1983).

Marie de France, *The Lais of Marie de France*, trans. Glyn S. Burgess and Keith Busby (London: Penguin, 1986).

Marmion, Shakerley, *Cupid and Psiche, or an Epick Poem of Cupid, and his Mistress*, in *Minor Poets of the Caroline Period*, ed. George Saintsbury, 3 vols. (Oxford: Clarendon, 1906).

Martianus Capella, *Martiani Minei Felicis Capellæ Afri Carthaginensis de nuptiis Philologiæ et Mercurii* (Vicenza: Henricus de Sancto Vrso, 1499).

—— *Martianus Capella*, ed. James Willis (Leipzig: Teubner, 1983).

—— *Martianus Capella and the Seven Liberal Arts*, trans. William Harris Stahl, Richard Johnson, and E. L. Burge, 2 vols. (New York: Columbia UP, 1971–7).

Martianus Capella, *Iohannis Scotti annotationes in Marcianum*, ed. Cora E. Lutz (Cambridge, Mass.: Mediaeval Academy of America, 1939).

—— *Dunchad glossae in Martianum*, ed. Cora E. Lutz (Lancaster, Pa.: APA, 1944).

—— *Remigii Autissiodorensis commentum in Martianum Capellam*, ed. Cora E. Lutz, 2 vols. (Leiden: Brill, 1962–5).

—— *The Berlin Commentary on Martianus Capella's 'De nuptiis Philologiae et Mercurii'. Book I*, ed. Haijo Jan Westra with the assistance of Christina Vester, Mittellateinische Studien und Texte 20 (Leiden: Brill, 1994).

—— *The Berlin Commentary on Martianus Capella's 'De nuptiis Philologiae et Mercurii'. Book II*, ed. Haijo Jan Westra and Tanja Kupke, Mittellateinische Studien und Texte 23 (Leiden: Brill, 1998).

Matthew of Vendôme, *Mathei Vindocinensis Opera*, 3 vols., ed. Franco Munari (Rome: Storia e letteratura, 1977–88).

Met(h)amorphosis Golye episcopi, text in R. B. G. Huygens, 'Mitteilungen aus Handschriften', *Studi medievali* 3 (1962), 747–72.

Miglio, Massimo, ed., *Giovanni Andrea Bussi: Prefazioni alle edizioni di Sweynheym e Pannartz prototipografi Romani*, Documenti sulle arti del libro 12 (Milan: Edizioni il Polifilo, 1978).

Milton, John, *Complete Prose Works of John Milton*, gen., ed. Don M. Wolfe, 10 vols. (New Haven: YUP, 1953–82).

—— *The Poems of John Milton*, ed. John Carey and Alistair Fowler (London: Longman, 1968; repr. 1972).

Moffet, Thomas, *The Silkewormes and their Flies* (1599), facs., ed. and introd. V. H. Houliston, MRTS 56 (Binghamton, NY: Medieval & Renaissance Texts & Studies, 1989).

Montgomerie, Alexander, *The Poems of Alexander Montgomerie*, ed. David J. Parkinson, STS, 4th ser. 28–9, 2 vols. (Edinburgh: Scottish Text Soc., 2000).

More, Thomas, *The Complete Works of St. Thomas More*, iii/2, ed. Clarence H. Miller et al. (New Haven: YUP, 1984).

—— *The Correspondence of Sir Thomas More*, ed. Elizabeth Frances Rogers (Princeton: PUP, 1947).

Morlini, Girolamo, *Hieronymi Morlini Parthenopei novellae, fabulae, comoedia* (Naples: Joan. Pasquet de Sallo, 1520).

—— *Novelle e favole*, ed. Giovanni Villani, Novellieri italiani (Rome: Salerno, 1983).

Muret, Marc-Antoine de, *M. Antonii Mureti, presbyteri, J. C. et civis Rom. Orationum volumina duo. Quorum primum ante aliquot annos in lucem prodijt, secundum vero recens est editum* (Cologne: Anton Hierat, 1614).

Muth, Konrad, *Der Briefwechsel des Conradus Mutianus*, ed. K. Gillert (Halle: Hendel, 1890).

Nashe, Thomas, *The Works of Thomas Nashe*, 5 vols., ed. Ronald B. McKerrow (London: A. H. Bullen/Sidgwick & Jackson, 1904–10).

Nizzoli, Mario, *Nizolius sive Thesaurus Ciceronianus*, ed. Marcello Squarcialupo of Piombino (Basle: Eusebius Episcopius, 1576).

Nonnius, *Nonii Marcelli de compendiosa doctrina libros XX*, ed. Wallace M. Lindsay, vol. i (Leipzig: Teubner, 1903).

Origen, *Origen on First Principles: Being Koetschau's Text of the 'De Principiis'*, trans. G. W. Butterworth (London: SPCK, 1936).

Painter, William, *The Palace of Pleasure: Elizabethan Versions of Italian and French Novels from Boccaccio, Bandello, Cinthio, Straparola, Queen Margaret of Navarre and Others*, ed. Joseph Jacobs, 3 vols. (London: David Nutt, 1890).

Partalopa Saga, ed. Lise Praestgaard Andersen, Editiones Arnamagaeanae, Ser. B, 28 (Copenhagen: Reitzels, 1983).

Partonope, *The Middle-English Versions of 'Partonope of Blois'*, ed. A. Trampe Bödtker, EETS, ES 109 (London: OUP, 1912 for 1911).

Partonopeu de Blois: A French Romance of the Twelfth Century, ed. J. Gildea, 2 vols. (Villanova: Villanova UP, 1967–70).

Perotti, Niccolo, *Nicolai Perotti Cornu copiae seu linguae Latinae commentarii*, ed. Jean-Louis Charlet and Martine Furno, introd. Sesto Prete, 8 vols. (Sassoferrato: Istituto internazionale di studi Piceni, 1989–2001).

Peter of Blois, *Petri Blesensis Carmina*, ed. C. Wollin, CCCM 128 (Turnhout: Brepols, 1998).

Petrarca, Francesco, *Francisci Petrarchæ Florentini, philosophi, oratoris, & Poëtæ, clarissimi, reflorescentis literaturæ Latinæqúe linguæ, aliquot seculis horrenda barbarie inquinatæ ac penè sepultæ, assertoris & instauratoris, Opera quæ extant omnia* (Basle: Henrichus Petrus, 1554).

—— *Edizione nazionale delle opere di Francesco Petrarca*, gen. ed. Vittorio Rossi (Florence: Sansoni, 1926–).

—— *Invectives*, ed. and trans. David Marsh, The I Tatti Renaissance Library 2 (Cambridge, Mass.: HUP, 2003).

—— *Petrarch's Book without a Name*, trans. N. P. Zacour (Toronto: PIMS, 1973).

Petrus Pictor, *Petri Pictoris carmina nec non Petri de Sancto Audemaro librum de coloribus faciendis*, ed. L. van Acker, CCCM 25 (Turnhout: Brepols, 1972).

The Phoenix Nest 1593, ed. H. R. Rollins (Cambridge, Mass.: HUP, 1931).

Pick, Samuel, *Festum Uoluptatis, or The banquet of pleasure furnished with much variety of speculations, wittie, pleasant, and delightfull. Containing divers choyce love-posies, songs, sonnets, odes, madrigals, satyrs, epigrams, epitaphs and elegies. For varietie and pleasure the like never before published* (London: E[lizabeth] P[urslowe] for Bernard Langford, 1639).

Pico the Younger (Giovanni Francesco Pico della Mirandola), *De Venere et Cupidine expellendis carmen* (Rome: Jacobus Mazochius, 1513).

Pinciano, Alonso López, *Philosophia antigua poetica* (Madrid: Thomas Iunti, 1596).

Pins, Jean de, *Vita Philippi Beroaldi Bononiensis*, in *Vitae summorum dignitate et eruditione virorum*, ed. J. G. Meuschen, 4 vols. (Coburg: Jo. Georgius Steinmarck, 1735–41), i. 123–51.

Platina, Bartolomeo, [*Platinae Historici liber De uita Christi: ac Pontificum omnium: qui hactenus ducenti et uigintiduo fuere*] ([Venice]: [Johannes de Colonia & Johannes Manthen], [11 June 1479]).

Platina, Bartolomeo, *Hystoria de vitis pontificum periucunda, diligenter recognita, & nunc tantum integre impressa* (Venice: Philippus Pincius Mantuanus, 1504).

—— *Platynae Historici Liber de vita Christi ac omnium pontificum*, ed. Giacinto Gaida, Rerum italicarum scriptores 3/1 (Città di Castello: Lapi, 1913–32).

—— *The Lives of the Popes*, [anon. Eng. trans., ed. Sir Paul Rycaut, 1685.], ed. Rev. W. Benham, 2 vols. (London: Griffith, Farran, Okeden & Welsh, 1888).

—— *Platina, on Right Pleasure and Good Health: A Critical Edition and Translation of 'De honesta voluptate et valetudine'*, ed. and trans. Mary Ella Milham, MRTS 168, Renaissance Texts Series 17 (Tempe, Ariz.: Medieval & Renaissance Texts & Studies, 1998).

Poggio Bracciolini, *Poggii Florentini oratoris eloquentissimi ac Secretarii Apostolici || Facetiarum liber || accessit Lucii Philosophi Syri Comœdia lepidissima, quæ ASINVS intitulatur, ab ipso è Græco in Latinum traducta* (Cracow: n.pub., 1592).

Pomponio Leto, *Opera Pomponii Laeti. Romanae historiae compendium, ab interitu Gordiani Iunioris vsq(ue) ad Iustinum tertium. Pomponivs. De Romanorum Magistratibus. De Sacerdotiis. De Iurisperitis. De legibus ad M. Pantagathum. Item. De Antiquitatibus vrbis Romae libellus, ... Epistolae aliquot familiares. Pomponij vita, per M. Antonium Sabellicum* (Strasbourg: Matthias Schürer, 1515).

Prynne, William, *Histrio-Mastix. The Players Scovrge, or Actors Tragædie, Divided into Two Parts. Wherein it is largely evidenced, by divers Arguments... That popular Stage-playes (the very Pompes of the Divell which we renounce in Baptisme, if we beleeve the Fathers) are sinfull, heathenish, lewde, ungodly Spectacles, and most pernicious Corruptions* (London: for Michael Sparke, 1633).

Psellos, Michael, ed. C. N. Sathas, 'Fragments inédits des historiens grecs', *Bulletin de correspondance hellénique* 1 (1877), 121–33 and 309–20.

—— *Michaelis Pselli philosophica minora*, ed. J. M. Duffy and D. J. O'Meara, 2 vols. (Stuttgart: Teubner, 1989–92).

(Pseudo-)Acro, *Pseudacronis scholia in Horatium vetustiora*, ed. Otto Keller, 2 vols. (Leipzig: Teubner, 1902–4).

Rabelais, François, *Pantagruel's Voyage to the Oracle of the Bottle, Being the Fourth and Fifth Books of the Works of Francis Rabelais, M.D.*, trans. Peter le Motteux (London: Richard Baldwin, 1694).

Reardon, B. P., ed., *Collected Ancient Greek Novels* (Berkeley and Los Angeles: U of California P, 1989) [= *CAGN*].

Registrum Anglie de libris doctorum et auctorum veterum, ed. Richard H. Rouse, Mary A. Rouse, and R. A. B. Mynors, Corpus of British Medieval Library Catalogues 2 (London: British Library in assoc. with British Academy, 1991).

Ridderikhoff, Cornelia M., with Hilde De Ridder-Symoens, eds., *Premier Livre des procurateurs de la nation germanique de l'ancienne université d'Orléans, 1444–1546* (Leiden: Brill, 1971).

Ridevall, John, *Fulgentius Metaforalis: Ein Beitrag zur Geschichte der antiken Mythologie im Mittelalter*, ed. Hans Liebeschütz (Leipzig: Teubner, 1926).

Rollins, H. R., ed., *A Poetical Rhapsody 1602–1621*, 2 vols. (Cambridge, Mass.: HUP, 1931).

Sabellico, Marcantonio (Coccio), *Liber de Venetae urbis situ liber primus . . . Marci Antonii Sabellici Dialogus que et latinae linguae reparatio inscribitur* (Venice: Damianus de Mediolana de Gorgonzola, *c.*1494).

——— ed., *Annotationes veteres et recentes. In hoc volumine hec continentur. Marci Antonii Sabellici Annotationes veteres [et] recentes: ex Plinio: Liuio: [et] pluribus authoribus. Philippi Beroaldi Annotationes centum. . . . Eiusdem castigationes in Plinium. . . . Joannis Baptiste pii Bononiensis Annotationes. . . . Domitii Calderini Observationes quedam. . . . Joa[n]. Baptiste Egnatii Veneti Racemationes* (Venice: Ioannes Tacuinus de Tridino, 1508).

——— *De latinae linguae reparatione*, ed. Guglielmo Bottari, Percorsi dei classici 2 (Messina: Centro interdipartimentale di studi umanistici, 1999).

Sallustius, *Concerning the Gods and the Universe*, trans. A. D. Nock (Cambridge: CUP, 1926).

Salutati, Coluccio, *Colucii Salutati De laboribus Herculis*, 2 vols., ed. B. L. Ullman (Zurich: Thesaurus Mundi, 1951).

——— *Epistolario di Coluccio Salutati*, ed. Francesco Novati, 4 vols. (Rome: Istituto storico italiano, 1891–1911).

Scalamonti, Francesco, *Vita viri clarissimi et famosissimi Kyriaci Anconitani*, ed. and trans. Charles Mitchell and Edward W. Bodnar (Philadelphia: American Philosophical Soc., 1996).

Scaliger, Julius Caesar, *Iulii Cæsaris Scaligeri, uiri clarissimi, Poetices libri septem* (Lyons: Antonius Vincentius, 1561).

Schott, Andreas, *And. Schotti Societatis Iesu Tullianarum quæstionum de instauranda Ciceronis imitatione libri IIII* (Antwerp: Jan Moretus, 1610).

Scot, Reginald, *The Discoverie of Witchcraft*, ed. Bradley Nicholson (London: Elliot Stock, 1886).

Scriptores Historiae Augustae, vol. i, ed. Ernestus Hohl (Leipzig: Teubner, 1965).

Shakespeare, William, *A Midsummer Night's Dream*, ed. Harold F. Brooks, Arden Shakespeare (London: Methuen, 1979).

Shelley, Mary, *Mary Shelley's Literary Lives and Other Writings*, vol. iv, Pickering Masters, gen. ed. N. Crook (London: Pickering & Chatto, 2002).

Sherry, Richard, *A Treatise of the Figures of Grammer and Rhetorike* (London: Richard Tottel, 1555).

Sidney, Sir Philip, *An Apology for Poetry*, ed. Geoffrey Shepherd (Manchester: Manchester UP, 1973).

——— *A Defence of Poetry*, in *Miscellaneous Prose of Sir Philip Sidney*, ed. Katherine Duncan-Jones and Jan van Dorsten (Oxford: Clarendon, 1973).

——— *The Countess of Pembroke's Arcadia (The Old Arcadia)*, ed. Jean Robertson (Oxford: Clarendon, 1973). [= *OA*]

——— *The Countess of Pembroke's Arcadia (The Old Arcadia)*, ed. Katherine Duncan-Jones, World's Classics (Oxford: OUP, 1985).

——— *The Countesse of Pembrokes Arcadia* (London: John Windet for William Ponsonbie, 1590).

Sidney, Sir Philip, *The Countess of Pembroke's Arcadia (The New Arcadia)*, ed. Victor Skretkowicz (Oxford: Clarendon, 1987). [= *NA*]

—— *The Countesse of Pembrokes Arcadia. ...Now since the first edition augmented and ended*, prefaced H[ugh] S[anford] (London: William Ponsonbie, 1593).

—— *The Poems of Sir Philip Sidney*, ed. W. A. Ringler (Oxford: Clarendon, 1962).

Sidonius Apollinaris, *C. Sollius Apollinaris Sidonius*, ed. Paulus Mohr (Leipzig: Teubner, 1895).

—— *The Letters of Sidonius*, trans. O. M. Dalton, 2 vols. (Oxford: Clarendon, 1915).

Spenser, Edmund, *The Faerie Queene*, ed. Thomas P. Roche, Jr. and C. Patrick O'Donnell, Jr. (Harmondsworth: Penguin, 1978; repr. 1984).

—— *The Yale Edition of the Shorter Poems of Edmund Spenser*, ed. William A. Oram et al. (New Haven: YUP, 1989).

Tasso, Torquato, *Gerusalemme liberata*, introd. Giorgi Petrocchi (Basiano: Bietti, 1968).

—— *Jerusalem Delivered*, trans. Edward Fairfax (1600), ed. and introd. Roberto Weiss (London: Centaur, 1962).

—— *Tasso: Discourses on the Heroic Poem*, trans. M. Cavalchini and I. Samuel (Oxford: Clarendon, 1973).

Tertullian, *Quinti Septimii Florentis Tertulliani De praescriptione haereticorum ad martyras: ad scapulam*, ed. T. Herbert Bindley (Oxford: Clarendon, 1893).

—— *De anima*, ed. J. H. Waszink (Amsterdam: North-Holland, 1947).

—— *Adversus Valentinianos*, ed. E. Kroymann, in *Quinti Septimi Florentis Tertulliani opera, Pars II: Opera Montanistica*, CCSL 2 (Turnhout: Brepols, 1954).

—— *The Writings of Tertullian*, trans. Peter Holmes, *Ante-Nicene Christian Library: Translations of the Fathers down to A. D. 325*, vol. xv/2 (Edinburgh: Clark, 1870).

Thomas, Thomas, *Dictionarium linguæ Latinæ et Anglicanæ* (Cambridge, [1587]), facs. edn., ed. R. C. Alston, English Linguistics 1500–1800: A Collection of Facsimile Reprints 330 (Menston: Scolar P, 1972).

Tofte, Robert, *The Poetry of Robert Tofte, 1597–1620*, ed. J. N. Nelson (New York: Garland, 1994).

Tomkis, Thomas, *Albumazar, A comedy presented before the Kings Maiestie at Cambridge, the ninth of March. 1614. By the Gentlemen of Trinitie Colledge* (London: Nicholas Okes for Walter Burre, 1615).

Underdowne, Thomas, trans., *An Æthiopian Historie, written in Greeke by Heliodorus, no less wittie then pleasant: Englished by Thomas Underdowne, and newely corrected and augmented, with diuers and sundrie new additions by the saide Authour* (London: Frauncis Coldocke, 1577).

Valeriano, Pierio, *Ioannis Petri Valeriani præludia quædam* (Venice: Io. Tacuinus, 1509).

—— *Hexametri, odae et epigrammata* (Venice: Gabriel Giolito di Ferrariis, 1550).

—— *Hieroglyphica, siue de sacris aegyptiorum, aliarumque gentium literis commentarij Ioannis Pierii Valeriani Bolzanij Bellunensis* (Basle: Thomas Guérin, 1567).

—— *De litteratorum infelicitate*, trans. Julia Gaisser, in her *Pierio Valeriano on the Ill Fortune of Learned Men: A Renaissance Humanist and his World* (Ann Arbor: U of Michigan P, 1999).

—— *Dialogo della volgar lingua*, in *Discussioni linguistiche del Cinquecento*, ed. Mario Pozzi, Classici italiani (Turin: Unione tipografico-editrice torinese, 1988), 39–93.

Valla, Lorenzo, *On pleasure = De voluptate*, trans. A. Kent Hieatt and Maristella Lorch, introd. Maristella de Panizza Lorch, Janus series 1 (New York: Abaris Books, 1977).

—— *Laurentii Vallæ elegantiarum libri sex. Item Adnotationes in Antonium Raudensem* (Strasbourg: Hulderichus Morhadus (= Ulrich Morhart), 1521).

Vatican Mythographers, *Scriptores rerum mythicarum Latini tres Romae nuper reperti. Ad fidem codicum MSS. Guelferbytanorum Gottingensis Gothani et Parisiensis*, ed. George Henry Bode (Cellis: E. H. C. Schulze, 1834).

—— *Mythographi Vaticani I et II*, ed. Péter Kulcsár, CCSL 91 (Turnhout: Brepols, 1987).

—— *Le Premier Mythographe du Vatican*, ed. Nevio Zorzetti, trans. Jacques Berlioz (Paris: Les Belles Lettres, 1995).

Vincent of Beauvais, *Speculi maioris Vincentii Burgundi praesulis Beluacensis, ordinis praedicatorum, theologi ac doctoris eximii tomi quatuor* (Venice: Dominicus Nicolinus, 1591).

Vitalis of Blois, *Geta*, in *Three Latin Comedies*, ed. Keith Bate (Toronto: Centre for Medieval Studies, 1976).

Vives, Juan Luis, *Ioannis Lodovici Vivis Valentini Veritas fucata, sive de licentia poetica, quantum poetis liceat a veritate abscedere* (Louvain: Theodornecus Martinus Alostensis, 1523).

—— *St. Augustine, Of the citie of God vvith the learned comments of Io. Lod. Viues. Englished by I. H.* (London: George Eld, 1610). (EEBO)

—— *De conscribendis epistolis*, ed. and trans. Charles Fantazzi (Leiden: Brill, 1989).

—— *Early Writings*, ed. C. Matheeussen, Charles Fantazzi, and E. George (Leiden: Brill, 1987).

—— *De disciplinis libri XII. Septem de corruptis artibus; quinque de tradendis disciplinis* (Leiden: Joannes Maire, 1636).

—— *De officio mariti* (Bruges: [De Molendino?], 1529).

—— *The Office and Duetie of an Husband*, trans. Thomas Paynell (London: John Cawood, *c.*1558).

Waleys, Thomas, *Diui Aurelij Augustini hipponensis episcopi ad Marcellinum: de Ciuitate dei contra paganos Libri duo et viginti: opus dignissimum: humanarum diuinarumque litterarum disciplinis clarissime refertum. Cum commentarijs Thomæ Valois et Nicolai Triueth: necnon additionibus Jacobi Passauantij: atque Theologicis veritatibus Francisci Maronis* (Basle: Adam Petri, 1515).

Watson, Thomas, *The hekatompathia or Passionate centurie of loue diuided into two parts: whereof, the first expresseth the authors sufferance in loue: the latter, his long farewell to loue and all his tyrannie* (London: John Wolfe for Gabriell Cawood, 1582), sig. K2^r.

—— *The Complete Works of Thomas Watson, 1556–1592*, ed. Dana F. Sutton, 2 vols. (Lewiston, NY; Lampeter: Edwin Mellen P, 1996).

Wier, Johann, *Ioannis VVieri de praestigiis daemonum, & incantationibus ac ueneficiis libri sex, postrema editione quinta aucti & recogniti* (Basle: Ex officina Oporiniana, 1577).

Wilkinson, Edward, *E. W. his Thameseidos Deuided into three bookes, or cantos* (London: W. W[hite] for Simon Waterson, 1600).

William of Malmesbury, *Gesta regum anglorum, The History of the English Kings*, ed. and trans. R. A. B. Mynors, R. M. Thompson, and M. Winterbottom, 2 vols. (Oxford: Clarendon, 1998–9).

Wilson, Thomas, *The arte of rhetorique for the vse of all suche as are studious of eloquence* ([London]: Richard Grafton, 1553).

Zacharias Scholasticus, *Vita Severi*, in *Sévère Patriarche d'Antioche 512–518: Textes syriaques publiés, traduits et annotés*, ed. and trans. M.-A. Kugener, 2 vols., Patrologia Orientalis 2 (Paris: Firmin-Didot, 1907).

Secondary Sources

Accademia nazionale virgiliana, *Leon Battista Alberti: Architettura e cultura: Atti del convegno internazionale, Mantova, 16–19 novembre 1994*, Series Miscellanea (Accademia nazionale virgiliana) 7 (Florence: Olschki, 1999).

Accardo, Pasquale, *The Metamorphosis of Apuleius: Cupid and Psyche, Beauty and the Beast, King Kong* (Madison, NJ: Fairleigh Dickinson UP; London: Associated University Presses, 2002).

Acocella, Mariantonietta, *L'Asino d'oro nel Rinascimento: Dai volgarizzamenti alle raffigurazioni pittoriche*, Memoria del tempo 21 (Ravenna: Longo, 2001).

Alföldi, Andreas, *A Festival of Isis under the Christian Emperors of the IVth Century* (Budapest: Pázmány U, 1937).

—— *Die Kontorniaten: Ein verkanntes Propagandamittel der stadtrömischen heidnischen Aristokratie in ihrem Kampfe gegen das christliche Kaisertum* (Budapest/Leipzig: Harrassowitz, 1942–3).

—— *A Conflict of Ideas in the Later Roman Empire* (Oxford: Clarendon, 1952).

Alimonti, Terenzio, 'Apuleio e l'arcaismo in Claudiano Mamerto', in *Forma futuri: Studi in onore del Cardinale Michele Pellegrino* (Turin: Bottega d'Erasmo, 1975), 189–228.

—— *Struttura, ideologia ed imitazione virgiliana nel 'De mortibus boum' di Endelechio* (Turin: Giappichelli, 1976).

Allen, Don Cameron, 'On Spenser's *Muiopotmos*', *SP* 53 (1956), 141–58.

—— *Image and Meaning: Metaphoric Traditions in Renaissance Poetry* (Baltimore: Johns Hopkins P, 1960; rev. edn., 1968).

—— *Doubt's Boundless Sea: Skepticism and Faith in the Renaissance* (Baltimore: Johns Hopkins P, 1964).

—— *Mysteriously Meant: The Rediscovery of Pagan Symbolism and Allegorical Interpretation in the Renaissance* (Baltimore: Johns Hopkins P, 1970).

Amory, Frederic, 'Things Greek and the *Riddarasögur*', *Speculum* 59 (1984), 509–23.

Andersen, Lise Præstgaard, '*Partalopa saga*, homologue d'*Eros et Psyché*', *Revue des langues romanes* 102 (1998), 57–64.

Arata, Alda, *Niccolò da Correggio nella vita letteraria e politica del tempo suo, 1450–1508* (Bologna: Zanichelli, 1934).

Armas Wilson, Diana de, 'Homage to Apuleius: Cervantes' Avenging Psyche', in *Search for the Ancient Novel*, ed. Tatum, 88–100.

Ayscough, Samuel, *A Catalogue of the Manuscripts Preserved in the British Museum hitherto Undescribed ... Including the Collection of Sir Hans Sloane* (London: Ayscough, 1782).

Babinger, F., 'Notes on Cyriac of Ancona and Some of his Friends', *JWCI* 25 (1962), 321–3.

Bajoni, Maria Grazia, 'La novella del *Dolium* in Apuleio *Metamorfosi* IX, 5–7 e in Boccaccio, *Decameron* VII, 2', *Giornale storico della letteratura italiana* 171 [III: 554] (1994), 217–25.

Baldwin, Anna, 'From the *Clerk's Tale* to *The Winter's Tale*', in *Chaucer Traditions: Studies in Honour of Derek Brewer*, ed. Ruth Morse and Barry Windeatt (Cambridge: CUP, 1990), 199–212.

Baldwin, Barry, *Studies in Lucian* (Toronto: Hakkert, 1973).

—— 'Vergilius Graecus', *AJP* 97 (1976), 361–8.

—— 'Fulgentius and his Sources', *Traditio* 44 (1988), 37–57.

—— 'Apuleius and the Christians', *LCM* 14/4 (Apr. 1989), 55.

Baldwin, T. W., *William Shakspeare's Small Latine and Lesse Greeke*, 2 vols. (Urbana: U of Illinois P, 1944).

Barkan, Leonard, 'The Beholder's Tale: Ancient Sculpture, Renaissance Narratives', *Representations* 44 (Autumn 1993), 133–66.

—— *Unearthing the Past: Architecture and Aesthetics in the Making of Renaissance Culture* (New Haven: YUP, 1999).

—— *The Gods Made Flesh: Metamorphosis and the Pursuit of Paganism* (New Haven: YUP, 1986).

Barnes, T. D., *The Sources of the 'Historia Augusta'*, Collection Latomus 155 (Brussels: Latomus, 1978).

—— 'Augustine, Symmachus and Ambrose', in *Augustine: From Rhetor to Theologian*, ed. Joanne McWilliam (Waterloo, Ont.: Wilfrid Laurier UP, 1992), 7–13.

Barolini, Helen, *Aldus and his Dream Book: An Illustrated Essay* (New York: Italica, 1992).

Barton, Monika, *Spätantike Bukolik zwischen paganer Tradition und christlicher Verkündigung—Das Carmen 'De mortibus boum' des Endelechius*, Bochumer Altertumswissenchaftliches Colloquium 48 (Trier: Wissenschaftlicher Verlag Trier, 2000).

Bassett, Sarah Guberti, '*Historiae Custos*: Sculpture and Tradition in the Baths of Zeuxippos', *American Journal of Archaeology* 100 (1996), 491–506.

Bate, K. A., 'Walter Map and Giraldus Cambrensis', *Latomus* 31 (1972), 860–75.

Baxandall, Michael, 'A Dialogue on Art from the Court of Leonello d'Este: Angelo Decembrio's *De Politia Litteraria* Pars LXVIII', *JWCI* 26 (1963), 303–26.

Baxandall, Michael, and E. H. Gombrich, 'Beroaldus on Francia', *JWCI* 25 (1962), 113–15.

Bebb, Philip Norton, 'The Lawyers, Dr. Christoph Scheurl, and the Reformers in Nürnberg', in *The Social History of the Reformation*, ed. Lawrence P. Buck and Jonathan W. Zophy (Columbus: Ohio State UP, 1972), 52–72.

Becker, Reinhard Paul, *A War of Fools. The Letters of Obscure Men: A Study of the Satire and the Satirized*, New York University Ottendorfer series 12 (Bern: Lang, 1981).

Bek, Lisa, 'The Changing Architectonic Aspect of the Ideal City in the Early Renaissance', *Acta Conventus Neo-Latini Hafniensis: Proceedings of the Eighth International Congress of Neo-Latin Studies*, ed. Rhoda Schnur et al. (Binghamton, NY: MRTS, 1994), 143–53.

Benton, J. F., 'The Court of Mary of Champagne as a Literary Centre', *Speculum* 36 (1961), 551–91.

Bernardo, Aldo S., and Saul Levin, eds., *The Classics in the Middle Ages*, MRTS 69 (Binghamton, NY: Center for Medieval & Early Renaissance Studies, 1990).

Berrigan, Joseph R., 'The Prehumanism of Benzo d'Alessandria', *Traditio* 25 (1969), 249–63.

Biasuz, Giuseppe, 'Le probabili relazioni di Pierio Valeriano e Gio. Battista Scita con l'autore del Polifilo', *Archivo storico de Belluno, Feltro e Cadore* 31 (1960), 148–9.

Bietenholz, Peter G., *Contemporaries of Erasmus: A Biographical Register of the Renaissance and Reformation*, 3 vols. (Toronto: U of Toronto P, 1985).

Billanovich, Giuseppe, *Petrarca letterato*, vol. i. *Lo scrittoio del Petrarca*, Storia e Letteratura 16 (Rome: Edizioni di storia e letteratura, 1947).

—— *Restauri Boccacceschi* (Rome: Edizioni di storia e letteratura, 1947).

—— *I primi umanisti e le tradizioni dei classici latini: prolusione al corso di letteratura italiana detta il 2 febbraio 1951* (Fribourg: Edizioni universitarie, 1953).

—— 'Zanobi da Strada tra i tesori di Montecassino', *RANL: Classe di scienze morali, storiche e filologiche*, 9th ser. 7/3 [= 393] (1996), 653–63.

—— 'Biografia e opere del Petrarca tra miti e realtà da Senuccio del Bene a Laura', *RANL: Classe di scienze morali, storiche e filologiche*, 9th ser. 8/4 [= 394] (1997), 627–31.

Billanovich, Myriam, 'Francesco Colonna, il *Polifilo* e la famiglia Lelli', *IMU* 19 (1976), 419–28.

Binns, J. W., *Intellectual Culture in Elizabethan and Jacobean England: The Latin Writings of the Age* (Leeds: Francis Cairns, 1990).

—— ed., *Latin Literature of the Fourth Century* (London: RKP, 1974).

Biondi, Laura, '*Hara*: Nuove considerazione sul problema', *ACME* 54/1 (2001), 59–84.

—— 'Apuleius, *De nota aspirationis* e *De diphthongis*: Ricognizioni su modelli strutturali e teorici in due testi medievali sull'ortografia latina', *ACME* 54/3 (2001), 73–111.

Blanchard, Harold H., 'Imitations of Tasso in the *Faerie Queene*', *SP* 22 (1925), 198–221.

—— 'Spenser and Boiardo', *PMLA* 40 (1925), 828–51.

Blavatsky, H. P., *Isis Unveiled: A Master-key to the Mysteries of Ancient and Modern Science and Theology*, 2 vols. (London: J. W. Bouton, 1877).

Bloch, Herbert, 'The Pagan Revival in the West at the End of the Fourth Century', in *The Conflict between Paganism and Christianity in the Fourth Century*, ed. Arnaldo Momigliano (Oxford: Clarendon, 1963), 193–218.

—— 'The Bombardment of Monte Cassino (February 14–16, 1944): A New Appraisal', *Benedictina* 20 (1973), 383–424.

—— *Monte Cassino in the Middle Ages*, 3 vols. (Cambridge, Mass.: HUP, 1986).

—— ed., *The Atina Dossier of Peter the Deacon of Monte Cassino: A Hagiographical Romance of the Twelfth Century*, Studi e testi 346 (Vatican City: Biblioteca Apostolica Vaticana, 1998).

Blunt, Anthony, 'The *Hypnerotomachia Poliphili* in 17th Century France', *JWI* 1 (1937–8), 117–37.

—— *Artistic Theory in Italy 1450–1600* (Oxford: Clarendon, 1940; repr. 1956).

Bober, Phyllis Pray, 'The *Coryciana* and the Nymph Corycia', *JWCI* 40 (1977), 223–39.

Bødtker, A. Trampe, '*Parténopeus* in Catalonia and Spain', *MLN* 21 (1906), 234–5.

Boitani, Piero, *Chaucer and Boccaccio* (Oxford: Society for the Study of Mediaeval Languages and Literature, 1977).

—— ed., *Chaucer and the Italian Trecento* (Cambridge: CUP, 1983).

Bolgar, R. R., *The Classical Heritage and its Beneficiaries* (Cambridge: CUP, 1954).

Bonner, Gerald, *St Augustine of Hippo: Life and Controversies*, 3rd edn. (Norwich: Canterbury P, 2002).

Borsa, Mario, 'The Correspondence of Humphrey Duke of Gloucester and Pier Candido Decembrio', *EHR* 19 (1904), 509–26.

Branca, Vittore, *Boccaccio medievale* (Florence: Sansoni, 1956).

Brancaleone, Francesca, 'Considerazioni sulle citazioni apuleiane e pseudo-apuleiane nel *Cornu Copiae* di Perotti', *SUP* 14 (1994), 49–54.

Brehaut, Ernest, *An Encyclopedist of the Dark Ages: Isidore of Seville* (New York: Columbia UP, 1912; repr. New York: B. Franklin, 1964).

Brinkley, Robert A., 'Spenser's *Muiopotmos* and the Politics of Metamorphosis', *ELH* 48 (1981), 668–72.

British Library, *Catalogue of Manuscripts in the British Museum, New Series, Volume I, Part II: The Burney Manuscripts* (London: British Museum, 1840).

Brooks, Harold F., ed., *Shakespeare: A Midsummer Night's Dream*, Arden Shakespeare (London: Methuen, 1979).

Brown, Eric C., 'The Allegory of Small Things: Insect Eschatology in Spenser's *Muiopotmos*', *SP* 99 (2002), 247–67.

Brown, Louise Fargo, 'On the Burning of Books', in *Vassar Mediæval Studies*, ed. Christabel Forsyth Fiske (New Haven: YUP, 1923), 249–71.

Brown, Patricia Fortini, *Venice & Antiquity: The Venetian Sense of the Past* (New Haven: YUP, 1996).

Brown, Peter, *Augustine of Hippo: A Biography* (London: Faber, 1967).

Brown, Thomas H., 'The Relationship between *Partonopeus de Blois* and the Cupid and Psyche Tradition', *Brigham Young University Studies* 5/3–4 (Spring–Summer 1964), 193–202.

Bruckner, Matilda Tomaryn, 'When the Empress of Byzantium Plays Cupid to a French Knight's Psyche in the Upside-Down World of *Partonopeu de Blois*', ICAN2 paper, abstracted in *The Ancient Novel*, ed. Tatum and Vernazza, 125–6.

Buchanan, Milton A., '*Partinuplés de Bles*. An Episode in Tirso's *Amor por Señas*. Lope's *La viuda valenciana*', *MLN* 21/1 (Jan. 1906), 3–8.

Bullough, Donald A., 'Charlemagne's Court Library Revisited', *Early Medieval Europe* 12 (2003), 339–63.

Burckhardt, Jacob, *The Civilization of the Renaissance in Italy*, trans. S. G. C. Middlemore, 2 vols. (London: C. K. Paul, 1878).

Burnett, Mark Thornton, 'The "Trusty Servant": A Sixteenth-Century English Emblem', *Emblematica* 6/2 (1992), 1–17.

Busby, Keith, '*Cristal et Clarie*: A Novel Romance?', in *Convention and Innovation in Literature*, ed. Theo D'haen, Rainer Grübel, and Helmuth Lethen, Utrecht Publications in General and Comparative Literature 24 (Amsterdam: Benjamins, 1989), 77–103.

Butler, H. E., and A. S. Owen, eds., *Apulei Apologia sive Pro se de Magia Liber* (Oxford: Clarendon, 1914).

Bynum, Caroline Walker, 'Metamorphosis, or Gerald and the Werewolf', *Speculum* 73 (1998), 987–1013.

—— *Metamorphosis and Identity* (New York: Zone Books, 2001).

Cabaillot, Claire, 'La *Mavortis miles*: Petrarca in Boccaccio?', in *Gli Zibaldoni di Boccaccio: Memoria, scrittura, riscrittura. Atti del Seminario internazionale di Firenze-Certaldo (26–28 aprile 1996)*, ed. Michelangelo Picone and Claude Cazalé Bérard (Florence: Cesati, 1998), 129–39.

Calvesi, Maurizio, *Il Sogno di Polifilo prenestino* (Rome: Officina, 1980).

—— '*Hypnerotomachia Poliphili*: Nuovi riscontri e nuove evidenze documentarie per Francesco Colonna signore di Praeneste', *Storia dell'arte* 60 (1987), 85–136.

—— 'Il gaio classicismo Pinturicchio e Francesco Colonna nella Roma di Alessandro VI', in *Roma, centro ideale della cultura dell'Antico nei secoli XV e XVI: Da Martino V al sacco di Roma, 1417–1527*, ed. Silvia Danesi Squarzina (Milan: Electa, 1989), 71–101.

Cameron, Alan, 'The Date and Identity of Macrobius', *JRS* 56 (1966), 25–38.

—— 'Paganism and Literature in Late Fourth Century Rome', in *Christianisme et formes littéraires de l'Antiquité tardive en Occident: huit exposés suivis de discussions par Alan Cameron*... [et al.]*; avec la participation de Helena Junod-Ammerbauer et François Paschoud; entretiens préparés et présidés par Manfred Fuhrmann*, Entretiens sur l'antiquité classique 23 (Geneva: Fondation Hardt, 1977), 1–30.

Campbell, Killis, 'A Study of the Romance of the Seven Sages with Special Reference to the Middle English Versions', *PMLA* 14/1 (1899), 1–107.

Carey, John, *John Donne: Life, Mind and Art*, 2nd edn. (London: Faber, 1990).

Carver, Robert H. F., 'The Protean Ass: The *Metamorphoses* of Apuleius from Antiquity to the English Renaissance' (University of Oxford D.Phil. Thesis, 1991).

—— '"Valiant Aristomenes": A Messenian Hero in Sidney's *Old Arcadia*', *N&Q* 239 (1994), 26–8.

—— '"Sugared Invention" or "Mongrel Tragi-comedy": Sir Philip Sidney and the Ancient Novel', *GCN* 8 (1997), 197–226.

—— ' "Transformed in Show": The Rhetoric of Transvestism in Sidney's *Arcadia*', *ELR* 28 (1998), 323–52.

—— 'A New Source for Sidney's *Arcadia*: Pierio Valeriano's *Leucippus* (Text, Translation, and Commentary)', *ELR* 28 (1998), 353–71.

—— 'The Rediscovery of the Latin Novels', in *Latin Fiction: The Latin Novel in Context*, ed. Heinz Hofmann (London: Routledge, 1999), 253–68.

—— ' "True Histories" and "Old Wives' Tales": Renaissance Humanism and the "Rise of the Novel" ', *Ancient Narrative* 1 (2000–1), 322–49.

—— '*Quis ille?* The Role of the Prologue in Apuleius' *Nachleben*', in *A Companion to the Prologue of Apuleius' 'Metamorphoses'*, ed. Ahuvia Kahane and Andrew Laird (Oxford: OUP, 2001), 163–74.

Casella, Maria Teresa, and G. Pozzi, *Francesco Colonna: Biografia e opera*, 2 vols. (Padua: Antenore, 1959).

Caspar, Erich L. E., *Petrus Diaconus und die Monte Cassineser Fälschungen: Ein Beitrag zur Geschichte des italienischen Geisteslebens im Mittelalter* (Berlin: Springer, 1909).

Cavallo, Guglielmo, *L'età dell'abate Desiderio*, 3 vols. (Montecassino: Pubblicazioni Cassinesi, 1989–92).

Cavallo, Jo Ann, *Boiardo's 'Orlando innamorato': An Ethics of Desire* (Rutherford: Fairleigh Dickinson UP, 1993).

Cave, Terence, *The Cornucopian Text: Problems of Writing in the French Renaissance* (Oxford: Clarendon, 1979).

Celenza, Christopher S., 'Creating Canons in Fifteenth-Century Ferrara: Angelo Decembrio's *De politia litteraria*, 1/10', *RQ* 57 (2004), 43–98.

Charlet, Jean-Louis, 'Sur dix citations d'auteurs antiques dans le *Cornu copiae* de Niccolò Perotti: Remarques méthodologiques', *RPL* 13 (1990), 41–7.

Chastel, André, *The Sack of Rome, 1527*, trans. Beth Archer, Bollingen Series 35: The A. W. Mellon Lectures in the Fine Arts, 1977, The National Gallery of Art, Washington DC, 26 (Princeton: PUP, 1983).

Chavasse, Ruth, 'The Reception of Humanist Historiography in Northern Europe: M. A. Sabellico and John Jewel', *RS* 2 (1988), 327–38.

—— 'The *studia humanitatis* and the Making of a Humanist Career: Marcantonio Sabellico's Exploitation of Humanist Literary Genres', *RS* 17 (2003), 27–38.

Chomarat, Jacques, 'Erasme lecteur des *Elegantiae* de Valla', in *Acta Conventus Neo-Latini Amstelodamensis: Proceedings of the Second International Congress of Neo-Latin Studies, Amsterdam, 19–24 August 1973*, ed. P. Tuynman, G. C. Kuiper, and E. Kessler (Munich: Fink, 1979), 206–43.

Clarke, John R., 'Metamorphosis in the Twelfth-Cenury *Metamorphosis Golye Episcopi*', in *Classical Texts and their Traditions: Studies in Honour of C. R. Trahman*, ed. D. F. Bright and E. S. Ramage (Chico, Calif.: Scholars P, 1984), 7–12.

—— 'Love and Learning in the *Metamorphosis Golye Episcopi*', *Mittellateinisches Jahrbuch* 21 (1986), 156–71.

Coates, Alan, Kristian Jensen, Cristina Dondi, Bettina Wagner, and Helen Dixon, *A Catalogue of Books Printed in the Fifteenth Century now in the Bodleian Library, Oxford*, 6 vols. (Oxford: OUP, 2005).

Cochrane, C. N., *Christianity and Classical Culture* (London: OUP, 1940).

Collins, S. T., 'Who was Ysopullus?', *Speculum* 23 (1948), 112.

Colton, Robert E., *Some Literary Influences on Sidonius Apollinaris*, Classical and Byzantine Monographs 47 (Amsterdam: Hakkert, 2000).

Connell, Dorothy, *Sir Philip Sidney: The Maker's Mind* (Oxford: Clarendon, 1977).

Cooke, Thomas D., and Benjamin L. Honeycutt, eds., *The Humor of the Fabliaux: A Collection of Critical Essays* (Columbia: U of Missouri P, 1974).

Copinger, W. A., *Supplement to Hain's Repertorium Bibliographicum or Collections towards a New Edition of that Work*, Part II, vol. i (1898; Milan: Görlich, 1950).

Cosenza, Mario Emilio, *Biographical and Bibliographical Dictionary of the Italian Humanists and of the World of Classical Scholarship in Italy, 1300–1800*, 6 vols. (Boston: Hall, 1962–7). [= *BBDIH*]

—— *Biographical and Bibliographical Dictionary of the Italian Printers, and of Foreign Printers in Italy from the Introduction of the Art of Printing into Italy to 1800* (Boston: Hall, 1968). [= *BBDIP*]

Costanza, Salvatore, *La fortuna di L. Apuleio nell' età di mezzo* (Palermo: Scuola Salesiana del libro, 1937).

Coulter, Cornelia C., 'Boccaccio and the Cassinese Manuscripts of the Laurentian Library', *CP* 43 (1948), 217–30.

Courcelle, Pierre, *Les Confessions de Saint Augustin dans la tradition littéraire: Antécédents et postérité* (Paris: Études augustiniennes, 1963).

Court, F. E., 'The Theme and Structure of Spenser's *Muiopotmos*', *SEL* 10 (1970), 1–15.

Coville, A., 'Une correspondance à propos d'Apulée, 1371–1375', *Humanisme et renaissance* 2 (1935), 203–15.

Cowdrey, H. E. J., *The Age of Abbot Desiderius: Monte Cassino, the Papacy, and the Normans in the Eleventh and Early Twelfth Centuries* (Oxford: Clarendon, 1983).

Cox, Virginia, 'Rhetoric and Humanism in Quattrocento Venice', *RQ* 56 (2003), 652–94.

Coxe, H. O., *Bodleian Library Quarto Catalogue, II: Laudian Manuscripts* (1858–1885), corr. edn., ed. and introd. R. W. Hunt (Oxford: Bodleian Library, 1973).

Cranz, F. Edward, *Nicholas of Cusa and the Renaissance*, ed. Thomas M. Izbicki and Gerald Christianson (Aldershot: Ashgate, 2000).

Creighton, Mandell, *A History of the Papacy during the Period of the Reformation*, 5 vols. (London: Longmans, Green, 1882–94).

Croce, Benedetto, 'Pierio Valeriano e la controversia sulla lingua', in his *Poeti e scrittori del pieno e del tardo Rinascimento*, Scritti di storia letteraria e politica 36, 2nd edn., 3 vols. (Bari: Laterza, 1958–70), ii. 74–84.

Croll, Morris W., *'Attic' and Baroque Prose Style: The Anti-Ciceronian Movement*, ed. J. Max Patrick, Robert O. Evans, and John M. Wallace (Princeton: PUP, 1966; repr. 1969).

Cummings, R. M., 'A Note on the Arithmological Stanza: *The Faerie Queene* ii. ix. 22', *JWCI* 30 (1967), 410–14.

Cunningham, J. G., trans., *Letters of Saint Augustine, Bishop of Hippo*, 2 vols. (Edinburgh: T. & T. Clark, 1872–5).

Curran, Brian, 'The *Hypnerotomachia Poliphili* and Renaissance Egyptology', in *Garden and Architectural Dreamscapes*, ed. Leslie and Hunt, 156–85.

Curran, John R., *Pagan City and Christian Capital: Rome in the Fourth Century* (Oxford: OUP, 2000).

Curtius, Ernst Robert, *European Literature and the Latin Middle Ages*, trans. Willard R. Trask (London: RKP, 1953; repr. 1979). [*ELLMA*]

D'Amico, John F., *Renaissance Humanism in Papal Rome: Humanists and Churchmen on the Eve of the Reformation* (Baltimore: Johns Hopkins UP, 1983).

—— 'The Progress of Renaissance Latin Prose: The Case of Apuleianism', *RQ* 37 (1984), 351–92.

—— 'Humanism in Rome', in *Renaissance Humanism: Foundations, Forms, and Legacy*, ed. Rabil, i. 264–95.

Danesi Squarzina, Silvia, 'Francesco Colonna, principe, letterato, e la sua cerchia', *Storia dell'arte* 19 [60] (1987), 137–54.

Davies, Martin, 'Juan de Carvajal and Early Printing: The 42-line Bible and the Sweynheym and Pannartz Aquinas', *The Library* 18/3 (1996), 193–215.

Deitz, Luc, 'Ioannes Wower of Hamburg, Philologist and Polymath. A Preliminary Sketch of his Life and Works', *JWCI* 58 (1995), 132–51.

DellaNeva, JoAnn, 'Reflecting Lesser Lights: The Imitation of Minor Writers in the Renaissance', *RQ* 42 (1989), 449–79.

Dempsey, Charles, '*Mercurius Ver*: The Sources of Botticelli's *Primavera*', *JWCI* 31 (1968), 251–73.

De Smet, Ingrid A. R., 'Amatus Fornacius, *Amator Ineptus* (Palladii, 1633): A Seventeenth-Century Satire', *HL* 38 (1989), 238–306.

—— *Menippean Satire and the Republic of Letters, 1581–1655* (Geneva: Droz, 1996).

Dessau, H., 'Über Zeit und Persönlichkeit der *SHA*', *Hermes* 24 (1889), 337–92.

DiGangi, Mario, 'Asses and Wits: The Homoerotics of Mastery in Satiric Comedy', *ELR* 25 (1995), 179–208.

Dilts, Dorothy A., 'John Gower and the *De Genealogia Deorum*', *MLN* 57/1 (Jan. 1942), 23–5.

Dionisotti, Carlo, 'G. B. Pio e M. Equicola', in his *Gli umanisti e il volgare fra Quattro e Cinquecento*, Bibliotechina del saggiatore 29 (Florence: Le Monnier, 1968), 78–130.

Dizionario biografico degli italiani (Rome: Istituto della Enciclopedia italiana, 1960–).

Doody, Margaret Anne, *The True Story of the Novel* (London: HarperCollins, 1997).

Douce, Francis, *Illustrations of Shakspeare and of Ancient Manners*, 2 vols. (London: Longman, Hurst, Rees, & Orme, 1807).

Dowden, Ken, Review of Fehling, *CR*, NS 29 (1979), 314.

—— 'Eleven Notes on the Text of Apuleius' *Metamorphoses*', *CQ* 30 (1980), 218–26.

—— 'Psyche on the Rock', *Latomus* 41 (1982), 336–52.

Draper, John W., 'Classical Coinage in the *Faerie Queene*', *PMLA* 47 (1932), 97–108.

Dronke, Peter, *Fabula: Explorations into the Use of Myth in Medieval Platonism* (Leiden: Brill, 1974).

Dronke, Peter, 'William of Conches's Commentary on Martianus Capella', in *Études de civilisation médiévale (IXe–XIIe siècles): Mélanges offerts à Edmond-René Labande* (Poitiers: CÉSCM, 1974), 223–35.

—— 'Profane Elements in Literature', in *Renaissance and Renewal in the Twelfth Century*, ed. Robert L. Benson and Giles Constable (Oxford: Clarendon, 1982), 569–612.

—— , introd., *Francesco Colonna: Hypnerotomachia Poliphili (Venetiis, Aldo Manuzio, 1499)*, facs. edn. (Saragossa: Ediciones de Pórtico, 1981).

Duncan, Douglas, *Ben Jonson and the Lucianic Tradition* (Cambridge: CUP, 1979).

Dundas, Judith, '*Complaints: Muiopotmos, or The Fate of the Butterflie*', in *Spenser Encyclopedia*, ed. Hamilton, 186–7.

Dunston, A. J., 'A Student's Notes of Lectures by Giulio Pomponio Leto', *Antichthon* 1 (1967), 86–94.

—— 'Pope Paul II and the Humanists', *Journal of Religious History* 7 (1973), 287–306.

Durling, Robert M., 'The Bower of Bliss and Armida's Palace' *CL* 6 (1954), 335–47.

Earle, T. F., *Theme and Image in the Poetry of Sá de Miranda* (Oxford: OUP, 1980).

Edwards, M. J., 'The Tale of Cupid and Psyche', *ZPE* 94 (1992), 77–94.

Edwards, Robert, 'The Heritage of Fulgentius', in *The Classics in the Middle Ages*, ed. Bernardo and Levin, 141–51.

Eliot, George, *Middlemarch* (1871–2), ed. W. J. Harvey (Harmondsworth: Penguin, 1965).

Elsom, Helen E., 'Apuleius in Erasmus' *Lingua*', *SUP* 8 (1988), 125–34.

Emison, Patricia, 'Asleep in the Grass of Arcady: Giulio Campagnola's Dreamer', *RQ* 45 (1992), 271–92.

Evans, Robert C., *Habits of Mind: Evidence and Effects of Ben Jonson's Reading* (Lewisburg: Bucknell UP; London: Associated University Presses, 1995).

Faucon, Maurice, *La Librairie des Papes d'Avignon: Sa formation, sa composition, ses catalogues (1316–1420) d'après les registres de comptes et d'inventaires des archives vaticanes*, Bibliothèque des Écoles françaises d'Athènes et de Rome 43 and 50, 2 vols. in 1 (Paris: Thorin, 1886–7).

Fehling, Detlev, *Amor und Psyche: Die Schöpfung des Apuleius und ihre Einwirkung auf das Märchen, eine Kritik der romantischen Märchentheorie*, Abhandlungen der Geistes-und Sozialwissenschaftlichen Klasse, Jarhung 1977, Nr. 9 (Mainz: Akademie der Wissenschaften und der Literatur, 1977).

Feld, M. D., 'Sweynheim and Pannartz, Cardinal Bessarion and Neoplatonism: Two Early Printers' Choice of Texts', *HLB* 30 (1982), 282–335.

—— 'A Theory of the Early Italian Printing Firm, Part I: Variants of Humanism', *HLB* 33 (1985), 341–77.

—— 'The First Roman Printers and the Idioms of Humanism', *HLB* 36/1 (1988) (special issue).

Feo, Michele, 'The "Pagan Beyond" of Albertino Mussato', in *Latin Poetry and the Classical Tradition*, ed. Godman and Murray, 115–47.

Feuer-Toth, Rozsa, *Art and Humanism in Hungary in the Age of Matthias Corvinus*, trans. Györgyi Jakobi, Studia humanitatis 8 (Budapest: Akadémiai Kiadó, 1990).

Fiorilla, Maurizio, 'La lettura apuleiana del Boccaccio e le note ai manoscritti Laurenziani 29,2 e 54,32', *Aevum* 73 (1999), 635–68.

Fisher, Fay, *Narrative Art in Medieval Romances* (Cleveland, Oh.: n.pub., 1938).

Fitzgerald, Allan D, gen. ed., *Augustine through the Ages: An Encyclopedia* (Grand Rapids, Mich.: Eerdmans, 1999).

Flood, John L., 'Hans von Laude(n)bach "who printed the first books in Rome"', in *The Italian Book 1465–1800: Studies Presented to Dennis E. Rhodes on his 70th Birthday*, ed. Denis V. Reidy (London: British Library, 1993), 11–19.

Floriani, Piero, *Bembo e Castiglione: Studi sul classicismo del Cinquecento*, Analisi letteraria 15 (Rome: Bulzoni, 1976).

—— 'La "Questione della Lingua" e il "Dialogo" di P. Valeriano', *GSLI* 155 (1978), 321–45.

Fontaine, Jacques, *Isidore de Séville et la culture classique dans l'Espagne wisigothique*, 3 vols. (Paris: Études augustiniennes, 1959–83).

Forcione, A. K., *Cervantes, Aristotle, and the 'Persiles'* (Princeton: PUP, 1970).

Fourrier, Anthime, *Le Courant réaliste dans le roman courtois en France au moyen-âge* (Paris: Nizet, 1960).

Fowler, Alastair, *Triumphal Forms: Structural Patterns in Elizabethan Poetry* (Cambridge: CUP, 1970).

Fraenkel, Eduard, 'A Sham Sisenna', *Eranos* 51 (1953), 151–4.

Françon, Maurice, 'Francesco Colonna's *Poliphili Hypnerotomachia* and Rabelais', *MLR* 50 (1955), 52–5.

Frye, Northrop, *Anatomy of Criticism: Four Essays* (Princeton: PUP, 1957; repr. 1973).

—— *The Secular Scripture: A Study of the Structure of Romance* (Cambridge, Mass.: HUP, 1976).

Fubini, Riccardo, *Umanesimo e secolarizzazione da Petrarca a Valla* (Rome: Bulzoni, 1990).

Fumagalli, Edoardo, Review of Pozzi and Ciapponi, *Aevum* 55 (1981), 571–83.

—— 'Francesco Colonna lettore di Apuleio e il problema della datazione dell'*Hypnerotomachia Polphili*', *IMU* 27 (1984), 233–66.

—— *Matteo Maria Boiardo volgarizzatore dell' 'Asino d'Oro': Contributo allo studio della fortuna di Apuleio nell'umanesimo*, Medioevo e umanesimo 70 (Padua: Antenore, 1988).

—— 'Due esemplari dell' *Hypnerotomachia Poliphili* di Francesco Colonna', *Aevum* 66 (1992), 419–32.

Gairdner, James, ed., *Letters and Papers Illustrative of the Reigns of Richard III and Henry VII*, Rerum britannicarum medii aevi scriptores 24, 2 vols. (London: Longman, Green, Longman, and Roberts, 1861–3; repr. 1891).

Gaisser, Julia Haig, 'The Rise and Fall of Goritz's Feasts', *RQ* 48 (1995), 41–57.

—— *Pierio Valeriano on the Ill Fortune of Learned Men: A Renaissance Humanist and his World* (Ann Arbor: U of Michigan P, 1999).

—— 'Teaching Classics in the Renaissance: Two Case Histories', *TAPA* 131 (2001), 1–21.

Gaisser, Julia Haig, 'Reading Apuleius with Filippo Beroaldo', in *Being there Together: Essays in Honor of Michael C. J. Putnam*, ed. Philip Thibodeau and Harry Haskell (Afton, Minn.: Afton Historical Soc. P, 2003), 24–42.

—— 'Allegorizing Apuleius: Fulgentius, Boccaccio, Beroaldo, and the Chain of Receptions', in *Acta Conventus Neo-Latini Cantabrigiensis*, ed. Rhoda Schnur et al., MRTS 259 (Tempe, Arizona: Arizona Center for Medieval and Renaissance Studies, 2003), 23–41.

—— 'Filippo Beroaldo on Apuleius: Bringing Antiquity to Life', in *On Renaissance Commentaries*, ed. Marianne Pade, Noctes Neolatini: Neo-Latin Texts and Studies 4 (Hildesheim: Olms, 2005), 87–109.

Gardner, Edmund G., *Dukes and Poets in Ferrara: A Study in the Poetry, Religion, and Politics of the Fifteenth and Early Sixteenth Centuries* (London: Constable, 1904).

Garrard, Mary D., 'Leonardo da Vinci: Female Portraits, Female Nature', in *The Expanding Discourse: Feminism and Art History*, ed. Norma Broude and Mary D. Garrard (New York: IconEditions, 1992), 58–86.

Geanakoplos, Deno John, *Constantinople and the West: Essays on the Late Byzantine (Palaeologan) and Italian Renaissances and the Byzantine and Roman Churches* (Madison: U of Wisconsin P, 1989).

Geffcken, Johannes, *The Last Days of Greco-Roman Paganism*, rev. and trans. Sabine MacCormack (Amsterdam/Oxford: North Holland, 1978).

Geiger, Joseph, 'Some Latin Authors from the Greek East', *CQ* 49 (1999), 606–17.

Generosa, Sister M., 'Apuleius and *A Midsummer Night's Dream*: Analogue or Source, Which?', *SP* 42 (1945), 198–204.

Gesamtkatalog der Wiegendrucke, vol. ii (Alfarabius-Arznei) (Leipzig: Hiersemann, 1926).

Gesner, Carol, *Shakespeare and the Greek Romance: A Study of Origins* (Lexington: UP of Kentucky, 1970).

Gianola, Giovanna Maria, 'La raccolta di biografie come problema storiografico nel *De viris* di Giovanni Colonna', *Bullettino dell'Istitutostorico italiano per il medio evo e Archivio Muratoriano* 89 (1982 for 1980–1), 509–40.

Giarratano, Caesar, ed., *Apulei Metamorphoseon Libri XI*, 2nd edn, ed. Paulus Frassinetti (Turin: Corpus Scriptorum Latinorum Paravianum, 1960).

Gil, Juan, 'Apuleyo en la Sevilla renacentista', *Habis* 23 (1992), 297–306.

Gill, Christopher, and T. P. Wiseman, eds., *Lies and Fiction in the Ancient World* (Exeter: U of Exeter P, 1993).

Gillam, S. G., et al., *The Douce Legacy* (Oxford: Bodleian Library, 1984).

Godman, Peter, 'Literary Classicism and Latin Erotic Poetry of the Twelfth Century and the Renaissance', in *Latin Poetry and the Classical Tradition*, ed. Godman and Murray, 149–82.

—— ed., *Poetry of the Carolingian Renaissance* (London: Duckworth, 1985).

—— and Murray, Oswyn, eds., *Latin Poetry and the Classical Tradition: Essays in Medieval and Renaissance Literature* (Oxford: Clarendon, 1990).

Gombrich, E. H., 'Hypnerotomachiana', *JWCI* 14 (1951), 119–25; repr. in his *Symbolic Images*.

Gombrich, E. M., *Symbolic Images: Studies in the Art of the Renaissance* (London: Phaidon, 1972).

—— 'Architecture and Rhetoric in Giulio Romano's Palazzo del Te', in his *New Light on Old Masters* (Chicago: U of Chicago P, 1986), 161–70.

Gouwens, Kenneth, 'Ciceronianism and Collective Identity: Defining the Boundaries of the Roman Academy, 1525', *JMRS* 23 (1993), 173–95.

Grafton, Anthony, 'On the Scholarship of Politian and its Context', *JWCI* 40 (1977), 150–88.

—— *Commerce with the Classics: Ancient Books and Renaissance Readers* (Ann Arbor: U of Michigan P, 1997).

—— *Cardano's Cosmos: The Worlds and Works of a Renaissance Astrologer* (Cambridge, Mass.: HUP, 1999).

—— and Lisa Jardine, *From Humanism to the Humanities: Education and the Liberal Arts in Fifteenth- and Sixteenth-Century Europe* (London: Duckworth, 1986).

Greenlaw, Edwin, 'Some Old Religious Cults in Spenser', *SP* 20 (1923), 216–43.

—— Charles Grosvenor Osgood, and Frederick Morgan Padelford, eds., *The Works of Edmund Spenser: A Variorum Edition*, 11 vols. (Baltimore: Johns Hopkins P, 1932–57).

Grendler, Paul F., 'The Rejection of Learning in Mid-*Cinquecento* Italy', *Studies in the Renaissance* 13 (1966), 230–49; repr. in his *Culture and Censorship in Late Renaissance Italy and France* (London: Variorum Reprints, 1981), 230–49.

Griffin, Clive, 'Aldus Manutius's Influence in the Hispanic World', in *Aldus Manutius and Renaissance Culture*, ed. Zeidberg and Superbi, 323–33.

Griffiths, J. Gwyn, *Apuleius of Madauros: The Isis-Book (Metamorphoses, Book XI)* (Leiden: Brill, 1975).

Griggs, Tamara, 'Promoting the Past: The *Hypnerotomachia* as Antiquarian Enterprise', in *Garden and Architectural Dreamscapes*, ed. Leslie and Hunt, 17–39.

Grignaschi, Mario, 'Lo Pseudo Walter Burley e il *Liber de vita et moribus philosophorum*', *Medioevo: Rivista di storia della filosofia medievale* 16 (1990), 131–90.

—— '*Corrigenda et addenda* sulla questione dello Ps. Burleo', *Medioevo* 16 (1990), 325–54.

Grimal, Pierre, 'A la recherche d'Apulée', *REL* 47 (1969), 94–9.

Grossmann, Maria, *Humanism in Wittenberg 1485–1517*, Bibliotheca humanistica et reformatorica 11 (Nieuwkoop: De Graaf, 1975).

Grünberg-Dröge, Monika, 'Peutinger, Konrad', *Biographisch-Bibliographischen Kirchenlexikons* 7 (1994), 392–7.

Gual, Carlos García, 'Sobre la version espanola de *El asno de oro* por Diego Lopez de Cortegana', in *Homenaje al profesor Antonio Vilanova*, ed. Adolfo Sotelo Vázquez and Marta Cristina Carbonell, 2 vols. (Barcelona: Dept. de Filol. Espanola, U of Barcelona, 1989), i. 297–307.

Gualandri, Isabella, and Giovanni Orlandi, 'Commedia elegiaca o commedia umanistica? Il problema del *De Cavichiolo*', in *Filologia e forme letterarie: Studi offerti a Francesco Della Corte*, ed. Sandro Boldrini et al., 5 vols. (Urbino: Università degli Studi di Urbino, 1987), v. 335–56.

Guillemain, Bernard, *La Cœur pontificale d'Avignon 1309–1376: Étude d'une société* (Paris: Boccard, 1966).

Guyer, Foster Erwin, *Chrétien de Troyes: Inventor of the Modern Novel* (London: Vision, 1960).

Häfner, Ralph, 'Ein schoenes Confitemini. Johann Sieders Übersetzung von Apuleius' *Goldenem Esel*: Die Berliner Handschrift Germ. Fol. 1239 aus dem Jahr 1500 und der erste Druck von 1538', *Beiträge zur Geschichte der deutschen Sprache und Literatur* 125/1 (2003), 94–136.

Hagendahl, Harald, *Latin Fathers and the Classics: A Study on the Apologists, Jerome and other Christian Writers* (Göteborg: [Elanders boktr. aktiebolag; distr.: Almqvist & Wiksell, Stockholm], 1958).

—— *Augustine and the Latin Classics*, 2 vols., Studia Graeca et Latina 20 (Göteborg: Acta Universitatis Cothoburgensis, 1967).

Hägg, Tomas, *The Novel in Antiquity* (Oxford: Blackwell, 1983).

Hagstrum, Jean H., 'Eros and Psyche: Some Versions of Romantic Love and Delicacy', *Critical Inquiry* 3 (1977), 521–42.

Haight, Elizabeth H., *Apuleius and his Influence* (London: Harrap, 1927).

—— 'Apuleius and Boccaccio', in her *More Essays on Greek Romances* (New York: Longmans, Green, 1945), 113–41.

Hain, Ludwig, *Repertorium Bibliographicum in quo libri omnes ab arte typographica inventa usque ad annum MD. typis expressi, ordine alphabetico vel simpliciter enumerantur vel adcuratius recensentur*, 4 vols. (Stuttgart: J. G. Cotta, 1826–38).

Hale, William Gardner, 'Benzo of Alexandria and Catullus', *CP* 5 (1910), 56–65.

Hall, Jennifer, *Lucian's Satire* (New York: Arno P, 1981).

Halstead, W. L., 'Dekker's *Cupid and Psyche* and Thomas Heywood', *ELH* 11/3 (Sept. 1944), 182–91.

Hamilton, A. C., 'Spenser's Treatment of Myth', *ELH* 26 (1959), 335–54.

—— *The Structure of Allegory in 'The Faerie Queene'* (Oxford: Clarendon, 1961).

—— *Sir Philip Sidney: A Study of his Life and Work* (Cambridge: CUP, 1977).

—— ed., *Edmund Spenser: The Faerie Queene* (London: Longman, 1977; repr. 1980).

—— ed., *The Spenser Encyclopedia* (Toronto: U of Toronto P, 1990).

Hanning, R. W., *The Individual in Twelfth-Century Romance* (New Haven: YUP, 1977).

—— and David Rosand, eds., *Castiglione: The Ideal and the Real in Renaissance Culture* (New Haven: YUP, 1983).

Hardin, R. F., Review of *SFN* by Tobin, *RPL* 8 (1985), 297–9.

Harran, Marilyn J., ed., *Luther and Learning: The Wittenburg University Luther Symposium* (Selinsgrove: Susquehanna UP; London: Associated University Presses, 1985).

Harries, Jill, *Sidonius Apollinaris and the Fall of Rome, AD 407–485* (Oxford: Clarendon, 1994).

Harrison, S. J., 'The Milesian Tales and the Roman Novel', *GCN* 9 (1998), 61–73.

—— *Apuleius: A Latin Sophist* (Oxford: OUP, 2000).

—— ed., *Oxford Readings in the Roman Novel* (Oxford: OUP, 1999).

Havely, N. R., ed. and trans., *Chaucer's Boccaccio: Sources of 'Troilus' and the Knight's and Franklin's Tales: Translations from the 'Filostrato', 'Teseida' and 'Filocolo'* (Cambridge: Brewer; Totowa, NJ: Rowman & Littlefield, 1980).

Hays, Gregory, 'The Date and Identity of the Mythographer Fulgentius', *Journal of Medieval Latin* 13 (2003), 163–252.

—— '*Romuleis Libicisque Litteris*: Fulgentius and the "Vandal Renaissance" ', in *Vandals, Romans and Berbers: New Perspectives on Late Antique North Africa*, ed. A. H. Merrills (Aldershot: Ashgate, 2004), 101–32.

Hellinga, Wytze, and Lotte Hellinga, *The Fifteenth-Century Printing Types of the Low Countries*, vol. i. (Amsterdam: Menno Hertzberger, 1966).

Herrmann, Léon, 'Le Fragment obscène de l'*Âne d'or* (X, 21)', *Latomus* 10 (1951), 329–32.

Hibbert, Christopher, *Rome: The Biography of a City* (Harmondsworth: Viking, 1985).

Hieatt, A. Kent, and Anne Lake Prescott, 'Contemporizing Antiquity: The *Hypnerotomachia* and its Afterlife in France', *Word & Image* 8 (1992), 291–321.

Hijmans, B. L., and R. Th. van der Paardt, eds., *Aspects of Apuleius' 'Golden Ass'* (Groningen: Bouma, 1978).

Hinds, Stephen, *Allusion and Intertext: Dynamics of Appropriation in Roman Poetry* (Cambridge: CUP, 1998).

Hoffmann, Adolf, *Das Psyche-Marchen des Apuleius in der englischen Literatur* (Strasbourg: Huber, 1908).

Hofmann, Heinz, ed., *Latin Fiction: The Latin Novel in Context* (London: Routledge, 1999).

Holford-Strevens, Leofranc, 'Humanism and the Language of Music Treatises', *RS* 15 (2001), 415–49.

Hollander, Robert, *Boccaccio's Two Venuses* (New York: Columbia UP, 1977).

Holmer, J., 'Internal Evidence for Dating William Browne's *Britannia's Pastorals*, Book III', *PBSA* 70 (1976), 347–64, at 362–4.

Höltgen, Karl Josef, 'Sir Robert Dallington (1561–1637): Author, Traveler, and Pioneer of Taste', *HLQ* 47 (1984), 147–77.

Horsfall Scotti, Mariateresa, 'Apuleio tra magia e filosofia: La riscoperta di Agostino', in *Dicti studiosus: Scritti di filologia offerti a Scevola Mariotti dai suoi allievi* (Urbino: QuattroVenti, 1990), 297–320.

—— 'The *Asclepius*: Thoughts on a Re-opened Debate', *Vigiliae Christianae* 54 (2000), 396–416.

Hough, Graham, *A Preface to 'The Faerie Queene'* (London: Duckworth, 1962; repr. 1983).

Huet, G., 'Le Roman d'Apulée était-il connu au moyen âge?', *Le Moyen Âge*, 2nd ser. 13 (1909), 23–8.

Humphreys, K. W., 'The Library of John Erghome and Personal Libraries of the Fourteenth Century in England', *Proceedings of the Leeds Philosophical and Literary Society* 18 (1982), 106–23.

Hunink, Vincent, 'The Prologue of Apuleius' *De Deo Socratis*', *Mnemosyne* 48 (1995), 292–312.

Hunink, Vincent, 'Apuleius and the *Asclepius*', *Vigiliae Christianae* 50 (1996), 288–308.

—— '*Apuleius, qui nobis afris afer est notior*: Augustine's Polemic against Apuleius in *De Civitate Dei*', *Scholia: Studies in Classical Antiquity*, NS 12 (2003), 82–95.

—— 'The *spurcum additamentum* (Apul. *Met.* 10,21) once again', in *Lectiones Scrupulosae*, ed. Keulen, et al. 266–79.

Hunt, A., 'Chrétien and Macrobius', *Classica et Mediaevalia* 33 (1981), 211–27.

Hutson, Lorna, *Thomas Nashe in Context* (Oxford: Clarendon, 1989).

Huygens, R. B. G., 'Mitteilungen aus Handschriften', *Studi medievali* 3 (1962), 747–72.

Hyma, Albert, *The Life of Desiderius Erasmus* (Assen: Van Gorcum, 1972).

Ife, W. B., *Reading and Fiction in Golden Age Spain: A Platonic Critique and Some Humanist Replies* (Cambridge: CUP, 1985).

Ijsewijn, Jozef, *Companion to Neo-Latin Studies*, 2nd edn., 2 vols. (Leuven: Leuven UP, 1990–8).

—— 'De *huius nympha loci* (*CIL* VI/5, 3$^+$ e) eiusque fortuna poetica syntagmation', *Arctos (Acta philologica fennica)*, suppl. II: Studia in honorem Iiro Kajanto (1985): 61–7.

Isbell, Harold, 'Decimus Magnus Ausonius: The Poet and his World', in *Latin Literature of the Fourth Century*, ed. Binns, 22–57.

James, Montague Rhodes, *A Descriptive Catalogue of the Manuscripts in the Library of Eton College* (Cambridge: CUP, 1895).

—— *A Descriptive Catalogue of the Manuscripts other than Oriental in the Library of King's College, Cambridge* (Cambridge: CUP, 1895).

—— *On the Abbey of S. Edmund at Bury*, Cambridge Antiquarian Soc. Octavo Publications 28 (Cambridge: Cambridge Antiquarian Soc., 1895).

—— 'The Catalogue of the Library of the Augustinian Friars at York, now first edited from the Manuscript at Trinity College, Dublin', in *Fasciculus Ioanni Willis Clark dicatus* (Cambridge: CUP, 1909), 2–96.

Jocelyn, H. D., 'L. Caecilius Minutianus Apuleius', in *Homo sapiens, homo humanus*, ed. Giovannangiola Tarugi, Centro di studi umanistici 'Angelo Poliziano', 2 vols. (Florence: Olschki, 1990), i. 207–18.

Jones, C. P., *Culture and Society in Lucian* (Cambridge, Mass.: HUP, 1986).

Jong, Jan. L. de, 'Renaissance Representations of Cupid and Psyche: Apuleius versus Fulgentius', *GCN* 2 (1989), 75–87.

—— '*Il pittore a le volte è puro poeta*: Cupid and Psyche in Italian Renaissance Painting', in *Aspects of Apuleius' 'Golden Ass'*, vol. ii. *Cupid and Psyche*, ed. M. Zimmerman, et al. (Groningen: Forsten, 1998).

Judson, Alexander C., *The Life of Edmund Spenser* (Baltimore: Johns Hopkins P, 1945); repr. 1947).

Jullien de Pommerol, Marie-Henriette, and Jacques Monfrin, *La Bibliothèque pontificale à Avignon et à Peñiscola pendant le grand schisme d'occident et sa dispersion*, 2 vols. (Rome: École française de Rome, 1991).

Jusserand, J. J., 'Did Chaucer Meet Petrarch?', *Nineteenth Century* 39 (1896), 993–1005.

Kahane, Ahuvia, and Andrew Laird, eds., *A Companion to the Prologue of Apuleius' 'Metamorphoses'* (Oxford: OUP, 2001).

Kahane, Henry, Renee Kahane, and Angelina Pietrangeli, 'On the Sources of Chrétien's Grail Story', in *Festschrift Walther von Wartburg zum 80. Geburstag*, ed. Kurt Baldinger (Tübingen: Niemeyer, 1968), 191–233.

Kawczynski, Maximilien, 'Ist Apuleius im Mittelalter bekannt gewesen?', in *Bausteine zur romanischen Philologie: Festgabe für Adolfo Mussafia* (Halle: Niemeyer, 1905), 193–210.

Keefer, M. H., 'Agrippa's Dilemma: Hermetic Rebirth and the Ambivalences of *De Vanitate* and *De Occulta Philosophia*', RQ 41 (1988), 614–53.

Kelly, Douglas, 'The Source and Meaning of *Conjointure* in Chrétien's *Erec* 14', *Viator: Medieval and Renaissance Studies* 1 (1970), 179–200.

Kenney, E. J., 'The Character of Humanist Philology', in *Classical Influences on European Culture, A.D. 500–1500*, ed. R. R. Bolgar (Cambridge: CUP, 1971), 119–28.

—— *The Classical Text: Aspects of Editing in the Age of the Printed Book* (Berkeley and Los Angeles: U of California P, 1974).

Kenny, Neil, *The Palace of Secrets: Béroalde de Verville and Renaissance Conceptions of Knowledge* (Oxford: Clarendon, 1991).

Kermode, J. F., 'The Mature Comedies', in *Stratford-upon-Avon Studies 3: Early Shakespeare*, ed. J. R. Brown and B. Harris (London: Arnold, 1961), 211–27.

—— 'The Banquet of Sense', *BJRL* 44 (1961–2), 68–99.

Keulen, W. H., R. R. Nauta, and S. Panayotakis, eds., *Lectiones Scrupulosae: Essays on the Text and Interpretation of Apuleius' 'Metamorphoses' in Honour of Maaike Zimmerman, Ancient Narrative*; suppl. 6 (Groningen: Barkhuis/ Groningen University Library, 2006).

Klibansky, Raymond, *The Continuity of the Platonic Tradition during the Middle Ages* (Millwood, NY: Kraus, 1982).

Knowles, David, *The Evolution of Medieval Thought*, 2nd edn., ed. D. E. Luscombe and C. N. L. Brooke (London: Longman, 1988).

Koff, Leonard Michael, and Brenda Deen Schildgen, eds., *The 'Decameron' and the 'Canterbury Tales': New Essays on an Old Question* (Madison, NJ: Fairleigh Dickinson UP; London: Associated University Presses, 2000).

Kohl, Benjamin G., and Nancy G. Siraisi, 'The *De Monarchia* attributed to Apuleius', *Mediaevalia* 7 (1984 for 1981), 1–39.

Kolsky, Stephen, 'Culture and Politics in Renaissance Rome: Marco Antonio Altieri's Roman Weddings', *RQ* 40 (1987), 49–90.

—— *Mario Equicola: The Real Courtier* (Geneva: Droz, 1991).

Korkowski, Eugene, 'Agrippa as Ironist', *Neophilologus* 60 (1976), 594–607.

Krautter, Konrad, *Philologische Methode und humanistische Existenz: Filippo Beroaldo und sein Kommentar zum Goldenen Esel des Apuleius*, Humanistische Bibliothek, Reihe 1: Abhandlungen; Bd. 9 (Munich: Fink, 1971).

Krill, R. M., 'The "Vatican Mythographers": Their Place in Ancient Mythography', *Manuscripta* 23 (1979), 173–7.

Kurz, Otto, '*Huius nympha loci*: A Pseudo-Classical Inscription and a Drawing by Dürer', *JWCI* 16 (1953), 171–7.

Labowsky, Lotte, *Bessarion's Library and the Biblioteca Marciana: Six Early Inventories* (Rome: Edizioni di storia e letteratura, 1979).

Laistner, M. L. W., 'Fulgentius in the Carolingian Age', in his *The Intellectual Heritage of the Early Middle Ages* (Ithaca, NY: Cornell UP, 1957), 202–15.

Lanciani, Rodolfo, *Pagan and Christian Rome* (London: Macmillan, 1892).

Lane Fox, Robin, *Pagans and Christians* (Harmondsworth: Viking, 1986).

Lathrop, H. B., *Translations from the Classics into English from Caxton to Chapman, 1477–1620* (Madison: U of Wisconsin, 1933; New York: Octagon, 1967).

Laude, S. De., 'La *spola* di Bartolomeo de'Bartoli: Sull'esperimento metrico di una canzone illustrata del Trecento', *Anticomoderno* 2 (1996), 201–18.

Lawn, Brian, *The Salernitan Questions: An Introduction to the History of Medieval and Renaissance Problem Literature* (Oxford: Clarendon, 1963).

Leccisotti, Tommasso, *Monte Cassino*, ed. and trans. Armand O. Citarella (Monte Cassino: Abbey of Monte Cassino, 1987).

Lee, Egmont, *Sixtus IV and Men of Letters,* Temi e testi 26, (Rome: Edizioni di storia e letteratura, 1978).

Leedham-Green, E. S., *Books in Cambridge Inventories: Book-Lists from Vice-Chancellor's Court Probate Inventories in the Tudor and Stuart Periods,* 2 vols. (Cambridge: CUP, 1986).

Lefaivre, Liane, *Leon Battista Alberti's 'Hypnerotomachia Poliphili': Re-cognizing the Architectural Body in the Early Italian Renaissance* (Cambridge, Mass.: MIT P, 1997).

Lehmberg, Stanford E., *Sir Thomas Elyot: Tudor Humanist* (Austin: U of Texas P, 1960).

Le Maitre, Henri, *Essai sur le mythe de Psyché dans la littérature française des origines à 1890,* Études de littérature étrangère et comparée 16 (Paris: Boivin, n.d.).

Lemmi, Charles W., 'The Influence of Trissino on the *Faerie Queene*', *PQ* 7 (1928), 220–3.

—— 'Symbolism in the Classical Episodes in the *Faerie Queene*', *PQ* 8 (1929) 270–87.

—— 'The Allegorical Meaning of Spenser's *Muiopotmos*', *PMLA* 45 (1930), 732–48.

—— 'Astery's Transformation in *Muiopotmos*', *PMLA* 50 (1935), 913–14.

Leslie, Michael, and John Dixon Hunt, eds., *Garden and Architectural Dreamscapes in the 'Hypnerotomachia Poliphili'*, *Word & Image* 1 & 2 (1998) (special issue).

Lev Kenaan, Vered, '*Fabula anilis*: The Literal as a Feminine Sense', in C. Deroux, ed., *Studies in Latin Literature and Roman History,* vol. x (Brussels: Latomus, 2000), 370–91.

Levao, Ronald, *Renaissance Minds and their Fictions: Cusanus, Sidney, Shakespeare* (Berkeley and Los Angeles: U of California P, 1985).

Lewis, C. S., *The Allegory of Love* (Oxford: Clarendon, 1936).

—— *English Literature in the Sixteenth Century Excluding Drama* (Oxford: Clarendon, 1954).

Lewy, Hans, *Chaldaean Oracles and Theurgy: Mysticism, Magic and Platonism in the Later Roman Empire*, 2nd edn., rev. Michel Tardieu (Paris: Études augustiniennes, 1978).

Limone, Oronzo, 'L'opera agiografica di Guaiferio di Montecassino', in *Monastica III: Scritti raccolti in memoria del XV centenario della nascita di S. Benedetto (480–1980)*, Miscellanea Cassinese 47 (Monte Cassino: Pubblicazioni cassinesi, 1983), 77–130.

Lindsay, W. M., 'The Abstrusa Glossary and the *Liber Glossarum*', *CQ* 11/3 (July 1917), 119–31.

—— 'The St. Gall Glossary', *AJP* 38 (1917), 349–69.

—— 'The "Abolita" Glossary (Vat. Lat. 3321)', *Journal of Philology* 34 (1918), 267–82.

—— and H. J. Thomson *Ancient Lore in Medieval Latin Glossaries*, St Andrews University Publications 13 (London: St Andrews U, 1921).

Loewe, Gustav, *Prodromus corporis glossariorum Latinorum: Quaestiones de glossariorum Latinorum fontibus et usu* (Leipzig: Teubner, 1876).

Lotspeich, H. G., *Classical Mythology in the Poetry of Edmund Spenser* (Princeton: PUP, 1932).

Lowe [Loew], E. A., *The Beneventan Script: A History of the South Italian Miniscule* (Oxford: Clarendon, 1914).

—— 'The Unique Manuscript of Apuleius' *Metamorphoses* (Laurentian. 68.2) and its Oldest Transcript (Laurentian. 29.2)', *CQ* 14 (1920), 150–5.

—— 'On the Oldest Extant MS. of the Combined *Abstrusa* and *Abolita* Glossaries', *CQ* 15 (1921), 189–91.

—— 'The Unique Manuscript of Tacitus' *Histories* (Florence Laur. 68.2)', in *Casinensia: Miscellanea di studi Cassinesi* (Monte Cassino: Monte Cassino, 1929). 257–72; repr. in his *Palaeographical Papers, 1907–1965*, ed. Ludwig Bieler, 2 vols. (Oxford: Clarendon, 1972), i. 289–302.

Lowry, Martin J. C., 'The "New Academy" of Aldus Manutius: A Renaissance Dream', *BJRL* 58 (1976), 378–420.

—— *The World of Aldus Manutius: Business and Scholarship in Renaissance Venice* (Oxford: Blackwell, 1979).

Luttrell, Claude, *The Creation of the First Arthurian Romance: A Quest* (London: Edward Arnold, 1974).

Lutz, Cora E., 'Aesticampianus' Commentary on the *De Grammatica* of Martianus Capella', *RQ* 26.2 (1973), 157–66.

—— 'Walter Burley's *De vita et moribus philosophorum*', in her *Essays on Manuscripts and Rare Books* (Hamden, Conn.: Archon Books, 1975), 51–6.

Lytle, Ephraim, 'Apuleius' *Metamorphoses* and the *Spurcum Additamentum* (10. 21)', *CP* 98 (2003), 349–65.

McCobb, Lilian M., 'The Traditional Background of *Partonopeu de Blois*: An Additional Note', *Neophilologus* 60 (1976), 608–10.

—— 'The English *Partonope of Blois*, its French Source, and Chaucer's Knight's Tale', *Chaucer Review* 11 (1977), 369–72.

McKerrow, R. B., gen. ed., *A Dictionary of Printers and Booksellers in England, Scotland and Ireland, and of Foreign Printers of English Books, 1557–1640* (London: Bibliographical Soc., 1910).

McLachlan, Elizabeth Parker, *The Scriptorium of Bury St. Edmunds in the Twelfth Century* (New York: Garland, 1986).

Maclean, Hugh, ed., *Edmund Spenser's Poetry*, 2nd edn. (London: Norton, 1982).

MacMullen, Ramsay, *Christianity and Paganism in the Fourth to Eighth Centuries* (New Haven: YUP, 1997).

McPeek, James A. S., 'The Psyche Myth and *A Midummer Night's Dream*', *SQ* 23 (1972), 69–79.

McPherson, David, 'Aretino and the Harvey-Nashe Quarrel', *PMLA* 84 (1969), 1551–8.

Maggiulli, Gigliola, and M. Franca Buffa Giolito, *L'altro Apuleio: Problemi aperti per una nuova edizione dell'Herbarius*, Studi latini 17 (Naples: Loffredo, 1996).

Magnaldi, Giuseppina, and Gian Franco Gianotti, eds., *Apuleio: Storia del testo e interpretazioni* (Alessandria: Edizioni dell'Orso, 2000).

Mal-Maeder, Danielle van, '*Lector, intende: laetaberis*: The Enigma of the Last Book of Apuleius' *Metamorphoses*', *GCN* 8 (1997), 87–118.

Mancini, M., 'Intorno alla lingua del *Polifilo*', *Roma nel Rinascimento, Bibliografie e note* 6 (1989), 29–48.

Manetti, Aldo, 'Nota su Dante e Apuleio', *L'Alighieri: Rassegna bibliografica dantesca* 22/2 (July–Dec. 1981), 61–2.

Maniscalco, Silvana, 'Criteri e sensibilità di Agnolo Firenzuola, traduttore di Apuleio', *La rassegna della letteratura italiana* 82 (1978), 88–109.

Manitius, Max, *Philologisches aus alten Bibliothekskatalogen (bis 1300)*, Rheinisches Museum für Philologie, NS 47 (Frankfurt: Sauerländer, 1892).

—— *Geschichte der lateinische Literatur des Mittelalters*, 3 vols. (Munich: Beck, 1911–31).

—— and Karl Manitius, *Handschriften antiker Autoren in mittelalterlichen Bibliothekskatalogen*, Zentralblatt für Bibliothekswegen 67 (Leipzig: Harrassowitz, 1935).

Marchesi, Concetto, 'Giovanni Boccaccio e i codici di Apuleio', *Rassegna bibliografica della letteratura italiana* 20 (1912), 232–4; repr. in his *Scritti minori di filologia e di letteratura*, 3 vols, Opuscoli accademici 13, (Florence: Olschki, 1978), iii. 1010–11.

Mare, A. C. de la, *The Handwriting of Italian Humanists*, vol. i, fas. i (Oxford: OUP for Association internationale de bibliophilie, 1973).

Marenbon, John, *From the Circle of Alcuin to the School of Auxerre: Logic, Theology, and Philosophy in the Early Middle Ages* (Cambridge: CUP, 1981).

—— 'Carolingian Thought', in *Carolingian Culture: Emulation and Innovation*, ed. Rosamond McKitterick (Cambridge: CUP, 1994), 171–92.

Mariotti, Scevola, 'Lo *Spurcum Additamentum* ad Apul. *Met.* 10, 21', *SIFC* 27–8 (1956), 229–50.

Markus, R. A., 'Paganism, Christianity and the Latin Classics in the Fourth Century', in *Latin Literature of the Fourth Century*, ed. Binns, 1–21.

Marrou, Henri Irénée, 'La Vie intellectuelle au Forum de Trajan et au Forum d'Auguste', *Mélanges d'archéologie et d'histoire de l'École française de Rome* 49 (1932), 93–110.

Marsh, David, 'Alberti and Apuleius: Comic Violence and Vehemence in the *Intercenales* and *Momus*', in *Leon Battista Alberti: Actes du Congrès International de Paris (Sorbonne-Institut de France-Institut culturel italien-Collège de France, 10–15 avril 1995) tenu sous la direction de F. Furlan, P. Laurens, S. Matton*, ed. Francesco Furlan, Anna Pia Filotico, et al., 2 vols. (Paris: Librairie Philosophique J. Vrin; Turin: Nino Aragno, 2000), i. 405–26.

Martellotti, Guido, *Le due redazione delle 'Genealogie' del Boccaccio*, Note e discussioni eruditi 1 (Rome: Edizioni di storia e letteratura, 1951).

Martin, René, 'Apulée dans les *Géoponiques*', *Revue de philologie* 46 (1972), 246–55.

—— 'Apulée, Virgile, Augustin: Réflexions nouvelles sur la structure des *Confessions*', *REL* 68 (1990), 136–50.

Martindale, Charles, and Michelle Martindale, *Shakespeare and the Uses of Antiquity: An Introductory Essay* (London: Routledge, 1990).

Martos, Juan, ed. and trans., *Apuleyo de Madauros: Las Metamorfosis o El Asno de Oro. Introducción, Texto Latino, Traducción y Notas*, 2 vols. (Madrid: Consejo Superior de Investigaciones Científicas, 2003).

Mass, Edgar, 'Tradition, und Innovation im Romanschaffen Boccaccios: Die Bedeutung des *Goldenen Esel* für die Erneuerung des Prosaromans durch die *Elegia di Madonna Fiammetta* (1343/4)', *GCN* 2 (1989), 87–107.

Mather, F. J., 'On the Asserted Meeting of Chaucer and Petrarch', *MLN* 12 (1897), cols. 1–18.

Mathisen, Ralph W., 'Epistolography, Literary Circles and Family Ties in Late Roman Gaul', *TAPA* 111 (1981), 95–109.

Matthews, J. F., 'The Historical Setting of the *Carmen contra paganos* (Cod. Par. Lat. 8084)', *Historia* 19 (1970), 464–79.

—— 'Symmachus and the Oriental Cults', *JRS* 63 (1973), 174–95.

—— 'The Theme of Literary Decline in Late Roman Gaul', *CP* 83 (1988), 45–52.

Mattiacci, Silvia, 'Apuleio in Fulgenzio', *SIFC*, 4th ser. 1 (2003), 229–56.

May, Regine, 'The Prologue to Apuleius' *Metamorphoses* and Coluccio Salutati: MS Harley 4838 (With an Appendix on Sozomeno of Pistoia and the Nonius Marginalia)', in *Lectiones Scrupulosae*, ed. Keulen, et al., 280–312.

Mayor, J. E. B., 'Latin-English and English-Latin Lexicography', *Journal of Classical and Sacred Philology* 4 (1859), 1–44.

Mazzarino, Antonio, *La Milesia e Apuleio* (Turin: Chiantore, 1950).

Mazzola, E., 'Spenser, Sidney, and Second Thoughts: Mythology and Misgiving in *Muiopotmos*', *Sidney Journal* 18/1 (2000), 57–81.

Merkelbach, Reinhold, 'La nuova pagina di Sisenna ed Apuleio', *Maia* 5 (1952), 234–41.

Miglio, Massimo, ed., *Giovanni Andrea Bussi: Prefazioni alle edizioni di Sweynheym e Pannartz prototipografi Romani* (Milan: Edizioni il Polifilo, 1978).

Miller, C. William, 'A Bibliographical Study of *Parthenissa* by Roger Boyle, Earl of Orrery', *SB* 2 (1949), 115–37.

Mitchell, Charles, 'Archaeology and Romance in Renaissance Italy', in *Italian Renaissance Studies*, ed. E. F. Jacobs (London: Faber, 1960), 455–83.

Momigliano, Arnaldo, ed., *The Conflict between Paganism and Christianity in the Fourth Century* (Oxford: Clarendon, 1963).

Mondin, Luca, 'Note all'*Apulegio volgare* di Matteo Maria Boiardo', *Lexis* 4 (1989), 77–105.

Monfasani, John, *George of Trebizond: A Biography and a Study of his Rhetoric and Logic* (Leiden: Brill, 1976).

—— 'Il Perotti e la controversia fra platonici ed aristotelici', *RPL* 4 (1981), 195–231.

—— '*Bessarion Latinus*', *Rinascimento*, NS 21 (1981), 165–209.

—— 'Still More on *Bessarion Latinus*', *Rinascimento*, NS 23 (1983), 217–35.

—— 'The First Call for Press Censorship: Niccolò Perotti, Giovanni Andrea Bussi, Antonio Moreto and the Editing of Pliny's *Natural History*', *RQ* 41 (1988), 1–31.

—— 'Platonic Paganism in the 15th Century', in *Reconsidering the Renaissance*, ed. M. A. di Cesare (Binghamton, NY: CMERS, 1992), 45–61; repr. in his *Byzantine Scholars in Renaissance Italy*, no. X.

—— *Byzantine Scholars in Renaissance Italy: Cardinal Bessarion and Other Emigrés: Selected Essays* (Aldershot: Ashgate, 1995).

Moorman, Frederick, *William Browne: His 'Britannia's Pastorals' and the Pastoral Poetry of the Elizabethan Age* (Strasbourg: Trübner, 1897).

Moreschini, Claudio, 'Sulla fama di Apuleio nella tarda antichità', in *Romanitas et Christianitas: studia Iano Henrico Waszink A.D. VI Kal. Nov. A. MCMLXXIII, XIII lustra complenti oblata*, ed. Willem den Boer et al. (Amsterdam: North-Holland Pub. Co., 1973), 243–8.

—— 'Sulla fama di Apuleio nel medioevo e nel rinascimento', in *Studi filologici letterari e storici in memoria di Guido Favati*, ed. Giorgio Varanini and Palmiro Pinagli, Medioevo e Umanesimo 28–9, 2 vols. (Padua: Antenore, 1977), 457–76.

—— *Apuleio e il Platonismo*, Accademia toscana di scienze et lettere 'la Colombaria', 'studi' 51 (Florence: Olschki, 1978).

—— *Il mito di Amore e Psiche in Apuleio: Saggio, testo di Apuleio, traduzione e commento* (Naples: D'Auria, 1994).

—— 'Towards a History of the Exegesis of Apuleius: The Case of the "Tale of Cupid and Psyche"', in *Latin Fiction*, ed. Hofmann, 215–28.

Morey, James H., 'Spenser's Mythic Adaptations in *Muiopotmos*', *Spenser Studies* 9 (1988), 49–59.

Morgan, Gerald, 'Chaucer's Adaptation of Boccaccio's Temple of Venus in *The Parliament of Fowls*', *RES*, NS 56 (2005), 1–32.

Munby, A. L. N., 'Notes on King's College Library in the Fifteenth Century', *Transactions of the Cambridge Bibliographical Society* 1 (1949–53), 280–4.

Munk Olsen, Birger, *L'Étude des auteurs classiques aux XIe et XIIe siècles*, 3 vols. (Paris: Centre national de la recherche scientifique, 1982–9).

Mynors, R. A. B., 'The Latin Classics Known to Boston of Bury', in *Fritz Saxl: 1890–1948: A Volume of Memorial Essays from his Friends in England*, ed. D. J. Gordon (London: Nelson, 1957), 199–217.

Nelson, William, *Fact or Fiction: The Dilemma of the Renaissance Storyteller* (Cambridge, Mass.: HUP, 1973).

Newman, W. L., 'The Correspondence of Humphrey, Duke of Gloucester, and Pier Candido Decembrio', *EHR* 20 (1905), 484–98.

Newstead, Helaine, 'The Traditional Background of *Partonopeus de Blois*', *PMLA* 61 (1946), 916–46.

Newton, Francis, 'The Desiderian Scriptorium at Monte Cassino: The Chronicle and Some Surviving Manuscripts', *Dumbarton Oaks Papers* 30 (1976), 37–54.

—— *The Scriptorium and Library at Monte Cassino, 1058–1105*, Cambridge Studies in Palaeography and Codicology 7 (Cambridge: CUP, 1999).

Nicholl, Charles, *A Cup of News: The Life of Thomas Nashe* (London: RKP, 1984).

Nightingale, Jeanne A., 'Chrétien de Troyes and the Mythographical Tradition: The Couple's Journey in *Erec et Enide* and Martianus' *De Nuptiis*', in *King Arthur through the Ages*, ed. Valerie M. Lagorio and Mildred Leake Day, Garland Reference Library of the Humanities 1269, 2 vols. (New York: Garland, 1990), i. 56–79.

Nolhac, Pierre de, *La Bibliothèque de Fulvio Orsini: Contributions à l'histoire de collections d'Italie et à l'étude de la Renaissance*, Bibliothèque de l'École des hautes études, Sciences philologiques et historiques 47 (Paris: Vieweg, 1887).

Norden, Eduard, *Die antike Kunstprosa vom VI. Jahrhundert v. Chr. bis in die Zeit der Renaissance*, 2nd edn., 2 vols. (Leipzig: Teubner, 1909).

Nurmela, T., 'La Misogynie chez Boccacce', in *Boccaccio in Europe: Proceedings of the Boccaccio Conference, Louvain, December 1975*, ed. Gilbert Tournoy (Leuven: Leuven UP, 1977), 191–6.

Nuttall, A. D., *The Stoic in Love: Selected Essays on Literature and Ideas* (London: Harvester Wheatsheaf, 1989).

—— *Dead from the Waist Down: Scholars and Scholarship in literature and the Popular Imagination* (New Haven: YUP. 2003).

Oberhuber, Konrad, 'Raphael's Drawings for the Loggia of Psyche in the Farnesina', in *Raffaello a Roma: Il convegno del 1983*, ed. Christophe Luitpold Frommel and Mathias Winner (Rome: Elefante, 1986), 189–208.

O'Connell, John J., *Amadis de Gaule and its Influence on Elizabethan Literature* (New Brunswick, NJ: Rutgers UP, 1970).

O'Daly, Gerald, *Augustine's 'City of God': A Reader's Guide* (Oxford: Clarendon, 1999).

O'Donnell, James, 'The Demise of Paganism', *Traditio* 35 (1979), 45–88.

Oldfather, W. A., H. V. Canter, and B. E. Perry, *Index Apuleianus* (Middletown, Conn.: American Philological Association, 1934).

Oldoni, Massimo, 'Streghe medievali e intersezioni da Apuleio', in *Semiotica della novella latina: Atti del Seminario interdisciplinare 'La novella latina', Perugia 11–13 aprile 1985* (Rome: Herder, 1986), 267–79.

Oliver, Revilo P., ' "New Fragments" of Latin Authors in Perotti's *Cornucopiae*', *TAPA* 78 (1947), 376–424.

Orlandi, Giovanni, 'Classical Latin Satire and Medieval Elegiac Comedy', in *Latin Poetry and the Classical Tradition*, ed. Godman and Murray, 97–114.

Ormerod, David, '*A Midsummer Night's Dream*: The Monster in the Labyrinth', *Shakespeare Studies* 11 (1978), 39–52.

Osgood, Charles G., *A Concordance to the Poems of Edmund Spenser* (Washington: Carnegie Institute, 1915).

Ott, Martin, *Die Entdeckung des Altertums: Der Umgang mit der römischen Vergangenheit Süddeutschlands im 16. Jahrhundert*, Münchener Historische Studien. Abteilung Bayerische Geschichte 17 (Kallmünz: Lassleben, 2002).

Ottman, Jennifer, and Rega Wood, 'Walter of Burley: His Life and Works', *Vivarium* 37 (1999), 1–23.

Ozment, Steven, *Flesh and Spirit: Private Life in Early Modern Germany* (New York: Viking, 1999).

Painter, George D., *The 'Hypnerotomachia Poliphili' of 1499: An Introduction on the Dream, the Dreamer, the Artist, and the Printer* (London: Eugrammia P, 1963).

Palermino, R. J., 'The Roman Academy, the Catacombs and the Conspiracy of 1468', *Archivum historiae pontificiae* 18 (1980), 117–55.

Panayotakis, Stelios, Maaike Zimmerman, and Wyste Keulen, eds., *The Ancient Novel and Beyond*, Mnemosyne suppl. 241 (Leiden: Brill, 2003).

Panofsky, Erwin, *Studies in Iconology: Humanistic Themes in the Art of the Renaissance*, 1st Torchbook edn. (New York: Harper & Row, 1962).

—— *Renaissance and Renascences in Western Art* (London: Paladin, 1960; repr. London: Harper & Row, 1970).

Pastor, Ludwig, *The History of the Popes from the Close of the Middle Ages*, ed. and trans. Frederick Ignatius Antrobus, vol. iv (1899; 4th edn., London: Kegan Paul, Trench, Trubner & Co., 1923).

Pastore Stocchi, M., 'Il "Somnium" di Albertino Mussato', in *Studi in onore di Vittorio Zaccaria*, ed. Marco Pecoraro (Milan: Unicopli, 1987), 41–63.

Payne, F. Anne, *Chaucer and Menippean Satire* (Madison: U of Wisconsin P, 1981).

Pecere, Oronzo, 'Esemplari con *subscriptiones* e tradizione dei testi latini l'Apuleio Laur. 68.2', in *Atti del convegno internazionale: Il libro e il testo (Urbino, 20–24 settembre 1982)*, ed. Cesare Questa and Renato Raffaelli (Urbino: Università degli studi di Urbino, 1984), 111–38.

—— 'Qualche riflessione sulla tradizione di Apuleio a Montecassino', in *Le strade del testo*, ed. Guglielmo Cavallo (Bari: Adriatica, 1987), 99–124.

—— and Antonio Stramaglia, *Studi apuleiani*, updated by Luca Graverini (Cassino: Edizioni dell' Università degli studi di Cassino, 2003).

Penella, Robert J., 'An Overlooked Story about Apollonius of Tyana in Anastasius Sinaita', *Traditio* 34 (1978), 414–15.

Perry, Ben Edwin, 'On Apuleius' *Hermagoras*', *AJP* 48 (1927), 263–6.

—— *The Ancient Romances: A Literary-Historical Account of their Origins* (Berkeley and Los Angeles: U of California P, 1967).

Petoletti, Marco, 'Montecassino e gli umanisti, III: I *Florida* di Apuleio in Benzo d'Alessandria', in *Libro, scrittura, documento della civiltà monastica e conventuale nel basso medioevo (secoli XIII–XV): Atti del convegno di studio, Fermo (17–19 settembre 1997)*, ed. G. Avarucci, R. M. Borraccini Verducci, and G. Borri, Studi e ricerche 1 (Spoleto: Centro italiano di studi sull'alto medioevo, 1999), 183–238.

Pfeiffer, Rudolf, *History of Classical Scholarship, 1300–1850*, 2 vols. (Oxford: Clarendon, 1968–76).

Pigman III, G. W., 'Imitation and the Renaissance Sense of the Past: The Reception of Erasmus' *Ciceronianus*', *JMRS* 9/2 (1979), 155–77.

—— 'Versions of Imitation in the Renaissance', *RQ* 33 (1980), 1–32.

Pinotti, Giorgio, 'Curio Lancillotto Pasio e la *Bucolicorum Mimesis* dedicata a Niccolò da Correggio', *HL* 32 (1983), 165–96.

Pittaluga, S., 'Narrativa e oralità nella commedia mediolatina (e il fantasma di Apuleio)', in *Der antike Roman und seine mittelalterliche Rezeption*, ed. Michelangelo Picone and Bernhard Zimmermann (Basle: Birkhäuser, 1997), 307–20.

Plank, Birgit, *Johann Sieders Übersetzung des 'Goldenen Esels' und die frühe deutschsprachige 'Metamorphosen'-Rezeption: ein Beitrag zur Wirkungsgeschichte von Apuleius' Roman* (Tübingen: Niemeyer, 2004).

Poeschel, Sabina, 'A Hitherto Unknown Portrait of a Well-Known Renaissance Humanist', *RQ* 43 (1990), 146–54.

Poole, R. L., 'The Masters of the Schools at Paris and Chartres in John of Salisbury's Time', *EHR* 35 (1920), 336–42.

Powell, Jonathon G. F., 'Some Linguistic Points in the Prologue', in *Companion to the Prologue*, ed. Kahane and Laird, 27–36.

Pozzi, Giovanni, and Lucia A. Ciapponi, eds., *Francesco Colonna: Hypnerotomachia Poliphili. Edizione critica e commento*, 2 vols., 2nd edn. (Padua: Antenore, 1980).

Præstgaard Andersen, Lise, '*Partalopa saga*, homologue scandinave d'*Eros* et *Psyché*', *Revue des langues romanes* 102 (1998), 57–64.

Praz, Mario, 'Il Polifilo e Aubrey Beardsley', in his *Storia della letteratura inglese* (Florence: Sansoni, 1946).

—— 'Some Foreign Imitators of the *Hypnerotomachia Polyphili*', *Italica* 24 (1947), 20–5.

—— *The Romantic Agony*, trans. Angus Davidson, 2nd edn. (London: OUP, 1951).

Prelog, Jan, 'Die Handschriften und Drucke von Walter Burleys *Liber de vita et moribus philosophorum*', *Codices manuscripti* 9 (1983), 1–18.

Prete, Sesto, 'La questione della lingua latina nel Quattrocento e l'importanza dell'opera di Apuleio', *GCN* 1 (1988), 123–40.

Prinsac, Annie-Paule de, 'La Métamorphose de Bottom et *L'Âne d'or*', *Études anglaises* 34 (1981), 61–71.

Prouty, C. T., *George Gascoigne: Elizabethan Courtier, Soldier, and Poet* (New York: Columbia UP, 1942).

Purser, L. C., 'Laud's Manuscript of Apuleius', *Hermathena* 35 (1909), 425–37.

Raab, Felix. *The English Face of Machiavelli: A Changing Interpretation* (London: RKP, 1964).

Rabil, Albert, Jr., ed., *Renaissance Humanism: Foundations, Forms, and Legacy*, 3 vols. (Philadelphia: U of Pennsylvania P, 1988).

—— 'Significance of "Civic Humanism" in the Interpretation of the Italian Renaissance', in *Renaissance Humanism: Foundations, Forms and Legacy*, ed. Albert J. Rabil Jr., 3 vols. (Philadelphia: U of Pennsylvania P, 1988), i. 141–79.

Radcliff-Umstead, Douglas, *The Birth of Modern Comedy in Renaissance Italy* (Chicago: U of Chicago P, 1969).

Raimondi, Ezio, *Codro e l'umanesimo a Bologna* (Bologna: Zuffi, 1950; repr. Bologna: Il Mulino, 1987).

Reeve, M. D., 'The Rediscovery of Classical Texts in the Renaissance', in *Itinerari dei testi antichi*, ed. Oronzo Pecere, Saggi di storia antica 3 (Rome: 'L'Erma' di Bretschneider, 1991), 115–57.

Regoliosi, Mariangela, 'Umanesimo lombardo: La polemica tra Lorenzo Valla e Antonio da Rho', in *Studi di lingua e letteratura lombarda offerti a Maurizio Vitale*, 2 vols. (Pisa: Giardini, 1983), i. 170–9.

Reid, Jane Davidson, with the assistance of Chris Rohmann, *The Oxford Guide to Classical Mythology in the Arts, 1300–1990s*, 2 vols. (New York: OUP, 1993).

Reinhold, J., 'Quelques remarques sur les sources de *Floire et Blancheflor*', *Revue de philologie française* 19 (1905), 153–75.

Relihan, Joel C., *Ancient Menippean Satire* (Baltimore: Johns Hopkins UP, 1993).

Reynolds, L. D., and N. G. Wilson, *Scribes and Scholars: A Guide to the Transmission of Greek and Latin Literature*, 3rd edn. (Oxford: Clarendon, 1991). [*S&S3*]

—— ed., *Texts and Transmission: A Survey of the Latin Classics* (Oxford: Clarendon, 1983).

Rhodes, Dennis E., *A Catalogue of Incunabula in all the Libraries of Oxford University outside the Bodleian* (Oxford: Clarendon, 1982).

Rhodes, Neil, *Elizabethan Grotesque* (London: RKP, 1980).

Ribner, Rhoda M., 'The Compasse of This Curious Frame: Chapman's *Ovids Banquet of Sence* and the Emblematic Tradition', *SR* 17 (1970), 233–58.

Ricapito, Joseph V., '*The Golden Ass* of Apuleius and the Spanish Picaresque Novel', *Revista hispanica moderna* 40 (1978), 77–85.

Rigg, A. R., *A History of Anglo-Latin Literature, 1066–1422* (Cambridge: CUP, 1992).

Riggan, William, 'The Reformed Picaro and his Narrative: A Study of the Autobiographical Accounts of Lucius Apuleius, Simplicius, Simplicissimus, Lazarillo de Tormes, Guzmán de Alfarache and Moll Flanders', *Orbis Litterasum* 30 (1975), 165–86.

Riley, E. C., *Cervantes's Theory of the Novel* (Oxford: Clarendon, 1962).

Roberts, C. H., and T. C. Skeat, *The Birth of the Codex* (London: OUP for the British Academy, 1983).

Roberts, Michael, 'Paulinus Poem 11, Virgil's First *Eclogue*, and the Limits of *Amicitia*', *TAPA* 115 (1985), 271–82.

Robertson, D. S., 'The Manuscripts of the *Metamorphoses* of Apuleius', *CQ* 18 (1924), 27–42, 85–99.

—— 'The Assisi Fragments of the *Apologia* of Apuleius', *CQ*, ns 6 (1956), 68–80.

Robertson, Edward, *Aldus Manutius: The Scholar Printer, 1450–1515* (Manchester: MUP, 1950).

Robinson, F. N., ed., *The Works of Geoffrey Chaucer*, 2nd edn. (London: OUP, 1957).

Roche, Thomas P., *The Kindly Flame: A Study of the Third and Fourth Books of Spenser's 'Faerie Queene'* (Princeton: PUP, 1964).

Rodgers, R. H., 'The Apuleius of the *Geoponica*', *CSCA* 11 (1978), 197–207.

Rollo, David, 'From Apuleius' Psyche to Chrétien's Erec and Enide', in *The Search for the Ancient Novel*, ed. Tatum, 347–69.

Romei, Danilo, 'L'alfabeto segreto di Agnolo Firenzuola', revised version of a paper delivered at a conference to mark the 500th anniversary of Firenzuola's birth (Prato 25 September 1993). http://www.nuovorinascimento.org/n-rinasc/saggi/html/romei/firenz93.htm

Rouschausse, Jean, *Erasmus and Fisher: Their Correspondence 1511–1524* (Paris: Librairie Philosophique J. Vrin, 1968).

Rouse, R. H., 'Bostonus Buriensis and the Author of the *Catalogus Scriptorum Ecclesiae*', *Speculum* 41 (1966), 471–99.

—— 'Manuscripts belonging to Richard de Fournival', *Revue d'histoire des textes* 3 (1973), 253–69.

Rowland, Ingrid D., 'Revenge of the Regensburg Humanists, 1493', *SCJ* 25 (1994), 307–22.

—— *The Culture of the High Renaissance: Ancients and Moderns in Sixteenth-Century Rome* (Cambridge: CUP, 1998).

Rubio, Francisco Pejenaute, 'La traducción española del *Asinus Aureus* de Apuleyo de Diego López de Cortegana', *Livius: Revista de estudios de traducción* 4 (1993), 157–68.

Ruffo-Fiore, Silvia, *Niccolò Machiavelli* (Boston: Twayne, 1982).

Ryan, Lawrence V., *Roger Ascham* (London: OUP, 1963).

Sabbadini, Remigio, *Storia del Ciceronianismo e di altre questioni letterarie nell'età della rinascenza* (Turin: Loescher, 1886).

—— *Le scoperte dei codici latini e greci ne' secoli xiv e xv*, 2 vols. (Florence: Sansoni, 1905–14), repr. with corr., ed. Eugenio Garin (Florence: Sansoni, 1967).

—— 'Giovanni Colonna biografo e bibliografo del sec. XIV', *ARAST* 46 (1911), 830–60.

Salzman, Paul, *English Prose Fiction, 1558–1700: A Critical History* (Oxford: Clarendon, 1985).

Sammut, Alfonso, *Unfredo duca di Gloucester e gli umanisti italiani* (Padua: Antenore, 1980).

Sandy, G. N., 'Knowledge and Curiosity in Apuleius' *Metamorphoses*', *Latomus* 31 (1971), 179–83.

—— 'Recent Scholarship on the Prose Fiction of Classical Antiquity' *CW* (1974), 321–60.

—— '*Serviles Voluptates* in Apuleius' *Metamorphoses*', *Phoenix* 28 (1974), 234–44.

—— 'Book 11: Ballast or Anchor?', in *Aspects of Apuleius' 'Golden Ass'*, ed. Hijmans and van der Paardt, 123–37.

—— 'Ancient Prose Fiction and Minor Early English Novels', *Antike und Abendland* 25 (1979), 41–55.

—— 'Classical Forerunners of the Theory and Practice of Prose Romance in France: Studies in the Narrative Form of Minor French Romances of the Sixteenth and Seventeenth Centuries', *Antike und Abendland* 28 (1982), 169–91.

—— *The Greek World of Apuleius: Apuleius and the Second Sophistic* (Leiden: Brill, 1997).

Sandys, John Edwin, *Harvard Lectures on the Revival of Learning* (Cambridge: CUP, 1905).

—— *A History of Classical Scholarship*, 3 vols. (Cambridge: CUP, 1908–21).

Sanguineti White, Laura, *Boccaccio e Apuleio: Caratteri differenziali nella struttura narrativa del 'Decameron'* (Bologna: Edizioni italiane moderne, 1977).

Scarpa, L. ed., *Macrobii Ambrosii Theodosii commentariorum in Somnium Scipionis libri duo* (Padua: Liviana, 1981).

Schlam, Carl C., 'The Scholarship on Apuleius since 1938', *CW* 64 (1971), 285–309.

—— *Cupid and Psyche: Apuleius and the Monuments* (University Park, Pa,: American Philological Association, 1976).

—— Review of Fehling, *CP* 76/2 (Apr. 1981), 164–6.

—— 'Apuleius in the Middle Ages', in *The Classics in the Middle Ages*, ed. Bernardo and Levin, 363–9.

—— *The 'Metamorphoses' of Apuleius: On Making an Ass of Oneself* (London: Duckworth, 1992).

Schloderer, J. V. et al., eds., *Catalogue of Books Printed in the Fifteenth Century now in the British Museum. Part IV: Subiaco and Rome* (London: British Museum, 1916).

Schloderer, Victor, *Fifty Essays in Fifteenth- and Sixteenth-Century Bibliography*, ed. Denis E. Rhodes (Amsterdam: Hertzberger, 1966).

Schulz, J., 'Pinturicchio and the Revival of Antiquity', *JWCI* 25 (1962), 35–55.

Schmidt, W., 'Endelechius', in *Reallexikon für Antike und Christentum: Sachwörterbuch zur Auseinandersetzung des Christentums mit der antiken Welt*, ed. Theodor Klauser, vol. v (Stuttgart: Hiersemann, 1962).

Scobie, Alexander, *Aspects of the Ancient Romance and its Heritage: Essays on Apuleius, Petronius, and the Greek Romances* (Meisenheim am Glan: Anton Hain, 1969).

—— *More Essays on the Ancient Romance and its Heritage* (Meisenheim am Glan: Anton Hain, 1973).

—— 'The Influence of Apuleius' *Metamorphoses* in Renaissance Italy and Spain', in *Aspects of Apuleius' 'Golden Ass'*, ed. Hijmans and van der Paardt, 211–25.

—— *Apuleius and Folklore: Toward a History of ML3045, AaTh567, 449A* (London: Folklore Soc., 1983).

Severs, J. Burke, *The Literary Relationships of Chaucer's 'Clerkes Tale'*, Yale Studies in English 96 (New Haven: YUP, 1942).

Seznec, Jean, *The Survival of the Pagan Gods: The Mythological Tradition and its Place in Renaissance Humanism and Art*, trans. Barbara F. Sessions (Princeton: PUP, 1953; repr. 1972).

Shanzer, Danuta, *A Philosophical and Literary Commentary on Martianus Capella's 'De Nuptiis Philologiae et Mercurii' Book I* (Berkeley and Los Angeles: U of California, 1986).

Sharpe, Richard, 'Reconstructing the Medieval Library of Bury St Edmunds: The Lost Catalogue of Henry of Kirkstead', in *Bury St Edmunds: Medieval Art, Architecture, Archaeology and Economy*, ed. Antonia Gransden (Leeds: British Archaeological Assoc., 1998), 204–18.

Shepherd, G. T., 'The Emancipation of Story in the Twelfth Century', in *Medieval Narrative: A Symposium*, ed. Hans Bekker-Nielson et al. (Odense: Odense UP, 1979), 44–57.

Sheppard, L. A., 'A Fifteenth-Century Humanist, Francesco Filelfo', *The Library*, 4th ser. 16 (1936), 1–26.

—— *Catalogue of XVth Century Books in the Bodleian Library* (Oxford: Bodleian Library, 1973).

Shumate, Nancy, *Crisis and Conversion in Apuleius' 'Metamorphoses'* (Ann Arbor: U of Michigan P, 1996).

Simons, Penny, and Penny Eley, 'Male Beauty and Sexual Orientation in *Partonopeus de Blois*', *Romance Studies* 17 (1999), 41–56.

Singer, Charles, *From Magic to Science: Essays on the Scientific Twilight* (London: Ernest Benn, 1928; repr. New York: Dover, 1958).

Sisson, C., 'Henslowe's Will Again', *RES* 5 (1929), 308–11.

Skinner, Quentin, 'Moral Ambiguity and the Renaissance Art of Eloquence', *Essays in Criticism* 44 (1994), 267–92.

Skretkowicz, Victor, 'Sidney and Amyot: Heliodorus in the Structure and Ethos of the *New Arcadia*', *RES* 27 (1976), 170–4.

—— 'Sidney's Tragic *Arcadia* and the Ancient Novel', ICAN II paper, abstracted in *The Ancient Novel*, ed. Tatum and Vernazza, 52.

Smalley, Beryl, *The English Friars and Antiquity in the Early Fourteenth Century* (Oxford: Blackwell, 1960).

Smith, William, and Samuel Cheetham, *A Dictionary of Christian Antiquities*, 2 vols. (London: John Murray, 1875).

Spitz, Lewis W., *Conrad Celtis: The German Arch-Humanist* (Cambridge, Mass.: HUP, 1957).

—— 'Mutian—Intellectual Canon', in his *The Religious Renaissance of the German Humanists* (Cambridge, Mass.: HUP, 1963), 130–54.

—— 'Luther and Humanism', in *Luther and Learning*, ed. Harran, 69–94.

—— and Barbara Sher Tinsley, *Johann Sturm on Education: The Reformation and Humanist Learning* (St Louis, Mo.: Concordia, 1995).

Stadter, Philip, 'Fictional Narrative in the *Cyropaideia*', *AJP* 112 (1991), 461–91.

Stahl, William Harris, trans. and introd., *Macrobius: Commentary on the Dream of Scipio* (New York: Columbia UP, 1952).

—— Richard Johnson, and E. L. Burge, *Martianus Capella and the Seven Liberal Arts*, 2 vols. (New York: Columbia UP), 1971–7.

Starnes, D. T., 'Shakespeare and Apuleius', *PMLA* 60 (1945), 1021–50.

—— and E. W. Talbert, *Classical Myth and Legend in Renaissance Dictionaries* (Chapel Hill: U of North Carolina P, 1955).

Steadman, J. M., 'Una and the Clergy: The Ass Symbol in *The Faerie Queene*', *JWCI* 21 (1958), 134–7.

Steegmuller, Francis, *Flaubert and 'Madame Bovary': A Double Portrait* (London: Robert Hale, 1939).

Stephens, Walter, 'Tasso's Heliodorus and the World of Romance', in *The Search for the Ancient Novel*, ed. Tatum, 67–87.

Stern, Virginia F., *Gabriel Harvey: His Life, Marginalia and Library* (Oxford: Clarendon, 1979).

Stewering, Roswitha, 'The Relationship between World, Landscape, and Polia in the *Hypnerotomachia Poliphili*', in *Garden and Architectural Dreamscapes*, ed. Leslie and Hunt, 2–10.

Stichel, Dorothea, 'Reading the *Hypnerotomachia Poliphili* in the Cinquecento: Marginal Notes in a Copy at Modena', in *Aldus Manutius and Renaissance Culture*, ed. Zeidberg and Superbi, 217–36.

Stigall, John O., 'The Manuscript Tradition of the *De vita et moribus philosophorum* of Walter Burley', *M&H* 11 (1957), 44–57.

Stock, Brian, *Myth and Science in the Twelfth Century: A Study of Bernard Silvester* (Princeton: PUP, 1972).

Stramaglia, Antonio, 'Apuleio come *auctor*: Premesse tardoantiche di un uso umanistico', *SUP* 16 (1996), 137–61.

Stupperich, Reinhold, 'Das Statuenprogramm in den Zeuxippos-Thermen: Überlegungen zur Beschreibung des Christodoros von Koptos', *Istanbuler Mitteilungen* 32 (1982), 210–35.

Sullivan, Mark W., *Apuleian Logic: The Nature, Sources, and Influence of Apuleius' 'Peri Hermeneias'* (Amsterdam: North-Holland Pub. Co., 1967).

Swahn, Jan-Öjvind, *The Tale of Cupid and Psyche (Aarne-Thompson 425 & 428)* (Lund: Gleerup, 1955).

Synan, Edward A., 'The Classics: Episcopal Malice and Papal Piety', in *The Classics in the Middle Ages*, ed. Bernardo and Levin, 379–402.

—— 'A Goliard Witness: The *De nuptiis Philologiae et Mercurii* of Martianus Capella in the *Metamorphosis golye episcopi*', *Florilegium: Carterton University Annual Papers on Classical Antiquity and the Middle Ages* 2 (1980), 121–45.

Tatlock, J. S. P., 'Chaucer's "Merchant's Tale"', *Modern Philology* 33/4 (May 1936), 367–81.

Tatum, James, *Apuleius and 'The Golden Ass'* (Ithaca: Cornell UP, 1979).

—— Review of Fehling, *AJP* 101 (1980), 109–11.

—— *Xenophon's Imperial Fiction: On the Education of Cyrus* (Princeton: PUP, 1989).

—— and Gail M. Vernazza, eds., *The Ancient Novel: Classical Paradigms and Modern Perspectives (Proceedings of the International Conference on the Ancient Novel, 1989)* (Hanover, NH: Dartmouth College/NEH, 1990).

—— ed., *The Search for the Ancient Novel* (Baltimore: Johns Hopkins UP, 1994).

Teeuwen, Mariken, *Harmony and the Music of the Spheres: The 'Ars musica' in Ninth-Century Commentaries on Martianus Capella*, Mittellateinische Studien und Texte 30 (Leiden: Brill, 2002).

Thomas, D. F. S., 'The Latinity of Erasmus', in *Erasmus*, ed. T. A. Dorey, (London: RKP, 1970), 115–37.

Thompson, C. R., *The Translations of Lucian by Erasmus and St. Thomas More* (Ithaca, NY: n.pub., 1940).

Thompson, N. S., *Chaucer, Boccaccio, and the Debate of Love: A Comparative Study of the 'Decameron' and the 'Canterbury Tales'* (Oxford: Clarendon, 1996).

Thomson, Rodney M., 'The Library of Bury St Edmunds Abbey in the Eleventh and Twelfth Centuries', *Speculum* 47 (1972), 617–45.

—— 'The Satirical Works of Berengar of Poitiers: An Edition with Introduction', *Mediaeval Studies* 42 (1980), 89–138; repr. in his *England and the 12th-Century Renaissance* (Aldershot: Ashgate, 1998), no. XIII.

Thorndike, Lynn, *A History of Magic and Experimental Science*, 8 vols. (New York: Macmillan, 1923–58).

Tobin, J. J. M., 'Spenserian Parallels', *EC* 29 (1979), 264–9.

—— 'Apuleius and Milton', *RPL* 7 (1984), 181–91.

—— *Shakespeare's Favorite Novel: A Study of 'The Golden Asse' as Prime Source* (Lanham, Md.: UP of America, 1984). [*SFN*]

—— 'Apuleius', in *Spenser Encyclopedia*, ed. Hamilton, 49.

Toynbee, J. M. C., Review of Alföldi, *Die Kontorniaten*, *JRS* 35 (1945), 115–21.

Traube, Ludwig, 'O Roma nobilis. Philologischen Untersuchungen aus dem Mittelalter', *Abhandlung der philosophisch-philologischen Classe der königlich Bayerische Akademie der Wissenschafter* 19 (1891), 299–395.

Trippe, Rosemary, 'The *Hypnerotomachia Poliphili*, Image, Text, and Vernacular Poetics', *RQ* 55 (2002), 1222–58.

Tristano, Caterina, 'Le postille del Petrarca nel Vaticano Lat. 2193 (Apuleio, Frontino, Vegezio, Palladio)', *IMU* 17 (1974), 365–468.

Trout, Dennis E., *Paulinus of Nola: Life, Letters, and Poems,* The Transformation of the Classical Heritage 27 (Berkeley and Los Angeles: U of California P, 1999).

Uitti, Karl D., 'Vernacularization and Old French Romance Mythopoesis with Emphasis on Chrétien's *Erec et Enide*', in *The Sower and his Seed: Essays on Chrétien de Troyes*, ed. Rupert T. Pickens (Lexington, Ky.: French Forum, 1983), 81–115.

Ullman, Berthold L., *The Humanism of Coluccio Salutati*, Medioevo e umanesimo 4 (Padua: Antenore, 1963).

—— *Studies in the Italian Renaissance* (Rome: Edizioni di storia e letteratura, 1973).

—— and Philip A. Stadter, *The Public Library of Renaissance Florence: Niccolò Niccoli, Cosimo de' Medici, and the Library of San Marco* (Padua: Antenore, 1972).

Van der Paardt, R. Th., ed., *L. Apuleius Madaurensis: The Metamorphoses: A Commentary on Book III with Text and Introduction* (Amsterdam: Hakkert, 1971).

Vecce, Carlo, 'Bembo e gli antichi: Dalla filologia ai classici moderni', in *'Prose della volgar lingua' di Pietro Bembo: Gargnano del Garda (4–7 ottobre 2000)*, ed. S. Morgana, M. Piotti, and M. Prada (Milan: Cisalpino (Istituto editoriale universitario), 2000), 9–22.

Verheyen, Egon, with plans by Diane Finiello Zervas, *The Palazzo del Te in Mantua: Images of Love and Politics* (Baltimore: Johns Hopkins UP, 1977).

Vertova, Luisa, 'Cupid and Psyche in Renaissance Painting before Raphael', *JWCI* 42 (1979), 104–21.

Vidmanová, Anežka, 'La Formation de la second rédaction des *Vite philosophorum* et sa relation à l'œuvre originale', *Medioevo* 16 (1990), 253–72.

Vio, Gianluigi, 'Chiose e riscritture apuleiane di Giovanni Boccaccio', *Studi sul Boccaccio* 20 (1992), 139–65.

Voigt, Ludwig Georg, *Pétrarque, Boccace et les débuts de l'humanism en Italie, d'après la Wiederbelebung des classischen Alterthums*, trans. M. A. Le Monnier (Paris: Welter, 1894).

Wadsworth, James B., 'Filippo Beroaldo the Elder and the Early Renaissance in Lyons', *M&H* 11 (1957), 78–89.

Wallace, David, *Chaucer and the Early Writings of Boccaccio* (Woodbridge: Brewer, 1985).

Wallace, Nathanial, 'Architextual Poetics: The *Hypnerotomachia* and the Rise of the European Emblem', *Emblematica* 8/1 (1994 [= 1996]), 1–27.

Walsh, P. G., *The Roman Novel: The 'Satyricon' of Petronius and the 'Metamorphoses' of Apuleius* (Cambridge: CUP, 1970).

—— ed. and trans. *Andreas Capellanus on Love* (London: Duckworth, 1982).

Weiner, Andrew D., 'Spenser's *Muiopotmos* and the Fates of Butterflies and Men', *JEGP* 84 (1985), 203–20.

Weir, Robert, 'Apuleius Glosses in the Abolita Glossary', *CQ* 15/1 (Jan. 1921), 41–3.

—— 'Addendum on Apuleius Glosses in the "Abolita" Glossary', *CQ* 15/2 (Apr. 1921), 107.

Weiss, James Michael, '*Kennst Du das Land wo die Humanisten blühen?*: References to Italy in the Biographies of German Humanists', in *Germania latina / latinitas Teutonica: Politik, Wissenschaft, humanistische Kultur vom späten Mittelalter bis in unsere Zeit*, ed. Eckhard Kessler and Heinrich C. Kuhn, Humanistische Bibliothek. Reihe 1, Abhandlungen; Bd. 54 (Munich: Fink, 2003) 439–55.

Weiss, Roberto, *Un umanista veneziano: Papa Paolo II* (Venice: Istituto per la collaborazione culturale, 1958).

—— *The Spread of Italian Humanism* (London: Hutchinson UP, 1964).

—— *Humanism in England during the Fifteenth Century*, 3rd edn. (Oxford: Basil Blackwell, 1967).

Wetherbee, Winthrop, *Platonism and Poetry in the Twelfth Century: The Literary Influence of the School of Chartres* (Princeton: PUP, 1972).

Whibley, Charles, introd., *The Golden Ass of Apuleius: Translated out of the Latin by William Adlington*, ed. W. E. Henley, Tudor Translations 4 (London: David Nutt, 1893).

Whitman, Jon, *Allegory: The Dynamics of an Ancient and Medieval Technique* (Oxford: Clarendon, 1987).

Whittaker, Thomas, *Macrobius, or Philosophy, Science and Letters in the Year 400* (Cambridge: CUP, 1923).

Wilkins, Ernest H., 'Petrarch's Ecclesiastical Career', *Speculum* 28 (1953), 754–75.

—— *Studies in the Life and Works of Petrarch* (Cambridge, Mass.: Mediaeval Academy of America, 1955).

Wilks, Michael, ed., *The World of John of Salisbury* (Oxford: Ecclesiastical History Soc., 1984).

Williams, F. B., Jr., *Index of Dedications and Commendatory Verses in English Books before 1641* (London: Bibliographical Soc., 1962).

Wilson, John Dover, *Shakespeare's Happy Comedies* (London: Faber, 1962).

Wilson, N. G., *Scholars of Byzantium* (London: Duckworth, 1981).

Wind, Edgar, *Bellini's Feast of the Gods: A Study in Venetian Humanism* (Cambridge, Mass.: HUP, 1948).

—— *Pagan Mysteries in the Renaissance*, rev. edn. (Oxford: Clarendon, 1980).

Windeatt, Barry, 'Chaucer and Fifteenth-Century Romance: *Partonope of Blois*', in *Chaucer Traditions: Studies in Honour of Derek Brewer*, ed. Ruth Morse and Barry Windeatt (Cambridge: CUP, 1990).

Winkler, John J., 'The Mendacity of Kalasiris and the Narrative Strategy of Heliodoros' *Aithiopika*', *Yale Classical Studies* 27 (1982), 93–158.

—— *Auctor & Actor: A Narratological Reading of Apuleius's 'The Golden Ass'* (Berkeley and Los Angeles: U of California P, 1985).

Witt, R. E., *Albinus and the History of Middle Platonism* (Cambridge: CUP, 1937).

Wolff, Samuel Lee, *The Greek Romances in Elizabethan Prose Fiction* (New York: Columbia UP, 1912).

Woodhouse, C. M., *George Gemistos Plethon: The Last of the Hellenes* (Oxford: OUP, 1986).

Wormald, Francis, and C. E. Wright, eds., *The English Library before 1700: Studies in its History* (London: U of London, 1958).

Wright, Cyril E., 'The Dispersal of the Libraries in the Sixteenth Century', in *The English Library before 1700*, ed. Wormald and Wright, 148–75.

—— *Fontes Harleiani: A Study of the Sources of the Harleian Collection of Manuscripts Preserved in the Department of Manuscripts in the British Museum* (London: British Museum, 1972).

Wright, Herbert G., *Boccaccio in England from Chaucer to Tennyson* (London: U of London, Athlone P, 1957).

Wright, J. R. G., 'Folk-Tale and Literary Technique in *Cupid and Psyche*', *CQ*, NS 21 (1971), 273–84.

Wright, Thomas, ed., *Latin Poems Commonly attributed to Walter Mapes* (London: Camden Soc., 1841).

Yates, Frances A., *Giordano Bruno and the Hermetic Tradition* (London: RKP, 1964).

Zabughin, Vladimiro, *Giulio Pomponio Leto: Saggio critico*, 3 vols. (Rome: La vita letteraria, 1909–12).

Zeidberg, David S., and Fiorella Gioffredi Superbi, eds., *Aldus Manutius and Renaissance Culture: Essays in Memory of Franklin D. Murphy (Acts of an International Conference, Venice and Florence, 14–17 June 1994)* (Florence: Olschki, 1998).

Zimmerman, Maaike, ed., *Apuleius Madaurensis Metamorphoses Book X*, GCA (Groningen: Forsten, 2000).

Index Manuscriptorum

Index Locorum

9. 2: 53
10. 312 ff.: 78
10. 473–4:
      97 n. 142
10. 710 ff.: 389
11. 416–7: 222 n. 134
14. 597: 106
14. 695–764: 231

Tristia
2. 413–4: 216 n. 25
3. 5. 14: 83 n. 95

PETRONIUS

Satyrica
31: 449

SENECA

Epistulae ad Lucilium
1. 2. 5: 142

VERGIL

Aeneid
2. 1: 6
3. 27–42:
      405 n. 63
6. 268–899: 393
6. 337–83:
      123 n. 65

Georgics
4. 67–84: 393
4. 405–10: xv

Index verborum Apuleianorum

Index nominum et rerum